The Last of the Doughboys

Also by Richard Rubin

CONFEDERACY OF SILENCE:
A TRUE TALE OF THE NEW OLD SOUTH

The Last

of the

Doughboys

✯ ✯ ✯ ✯ ✯ ✯ ✯ ✯ ✯ ✯

The Forgotten Generation and Their Forgotten World War

Richard Rubin

HOUGHTON MIFFLIN HARCOURT

BOSTON   NEW YORK

Copyright © 2013 by Richard Rubin

All rights reserved

For information about permission to reproduce selections from this book,
write to Permissions, Houghton Mifflin Harcourt Publishing Company,
215 Park Avenue South, New York, New York 10003.

www.hmhbooks.com

Library of Congress Cataloging-in-Publication Data
Rubin, Richard.
The last of the doughboys : the forgotten generation and their forgotten world war /
Richard Rubin.
pages cm
Includes index.
ISBN 978-0-547-55443-3
1. World War, 1914–1918 — Veterans — United States. 2. World War, 1914–1918 —
Personal narratives, American. 3. Soldiers — United States — Biography.
4. Veterans — United States — Biography. 5. Centenarians — United States — Biography.
I. Title.
D639.V48U67 2013
940.4'12730922 — dc23   2013000614

Book design by Melissa Lotfy
Maps by Chris Robinson

Printed in the United States of America
DOC 10 9 8 7 6 5 4 3 2

Excerpts from *Company K* by William March (University of Alabama Press) used by
permission of Harold Ober Associates Incorporated.

To them
and those they represent

Contents

Maps

Oostvleteren

Ypres

Passchendaele

Lys R.

Scheldt R.

Brussels

B E L G I U M

Vimy

Arras

Beaumont-
Hamel

La Boiselle

Albert

Amiens

Cambrai

St. Quentin

Somme R.

Rhine R.

Mosel R.

LUXEMBOURG

Sedan

*Chemin-
des-Dames*

Aisne R.

Soissons

Reims

Séchault

Consenvoye

Douaumont

Verdun

G E R M A N Y

Metz

Paris

Marne R.

*Saint-Mihiel
Salient*

Saint-Mihiel

Meuse R.

Nancy

Moselle R.

Seine R.

Landeville

Neufchâteau

Chaumont

Bourbonne-
les-Bains

V O S G E S   M O U N T A I N S

Rhine R.

Colmar

F R A N C E

Mulhouse

Loire R.

Allerey

S W I T Z E R L A N D

Western Front, 1914–1918

- – ·· – ·· – International Boundaries
              on Aug 1, 1914
- ·········· Line of Oct. 1, 1914
- – – – – – Line of Jan 1, 1916
- ———— Line of June 30, 1916
- ● ● ● ● ● Line of Apr 6, 1917
- – – – – – Line of May 26, 1918
- ———— Line of Nov 11, 1918

0   25   50   75 Miles

Nantua

N

No Man's Land

B EFORE THE NEW AGE and the New Frontier and the New
Deal, before Roy Rogers and John Wayne and Tom Mix, before
Bugs Bunny and Mickey Mouse and Felix the Cat, before the
TVA and TV and radio and the Radio Flyer, before *The Grapes of Wrath*
and *Gone with the Wind* and *The Jazz Singer*, before the CIA and the
FBI and the WPA, before airlines and airmail and air conditioning, be-
fore LBJ and JFK and FDR, before the Space Shuttle and Sputnik and
the *Hindenburg* and the *Spirit of St. Louis*, before the Greed Decade
and the Me Decade and the Summer of Love and the Great Depression and Prohibition, before Yuppies and Hippies and Okies and Flap-
pers, before Saigon and Inchon and Nuremberg and Pearl Harbor and
Weimar, before Ho and Mao and Chiang, before MP3s and CDs and
LPs, before Martin Luther King and Thurgood Marshall and Jackie
Robinson, before the pill and Pampers and penicillin, before GI surgery and GI Joe and the GI Bill, before AFDC and HUD and Welfare
and Medicare and Social Security, before Super Glue and titanium and
Lucite, before the Sears Tower and the Twin Towers and the Empire
State Building and the Chrysler Building, before the In Crowd and the
A Train and the Lost Generation, before the Blue Angels and Rhythm
& Blues and *Rhapsody in Blue*, before Tupperware and the refrigerator
and the automatic transmission and the aerosol can and the Band-Aid
and nylon and the ballpoint pen and sliced bread, before the Iraq War
and the Gulf War and the Cold War and the Vietnam War and the Ko-
rean War and the Second World War, there was the First World War,
World War I, the Great War, the War to End All Wars.

. . .

It wasn't the biggest Veterans Day parade in New England, or in Massachusetts, or even on Cape Cod, for that matter. In fact, it was rather modest: a handful or two of old soldiers and sailors in uniform, a half-dozen large flags, a few cars, a couple of cops on motorcycles, and a fife-and-drum corps comprising two or three dozen area schoolchildren dressed like Continental soldiers and playing Revolutionary War–era tunes. There were short speeches at the war memorial, salutes at the Civil War monument, and hot dogs at the American Legion Hall. All told, this celebration of Veterans Day, 2003 — a holiday that was first established by Congress in 1926 as Armistice Day, an observance of the truce that ended World War I at 11:00 a.m. on November 11, 1918 — lasted about an hour.

But the procession, modest as it was, had something else that made it unique among Veterans Day parades throughout the United States that year: Corporal Jesse Laurence Moffitt, a bona fide World War I veteran, a man who was then 106 years, eight months, and five days old. He had joined the Connecticut National Guard in February, 1917; when America entered the war, two months later, his unit became the 102nd Infantry Regiment, which was in turn part of the 26th Division, the "Yankee Division," so called because it was composed entirely of regiments from New England. That summer, he shipped out for France, where he would, eventually, fight in one terrible battle after another — until, on November 11, 1918, as he recalled, "all firing stopped. Complete silence — there wasn't a sound at eleven o'clock. And we were able to go out of our dugouts and trenches without our helmets or gas masks, which was the first time we'd been able to do that since we first went to the front."

Exactly eighty-five years later, he rode in a parade in the picturesque seaside town of Orleans, Massachusetts, to mark the anniversary of that day, just as he did every year. Afterward, I asked him why, at his age, he made a point of doing so.

"People like to see a World War I exhibit," he replied. "I would assume that it means something to people to see a World War I veteran, because there's not many of us around, as you know. Just to be able to say that you have seen a 106-year-old is satisfying to some people. After all, it's not an everyday event for most people."

I couldn't argue with that; if anything, it was a serious understatement. It had taken me several months of intensive searching to find just such a man, and several more before I found myself here, witnessing this historic occasion. And yet, as remarkable as all this was to me, I would not grasp the occasion's true significance for some time to come. None of us who lined the road that morning could have known that what we were actually witnessing there in Orleans was the last small-town Veterans Day parade anywhere to feature a living American veteran of World War I.

I write these words on the island of Manhattan, the center of a city older than Boston and Philadelphia, a city that is richer in history than perhaps any other in America. That this is so often comes as a surprise to people, because New York is and always has been about what is new, not what is old; about what will be rather than what was. But just a few blocks from where I sit, mounted on the front of a small, vest-pocket Presbyterian church, there is a very large plaque listing the names of 136 members of that congregation who went off to fight in the First World War, including five who never returned. Three blocks away, inside a large Catholic church, another plaque lists the names of thirty-eight men from the parish who were killed in the same war. Across the park, almost to the East River, is York Avenue; most New Yorkers assume it is named, as is their city, for the Duke of York, but it is actually an homage to Sergeant Alvin C. York, a pacifist from the mountains of eastern Tennessee who was drafted and sent off to France, where, on the night of October 8, 1918, he single-handedly killed seventeen German soldiers and captured 132 more, a feat for which he was awarded the Congressional Medal of Honor, the French Légion d'Honneur, and several other high honors. Farther uptown, at the spot where Broadway and St. Nicholas Avenue converge, you will find a large bronze statue of doughboys struggling on a battlefield, mounted atop a granite monument to neighborhood boys who did the same. And up at the tip of the island, in the neighborhood known as Inwood, there are streets named for local sons who never returned from the trenches. Their last names, and the war they served in, are all that is remembered of them today.

And that's just what I can think of off the top of my head, for the top half of the island. There are statues, monuments, and plaques commemorating World War I all over this city that often doesn't seem to care about history — in parks and squares and libraries, in the South Bronx and Times Square and the Lord & Taylor department store on Fifth Avenue. I'm not sure I could direct you to three World War II monuments within the five boroughs, and believe me, I pay attention to these sorts of things. But World War I is everywhere.

And not just in New York. In Memphis, where I lived in the early 1990s, the city's most revered old park is dominated by a massive green statue of a doughboy charging up a hill, lips pursed in a grim scowl, bayonet thrust out to skewer the Hun. I can think of only two Civil War monuments in the entire city, which was occupied by the Yankees for three years before Appomattox.

Most of these statues, monuments, plaques, and memorials were commissioned, produced, and dedicated within about a decade of November 11, 1918. For ten years or so — maybe a bit longer in some cities or regions, a bit less in others — it seemed terribly important, at least to a certain type of person, that America remember that war and the people who fought it. Those who weren't a certain type of person had already set out to forget the war years earlier, in some cases even before the troops had all returned home. They were traumatized or embittered veterans; or men and women who had lost a boy Over There, or were caring for one who was now an invalid; or those whose businesses or marriages hadn't survived the experience; or just people, most of them good at heart, who'd had enough and didn't want to hear or think about it anymore. And then the Great Depression came along, and then World War II, and between those two events, even a certain type of person had other, more pressing things to think about. And by the by, America just forgot about World War I — did it so thoroughly, in fact, that after a while it became difficult to conceive that it had ever remembered it in the first place, that there had once been a time when that war hadn't seemed like very distant history.

Those statues and monuments and plaques and memorials commissioned back in the 1920s, though — they were big and elaborate, well made and well placed. They are still there, still everywhere, still striking and arresting and as legible as the day they were cast or chiseled. They still proclaim their stories as clearly as ever. And it's not just them: There are murals in old buildings, markers in front of old trees, ships and highways and public spaces named for World War I generals or battles or heroes or casualties; they talk a bit more softly, perhaps, but if you're attuned to them they can tell you a great deal. Go to any flea market in the continental United States and you will find reams of old World War I sheet music, and stacks of old World War I 78s, both selling for pocket change. They are as common as they are cheap. And of course, they speak, too.

And surprising as all of that may seem, you may be more surprised yet to learn that, well into the first decade of the twenty-first century, you could, if you were really determined, still track down a remnant of World War I capable of speaking to you more effectively and compellingly than all of the aforementioned put together: an actual veteran.

One day in the mid-1970s, when I was perhaps seven or eight years old, I was riding into the city with my mother when she pointed out the Bronx VA hospital, up on a hill, and told me that there were still in residence there veterans of World War I, including some who had never recovered from being gassed at the front.

I just stared at her. How could such a thing possibly be true? World War I! It felt so distant, relegated to an era of black-and-white and silence. Back then our allies were a King, a Crown Prince, and a Czar, our enemies a Kaiser, an Emperor, and a Sultan. How, I wondered, could warriors from such a remote past still be among us? It seemed unthinkable.

It seemed unthinkable because the Great War had already attained mythic status. It was an epic conflict, of course, by far the largest — in scope, casualties, and almost any other measure you can think of — the world had ever seen. The slaughter was terrific: In just one of the war's hundreds of battles — the Somme — more than a million men were lost, among them some 14,000 British soldiers who fell in the first *ten minutes* of battle. And yet, so often the images of that war that come to mind are curiously romantic: dashing aviators in leather jackets and long white scarves, genially sharing a bottle of cognac with a recently downed enemy pilot; colorfully clad regiments majestically marching off to battle, singing songs written specially for the occasion; soldiers crouching in trenches, writing poetry (and really good poetry, at that) while ducking enemy fire; troops kicking out soccer balls as they went "over the top" to the sound of bagpipes. Countless men were killed by artillery fired from miles away, after fighting, hand to hand and month after month, over the same few yards of rotten ground. Armies still observed age-old codes of chivalrous conduct toward the enemy, yet also unleashed upon them awful new weapons, chemical and biological agents so horrible that after the war they were banned forever.

Such paradoxes could exist because the Great War occurred at, and in many ways created, a great crossroads in the history of man. It changed the Western world — and much of the rest of the world, too — more than any other war had, or has. The Austro-Hungarian and Ottoman Empires, which had dominated large chunks of Europe and Asia for centuries, ceased to exist. Russia lost the monarchy that had ruled it for nearly a thousand years. Germany lost its ruler and plunged into an era of unprecedented political chaos culminating in the horror of the Third Reich. Much of France was destroyed. England lost an entire generation of young men. The United States — which sat out the first two and a half years of the war — lost more than one hundred thousand men; and though, in the process of fighting the war, it rose to the top tier of powerful nations for the very first time, it was so traumatized by the experience that it withdrew into a reactionary, isolationist cocoon, deporting hundreds and closing the door to several generations of immigrants. On the field of American memory, World War I occupies the slim No Man's Land between the archaic and the modern.

Other conflicts, though, hold much more prominent positions on that battleground. In the spring of 2003, I heard someone on the radio declare, in a tone of great urgency, that as many as a thousand World War II veterans were dying every day, and that we must harvest their stories now, while we still can; and, having always been a sucker for things — and people, and places, and facts, and stretches of history — overlooked and underappreciated, it occurred to me that no one was even bothering to seek out surviving veterans of World War I, since almost everyone assumed that anyone who fought in that earlier conflict was long dead. I did the math in my head, figuring that a man who was 21 at the war's end would now be 106 years old. People did occasionally live to be that old, I knew, and even a bit older. I had no idea how I might find such a person; but I was able to find a webpage for the

Department of Veterans Affairs featuring an actuarial table, compiled a couple of years earlier, which projected that there were still nearly fifteen hundred veterans of the First World War living in America. I set out to find some.

The VA, the source of that promising statistic, seemed a logical place to start looking; but no one there — at least, no one I spoke to that spring — seemed to have any idea at all who any of these fifteen hundred people were, much less where they might be. And try as I might, I couldn't get any of them to look into the matter, either. Eventually, perhaps spurred on by a few months' worth of my phone and email inquiries, they did do one thing: they revised their original projection down from fifteen hundred to "fewer than two hundred."

I didn't have any more luck with organizations like the Veterans of Foreign Wars or the American Legion, neither of which, I was told, kept centralized records; "Let us know if you find any!" was, typically, the last thing the people I spoke to at local chapters said by way of goodbye. VA hospitals, state veterans' agencies, regional veterans' homes, assisted-living facilities, nursing homes: No one had seen a World War I veteran in years, maybe decades. I started to wonder if that actuarial table might be the only place they still existed.

And then, hope — and help — came from an unexpected source.

In 1998, French president Jacques Chirac had announced that his country would grant its highest military award, the Légion d'Honneur, to any living American veteran who had served on French soil during World War I. There were a few other requirements — the most notable one being the lack of a criminal record — but overall the program was designed to make sure that as many American veterans as possible actually receive the award, and as quickly as possible: Another stipulation held that it could not be awarded posthumously.

The French government went to remarkable lengths to track down potential awardees, and always made a point, once it did so and had processed the necessary paperwork, of having some official representative of that government present the award — a handsome little medal, coupled with a large and ornate certificate — in a formal ceremony, whether before an auditorium full of spectators or a few family members crowded around a hospital bed. (On a few occasions, President

Chirac presented the award personally.) As a result, the government of France typically knew much more about America's surviving dough-boys than Americans did.

On almost every occasion, the presentation ceremony merited an article in the local newspaper, which is how I first learned of the program. Unfortunately, in many cases I read about it only in the honored veteran's obituary. Many of them, it seemed, did not long outlive the occasion. (One, I would later learn, died the very next day.) There were even a few reported cases of men who, sadly, died before the presenting officials could reach them. Nevertheless, one day I went to the French Embassy's official website in search of more information about the program, and there got my first big break in the search: a complete list of the American men and women — more than five hundred — to whom France had presented the Legion of Honor in the past five years, complete with their hometowns. It came out to twenty-four pages. I carried it around with me for days, reading the names over and over again.

Now, the program was already five years old by the time I heard about it, and most of those Legions of Honor had been awarded in 1998 or 1999; perhaps one person in twenty on that list was still living in 2003. There was no way to locate that one in twenty that didn't involve having nineteen at least slightly awkward telephone conversations. And some were more than just slightly. One woman, for example, responded to my query by asking me why I wanted to talk to the man in question. "I'd like to interview him about his experiences in the war," I explained.

"Well, you're barking up the wrong tree — he's dead!" she replied, and slammed down the handset.

A bit shaken, I tried to rephrase my inquiry for the next name on the list, but dialed the number before I'd taken enough time to think the matter through. Inquiring after the veteran in question, I stammered, "Is he, uh, *still around?*"

"No," the woman replied calmly. "He died a little over a year ago. And for future reference, you might just want to ask, 'Is he still living?'"

Good advice. I adopted that phrasing for future calls, posing that question again and again and again; and one day, I got a yes. And then another. Eventually, I would find quite a few veterans off what I came to think of as the French List.

William Edward Campbell was born in Mobile in 1893, left school at fourteen to work in a lumber mill, returned later to study law at the University of Alabama, and was working as a clerk at a law firm in Manhattan when America entered the war. He enlisted in the Marines, was sent to France, was shot and gassed at Belleau Wood, and returned to the front in time to see more battles before the war ended. He fought bravely: For valor he was awarded both the American Distinguished Service Cross and the French Croix de Guerre. Returning home, he went to work for a steamship company and, in short order, rose to become its vice president. But the war haunted him; he was plagued by depression and anxiety. Today we would recognize that as posttraumatic stress disorder; back then, to a proud and decorated ex-Marine, it was just a shameful, inexplicable weakness. But instead of turning to drink or some other form of self-medication, Campbell started to write. He wrote about the war, what he had seen and done, about those who had been killed and those whose lives had otherwise been destroyed. It came out in the form of a novel, the story of a fictional company of Marines, in which every man, living or dead, gets his own chapter to tell a story, short or long. He wrote under the pen name William March, and called his book *Company K*. When it was published, in 1933, it garnered tremendous critical acclaim; today it is as forgotten as the war itself.

The first Marine to speak in *Company K* is Private Joseph Delaney. The war has ended; he sits on his front porch with his wife, having just completed, he tells us, writing a book called *Company K*. "I have finished my book at last," he says, "but I wonder if I have done what I set out to do?"

Then I think: "This book started out to be a record of my own company, but I do not want it to be that, now. I want it to be a record of every company in every army. If its cast and its overtones are American, that is only because the American scene is the one that I know. With different names and different settings, the men of whom I have written could, as easily, be French, German, English or Russian for that matter."

I think: "I wish there were some way to take these stories and pin them to a huge wheel, each story hung on a different peg until the circle was completed. Then I would like to spin the wheel, faster and faster, until the things of which I have written took life and were re-created, and became part of the wheel, flowing toward each other, and into each other; blurring, and then blending together into a composite whole, an unending circle of pain. . . . That would be the picture of war. And the sound that wheel made, and the sound that the men themselves made as they laughed, cried, cursed or prayed, would be, against the falling of walls, the rushing of bullets, the exploding of shells, the sound that war, itself makes . . ."

Obscure as it is today, *Company K* is easily one of the best American war novels ever written, and one of the great war novels of modern times. Whenever I reread it I find, every few pages, something new and profound that stops me cold. And yet I always return, in the end, to Private Delaney's wish to take the disparate stories of the men in his company and spin them together until they melt into a great collage that tells one tale of undeniable truth. And I wonder: Can I somehow do the same, all these many years later, with the detritus that remains in our midst?

When I discovered that actuarial table on the VA's website I realized, to my astonishment, that I didn't have just inanimate detritus to work with. I still had, in 2003, the same resource William March had had in 1933: the actual people who fought that war, lived through it, and returned home afterward to get on with the business of life as best they could. I didn't know, at first, how many there still were, or what they might have to say; for a while, until I discovered the French List, their existence was, to me, nothing more than theoretical. But then, thanks to that resource and others, I did find one, and then another, and another. I had hoped, in the beginning, to find perhaps a half-dozen. Eventually I found several times that number. And every one of them had unique stories to tell, surprising, stunning, a few inconceivable, stories the likes of which I had never heard or read before, stories they hadn't told in fifty, sixty years. Stories they'd never told. These men and women did more than pin things to a wheel; they built the wheel, and spun it, and showed me five or six different vantage points where I might stand and behold something entirely new in it. Like the individual Marines in *Company K,* each one told, at the last possible moment, a story that was complete in and of itself and yet also a part of some greater whole, composed of other stories and artifacts and observations accumulated almost at random. That greater whole is what you now hold in your hands: a mosaic that tells a story about the United States of America and the First World War.

I cannot claim that it is the complete truth; I doubt a complete history of that war has ever been written, or ever will be. It was too vast, and too strange, to be knowable in its entirety. And this is not a conventional history of it. This is a book about America's experience of that war, at the front, behind the lines, and at home; how it infiltrated, influenced, shaped, and determined every last facet of life in the United States, no matter how small or seemingly removed; and how it continues to do so to this day, and perhaps always will, no matter how little evidence of that we think we can perceive, or how much we think we have forgotten. It is about the generation that fought that war — people who grew up without electricity or automobiles, who never left the county in which they'd been born until they were swept up in something that had previously existed for them only in the newspaper, something that carried them across an ocean to fight with and against soldiers from distant, exotic places, some of which they'd never even heard of; people who, having triumphed, came home and quietly set about trying to rebuild their lives. And were forgotten.

Most of all, it is about how much of that we can still find, and see, and hear, and touch, if we just open our eyes and understand where, and how, to look. Because it really is everywhere — even now that the last of the doughboys have left us.

The Last of the Doughboys

1

Wolves on the Battlefield

I'LL ADMIT: I was nervous. How do you talk to a 107-year-old man?

And I'll admit: After that day — July 19, 2003 — I interviewed many more World War I veterans, men and women ranging in age from 101 to 113 years old, and every single time I was nervous beforehand. But never as nervous as I was that first time.

I had never met anyone that old before. I didn't even know anyone who had. I had no idea what to expect.

Well, that's not quite true; I had a few ideas, all of which turned out to be wrong. For instance, for some reason I thought a 107-year-old man would live in a 107-year-old house filled with 107-year-old things. But that day, as I turned onto Anthony Pierro's street in Swampscott, Massachusetts — a North Shore suburb of Boston — I could see right away that there weren't any houses there even half that old. And his was downright modern. Strange, I mused: A man could be born in 1896 and yet live in a house with central heat and air conditioning, high-definition satellite television, and broadband Internet access.

"His" house was really his nephew Rick's. Rick Pierro's father, Nicholas, was Anthony's baby brother. Nicholas was ninety-four.

I didn't even know what a 107-year-old man might look like. In my mind I tried to add twenty-five years to the octogenarians I knew already, but I just couldn't summon up such an image. The octogenarians I knew were spry and sharp, for the most part, but they also looked pretty old. Maybe they'd lived too hard and breathed in too much dirty Manhattan air, but I didn't think any of their bodies could take on another quarter century without crumbling to dust.

Yet here was a man who could have been their father. I ran through a history-buff exercise in my head: Born in 1896. In 1896, Grover Cleveland was president. William Jennings Bryan ran to succeed him. Utah was admitted to the Union as the forty-fifth state. The Wright brothers were still tinkering around with bicycles. George Burns was born. The tallest building in the world was eighteen stories high. . . .

I had carried on like this right up until I pulled onto the street and took notice of the modern houses.

Rick Pierro answered the door, shook my hand, and led me into the living room, where another man sat upright, dozing on the couch; completely bald, he wore a bright green golf shirt under a dark blue cardigan sweater. Tortoiseshell eyeglasses perched on the bridge of his nose. Rick walked over to him, placed his hand gently on the man's shoulder, and leaned over to his ear. "Uncle!" he said loudly, rubbing the sleeping man's shoulder. "Uncle! This man's here to see you!"

The man opened his eyes, waited a moment for them to come into focus, looked at his nephew, then at me, then at his nephew again. "What?" he asked.

"This man came all the way here from New York to see you!"

Anthony Pierro turned to me again and smiled faintly. He looked about twenty-five years younger than I knew he was. "Hello," he said, nodding his head, the same head that, in the distant past, he had tucked under his arms during a particularly severe artillery barrage, so that he might survive the day, and the war, and another eighty-five years.

When the French government was handing out all those Légions d'Honneur in 1998 and 1999, somehow they missed Anthony Pierro. Actually, the oversight was his; the French invited American World War I veterans to apply for the award, and while they did everything they could to get the word out, working with both government agencies and private organizations, the ultimate responsibility rested upon the veterans themselves. They had to apply for it, had to prove that they had served on French soil before the armistice and that they had not acquired a criminal record since then. Anthony Pierro certainly qualified, yet for some reason he hadn't applied.

But in early 2003, someone at a local veterans' organization discovered the oversight and contacted the French Embassy, which hadn't awarded any World War I Légions d'Honneur in a few years and hadn't expected to award any more. Delighted, the embassy dispatched an attaché up to Swampscott, staged a little ceremony, and presented France's premier honor to a man who was one of the last living participants in what is arguably the worst thing that has ever happened there. A reporter wrote the affair up for a local weekly newspaper; a couple of months later, I came upon this article and hurriedly reached for the telephone.

In several years of interviewing extremely old men and women, my routine scarcely changed. I would show up at the subject's home or apartment or room and introduce myself to them and their child or grandchild or niece or nephew or old family friend or caregiver. Immediately after that, I would start setting up, a process that involved figuring out where the subject and I would sit; opening as many blinds, and turning on as many lights, as possible; unfolding and positioning a tripod; and fixing a mini DV camcorder to it. (For the first half-dozen or so interviews, until I came to trust my camcorder, I also set up a regular analog tape recorder, complete with two handheld microphones, and ran it simultaneously.) When everything was in place, I sat down, pressed the record button, announced the date and the location, and, every single time, started with the same question.

"What's your name?"

"My name?" this particular 107-year-old man said in response. "Well, it's a simple name: Anthony Pierro." He spoke these last two words with strength and clarity and pride, stressing every syllable of his surname equally. I laughed softly, in wonder at the whole thing.

"Where were you born?" I asked.

"I was born in Italy," he said. "Forenza, Provincia di Potenza."

"And what day were you born?"

"Ahh," he said, shaking his head in exasperation. "Doggone if I can remember."

"February fifteen," his nephew called out. "Eighteen ninety-six."

"Eighteen ninety-six?" I said.

"That's what he says," Anthony Pierro replied. "He knows more than I do."

· · ·

One thing you quickly learn in doing this kind of research is that for most of human history, record keeping has been neither an art nor a science but merely something that most people didn't want to be bothered with. We assume, for instance, that for every living person — or at least, for every living person in an industrialized country — there is a birth certificate. This, however, is not true, and in 1896 it was quite far from true. Back then, there was no centralized, standard method of recording births; how your birth was recorded — if it was recorded at all — was determined by where you lived, who your parents were, and quite possibly what church they attended. The state of Louisiana, for example, didn't start keeping birth records — or, for that matter, death records — until 1918; and since very few towns or parishes in Louisiana recorded them, either, if you want to find or confirm a specific date of birth for someone born in Louisiana before 1918, your best bet would be to hope that they were a baptized Catholic, since Catholic churches in Louisiana typically (though not always) listed a date of birth on their certificates of baptism, and typically (though not always) kept a copy of those certificates for their records. Of course, sometimes those churches moved and in the process misplaced or lost or discarded their old records, and sometimes those churches and everything in them burned to the ground or washed away in floods or just crumbled with age. And sometimes those certificates didn't get lost or tossed out or burned up but simply fell apart or faded over the decades to the point where they appeared to be merely blank pages.

In 1896, few of the nation's forty-five states — very few — recorded all births within their borders. If you weren't in one of them, maybe your county or your city or town did, though probably not; and maybe your church did somewhere, though again, the odds are against it. Maybe your parents recorded it in the family Bible, if they had one. If they didn't — and if their church or town or county or state didn't record it, either — well, then, everyone just did their best to remember what day of what month of what year you were born on, at least until they could tell you and you could assume the burden of remembering for yourself. I like to think that they (and you) usually did a pretty good job, although sometimes one has to wonder. When I was a child, I believed, as did everyone else in my family, that my paternal grandmother had been born in Stamford, Connecticut, on December 23,

1899. But after she died, in 1990, someone managed to dig up a birth certificate — apparently Stamford, Connecticut, did keep these records back then — and we discovered, to our astonishment, that she was actually born in 1898. On December 26.

In other words: It's all a mess. And Italy certainly wasn't any better in 1896, at least not as far as record keeping is concerned. So it's understandable that Anthony Pierro might be confused about his own birthday. His brother and nephew believed he was born on February 15, 1896. Other researchers have claimed it was February 12, or 17, or 22 of that year. No one, though, disputes that he was born Antonio Pierro in Forenza, Italy, in February, 1896.

Italy had only become a unified nation in 1873; though it had a glorious distant past, in 1896 it was, like the United States, a largely rural, agricultural country with pronounced regional divisions. It was a center of the arts, of course; the same month that Antonio Pierro was born in Forenza, Giacomo Puccini premiered his grand opera *La Bohème* at the Teatro Regio in Turin. But Turin was a different Italy than Forenza. It was industrial, cosmopolitan, rich. In Italy, it was the exception. Forenza — rural, agricultural, poor — was the rule. It was also, like thousands of other poor towns throughout Italy and the rest of southern and eastern Europe, increasingly sending its own off to America. One of them was Antonio Pierro's father, Rocco. Or, as his son always said the name, even when he was well over a century old: "Rrrrocco!"

Like most people in Forenza, Rocco Pierro worked the land, but it was a hard living, and at some point, most likely after his son Antonio was born, he discovered that he could earn more for himself and his family by working someone else's land, if he were willing to travel — to America. Which he did. As his sons and grandson explained it to me more than a century later, Rocco Pierro came to Massachusetts and found work as a landscaper for affluent Yankee families in Swampscott. I say "came to Massachusetts" rather than "immigrated" because he didn't immigrate, not really — at least not until decades after he first arrived. Many immigrants back then came to America not to stay forever but to work good jobs, save their pay, and ultimately return home with a healthy bankroll. Rocco Pierro did, too — except, unlike most, he did it *every year*. As Rick Pierro explained it to me, once a year his grandfather would leave Swampscott, return to his wife and children in Forenza, tend to his affairs there, and, after a certain amount of time — typically a month or so — depart once again for Swampscott, leaving behind those same children and that same wife, who was invariably, at the end of one of those annual visits, pregnant. "Between children," his son Anthony recalled, "having children, you know, he used to come here. Load up with all kinds of money that he had earned. And he'd come back. When that money was gone, he'd come back here again. Honestly, he was back and forth, back and forth. Every child. Between children."

No one's sure exactly when Rocco Pierro started his annual transatlantic commute, but in 1914, Antonio, now eighteen, made the trip with his father and, not having started a family of his own yet, stayed. As it happened, his timing was good: While he was getting settled in to America, Europe was collapsing into the biggest war it had ever seen. Italy managed to stay out of it for eight months or so, until the Allies lured the Italians into it by promising them several Austro-Hungarian provinces once that old empire was defeated and dismantled. There was a good bit of fighting in Italy — at one point, the Austrians made it almost to Venice — but it never got close to Forenza. And it never got close to Antonio Pierro, safely across the ocean, mowing lawns and pruning shrubs in Swampscott.

Until, that is, America entered the war and decided that, though he'd only been here a few years and wasn't yet a citizen, they needed him anyway. They made it easy for him, too; he didn't even have to make a trip down to the local recruiter's office. "I didn't have to do anything," he told me. "They just drafted me in." He was twenty-one years old, the minimum age for Selective Service in 1917.

He was sent to boot camp at Camp Gordon, in Georgia, where he learned to play checkers and was assigned to an artillery unit. Someone discovered that he was good with horses; in Italy, he recalled, "I loved the horses. Whenever I had a chance I'd take a horse and go to the public forest and get a load of wood for the people." So they made him an orderly to a lieutenant. Many artillery units had been recently converted from old cavalry units, and officers were still mounted. As an orderly, Private Pierro was responsible for taking care of the lieutenant's horse. They gave him a horse, too, so he could keep up. He liked the work. "I used to mount the horse like a monkey," he said with a chuckle. "I used to hop on a horse, no problem at all. Right from the ground up."

Horses run through just about all of Anthony Pierro's memories of the war. If you ever need a quick way to remind yourself how long ago the First World War happened, and how much the world has changed since then, think of this: There were still horses everywhere, carrying scouts, towing heavy artillery from place to place, pulling supply wagons. By the next big war they were all but gone. (The Polish cavalry famously squared off against the mechanized Nazi *Wehrmacht* in the opening hours of that war; it did not fare well.) But in World War I, horses were essential. And they weren't sheltered, either, kept far behind the lines and consigned to light work. They were in the thick of it, often getting killed — and even, occasionally, doing the killing. "Some of them were wild," Anthony Pierro recalled. "And the city kids, they didn't know anything about a horse or anything. No, they couldn't even mount a horse. They had to crawl up there like a cat." This is not a good way to approach a horse, especially one that has already been rendered skittish by a steady diet of bursting shells. "[If] he can't see you, or who it is — he'll kick you." One city kid in Private Pierro's unit learned this lesson too late. "He goes and puts his hands on the back part of the horse," Mr. Pierro recalled. "The horse didn't see him in the front, so, woo, he killed him. So, whenever you want to caress a horse, you go at the neck and then stay there. Yeah, animals are — I learned a lesson."

Much more typically, though, horses were the casualties. A boat full of them, part of the convoy that carried Private Pierro and thousands of other American soldiers across the Atlantic, was sunk by a bomb-dropping German airplane (or "aeroplane," as flying machines were then called) as it approached the French coast. (It was, apparently, a very large convoy: "A whole division went [over] together," he recalled. "It looked like a village.") And one time, in France, when he was walking up a road behind a horse, an H.E. (high explosive) shell came screaming in and burst in front of them; the horse was killed, but its body shielded Private Pierro from the explosion and shrapnel, saving his life. "Oh, well," he told me, "the horses, they got killed, yeah. But the only thing that we could do is dig a trench and bury them. Because leaving them outside, they would have had wolves eating it up." Yes: wolves on the battlefield.

Mr. Pierro didn't just tend to horses in France. "I was a driver," he told me. "I rode a horse attached to the carriage, to take the supply around." What he didn't tell me was that he would ride up to the front lines with a wagon loaded with supplies, drop them off with the troops, and ride back with another load: the bodies of slain infantrymen. I learned that part of the story much later, by which time I was no longer surprised that someone might leave it out in the retelling. Some memories, I had since learned, don't grow easier to recount even with the passage of eighty-five years.

In fact, though his nephew later confirmed that his uncle had, indeed, told him in the past that he had often carried bodies back from the front lines, when I spoke to Anthony Pierro in 2003, he remembered it differently. "We didn't take no bodies," he told me. "We buried them in the—at the front line. Wherever they died, that's where we dug a hole and buried his body. Yeah. And the—the cross would be in the cemetery, but the body would be where he died." However he remembered it, disposing of dead bodies was a regular event.

And there were a lot of them. In World War I, artillery was responsible for more deaths than anything else, more than bullets and bayonets, more than tanks and aeroplanes, more than poison gas and barbed wire. Naturally, this made artillery units on both sides a favorite target of the enemy, and Private Pierro frequently found himself under fire. "The shells used to come pretty often," he said. "That's terrific. Shells are coming your way, and you don't know where to duck." Fortunately, soldiers would often be alerted that a barrage was about to begin by the sight of an enemy aeroplane overhead. "They'd send a plane to locate the enemy's [position] . . . and that's how they got the distance to shoot . . . oh, they'd kill quite a few soldiers."

The sound of an aeroplane overhead may have filled doughboys with dread, but at least it served as a warning to take cover, as did the noise the shells made when they were coming in. "They used to make a whistle when the shell was flying," Mr. Pierro recalled, and whistled himself to mimic the sound. "They went *weeeeeee, ba-BOOM!* when it hit the ground and exploded." It was such a regular event that some soldiers developed their own routines in response.

"I had one tree — I used to duck underneath that tree," Mr. Pierro told me. And one day, like that unfortunate horse, this tree saved his life. "I was lucky," he said. "I was ducking underneath a tree. It got hit. But it didn't — the shell didn't explode." He turned his gaze toward the ceiling and said, in the voice of a twenty-two-year-old private: "Oh, boy. Thank you, God."

The incoming shell had gotten caught in the tree's branches; if it had hit the trunk, or passed through and hit the ground below, it would have killed him. But it didn't. "That's what saved me," he told me. "It was a tree. The shell landed in the tree. And it didn't explode."

Private Pierro knew how lucky he was; he immediately ran to find his captain, hunkering down in a dugout, and told him the story. The captain just looked at Private Pierro and said: "Bring it over."

It: the unexploded shell. Anthony Pierro couldn't believe what he was hearing, but an order is an order. "So I brung it over," he recalled. He ran back to that tree, climbed up, retrieved the unexploded shell, and carried it — "oh, boy, nice and easy; if the thing went off, I wouldn't be here, telling you" — to the captain's dugout.

The captain, seeing the private return to the dugout carrying a live shell, must have been just as stunned as the private had been when the captain had ordered him to fetch it from the tree; perhaps the order had merely been a joke that was just a shade too subtle. "Here's the shell," Pierro said to the wide-eyed captain. The captain's response, he recalled, was to cry: "Get it out of here! Take it away from here!"

"Where do you want to put it?" the private asked.

"Just lay it down there!" the captain replied, pointing at a spot far away.

And eighty-five years later, the private added: "Oh, boy."

And this coda: "You know, a foolish thing to do. Pick it up from the tree where it was stuck."

Although he had a couple of close brushes with death, the war stories Anthony Pierro returned to most frequently and with the most fondness that day were not tales of combat, and they didn't take place anywhere near the front. There was the time, for instance, when, he said, on his way over to France, his unit passed through England and marched in parade for a special audience. "The king and the queen," he recalled. "They were way up on the balcony while we were passing by." Someone barked out an order: *Eyes right!* "So, you march and you look at the king and the queen," he said.

And then there was Madeleine. Private Pierro met her when he was stationed in Bordeaux after the armistice, and he confirmed, eighty-five years later, that she was very pretty and that they would go dancing "every night." He became close with her parents, too. "I used to go to their house," he said. "They had some goodies, and they put it out." French fathers typically sought to keep their daughters clear of soldiers — especially Americans, who had been through less of the war and were very far from home, two factors that helped give them a reputation of being a bit wilder than French or British troops — but Anthony Pierro found a way to win over Madeleine's father: "I used to bring him a bottle of wine . . . cigarettes, too. He would — he used to smoke, but it was hard to get the stuff at the store." He smiled at the memory. "Oh, I got along fine," he explained. But he got along best with Madeleine. "We used to dance, and this girl, Madeleine, every night, we'd go out dancing," he recalled. "What else there was?"

Actually, in most fair-sized towns in France, including Bordeaux, there was quite a lot else. While Private Pierro's relationship with Madeleine was mostly innocent, the same could not be said of the dance-halls they frequented. On street level, everything looked normal, if a bit empty — a dance floor, maybe a small band or a man and a piano or perhaps just a gramophone, and a girl or two standing around, waiting for a dance with a soldier; but upstairs, almost always, was a bordello. "That's the business," Pierro explained. "One girl was down on the main floor. Upstairs were the other girls." He smiled as he recalled the phrase that the downstairs girls had learned and repeated often: "Upstairs, two dollars."

"And did you go up?" Rick asked him, already knowing the answer; they had had this conversation many times before.

"No," his uncle replied. "I was afraid to get sick." He thought again about the woman who worked downstairs, on the dance floor. "She had a skirt up to here. Yeah, she was sending the business from down the main floor upstairs. 'Upstairs, two dollars.'"

Two dollars was not an insignificant sum to an enlisted man in the American Expeditionary Forces, or AEF, in 1918, but these places did a brisk business, anyway — so brisk, in fact, that the matter became a cause for alarm, both in the Army and on the Home Front, where a new book titled *First Call: Guideposts to Berlin* was in wide circulation; its author, an American returned from serving in France, intended *First Call* as a primer on what newly minted soldiers, future soldiers, and their loved ones back home might expect from the war. In chapter 2, "For the Mothers," the author, anticipating that the expression "Upstairs, two dollars" might soon work its way back to the Home Front, writes:

> I wish to impress upon you the fact that there is certain propaganda in the United States (if its source is traced it will be found that it is of pro-German origin), spreading the report that our boys, when they reach France, will have ample opportunity to mingle with women of questionable character. Nowhere in the world is a stronger line drawn between soldiers and this class of women than in France. In fact, when soldiers are quartered in cities, towns or villages, it is a court-martial offense for them to be found in certain segregated districts. This order or regulation is strictly enforced by provost guard and patrols, which constantly watch these districts and arrest all soldiers found within the prohibited zones, unless they have documentary evidence to prove that they are there on a specific military duty. So, Mothers, do not let this worry you in any way, no matter what stories to the contrary you may hear in the United States.

The author, a man of some intelligence, undoubtedly knew from his own time in France that this entreaty to the reader was bushwah of the purest form. Every soldier who'd been there would have.

"The best part of it was being in Bordeaux," Anthony Pierro said later, toward the end of our conversation. "The girls used to say, 'Upstairs, two dollars.'"

"But you didn't go upstairs," his nephew added.

"I didn't have the two dollars," the old man replied with a shrug.

• • •

On the morning of November 11, 1918, Anthony Pierro was guarding German prisoners in the Argonne Forest—"a whole bunch of them, we had them all fenced in"—when a messenger brought the news: The war was over. "Everybody was dancing," Mr. Pierro recalled. "Hurray!" And then: "Who won? Who won?"

Eventually Private Pierro sailed back home again, arriving in New York on May 9, 1919, 356 days after he'd sailed off for France. Six days after his return, he was discharged at Camp Dix, New Jersey. He returned to Swampscott and went back to work, landscaping for the same people he had left when he was drafted, a family named Waters. He got married and went to work at a shoe factory, trimming leather edges; then for a brother-in-law in the service department of a Pontiac dealership, where he did everything from straightening car frames to painting pinstripes; then at General Electric, where he worked on prototypes of engines for fighter planes. At some point, facing anti-Italian prejudice, he changed his last name to "Pierre" (anti-French prejudice, apparently, was less acute at the time), but later changed it back. He never had children. "My wife's parents had ten children," he told me ruefully, "and she couldn't have any. Just—just couldn't have any. That's all." He retired in 1961. She died in 1964. Thirty-nine years later, we met.

"Why do you think you've lived so long?" I asked him. "Do you have a secret?"

"No secret about it," he replied. "Just healthy, and—you live. Something bothers you, you better get rid of it if you can."

"Other than hard of hearing, he takes no medication, prescribed medication," his nephew said. "I give him Tylenol for his arthritis, and two multivitamin pills a day. That's it. Every morning, he gets up and takes—he has an egg for breakfast, toast. He eats like a horse. Uses a lot of salt. He lived by himself until he was a hundred."

We talked a bit more, and then I turned off the camera and tape recorder and packed them up. Rick Pierro went off to find a copy of his uncle's discharge papers; his uncle appeared to be dozing upright on the couch. I looked over some of the old pictures Rick had dug out in anticipation of my visit. There was one of Anthony Pierro in his uniform in 1918; he was handsome—really handsome, what they used to call matinee-idol handsome. I looked at the man on the couch, then back at the picture. Several times.

Behind me, propped up on a shelf, was a large framed color photograph of a rustic town spread out in shades of brown and white and green across a rocky hill. I walked over to it and examined it closely; the picture was taken at a distance, so the whole town was visible, although I couldn't discern any people, animals, or even cars, which made me feel like I was looking at a scale model. I had an idea of what it was.

"That's Forenza," said a voice right behind me. Anthony Pierro, now very much awake, raised his hand and touched a finger to the glass, pointing out the house where he had lived a century earlier, and the church he had attended as a child. That moment was, I sensed, the closest he had felt that morning to his distant past. There were a few points, during our conversation, when he punctuated a war story with phrases like "I hope it will never happen again" and "It wasn't worth it," but for the most part, whether he was talking about dancing with Madeleine or that shell hitting the tree or his wife's infertility, his mood stayed the same, calm and detached, with faint hints of wonder or amusement here and there. But standing there next to me, softly pressing his finger to that glass, gazing through spectacles at the home he'd left forever at eighteen, he seemed to change just a little bit, to soften just enough for me to see a hint of that eighteen-year-old's flame inside a 107-year-old body. He was very, very old, but he was still a man, the same man who had done all those things so long ago.

Rick returned with the discharge papers. I was surprised at how much information one double-sided sheet contained, recorded in beautiful penmanship — not simply name, rank, serial number, age at enlistment, height (5'4½"), eye color (brown), hair color (dark), and complexion (medium), but occupation ("Laborer"), unit (Battery "E" of the 320th Field Artillery), the date and location of his enlistment (October 4, 1917, Swampscott, Massachusetts), his level of marksmanship ("Not Qualified") and horsemanship ("Not Mounted" — I imagined the anonymous clerk hadn't actually asked Private Pierro about that), the dates of his typhoid vaccines, his marital status, his character ("Excellent"), and the dates of his departure, return, and discharge.

In the middle of the back side of the paper was an entry, with three blank lines, for "battles, engagements, skirmishes, expeditions." In this case, the clerk had to use all three lines:

Oise-Aisne, from August 21, 1918 to September 11, 1918
St. Mihiel, from September 12, 1918 to September 16, 1918
Meuse-Argonne, from September 26, 1918 to November 11, 1918

I couldn't believe it. These were three of the largest battles in which Americans had fought in that war; in the last of them, the Meuse-Argonne Offensive, more than twenty-six thousand Americans had been killed. Private Anthony Pierro had spent much of the final three months of the war under terrible fire. And yet, the war he'd spoken of had presented only random and anecdotal dangers — shells, and bullets, and kicking horses. "It's a miserable life," he said of the Army at one point, explaining: "You can't do anything . . . on your own. They tell you what to do." If you'd polled the men of Battery E of the 320th Field Artillery in the fall of 1918, I imagine that "being told what to do" would have fallen near the bottom of their list of complaints, well below getting bombarded and gassed, scurrying for cover in the dark, sleeping in the mud, dodging rats and lice, burying your dead comrades, literally keeping the wolves at bay, and, of course, army food. I wonder what Private Pierro would have said, though. It seems to me entirely possible that he would have given the same answer in 1918 as he did in 2003. I don't know if he really was able to shut out the fear, the terror, the sense that a horrible death could literally fall upon you from the sky at any moment, or if he'd felt it at the time but was somehow able to leave it behind when he sailed for home, and never let it find him again. Whichever it was, I am sure it was part of something greater within him, an equanimity that helped him make it to the age of 107.

He and Rick both showed me to the door. Walking to my car, I heard something, turned, and saw Anthony Pierro standing on the porch, alone. He was waving to me and calling out: "Adios, amigos! Adios, amigos!"

As I drove off, I saw in my rearview mirror that he was still waving. And I thought: *I will probably never see this man again.*

2

Over the Top

THE AUTHOR OF *First Call*, the book that offered the cheerful (or depressing, depending upon your perspective) assessment of the state of vice in France, was a man named Arthur Guy Empey. *First Call* was actually Empey's second book, and that one passage tells you pretty much all you need to know about it. His first book, though — *Over the Top* — well, now, that one was really something.

Almost from the moment it was published, in June, 1917, *Over the Top* was a tremendous success. In its March, 1918, issue, *The Bookman*, a trade journal for the publishing industry, reported that the book "has been selling at the rate of two hundred and fifty copies every business hour since its publication last June." If you do the math, you come up with the figure of nearly four hundred thousand copies in print at that point — this at a time when the population of the United States was less than a third of what it is today, and literacy rates were significantly lower, too. By the time the war ended that autumn, more than a million copies of *Over the Top* were in print. If you want to know what one book almost all Americans were reading back in 1917 and 1918, what single volume most informed their vision of what that war was really like for the men in the trenches of France, this is it. It shares, in a voice that even today sounds surprisingly modern, a tale that most returning soldiers did not care to.

Writers love to grouse about the undeserved success of best-selling authors, but *Over the Top* is, in fact, a wonderful book — interesting, compelling, well written, and even, in spots, very funny. Still, as is so often the case, its success was due, in large part, to good timing: It was published just two months after America entered the war, and weeks after Congress passed the Selective Service Act, effectively establishing the first draft since the Civil War. Americans were excited, apprehensive, and above all hungry to learn about this war they were now in. Empey, as it happened, was the man to feed that hunger. A fellow American, he'd lost patience when the sinking of the *Lusitania* did not propel his country into the war, so he made his way over to England, convinced the British Army to let him enlist, shipped out for France, saw a good bit of action in the trenches, and was badly wounded at the Somme, so badly that he was not expected to live. But he did live, and was eventually discharged and shipped back home, where he got to work on a book about his experiences. He didn't plan the timing of its release, but if he had he certainly couldn't have done any better. The convergence linked Arthur Guy Empey with the Great War in the minds of millions of Americans; and eventually, when that war was forgotten, he was, too.

In 1917, when *Over the Top* began to sell, Empey gave some newspaper interviews, and the few that survive and can be found today are among the only sources of any information about his early life. To call them "interviews," though, takes a good bit on faith, as they were all printed as soliloquies, and you get the sense, in reading them, that Empey (or perhaps a publicist) wrote them in full beforehand and just sent them out to be published as they were. They certainly serve to help create the legend he wished to proliferate. "When I first opened my eyes, I breathed the air of the Rockies," he declares. "It is with pride that I state that I am a pure, unadulterated American."

He was born on December 11, 1883, in Ogden, Utah, and his adventurous spirit, he claims, first manifested itself when he was four; the family was then living in Cheyenne, Wyoming. "I took it into my head to explore the sandhills," he tells us, "and after a frantic twelve-hour search by my parents, was brought back to the fold." His parents then put up a locked gate, which did manage to keep him in, as did the fact that, on several occasions, his father caught him trying to pick the lock, and, in the splendid parlance of the day, "applied the slipper" to his son. Thus was young Empey's wanderlust stifled, or perhaps merely channeled through that of his family, which eventually moved to Virginia, then Canada, then New York. Empey enrolled in Brooklyn's Manual Training High School, where he played left halfback on the football team ("the most worthy thing I did in high school"), and where his adventurousness resurfaced. "While in high school I took a notion to go to sea," he declares. "I ran away and shipped as second cook on the tramp steamer *Cuzco*." Nearly seven months later, he tells us, having "put in at twenty-six different ports and peeled eleven million barrels of 'spuds,'" he returned to New York with "a monkey, a parrot and about $8 in silver."

Empey was only home for a couple of weeks before boredom drove him to join Brooklyn's 47th National Guard Regiment, where, he says, he made sergeant before choosing to return to sea, this time with the United States Navy. He was assigned to "the USS *Missouri, or Misery, as we called her.*" It was an ill-fated post: The *Missouri* rammed and nearly sank another American battleship in Guantánamo Bay, Cuba, and later, on April 13, 1904, caught fire during target practice. Thirty-six sailors were killed; "I barely escaped with my life," Empey declares.

So he returned to the Army, this time to the 12th United States Cavalry; records show he enlisted on July 10, 1905, giving his height as five feet four and a half inches, and his occupation as "lifeguard." He was, he tells us, eventually promoted to the rank of sergeant major, although the highlight of his service in the 12th was giving "exhibitions of rough riding at the Jamestown exposition" of 1907. On July 15, 1908, he reenlisted, this time with the 11th United States Cavalry — the 1910 census lists him as a corporal stationed at Fort Oglethorpe, Georgia — but on July 2, 1910, the record shows, he went absent without leave, or AWOL (the original designation — desertion — is crossed out on the form), surrendering to military authorities thirteen days later. He was ultimately discharged at San Antonio on July 25, 1911, presumably honorably; the record notes him as "reformed." Empey understandably omits this episode from his account of his time with the 11th, stating only that he "did duty with them on the Mexican border during the trouble in 1911." There was a lot of "trouble" along the border in those days; a few years later, General John J. Pershing would lead his own troops across it in search of Mexican revolutionary Pancho Villa, only to return empty-handed.

By his own account, Empey served a total of six years in the cavalry. Upon discharge, he returned to New York, where he joined a mounted

National Guard unit, and then, when his term of service expired, joined another. He also, depending upon which account you read, "started in business for myself" (business unspecified) or went to work for "a well-known detective agency" (job title unspecified). But with the coming of the war, his wanderlust apparently returned. Records show that he applied for a passport on October 18, 1915, in New York, now listing his height as five feet five, his hair and eyes as brown, his nose as straight, his forehead as high, mouth large, chin square, complexion dark. He gives his occupation as "private investigator," and claims he wishes to travel abroad — specifically, to France and England — for the purpose of "legal investigations." He does not confirm or even mention any of this in his later accounts; rather, he tells us: "I thought I would take a peep at France, so I shipped on the horse ship *La Gascogne* as assistant veterinarian, and after ducking the submarines we landed thirteen hundred horses for the French artillery at Bordeaux, France." He returned right home, he says, but shortly after his arrival, while walking down Broadway, "I heard a German pass the remark about the Americans being too proud to fight, so I went to London and joined the British army."

I won't speculate on how much of this autobiography is factual, except to note that in *Over the Top*, Empey tells a different version of the story of how he came to enlist. He was working in Jersey City, he writes, when word came into his office of the sinking of the *Lusitania*. He and his office-mate, a lieutenant in the New Jersey National Guard, immediately break out the muster rolls, expecting a declaration of war to come at any moment. "We busied ourselves till late in the evening," he recalls, "writing out emergency telegrams for the men to report when the call should come from Washington." But the call never came. "Months passed," he writes, "the telegrams lying handy, but covered with dust"; eventually, he and the lieutenant threw them away. "He was squirming in his chair and I felt depressed and uneasy," Empey confesses. And then:

> The telephone rang and I answered it. It was a business call for me requesting my services for an out-of-town assignment. Business was not very good, so this was very welcome. After listening to the proposition, I seemed to be swayed by a peculiarly strong force within me,

and answered, "I am sorry that I cannot accept your offer, but I am leaving for England next week," and hung up the receiver. The Lieutenant swung around in his chair, and stared at me in astonishment. A sinking sensation came over me, but I defiantly answered his look with, "Well, it's so. I am going." And I went.

Arthur Guy Empey was by no means the first American to join the fight. Since the war had begun in Europe in 1914, American citizens had been sailing off to England, or making their way up to Canada, to get around their own country's neutrality and get in their own shot at the Kaiser. (Or possibly to fight *for* the Kaiser, though I've never read about any such men.) Empey, though, writes as if he were the only one, and the early sections of *Over the Top* are filled with comic scenes of Englishmen encountering a Yank for the very first time and not knowing quite what to make of him. He has difficulty getting someone to let him enlist, more difficulty getting someone to give him something to do, more difficulty still getting anyone to agree that he should be allowed to fight. And when at last he does manage to get himself sent to training camp, misunderstandings compound misunderstandings. (He never quite tells us which unit he joined, just that they were part of the Royal Fusiliers; if you hold a magnifying glass up to the photo he includes of his arm and identification disk, though, you can make out that he was a private in the Machine Gun Company of the 167th Brigade, 56th Division.) They find his brand of English incomprehensible, and we quickly come to understand, by way of his phonetically rendered cockney accents — you could call it a bad movie brogue, but movies were still silent then — that the feeling is mutual. Empey, the proud autodidact, eagerly shares what he learns regarding regulations, equipment, terminology, slang. But then he gets sent to France, and at this point the experience changes for the reader as quickly and dramatically as it did for him:

The odor from a dug-up, decomposed human body has an effect which is hard to describe. It first produces a nauseating feeling, which, especially after eating, causes vomiting. This relieves you temporarily, but soon a weakening sensation follows, which leaves you limp as a dish-rag. Your spirits are at their lowest ebb and you

feel a sort of hopeless helplessness and a mad desire to escape it all
. . . a vague horror of the awfulness of the thing and an ever-recurring
reflection that, perhaps I, sooner or later, would be in such a state.

The dead body in this instance — and there are a lot of them in *Over
the Top* — is that of a German soldier, stumbled upon by a member of
Empey's digging party when, in the darkness, he inadvertently thrusts
his pick into its lifeless chest. "One of the men fainted," Empey reports,
adding, gamely: "I was that one."

When you read something like that, the question of why Empey's
book became such a sensational bestseller just disintegrates in your
mind. But it is soon replaced by another: How did something like this
even manage to be published at all in 1917, given that the country had
just entered that same war? Because Empey wasn't just relating the
horrors of war; he was testifying to the rank stupidity of the men in
charge of waging it.

Take this description of a nighttime mission assigned to Empey and
a few others shortly after they arrived in the trenches — that is, long,
muddy ditches filled with rats and vermin and separated from the enemy's long, muddy ditches by no more than a few hundred yards of
shell-ravaged earth known, for good reason, as No Man's Land:

> All we had to do was crawl out into No Man's Land, lie on our bellies
> with our ears to the ground and listen for the tap tap of the German
> engineers or sappers who might be tunneling under No Man's Land
> to establish a mine-head beneath our trench.
>
> Of course, in our orders we were told not to be captured by Ger-
> man patrols or reconnoitering parties. Lots of breath is wasted on
> the Western Front giving silly cautions.

Ill-conceived as this assignment is, Empey and the other men do
it anyway, and without question, or at least uttered question. At one
point, lying there completely exposed, they are very nearly discovered
by a German patrol.

> A dark form suddenly loomed up in front of me, it looked as big as
> the Woolworth Building. I could hear the blood rushing through my
> veins and it sounded as loud as Niagara Falls.

Forms seemed to emerge from the darkness. There were seven of them in all. I tried to *wish* them away. I never wished harder in my life. They muttered a few words in German and melted into the blackness. I didn't stop wishing, either.

That time, everyone made it back. "The next morning I was stiff as a poker and every joint ached like a bad tooth," Empey tells us, "but I was still alive, so it did not matter."

Another night — the hard work, it seems, was always done under cover of darkness — Empey is sent out to inspect the enemy's barbed wire fence. He manages to complete this portion of the mission, but becomes disoriented while returning to his trench and nearly crawls into a German trench, instead; he is discovered, leaps to his feet, and sprints back toward his own lines. "The bullets were biting all around me," he tells us, "when bang! I ran smash into our wire." He is nearly shot by a British sentry.

Despite that, he remains quite fond of "Tommy," or the typical British soldier; he also develops a grudging but firm respect for the enemy — and even, in some cases, affection. Prussian and Bavarian units usually gave Tommy "a hot time of it," but the Saxons were, in Empey's view, much more civilized. When Saxon and English units faced each other, he writes, "both sides would sit on the parapet and carry on a conversation." They would chat genially; then, "when the Saxons were to be relieved by Prussians or Bavarians, they would yell this information across No Man's Land and Tommy would immediately tumble into his trench and keep his head down." The Saxons did the same when the English called out that they were about to be replaced by feared Irish troops. "The Boches," Empey explains, invoking a popular ethnic epithet of the day, "hate the man from Erin's Isle."

One night, Empey offers some newly captured German prisoners a drink, and is surprised when one responds, "Thank you, sir, the rum is excellent and I appreciate it, also your kindness." They strike up a conversation: "He told me his name was Carl Schmidt, of the 66th Bavarian Light infantry," Empey recounts. "That he had lived six years in New York (knew the city better than I did), had been to Coney Island and many of our ball games. He was a regular fan. I couldn't make him believe that Hans Wagner wasn't the best ballplayer in the world."

Later, after an escort comes to take the prisoners to the rear, Empey confesses: "I liked that prisoner, he was a fine fellow and had an Iron Cross, too. I advised him to keep it out of sight, or some Tommy would be sending it home to his girl in Blighty as a souvenir."

It's not all horror and drudgery and moral dilemmas. Empey writes entire chapters on the things soldiers do when they aren't dodging bullets and artillery and poison gas, or being sent on suicidal missions, or trying not to become too fond of enemy prisoners. He discusses, at some length, tea and rum, cards and dice, inspection and drills and church services and parades, a musical play he and some friends write and perform for their fellow troops at a makeshift theater "situated corner of Sand Bag Terrace and Ammo Street." They even, somehow, manage to print up elaborate playbills.

But in war, even tales that begin happily often end in tragedy. At one point, after a particularly long and hazardous spell in the trenches, Empey's unit is relieved and sent back behind the lines; then, to his great surprise and joy, he and forty other men are awarded leave time in England. They climb aboard trucks and travel overland for a couple of hours until they reach a rail station, where they wait for the train that will take them to the port of departure. When it arrives, five hours late, they are loaded onto boxcars, which take two days to reach the port. Before they can board their ship, though, they are stopped by an officer, who informs them that all leave has been canceled, and that they will have to get right back in those boxcars and return whence they came. "Beastly rotten, I know," he says by way of consolation. "If you had been three hours earlier you would have gotten away."

Empey and the others, it seems, are needed for an attack that's about to begin. "Seventeen of the forty-one will never get another chance to go on leave," he tells us. "They were killed in the attack."

That, though, is only the beginning of this awful tale. For in the attack, Empey and his machine gun company charge across No Man's Land and occupy a German trench that has already been shelled heavily. "I never saw such a mess in my life," he reports:

. . . bunches of twisted barbed wire lying about, shell-holes everywhere, trench all bashed in, parapets gone, and dead bodies, why, that ditch was full of them, theirs and ours. . . . Some were mangled horribly from our shell fire, while others were wholly or partly buried in the mud, the result of shell explosions caving in the wall of the trench. One dead German was lying on his back, with a rifle sticking straight up in the air, the bayonet of which was buried to the hilt in his chest. Across his feet lay a dead English soldier with a bullet hole in his forehead. This Tommy must have been killed just as he ran his bayonet through the German. . . .

At one point, just in the entrance to a communication trench, was a stretcher. On this stretcher a German was lying with a white bandage around his knee, near to him lay one of the stretcher-bearers, the red cross on his arm covered with mud and his helmet filled with blood and brains. Close by, sitting up against the wall of the trench, with head resting on his chest, was the other stretcher-bearer. He seemed to be alive, the posture was so natural and easy, but when I got closer, I could see a large, jagged hole in his temple. The three must have been killed by the same shell-burst.

I have only rarely come across a description of combat as graphic as this one. And I've never read anything like it from this period, a time when a certain genteel sensibility still reigned over the American consciousness. But Empey just shatters that sensibility; or at least seems entirely unaware of its existence. This passage, like many others in *Over the Top*, is more modern, in that sense, than most of what would be written on the subject for thirty or forty years afterward.

This, though, is not even Empey's most impressive accomplishment; that would have to be the fact that throughout the book, without diluting or minimizing the horror of what he sees and experiences, he manages to maintain a sense of humor and a tone just light enough to keep you from putting his book down and pouring yourself a stiff drink. To tell you the truth, I have no idea how he does it; but he does, even while telling this particular story. Taking the trench was easy, he reports, but holding it is another matter; three of his men are killed just trying to set up their machine gun. "One of the legs of the tripod was resting on the chest of a half-buried body," he recounts. And then, as if that weren't bad enough, he makes a discovery:

Three or four feet down the trench, about three feet from the ground, a foot was protruding from the earth; we knew it was a German by the black leather boot. One of our crew used that foot to hang extra bandoliers of ammunition on. This man always was a handy fellow; made use of little points that the ordinary person would overlook.

Despite being shelled and shot at throughout six straight days — all the while crouching among the unburied dead, watching "their faces become swollen and discolored," while "the stench was fierce" — Empey managed to develop a strange fixation:

What got on my nerves the most was that foot sticking out of the dirt. It seemed to me, at night, in the moonlight, to be trying to twist around. Several times this impression was so strong that I went to it and grasped it in both hands, to see if I could feel a movement.

I told this to the man who had used it for a hat-rack just before I lay down for a little nap. . . . When I woke up the foot was gone. He had cut it off with our chain saw out of the spare parts' box, and had plastered the stump over with mud.

During the next two or three days, before we were relieved, I missed that foot dreadfully, seemed as if I had suddenly lost a chum.

Empey's sense of humor comes in particularly handy when he reflects on the subject of military discipline. It was, to say the least, draconian; Jefferson Davis once famously declared that the poorest use of a soldier is to shoot him, but a half century later, the British Army still hadn't caught up with the late Confederate president. If you need another reminder of how much things have changed since World War I, consider this: Men could be, and often were, shot by their own for any number of offenses, including, but not limited to, by Empey's account, "desertion, cowardice, mutiny, giving information to the enemy, destroying or willfully wasting ammunition, looting, rape, robbing the dead, forcing a safeguard, striking a superior, etc." (In one notorious instance that came to light after the war, a cat, which had taken to scurrying back and forth between the lines in search of food, was shot as a spy by the French after some German soldiers strapped a collar, bearing a note with greetings in pidgin French, around its neck.)

And if you weren't put in front of a firing squad, you might well have ended up wishing you had been. As Empey tells us, in cases where "there is a doubt as to the willful guilt of a man who has committed an offence punishable by death" — say, if he wasted ammunition by accident, perhaps due to poor aim — he was often sentenced, instead, to spend sixty-four days in a front-line trench, ineligible for relief, and bound "to engage in all raids, working parties in No Man's Land, and every hazardous undertaking that comes along. If you live through the sixty-four days," Empey says, "you are indeed lucky." And for "repeated minor offences," one could draw what was officially known as "Field Punishment No. 1," for which, Empey recounts, "a man is spread eagled on a limber wheel, two hours a day, for twenty-one days" — and also, in what seems like an afterthought, restricted to a diet of water, hard biscuits, and something called "bully beef." The unofficial term for Field Punishment No. 1 was "crucifixion," and the British, it seems, doled it out about as liberally as the Romans had.

Executions were shockingly common, too, especially for the crime of "cowardice," whose broad definition embraced everything from hesitating before going "over the top" — that is, climbing up out of a trench and charging into No Man's Land — to what, in the next war, would come to be regarded as "shell shock." In the 1980s, what had once been a capital offense was officially reclassified as posttraumatic stress disorder; but it wasn't until 2006 that the British Army began apologizing to the descendants of soldiers executed for a transgression that is now universally recognized as a psychiatric syndrome.

That was nine decades too late for Arthur Guy Empey, who was, as he writes, once awakened at 2:00 a.m. by a regimental sergeant major, with orders for the sleeping man to get dressed and equipped and, without a word, follow him out into the rainy night. Empey is led to a barn and told to sit there in silence. There are men there already, sitting in the darkness, and while they wait quietly, more are led in, until there are a dozen of them in all, none of whom Empey recognizes. They are then led out and marched for an hour until they find themselves in a courtyard, standing before four stacks of rifles. "Men, you are here on a very solemn duty," an officer tells them. "You have been selected as a firing squad for the execution of a soldier, who, having been found guilty of a grievous crime against King and Country, has been regularly and duly tried and sentenced to be shot at 3:28 a.m. this date." The officer informs the firing squad that one of the twelve rifles has a blank cartridge in it, but that "every man is expected to do his duty and fire to kill."

"My heart was of lead and my knees shook," Empey confesses. "After standing at 'Attention' for what seemed like a week, though in reality it could not have been over five minutes," the men hear whispers and footsteps, and then, against a far wall, Empey spots "a dark form with a white square pinned on its breast. We were supposed to aim at this square." Empey, though, decides to aim at a white spot on the wall, instead. When he fires, he tells us, "I could see the splinters fly. Someone else had received the rifle containing the blank cartridge, but my mind was at ease, there was no blood of a Tommy on my hands." When it is all over, the men are ordered to "return, alone, to your respective companies, and remember, no talking about this affair, or else it will go hard with the guilty ones."

"We needed no urging to get away," Empey says. He never learns the dead man's name, nor the offense for which he was sentenced to die; and, as a compassionate gesture, the army that executed the unfortunate soldier will tell his family even less. "In the public casualty lists," Empey tells us, "his name will appear under the caption 'Accidentally Killed,' or 'Died.'"

And perhaps, in the end, he wasn't much worse off than his friends still in the trenches; odds were good they would get shot, too, or shelled, or gassed, or find some other way to die before they could make it back home. In one of the finest memoirs of that war, Robert Graves's *Good-Bye to All That* (first published in 1929), almost every fellow soldier Graves mentions somewhere — officers and enlisted men, aristocrats and commoners, in scores of anecdotes that occupy pages or merely half a sentence — is, in the end, killed at the front. It is so common an experience, really, that at a certain point it starts to feel like Graves only mentions their deaths as a way to punctuate the end of a sentence; you get the sense that everyone who served in the trenches long enough arrived at the understanding that he would probably not live to see the war's end. Graves, a lieutenant in the British Army, barely did himself; he was wounded so badly at the Somme that he was not expected to live, and his colonel wrote his parents and told them he had died. It was only after his aunt accidentally came across him while visiting someone else at the hospital where he was recovering that Graves's family discovered the error.

The Somme lasted four months and claimed more than a million casualties. Nearly twenty thousand British soldiers were killed on the first day alone, their army's worst day in history. The battle had been planned by the Allies for months, and the buildup was massive. Empey describes a "never-ending stream of men, supplies, ammunition and guns pouring into the British lines." When massive howitzers would pass, he writes, "a flush of pride would mount to my face, because I could plainly read on the name plate, 'Made in the U.S.A.,' and I would remember that if I wore a name plate it would also read, 'Made in the U.S.A.' Then I would stop to think how thin and straggly that mighty stream would be if all the 'Made in the U.S.A.' parts of it were withdrawn."

Ten hours before the battle promptly commenced, at 7:30 a.m. on July 1, 1916, Empey and nineteen other men volunteered for a nighttime mission: They were to sneak across No Man's Land, raid an enemy trench at a certain point in their front line, snatch up a couple of German soldiers, and bring them back to British lines, where the Germans would be interrogated for intelligence purposes. Specifically, the British command hoped to learn the precise location of a couple of German machine guns that British artillery had failed to silence. HQ presented it as a straightforward exercise, but Empey wasn't so sure: "I had a funny sinking sensation in my stomach, and my tin hat felt as if it weighed about a ton," he tells us. His commander's instructions didn't do much to raise his spirits:

"Take off your identification disks, strip your uniforms of all numerals, insignia, etc., leave your papers with your captains, because I don't want the Boches to know what regiments are against them . . . and I don't want any of you to be taken alive. What I want is two prisoners and if I get them I have a way which will make them divulge all necessary information as to their guns. You have your choice of two weapons — you may carry your 'persuaders' or your knuckle knives." . . .

A persuader is Tommy's nickname for a club. . . . It is about two feet long, thin at one end and very thick at the other. The thick end is studded with sharp steel spikes, while through the center of the club there is a nine-inch bar, to give it weight and balance. When you get a prisoner all you have to do is just stick this club up in front of him, and believe me, the prisoner's patriotism for *Deutschland ueber Alles* fades away and he very willingly obeys the orders of his captor. If, however, the prisoner gets high-toned and refuses to follow you, simply "persuade" him by first removing his tin hat, and then — well, the use of the lead weight in the persuader is demonstrated, and Tommy looks for another prisoner.

The knuckle knife is a dagger affair, the blade of which is about eight inches long with a heavy steel guard over the grip. This guard is studded with steel projections. At night in a trench, which is only about three to four feet wide, it makes a very handy weapon. One punch in the face generally shatters a man's jaw and you can get him with the knife as he goes down.

Then we had what we called our "come-alongs." These are strands of barbed wire about three feet long, made into a noose at one end; at the other end, the barbs are cut off and Tommy slips his wrist through a loop to get a good grip on the wire. If the prisoner wants to argue the point, why just place the large loop around his neck and no matter if Tommy wishes to return to his trenches at the walk, trot or gallop, Fritz is perfectly agreeable to maintain Tommy's rate of speed.

I cannot even imagine the reaction of the typical American who read these words in the summer or fall of 1917; certainly, persuaders, knuckle knives, and come-alongs were never featured on the British fundraising and propaganda posters that somehow, despite the official American posture of neutrality, managed to make their way onto walls throughout the United States. It was a bloody war, to be sure, but a civilized one, conducted under the time-honored codes of chivalry — wasn't it?

Back in the trenches, Empey and his fellow volunteers, equipped additionally with four hand grenades apiece ("these to be used only in case of emergency"), their hands and faces blackened to help conceal them in the light of German flares, or "star shells" ("In a trench raid there is quite sufficient reason for your face to be pale. If you don't believe me, try it just once"), go over the top and slowly crawl through No Man's Land, communicating with each other through a series of coded taps. After about a half hour, they arrive at the Germans' front trenches, or, more accurately, at the barbed wire just in front of them. "Then," Empey says, "the fun began."

> I was scared stiff as it is ticklish work cutting your way through wire when about thirty feet in front of you there is a line of Boches looking out into No Man's Land with their rifles lying across the parapet, straining every sense to see or hear what is going on in No Man's Land. . . . There is only one way to cut a barbed wire without noise and through costly experience Tommy has become expert at doing this. You must grasp the wire about two inches from the stake in your right hand and cut between the stake and your hand. . . .
>
> During the intervals of falling star shells we carried on with our wire cutting until at last we succeeded in getting through the German barbed wire. At this point we were only ten feet from the German trenches. If we were discovered, we were like rats in a trap. Our way out was cut off unless we ran along the wire to the narrow lane we had cut through. With our hearts in our mouths we waited for the three-tap signal to rush the German trench. Three taps had gotten about halfway down the line when suddenly about ten to twenty German star shells were fired all along the trench and landed in the barbed wire in rear of us, turning night into day and silhouetting us against the wall of light made by the flares. In the glaring light we were confronted by the following unpleasant scene.
>
> All along the German trench, at about three-foot intervals, stood a big Prussian guardsman with his rifle at the aim. . . . About three feet in front of the trench they had constructed a single fence of barbed wire and we knew our chances were one thousand to one of returning alive. We could not rush their trench on account of this second defence. Then in front of me the challenge, "Halt," given in English rang out, and one of the finest things I have ever heard on the western front took place.
>
> From the middle of our line some Tommy answered the challenge with, "Aw, go to hell." . . . He wanted to show Fritz that he could die game.

The Germans, unimpressed, open fire with their machine guns while also throwing grenades. "The Boche in front of me was looking down his sight," Empey says. "Then came a flash in front of me, the flare of his rifle — and my head seemed to burst. A bullet had hit me on the left side of my face about half an inch from my eye, smashing the cheek bones. I put my hand to my face and fell forward, biting the ground and kicking my feet. I thought I was dying. . . . The blood was streaming down my tunic, and the pain was awful." He loses consciousness for a moment, then comes to and tells himself, "Emp, old boy, you belong in Jersey City and you'd better get back there as quickly as possible." This was no mere exhibition of roughriding.

He crawls away under the machine-gun fire, looking for the hole he'd cut in the barbed wire; but before he gets there,

> I came to a limp form which seemed like a bag of oats hanging over the wire. In the dim light I could see that its hands were blackened, and knew it was the body of one of my mates. I put my hand on his head, the top of which had been blown off by a bomb. My fingers sank into the hole. I pulled my hand back full of blood and brains, then I went crazy with fear and horror and rushed along the wire.

He finds the gap, but as he rises to his feet, a voice in his head tells him to look around; as he does, a bullet hits him in the left shoulder. "It did not hurt much," he says, but "then my left side went numb. My arm was dangling like a rag. I fell forward in a sitting position. But all fear had left me and I was consumed with rage and cursed the German trenches." With his good hand he grabs a grenade, pulls the pin with his teeth, and "blindly" throws it toward the German trench. Seeing it explode, and once again "seized with a horrible fear, I dragged myself . . . through the barbed wire, stumbling over cut wires, tearing my uniform, and lacerating my hands and legs." He is just about to make it through to No Man's Land when that same voice in his head tells him to turn around; again he obeys, and another bullet hits him in the same shoulder. "Then it was taps for me," he says. "The lights went out."

He wakes up in a shell hole in No Man's Land; "How I reached this hole I will never know," he tells us. Bullets are still flying just overhead. He is in great pain, soaked in his own blood, "and a big flap from the wound in my cheek was hanging over my mouth. The blood running from this flap choked me. Out of the corner of my mouth I would try and blow it back but it would not move." He tries to wrap a makeshift bandage around the wound, but fails. "You would have laughed if you had seen my ludicrous attempts at bandaging with one hand," he assures us, though I doubt it. He wasn't laughing, either. "I had an awful horror of bleeding to death and was getting very faint. . . . The pains in my wounded shoulder were awful and I was getting sick at the stomach." He passes out again, for an indeterminate spell.

"When I came to," he recalls, "hell was let loose." The Battle of the Somme was under way.

"An intense bombardment was on, and on the whole my position was decidedly unpleasant," he explains. But then, from the friendly trenches somewhere beyond his shell hole, a cheer rises up, and the British come storming over the top. The first wave are "Jocks," or Scots, in full regalia. They were known to kick soccer balls ahead of them as they charged up out of the trenches; Empey doesn't report seeing this, but still, he says,

> They were a magnificent sight, kilts flapping in the wind, bare knees showing, and their bayonets glistening. In the first wave that passed my shell hole, one of the "Jocks," an immense fellow, about six feet two inches in height, jumped right over me. . . . One young Scottie, when he came abreast of my shell hole, leaped into the air, his rifle shooting out of his hands, landing about six feet in front of him, bayonet first, and stuck in the ground, the butt trembling. This impressed me greatly.
>
> Right now I can see the butt of that gun trembling. The Scottie made a complete turn in the air, hit the ground, rolling over twice, each time clawing at the earth, and then remained still, about four feet from me, in a sort of sitting position. I called to him, "Are you hurt badly, Jock?" but no answer. He was dead. A dark, red smudge was coming through his tunic right under the heart. The blood ran down his bare knees, making a horrible sight. On his right side, he carried his water bottle. I was crazy for a drink and tried to reach this, but for the life of me could not negotiate that four feet. Then I became unconscious. When I woke up I was in an advanced first-aid post. I asked the doctor if we had taken the trench. "We took the trench and the wood beyond, all right," he said, "and you fellows did

your bit; but, my lad, that was thirty-six hours ago. You were lying in No Man's Land in that bally hole for a day and a half. It's a wonder you are alive."

How he got from that shell hole to the first-aid station — how anyone seeing him there even knew he was still alive — Empey does not say. Maybe he never knew. They do tell him that seventeen of the twenty men in his raiding party were killed that night; the officer who led it died while trying to crawl back to his trench. Only one of the twenty returned unharmed. The official communiqué on his trench raid began "All quiet on the Western front," Empey tells us, and thus did American readers encounter for the first time a phrase that, a dozen years later, Erich Maria Remarque would enlist for the title of the most celebrated novel ever written about that war.

For Empey, that communiqué marks the end of his war. He spends four months in an English hospital, witnesses daily unheralded acts of great courage, selflessness, and altruism, is discharged as "physically unfit for further war service," and is sent home on the American ship *New York*, which, records show, left Liverpool on November 11, 1916, arriving at its eponymous port nine days later. As it pulls into the harbor and he spots the Statue of Liberty, he says, "Though it may seem strange, I was really sorry not to be back in the trenches with my mates. War is not a pink tea but in a worthwhile cause like ours, mud, rats, cooties, shells, wounds, or death itself, are far outweighed by the deep sense of satisfaction felt by a man who does his bit."

And then he wrote a book about it.

That was just the beginning. There was to be a film version, for one thing, shot at Camp Wheeler, Georgia, the War Department graciously offering the production company use of its training trenchworks as locations, not to mention thousands of soldiers of the 82nd Division as extras. Empey himself wrote the screenplay; he also landed the starring role. Like the book, it was a hit, though Empey scarcely had time for red-carpet appearances, occupied as he was with speaking engagements, Liberty Bond rallies, and live demonstrations of trench warfare, staged at some of the country's largest and most prestigious venues, including, on a half-dozen occasions, Carnegie Hall. They never failed to sell out. He even wrote and published several patriotic songs; my favorite is an anthem of love and trench warfare called "Your Lips Are No Man's Land but Mine."

Somehow, "while trekking back and forth over this country," as he wrote in its afterword, he managed to write *First Call,* a very different kind of book that enjoyed much more modest success than had *Over the Top.* In the years following the war he published several more books, all of them novels; none did well. In the 1920s, he moved out to California, hired a publicist, and wrote a bunch of screenplays, some of which were produced; none did well. He turned to pulp monthlies, churned out action and adventure and combat stories — "Bulldogging the Boche" and "Horsehair Ropes a Heinie" and "Stretcher Bearers Up!" and "Lay That Wire!" and "When Gunmen Turned Soldiers" and "Cannon Fodder" and "Sealed Orders" and "Two Doughs in a Dungeon" and "Curse of the Iron Cross" and "To the Front in a Hearse" and "Buck Privates Commanding" and "All Quit on the Western Front" and more than a hundred others — until the next war killed both format and genre. In 1943, a reporter for the Associated Press discovered Empey working as a security guard at an aircraft plant. Twenty years later, when he died at a veterans' hospital in Leavenworth, Kansas, the same wire service misspelled his name "Emtey" in his brief obituary. Five times.

The depth of his fall, though, does not diminish the accomplishment that initially carried him to the heights from which he later plummeted. I don't mean selling a million copies of his first book; lots of people make and lose fortunes in short order. But more than any other volume ever published, that first book, *Over the Top,* brought the war to America, and shaped Americans' understanding of the conflict; and somehow, while doing all that, Empey managed to assure new doughboys' families back home that it was OK to laugh. Most important, he simultaneously managed to assure those new doughboys that it was OK to be afraid. As he writes in the book's final passage:

> There is one thing which my experience taught me that might help the boy who may have to go. It is this — anticipation is far worse than realization. In civil life a man stands in awe of the man above him, wonders how he could ever fill his job. When the time comes he rises

to the occasion, is up and at it, and is surprised to find how much more easily than anticipated he fills his responsibilities. It is really so "out there."

He has nerve for the hardships; the interest of the work grips him; he finds relief in the fun and comradeship of the trenches and wins that best sort of happiness that comes with duty done.

The same month those words first appeared in print, hundreds of thousands of draft notices, the first of the war, were sent out; and soon, very soon, a great many young men — draftees, like Antonio Pierro, a poor, struggling immigrant who had just managed to establish a toe-hold in America and was now being sent back to the continent whence he had escaped; and volunteers, like a twenty-year-old Connecticut Yankee named J. Laurence Moffitt who had seen the storm coming and had already enlisted to do his part — would have the chance to measure Empey's final sentiment against their own experiences Over There.

3

The American Sector

J. LAURENCE MOFFITT IS directly responsible for the fact that you are holding this book in your hands. Not that he had anything to do with your choosing this title over, say, something by Jane Austen or Louis L'Amour; but were it not for J. Laurence Moffitt, I'm pretty sure this book wouldn't exist.

Let me explain. I first met Mr. Moffitt at his home in Orleans, Massachusetts, right at the elbow of Cape Cod, on July 20, 2003. It was the day after my conversation with Anthony Pierro. But that word, "conversation," is, to be frank, a term that masks the problem that left me terribly discouraged afterward. Yes, I asked Mr. Pierro questions, and he answered them. But it was not a conversation of the type you and I might have if we found ourselves in the same place and were inclined to talk to each other. It was, rather, a bit like a complex game of pinball: There were times when a question would hit a bumper and get a response, or land in a hole and get a big response; but more often it would just fall, freely, striking and setting off nothing but a look of mild bemusement. When this happened I always tried to bat it up again and get different results, but again, more often than not, it would just fall, and eventually I wouldn't be able to bat it up anymore and I'd just have to move on to the next ball. If I asked the right question, something that would spark in Anthony Pierro the memory of a favorite anecdote — and I received a lot of guidance from Rick Pierro in this regard — then I would get to hear it. But there wasn't a lot of telling done beyond those favorite old anecdotes. Perhaps the most frustrating part of it was the fact that there were, apparently, some very interesting old stories that Anthony Pierro had forgotten completely, like the one Rick tried to get him to tell me about the time he went back on the chow line for seconds and another soldier, angered by this for some reason, called him a greedy Wop, and a brawl ensued. I would have liked to have heard that one.

In any event, as much as I had enjoyed meeting and talking with Anthony Pierro — and as grateful as I was that a 107-year-old man who knew nothing about me would take a couple of hours out of his life to talk with me in the first place — I left his house that day with grave doubts about this endeavor I had undertaken. Was I just kidding myself in thinking that I could really converse with World War I veterans, and they with me, and come away with something real and true?

Those doubts lasted exactly one day. They evaporated a few minutes into my first conversation with J. Laurence Moffitt. He had just told me that he had been born in the small northeastern Connecticut town of Lebanon, when I asked him if he had gone to high school there, too. Here is his response:

I went to high school from Lebanon. That high school was in Willimantic, which was about two miles from home. And then, I was directed to an insurance company in Hartford for a position and accepted. And I spent my life in insurance. I was hired by two companies, one then another. And I went to World War I. I graduated from high school in 1914. I went in the Army in 1917, in April of 1917, just before war was declared. And I was in the Army for two years; eighteen months in France, in the first division to go to France. The division was the 26th Division, made up of the National Guard of the six New England states. There are four infantry regiments in a division, and artillery batteries, with which I am not acquainted. And the 101st Infantry Regiment was made up of the Massachusetts National Guard. The 102nd was made up of the Connecticut National Guard; that's where I was, in the 102nd Infantry. The 103rd Infantry Regiment was from Maine, and the 104th from New Hampshire and Vermont, and artillery mostly from Rhode Island.

And we were, in Connecticut we were assembled at New Haven. All the different National Guard companies of Connecticut were assembled in New Haven, in 1917, July. And from there we went — it was so early in the war there were no transports. We went to — my company, and I don't know how many others — went by train, the

CV, Central Vermont, to Montreal, and then embarked there and sailed down the St. Lawrence to Halifax, where we joined several other National Guard companies that were ready to go across, and went across to Liverpool. A nine-day trip, it was. And then across the Channel to France, and then across France to a certain area, Lande-ville, and the regiment trained for four months there. And in Febru-ary we were sent to the front. At that time the Allies, Britain and France and Belgium and others, they were, had been in the war since 1914. And we joined them in 1917, and went to the front in February of 1918.

So, the first sector was, the Allies at that time were defending themselves against the attacks of Germany. And we were just in de-fensive action. I was in the Headquarters [Company] of the infantry regiment, and on the staff of the colonel, along with others. I had the rank of a corporal. And I escaped the front line, trench warfare, but I was subject to constant artillery fire. I spent my twenty-first birthday in the front line, March sixth of 1918. And I went out on patrol with a patrol group that night. And we spent two months in that sector, which was the Chemin des Dames. . . .

Well, that was our first sector. Two months later we were moved to another sector, the Toul Sector. And then came Château-Thierry in the summer of 1918, and then the closing war at Saint-Mihiel and Verdun, and the war was over, as you know, on November eleventh of 1918. . . . And President Wilson paid our company a visit while we were there. And talked to us, and that might have . . . I, I don't re-member . . . don't recall now just when that was, or what the occasion was. But it was maybe a holiday.

Mr. Moffitt was 106 years old at the time; he was talking about things that had happened eighty-five years earlier. And not only did he remember these things precisely — he offered up, unsolicited, details like the composition of various regiments of the 26th Division, and the name of the railroad that carried him to Montreal.

And he was just getting started.

J. Laurence Moffitt: He was the first veteran I found off the French List. He was actually listed in the phone book. This proved encour-aging, though not quite exciting; lots of people remain in the phone book long after they have died. But when I dialed the number and a woman — I would soon learn she was his daughter, Janet — answered the phone and I asked her my now-refined "Is he still living?" she actually answered, "Yes. Would you like to speak with him?"

I said I would, and there was silence for what seemed like a very long time, though in fact it was probably just a minute or two. And then another voice came on the line and said: "Hello." It wasn't frail; it didn't quaver. But it came wrapped in an accent I had never heard before, one that had all but vanished before I'd been born. Though he now lived in Orleans, Massachusetts, this man was a true Connecticut Yankee, a relic of a time when Connecticut was a state of farms, not tony suburbs and enormous Indian casinos.

We met just a couple of weeks after that. Like most of Cape Cod, Orleans had long since metamorphosed from an old fishing village to an expensive summer destination, a place of large second homes. J. Laurence Moffitt had retired there after decades working in insurance, traveling throughout Connecticut and taking the train into Manhattan. His was a small house, set back in some woods; it didn't get much light. There was only one armchair in the living room on the day I visited, and it was offered to me. I, in turn, offered it back to him, and took for myself the only other seat in the house: his wheelchair. We sat like that for two hours — and, when I returned to see him a few months later, did it again. He was a small man, and thin; on that first day he wore a baggy yellow short-sleeved golf shirt with a button-down pocket, and very large eyeglasses. Exuberant tufts of white hair sprang out from all over his head, a bit more thinly in the middle of it, but still there nonetheless. He spoke very slowly — not that the words came out of his mouth haltingly, but he was prone to taking frequent pauses, sometimes several per sentence, during which, more often than not, he hummed softly. I liked him immediately.

"I was born in Lebanon, Connecticut," he told me at the beginning of our conversation that first day. "In a small town in which my grandfather Moffitt had retired from his manufacturing business in Providence in eighteen hundred and sixty-nine. My father was then nine years old. And across the road, a little bit away from ours, was another farm by the name of Cod, and that was my mother's family. And my father married the daughter of the Cods."

"And what day were you born?" I asked him.

"March sixth," he replied.

"And the year?"

"Eighteen ninety-seven." He must have sensed how odd that number struck me, sitting there in 2003, because at one point, he said: "You know, you hear about long-time memory and short-time memory. My long-time memory is good. I can remember names from back when I was in high school, and where I worked and who I visited; and I can't remember what happened last week, maybe, or last year. Your short memory, at my age, gets weak. But my long-time memory is good. Yes, I can remember lots of things."

Toward the end of that day, after the strangeness had worn off, he conceded that perhaps he had fared better than many. "A lot of people do not retain their memory or their mind as they age," he stated. "As you see, I have no problem in this. And my mind seems to be clear, and I keep up with things and world news.

"And I read the paper," he added, matter-of-factly.

J. Laurence Moffitt: He never used his first name, Jesse. Years later, rooting around in old census records, I learned that he had been named for his paternal grandfather. The elder Jesse Moffitt had been born in Connecticut in 1828, and by 1850 was married — his wife, Maria, was a couple of years older — and living in Cumberland, Rhode Island, working as a hired hand on a farm owned by an elderly widow named Parmelia Peck. (Don't you just love those old names?) The 1870 census counts him twice — once in Pawtucket, Rhode Island, where he is listed as being a machinist; and once in Lebanon, Connecticut, where he is noted as a farmer, with a net worth of $10,000. His farm, the record shows, was worth $6,000; Parmelia Peck's had only been valued at $1,000. In just two decades, Jesse Moffitt had done quite well for himself, had achieved the American Dream, thanks, no doubt, to New England thriftiness, a lot of elbow grease, and perhaps a few other nineteenth-century values that we now think of as timeworn clichés and yet miss terribly.

By 1900, Jesse's son Edward was living and farming in the land of the Cods. He and his wife, Nellie, had four children, the youngest of whom, a three-year-old boy, had been named for Edward's father. One hundred and three years later, that little boy, Jesse — though from now on we'll call him Laurence, as he preferred — told me that his earliest memory was "being out in our yard and seeing my grandfather Moffitt, with a long white beard, in the yard of the barn, across the road from our house." The old man still lived and farmed there, next door to his son's in-laws, the Cods. Except they weren't; as I also discovered while searching through those census records, they were, in fact, the "Cards." This was Laurence Moffitt's old Connecticut accent. Good luck finding anyone there who still speaks that way.

Jesse Moffitt may have set himself up as a gentleman farmer in 1869, but his grandson and namesake grew up on a working farm, and he didn't much care for it. "What kind of farm was it?" I asked him in July, 2003.

"Milk and vegetables," he said. "Dairy. We had about fifteen cows. And then there was, always, vegetables, carrots and onions and turnips that my father harvested and took into Willimantic and sold. And the milk was in cans and picked up daily by some organization . . . and of course we had our own milk."

"Did you work on the farm when you were a boy?"

"I did, exactly, and hated it. I hoed and weeded rows of carrots and onions, turnips . . . it was no fun being on your knees all day long and pulling weeds."

He liked school much better — because it wasn't the farm, and because, despite the fact that it was almost as rural and remote as the farm, he managed to see there a bit more of the world, the new. "In the country," he recalled, "one-room country schoolhouse, whenever there was a car heard coming, kids were allowed to run to the window and watch the car go by."

As he said, he went into Willimantic, a town of some size (at least compared to Lebanon), for high school; then, after graduation in 1914, off to Hartford, where he worked in insurance. He was still there in early 1917, and might never have left were it not for a growing sense that his country was about to be drawn into the war that was tearing through much of the rest of the world.

Eighty-six years later, he explained: "Germany had continued to sink ships, and including the *Lusitania*, which was a British ship. . . . And on it, there were two hundred Americans on it. And our president, President Woodrow Wilson, registered his complaint to the Kaiser, to Germany. And he got some response, but the sinking of ships by submarines continued through 1916 and '17, so much so that the National Guard troops were what was called 'called out.' And obviously there was news of what Germany had been doing to us, and aroused the Americans. So the National Guard, the National Guard of Connecticut, and of other states, were called out. And when they were is when I joined the National Guard. Now I left my job in the insurance company and went and joined the National Guard. And then we were formed into a division, and Connecticut was the 102nd Infantry. From all of the companies, the National Guard companies in Connecticut, were formed into the 102nd Infantry."

"So you joined up because you knew that America was going to go to war," I said, "and they needed soldiers?"

"Yes, that's right," he replied. "And when I went home and told my mother I joined the Army, after she got over the shock, she said 'Well, I'm thankful you didn't join the Navy.' Because at that time it looked like it was to be a naval war. Well, she was wrong."

There were actually 139 Americans on the *Lusitania*, 128 of whom went down with the ship on May 7, 1915. Not quite 200, but plenty; and despite certain mitigating circumstances — that Germany had warned Americans against booking passage on the ship, had gone so far as to take out ads in American newspapers warning that they might well sink it, that "travelers sailing in the war zone on ships of Great Britain and her allies do so at their own risk" because, Germany rightfully suspected, passenger ships like the *Lusitania* were sometimes being used, secretly and against the laws of war, to ferry arms and ammunition through U-boat-infested waters — Americans were outraged. Many called for war with Germany.

Many others, though, called for restraint — most importantly among them, President Wilson. "There is such a thing as a man being too proud to fight," he said. "There is such a thing as a nation being so right that it does not need to convince others by force that it is right." Instead, working through diplomatic channels, he secured promises that Germany would ease up on its campaign of submarine warfare.

Which it did, for more than a year; some historians have argued that doing so cost it the war. By early 1917, the Allied blockade, unchecked by German U-boats, had brought Germany close to starvation. Desperate, the country's leaders concluded they had no choice but to do what they could to curtail the Allies' advantage. So if American merchant ships, sailing under flags of neutrality, were going to continue supplying the Allies with the food and arms Germany no longer had access to, Germany decided it would have to start sinking those ships, even though they knew it could mean war with America.

Which it did, especially once British intelligence shared with Washington a cable it had intercepted from German Foreign Secretary Arthur Zimmermann, intended for Germany's ambassador in Mexico, Heinrich von Eckardt, instructing the latter to approach the Mexican government with a proposal for Mexico to enter the war on Germany's side, in exchange for the return to Mexico of Texas, New Mexico, and Arizona once victory was secured. That note — now remembered, with great notoriety, as the Zimmermann Telegram — was a response to the growing understanding that Germany and America would soon be at war with one another. So was Laurence Moffitt's enlistment, right around his twentieth birthday, in the Connecticut National Guard. Two months later, war having been declared, the Connecticut National Guard was nationalized and converted to the 102nd Infantry Regiment of the 26th Division, the "Yankee Division." Mr. Moffitt was then a private. "Or as we used to call it," he told me, "a 'buck private.'"

The Yankee Division, or "YD" as it was known by those who served in it, arrived in France on October 9, 1917. With them was one Frank P. Sibley, a reporter for the *Boston Globe*. When the division was mobilized, the *Globe*, the largest daily newspaper in New England, hit upon the idea of sending a reporter along just to cover its actions. Sibley had gone to the Mexican border with Massachusetts National Guard troops the previous year, and he was, you might say, a real booster. So eager was he to go overseas with the division that when the War Department denied him accreditation — the *Globe's* request was apparently so novel that no one in Washington knew what to make of it — Sibley went anyway, without any credentials at all. "My mission," he writes in his 1919 memoir, *With the Yankee Division in France*, was "to keep the families at home informed of the experiences of their boys in France.

The *Boston Globe* was thoroughly protected by news services, by special correspondents, and by every obtainable agent, as to the progress of the war as a whole. I was to write only what was happening to the New England boys." It's safe to say that Sibley actually considered himself one of the troops, referring to them, unfailingly, as "we" rather than "they." He even claimed credit for coining the name "Yankee Division."

And he advocated for the YD tirelessly. He surely felt they needed it; according to Sibley, the YD was probably the most embattled, underappreciated, and maligned outfit in all of the American Expeditionary Forces. "The Twenty-Sixth . . . did not stand well with the American higher command," Sibley writes. For example, when the YD was pulled out of the Chemin des Dames Sector in March, 1918, he says, "Misgivings were heavy upon us . . . because of what we were sure was mismanagement of us and prejudice against us."

Suspect as that sentiment sounds today, Sibley may actually have had it right. And this is where the story gets a bit strange.

There were a lot of big egos in the AEF, and the big ego at the top of the YD — General Clarence Ransom Edwards — didn't get along with some of the Army's other big egos, including the biggest of them all, General John Joseph "Black Jack" Pershing. Edwards was fifty-eight years old when America entered the war, a West Point graduate and career soldier who had served in the Spanish-American War and the Philippine Insurrection; his last posting had been as commander of all American troops in the Panama Canal Zone. When Wilson declared war on Germany, Edwards was hastily recalled to the States, promoted to major general, and put in charge of the nascent 26th Division.

Edwards had a reputation for being sharp-tongued, which may account for his unpopularity. He was also, apparently, pretty full of himself, which probably didn't help. In his memoirs, Major General William Lassiter, who also served in France and later became commander of all American troops in the Hawaiian Department, called Edwards "the most egocentric person I have ever known. He thought so much and talked so much about himself that his job always became a secondary consideration. . . . He spent his time criticizing all and sundry in the hierarchy above him and making his men feel they were not being given a fair share."

Whether Laurence Moffitt, the last surviving member of the YD from World War I, felt this way, I do not know; he certainly never hinted at it. He was, to be sure, extremely proud of the association — for many years after the war, he even had a special license plate on his car, YD29 — and, while most of that is probably the pride any soldier feels for his unit, I suspect that some small part of it may be due to a special distinction the YD held during that war, one for which General Edwards was entirely responsible.

Edwards, you see, decided that he wanted his 26th to be the first full division to serve in France. Trouble was, there were three full Regular Army divisions — the 1st, 2nd, and 3rd — with seniority over his, and Edwards, likely not helped by his reputation, couldn't seem to secure the orders that would realize his ambition. So, in September, 1917, Edwards just shipped the entire 26th Division, some twenty-five thousand men in all, to France anyway.

Without orders.

The Army was not impressed. The French, however, were. Everyone seems to agree that the YD and the people of France fell in love with each other quickly. As the first full US Army division in France, they were a symbol of hope as much as anything else. By the time the YD arrived in France that fall, the French had endured more than three years of fighting on their own soil — thirty-eight months of unstanched hemorrhaging, of dead sons and husbands, of blasted houses and farms, of destroyed villages, of colossal battles, some of them the greatest in history. Yet despite it all, in three years the battle lines had scarcely moved. The Germans had snatched up a fair chunk of France back in August and September of 1914, the first two months of the war, and had managed to hold it ever since. It wasn't easy, or cheap; the French, under orders to attack constantly, did just that. In the process, they managed to kill many Germans, and to lose just as many of their own. The war was an extremely deadly stalemate. The French, exhausted, depopulated, living in occupied ruins, nevertheless retained their anger and their pride. They swore they would never surrender to the hated Boche. But how could they prevail?

Then, in the spring of 1917, the news: Millions of Americans would be coming soon. Or eventually, anyway. It took months for them to even start showing up; for many French men and women, the soldiers of the YD were the first physical indication that yes, this really was going to happen, that the war might just end someday. "The vast majority [of French] . . . welcomed the Americans as saviors. They looked on our men as crusaders, who had left their homes to fight for an ideal, as the force which was destined to cause the triumph of right and justice," writes Emerson Gifford Taylor in *New England in France*, the definitive history of the YD in World War I, first published in 1920. Taylor, as it happened, was Laurence Moffitt's captain. "A Yale man," as Mr. Moffitt recalled. "A good man." One time, he told me, "I was on what we called kitchen duty, and the only phone in the regiment, our company phone, was on a post in the kitchen. And a call came in for Captain Taylor. . . . So I stepped out of the tent and I yelled to Captain Taylor, 'Telephone!' And he very kindly says, 'You don't yell to a captain, to an officer. You come up and salute and you give your message.'"

Captain Taylor had already made a name for himself as a writer of Victorian grippers like *A Daughter of Dale* and *The Upper Hand*. Yet if he had a weakness for purple prose, he didn't overstate the level of hospitality with which the YD were greeted almost everywhere they went in France. Laurence Moffitt told me he often visited French homes when he was Over There. "They had you for dinner?" I asked him.

"That's right, they did," he replied. "They were quite cordial to us."

"The women-folk liked the Yankees well," Taylor writes in *New England in France*. "How about the girls?" I asked his corporal — he hadn't stayed a buck private for long — eight decades later.

"A buddy of mine dated a couple of French girls," Corporal Moffitt told me. "And I kept in touch with one of them . . . and she wrote beautiful love letters to me . . . and I kept it up by letter for a while after I came home." Until, that is, he met the woman who would eventually become his wife of seventy-five years; then, he said, "I basically discontinued it."

The YD spent their first four months abroad training under the French, and, apparently, learning a great deal. "The Yankees had the sense to appreciate the French officers who formed their mission," Sibley asserts. "And it was largely because the Division was capable of learning from them that their fine record was made." Taylor, for his part, credits "the generally rapid and satisfactory progress of the troops" to "the tireless and intelligent assistance of the French." By the first week of February, 1918, they were deemed combat-ready, and put into action in the Chemin des Dames Sector. Among the many French soldiers serving there at around this time was an artillery officer named Alfred Dreyfus. Yes, *that* Alfred Dreyfus. Of *L'Affaire*.

Chemin des Dames was a line in the northern Champagne region that had been the site of brutal fighting for several years; in the spring of 1917, when America was just entering the war, the French Army took so many casualties there (due, in large part, to the ineptitude of then commander in chief Robert Nivelle) that it was beset by large-scale mutinies afterward. By February, 1918, though, it was relatively quiet, with both sides mostly taking shelter in underground bunkers and quarries. (The Germans had occupied their defensive positions there for so long that they had actually electrified their bunkers; you can still see their wiring today.) The YD stayed at Chemin des Dames for about six weeks, scratching out impressive graffiti (also still visible) on the subterranean walls; then they were shipped to the Toul Sector, another "safe" area, to further their education. And it was there, in the town of Seicheprey, that they — and by extension, the AEF — had their first major encounter with the German Army.

In a clearing in the woods not far from Seicheprey, in the region of Lorraine in northeastern France, you will find a section of German trench, complete with concrete walls and steps and iron handgrips. These are common in this part of the country, but this particular section is so well preserved that at some point in recent years someone thought to put up a kiosk commemorating the fighting that took place in and around it. Toward the bottom of that kiosk you can see an old greenish photograph; it looks very familiar: long rows of doughboys in puttees and tin hats, sitting cross-legged, kneeling, standing. It seems just like any number of official platoon or company portraits, those stretched-out panoramic shots you sometimes find in attics, their elongated frames caked in dust. Look closely at this particular photograph, though, and its strangeness starts to reveal itself. It's a bit grainy, for one thing; the photographer probably wasn't a professional. The soldiers aren't in camp or the field, but sitting and standing in front of some sort of quasi-official-looking edifice. And none of them — not a single one — is smiling. Many are looking down at the ground; a few are even hiding their faces. Those faces that are clearly visible can fairly be described as hangdog.

Their stay in the Toul Sector had started inauspiciously. They had arrived at the end of March, wet and exhausted, to find the place quite literally a mess. They were replacing American troops of the 1st Division commanded by Major Theodore Roosevelt Jr., son of the former president. "He was found to be a pleasant, congenial fellow," recalled Captain Daniel W. Strickland in his account, *Connecticut Fights: The Story of the 102nd Regiment,* published in 1930. "When the relieving officers came upon him he was busily writing at a make-shift desk in his dugout, with water up to his ankles, and he reached up occasionally either to scratch his back or tear a hunk from a loaf of stale bread." As much of a treat as this encounter may have seemed, TR Jr. wasn't quite ready to move his troops out yet, meaning that the men of the 102nd could not rest, but rather "must then rot in the decay of ancient, vermin-infested billets and shelters that had not been cleaned for years" for a while longer. "The sector," Strickland explains, "had become known as 'the American Sector' or the 'Toul Sector,' and had achieved much notoriety because of being the first sector held entirely by United States troops."

Seeing the words "American Sector" on a battle map must have given the AEF no small measure of pride, but the men of the Yankee Division no doubt would have rather been elsewhere just then. Strickland sets the scene:

> When the Americans took over this sector one of the outstanding features was its run-down condition. Winter was just over; the rainy season was in progress. . . . The low country in which lay the forward positions was full of marshes and tiny streams. . . . Long stretches of trench contained water one or two feet deep, over soft mud, into which a man would sink nearly to the waist. . . . Thousands of yards of telephone wire were fastened to the trench walls — all unused — the evident principle having been that it was simpler to string new wire than to repair the old. . . . Often wounded had to be carried over the top. . . . In many places it was impossible to proceed for any great distance in a trench without climbing onto the parapet and walking

there. . . . No latrine system was established, so that all trenches were polluted.

This is a side of that war you rarely hear about: the mess. Sure, there was the mess of getting shot by machine-gun bullets, of having your arm or leg or head blown off by an artillery shell, of having your intestines snagged on barbed wire or your lungs broken down and spit up after exposure to poison gas. But when you think of World War I, you don't think of sinking up to your waist in a gumbo of mud and human filth and, for good measure, old telephone wire. Somehow, I imagine troops in such a spot would find that last ingredient particularly galling. What a tease.

Up to that point, the Americans hadn't had much of a war. They had fired a few shots at the Germans, and the Germans had fired a few back. A handful had been killed; a few captured. But for the most part, American soldiers spent their first year of the war training and observing, both at a safe-enough reserve.

This was more than simply good luck. The French and British, delighted and relieved that America was finally getting into this thing, would have liked nothing more than to use the promised millions of fresh American troops the way they had used the Canadians and the Australians and New Zealanders, the Indochinese and Senegalese: to draw German fire away from them, to give them a break, some relief. A cynic might liken that type of assignment to being used as cannon fodder — Newfoundlanders, for instance, whose only regiment suffered 90 percent casualties during the first half hour of the Battle of the Somme. General Pershing, knowing that tale and so many others, refused to allow American units to be split up and deployed piecemeal under British or French command. This didn't make Pershing terribly popular with the French and British high commands; they — especially the British — put a tremendous amount of pressure on him to change his mind. But Pershing held firm, and the British and French decided they'd rather give the Americans their own sectors than have them sit out the fight any longer. At this point — the early spring of 1918 — there still weren't all that many Americans in France; better to find out what they were capable of before the bulk of them showed up.

So here they were, the Yankee Division, having shipped across without orders, the first American division to arrive in full, taking over the newly rechristened American Sector. In addition to the mess, they had to deal with other nuisances no Americans had faced to date in France, like a German Army that was quite close by and eager to terrify, humiliate, and demoralize them. The Germans had been entrenched in their positions since 1914; they held, for the most part, the better ground, and took shelter in trenches and bunkers that were made of concrete, not dirt. (They had much better drainage and latrine systems, too.) They had built a large yet efficient network of infirmaries, hospitals, and rest camps, all of it electrified, connected by tunnels and supplied by narrow-gauge railroad. On the other hand, the French, who'd been trying to take the territory back since 1914, refused to build anything permanent, for philosophical reasons: Constructing concrete trenches, not to mention hospitals, implied that it might take you a while to recover what you'd lost. This was considered to be bad for morale — worse, apparently, than crumbling trenches and greatly delayed medical care. The new troops had to adjust to this prevailing mindset, and their surroundings, very quickly; they were facing an enemy with much more experience and much greater knowledge of the area, an enemy who was better rested than they were and eager to attack before the YD could get established there.

And attack the enemy did, almost immediately. On April 1 they began a withering artillery barrage; for more than two weeks they fired H.E. and gas shells at the Americans day and night. They jabbed at the American lines at Bois Brulé and Apremont. They ambushed American patrols, bombarded American field kitchens when they knew meals were being prepared, and even hijacked an American supply wagon, shooting all the mules and a couple of soldiers, carrying off the rations and a wounded American sergeant, and leaving that day's mail delivery scattered in the mud. "Much is said about men who face the enemy in hand to hand conflict," Strickland writes, "but too little is recorded of those men on the escort and ammunition wagon who with black snake whip in one hand, reins in the other, with a smothering gas mask on, with foot on the brake and without lights of any kind save the glare of shell and battery guns, lashed their teams through the teeth of the barrage, or drum fire to bring grub, hot coffee, and grenades to their dependant comrades up forward." No one in this "safe" sector was ever really safe.

Not even in camp. "An irritating feature of the sector," Strickland writes with measured understatement, "was the constant belief that enemy spies were moving freely among the troops." Everyone, it seemed, had a story about someone — a French officer or American soldier, always from a nearby unit, close but not so close as to be familiar — who showed up asking questions about which units were in the area, what their strength was, who was in charge, the state of fortifications, and anything else they could find out. Often, no one considered the matter suspicious until after they had left, although just enough spies did get caught to foment a certain level of paranoia. "Germans had put on American uniforms and mingled freely with our men at mess and in the rear areas," Strickland explains; the source of this knowledge was captured German soldiers. "Some of our men captured were called by name and nickname by the Bosche. They then knew that, posing as telephone men and runners from other units, the Germans had been able to pass freely and gather any information they chose. . . . On one occasion two strangers, one uniformed as a colonel and the other as a major, passed up and down the front line trenches for an entire forenoon unchallenged, the troops believing them to be inspecting officers until an American officer, noticing that the colonel's eagles were pinned on upside down, reported the pair to regimental headquarters and they were apprehended and passed back to higher authority for examination. No one ever learned what became of the case."

Men became wary about talking even to one another. Clearly, something big was in the works.

"Midnight of the nineteenth–twentieth of April was as clear and quiet a night as one could ask for on the Toul front," Strickland writes. "One of those clear, dreamy moonlight nights when the war seemed far away." When someone writes something like that, you know it won't last:

> Then at 3:16 o'clock all hell was let loose! Just as the mist and fog had begun to settle along the bottom lands the Boche tore out with

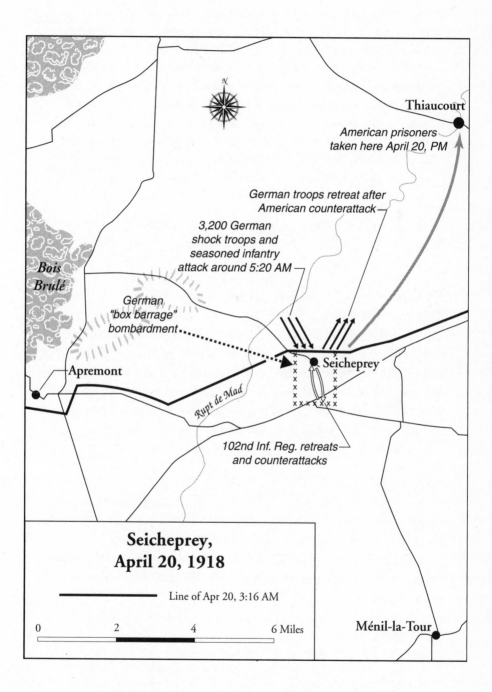

Thiaucourt

American prisoners
taken here April 20, PM

German troops retreat after
American counterattack

3,200 German
shock troops and
seasoned infantry
attack around 5:20 AM

*Bois
Brulé*

German
"box barrage"
bombardment

Apremont

Seicheprey

Rupt de Mad

102nd Inf. Reg. retreats
and counterattacks

Seicheprey,
April 20, 1918

——————— Line of Apr 20, 3:16 AM

0   2   4   6 Miles

Ménil-la-Tour

his barrage, the most terrific the 102nd had yet faced. A belt of artillery fire was laid on the front line fire trenches to annihilate the defenders there. Another belt cut off the front lines from support, while the trenches occupied by support platoons were pounded so unmercifully that almost every man was killed or wounded. Another band of fire swept the lateral road along Beaumont Ridge to prevent regimental or division reserve from coming to the assistance of Seicheprey. Still other bands of enemy fire were directed between the front line units to prevent communication. . . . It was a wonderfully planned piece of artillery work by the Germans . . . which made it impossible for troops or even messengers to pass through alive.

The men of the 102nd — under the command of Colonel John Henry "Machine Gun" Parker, so nicknamed because, as Taylor put it, he "had achieved a wide distinction as an exponent of advanced ideas on the tactical employment" of that weapon — were isolated and boxed in at Seicheprey; the only way out was straight forward, into the German lines. But that gap was quickly filled by a dense column of German troops, at the head of which were a frenzy of the dreaded *Stosstruppen,* German storm troopers, hundreds of them. The literal translation of *Stosstruppen* is "shock troops," and that was their job: to charge without warning (unless you consider a massive artillery barrage a warning) into an enemy area, shrieking and throwing grenades everywhere and firing off rifles when they weren't throwing grenades, their objective being to shock and disorient the entrenched enemy, thus softening them up for the much larger force of infantry following close behind. On this particular morning, they charged in before dawn after more than an hour of H.E. and gas shells raining down from above, many of them armed with flamethrowers. The Americans had never seen *Stosstruppen* or flamethrowers before; it's safe to say the Germans achieved their initial objective — to stun the doughboys of the 102nd. It was bedlam, shrieking chaotic death with guttural accents. And it was everywhere.

Strickland:
> Through the mist and fog overhead droned a black enemy plane, almost touching the house-tops, with absolute precision signaling the enemy artillery the location of each little group of defenders.

Sibley:

Almost immediately all telephone wires were cut by the artillery fire; the radio station at Seicheprey was knocked out, and trench shelters all over the front were caved in. Batteries and support positions were thoroughly gassed, besides being shelled.

Strickland:

Screams and screeches that made the blood run cold came from the throats of half drunken Germans as they hurled their deadly "potato masher" grenades at every American that appeared.

Sibley:

After the first rush, the entire fight at Seicheprey was a matter of small group combats. Nowhere did more than a platoon fight in one body, and in most places there were not more than twenty men in a bunch.

Strickland:

From the right of the town came screams and groans of agony as the Boche poured a stream of liquid fire into a "pill box" of 102nd machine gunners. Boxes of high explosive set off at dugout doors and alongside shelters brought down tons of mortar and debris on help-less doughboys.

Sibley:

The combat group in the extreme left of the Sibille trench was cap-tured intact. A young officer, in charge of this group, put his men into the trench shelters when the bombardment began. The Germans came so suddenly that they caught the platoon napping.

Strickland:

Chunks of stone and mortar, picks and shovels, clubbed rifles, were being used for weapons, while here and there grey clad forms rolled over and over in the death-lock with khaki.

Sibley:

The next group to the right fought until every man was either killed, wounded or captured. . . . Captain Locke of Company M . . . fought straight on, even after he was summoned to surrender. He managed to get three revolver clips of cartridge home, one after the other, in the faces of the Boches before they dared rush him; he was reloading for the fourth time when they closed in and killed him.

Strickland:
Carl Jacobs, the mess sergeant of Company "D", and his kitchen police . . . fought off the crew of the liquid fire gun with cleavers and butcher knives.

Sibley:
The crew of the kitchen were all dead or wounded; they had fought to a finish with the Germans, even when so surprised that one man fought with a cleaver. He did good work with the weapon, splitting a German right down through the head to the very shoulders.

Strickland:
The sector ammunition dump was afire so that cartridges, trench mortar shells, rockets and other combustibles were exploding in every direction.

Sibley:
Private Parker L. Polson of the 101st Signal Corps . . . was at the wireless station of the 102nd Infantry, and the aerials kept getting themselves shot away. Three times Polson climbed up into the tree which supported them, thirty feet up in the shower of flying fragments of steel, to repair the aerials. It should be remembered that Fritz paid constant and particular attention with his artillery to this wireless station, whose position and importance he knew very well.

Strickland:
Men were dying for lack of surgical attention, because the entire medical platoon had been killed or captured save one man, John R. Cannon. Several runners were killed in attempting to get more information back to Colonel Parker.

Sibley:

[Colonel Parker came across] two men of the 102nd Machine Gun Battalion, dead across their gun. . . . They had sold out dearly; there was a ring of dead Germans in front of them, scattered in the gully. At the end, they had evidently been killed in hand-to-hand fighting. In front of one of them lay two dead Germans, in front of the other three.

Strickland:

Both [companies] "C" and "D" had received orders that in case of attack . . . there was to be no falling back. And there had been no falling back. The men of Connecticut held the line until annihilated! There they were, dead — in windrows almost, out in front of the fire trenches that which by reason of the mud made poor places from which to fight. The heavy shock had been met by those that survived the awful shelling and grenading, and they accounted for themselves as men do who know that there is to be no retreat.

Taylor:

In Remieres Wood . . . were found two men of a machine-gun crew, killed — one with his finger on the trigger, the other with a feed strip in his hand, all ammunition exhausted, but with a heap of dead Germans in front of them, stopped by the two in their attempt to rush the gun. . . . In other centers combat groups were killed, fighting to the last man, at their posts. Surrounded, there was many a lad who, summoned to surrender, fought with clubbed and broken rifle, and when overpowered, still struggled with his captors — as was told by the Germans themselves months later. For every prisoner taken, the enemy paid in good measure.

His leadership of the 102nd on that day earned Machine Gun Parker a Distinguished Service Cross, a decoration second only to the Congressional Medal of Honor. Even so, after Seicheprey, the Yankee Division was criticized — for giving up ground, no matter how briefly ("By 6 a.m.," Sibley writes, "the enemy was entirely out of Seicheprey, having stayed less than forty minutes"), and for failing to follow up with a strong counterattack (generally blamed on the dithering of one officer, the ironically named Major Gallant, who afterward, Sibley reports, was promptly "arrested and tried by court-martial for disobedience of orders, and the Division never saw him again"). But mostly, they were criticized for their losses: not for the two hundred or so men who were killed, or the six hundred or so who were wounded, but for that third category. "The Germans said they considered our men crazy because when surrounded and outnumbered they refused to surrender and continued fighting, regardless of odds, until physically overpowered or killed," Sibley relates with pride. And if you peruse the accounts, you can't help but notice that the Germans went to an awful lot of trouble to overpower and capture Americans when it would have been much easier just to kill them. If the Germans didn't achieve their primary objective of taking and holding Seicheprey, they did manage to achieve another type of victory: They captured 150 fresh doughboys, most of them from Connecticut.

Later that morning they marched their new trophies to the nearby town of Thiaucourt, lined them up in rows, and took the photograph that today graces that kiosk in the French woods, above the caption: *Les prisonniers américains du 20 avril photographiés dans Thiaucourt.* The American prisoners of April 20, photographed in Thiaucourt. It was a public relations coup. *This is how we dealt with the first of your soldiers*, the Germans were saying. *Bring on the rest.*

In fact, the men of the 102nd had acquitted themselves very well: Surprised and overwhelmed by veteran German troops with superior numbers, weapons, and experience, the troops from Connecticut nevertheless fought them off, killing quite a few (in one case, with a meat cleaver) in the process; most reports echo Sibley's sentiments when he says, "In its essence, the result of Seicheprey was this: the enemy came over prepared to stay and didn't succeed in doing so. His losses were heavier than ours. So . . . at least we had the best of it."

And yet: those prisoners. People just couldn't get over that. Even the men of the 102nd who fought off the *Stosstruppen* and *Infanteristen*, beat them back with rifle butts and cobblestones and meat cleavers — even they came to view Seicheprey through that lens. Eighty-five years later, this is all the very last survivor of that battle — during which the German shock troops penetrated so far, so fast that there was even frantic fighting at the regiment's headquarters — could bring himself to say about it:

"Seicheprey. That was our first battle. In April of 1918. The Germans came over at us, captured quite a few, and took the city, where some of our troops were. And then, after, we turned and took the city back."

That's it.

"As I told my mother, she had reason to worry all the time about her son," Corporal Moffitt explained to me in his living room on Cape Cod. "I worried only when I was in danger, and I wasn't in danger most of the time. I was perfectly safe in the dugouts or in trenches. The people at home had reason to worry — they didn't know when I was safe and when I wasn't safe."

J. Laurence Moffitt: Nothing was a big deal to him. I asked him at one point what it was like to remember things that had happened almost a century earlier; he said his memories of 1918 were no different to him than my memories of 1993 were to me. "They're mine, they're yours," he said. "I'm not impressed or affected by it." A lot of people made a fuss over the fact that he was 106 years old, but he wasn't one of them. "My wife and I never gave any thought to age at all," he said; his wife, Flo, had died at ninety-seven, two weeks shy of their seventy-sixth wedding anniversary. "I don't care anything about age. It doesn't give me a thought. I just live, and age is never in my mind. I don't know why people make so much of age." His granddaughter, he told me, had recently complained to him that she was feeling old; she'd just turned forty-eight.

It wouldn't have occurred to her grandfather to complain on his forty-eighth birthday, or any birthday. "I take things as they are, and I don't let problems bother me. I never have problems," he told me when I asked him for the secret of his longevity. Several months later, when I visited him again and asked him if it had been difficult for him to adjust to civilian life after the war, he replied, "Nothing has ever been hard for me. I just live."

The war, though, couldn't have been easy for him. Being in HQ Company did not spare him, or anyone, what the rest of the regiment was enduring. Everyone took their turns in the front-line trenches, and, as at Seicheprey, the fighting often came right up to HQ; after artillery and machine guns, it was the enemy's top target. And in all their time in France — more than a year, between their arrival and the armistice — the YD spent only one month away from the front lines. They were moved around a lot, shuttling back and forth in boxcars between sectors. "There'd be maybe twenty-five or thirty, maybe more, in a single car," Laurence Moffitt told me. "No chairs, no anything, except the floor."

"Was that an uncomfortable way to travel?" I asked him.

"Well," he replied, "everything was uncomfortable, obviously . . . you're sitting on the ground or the floor. And you didn't mind the discomfort. You took it as part of the job. Yep."

After the Toul Sector they were shipped to Château-Thierry, just ninety kilometers from Paris, where, among other feats, they liberated the town of Belleau. The battle of Belleau Wood is remembered as a triumph for the Marines, and it was, but the YD fought in the immediate area just weeks later, and it wasn't a safe — or pleasant — place for anyone. "Apart from the hourly peril of the place, with its constant visitations from shell-fire, gas, and machine-gun bursts, the woods themselves were full of horror," Taylor writes. "Shapeless fragments of what once were men hung in the jagged branches of the trees, blown there by shells. . . . A grisly odor of death hung heavy in the summer air . . . and men there came to move and talk as when they know that ghosts are watching them."

If the Germans made things particularly hard for the YD in the summer of 1918, it was because they knew what was at stake. At that point, there were still not very many American divisions in France, and the Germans had taken a big risk, overstretching themselves in a grand offensive that they hoped would end the war before the Americans could arrive in force. The risk didn't pay off; ultimately, the Germans failed to destroy the fledgling AEF. Many historians credit that failure with mortally wounding the German war machine, starting a decline that would culminate four months later. But if the Germans didn't manage to kill off the American Army at that point, they did nevertheless kill off quite a few American soldiers, and wounded many more so badly that they had to be sent back to America, perhaps never to recover. By his own account, Laurence Moffitt had a number of close calls. "I was very lucky," he said, typically. "I was hit once by shrapnel, not severely." He said it had occurred around Château-Thierry.

"What happened?" I asked him.

"Well, I was hit in the leg, in the hip. It wasn't severely. It hit my leg, and it dropped, the shrapnel dropped to the ground and I reached down and picked it up and it was very hot. So I dropped it, and waited for it to cool, then picked it up. But I have it, still have it . . . a piece of shrapnel about that long." He held a thumb and forefinger about two inches apart; it didn't look like much, until you imagined a jagged, red-hot piece of iron that size tearing through your bowels or chest or head. So much of it fell on Lorraine that it still pops up today every time a field there is plowed. In just minutes one morning, strolling casually, I found enough of it in a field outside Seicheprey to fill a large grocery bag, including some pieces that were a foot or longer.

"Did you come under artillery fire often?" I asked him.

"All the time," he replied. "We lived under it."

"What was that like?"

"Well, after a while you disregarded it. You didn't worry about it. You felt, *If I get it, I get it. If I don't, I don't.* And you just paid no attention to it, the shells dropping about you. You couldn't worry about it all the time."

Coming from another man, a younger man, I would have taken this statement as merely bravado. But I could tell that Laurence Moffitt was speaking what was, to him, merely the plain truth. As I said, nothing was a big deal to him; that, I suspect, is part of the reason he made it to 106.

"Did you ever come under gas attack?" I asked him.

"All the time," he replied. "There was gas in all the shells, practically. And yes, I was severely gassed several times, but I never went to medical for it. I just lost my voice and eventually it would come back."

Although it was responsible for far fewer deaths than bullets, bombs, or bayonets (though probably more than meat cleavers), poison gas is remembered today as *the* weapon of World War I, primarily because of the horrible things even a little of it could do to you: blind you, cover your skin with blisters and sores, break down your lungs in a hurry, bleed you out internally, drown you in your own bodily fluids. "So you were very lucky?" I asked.

"Yes, I was," he replied. "Very."

Still, it wasn't as if he'd been unprepared. "We were trained to put on the gas masks," he explained. "As I remember, six seconds was the time it would take you to put on the gas mask. And when the shells started coming over, you would use those six seconds to get the gas mask on. And after a while, you didn't bother to put the gas mask on. You smelled the gas" — it smelled, he said, like mustard — "and if it wasn't severe, you didn't bother to put your gas mask on. And we lived with that."

Only, a lot of men in Corporal Moffitt's regiment didn't live. Throughout the summer of 1918 and on into the fall, the Yankee Division, including the 102nd Regiment, went from fight to fight to fight. As at Seicheprey, they acquitted themselves very well; and, as at Seicheprey, some of them died in the process. Major George Rau of Hartford, who had commanded the defense of Seicheprey and been highly decorated for it afterward, was killed by a German shell three months later, near Château-Thierry; during that same week, July 18–25, Sibley claims the YD, in a counteroffensive against the Germans, "lost 4,108 men in killed, wounded, gassed and missing." According to Strickland, "About 9,000 officers and men passed through the ranks of the [102nd] regiment during the war"; of those, official records indicate, 476 were killed in battle, 1,765 were wounded, and 1,909 were gassed — a total of 4,150, nearly half the regiment.

Laurence Moffitt would have known those figures better than just about anyone in the 102nd; his job, he told me, was "personnel of the regiment . . . I was in charge of service records of the twelve companies in the regiment . . . about two hundred men each." Regimental HQ "was just a short distance in back of the front lines," he explained. "Maybe a hundred yards, more or less." The Germans always had HQ in their sights; and, as I mentioned earlier, everyone who served there had to take their turn in the front-line trenches, too. The first time I interviewed Laurence Moffitt, he played down the danger he faced in France; but when I returned a few months later and asked him again, he conceded: "I was in danger always when going from one dugout to another, or one trench to another. The trenches were all open space, and they were always a dangerous place to be." Then there were the "German airplanes flying up our regiment, dropping bombs. That's right. Some of those bombs included gas, as well as artillery bombs. . . . That was a constant and regular occurrence." But the greatest threat came from big German guns lobbing artillery shells — like the one that had hurled that piece of shrapnel against his leg, if not through it.

"Were you caught in a lot of artillery barrages?" I asked.

"I'd say not a lot," he replied, of course. "But the artillery fired regularly at the different positions."

"How," I asked him a bit later, "did you cope with it?"

"You just lived with it," he said. "It was a dangerous situation and you figured if you got killed, you wouldn't know it. Other people would know it, but you wouldn't. So you just lived like in any dangerous situation. You just ignore the danger."

During that first interview, I asked Mr. Moffitt if he'd seen anyone killed in action. He said no, he hadn't, but said it in a way that made me wonder if he really hadn't, or if he just didn't want to think about it too hard, to summon up a memory he had long since put away. After interviewing a dozen or so other veterans, and then talking to him again about the danger he and the rest of the YD were in from day to day, I decided to ask him again. "Did you see anyone get wounded or killed in battle?"

"Yes, plenty," he said, just like that. "Some young fellow along while I was going . . ." His voice trailed off for a moment. "It's hard for me to remember where I was, where we went and why. . . . My company commander knew why. Us small units only did what they were told."

"But you were telling me about a fellow you saw get killed."

"Yes. His face was all blown off. I leaned down over him to tell him that his gas mask was off. Then I saw that his face was mutilated, and so I just left him for the fellows whose job it was to take care of the wounded."

I asked him if he'd seen anybody else get wounded or killed. "I saw fellows who were wounded frequently, yes . . . by shell fire, the three-inch, 75-millimeter shells the Germans kept sending over. You were always exposed to those, that artillery. And the Germans sent it over for a purpose."

I asked him if that fellow he had seen that day was the only fatality he personally witnessed. "Probably the only one that I leaned over in the war and looked at," he said.

"Did you see him fall?"

"No," he said. "He was back in the ditch on the ground. And I leaned over him to tell him his gas mask was off, and I saw his face was all mutilated."

If he hadn't remembered it before, he certainly did now; and I felt bad for asking him again. This man before me, this small, very old man still dressed up from his Veterans Day parade in a salmon blazer and deep blue tie and wearing his helmet, his actual helmet with its scarcely faded little square painting of the Connecticut Charter Oak, the symbol of the 102nd, this man who said that nothing was ever hard for him, who didn't mind the mud or the boxcars or army food — this man had once seen something truly horrific. And no doubt much more than once.

Exactly eighty-five years earlier to the day, something remarkable — perhaps the most remarkable thing in J. Laurence Moffitt's very long life — happened. This, again, is how he described it, simply: "All firing stopped. Complete silence. There wasn't a sound at eleven o'clock. And we were able to go out of our dugouts and trenches without our helmets or gas masks, which was the first time we had been able to do that since we first went to the front." He added that, most likely, he "yelled and rejoiced that the war was over."

I have a large old poster of that scene — a solitary doughboy standing next to a trench, helmet in hand, gas mask hanging from around his neck, eyes turned skyward; his expression is a mixture of awe and relief. The poster is an advertisement for the YD Fund, which offered support to soldiers making the difficult transition to life back home after all they'd seen and done Over There.

Which was quite a bit: After a long summer at Belleau and Château-Thierry and Oise-Aisne, they were sent back east to the Toul Sector, where they played a critical role in the Battle of Saint-Mihiel, a two-day affair that quickly turned into a rout of the Germans and set the stage for the Meuse-Argonne Offensive, the last great battle of the war. The YD was assigned to a sector on the right flank, near Verdun.

And then, four weeks into that huge campaign, the high command decided they'd finally had enough of General Clarence Edwards. On October 22, 1918, they yanked him from the Yankee Division and sent him back to Boston. The pretext was that he had allowed his men to fraternize with the enemy.

Shocked? Don't be. There was plenty of precedent. Unlike their French allies, the British and American soldiers didn't particularly hate the Germans; in some cases, quite the opposite. "We regarded them very highly," Laurence Moffitt told me. "They were very well-trained, very strict, very rigid, very straight. And their movements were all very orderly. Even outside of our organization, organized activities, even alone, individually they maintained a high degree of dignity."

"Was there mutual respect between the Allied soldiers and the German soldiers?" I asked him.

"To some extent, yes," he replied. "Exactly that."

In many cases, it went beyond simply mutual respect; long before America entered the war, quite a few British and German units adopted unofficial policies of "live and let live" toward one another, wherein they wouldn't try very hard to kill each other. Often, it meant nothing more than a tacit agreement that you wouldn't shell each other during mess, target each other's supply trains, and so on; but there are tales of one side warning the other when a barrage was about to begin, even going so far as letting them know where they might seek shelter. The most famous episode is the Christmas Truce of 1914, when British and German troops decided spontaneously to celebrate the holiday together, sharing food, drink, and tobacco from home, and even hosting international soccer matches.

Sibley reports that the incident that ultimately cost General Edwards his job occurred on October 20, 1918, when a unit of Saxons called out across a hundred yards of No Man's Land and asked that a couple of Americans come over to their trench. They did, and were promptly surrounded by several dozen eager (and unarmed) Germans. Their spokesman said: "We want you to stop shooting at us . . . we are not barbarians, and we don't want to kill unnecessarily. . . . We don't want to kill Americans. We have had plenty of chances to shoot you in the last few days, and haven't done it. When we have been ordered to fire by our officers, we have fired high, purposely."

According to Sibley, the Americans replied that the only ways the Saxons could avoid being fired upon were to surrender or retreat. The Saxons countered that they could do neither. The Americans went back to their trench and reported the conversation to their superiors; it went up the line until it was decided, as Sibley puts it, "to put down a heavy concentration of artillery fire on that spot next day — which was done. As the reporting officer put it, being of a literary turn, 'the concentration was placed on certain German soldiers who had expressed a desire to meet some of our men as individuals for the purpose of discussing a possible cessation of hostilities.'" So much for live and let live.

Two days later, General Edwards was relieved of his command. The episode of "fraternization" cited as cause was most likely a pretext; a better-liked man would probably have received only a mild reprimand, if that, for something that was not at all uncommon at the time. I don't know if Edwards was really that obnoxious, or if he was just another outspoken general who had made some poor choices in his alliances. Historians have made strong cases on both sides of the question; I've even heard it suggested that the Army's top brass, many of whom were southerners, wouldn't have cottoned to anyone leading a self-proclaimed Yankee Division. Deserved or not, though, Edwards's unpopularity stigmatized his men.

Laurence Moffitt never expressed any bitterness to me about the way his division was treated. But then, he wouldn't have; I doubt he'd ever felt it. It wasn't in him to do so. He did let on that he was a little disappointed about not going home immediately after the armistice. "With the war ending in November, we foolishly were sure we would be home by Christmas," he recalled. "We forgot there were two million other troops over there. We didn't leave for home until the last part of March in 1919."

But a strange thing happened to the beleaguered, maligned YD in their last few months in France: Somehow it was decided that they should, at last, be recognized and honored for their service. So now, instead of being criticized as sloppy and inconsistent, they were lauded as determined, effective, brave. They were even chosen, from among all the American divisions in France, to be reviewed by President Wilson on Christmas Day, 1918. "We were quite impressed to be able to see our president, and quite honored that he came to our regiment," Corporal Moffitt recalled. But even here, there were, shall we say, issues. "The whole regiment was lined up along the side of the road. And we were stationed there at twelve o'clock, at noon, and he didn't show until four o'clock in the afternoon. And we were four hours waiting for him to come and inspect us. But he came, and then we had lunch. But it was not until after he came that we had lunch." By which time, I imagine, they were pretty hungry. And cold.

"Did he talk to you?" I asked.

"Not to me," he said, "but one of the fellows in my company, he was right near him. And he [President Wilson] asked him how conditions were. And the fellow, as usual, said 'lousy.' And he got reprimanded for that."

I couldn't tell, from Mr. Moffitt's tone, whether or not he approved of the man's response, but he certainly didn't agree with him. "Actually, they were not lousy," he asserted. "For the Army they were pretty good. . . . Some had better care in the Army than they ever got at home, and better food. Because it's surprising how good the food was. Even beef stew. That was the standard meal, beef stew." And, he added: "Always enough. Never without it. Right." Perhaps this is another key to living to 106: no complaints, not even about army food.

Life got a lot easier after the armistice. And better. "The girls were very hungry for male companions, because the youths were killed off pretty much in France," Corporal Moffitt recalled, and left it at that. The rest of the time, "we just hung around. There were regular military exercises, and there would be hiking trips day after day, just for the troops to do something, you know . . . entertainment had to be planned. . . . And there were games of baseball and boxing, and probably other sports. . . . And I got a leave . . . I guess a ten-day . . . and I went down with other troops, down to a nice mountain resort area for a week, Aix-les-Bains. Do you know French? It's a bath, as you know."

Nevertheless, he and the rest of the Yankee Division were eager to get home, which they did in April, 1919 — one of the first divisions to be repatriated. "Had a big parade in Boston," he told me. "And then more parades in Connecticut for our Connecticut regiment. And everything was veterans." And then, to hear him tell it, life started right back up again. At least, his did; he was one of the fortunate ones in that regard. And he knew it. "As I said, I started working at an insurance company when I was right out of high school. And the company took us all back. They held our positions; they filled them with girls, mostly. But they took us all back. In my case, I had a job waiting for me when I came back. That was not true with everyone who was in World War I, unfortunately. So, I was hired by another company for certain reasons, and then . . . in 1921, I was hired by a New York [insurance] group, Crum and Forster. . . . I was hired by that company to represent them in Connecticut, out of Hartford, which I did for forty-two years. . . . It so happens I went to work for that company the year I was married." His new wife had been one of the girls hired to replace him and his coworkers during the war.

He had a good life, rising high in the company, traveling frequently to New York, where he belonged to two clubs, the kind of places that men like him — insurance men, New England Yankees, veterans — joined. In the late 1940s, he was elected president of the Connecticut Field Club, a state insurance organization. He was happily married, had four children and nine grandchildren and eight great-grandchildren, all of whom adored him; his wife, Flo, had been a woman of "real class, not real sexy, but real class. Everybody admired her, loved her, loved to talk with her." His job, he said, had been "very comfortable, no problem, no stress, never, never any pressure. It was just, develop a business to work with agents, helping agents, solving problems." He retired at sixty-six, moved to Cape Cod, had another third of a century with his wife, and still belonged to several weekly clubs until his hearing grew so faint that he could no longer participate fully in their talks. He never disliked anything, it seems, except farm work.

Maybe it's true: Nothing ever was hard for him. Even the war. Especially the war. After our first visit, I actually came away with the impression that it was — or at least that he believed it was — the best thing that had ever happened to him.

"Was your service in the Army a very important part of your life?" I asked him at one point.

"Yes," he said without hesitating. "Most important, all my life. That's right." And long after it had ended, it remained a major component of his social life. "Our original company . . . had annual meetings. Then our regiment, the 102nd Infantry, would have its regular meetings, monthly meetings. And . . . the 26th Division . . . would have its annual meetings, and some in between. And our Army veterans' service unified us for many, many years . . ." There was the American Legion, too. And those YD license plates. "Any car you saw with a YD on it, you knew was owned and operated by a member of your division. And you would give him a toot, and he would give you a toot." The division was reactivated in 1941, sent to Europe, fought at the Bulge, drove on into France and Germany, and helped capture Hitler's hometown of Linz, Austria, before the war ended. And yet today, few people who aren't military buffs or historians know anything at all about the Yankee Division. And when I met its last surviving World War I veteran, the division didn't know about him, either.

But what luck for me that I found him. And that I found him as early as I did. As I've said, without him this book wouldn't exist — not just because I probably would have become too discouraged to seek out a third and fourth and fifth veteran, but because, without Laurence Moffitt, I might never have encountered the Yankee Division; and without them, well, I'm not sure I would have come to understand fully just what this war was to Americans.

The YD's crucible, Seicheprey, is very quiet now. Like almost every other village in the area, it was completely destroyed; unlike some, it was rebuilt afterward, just where it had stood before, and looks, I would guess, very much like it did in 1914. But I sense there is much less to it these days; like their American counterparts, French small towns have been shriveling up for a long time now. I suspect the process actually started that day in the spring of 1918; that some people, maybe quite a number, never bothered to return to their destroyed houses and shops and farms, never even tried to rebuild. I visited Seicheprey on a sunny, warm June afternoon, yet I never spotted a single resident walking about there; as far as I could see, there were no shops or commercial establishments for them to walk to. The houses are modest, and appear much older than they are. The church is pretty but small. The village's Great War memorial is small, too, smaller than most I saw in France; but it is very well kept, with bright gold leaf still filling the engraved names of the local war dead, eleven of them in all. Underneath the list, someone had attached a slab of slate with a small, chipped photograph of a handsome man: *A la memoire de Jean Paul Fourriere, victime de la barbarie Nazie, mort pour la France* about six weeks before D-day, a reminder that the Germans successfully took the Toul Sector, and the rest of the country, the next time around. On a separate side of the memorial's base, a generation earlier, another family had mounted a bright porcelain slab, bordered in more gold leaf, a grainy (but not chipped) photograph and likenesses of his medals: *A la memoire de mon Papa regretté Lucien Petit, mort pour la France 11 Septemb. 1914.* The long war had been barely a month old then.

In the same little green space you'll find a small fountain that has not been maintained nearly so well. Water hasn't flowed from its spout for a long time; its bronze plaque has grown dark and discolored. You have to get very close in order to read it:

TO THE COMMUNE OF SEICHEPREY
TO COMMEMORATE THE SERVICE
OF THE 102D INFANTRY, 26TH DIVISION,
A REGIMENT OF THE AMERICAN ARMY
RECRUITED FROM THE CITIZENS OF CONNECTICUT
DEFENDERS OF SEICHEPREY APRIL 20, 1918.
IN THE FIRM BELIEF THAT THE FRIENDSHIP
OF FRENCHMEN AND AMERICANS SEALED
IN THIS PLACE IN BATTLE SHALL SERVE
THE CAUSE OF PEACE AMONG ALL NATIONS
THIS MEMORIAL IS PRESENTED BY THE
MEN AND WOMEN OF CONNECTICUT
1923

Of all the places they fought and died — Belleau, Château-Thierry, Oise-Aisne, Saint-Mihiel, Meuse-Argonne — this is the place the soldiers of the 102nd, and the widows and parents they'd left behind in Connecticut, chose to store on the highest shelf of their memory. Just as I wouldn't have fully understood the war without them, it seems they wouldn't have fully understood it without Seicheprey.

• • •

About ninety minutes into my first visit with Laurence Moffitt, his daughter, Janet, who had been here and there in the house up until that point, sometimes listening in, more often not, told me she had to leave to go pick up her granddaughter. Suddenly, I was filled with an irrational but potent sense of dread: What if her father should die while she was gone? The man was 106 years old, after all; he looked fine, but who knows? So, although we were then nearing the end of the interview, I decided to stay until she returned. Mr. Moffitt seemed tired, but, in keeping with his stoicism, he didn't let on; and when we finished talking about the war, we talked about everything else: his career, his marriage, his life. He told me he'd voted for the first time in 1920, for Warren G. Harding, and had voted in every election, national and local, since. He was a Republican; his father had been a Democrat. He said he participated in every parade they had in Orleans — Memorial Day, July Fourth, Veterans Day, whatever. "I've never missed an Armistice Day parade," he said, "and I don't expect to miss this one."

"Do you march?" I asked.

"No, I ride," he replied, without making me feel stupid for asking. "In fact," he added, "the World War II veterans no longer march. They ride in a car." He rode in Janet's Japanese sedan; for the occasion, they slapped a magnetic sign reading WORLD WAR I VETERAN on the door. No one ever oohed or aahed.

On the occasion of his 104th birthday, he'd received a letter from President George W. Bush, congratulating him. It did not mention his service. He kept it in a scrapbook, which he invited me to flip through; there was also in there a letter from a prominent gerontologist, thanking Mr. Moffitt for agreeing to leave his body to science.

He showed me his Légion d'Honneur; it was a beautiful, colorful medal, and came with a large certificate signed by President Chirac. He'd had it mounted in a simple frame, from which a very large, jagged piece of glass — almost half the entire thing — had since broken out. It sat on the floor, leaning up against a piece of furniture.

We talked about his family, his siblings, his parents and grandparents. After he reiterated that he made a point of keeping up with the news and world affairs, I asked him if he'd ever been on the Internet.

"No, and I don't know what the Internet is," he stated. "And maybe you can tell me. How do I get on the Internet? Do I have to join?"

"You have to have a computer," I told him.

"Well, I have a computer," he replied.

"You don't have to join," I explained. "It's just that you have to — you have to subscribe. It's like a service."

"Oh."

"And you pay a certain amount of money every month, ten dollars or twenty dollars, and you connect through the telephone line, go through your computer, and then you can connect with millions of different, what they call websites, all over the world. Information, and news, and music, and everything you can imagine. Pictures. It's — I think you would like it very much."

He was quiet for a moment. "I have plenty to do," he said, finally. "Do I need it?"

"No," I told him. "You don't."

He said he couldn't remember what his grandfather had manufactured. I asked if he had fought in the Civil War. "No," he said. "We had nobody in the Civil War. I don't know why. Lots of my ancestors were in the Revolutionary War."

"How do you feel," I asked him, "about being the last World War I veteran that many people will meet?"

"Actually, you don't feel any of those things," he replied. "The last this, the first this. Actually, you don't give it a thought any more than you live every day."

A few months later, I returned to Orleans to watch him ride in that parade and interview him a second time. When we were done talking, he and Janet told me they had a tradition of going out to lunch on Veterans Day, and invited me to join them. I considered for a moment, thought about the traffic I might hit on the way home, and demurred. They seemed disappointed; I said I would come back again sometime soon, maybe in the spring. Why not?

Somehow, the fear that had gripped me a few months earlier, when Janet Moffitt had left to go pick up her granddaughter, had since left me entirely. It didn't occur to me that her father might not still be around come spring.

He wasn't. He died on February 7, 2004, a month shy of his 107th birthday. Had some trouble with his heart, went into the hospital and never emerged. He was a corporal in HQ Company, the keeper of the roll for the 102nd Infantry Regiment of the 26th Division of the United States Army. The rest of the regiment — and the division — having moved on, he closed the register and did, too.

4

Cheer and Laughter and Joyous Shout

There isn't any girl in France, dear
who in any way compares with you
I crossed the sea to take my chance, dear
with our own Red, White, and Blue
If they'll carry me back to old New England
now that the war is through,
They can keep all the Frenchies for the French laddies
but I'm coming back to you.

    —from "Yankee Girl, I'm Coming Back to You"
    by Jack O'Brien and Billy Timmins
    Dedicated to General Clarence R. Edwards and the 26th Division

NOT EVERYTHING OLD IS VALUABLE. Sure, some people are willing to pay a lot for certain things that have absolutely no practical or aesthetic merit, like those little glass insulator caps that fall off the tops of old power lines; no matter how long I may live, I'll never understand the allure of those. But there is an awful lot of old stuff out there that people are just dying to unload, and if you should cross their path at the right moment, they will happily unload it upon you rather than haul it to the dump.

Take 78 rpm records. They're heavy, ungainly, fragile, and hopelessly obsolete. They also take up an awful lot of space, and generally age pretty poorly. In my early twenties, though, none of that mattered to me. I bought them in bulk, a hundred or two at a time, for what typically worked out to about a nickel apiece. I knew their resale value was even less, but I didn't care; I had started collecting Victrolas, and needed something to play on them.

This was the early 1990s, before *Antiques Roadshow* and eBay conspired to obliterate the joy of finding things serendipitously. I was living in Memphis in those days, and frequenting a flea market that sprang up monthly at the city's old fairgrounds. Scarcely a month would pass that didn't see me lugging home a few large and very heavy boxes of 78s. I had a ritual: crank up the Victrola, get a packet of needles, and spend the day listening to my finds. I didn't have space for all of them; a record had to be pretty special in some way for me to keep it.

One day I put an old Victor black-label disk on the platter, dropped the needle on it, and heard this:

> *Over in the trenches, up to their eyes in clay,*
> *Billy and Jack and Jimmie and Joe are singing all the day.*
> *When they see a German sticking up his snout*
> *They give him a chance to get out of France and then they shout:*
> *"Keep your head down, Fritzie boy,*
> *Keep your head down, Fritzie boy.*
> *Late last night in the pale moonlight*
> *I saw you! I saw you!*
> *You were fixing your barbed wire, when we opened rapid-fire.*
> *So if you want to see your Vater in the Vaterland,*
> *Keep your head down, Fritzie boy!"*

I played it over and over throughout that day. And many times thereafter.

A few years later, at another flea market on the Upper West Side of Manhattan, I came upon a copy of the sheet music to "Keep Your Head Down, Fritzie Boy." It was, to me at that moment, an astonishing discovery. The artwork was fairly crude — a young doughboy standing in uniform and holding a bayonet, rosy-cheeked and beaming, while other doughboys duke it out with Fritzie in the trenches behind him — but the object itself was, somehow, beautiful. I couldn't believe I had come across it. The record was extremely entertaining but also seemed a common artifact to me; this piece of sheet music struck me as exceedingly rare.

Actually, I had it backwards. World War I coincided with the apex of the American music-publishing industry, which was then known (and still is, by some) as Tin Pan Alley. Tin Pan Alley was, in fact, a real and specific place, though not an alley — actually, it was a stretch of West Twenty-eighth Street in Manhattan, between Fifth and Sixth Avenues, where a great many music publishers had their offices. It is not known why so many of them converged upon the same spot (a situation that presumably would have made intellectual espionage and theft a great deal easier), nor is it known why the place was nicknamed Tin Pan Alley (some have speculated that the term is a derogatory reference to the cacophonous effect of many different pianos playing many different songs at once). But to say that this little stretch of side street in a neighborhood that doesn't even have a name these days was once the epicenter of American music — maybe even culture — is defensible hyperbole. No one today seems to know exactly how many music-publishing houses were clustered there in 1917, but it was big business — the biggest. It made some men tremendously rich.

To really understand the importance of Tin Pan Alley, we have to reexamine our definitions of both "music" and "publishing." Yes, publishing houses bought the rights to songs peddled by itinerant songwriters, or "pluggers"; but more often, they wrote their own songs, sometimes three or four a day. Some houses were known to hang out signs declaring SONGS WRITTEN TO ORDER!, and they meant it. And that's where our reexamination of the term "music" comes in, because in those days, music was much more than merely entertainment: It was news. If something big happened — a great ship sank, or a train wreck occurred, or someone new was elected president or governor, or the stock market took a dip, or someone was assassinated — people started writing songs about it immediately, and sheet music hit the stores before the headlines had cleared the newspapers. And if something really, really big happened — like, say, America entered the greatest war the planet had ever seen — well, a lot of people started writing a lot of songs, and they didn't stop for a long time. There was a lot to tell.

• • •

I didn't raise my boy to be a soldier,
I brought him up to be my pride and joy.
Who dares to place a musket on his shoulder,
To shoot some other mother's darling boy?
Let nations arbitrate their future troubles,
It's time to lay the sword and gun away.
There'd be no war today, if mothers all would say,
"I didn't raise my boy to be a soldier."

"I Didn't Raise My Boy to Be a Soldier," written by Alfred Bryan and Al Piantadosi, was one of the biggest hits of 1915. At a time when reports of horrific bloodletting Over There occupied the front pages of American newspapers every day, an awful lot of people Over Here wanted absolutely nothing to do with it. Some were pacifists. Some were Irish, who had no desire to fight for (and alongside) the British. Some were Russian Jews, who had fled the czar's anti-Semitic regime and had no desire to go off and fight for the man. Some were Austrian or Hungarian and remembered their old emperor, and their empire, fondly; a great many were German, or at least of German descent (at the time, more Americans could trace their ancestors to Germany than to any other country), and resented being characterized as barbarians and Huns. And a great many more just thought the whole bloody thing had absolutely nothing to do with them. "If They Want to Fight, All Right," declared another song title from 1915, "but 'Neutral' Is My Middle Name."

It wasn't a universal sentiment; many sympathized with "Wake Up, America!" which became a hit the following year. *Must we be laughed at, America / while our swords turn weak with rust?* it asked. *Let us pray, God, for peace, but peace with honor / But let's get ready to answer duty's call.* Still, there was room, in 1916's America, for honest differences of opinion.

In April 1917, though, that all changed suddenly. "Uncle Sam's Awake" declared a 1917 response to 1916's musical plea; "America, Here's My Boy" announced another title from 1917, rebuking 1915's pacifist (or at least isolationist) hit. Suddenly, if you weren't for the war, you were against America. Like most of America's newspapers and politicians, its songwriters fell in line, whether because they actually believed it or simply believed it was good for business. I have come across many hundreds of pieces of World War I sheet music, but I have never seen one published after 1916 that didn't support the war. I doubt such a thing exists. And believe me, there is a bottomless well of American World War I sheet music.

In the twenty-aughts, it would be: Do this, or don't do that, and the terrorists win. In the late nineteen-teens, *the* terrorist, as far as Americans were concerned, was Friedrich Wilhelm Viktor Albrecht von Preussen, better known as Kaiser Wilhelm II, Emperor of Germany and King of Prussia, known better still as Kaiser Bill, Billy, Willie, or, simply, the Kaiser. This was the man, after all, who had started the war so he could conquer and own the world, who had personally ordered the sinking of the *Lusitania,* the rape and destruction of Belgium, and all kinds of atrocities in *la belle France.* Or so it was said, anyway. Americans just hated the man; a popular poster of the day portrayed him as a rabid gorilla wading onto an American shore wearing a spiked helmet (the Germans called it a *Pickelhaube*) labeled "militarism" while clutching a defiled maiden in one hand and a club labeled *Kultur* (the German word for "civilization") in the other, the charred ruins of Paris smoldering behind him, all under the slogan: DESTROY THIS MAD BRUTE. ENLIST.

Grotesque as this all might seem to us nearly a century later, it must be said that the Kaiser didn't exactly do much to help his image Over Here, or, come to think of it, anywhere. He was bellicose, petulant, blustering, racist, anti-Semitic, xenophobic, paranoid, egomaniacal, megalomaniacal, conniving, treacherous, greedy, and possessed of powerful inferiority and persecution complexes. He rarely appeared in public in civilian clothes, favoring some or other extravagant military uniform. His left arm, damaged at birth in a complicated breech delivery, was withered and virtually useless; during public appearances he kept it either behind his back or awkwardly posed in front and rigidly clutching some object, creating the impression that he was up to something. And he wore his thick, stiff mustache turned straight up at the ends. Few people can pull that look off; he wasn't one of them.

Still, I don't think he quite deserved the battering he took in Tin

Pan Alley, where he quickly became the man songwriters — and, by extension, the American people — loved to hate. Violently. Savagely. So much so that in some of their hands, the war to Make the World Safe for Democracy became the war to capture the Kaiser, do all kinds of unspeakable but horribly painful things to him, and then kill him. Several times, if possible.

You said you'd plaster Paris with your Hindenburg machine / but now it looks as if you're on the road to Paris Green, declares one song, "The Worst Is Yet to Come" by Sam M. Lewis, Joe Young, and Bert Grant. Not particularly menacing (or, for that matter, catchy), but the sheet music is adorned with a cover illustration of the Kaiser chained to a dungeon wall, cowering on a cot under a tattered blanket, while a strapping young doughboy, perched on the mattress with one foot on the Kaiser's chest, jabs a bayonet into the old man's face. That alone must have sold a few copies.

In many other cases, the title was probably enough. "We're Going to Hang the Kaiser Under the Linden Tree." "The USA Will Lay the Kaiser Away." "When the Yankees Yank the Kaiser off His Throne." "We'll Lick the Kaiser If It Takes Us Twenty Years." "We Are Out for the Scalp of Mister Kaiser Man." "We're All Going Calling On the Kaiser." (*And we'll bring him something good / A kimono made of wood.*) "The Kaiser Wanted More Territory, So We Gave Him Hell." (*Soon he'll sit on another throne / where he's sure to be right at home / Nice red uniform, and horns upon his dome.*) "I'd Like to See the Kaiser with a Lily in His Hand." Which is to say: embalmed and laid out in that kimono made of wood.

The cover for "We'll All Make Billy Pay the Bill He Owes" calls it "An Impressive War Song with a Punch in Every Line." I'm not sure I agree, though I really like the cover art, which features a stern Uncle Sam holding out, at arm's length, a document addressed to "Mr. Bill Hohenzollern" that reads: "Pay to the Order of the Allies, Suitable Indemnities to All Warring Nations and America's Demands, France's Demands, England's Demands, Belgium's Demands, Italian Demands, Serbia's Demands, Portugal's Demands . . ." (Portugal?) The Kaiser's expression betrays what would, decades later, become known as sticker shock.

My favorite song of this ilk, though, is "When the Kaiser Does the Goose-Step to a Good Old American Rag" by Jack Frost (really) and

Harold Neander. *They'll play it jerky / and make Bill "walk turkey" / and salute our grand old flag,* the song promises. *There'll be a jazz band from Dixie / and Bill won't dare say "Nix-ie," / when the Yankees say, "Come, William, dance that drag."* Not only does it manage to work in all kinds of contemporary musical references — everything from John Philip Sousa to the Six Brown Brothers (a vaudeville saxophone ensemble from Canada) to Alexander's Ragtime Band — but the song actually robs the Kaiser of something more precious to him than life: his dignity. Knowing what little I do about Wilhelm II, I suspect he might just rather have been hanged under the linden tree — particularly if, as the cover art speculates, he was forced to dance by being jabbed in the *tuchus* by bayonets.

Wilhelm II may have served as a lightning rod on Tin Pan Alley, but his country — and its people — were not spared, either. "Germany, You'll Soon Be No Man's Land." "It's a Long Way to Berlin but We'll Get There." "We Don't Want the Bacon — What We Want Is a Piece of the Rhine!" "When We Wind Up the Watch on the Rhine." "We'll Sing 'Hail! Hail! The Gang's All Here' on the Sidewalks of Berlin." "We'll Knock the Heligo — into Heligo — out of Heligoland" even tried to teach Americans a little geography. "Hunting the Hun," by Howard E. Rogers and Archie Gottler, featured a cartoonish cover illustration of the Yanks luring hapless Germans across No Man's Land — and into the stockade — with a barrel of "pilsner beer," a steaming plate of sauerkraut, and an even more aromatic Teutonic delicacy:

> You can capture them with ease
> All you need is just a little limburger cheese.
> Give 'em one little smell, they come out with a yell.
> Then your work is done.
> When they start to advance, shoot 'em in the pants.
> That's the game called Hunting the Hun.

It's tempting, if you've ever smelled Limburger cheese, to joke that you'd be shooting the Huns in the back, since the smell would make anyone flee; but by 1918, the war had taken its toll, and most Germans didn't have nearly enough to eat.

For pure, brazen bravado, though, you can't beat a 1918 composition by J. Keirn Brennan and Ernest R. Ball. The lyrics aren't what you'd call clever:

> *Say, Fritz, we knew we'd give you fits.*
> *With a million Yankee hits, we blew you into bits.*
> *Hey, Fritz, when you met Yankee wits,*
> *We pounded you until you knew you had to call it quits.*

The cover art features — who else? — Uncle Sam, pointing right at you, though instead of James Montgomery Flagg's famously stern "I Want You" Uncle Sam, this one seems to be stifling a chuckle behind his cocky grin. But what really makes this song special is its title: "You Can't Beat Us, For We've Never Lost a War."

Clearly, Uncle Sam is a Yankee, in every sense of the word.

For every anti-German song, you'll find another, equally passionate, pro-French song. Where the former were zippy, and often witty, the latter tended to be maudlin dirges. You wouldn't dance to them.

> *Lafayette, we hear you calling, Layfayette, 'tis not in vain*
> *That the tears of France are falling, we will help her to*
>   *smile again.*
> *For a friend in need is a friend in deed, do not think we shall*
>   *ever forget.*
> *Lafayette, we hear you calling, we are coming, Lafayette.*

Like Mary Earl did in "Lafayette (We Hear You Calling)," many pluggers followed the lead of General Pershing, who, shortly after arriving in France in June, 1917, made a special pilgrimage to the grave of George Washington's old aide-de-camp. (It was actually Pershing's aide-de-camp, Colonel Charles E. Stanton, who uttered the famous line that has since been attributed to his boss: "Lafayette, we are here.") Never mind the fact that America owed a similar debt to Germany, whence hailed the likes of General von Steuben and Baron de Kalb, men who arguably played an even greater role in America's military victory over Britain than had the Marquis de Lafayette. Suddenly, Americans collectively remembered that Lafayette was their man, that they owed him, and that the time had come to repay that debt by sailing over and saving his descendants' collective *derrières*. And even, perhaps, a bit more, as Jack Coogan promises in "France, We'll Rebuild Your Towns for You":

> *First we'll send our sons and our mighty guns,*
> *Then vic'try will come from above.*
> *We will re-plant each field, so it will yield*
> *The fruits of our brotherly love.*
> *All your shattered dreams we'll mend*
> *In America you'll find a friend*
> *And we'll send our gold across the ocean blue.*
> *France, we'll rebuild your towns for you.*

Lafayette wasn't the only dead French soldier summoned back to duty on Tin Pan Alley, either:

> *Joan of Arc, Joan of Arc, do your eyes from the skies see the foe?*
> *Don't you see the drooping Fleur-de-lis? Can't you hear the tears of Normandy?*
> *Joan of Arc, Joan of Arc, let your spirit guide us through.*
> *Come lead your France to victory; Joan of Arc, they are calling you.*
> — "Joan of Arc, They Are Calling You" by Alfred Bryan, Willie Weston, and Jack Wells

While many of the songs that deal with France wallow in that country's tremendous pool of suffering, others manage to find the bright side. France, after all, is full of French girls. It didn't matter that they couldn't speak English — in fact, as songs like "And He'd Say Ooh-La-La! Wee-Wee!," and "Wee, Wee, Marie (Will You Do Zis for Me)" make plain, the linguistic differences might even have been a plus. And it wasn't just doughboys who succumbed to the charms of their hosts:

> *Rosie Green was a village queen who enlisted as a nurse.*
> *She waited for a chance, and left for France with an ambulance.*
> *Rosie Green met a chap named Jean, a soldier from Paree.*
> *When he said "Par-le-vous, my pet,"*
> *She said, "I will, but not just yet."*
> — "Oh! Frenchy" by Sam Ehrlich and Con Conrad

If you must go off to war, France, it seems, is as good a place as any — for gander *and* goose.

Looking back on it, it appears that everyone was just playing catch-up. The best song of the whole singin' war was written right at the start.

Maybe it had to be that way. The most popular song of the war in England was written two years before the first shot was fired. "It's a Long, Long Way to Tipperary" isn't even about war; it's about an unsophisticated Irishman who goes off to London but, despite the excitement of the place, can't stop thinking about home, and about the girl he left behind. Like many songs of the day, its writers, Jack Judge and Harry Williams, built "Tipperary" upon a pejorative ethnic stereotype — in this case, that the Irish are, shall we say, a simple people:

> *Paddy wrote a letter to his Irish Molly O',*
> *Saying "Should you not receive it, write and let me know!*
> *If I make mistakes in 'spelling,' Molly, dear," said he,*
> *"Remember, it's the pen that's bad, don't lay the blame on me."*

Strangely, it was an Irish regiment, the Connaught Rangers, that first adopted it as a marching song; London *Daily Mail* war correspondent George Curnock reported seeing them do so in northern France in August, 1914, just a couple of weeks after the war began. By the end of the war, just about every soldier in Europe knew it.

Lots of other English war songs made it Over Here — the most famous, perhaps, being "Pack Up Your Troubles in Your Old Kit-Bag and Smile, Smile, Smile," by George Asaf and Felix Powell, a song that really makes you want to do what it tells you to — but when the United States finally got into the war, everyone in America knew that only American war songs would do from then on. And sure enough, America was soon drawing from that bottomless well of music on West Twenty-eighth Street, singing the output of pretty much every working songwriter in the country, famous or obscure. As many songs as they wrote, though — and as good as some of them were — they were all, as I said, trying to catch up. And none of them ever would.

The first big American song of the Great War — and the best — was written by a man too old to fight, a man who, many believed, had already seen his best days go by. The grandson of Irish immigrants, George Michael Cohan was born into show business in Providence, Rhode Island, on July 3, 1878. (Cohan would claim all his life that — like his creation, the Yankee Doodle Boy — he was actually born on the Fourth of July.) Almost immediately, his parents, vaudevillians, incorporated their new baby into the act; his older sister Josie was already in it. By the time he was a teenager, he was running the show, ending each performance with his trademark farewell: "My mother thanks you, my father thanks you, my sister thanks you, and I thank you." He published his first song at fifteen, and wrote, directed, and starred in his first Broadway show at twenty-three. In the first decade of the twentieth century, he wrote a string of classic American songs that helped define the era: In addition to "Yankee Doodle Boy," there were "You're a Grand Old Flag," "Give My Regards to Broadway," "Mary Is a Grand Old Name," and "Forty-Five Minutes from Broadway," to name just a few. One of the greatest Tin Pan Alley men of all time, George M. Cohan would publish more than three hundred songs.

But by 1917, it seemed to many that Cohan had passed his peak. Worse, his beloved sister Josie had died of heart disease at the age of forty the previous summer; on her deathbed in Manhattan, she had called for her brother, who raced in from Long Island but arrived a few minutes too late. His father, Jeremiah "Jere" Cohan, would die shortly after that.

And then, in early April, America entered the war. That same month, Cohan would later recount, he was riding the train into Manhattan from his home in suburban New Rochelle when the words and music just came to him:

> *Johnnie get your gun, get your gun, get your gun,*
> *Take it on the run, on the run, on the run;*
> *Hear them calling you and me;*
> *Ev'ry son of liberty.*
> *Hurry right away, don't delay, go today,*
> *Make your daddy glad to have had such a lad,*
> *Tell your sweetheart not to pine,*
> *To be proud her boy's in line.*
>
> *Over there, Over there,*
> *Send the word, send the word, over there,*

That the Yanks are coming,
The Yanks are coming,
The drums rum-tumming ev'rywhere.
So prepare, Say a pray'r,
Send the word, send the word, to beware.
We'll be over, We're coming over,
And we won't come back till it's over over there!

To say that it was the greatest American song of World War I is to say not nearly enough. It's clearly the best American war song ever written. Not that the competition is all that stiff. "Yankee Doodle"? "Battle Hymn of the Republic"? "Dixie"? "Boogie Woogie Bugle Boy"? "Don't Sit Under the Apple Tree (With Anyone Else but Me)"? Really? The best of the rest is probably "Bonnie Blue Flag," and frankly, I've never really understood that song. Who had a blue flag with one star, again?

"Over There" is simple. It's outrageously catchy. You can sing along with it the very first time you hear it. Like "Pack Up Your Troubles," it tells you exactly what to do and how to do it; unlike "Troubles," it's something you can actually do. You can get a gun; you can hurry, make your daddy proud, tell your girl to buck up. You can't really stuff a bunch of problems into a kit bag, and even if you could, would you want to? Won't you find enough troubles waiting for you at the front? What's more, "Over There" gives you a great beat — a zesty, motivating beat — to which to do it all. Its lyrics are so clever that, for decades to come, everyone from Irving Berlin (*Annie Get Your Gun*) to antiwar novelist Dalton Trumbo (*Johnny Got His Gun*) would rip them off. And its title became nothing less than a synonym for the war itself.

If the rest never did catch up, at least they tried. And tried, and tried, and tried. And often, they did quite well. C. Francis Reisner, Benny Davis, and Billy Baskette had a big hit with "Good-bye Broadway, Hello France!":

Good-bye Broadway, Hello France,
We're ten million strong.
Good-bye sweethearts, wives and mothers,
It won't take us long.

Don't you worry while we're there,
It's for you we're fighting too,
So good-bye Broadway, hello France,
We're going to square our debt to you.

I don't know where they got the figure ten million, except that maybe they reckoned it would roll off a singer's tongue more smoothly than four million, which was the actual number of men in the ranks of the military by war's end. (Only two million of them made it to France by the armistice; the rest were still stateside.) And I'm not sure why they chose Broadway, which gives one the impression that a bunch of theater types are heading off to the trenches. Perhaps it's less of a mouthful than "Main Street" or "Park Place"?

They were right on the money with the sweetheart thing, though, at least judging by how many other songwriters hoped to cash in on the heartbreak of a young man leaving his best girl behind while he runs off to take a shot at the Kaiser, cranking out the likes of "I May Be Gone for a Long, Long Time," "Send Me Away with a Smile," "Farewell, Little Girl of Mine," "Watch, Hope and Wait, Little Girl," and "Uncle Sammy Take Care of My Girl," among many others. I hope the fellow from "I'm Hitting the Trail to Normandy So Kiss Me Good-Bye" got what he wanted, even though he was way off on his destination. (American troops didn't fight in Normandy, at least not in that war.) In "I'm Goin' to Fight My Way Back to Carolina," the doughboy in question is talking about both his home state *and* his girl.

The girls answered back with songs like "Goodbye, My Hero" and "While You're Over There in No Man's Land, I'm Over Here in Lonesome Land." Presumably wiser heads are counseling them in "Set Aside Your Tears Till the Boys Come Marching Home" and "He's Well Worth Waiting For," which, apparently, some of the girls didn't take to heart, because someone had to go and write "Don't Try to Steal the Sweetheart of a Soldier." As we learn in "Don't Cry, Frenchy, Don't Cry," the boys were finding plenty of comfort Over There. If you thought the boys were the only ones given to bragging, "If He Can Fight Like He Can Love, Good Night Germany!" (*If he's half as good in a trench / as he was in the park on a bench*) and "Look What My Boy Got in France" will quickly disabuse you of that fallacy. (The latter, by the way, refers to a medal, not a social disease.) And, of course, the long-awaited happy ending: "Oh! What a Time for the Girlies (When the Boys Come Marching Home)," and "When I Come Back to You (We'll Have a Yankee-Doodle Wedding)."

Not all the girlies were satisfied to wait until the boys came marching home; the heroine of "I'm Going to Follow the Boys," for instance (*I've always had a lot of boys around me / Wherever boys were that's the place you found me*) decides to go Over There and become a nurse, thinking, I suppose, that she'd have the entire AEF to herself. Unfortunately for her, there was plenty of evidence that the boys had already fallen in love with other nurses, like "The Rose of No Man's Land" and "My Red Cross Girlie (The Wound Is Somewhere in My Heart.)"

Al Jolson had a big hit with "Hello, Central, Give Me No Man's Land," about a night when *Baby toddles up to the telephone* and tries to get ahold of daddy Over There — such a big hit, in fact, that soon a competitor came out with "Hello! Gen'ral Pershing (How's My Daddy To-Night?)," in which *Baby longs for daddy o'er the sea,* so *To the telephone, she toddles all alone.* I'm sure "Let Us Say a Prayer for Daddy" also spawned many imitations, although I've only ever seen one song like "Just a Baby's Letter (Found in No Man's Land)." Good thing, that; a person only has so many tears.

Of all the doughboy's loves, though, one occupied a perch high above all the others: dear old mom. One of the most popular songs of the time, "Break the News to Mother," tells of a lad who, dying on the field of battle, manages to gasp:

> *Just break the news to mother,*
> *She knows how dear I love her,*
> *And tell her not to wait for me,*
> *For I'm not coming home;*
> *Just say there is no other*
> *Can take the place of mother;*
> *Then kiss her dear, sweet lips for me,*
> *And break the news to her.*

The song was actually a hit during the Spanish-American War; the fact that it was revived, with great popularity, twenty years later tells you something about what kind of country America was then —

quite simply, a nation of fervent, unashamed mama's boys. So the fellows in Tin Pan Alley, who had mothers, too, wrote "When a Boy Says Goodbye to His Mother (And She Gives Him to Uncle Sam)," and "So Long, Mother," and "Hello! My Darling Mother," and "Don't Forget Your Dear Old Mother," and "Dreaming Sweet Dreams of Mother." Sometimes, the boys found surrogates Over There, as does the subject of "Little French Mother, Good Bye!" And sometimes, as in "He Sleeps Beneath the Soil of France" and "On a Battlefield in France (When I'm Gone Just Write to Mother)," their little French mothers couldn't protect them. But their real, American mothers always could, whether Over There or beyond. "I'll Be There, Laddie Boy, I'll Be There" ends:

> *When your comrades around are falling*
> *Then your mother will answer your pray'r.*
> *And if fighting you fall*
> *And the Master should call,*
> *I'll be there, laddie boy, I'll be there.*

On the other hand, the only World War I song I've ever seen that mentions dear old dad up front is "Cheer Up Father, Cheer Up Mother," and even there he has to share top billing.

Father's Day wouldn't become a national holiday until 1972.

As frequently as Mother turned up on the covers of sheet music in 1917 and 1918, she never even approached the Kaiser's numbers. Only one person ever came close to the old Hohenzollern in that regard, and, with few exceptions — my favorite being "Just Like Washington Crossed the Delaware, General Pershing Will Cross the Rhine" — his name rarely made it into song titles; perhaps pluggers were intimidated by General John Joseph Pershing's martial visage. Nevertheless, they put that visage on an awful lot of their sheet music. Whatever else you might have to say about the man, there is no disputing the fact that his face sold a lot of songs.

Historians ardently dispute pretty much everything else about him. Some revere him as the greatest supreme military commander the country ever produced, one of the finest military minds of modern times, an icon of dispassionate integrity, a pillar of determination who saved countless doughboys' lives by refusing in the face of tremendous pressure to allow the British and French to use them for cannon fodder, and nothing less than the savior of Europe. Others denigrate him as a martinet, so behind the times that he championed marksmanship in an age of artillery, a man so stubborn that his refusal to allow American troops to serve under British and French commanders drove America's allies insane with frustration and rage and (according to them) nearly cost them the war, so single-minded that, in the final days of the war, he sent a note to the Supreme War Council insisting that no armistice be signed with Germany short of unconditional surrender, and so inept that President Wilson was about to fire him, when the war ended and saved his command. Still others, a great many of them, stake out some territory in between the two. Entire books — lots of them — have been written on the subject, by people much more knowledgeable on the matter than I am, and still there is no universally embraced version of The Truth. I'm not going to posit one here, though I will tell you that General Pershing was tremendously popular back home, so much so that upon his return in 1919, he was promoted to General of the Armies of the United States, a rank so high it was created just for him. The only person to have achieved it since is George Washington, who was awarded it posthumously in 1976.

One of the reasons Pershing was so popular, I suspect, is that, like Robert E. Lee, it was (and is) hard to think of him as a real person. He had tremendous poise and self-control, at least in public, and he looked the part, too: firm jaw, razor-straight mustache, barrel chest, stern countenance. Filled out his uniform quite nicely. Not given to bluster or bravado. Classic strong, silent type. Possessed of an aura of quiet competence and determination, like U. S. Grant. Unlike Grant, smart enough not to let anyone draft him for president. And they tried.

He wasn't President Wilson's first choice for the job; that would have been General Fred Funston. Funston, though, committed the fatal error of suddenly dropping dead a few weeks before America entered the war. So Pershing it was. Until then, his highest-profile post had been along the United States' southern border, where he'd led the 8th Regiment in search of Pancho Villa. Unsuccessfully.

Pershing had been born in Linn County, Missouri, in 1860, less than a year before that state was transformed into a bitter battleground sandwiched between Union and Confederacy. It is believed the family's sympathies lay with the former. At the age of twenty, after two years of college, he applied to West Point because he thought it a better education than he could receive in Missouri; and it was free. He graduated in the middle of his class and was sent out West with the cavalry as a second lieutenant. After five years there (during which he may or may not have participated in the notorious massacre of Lakota Sioux at Wounded Knee Creek in South Dakota), he became an instructor of military tactics at the University of Nebraska, where he also earned a law degree. Returning to active duty, he was sent to Montana, promoted to first lieutenant, and put in charge of the 10th Cavalry Regiment. Buffalo Soldiers: black soldiers. Two years later, he was appointed an instructor of tactics at West Point. He was strict; the cadets didn't much care for him. They mocked his previous posting, dubbed him "Nigger Jack." Eventually, they toned it down to "Black Jack." He was said to be quite proud of the sobriquet.

In 1898, he was reunited with the 10th Cavalry, took his troops to Cuba, fought at San Juan Hill, earned a citation for bravery. Then on to the Philippines, where he fought guerrilla insurgents. Other postings followed. In 1905, at the age of forty-five, he married the daughter of a powerful Republican senator from Wyoming. That same year, after a stint as an observer in the Russo-Japanese War, he was made a brigadier general by President Theodore Roosevelt, a promotion that skipped several ranks and stoked some resentment among his colleagues.

In 1914, Pershing was assigned to Fort Bliss, on the Texas-Mexico border, where he served under General Funston; he left his family ensconced at the Presidio of San Francisco. A year later he sent for them to come join him, but before they could make the move, a fire swept through their living quarters, killing Pershing's wife and three of their four small children. It was the great trauma of his life. Among the letters of condolence he received was one from Pancho Villa. After the funerals, Pershing returned to Fort Bliss with his surviving child. He was fifty-five years old.

Then came the war.

The public certainly knew about Pershing's family trauma; whether or not that made him a more sympathetic figure in their eyes is hard to say. Pershing's clashes with French and British generals, his disdain for trench warfare, his refusal to allow his troops to serve under foreign commanders — to the extent to which these facets of his leadership became known to the public back home, they only made him more popular. After all, they certainly spared a great many American lives. Did people love him because he was the commander of the American Expeditionary Forces, or because he was Pershing? Again, it's hard to say. If pressed, I'd say it was both.

One thing is certain: If you were a music publisher, you would do just about anything to figure out a way to get his picture on the cover of your sheet music. No small number did.

While pluggers tried all kinds of gimmicks to get you to buy their songs, they could also be rather direct, especially when their intent was to get you — through patriotism, or shame, or some combination of the two — to pay up, as was the case in an awful lot of songs, like "Let's Keep the Glow in Old Glory, and the Free in Freedom, Too," and "Keep the Trench Fires Going for the Boys Out There." Will E. Dulmage and J. Fred Lawton's "Say — You Haven't Sacrificed At All!" demanded:

> *Have you had a gun upon your good right shoulder?*
> *Have you ever slept out in the mud?*
> *Have you performed your duties among the rats and cooties*
> *Have you ever shed a drop of blood for Uncle Sammy?*

A tad artless, to be sure, but almost subtle compared to Gus Kahn and Egbert Van Alstyne's "What Are You Going to Do to Help the Boys?":

> *What are you going to do for Uncle Sammy?*
> *What are you going to do to help the boys?*
> *If you need to stay at home while they're fighting o'er the foam,*
> *The least that you can do is buy a Liberty bond or two.*
> *If you want to be a sympathetic miser,*

The kind that only lends a lot of noise,
You're no better than the one who loves the Kaiser —
So, what are you going to do to help the boys?

The cover art for that sheet music actually says, in big red letters: "Buy a Liberty Bond!" Not in lieu of this song, of course. But still.

To its credit, though, for every musical guilt-trip it laid on the public, Tin Pan Alley produced dozens of wonderful pieces of light verse that people sang with pleasure for decades to come, like Charles McCarron and Carey Morgan's "The Russians Were Rushin', the Yanks Started Yankin'":

The Russians were rushin' the Prussians,
The Prussians were crushin' the Russians.
The Balkans were balkin' and Turkey was squawkin',
Rasputin disputin' and Italy scootin'.
The Boches all bulled Bolshevikis,
The British were skittish at sea.
But the good Lord I'm thankin', the Yanks started yankin',
And yanked Kaiser Bill up a tree.

And then there was the extremely popular song that posed, in its title, a question to the entire nation — a question that was both so catchy and so pertinent that long after the war ended, it lingered in the national consciousness: "How 'Ya Gonna Keep 'Em Down on the Farm After They've Seen Paree?" *They'll never want to see a rake or plow / And who the deuce can parley-vous a cow?* asked lyricists Joe Young and Sam M. Lewis.

The answers, as America would soon learn: Nobody. And ya ain't.

With *so many* songs — so many clever songs, catchy songs, funny or heartbreaking or offensive or ageless songs — it's strange to think that one of my favorite World War I songs is really none of those things. I heard it on wax long before I ever found a copy of the sheet music; it's a beautiful-looking disk, with a big Victor label in deep bold blue, and perfect, shimmering grooves, as if it had never been played before I stumbled upon it. It was recorded in 1918 by a Brooklyn-born baritone named Reinald Werrenrath. Like so many recording artists of that era, Werrenrath is now completely forgotten, but he had a good career once upon a time in music halls and studios. Like most of his colleagues, he turned his attention to patriotic fare during the war years; I own another Victor blue-label of him singing "The Star-Spangled Banner" on one side and "My Country 'Tis of Thee" on the other.

The first few times I listened to "The Americans Come!" (subtitled "An Episode in France in Year 1918"), I had no idea just what it was supposed to be. It's an unusual song, sort of an aria in the form of a father and son talking to each other, with Werrenrath singing both parts (and not altering his voice a bit as he switches back and forth). Thanks to the phenomenon of copyright expiration, I offer it to you here in full:

> [Blind Frenchman speaks to son:]
> *What is the cheering, my little one?*
> *Oh! That my blinded eyes could see!*
> *Hasten, my boy, to the window run,*
> *And see what the noise in the street may be.*
> *I hear the drums and the marching feet;*
> *Look and see what it's all about!*
> *Who can it be that our people greet*
> *With cheer and laughter and joyous shout?*
>
> [Son:]
> *There are men, my father, brown and strong,*
> *And they carry a banner of wondrous hue,*
> *With a mighty tread they swing along*
> *Now I see white stars on a field of blue!*
>
> [Father:]
> *You say that you see white stars on blue?*
> *Look, are there stripes of red and white?*
> *It must be, yes it must be true!*
> *Oh, dear God, if I had my sight!*
> *Hasten, son, fling the window wide;*
> *Let me kiss the staff our flag swings from*
> *And salute the Stars and Stripes with pride,*
> *For, God be praised, The Americans come!*

The song's composer and lyricist was a musician of some repute named Fay Foster. Her entry in the *Biographical Cyclopedia of American Women*, published in 1924, calls "The Americans Come!" "her greatest contribution," "the great rallying song of the last Liberty Loan Drive," a "stirring song, highly eulogized by Theodore Roosevelt and General Pershing. . . . When [famed Irish tenor] John McCormack entertained the heroes of the Château-Thierry, this song was the favorite, and he rendered it with the greatest feeling."

I don't know if any of that is true; to be sure, the song itself has an element of the fantastic. In France in the year 1918, fresh, unscathed, well-fed American troops were less likely to be greeted with cheer and laughter and joyous shout than with mute stares and hands too weak to clap. Many in the crowd — if there even was a crowd — must have been thinking about their own beautiful boys, brown and strong, who marched away four years earlier and were never seen again. "God be praised"? Maybe. "Where have you been?" Definitely. The soldiers at Château-Thierry would have known as much, too.

But really, none of that mattered. Whether they actually liked it or not, "The Americans Come!" wasn't written for the men, brown and strong, at Château-Thierry. In fact, it was written for pretty much everyone *but* them.

In those days, songwriters were often journalists as well as entertainers. And like so many newspapermen back then, the men and women of Tin Pan Alley, in reporting the news — or at least the news as they wished to report it — actually shaped it. And that was just to start. What they really did, in the end, was create their own reality. Fifteen years before Hollywood would successfully begin doing the same thing, songwriters told Americans who Americans were, what they were like as a people, and what kind of country they lived in — all in the context of this war they'd been swept into. And they did it so well that almost everyone else — mothers, wives, and sweethearts; John J. Pershing and Theodore Roosevelt; even the boys Over There — played along, no matter what they really believed as they lay in bed at night, hoping for sleep. They embraced the fantasy, forced themselves to ignore those prickling suspicions that it wasn't real, and to believe that every doughboy had someone — a mother, wife, sweetheart, child, or all of the above — who was sad to see him go, who pined for him, prayed for him, sent him a letter every day, awaited his safe return; that those men who couldn't fight gave all they had to give, and then found a way to give even more; that mothers were all proud to send their sons off to war, that wives were all bereft but making do, that sweethearts all stayed true, that children all remembered daddy every day; that German *Kultur* was no match for American grit, that the Hun was but a grim clown easily licked by simple country boys and savvy street urchins, that doughboys were going to march right into Berlin, grab the Kaiser by the ear, and make the man pay in all kinds of devilish ways; and that it would all be over soon, that the boys would be right back and none the worse for wear, that we'd all have a splendid time and even go to a Yankee-Doodle Wedding or two, that everything would be just as it had been.

So despite its many and sometimes grievous sins — I'll get to those a bit later — I have to give Tin Pan Alley its due. As much as bullets and shells, rifles and bayonets, barbed wire and big guns, aeroplanes and mustard gas, trenches and U-boats — as much as anything, really, except the men and women who fought it — songs *were* World War I. Don't get me wrong: I am certain that songwriters and publishers always had at least one eye on the dollars. But I think they also recognized that the news was handing them a rare opportunity to do well by doing good, and they didn't want to miss it. I have to believe that's why more songs were written about the First World War than about any other event in history.

Except Christmas.

Maybe.

5

The People Behind the Battle

OW DO I PUT THIS? If you spend enough time around the, uh, superannuated, you come to recognize certain portents that don't bode well for their continued longevity. For instance, a fall followed by a broken hip is usually bad news; otherwise-relatively-active men and women are suddenly rendered bedridden, and that kind of state can kill you any number of ways. The need for surgery is an ill omen; folks that age rarely come through a serious operation just fine. In fact, any kind of major change or minor illness can prove calamitous to the very elderly. (*I* don't deal with them particularly well, either.)

I say all this by way of explaining why I was so nervous during the three-hour drive up the western shore of Lake Michigan from Milwaukee to Kewaunee, Wisconsin, to meet 104-year-old Arthur Fiala. It was September 6, 2003, just two weeks since I had first made his acquaintance over the telephone, but in that short time the following things had happened: His wife of sixty-seven years suddenly died; he moved out of the farmhouse he had lived in for fifty-four years and into a local nursing home; and he contracted pneumonia. I felt like I was racing the grim reaper, and I didn't like my odds.

I'd found Mr. Fiala through both the French List and Google, but if I hadn't called his house exactly when I had, I might never have gotten to talk to him at all. As it happened, his granddaughter, Deb, was visiting that morning, and Deb was the only person who ever answered the phone in that house; Art Fiala and his wife, Adeline, were both too deaf to use it anymore. I got to talk to him a bit that morning anyway, then immediately booked tickets to Wisconsin.

To get to Kewaunee, I drove a couple of hours north to Green Bay (stopping in Sheboygan for a breakfast bratwurst), turned right on Route 29 (also known as the World War I Veterans Memorial Highway), and drove about thirty miles, past hamlets with names like Poland, Pilsen, and Krok (and a billboard for a bison farm named the Spunky Buffalo), until I reached the water: Lake Michigan. I know it's a lake, but in Kewaunee, it might as well be the ocean. The nearest landfall, in northern Michigan, is more than fifty miles east, well beyond the horizon. Kewaunee even has its own lighthouse, which from a distance looks like a little dollhouse sitting atop a pier. The town itself is quaint enough, possessed of an old-country feel; I soon learned that just about everyone in it was of Czech descent. Most of them couldn't believe I had no idea what a *kolache* was. (In case you're not Czech: It's a type of pastry.)

Arthur Fiala had taken up residence in a low, nondescript modern brick building on the outskirts of town. I met Deb in the lobby and followed her to her grandfather's room. The man didn't look good, lying there in a plaid shirt and gray chinos and enormous black eyeglasses, an oxygen hose hooked up to his nose. He seemed to be shrinking, withering within his own clothing. I soon discovered, though, that he was quite spunky—much more so, I imagined, than those ill-fated buffalo.

"I was out of a job, and I made up my mind, I decided to join the Army," he asserted before I had a chance to ask him any questions. Sick as he was, he remembered why I'd come and wanted to get right to it.

He was born in Kewaunee on February 17, 1899 (at least he thought so; the 1900 census says it was 1898). According to tradition, the family name was originally spelled "Fijala," and Arthur's father, Charlie, had been born somewhere on the Atlantic Ocean, during the middle passage of their immigration from what is now the Czech Republic. Charlie himself had told the census taker in 1900 that he'd been born in America in 1869, and listed his parents' birthplace as Bohemia. (His son later revealed that Charlie had lied about where he'd been born, afraid his employer, the post office, might fire him if they knew the truth.) Arthur's mother, Mary, was born in Wisconsin in 1872; her father was a German immigrant, her mother, depending upon the census, born in either Wisconsin or Bohemia.

Wherever he was born, Charles Fiala grew up in Kewaunee and worked there all his life. "When my dad got married, he was lighting streetlamps in Kewaunee for fifteen dollars a month," his son told me. "And then he got a job delivering groceries. Then he took an exam for a mail carrier. Rural. And he passed that, and he spent the next thirty years as a mail carrier."

"How did he get around?" I asked. "Did he have a horse and carriage?"

"Yeah," he said, "when he got that job, he had to buy a couple horses, a buggy, a cutter [a type of sleigh], and feed his animals, and feed our family, all in one."

Charlie's youngest child, Arthur, went through all of his schooling right there in Kewaunee. "Did you work also while you were in school?" I asked him.

"Not that I know of," he replied.

"So, then, you were telling me that you were looking for a job; this is how you came to go into the Army?"

"Listen," he said, "I got something to tell you first. I was in high school. And the principal was a dirty devil. And he asked me a question in algebra one day, and I didn't know it. He said to me, 'Art, if I were you I would pick up your books and go home and help your father earn a living.'" And he did. At least, he went home and never returned to school. He was fifteen or sixteen at the time, and wasn't too terribly upset about it. To hear him tell it, he had been granted parole.

"A neighbor of mine," he told me, "was a captain on a boat, and he offered me a job on the boat. And I went from Kewaunee to Milwaukee in a boat. And it was rough, and I was seasick the whole trip. When I got to Milwaukee, I jumped off the boat and went to Chicago. I had some relatives down there. And there I worked for a while. All I could tell, I don't. I can't tell you all the damn stories."

But he told me quite a few of them: How he left Chicago and headed up north, back to Wisconsin with a buddy, where they lived in a farmer's granary for a while and trapped. Eventually he made his way to Kenosha, Wisconsin, where he got work as an inspector at a Nash automobile plant — a good job, especially for a teenaged high school dropout. A much-coveted job, apparently. "One day a guy came up to me," he recalled more than eighty-five years later, "and he said, 'Don't come to work tomorrow.' He said, 'There's nobody going to come to-morrow.' And I stayed home." The fellow, he later learned, had been jealous of young Fiala's position, and had told the foreman that day that Art was actually trying to foment a strike. "And when I came back to work the next morning," he said, "the foreman kicked me out of the plant. I didn't have enough sense to talk up."

And he added: "That's when I joined the Army."

We spend so much time these days celebrating our men and women in service as selfless heroes — which, often, they are — that we fail to consider the fact that many of them joined up not, primarily, out of a sense of duty, but because it made good economic sense. If you can't find other work, the Army offers you a steady paycheck, free room and board, medical and dental care, transportation, and even a natty ward-robe. It also offers the promise of travel and adventure. Sure, these perks all come with the chance that you may be killed or maimed, but the possibility of being shot to death is better than the certainty of starving to death. Besides, those threats always seem remote at the enlistment center.

None of that, though, has any bearing on the fact that Private Fiala served honorably in France. Eighty years later, that service was recog-nized with the Legion of Honor. Mr. Fiala earned that medal. It doesn't matter that he enlisted, shortly before his nineteenth birthday, because he needed the work. As far as he was concerned, that fact only made his story more interesting; perhaps that's why he led off with it.

He told me he went to a recruitment center in Green Bay; they must have sent him to Columbus Barracks, Ohio, because that's where his discharge papers say he officially enlisted, on February 23, 1918. "Now, hear," he said. "When I enlisted, I didn't tell the recruiter what branch of service I wanted to get into. I said, 'That's up to you.' I said, 'Get me into an outfit that goes over to France quick.' And he put me into an engineer outfit, the 20th Engineers. And we had two weeks' train-ing . . . that was it."

They were in a hurry. The 20th Engineers was a special unit; though technically a regiment, it was not attached to any division, and in fact, by the end of the war, it comprised some thirty thousand soldiers, more than most divisions. A great many of them — perhaps a majority —

were lumberjacks. The 20th was charged, primarily, with providing the AEF with the timber it needed. And it needed a lot. Urgently. According to Alfred H. Davies, who wrote and published *Twentieth Engineers, France, 1917–1918–1919* shortly after the war, one of General Pershing's first cables from France called for lumbermen, saying that to send over infantry divisions before a good timber operation could be established would be fruitless. "If an army of the size contemplated was to be put at the front," wrote regimental chaplain Captain Howard Y. Williams in a foreword, "docks must be built; railroads laid; barracks, warehouses, hospitals, bakeries, refrigerator plants, and power plants provided; and trench timbers, dug-outs, and barb-wire stakes furnished. The basic factor in all these necessities was lumber and the Twentieth Engineers, detailed to this task, more than met their tremendous responsibility."

Captain Williams continues:

> It meant work; hard, monotonous, and unrelenting, but never did men respond more nobly. From these first days in the Fall of 1917 when I saw men hitched to wagons and pulling like horses because we had none; through those terrible spring days of 1918 when the Germans were driving on toward Paris and these men scattered from the Pyrenees to the Argonne toiled day and night to make possible our defense; down through the armistice until the last man came home, in all my experience across the seas I never saw more faithful and conscientious effort. Brave deeds abounded in France but equal in spirit to any of them was the persistent devotion to his task, so vitally essential but lacking in personal glory, of many a man in this largest regiment in history.

Brave deeds, though, don't always spare you the indignity of being forgotten. If not for Private Arthur Fiala, the last surviving veteran of the largest regiment in history, I would never even have heard of the 20th Engineers.

Which seems both odd and understandable. Understandable because you never really hear much about military engineers, unless you're related to one or happen to live near a place that floods a lot, like the Mississippi River delta; odd because the 20th was so very large, and served throughout France, from the front up in Lorraine down to the Spanish border. And because they were, at the time, considered so important by the AEF's high command. And because, quite simply, the war could not have been prosecuted without them. "All of the construction in the Service of Supplies were dependent upon lumber," Davies writes, expanding upon Captain Williams's introduction. "And the Front Lines required it for dugouts, trench construction entanglements, compounds for prisoners, bridges, and a great variety of other uses. Even coffin lumber was to be provided by the forest troops." Good thing France still had a lot of trees.

The 20th Engineer Regiment was officially established on September 9, 1917, on the campus of American University, in Washington, D.C. — or, as it was known during the war, Camp American University. Unlike other regiments, which were established all at once and had an enlistment cap, the 20th Engineers grew and grew. "For several reasons, principally those of clothing and shelter, it was found impossible to recruit and train the entire regiment at one time," Davies explains. Battalions were formed, trained, and shipped overseas in batches.

Arthur Fiala's batch, the 26th Company, part of the 9th Battalion, shipped out for France, aboard the transport *Mount Vernon*, on March 27 — just thirty-two days after he'd enlisted.

Somewhere in all that rush, the 9th Battalion of the 20th Engineers may have had an experience that, in America at least, was fairly singular to World War I. It was the last week of March, 1918. "We were supposed to go to New York to get on the boat," Private Fiala recalled eighty-five years later. "We had two boxcars full of barracks bags, with all the equipment that we were supposed to have when we got to our destination in France." He paused, then pounced: "It caught fire. And we think, I think it was sabotaged," he explained.

Yes: sabotage. For surreptitious skullduggery on American soil, no other war can touch that one.

The Germans, you see, were no fools; from the moment war broke out in Europe, they understood that there was no chance America might enter the conflict on their side. At best, they hoped, the United States would sit it out; at worst, it would throw its enormous manpower, wealth, and industrial might behind the Allied cause. Even America's muscular neutrality hurt the Germans: While all combatants' ships were "quarantined" at American ports at the outbreak of war, Britain, with its vastly larger fleet, could spare them much more easily than Germany could. And though Americans were free to trade with all combatant nations, Britain's tight blockade of Germany's small seacoast effectively meant that the United States could *really* only trade with the Allies. This, in turn, led to a sense, in America, that an Allied victory was inevitable, which disinclined American bankers to lend money to the Germans. Ninety-nine percent of all American money sent to combatants before 1917 went to Allied nations; if it belied American "neutrality," it was nevertheless good for business, since the United Kingdom spent fully half of its war budget in the United States. Of course, the fact that American banks loaned so much money to Allied nations made their victory all the more desirable to the United States, since, should they lose the war, all that money would be lost; so Americans loaned them yet more money, to enable them to buy more munitions. This vicious cycle was exacerbated by the fact that, at the war's outset, Britain cut Germany's undersea cable, which meant that all transcontinental news and information was conveyed to the United States through Allied channels alone.

And so Germany turned to espionage and sabotage. It developed an extremely sophisticated network in America, working out of German government offices at 45 Broadway, near Wall Street in lower Manhattan. The city of New York, even then the most ethnically diverse place in the world, was the perfect place to host an international spy ring. Foreign accents wouldn't stick out there; it had a large German and Austro-Hungarian population; and the rest of the city wasn't particularly amenable to the Allied cause, either. Irish New Yorkers, for instance, had no desire to go to war in support of the hated British, while Jewish immigrants, many of whom had fled the institutionalized anti-Semitism of the Russian Empire, weren't exactly enthused to risk their lives for the czar. Even after America entered the war, it continued to be unpopular in New York; the city's mayor, John Purroy Mitchel, was thrown out of office in November, 1917, for supporting it. Mitchel would go on to join the Army Air Corps, where he would fall out of a plane to his death during a training exercise, having failed to fasten his seat belt.

In America, German agents dabbled, mostly unsuccessfully, in early forms of germ warfare, spreading (or trying to spread) anthrax, poisoning livestock, spoiling crops. Some believe they tore up railroad tracks out West. Most often, though, they targeted munitions factories, and the ships that would carry those factories' output across the Atlantic. After all, they knew none of that stuff was making it to Germany. Probably the most famous incident happened on July 30, 1916, when saboteurs blew up a railroad yard and munitions depot (and, in the process, nine hundred tons of ammunition bound for the Western Front) on the small island of Black Tom, off the coast of Jersey City. The explosion, which was later estimated as the equivalent of an earthquake measuring 5.5 on the Richter scale, sent shrapnel and debris into the Statue of Liberty and blew out windows in Manhattan; it was felt in Philadelphia, and heard in Maryland.

The effect of all this activity was to create a sense of paranoia in an America that was completely unprepared for it. The Germans went from lingering beneath suspicion to being suspected of much more than they actually did; sabotage, and saboteurs, were now everywhere, even places they weren't, which was almost everywhere. So I don't know if German agents really burned Arthur Fiala's railroad car or not. In the end, it really doesn't matter: he thought they did. And his stuff was gone. All of it. "So when we got on the boat," he told me, "all we had was a pack, our pack sack with a couple blankets and a mess kit. That's all we had." That, and the clothes on their bodies.

"There were eleven boats in our convoy. The first four days out on the ocean were beautiful. I enjoyed the ride. Then I got seasick. I was sick for four days. And in the meantime, they wouldn't let us take our clothes off, so in case we got torpedoed, we had our clothes on. Well, and I was seasick for four days, and I decided to try to get something to eat. And I went down, I got in the galley, and I got half of a grapefruit. And I ate that, and then I was going to get another one, and then the abandon-ship alarm sounded. We had to all go up on deck. They thought we were going to be hit. Well, it so happened there wasn't any, uh . . ."

"U-boats?"

"U-boats, that's it. What came to meet us was subchasers. Oh, are they beautiful! . . . They're narrow and slick, and boy can they travel!

They were, see there were eleven boats in our convoy, and they were, they were just running between our boats."

"Pretty," Deb said. She'd served four years in the Navy herself.

"Pretty sight," her grandfather concurred.

The *Mount Vernon* landed at Brest on April 8, 1918. Their timing wasn't great. "When we landed, they marched us uphill about three miles," Private Fiala recalled. "So they said plunk these [packs] in the barracks. But we got up there, there was no barracks. There was nothing but a field with pup tents. And it was pouring, it was all mud. We couldn't sleep. Well, good thing, we were called out to go back down to the boat. And we worked there, we unloaded boats all night. We were pooped out. Then they took us back up this hill. And then the next day we were loaded on a train. Looked like boxcars. No seats in there, just lay down like a dog. And I don't know, over two or three days we were on, across France. Slow train!" Boxcars in France back then were labeled "40-8" — that is, forty men per car, or eight horses.

"Then," he told me, "we landed in a little town called La Cluse. And that was in the foothills of the Alps mountains. Here, I've got to tell you one thing about that: See, when we got there, we found out that our carload of food was lost. We were hungry, hungry as hell! So I thought, I'll take a walk uptown, and maybe I could buy something. I didn't have much money, but I found some figs." It was the first break he seemed to catch in a while. He even got a chance to laugh. "There was a Frenchman walking ahead of me," he said, "and he stopped by a big tree to take a pee. And while he was taking a pee, there was a woman coming down the street, and he was holding it in one hand and tipping his hat with the other hand. That was the first thing that struck me as funny."

Later that day, the cook managed to find some beans. "Boy, that tasted like ice cream, I'll tell you. That was good. Piece of bread and some of those beans."

The men marched another three miles up to a plateau, where they pitched camp by a creek. "And we didn't have our clothes off for nine days; we pulled off our clothes and jumped in the creek to wash off. And then a lot of the boys started fires around and everything." It was, after all, still cold up there. That night, they pitched tents and slept; in the morning, they awoke to snow. "Snow, snow, snow, everywhere . . .

we had no extra stockings, no nothing. Well, it snowed so damn hard we couldn't, we didn't know where to sleep. And there was a farmer up there, he let us sleep in the barn. So we all — can you picture two hundred and fifty guys —"

"No!" Deb said.

"— sleeping in a barn. Like sardines!" He added: "And by God, you know, nobody caught a cold."

Eventually, someone tracked down that boxcar full of food, but trucks couldn't make it up to camp in the snow, so 250 men had to trudge down the mountain and carry it back up by hand. Dinner that night was beef stew. "They gradually got a kitchen going and everything. And do you know what we were up there for? We were up there logging. We were making products, wood products, to be shipped to the front."

"Like what kinds of things?"

"Well, logs, railroad ties, camouflage poles, all kinds of stuff like that . . . There was about half of them guys in that outfit that were real lumberjacks. And we younger guys, we would go up in the woods, up in the woods in the mountains, and they would cut the logs down, and then we younger guys would chop the limbs off. They called us, we were 'swampers' . . . Well, anyway, then, here's the part: One day we were going down the mountain with a team of horses, there was about seven of us on the wagon, and the horses got wild and they jumped, they went off the side of the mountain. And we all went down the mountain. And lucky thing there was enough trees there to stop us. But anyway, I got, we all got hurt. I broke my wrist . . . so I didn't, I couldn't do anything for a while. And when my wrist got better, they gave me a job, to work around the kitchen."

And that's how Private Arthur Fiala became a cook.

It was a lucky break, as it were. Logging was dangerous work in peacetime; in war, with its accelerated pace and increased demands, it became very dangerous. "In the beginning, when we were there, they used to cut logs up in the mountains," Art Fiala explained to me. "And they would slide them down the mountain, and they would peel them, you know, so they were slippery. And a personal friend of mine, he got killed from a log, yeah, knocked him down. We had about eight guys I think got killed, died in the outfit . . . And one guy," he declared, "one guy was *murdered*. Somebody, we found one of our men under a bridge with a hole in his head. Somebody hit him."

Some of the men in his outfit were felled not by logs, but by disease, which, despite great medical advances since the last big war, still killed thousands of Americans in uniform during World War I. It even, almost, managed to kill Art Fiala.

It started in the kitchen. "For some reason or other," he recalled, "the ventilation was bad in that camp, and I got pleurisy." Pleurisy: an inflammation of the pleura, which line the lungs. Often caused by infection. It can make breathing very painful. It can also kill you any number of unpleasant ways. It's one of those diseases you don't hear about anymore; today it can be cured by a visit to a doctor's office and some over-the-counter drugs. Not then, though.

"I was sick," he told me, nodding gravely over the din caused by the machine that was pumping oxygen into his nose. "And I called the doctor. He came down, he looked at me, just put his head in the tent. He never touched me. He left a couple of aspirin tablets. That's all I got." He was sitting up now, looking disgusted, but lively.

"Well, here's the point," he continued. "On the edge of town, there was a woman living. She had about three little kids. She was taking care of a railroad crossing, I don't know what she had to do. She found out I was sick, she come to the tent, she brought hot tea to me. That woman *never failed*," he said emphatically. "Until I got well, she came in three times a day. And one day, one day she came with a plaster, plastered my chest even." His hands mimicked the act across his chest. "She was good."

"How nice!" Deb said.

"I'll never forget, never forget her," her grandfather asserted. "I give her a lot of credit. And here's the point: One day, one day I heard we were going to break up that camp. So at ten o'clock at night, when everybody was supposed to be in bed, I went to my kitchen. I took a flour sack; we used to get those tins of bacon, like that, like the big tin. I took, I gave her a can of that bacon, I gave her flour, sugar, coffee, all I could carry on my back. And I brought it to her that night. I woke them up at ten o'clock at night. Oh," he said, nodding his head earnestly, "you've never seen any happier people. They deserved it." Staples — not to mention luxuries like bacon — were scarce for civilians in France.

Laurence Moffitt had said that the men of the Yankee Division ate very well in France, many of them better than they'd ever eaten at home, and Art Fiala agreed, especially regarding the men in *his* outfit. Except, he admitted, once.

"One day, a couple of the boys, we decided we were going to take a trip, a trip uptown," he told me. "And maybe have a little fun for a change, see? And I didn't get back to camp to make supper. And when I got back up . . . my kitchen was all ripped to hell. They were, guys were hungry and broke in the kitchen and opened up all kinds of cans and all kinds of stuff. And the sergeant that was in charge of the camp, he come up to me and he says, 'You're fired!' On account of what I did, see.

"Well, the next day," he continued, "a motorcycle with a sidecar came down and picked me up and took me back to camp. I thought, 'Oh, boy, now I'm in for it. I'm going to get hell!' But when I got back to camp, I was greeted with open arms! And all the officers come up to me and said: 'You're promoted to officer's cook!'"

He smiled.

Art Fiala spent the rest of the war as a cook — at La Cluse, and Nantua, and in *la Forêt de Meyriat*. Though he, and the rest of the 20th Engineers, were behind the lines, the war managed to reach them anyway, this way or that. "One thing I never forgot," he told me, "in one camp, one of them camps where I was cooking, we got some casualties came there. And one guy come up to me and asked me if I could give him a job in the kitchen. And I said, 'Yes, I'll give you a job in the kitchen.' He was the principal from a high school." Considering his experience with his own high school principal back in Kewaunee, he must have enjoyed that.

All in all — unless you counted that broken wrist, that bout with pleurisy, and those long, soggy, exhausting first weeks in France — it sounded to me like Art Fiala had had a pretty good time Over There. He enjoyed the work (especially making pancakes), was well liked, well treated by his officers, and well fed. After the armistice, he was transferred to a camp in Bordeaux, where he only had to cook every third day. He scaled fences and hopped trains for free with his buddies, was once sent down to the Spanish border in a car to deliver food to some big shot, and enjoyed the company of French women more than he cared to discuss with me in detail, at least with his granddaughter around. "My wife used to throw that up to me all the time," he said with a hint of mock exasperation. "Say, Debbie, you haven't got that card there from that girl, have you?"

"No," she said.

"I got a card from a girl from France," he explained to me. "She said, 'We're all thinking about you, we all like you,' or something like that. I don't know. I wish," he said to Deb, "you would have had it."

"Well, I found it," she replied, "and then Grandma got mad."

"So tell me about meeting the girls over there," I said to him. "What was that like?"

"They were, they were pretty nice," he said with a big smile.

"Where did you meet them?"

"I don't know."

"Yes you do!" Deb declared with a laugh. "I won't tell, Dad."

"I don't know," he repeated. "I don't remember too much about that. But I remember, I remember I used to have one girlfriend I know of. Adeline always used to throw that up to me. 'You and your French girl!'" He couldn't recall her name; said she'd been in Nantua.

"So how would you meet them?" I asked him again.

"I don't know."

"Would you go into town?"

"Oh, hey, listen," he said, earnestly. "They were looking for Americans. Oh, hell!"

"Why was that?"

"I don't know. They wanted us. They liked us. They liked American boys."

"Were they pretty?"

"Oh, yeah." He nodded. "Some of them were pretty nice."

"What would you do?" I asked. "Would you go dancing?"

"No, just walk around . . . I don't know," he said.

After we'd talked for about an hour, Mr. Fiala suddenly said he was feeling very tired. He looked very tired. Honestly, he looked half dead.

I felt bad, but Deb assured me that her grandfather loved — *loved* — to talk. A few years earlier, when the French had come to Kewaunee to present him his Legion of Honor, they held a little ceremony at the high school auditorium, hosted by the mayor. Art was supposed to be escorted up to the podium, receive his medal, say thank you, and sit down. Except nobody told him that; instead, he spoke for a half hour. Without notes. He was 100 years old at the time.

We left him to rest for a couple of hours, and returned to find him awake and awaiting us. We talked about a lot of things: how the Army had gotten him hooked on cigarettes for the rest of his life; about the dancing that went on when the armistice took effect; how he'd sailed home on the SS *Luckenbach* in May, 1919, telling an officer to go to hell when he'd ordered Private Fiala to go work in the ship's galley; how he'd spent his first night back in America sleeping on a park bench in New York, just because he could. He made his way back to the Midwest, worked for a bit at a candy factory in Chicago (he was on an assembly line where peanuts were coated with chocolate), ran a taxi service in Kewaunee for a while, spent four years in northern Wisconsin just hunting and fishing, living for free at some rich man's lodge. He was a foreman at the Kewaunee Brewery for a while during Prohibition; it made liquid wort in those years. He told me that in 1920, he bought an old car and turned it into the world's first camper, so that he and his brother could take it hunting. Sold it four years later to a circus. He brewed chokecherry wine, showed me the recipe; it was written on a piece of Fiala's Taxi Service stationery. He dated his wife for eight years, married her at age thirty-seven. Eventually, they owned a one-hundred-acre farm; he told me farming was the best thing he ever did. They had one child, a son, Carl. They called him Carlie. Private Fiala said he'd been in the American Legion for so long that they paid his dues for him now; that the secret to his longevity was that he ate peanuts every day. He told me that one of his grandfathers had gotten him drunk at a very young age, and that the other one, whose name had actually been Klutz, had met his end while dumping garbage off a cliff into Lake Michigan. He'd fallen in.

Entertaining as it all was, I couldn't stop thinking about something that had happened earlier that morning, shortly before we'd stopped for a break. I'd just asked him again how he had come to serve in an engineering unit. "Well," he'd said, "I asked them to put me in an outfit that's going over quick. And they just happened to be making up that unit. And that's why I got into that."

"Why did you want to go over quick?"

"I don't know." He was quiet for a moment. "Cocky," he said, finally. "I wanted to win the war." He grew quiet again; there was no sound in the room at that moment but the groaning of the machine pumping oxygen into him. I turned off the camera.

And then, suddenly, without sitting up, he declared, loudly: "Listen! The people behind the battle were just as important as the people in the battle!" He took a few breaths, and continued: "I don't know why the hell they put me in with the engineers! I didn't ask them to do it! I wanted to be in the battle, but they put me in with engineering." It sounded almost as if he were crying.

Tell me, how could I ever forget something like that? Here was a man, for all he knew on his deathbed, thinking back to a war that had ended eight and a half decades earlier, and he's shouting, almost wailing, his regret, and maybe guilt, that in that war, the Great War, he hadn't served in combat. It was excruciating to behold; for a moment, I hated myself just for being there. I didn't press the matter that afternoon, when his spirits seemed to have recovered. We spent our time on other things.

An hour or so more of that and he was tired again. "Who am I that you should come here and talk to me? I'm nothing but a dummy," he said to me at one point. Yet he didn't want me to leave, either, said he wished I had come to see him before he'd gotten sick, that he could have told me much more. I couldn't imagine what more there could be, but I nodded. Just before I turned off the camera, I told him I'd come back and see him when he was feeling better. Even as I said it, though, I imagined I might get a phone call from Deb before I left Wisconsin, inviting me to her grandfather's funeral.

I didn't.

He was still alive a week later. And a month later. And a year later. At one point, influenza swept through the home, killing a number of residents. Not him. He rallied, recovered, thrived. And so, nineteen months after I first met him, I returned to Kewaunee to see him again.

He looked great. He'd put on weight; instead of lying flat on his back, he was sitting in a chair, wearing a bright white fishing T-shirt and a blue cardigan sweater. He had on new eyeglasses that seemed to cover half his face, and an enormous baseball cap that announced: US ARMY VETERAN. The only vestige of his previous illness was the oxygen hose under his nose. His son, Carl, who was with him that day, told me his dad didn't need it anymore, hadn't for a long time, but that he liked it. I guess no one at the nursing home cared to argue the point with him.

We covered pretty much the same ground we had the first time I'd been there; he elaborated on this point or that. And then something truly amazing happened.

He was telling me once again about their first night at camp in France, when they'd slept in tents and awoke to a heavy April snowfall — they were in the mountains, after all — and how a French farmer had let all 250 of them sleep in his barn. "I was all right, I slept up above. But some of the guys were down with the horses," he recalled with a wry grin. And then he added: "Say, that reminds me of something I didn't tell you last time."

To convey just how remarkable that statement was, and how stunned I was to hear it, I have to start by reiterating something J. Laurence Moffitt had told me the first time I met him: that his long-term memory was excellent, though his short-term memory was failing. Many of the veterans I interviewed — though not Mr. Moffitt — didn't recognize me the second time I visited (though of course they all had the good grace to fake it); they had completely forgotten our first meeting. Most of them, in fact, couldn't remember what they had eaten for breakfast that morning, even though they could recall quite vividly things they'd done and said eighty, ninety, a hundred years earlier. That's the way the human memory works: last in, first out.

But I hadn't seen Art Fiala in nineteen months. And the last time I had seen him, he'd been desperately ill, so weak he could only speak for an hour or so before he had to go to sleep. And yet, not only had he remembered our earlier visit — that was clear from the first moment I saw him again — but he actually remembered what he had and hadn't told me before. I couldn't do that, and I was almost seven decades younger than he. (He was also able to go off on long tangents — some that lasted twenty minutes or so — and somehow always return to the point of departure. Another skill that eludes me.)

"Say, that reminds me of something I didn't tell you last time. When we were situated up in that plateau," he recalled, "I had a little time, and I walked up the mountain farther and I struck a little town, a little town up there. And when I got up on top there, the first thing I noticed, the women had wooden shoes and had a stick across their shoulders carrying two pails of milk going across the road there. And like me, it didn't take me long to get acquainted with the people there, and they invited me into their home to see what they had there. And did you know that they had their cows in the same room in the house with them? There was a partition there, and you could go in the kitchen and sit there, talk and hear the cows mooing. That's the way it is. Oh, I'll tell you, it's so much different. And there was a guy that used to come up, they had logging, he would come up there with a double wagon of some kind and you know that man would come up there in the morning and go back in the evening with *one log*. Yes, that's all they had, a wagon and two parts and got that log on there. But just think of it, you work all day for that."

So Private Fiala goes off to France, and no sooner does he get there than he stumbles into an Alpine *Brigadoon*. That was him; and that was his war.

He passed away seven months later, just before Thanksgiving. He died where he'd been born, where he'd lived for just about every one of his 106 years, not far from every place he'd ever spent any considerable stretch of time. Except one, of course. Were it not for the Great War, he almost certainly would have never traveled to a place so distant, and strange, as France was to him.

"The first time I went into a restaurant [there]," he'd told me during that second visit, "we didn't know what to ask for. We started crowing like a chicken. And finally they know we wanted eggs. That's the way we got it."

"You just sat down in a restaurant and started crowing like a chicken?" I asked. "But what if they'd brought you a chicken instead?"

"Well," he said, "that would have been OK, too."

6

The Forgotten Generation

A T SOME POINT IN THE COURSE of reading this book, you may find yourself wondering: What's it like to hang out with a centenarian?

If so: I may be able to help you with that. In the process of tracking down and interviewing every American veteran of World War I that I could find, I had the opportunity to spend time with dozens of centenarians, including several supercentenarians (that is, people 110 years of age or older); as a group, their median age was 107 years old. Let me share just a bit of what I've learned.

Now, several societal imperatives — including political correctness, a general taboo against generalization, and the powerful writer's ethos that urges us to counter the conventional wisdom at every turn — demand that I tell you that centenarians are just like everyone else, only a bit older. However: I cannot. It isn't true. In fact, it's absurd. Centenarians belong to an elite and extremely small club, one composed entirely of men and women who have done something that the overwhelming majority of us will never be able to do. What's more, they did it without even trying. How can you try to live to be 100? You can't. Maybe you can try to live to be very old, but I'd wager that the effort, and the accompanying anxiety, would shave off more years than will simply leaving the egg yolks in your omelet. But these folks — not only did they live to be 100 and more, they passed most of those years in an era when cigarettes were believed to soothe your throat, red meat was an essential part of every meal, and seat belts were nonexistent. Many of their mothers smoked, drank alcohol, and consumed caffeine while carrying them in utero, too.

So no, centenarians are not like anyone else. It's not easy to live to be 100 or older. At present, only one living American in about 4,400 has made it.

Getting to know the very oldest among us forces you to reexamine your notions of what it means to be old. Before I started this project, I imagined it might be very difficult to have a conversation with any particular person that age, based on the octogenarians and nonagenarians I happen to know. When I finally did start finding and meeting veterans, I was astonished to discover that I was actually able to talk with them about 90 percent of the time. I won't say they were all good conversations — there was one fellow at the Soldiers Home and Colony in Orting, Washington, for instance, who kept asking me how the hell I thought he was supposed to remember things that had happened almost a century ago — but still: 90 percent! I don't even succeed at making toast 90 percent of the time.

My mistake was, once again, in assuming that centenarians were just like everyone else, only older. They are, in fact, different from the rest of us from birth, and probably from conception. It is encoded in their genes that, barring things like war and unfortunate jaywalking-related incidents, they will live much, much longer than their peers. Almost all of them had parents who lived to be very old, if not quite as old as they were; one fellow, who was then 105, told me that both his mother and her sister lived to be 109. They are impervious to the things that take down the rest of us — Alzheimer's, dementia, aggressive cancers. They do not get colds. They do not have to take a lot of medicine. Ever met one of those annoying people who brag that they've never been sick a day in their life? They're probably lying, but a centenarian who says so might just be telling you the truth. They also age much more slowly than the rest of us do. They look a great deal younger than they are — decades younger. It is as if their inner clocks run much more slowly than ours do. A year to us is nine or ten months to them.

Nothing I have just said applies to every last one of the centenarians I met. That fellow in Orting, for instance, had dementia, or so his caregiver told me after the unpleasant encounter. Frankly, I think he would have been a jerk anyway. (Did I mention he called me an idiot, too?) Some of them had survived cancer or other potentially terminal diseases, some did take medication, and a few did look their age, or pretty close. However, if you're a person who really needs to be able to break out an unassailably true generalization, say, at a cocktail party, I can tell you this: Every last centenarian I met was hard of hearing. At least. So if you're reading this and you plan to live to be 100, I can pretty much assure you that while you are teleporting yourself to Neptune and storing your head overnight in a jar, plan on doing so with hearing aids in your ears. Of course, by then they might be so small as to be barely noticeable. So there's that.

When I started finding and meeting veterans, I took a bit of a crash course in gerontology, the study of human aging. I read books, spoke to experts like Dr. Thomas T. Perls, of the New England Centenarian Study (the folks to whom Laurence Moffitt left his body), and Dr. L. Stephen Coles, of the California-based Gerontology Research Group. I learned quite a bit. For instance, although there are more female than male centenarians, male centenarians are more likely to have their mental faculties largely intact. No one is sure why this is so. No one is sure about much else when it comes to living that long, either. In fact, surprisingly little research has been done on the subject at all. Meanwhile, scientists keep studying vexing questions like whether or not reading makes you more informed, or consuming alcohol tends to make men and women appear more attractive to each other.

So I undertook my own study, by which I mean that I asked everyone I spoke with for the secret to their longevity. As you might expect, a lot of them offered up some version of Anthony Pierro's and Laurence Moffitt's claims that they don't sweat the small stuff, or the big stuff. Or anything. I'm inclined to take them at their word, in part because a 107-year-old man really doesn't need to lie to anybody, and in part because the people I met and interviewed were, almost to a person, extremely stoic. And they had very good reasons not to be. In addition to surviving the war, which often presented enough horrors in a single day to give the most jaded soul a severe case of posttraumatic stress disorder, they came of age in economically precarious times — the Panic of 1907, and coincident recession, cost millions their jobs and nearly broke Wall Street — without minimum wage, child labor, or workplace safety statutes. Jim Crow laws were unassailable. The concepts of "civil rights" and "social justice" concerned but a few quixotic souls. The infant mortality rate was quite high; children often died of things that today can be cured with one or two pills. So did adults. They also regularly died from fires, overwork, drinking befouled water, and breathing in things you don't even want to think about. Schools were overcrowded and underfunded — even more so than today — which was OK, actually, because a great many children had to drop out long before graduating in order to work so that their families might starve a little less quickly.

Then they went off to war.

And then, if they were lucky enough to come home, the fun really began.

Ever since 1998, when Tom Brokaw published his first book, it's been fashionable to sing the praises of what he dubbed the "Greatest Generation," the people who grew up during the Great Depression, then went off to fight, and win, World War II. Now, I'm certainly not going to denigrate, in any way, their achievements, but you only have to go back one generation to see that assigning a superlative like "greatest" to any of them is a dicey proposition at best. The parents of the Greatests — let's call them the "Forgotten Generation," since they are — grew up with all of the hardships I just listed, then went off to get the scalp of Mr. Kaiser Man, fighting in muddy, filthy trenches, battling tedium and lice as they ducked bullets, shells, and poison gas. If they made it through all that and managed to get back home, they often found their jobs gone, their farms laid to waste, their houses reclaimed by the bank. The GI Bill? Sorry; not until 1944. At least they could get drunk — for another year, anyway, until Prohibition outlawed that old reliable coping mechanism. By the time that was repealed, they were waist-deep in the aforementioned Depression, scrambling to feed, clothe, and shelter the Greatests. Who had time for a beer?

And yet: stoic. Almost to a person. At least the people I met. To be fair, one fellow with whom I spoke on the phone while I was still searching for my first interview, an older gentleman who worked at a facility in D.C., referred to World War I veterans as "the complainingest bunch of bastards I ever saw in my life." Maybe he was just having a bad day. Or maybe it's true, and the people I met just happened to all be stoic because you pretty much have to be that way if you're going to live to be 100.

Happily, not everyone told me that the secret to their longevity was just to relax and not worry; that would have been mighty boring. Art Fiala, for one, said at first that he had no secret. Then he said his secret was that he ate peanuts twice a day, every day. The next time I visited him, I asked him again; this time, when he started in about the peanuts, his son, Carl, broke in: "Well, I think it's brandy."

Apparently, a doctor had once told Art that every evening he, the doctor, took a shot of whiskey. "I thought, God damn it, that sounds pretty good. I'll try, too," Art explained. "He's been furnishing me with brandy for how many years . . . I get every night a little cup with so much brandy in there."

"It's a good few shots," Carl clarified.

On the other hand, there was the centenarian who volunteered: "You know why I'm here? I'm not a boozehound, and I never chased [women] around."

And here I must confess that asking people for the secret to their longevity is often not a very satisfying experience. "Use common sense and moderation in everything you do," one woman told me. "I didn't overeat," a man said; "I have always taken exercise," offered another. A few said "clean living." "I don't drink or smoke, so I think that helps a lot," one speculated; several others offered the same theory. "The organs of the body is what regulates the body," one supercentenarian explained, after offering that he, too, never smoked or drank. "You get them in bad shape, I don't care what the outside of the body is doing, it's just in bad shape." And then there was the fellow who elaborated: "I never abused my body. In fact, when I quit smoking [after thirty years!], it took me two years to get rid of the phlegm in my lungs." (I guess he figured it doesn't count as abuse until you've been smoking for thirty-*five* years.) "You've got to believe," offered someone else, also echoing what several others said, "first, in our Lord, our God. He's the master of all things. And when I say he's the master, he is *the* master of all things."

Not every centenarian I met was a goody two-shoes. A lot of them confessed that they had no idea why they had lived so long; "I couldn't tell you that for a million dollars," a supercentenarian reported, shaking his head. One woman confessed that she sometimes lay awake in bed at night, asking herself why God hadn't taken her yet. "Why am I staying here?" she wondered. "What am I to do before I leave?"

"I don't know, and nobody else knows," one gentleman stated. "There ain't any [secret], I guess," said another. One winked and just said, "It's a secret"; apparently, as much a secret to him as to anyone else. And that fellow in Orting, Washington — "I'll tell you what I tell everyone," he told me. "None of your Goddamn business!" He was kind enough to elaborate: "You've got to figure it out yourselves, because I ain't telling you nothing. Because I don't *want* to." He was a real peach, that guy.

"Well, I'd say good, clean living," one man offered with a hearty nod; then, after a pause — maybe he saw the pained expression on my face, or perhaps he just decided to come clean — he added: "Good whiskey." But then, for some reason, he reconsidered again. "Skip the good whiskey," he demurred — speaking, no doubt, to posterity. "I always figured a good, clean life." I asked him the same question again two years later. "I say it runs in the family," he replied, finally offering an explanation no one could argue with.

Several said they were "just lucky"; "If you live another day, you're lucky," one philosophized. "Eat what they give you, and that's all you can do," offered another. "I got a pretty good cook," yet another bragged.

"Get plenty of sleep and plenty of food," one man told me. "Don't worry about politics or who's winning the war in Asia [this was in 2004] or anything like that. Just keep a low profile and get plenty of sleep. And watch TV a lot." As much as I liked that response, my favorite — by which I mean, the only one I actually tried — came from a gentleman in upstate New York, who told me he ate bee pollen every day. *Ah,* I thought, *something I can actually do.* I went out and tracked some down, and immediately started eating a teaspoon of it every day — which, it turns out, may be harder than just plain clean living, because, as I quickly discovered, bee pollen tastes absolutely awful, and is textured so that you have to drink at least a full glass of water just to get it down. Nevertheless, I still eat it — when I remember to — because the person who offered me that advice happened, at the time, to be the oldest man in the entire country. Within a few months he would also be the oldest on the planet.

His name was Fred Hale Sr., and he was, in fact, *not* a World War I veteran, though not for lack of trying. When America entered the war, Fred Hale was working here and there — "everything I could find to do that I could get a little money from" — with a wife and three children to support. Yet he went down to the local Army recruiting station and offered his services. This was near his hometown of New Sharon, Maine, and the recruiter, knowing Fred and his family situation, sent him away, told him to "keep on doing as I was and they would call me." They never did. He signed up for the Maine National Guard anyway. They never activated him, either.

I met him in December, 2003, just two days after his 113th birthday; he was living then in Baldwinsville, New York, near Syracuse, having moved there at the age of 109 to be near his son Fred Jr. I had read something about his upcoming birthday in a newspaper a couple of weeks earlier, and since I was going to be in that area, I decided to see if I could come by and visit with him. I already knew he hadn't served in the war, but really, now — would you *not* visit with a 113-year-old man if given the chance?

I'd say that Fred Hale didn't look 113, but what exactly is a 113-year-old supposed to look like? He wore a tan plaid shirt (it always surprised me a little bit to see centenarians wear the same clothing as everyone else; I guess maybe I expected them to be dressed like Victorian chimney sweeps?) and large horn-rimmed glasses, and an air-hose under his nose, though he didn't appear to need it. He did seem tired, though; when I asked him if he had just had a birthday, he said, "Yeah, that's what ails me today." Apparently, there had been a bit of a celebration, and Mr. Hale was still recovering. "Too much excitement," Fred Jr. explained.

Fred Harold Hale Sr. had been born in New Sharon one month before the end of 1890. His father was named Fred C. Hale; when I asked what kind of work Fred C. had done back in 1890, his son replied, "Dug in the dirt, for all I know."

"He was a farmer?" I asked.

"No," he said, "he was everything."

His father did manage to keep a farm until his sons moved away; after that, it was too much work for him to continue it on his own. As a child, Fred took care of the sheep; "It was a pleasure," he said, even when he had to haul them around on horseback in the frigid winter air. He started working outside the house, too, when he was eight or nine. I asked him what he did for fun as a kid. "Tossed a ball around the house," he said. "That's all."

He went through school in New Sharon, then married Flora Mooers as soon as he graduated in 1910. "How old were you when you started dating your wife?" I asked him.

"Didn't really date," he answered. This is where the stereotype of Mainers as laconic and unflappable comes from: men who do anything and everything to scratch out a living, and don't date.

Flora's brother, John Mooers, was called up early in the war, went off to France, survived, and returned home. Eventually, Fred and Flora had five children, one of whom died in infancy of pneumonia. Fred's only brother became a doctor and moved to Massachusetts. In the 1920s, Fred got a job working as a mail clerk on the railroad, sorting letters on moving trains. He also worked as a handyman, retiring for good in 1957, when he was sixty-six years old. "What did you do to keep busy after you retired?" I asked him.

"Anything I could get my hands to," he replied.

"Were you very handy?"

"Handier than the other people." To say more than that might seem like boasting, or lying. So he didn't.

And now we get to the legend of Fred Hale. The term "legend," though, implies a lack of veracity, and everything I'm about to tell you is absolutely true.

From 1921 to 1937, Fred Hale rode his bicycle to work, a distance of five or six miles each way, every day. Year round. "Didn't make any difference if it was raining or snowing or what," his son explained. It snowed a lot in Maine. He did not own a car until he was in his late 40s.

He kept bees from the age of 12 until he was 107.

When he was in his late 80s, his wife, Flora, went to live in a nursing home a mile and a half away from their house. Fred walked there to visit her three times a day, for meals, then walked home after every meal. Often he had to wear snowshoes. He never missed a meal, even during an ice storm that crippled the state.

At 95, now a widower, he flew to Japan to visit his grandson, who was in the Navy. On his way home, he stopped in Hawaii, where he tried boogie boarding.

At 100, he went to Europe with his older son, Norman, to visit the sites where Norman had served during World War II.

When he was 103, the area was hit by a blizzard. After a few days, someone thought to go check on Fred to make sure he was OK. They found him shoveling snow — off his roof.

He continued to live alone, and to drive, until he was 107. Fred Jr. and Norman, concerned about their father, tried to force him to quit driving. "We went down to see the State Farm agent," Fred Jr. told me, "and said we don't want my father driving; when his insurance is due, cancel. They looked at us and said, 'Sorry, noncancelable, guaranteed renewable, as long as he wants it.'"

At 107, he went to live at the same nursing home where his wife had spent her last days twenty years earlier. The average resident lived ninety days after moving in.

At 109, he moved to New York.

At 108, he broke his hip, and had surgery on it. The next year, he broke the other one, and had surgery on it.

At 109, he had surgery to remove cataracts from one of his eyes. At 110, he had them removed from the other one.

Somewhere in there he also broke two ribs, had his tonsils removed, and had an operation on his prostate. He always recovered very quickly.

Fred Hale was, simply, a superman. I like to think I'm pretty hearty (perhaps even — forgive me — hale), especially for a writer, yet I'm six decades younger than he was when that blizzard hit, and I can't shovel a walkway without paying for it the next day, and maybe the day after that. I suspect State Farm is just dying to cancel my auto policy already. I don't ride my bicycle if it's drizzling out, much less in a snowstorm. I fall off boogie boards. Bees make me nervous.

Yes, Fred Hale was different from you and me. So were all of the other centenarians I met. Not necessarily better; I assure you that you can do things right now that none of them ever could, not even when they were your age. The difference is that it is highly unlikely that any of your things will inspire astonishment and awe in every last person who hears about them.

Don't feel too bad, though. Most of it just comes down to genes. Fred Hale's father lived to be 90, his mother 91. Unless science figures out a way to have you travel back in time and pick parents like his, you're probably going to have to stick with what everybody already knows: Eat more greens. Exercise every day. Cut the smokes and the booze. Baby aspirin. Wheat germ. Maybe, if scientific and medical trends continue, the average person may someday live to be Fred Hale's age. But they won't be Fred Hale; by then, whatever Fred Hales are walking among us will be 140. State Farm had better start pondering that prospect.

Talking with the very oldest among us is different than talking with anyone else. You have to speak louder around them, more slowly, and still you'll need to repeat yourself. Despite this, they are very good listeners. They are calmer than most people you meet. They are good talkers — having told a particular story so many times for so many decades, they can tell it very, very well. They're also willing to tell you stories they haven't told in decades, maybe ever, if you should happen to ask them the right questions. At this point, they have no reason not to tell you. In hundreds of hours of conversation, I believe I heard the phrase "I don't want to talk about it" only once. They speak slowly, pause often; perhaps there are physical reasons for this, but it gives the impression that they are more thoughtful than other people. It makes you want to hear everything they say, to lean in close and catch every word, to wait and make sure they are through before you say anything else. They have presence, effortless gravitas. They also have accents you may have heard only in old movies, and pronounce things differently, too, like the fellow who referred time and again to the Hawkeye State as "Ioway." Lots of people used to; most of them are dead now.

Not all the differences are in them, though; some of them will be in you. Perhaps you may find yourself unable, during such a conversation, to stop thinking, every few minutes: *I'm talking to a 107-year-old man!* I always caught myself, at some point or other, doing this weird mathematical/historical exercise that involved taking the person's age and subtracting it from the year in which he or she had been born —

for instance, subtract Laurence Moffitt's age (106) from his birth year (1897) and you get 1791, the year the Bill of Rights was ratified, when George Washington was just two years into his first term. That was quite something in itself, but when I did the same exercise for Fred Hale, I came up with something truly startling. He was born in 1890, and was 113 when I met him; using my little formula, you get to the year 1777 — the year of the Battle of Saratoga (take that, Burgoyne!), four years before Yorktown, six before the Paris Peace Treaty, a decade before the Constitutional Convention in Philadelphia. In other words, in his last years, Fred Hale's existence spanned more than half the life of the Republic.

I remember how astonished I felt when I first did that math while sitting in Fred Hale's room in that nursing home in Baldwinsville on that cold day back in December, 2003. As I drove back to Manhattan that night, through a sudden whiteout, I thought about that fact again and again; I couldn't believe it, couldn't believe that you could stick your arm into the barrel of American history, stretch it as far as you could, stretch until you imagine you can almost feel it coming out of its socket, stretch your fingers until it feels as if they've actually grown, and pull out — the Battle of Saratoga. Fred Hale's grandfather Christopher C. Hale had been born in 1824, only four years after Maine became a state. He could easily have known someone who had fought at Saratoga.

As the snow fell harder, I thought, too, about a question that had occurred to me only at the very end of my talk with Mr. Hale, after I'd asked him about things like when he'd first gotten electricity or voted, things he didn't care enough about to recall with precision. "Do you remember New Year's Eve nineteen hundred?" I asked him. "Do you remember the turn of the century?"

"Not so much," he answered. "I remember my minister speaking of it. That's all . . . it didn't sink in too deep, I guess."

"It was just another day in their life," his son explained.

Just another day. You worked, cared for the sheep, shoveled snow, did whatever else needed to be done. Every day. The birth of the twentieth century was no different than the passing of the nineteenth. Feeling otherwise is a luxury that we acquired as that era receded into the past and we started to look backwards at it. It is a luxury that came along with electricity, and automobiles, and farm machines, and anti-biotics. It is *our* luxury, just as the experience of talking to a 106-year-old man is *our* experience, not theirs. J. Laurence Moffitt really *didn't* give a thought to his age. He was inside it. His age, his wisdom, his insights, his experiences — they were all mine to take. He didn't even know he was giving.

I guess what I'm saying is this: Hanging out with centenarians is, in every sense of the word, awesome. I highly recommend it.

7

Give a Little Credit to the Navy

WHILE THEY MAY BE BEST remembered today for their rousing patriotic fight songs, the pluggers also cranked out plenty of sad World War I tunes, with titles like "He Sleeps Beneath the Soil of France" and lots of talk of kissing Mother's sweet lips one last time. As far as I'm concerned, though, none of them come close, in the matter of pathos, to a song by Bud de Sylva, Gus Kahn, and Albert Gumble that wasn't actually supposed to be sad at all. "Give a Little Credit to the Navy" is dedicated to a dignified-looking gentleman named William Buel Franklin, USNRF, commander of the US Naval Training Camp in Pelham Bay Park, New York — quite possibly the last man with such a resplendent monicker to tread upon the fair soil of the Bronx; its chorus goes:

> Give a little credit to the Navy,
> We took the boys across
> without a single loss.
> Ev'ry soldier is a fighting bear,
> but don't forget it,
> give us credit,
> we took 'em over there.
> Mothers of soldiers, sweethearts and wives,
> we'll take care of your boys, though it costs us our lives.
> So give a little credit to the Navy,
> the Navy will do its share.

Gee. I don't think it's very nice that somebody even had to write such a song. If you're a major branch of the United States military and you have to rely upon pluggers to make sure that you're not entirely ignored — in wartime, no less — well, something is seriously amiss. Maybe it's just because they often seem like the World War I of armed forces — that is, overlooked and underappreciated — but I am inclined to give a little credit to the Navy.

For one thing, they had their war stolen right out from under them. When America entered the fight in April, 1917, the conventional wisdom held that the Allies already had enough men, and that what they lacked were munitions, food, and, of course, money. The United States' main contribution, it was thought, would be guns and ammunition, wheat and corn — and the ships to carry it all across in the face of unrestricted submarine warfare. So little thought was given in those early days to raising an army, in fact, that the nation didn't even institute a draft until June, and only then after rigorous debate over the matter in Congress. Just as Art Fiala, looking to get into the war quickly, was directed toward the Engineers, other young men, looking for action, were encouraged to enlist in the Navy, where they would surely get in a shot or two at the hated *Unterseeboot,* or U-boat. This was to be a naval conflict, which explains why Laurence Moffitt's mother was relieved when she learned that her son had joined the Army National Guard.

It didn't work out that way. The notion that America's main role was to be played upon the high seas had been formed in a vacuum; when French and British representatives arrived in Washington toward the end of April, 1917, they quickly disabused the American military of it. What they really needed, it turned out, were more warm bodies in the trenches. And so, though the Navy would still be critical to the war effort, theirs would be more of a behind-the-scenes role. While the USN would offer battleships and destroyers to the British Navy to help keep the German fleet trapped in harbor, their primary role would be to shuttle men and materiel across the Atlantic. In the first three months of the war, a quarter of all American ships that headed off to Europe never returned. A quarter! With odds like those, it makes you wonder how the Navy got anyone to enlist at all.

Fortunately, those odds got better and better as the war progressed; you might say, even, that if the Navy had to go through such growing pains, it's best they did it at the beginning, before the boys were ready to go Over There. I say that by way of introducing perhaps the most remarkable statistic of the entire war: The Germans did not manage to sink a single American troop transport during a year and a half of war with the United States. Not a one. And America sent two million men across an ocean for the sole purpose of killing Germans.

So yes: Let's all try to give a little credit to the Navy. They really did take the boys across without a single loss. And it wasn't easy.

Among the veterans I met, seven of them had some direct connection to the Navy during the First World War.

There was 104-year-old Russell Buchanan, whom I visited in Cambridge, Massachusetts, on November 13, 2004. The son of immigrants from Prince Edward Island—his father, who died of some ailment ("You never hear of it today—I suppose they changed the name of that sickness") when Russell was three, had been a carpenter and, Russell added proudly, a Scottish piper—he had grown up in Cambridge. One day in 1916, while crossing Boston Common, he came across a Marine Corps recruiting station and tried to enlist. When they asked him his age, he made the mistake of telling them the truth: sixteen. They sent him home. He went up to Maine and worked on a farm for a while, built himself up; when America entered the war, he joined the United States Naval Reserve Force. "I was offering my service" is how he put it. They assigned him to an Eagle boat—a class of steel ship smaller than destroyers but larger, and with a longer range, than wooden submarine chasers—which patrolled the Atlantic coast from the Maritimes to the Carolinas. He was a signalman—flags, semaphores, lights. They never found any U-boats, though they did encounter some banana boats, and once got stranded at sea for a few days; eventually they were towed to Charleston, where Mr. Buchanan had his first encounter with racial segregation. "We went ashore," he recalled, "and we had a black chef, a cook, aboard the ship, and I was ashore with him. And we were going to the town proper, and a trolley car stopped. So we entered, and we took the first seats on the trolley." He laughed. "And the operator informed us, that he had to go back to the rear . . . So we both got off the trolley car, because we were insulted."

Like Russell Buchanan, David Byerly, whom I met in Newtown Square, Pennsylvania, on September 11, 2004, was 104 years old, born in 1900, and had lost his father at the age of three. But unlike Mr.

Buchanan, whose mother had to go to work as a judge's housekeeper, Mr. Byerly had grown up in somewhat less straitened circumstances in the town of Butler, about twenty-five miles from Pittsburgh. "The Byerlys were very well-known in Pennsylvania," he told me. His father, who had been in the oil business, had died, at the age of thirty, during a local epidemic of typhoid fever; "they drained the reservoir of the water," his son explained to me, and "found half a dozen cows in there." The family went to live with his widowed grandmother. One day in early 1916, his mother was at the bank when she ran into her local congressman, who made her a proposition: "Eunice," he said, "you have two boys. I've got an appointment for the Naval Academy. Would one of your boys be interested in it?"

"So my mother grabbed it," David Byerly recalled nearly ninety years later. "I think money was running a little shy at that time. And my older brother was already a freshman in college. And so the idea of a free education appealed to her." For his senior year in high school, his mother sent him to a special preparatory school in Annapolis, where he studied every past Naval Academy entrance exam since the Civil War, just to make sure he passed his. He did. Two months later, several of his friends from Butler High School enlisted in the Army. He tried to do the same, he said, but "they wouldn't take me. On account of I had already committed to the Naval Academy."

Classes didn't begin until September; he and the other five hundred members of his incoming class spent the summer drilling. At one point, he told me, "I was caught smoking and landed down on the Ship for two weeks." "The Ship" was a prison ship.

Once classes began, he explained, "we had a school routine. And the war didn't really intrude on it." In the summer of 1918, when classes were out, "they wanted us to get war experience. So they sent us out with the Atlantic Fleet . . . I served in a turret of a battleship . . . I was what was called the 'plug man.' In other words, I had seventeen and a half turns of this plug, to put the plug back into the breech of the gun. I did it every morning, all morning long."

The battleship, the USS *Wisconsin*, was already twenty years old; after the war it would be sold for scrap. "We were hiding up in the Chesapeake Bay," he recalled. "Actually, the York River . . . hiding from the German submarines." At night, he said, "I had to serve as a boat officer for a boat to patrol the net. We had a net down at the Chesapeake, and in the York River." The net was supposed to ensnare U-boats. "So every night I would go down with this boat. And my only armament was my .45 pistol."

"So if you had spotted a submarine —"

"I'd be firing bullets." Fortunately, he never spotted one.

And that was Midshipman Byerly's war.

It's a funny thing about revolutions: Sometimes, they can begin very subtly.

The Naval Reserve Act of 1916 started one not with a bold statement or action, but with an omission. What was omitted was any mention of the fact that you had to be a man to serve active duty in the Navy; by being omitted, it quietly ceased being a fact. So quietly, in fact, that Secretary of the Navy Josephus Daniels didn't even realize it until the following year. When he did, he made a decision that shocked many: He formally granted the Navy permission to start enlisting women. (The Navy already had a small Nurse Corps, but it was staffed by civilians without rank or benefits.) This was around the middle of March, 1917, several weeks before the United States entered the war, and three full years before American women would be granted the right to vote. By the end of April, nearly six hundred women had signed up. Their official designation was "Yeoman (F)," but most people called them Yeomanettes.

By the end of the war there would be more than eleven thousand of them in the Navy, which is kind of surprising to me because, as far as I can tell, the Yeomanettes didn't have it so good back then. All but five served stateside; no France for them. Almost all of them were confined to clerical work. Their uniforms were dowdy. They weren't assigned official ranks. The money wasn't very good. They didn't receive any benefits. They even had to pay their own room and board. You have to wonder: Why did they bother? If they really wanted to help the war effort, there were much easier ways of doing so; Rosie the Riveter was not an invention of World War II, even if her name was. So, why the Navy?

I was fortunate to locate and visit not one but two Yeomanettes in the first decade of the twenty-first century, the first being Ruth Elfean

Richardson, who was 107 years old when I met her on November 18, 2004. She was living then in a nursing home in Farnham, Virginia, just a few miles from the town of Lodge, where she'd been born. Both are on what is known as the Northern Neck, a rural peninsula that juts out into Chesapeake Bay about a hundred or so miles southeast of Washington. Her roots ran straight back in the Northern Neck; her father, George Washington Fisher, had been a farmer there. After high school, she went to work on the farm "crating tomatoes," she said, and didn't much care for it, so one day, after America had entered the war, she and a friend of hers named Myrtle Dawson decided to go up to Washington. "We thought that was just somewhere to go, and it would be nice, and we'd go to Washington, and, well, we thought we could have a good time, I guess," she recalled with a chuckle. They traveled there by steamboat. "I think we stayed on the boat all night," she told me.

They stayed for a bit with Myrtle's sister, "until we got a room that we wanted to be to ourselves. You know, have a good time, go to dances, and places. You know, like girls do." Somehow, they learned that the Navy was looking for women; she seemed to think a poster might have caught her eye: "Join the Navy and see the world," she remembered.

"Did that appeal to you?" I asked her.

"Yes!" she replied exuberantly.

So she and Myrtle went and signed up. They didn't have to drill, as she remembered it, though she also remembered "we marched up, when they had parades. We marched in the parade on Pennsylvania Avenue." One time, "we all got together and marched up from the Capitol to the White House in the uniform." That was for General Pershing, after the armistice.

Mostly, though, she said, "I worked in the Navy Department. I filed . . . I sorted papers and things. The usual things, you know, in an office that people do. . . . We went to dances, and things that girls do, you know, around that time, I guess."

Both she and Myrtle would meet their future husbands at dances. She mentioned them a lot; the more we talked, the more it became clear to me that these dances were her favorite thing about being in Washington. And her favorite thing about being in the Navy, it seemed, was that it got her to Washington. "If they wanted us to go to town and mail a letter for them, well, I did that, and I liked that because to get away, and go to town, you know, a girl liked to get away," she explained. "And I enjoyed that, that I was doing something, you know?" The Navy issued her two uniforms: a white one and a blue one. "I still have some of it," she told me, smiling. "At home, in my trunk."

Seventeen months later, I traveled to Boonsboro, Maryland, to meet another former Yeomanette named Charlotte Winters. She was 108 years old then. Boonsboro is near the Antietam battlefield, about sixty miles northwest of Washington, where Ms. Winters had grown up, and where she enlisted in the Navy in 1917. "Why did you join?" I asked her.

"I don't know," she said with a lilt in her voice. "I just loved the Navy." Later, she elaborated just a bit: "We lived in the part of Washington where everyone was in the Navy."

"Did you have any friends who joined the Navy?" I asked.

"I think so," she answered. "All of us girls joined the Navy."

Now, that's quite a statement, and to be honest, I don't know if it's accurate; Ms. Richardson's memory had been frail, but Ms. Winters's seemed faded almost to the point of irretrievability. I do know, from her obituary — she died about eleven months later — that her sister, Sophie, had also served in the Navy during the war; that, after the war, she was one of twenty women who helped found one of the first American Legion posts, in Washington, D.C.; and that she remained a member of the Legion for eighty years. From our conversation, I determined that her mother had died when she was very young, at which point her father's sister, her aunt Lottie, had moved in to help raise her; that her father had worked for the Navy as a civilian; that she had worked as a secretary at a factory — "the Naval Gun Factory," she said it was called — that produced artillery pieces for ships; that she met her husband there; and that she really liked her work. "I liked everything about the Navy," she told me, and it was obvious, almost ninety years later, that she still did. Thanks to the Navy, she was no longer confined to a sidestep realm where she could only watch from behind a glass as the world played out its script; the Navy put her out in the world, made her a player on the stage. She was doing something. Maybe that's why they all joined up, all eleven thousand of them — because Josephus Daniels had given them this fleeting chance to step out from behind that glass, and a lack of rank and benefits and room and board seemed a small price to pay for something most of them never could have imagined beforehand: a place in the wider world. Give a little credit to the Navy.

They were all released from active duty after the war ended, whether they wanted to be or not; perhaps, in the light of day after the fighting had stopped, the Navy reconsidered what was then a bold experiment. But the Yeomanettes did not just go back home and never mention their service again. Instead, they lobbied to upgrade their discharges from general to honorable — and won. They formed American Legion posts, sometimes with men, sometimes without. Many of them never stopped working at their jobs; they merely went home one day as Yeomanettes and returned the next as civilians.

I don't know if the notion of the Yeomanette piqued the popular imagination during World War I; I've never come across a song written about them, or even any mention of them in a newspaper from that time. It seems possible that the vast majority of Americans didn't even know they existed. But the military knew. And though the Yeomanettes were all discharged in 1919, and the Army and Navy returned to being single-sex institutions for more than twenty years, when World War II swept into America, they did not hesitate to welcome women into their ranks. In 1942, the Navy established Women Accepted for Volunteer Emergency Service, or WAVES; within a year it put some twenty-seven thousand women in uniform. The following year, the Army established the Women's Army Corps, and enlisted, by war's end, one hundred thousand WACs. And if their uniforms were spiffier, their nickname lacked the elegance of the one accorded to that earlier generation of servicewomen, the ones who'd blazed the trail.

Aside from the U-boats and a couple of battles, it wasn't much of a naval war. The first of those battles, near the Falkland Islands in 1914, was a sound defeat for the Germans, who lost an entire squadron, as well as the revered Vice Admiral Maximilian Graf von Spee. The second, fought two years later in the North Sea off the coast of Jutland, Denmark, was a draw; the Germans, tired of having their fleet bottled up in port, took it out to sea, confronted the British, and sank some ships, but not enough. The British could have pursued the retreating Germans and possibly destroyed their fleet once and for all, but they didn't. Both sides quickly returned to the status quo: the British ruling the open waters, blockading Germany; the Germans fighting back underwater.

Not the kind of naval war that might attract young American men seeking a lot of action, perhaps, but twenty-year-old William F. Cotton, of Corley, Arkansas — far away from any large body of water — chose to enlist in the Navy, nevertheless. "I was just looking for — for a life," he explained. "Kids today, I don't know what they look for."

He actually offered several different explanations. "I joined the Navy because we had a war comin' on," he told me at one point; then, a few minutes later, he said, "I joined the Navy, I guess, because I thought I was going to be drafted. So rather than do that, I had a choice . . . and the Navy, of course you had to go away to go to the Navy." Later still, he said: "I didn't particularly like the idea of the Army. But the Navy was kind of a lure."

They sent him to Boston — "coldest place in the United States," he called it — where they put him to work baking bread in a galley; back in Arkansas, he'd worked in a bakery on weekends. After the war, he and his brother, Herbert, moved to Alexandria, Louisiana (where he was still living when I visited him, on September 19, 2004), and bought a bakery. Eventually they owned several throughout the state.

From Boston he sailed off to Cork, Ireland, where he joined the crew of the USS *Oklahoma*, a battleship that escorted troop transports as they crossed the Atlantic for France. The *Oklahoma* was a new ship, one of only a few in the entire fleet to use oil instead of coal. On December 7, 1941, it was moored in Battleship Row at Pearl Harbor. It took five torpedo hits and was strafed until it capsized; 429 of its crew were lost.

"I was what they call a 'chief commissary,'" William Cotton recalled. That meant that when the *Oklahoma* docked in Brest, France, he had to go ashore and buy all the food for its crew — sixteen hundred men. And he didn't speak any French. It may not have been the adventure he'd thought he was signing up for back in Arkansas, but it was hard work; he particularly remembered buying yeast and flour, and strawberries from a large Frenchwoman, who impressed him. "She was the boss of a working crew," he remembered.

Unfortunately, he didn't remember much more about his service, at least not that he could convey to me; he was 107 when we met, and his memory seemed to have mostly slipped away by then. Lloyd Brown, though, was a different story.

Maybe it was because he was a mere 103 years old when we met, a couple of months after I'd visited William Cotton, but talking to Lloyd Brown was pretty much like talking to anyone else. He was a bit confused about his precise age, but that could have been because, when he enlisted in the Navy in 1917, he gave them 1899 as his birth year, when it seems much more likely that he was actually born in 1901, and had tacked on a couple of years at the time so as not to be turned away. Whatever the year, he was born on October 7, in Ozark County, Missouri, near the town of Lutie, which is no longer a town. He was the fourth of nine children, seven boys and two girls; the next in line was his brother Floyd. Lloyd and Floyd. Their father, Claud, had a small farm. "I used to pull weeds away from the plants," Lloyd recalled, "and take a hoe and dig around the plants, you know. Get all the weeds away from the plants, whatever we were growing, whether it's cabbage, corn, carrots, beans, whatever . . . I didn't mind. It was my duties as a kid. All the kids in the neighborhood did the same thing."

We sat in his living room in Charlotte Hall, Maryland, about an hour southeast of Washington; it was a mild, sunny autumn afternoon. His daughter Nancy was there, and some other family, too, and they chimed in liberally, sometimes disputing minor details, often sharing a hearty laugh. They were a loud, lively bunch. The patriarch spoke loudest of all; hesitated from time to time, but never for long. He had an accent that, like Laurence Moffitt's, seemed archaic, though his was harder to place. I'd say southern Missouri, but that would be cheating.

Around 1913, his father changed professions, "went to Chadwick [Missouri], and he went in business. Bought out a business, buying eggs and turkeys and processing them and plucking all the feathers off of them and putting them in barrels and shipping them to the Slipton Company, in St. Louis." Chadwick was a railroad town, bigger and busier than Lutie, and the business did well. Claud Brown needed help; good thing he had those nine kids. His son Lloyd left school after the eighth grade and never returned.

A year or two later, America entered the war, and Lloyd decided he wanted a part of it. "I don't know why I chose the Navy," he said, "but

I guess because it travels around different parts of the country." Like William Cotton, he was completely landlocked.

"He wanted to see things," Nancy added.

"Different parts of the world," he asserted. "That sounded good to me."

"How did your parents feel about it?" I asked.

"Oh, they weren't concerned very much," he said. "I was sixteen or seventeen years old." His oldest brother, Homer, went into the Army and off to France. Lloyd signed up in St. Louis; from there, "they sent me to Great Lakes, Illinois, for about a week or ten days," he recalled, "to learn to do a little marching, and row a boat. And then they put me on the *New Hampshire*."

Like the *Oklahoma*, the *New Hampshire* was a battleship, but though it was only eight years older than the *Oklahoma*, there was one significant difference between the two: The *New Hampshire* was powered by coal. When fuel ran low, Lloyd Brown recalled, "they had a big barge pull up, and it had a big" — he closed his hand to simulate a steel claw — "grab up coal, and drop it on our deck. And then our crew would shovel it down manholes. Had a manhole on the deck, take the cover off and shovel the coal down there, and it goes down in the engine room."

"Would that make a mess on deck?" I asked.

"Oh, yeah," he said, shaking his head. "It'd mess the ship up and the crew and everything. Had to wash everything, the walls, the ceiling, with soap and water." Then, he said, "you sprinkle sand on the wooden deck. And they had a brick, what they called a 'holey stone,' and they put that brick down there, and it had a hole in the middle of it, and you had something like a broom handle to push it back and forth. With the grain of the wood, of course."

"Was that very hard work?"

"You didn't have to press too hard. The weight of the brick would do the job. You would just have to push it back and forth."

"How long did it take you to clean up after you got a load of coal?"

"Oh, I'd say a couple of days, that's all." You can see why the new class of battleships were so popular with seamen. It wasn't so easy for the crew to get clean, either; on a ship that was at sea for weeks, even months, at a time, fresh water was a precious commodity. Lloyd Brown said that he and the other seamen were issued only about a quart of it every day at the canteen. In the shower, he explained, "usually you had enough fresh water to kind of get yourself soapy, and then you take a shower with seawater." And, he added, "you had to shave and brush your teeth" — also with fresh water. There wasn't much left over to actually drink. Fortunately, there was one fountain, located in the center of the ship, where anyone could go at any time and line up to drink their fill; it was known as the scuttlebutt. "You go to the scuttlebutt to get your drinking water. And gossip. Used to call it 'scuttlebutt news.'"

Hence the expression.

When he wasn't shoveling coal or scrubbing away coal dust, Seaman Second Class Brown was assigned to a gun crew. He was a loader. "You put the shell in, and then a bag of powder, and then close the breech and be ready to pull the trigger."

"How big was the shell?"

"It was about the size of a champagne bottle. Three inches in diameter."

"Did you ever actually have to fire the gun at sea?" I asked.

"Yeah," he said, "we fired the gun." And then, he added, almost casually: "We shot a hole through another ship, one of our own ships, by accident."

"Was that the gun you loaded?" I asked him.

"I believe it was," he replied.

"Where did that happen?"

"In the ocean there."

The rest of the family laughed. Lloyd didn't seem to mind.

"What were you supposed to be shooting at?" I asked.

"Germans," Nancy declared.

"Well," Lloyd answered, "we were supposed to be shooting at a submarine."

"Was there actually a submarine there?" I asked.

"There must have been not," Nancy offered.

"No," Lloyd said, "it turned out to be it was not a submarine, no." He said it was "a floating piece of framework, a discarded carton or something." U-boats were known to camouflage their periscopes by covering them with wooden crates, in the hopes that sailors would think they were just jetsam.

"Do you remember which ship it was that got hit?"

"No, I don't remember."

"Did it do a lot of damage?"

He considered for a moment. "No," he said.

"I guess they didn't shoot back at you, huh?" I asked.

"No," he said, and laughed. Most days, he explained, he did a four-hour tour on lookout up in the crow's nest. He described the system they had for splitting up the horizon into sectors; I asked him what he would do if he spotted something suspicious. "Well," he said, "I'd call my officer over the tube, call my boss, whoever he was — the watch-tower, I guess it was — tell him what I saw, and let him issue out the orders that would be suitable for it." On that particular day, he recalled, "I spotted what I thought was a submarine. It turned out to be a float-ing carton or something."

Wait a minute. "And then you called that down?" I asked.

"Yeah."

"And that's when they fired and hit the other ship?"

"Yeah."

"Oh!" I said. "So *you* were the beginning of that?"

"Yeah," he said, and everyone laughed, including him.

"Did you get in any trouble for that?" I asked him.

"No," he told me. "I gave them my — I described what I saw and left them to follow their own judgment."

And that was about as much excitement as he saw during the war, at least at sea. Ashore, especially in New York, he remembered, "we'd go chase girls together, things like that."

"Did you have any luck?" I asked him.

"Yeah," he said, his smile giving way to a laugh.

"Did they like the uniform?"

"Oh, yeah."

"That's why he joined," Nancy said.

"Yeah," her father added, "during the war we were very popular."

After the war he returned to Missouri, but soon found it bored him; a couple of years later, he enlisted in the Navy again. This time, he let them send him to music school — "It was better than scrubbing decks," he explained. He learned the cello, and was assigned to the *Seattle*, Admiral Robert Coontz's flagship, where he played in the admiral's orchestra. "We played for his parties," he recalled, "during his dinner hour." One of the perks, he said, was that "they serve you the same food they'd serve the admiral."

He also got to travel wherever the admiral went — Hawaii, Panama, Australia, New Zealand. It was a nice assignment. In 1925, after four years on the *Seattle,* he decided to leave the Navy for good; "my time was up, I guess," he explained. He moved to Washington, D.C., and got work as a fireman at Engine Company 16, a job that saw him through the Depression. After sixteen years there, he moved on to serve as a fireman at the city's National Airport, retiring in 1952.

He said he enjoyed all of the phases of his life a great deal, but I have reason to believe that his time on the *New Hampshire* was special to him. I know for a fact that it left a mark on him — literally. At one point, he rolled up his right sleeve and showed me, on the inside of his forearm, a large tattoo; it was faded and had blurred quite a bit, but still clear enough to read: USS NEW HAMPSHIRE.

It was eighty-six years old.

And that leaves Ernest Pusey. I first learned about him from an article in a Florida newspaper that didn't even mention his service. It was, rather, about how he was General Motors' oldest living pensioner. He was 109, and had been retired for forty-six years at that point. He had only worked at GM for thirty-two years. It pays to live a very long life.

He was living alone in a nice double-wide mobile home in Bradenton, Florida, when I met him; on the day I visited — June 15, 2004 — it was so steamy outside that when I walked into his air-conditioned home, the lens on my video camera fogged up.

As much as any veteran I met — maybe as much as any person I've met — Ernie Pusey just looked like a nice guy. He wore big glasses, had a big nose and big ears and big sprouts of pure white hair atop his big, oval head, but mostly his face was defined by a big, open-mouthed smile, which never really left it during the two hours I interviewed him, nor during the lunch he and his caregiver, Rose, insisted on treating me to after we had finished. His happiness would seem to favor the nature side of the old nature versus nurture debate, because his early life hadn't been an easy one. He'd been born in Washington, D.C., on

May 5, 1895; his father, already sick with tuberculosis, died just five years later. Ernie and his sister, Helen, were sent to live with their grandfather on N Street in Georgetown, but at some point his mother, who went to work for the telephone company, became afraid that her son would develop the consumption that had killed his father, so she sent him to live with two ladies — an elderly dowager and her unmarried middle-aged daughter — in Virginia. The mother, he remembered, "was bedridden, and they had to get her up and put her in a wheelchair every day. And her daughter taught school, and I went to the little school down the road." He spent years there — eight or nine, or maybe twelve, depending upon when you asked him about it — traveling back and forth to Washington on a side-wheeler steamboat.

The Washington of Ernie Pusey's childhood, at least the way he recalled it, sounded downright pastoral. The streets, he said, were still lit by gas lamps, "and they'd go around and light them every night." His grandfather Samuel Pusey had been a bookkeeper at a flour mill on the Potomac; Ernie would often visit, sometimes playing in a nearby swimming hole — really — and sometimes making the rounds with his grandfather. "He'd go around to the different companies and see what they needed of any kind of cookies, or what kind of flour they'd want. And he had a horse and buggy, and he'd take a nap every afternoon when he was on the route — he'd tie the horse and buggy across the street and take a nap."

They shared their backyard with a goat. Ernie also lived, some of the time, with his other grandparents, the Koeths, on A Street in Capitol Hill. He remembered that grandfather, Theodore Koeth, as being retired; in the 1900 census, Theodore Koeth is listed as a painter. "Their house there was a row house," he told me, "and all the sheds in the back were together. And they didn't want to let me out on the street because I'd run away a lot of times, so they'd put me in the backyard, and I'd get up there on the roof of those row houses, and I'd go down the street and see what everybody was doing. Sometimes they'd be having ice cream or something, I might get some." He laughed. "And then when I got home, I'd get a spanking, every time." It was worth it, he said.

Washington offered interesting employment opportunities for a boy.

"I was delivering telegrams when I was big enough, on a bike, to the embassies," he told me. "I must have been eight or nine years old." He also worked at Union Station. "I had a job of putting the tags for where each [bag] was going. Put [passengers] on the cars, so they know what car to get on. And they had steam engines then. Sometimes they'd have a hard time getting out of there; they'd put sand on the track." He said he saw the president — the first President Roosevelt — at the station many times. "They'd be on a special train," he explained. "He'd leave out of Washington and go to some other city." Later, he got a job as an oiler on a side-wheeler. The skipper often let him pilot it, he said.

And then, when he was twenty-one, he enlisted in the Navy. Or maybe he was twenty-two; America entered the war a month before his twenty-second birthday. "Why did you join the Navy?" I asked him.

"I had an uncle," he replied, "and he said, 'Join the Navy and you won't be in the trenches.'" That was an honest answer.

They assigned him to the USS *Wyoming*, where he served as a fireman, firing the ship's engines. "Two engines were fired with coal, and one engine was fired with oil," he explained. He worked shoveling coal into one of the engines — four hours on, four off, alongside eight or ten other men. It was very hot work. He wanted to put in for another job — "either oiler or water tender, something like that" — but never did.

The *Wyoming* was the lead ship in something called Battleship Division 9, a cluster of five Dreadnought-class battleships under the command of Admiral Hugh Rodman that the United States Navy essentially loaned to the British Grand Fleet for the duration of the war. They almost didn't make it; the weather was so bad during the transatlantic crossing that winds ripped the topmasts off all the ships, and one, the *New York*, nearly foundered. "All the way over, it was so rough, nobody was allowed topside," Ernie Pusey recalled eighty-seven years later. "And the destroyers were going along . . . as rough as it was, I think they only saw one German submarine." When that happened, he said, the destroyers "all rushed over there to drop the depth charges."

"Did they get it?" I asked.

"Who knows?" he said.

They finally made it to Scapa Flow, a stretch of water amid the

Orkney Islands, off the northern tip of Scotland, where they performed a series of maneuvers and exercises in relative safety. "It was fixed so the submarines couldn't come up in there," Ernie explained. "A couple of times we saw a submarine and the small ships would go right after them and drop depth charges."

"Did you yourself ever see one?" I asked him.

"Yeah," he said, "we saw one or two."

"What did they look like?"

"Well, they were just, had the snorkel out of the water, and of course, they weren't going to be up above, with the ships coming along, because they had six-inch guns they could fire out both sides."

"The battleship had six-inch guns?"

"Yeah."

"Did they ever fire them?"

"No, they'd only fire them in practice. And one time," he said, "they had twelve-inch guns, and they fired them in practice, and I remember we were looking out of the porthole, and thought they were going to fire the one up on the bow, and they fired the one right where we were looking out the porthole. My cap flew off the porthole. It deafened me." Things were pretty tense onboard the *Wyoming*. "Some of the men on there were so afraid of the submarines that they had to discharge them. . . . They just went all to pieces."

Since the *Wyoming* was frequently confined to port during its time at Scapa Flow, its seamen enjoyed a good bit of leave — "maybe four or five hours" at a time. "One time I went out," Mr. Pusey told me, "and a fellow says, 'Oh, I'm going so and so further,' so he went to Glasgow, and I went along. We met a couple of girls there, and I should've taken the train back that evening and I missed the train, and when I got back on ship, I didn't get any leave for six months."

The battleships of Division 9 left Scapa Flow on several occasions to escort critical supply convoys to and from Norway. It was hoped, by the fleet's high command, that the German fleet might attempt to intercept the convoy, thus giving the Allies an opportunity to destroy it once and for all; but that never happened. Instead, the ships sailed for the North Sea, where they performed still more exercises and maneuvers. According to its last surviving crew member, the men of the *Wyoming* spent most of their time there "waiting for the Germans to come out." He added, a bit ruefully: "They never came out."

Not until after the armistice was signed, anyway. On November 21, 1918, the British Grand Fleet, including US Battleship Division 9, collected in the North Sea, where they — 370 ships carrying ninety thousand seamen — formed two columns, through which passed the entire German fleet, en route to surrender. Admiral David Beatty, commander of the Grand Fleet, likened the procession to "sheep being herded by dogs to their folds." Admiral Rodman later wrote: "It was hard to realize that the ships which we had expected and hoped to engage, would all be given up without a struggle or fleet action, and surrender without a fight." In the end, the German fleet *was* sunk — by the Germans themselves. "They opened up valves down below," Mr. Pusey explained. "They sunk every one of them right there, in Scapa Flow. They're still there now."

Those 370 Allied ships weren't even there to see it; the armistice allowed the German Navy that small dignity. "The Fleet, my fleet, is brokenhearted," Admiral Beatty said afterward. Even Ernie Pusey, one of the most gentle-natured people I have ever met, felt that way, as I learned toward the end of our visit, when Rose handed me a letter he had written to his sister Helen on November 21, 1918:

> The German ships surrendered to us today so we went out about twenty five miles to meet them. Sorry we had to greet them in such a peaceful manner. What they really deserved was a twelve inch salvo. I guess you know what that is.

Despite the disappointment Admiral Beatty and Fireman Pusey and countless other seamen felt at the time, the fact is that, in successfully carrying supplies and munitions through U-boat-infested waters, in ferrying two million doughboys to France, in keeping the German fleet bottled up in harbor and conducting a blockade so effective that it literally starved Germany into submission, the Allied naval forces made an indispensable contribution to winning the war. Still, they never seemed to get even the little bit of credit that that old Tin Pan Alley song asked for. Even the French, who have done more than anyone in recent years to commemorate the efforts of those who fought and won the war, made service *on French soil* a requirement for receiving the

Légion d'Honneur. So Lloyd Brown and Ernest Pusey never received it; William Cotton did so only because he went ashore at Brest to buy supplies for the *Oklahoma*'s commissary.

I own hundreds of pieces of sheet music from World War I, hundreds of songs about every imaginable aspect of America's war experience. Exactly two of those songs mention the Navy.

We've already discussed the first. The second is one I first heard on a 1918 Columbia blue-label 78 I picked up, in a lot of a hundred or so, at a flea market in Memphis in the early 1990s. *"Over There,"* it starts off — borrowing, as so many songs back then did, from George M. Cohan — *we hear of heroes who've been fighting for you and me. / Ev'rywhere, we see our soldiers, decorated for bravery. / Tho' we are proud of them you bet, / Don't let that make us all forget:*

> *On the sea, we've other heroes, too,*
> *On the sea, our sailor boys in blue;*
> *With their swift Destroyers, "Submarine Annoyers,"*
> *They've been tried and true;*
> *God bless them!*
> *Now this war is over, "Over There,"*
> *We'll have to take our hats right off to Jack;*
> *Tho' the Army is the clover,*
> *'Twas the Navy took them over,*
> *And the Navy will bring them back!*

At the end of its second verse, the song, "The Navy Will Bring Them Back!" pleads: *We knew our boys were bound to win / But why not count the Navy in?* I don't know much about Yeoman Howard Johnson, USN, who is credited as the song's lyricist; I don't know if he, or any of the other Americans who served at sea in that war, ever got an answer to that question. For sure, no one ever had to ask it during the next war.

8

A Vast Enterprise in Salesmanship

THE WAR WAS BIG BUSINESS, not just for munitions plants and textile mills and Tin Pan Alley, but for just about everyone who could figure out a way to plug into it somehow. Doughboys, or at least their images, were recruited to sell untold numbers of items — pretty much everything you can imagine, including Cream of Wheat cereal, Wrigley's chewing gum, Yale padlocks, B. F. Goodrich tires, FTD flowers, Palmolive soap, Swift's Premium bacon, Hupmobile motorcars, Parker fountain pens, Gem razors, Colt firearms, Kodak film, Alvin silverware, Covert truck transmissions, AT&T telephone service, and just about every brand of near-beer then in existence. Showing a doughboy getting excited about a particular brand of silverware was probably a bit of a reach; about any kind of near-beer was just ridiculous.

In almost every regard, though — beauty, eloquence, audacity — it's hard to top a full-page, full-color advertisement that the Victor Talking Machine Company of Camden, New Jersey, manufacturer of both phonographs and records, ran in certain magazines in 1918. The central illustration features a sturdy Victrola IX in a dugout, resting atop its own shipping crate, around which sit a bunch of doughboys, cigarettes and smiles, at ease. Some are still wearing their helmets; one is smoking a pipe and cleaning his rifle. The dugout in the drawing looks quite nice, not a shelter clawed out of the dirt so much as a cozy (not to mention clean and dry) basement rumpus room. And a large one, at that, because there is space enough behind the Victrola for about a dozen elaborately costumed characters. The text, titled "Cheering Our Boys in France," explains:

> Caruso is singing in the trenches in France tonight. Alma Gluck is there, too, and John McCormack and Geraldine Farrar and Galli-Curci and all the glorious golden voices. The violin of Heifetz and Zimbalist, the piano of Paderewski are heard. Sousa's Band is there and the pathos and laughter of that sturdy, fighting Scotsman, Harry Lauder.
>
> Thousands of miles from home in a land torn by battle, our boys yet listen to the spiritual voice of Art. Through the Victrola, the mightiest artists in all the world sing to them the hymn of victory, cheer them with their wit and laughter, comfort and inspire them.
>
> "A singing army is a victorious army," says General Pershing. The great artists of the world are on the firing line, rallying our hosts about the banner of Freedom.

Now, I seriously question whether anyone actually lugged a forty-some-odd-pound Victrola IX (with no carrying handle) to France, much less into a dugout. And I'm not sure Galli-Curci and Alma Gluck and Heifetz and Paderewski would be the choices of a group of over-tired, underfed men squatting in the mud. But I don't doubt that the ad, which ran in American magazines, sold quite a few Victrolas back home, along with a good many Sousa and Zimbalist and John McCormack and Harry Lauder records. And a lot of "Keep Your Head Down, Fritzie Boy," too. So you can add Victor phonographs and records to that list of products. And while you're at it, add the many newspapers and magazines in which all of it was advertised, too.

But with the exception of the manufacturers of war materiel, printing presses probably did the biggest business of all during the war. They churned out sheet music, of course, and posters, and notices, and handbills, and leaflets, and Liberty Bonds, around the clock. But none of that kept them nearly as busy, I imagine, as did publishers — not simply with the aforementioned newspapers and magazines, but with mountains of books, and booklets, and pamphlets. If World War I produced a bottomless well of sheet music, it also generated, in the nineteen months Uncle Sam was at odds with the Kaiser, enough books to fill your local public library. And probably the one down at the high school, too.

Most of them went out of print shortly after the armistice, and were never reissued, a fact that conceals the tremendous amount of influence they exerted during those nineteen months. If you want to know what people were thinking on the Home Front in 1917 and 1918, just stroll through the stacks of the great World War I library and pull a few choice titles off the shelves.

Face to Face with Kaiserism, by James W. Gerard. New York: George H. Doran Company, 1918.

The title page identifies the author as "Late Ambassador to the German Imperial Court, Author of 'My Four Years in Germany.'" It's quite an understatement. Not only had James Watson Gerard served as the American ambassador to Germany, he had done so from late 1913 to early 1917, meaning that he had arrived there less than a year before the war began, and was recalled when the United States severed diplomatic ties with Germany as a prelude to declaring war on it. As an ally of Tammany Hall, Gerard had been elected to a seat on New York State's Supreme Court, and then worked hard to elect Woodrow Wilson, a fellow Democrat, to the presidency in 1912; more important, he donated a lot of money to Wilson's campaign. Diplomatic posts are often the reward of choice for this kind of largesse, and a few months later, Wilson offered to appoint him minister to Spain. Gerard held out until the title was upgraded to ambassador, then accepted, but before he had the chance to leave for Madrid, Wilson decided to send him to Berlin instead. Perhaps Wilson had discovered that Gerard had initially backed Theodore Roosevelt for the party's nomination; the president must have known that Spain would be a much easier post, with much better food.

As soon as Gerard returned to American soil — and maybe even before that — he set to work on his memoir, *My Four Years in Germany,* which would be published by Doran later that year. It reads, in part, like a diary: He spends a lot of words recounting the mundane functions of an ambassador in Edwardian Europe — ceremonies, conferences, tours — in part, I imagine, to give the reader a sense of what it was like to be an American in Germany just then, and in part to glorify his own memories. But the rest of the book is an analysis of Germany — its people, its government, its national character — and, let us just say, when Gerard ceased being a diplomat, he ceased being diplomatic. After spending so many years in Germany, he didn't seem to come away with anything good to say about the place or its people. Actually, from the beginning, he pretty much takes the stance that it and they are fit for nothing but to be destroyed. "We are warring against a nation whose poets and professors, whose pedagogues and whose parsons have united in stirring its people to a white pitch of hatred, first against Russia, then against England and now against America," he writes in the book's foreword, and ramps it up from there. (In the very next paragraph, he warns, with remarkable prescience: "Russia may either break up into civil wars or become so ineffective that the millions of German troops engaged on the Russian front may be withdrawn and hurled against the Western lines.")

Gerard outlines his assessment of the enemy on the same page:

> We are engaged in a war against the greatest military power the world has ever seen; against a people whose country was for so many centuries a theatre of devastating wars that fear is bred in the very marrow of their souls, making them ready to submit their lives and fortunes to an autocracy which for centuries has ground their faces, but which has promised them, as a result of the war, not only security but riches untold and the dominion of the world; a people which, as from a high mountain, has looked upon the cities of the world and the glories of them, and been promised these cities and these glories by the devils of autocracy and war.

You won't find a single "on the other hand" on any of *My Four Years'* 330 or so pages. Gerard is just relentless: He hates every last thing about Germany and its people. There's their educational system:

> The teachers in the schools are all government paid and teach the children only the principles desired by the rulers of the German people. There are no Saturday holidays in the German schools and their summer holidays are for only three to five weeks. You never see gangs of small boys in Germany. Their games and their walks are superintended by their teachers who are always inculcating

them in reverence and awe for the military heroes of the past and present.

And their culinary preferences:

Many of the doctors who were with me thought that the heavy eating and large consumption of wine and beer had unfavourably affected the German national character, and had made the people more aggressive and irritable and consequently readier for war. The influence of diet on national character should not be underestimated. Meat-eating nations have always ruled vegetarians.

And let's not even get into their notions of fun. Though he does:

In connection with court dancing it is rather interesting to note that when the tango and turkey trot made their way over the frontiers of Germany in the autumn of 1913, the Emperor issued a special order that no officers of the army or navy should dance any of these dances or should go to the house of any person who, at any time, whether officers were present or not, had allowed any of these new dances to be danced. This effectively extinguished the turkey trot, the bunny hug and the tango, and maintained the waltz and the polka in their old estate.

And, as a friend of such notable American Jews as Henry Morgenthau Sr., ambassador to the Ottoman Empire, and Adolph S. Ochs, owner of the *New York Times,* Gerard is offended by German anti-Semitism. "Jews are not admitted to court. Such Jews as have been ennobled and allowed to put the coveted 'von' before their names have first of all been required to submit to baptism in some Christian church," he tells us. "Jews have not much chance in government service." The only reason, he speculates, that Germany's POW hospitals are "in as good condition as could be expected" is "the fact that so many doctors in Germany are Jews. The people who are of the Jewish race are people of gentle instincts. In these hospitals a better diet was given to the prisoners."

It was certainly true back then that, in America, Jews could and did serve at very high levels in the government and diplomatic corps; Ambassador Morgenthau was evidence of that. Even so, the United States was far from devoid of institutionalized anti-Semitism in those days. So, for that matter, were America's allies Great Britain and France, while in yet another ally nation, czarist Russia, Jew-hatred was much worse — and more violent — than in Germany. And I'm no expert on the history of American education, but I suspect that the life of a schoolboy wasn't all that different in the United States at the time. (Except for the Saturday thing, of course; those Teutonic fiends!) And the United States wasn't exactly a nation of abstemious, teetotaling vegetarians back then, either, though Americans did enjoy a good bunny hug.

The book-buying public of 1917 didn't have much interest in second-guessing Gerard; America was at war with the Germans, and he had lots of juicy stories to tell about them. There's the one where, during a party, the German colonial minister "planted himself some distance away from me and addressed me in German saying, 'You are the American Ambassador and I want to tell you that the conduct of America in furnishing arms and ammunition to the enemies of Germany is stamped deep on the German heart, that we will never forget it and will some day have our revenge.'" Well! That's not very festive. The Kaiser himself tells Gerard, "America had better look out after this war," and "I shall stand no nonsense from America after the war." I guess he thought he was going to win.

The most despicable thing about Germany, though, as far as Gerard is concerned, is that they despise America. "I believe that to-day all the bitterness of the hate formerly concentrated on Great Britain has now been concentrated on the United States," he declares. We must crush them, he warns Americans, or they will crush us.

He wasn't the only one who believed that sort of thing back then. In September, 1914, with the war scarcely a month old, Walter Lippmann, a prominent American liberal intellectual and one of the founders of the *New Republic,* wrote to a friend, "If Germany wins . . . the whole world will have to arm against her — the U.S. included, for Germany quite seriously intends to dominate the World." By 1917, a great many books were being published about this country America was now at war with; I am perhaps most fond of one written by a journalist named D. Thomas Curtin, who managed to make his way into wartime Germany before the United States entered the conflict, then returned to write a memoir and analysis he called *The Land of Deepening Shadow*. Though its title is by far my favorite thing about it, the book itself is an entertaining read. Curtin is no fan of Germany — the title should tell you that much — but he at least has some pity for its people, whom he sees, to an extent, as victims:

> Unhealthy-looking little men are these German boys of from twelve to fifteen during the war. The overwork, and the lowering of their diet, has given them pasty faces and dark rings round their eyes. All games and amusements have been abandoned, and the only relaxation is corps marching through the streets at night, singing their hate songs and "Deutschland, Deutschland Über Alles."

Doesn't sound very relaxing. Of course, their teacher can spice things up for them in the classroom . . . can't he?

> Years before the war the Government corralled him for its own. It gave him social status, in return for which he would do his part to make the citizen an unquestioning, faithful and obedient servant of the State. As soon as he enters on his duties he becomes a civil servant, since the universities are State institutions. He takes an oath in which it is stipulated that he will not write or preach or do anything questioning the way of the State. His only way to make progress in life, then, is to serve the State, to preach what it wishes preached, to teach history as it wishes history taught.

Guess not. Surely, though, the church is a good foil to this program of indoctrination:

> The admixture of Biblical references and German boasting are typical of the lessons taught at German Sunday Schools, which play a great role in the war propaganda. The schoolmaster having done his work for six days of the week, the pastor gives an extra virulent dose on Sabbath. Sedan Day [a celebration of the great German victory in the Franco-Prussian War of 1870–71], which before the war was on the culmination of hate lessons, often formed the occasion of Sunday School picnics, at which the children sang new anti-French songs.

Well, that explains those *Gott Mit Uns* belt buckles German soldiers wore as part of their uniforms: "God is with us." Those were probably the single most-prized war souvenir for a doughboy. It was hard to get a German to part with one, at least while he was alive.

Curtin would call that kind of tenacity mindless; the typical Prussian, he argues, is little more than a drone at the service of the Kaiser, his generals, and his ministers. "The German, with his cast-in-a-mould mind, does not understand the trait developed among other peoples of seeing things for themselves. He is unacquainted with originality in human beings," Curtin explains. "The majority of Germans of all classes believe what they are officially instructed to believe, no more, no less. The overmastering self-hypnotism which leads the present-day German to believe that black is white, if it adds to his self-satisfaction, is one of the most startling phenomena in history." Of course, a case could be made that, in publishing his book, Curtin was hoping to instruct the American people on what to believe about Germany. For instance, Americans should hardly be surprised, he tells us, that Germany had spies in the United States even before the war began: "Spying is just as essential an ingredient of Prussian character as conceit, indifference to the feelings of others, jealousy, envy, self-satisfaction, conceit, industry, inquisitiveness, veneration for officialdom, imitativeness, materialism, and the other national attributes that will occur to those who know Prussia, as distinct from the other German States."

He tries, at least, to end the book on an optimistic note:

> It is part of the Prussian nature to push everything to extremes, a trait which has advantages and disadvantages. It has resulted in brilliant achievements in chemical and physical laboratories, and in gout, dyspepsia and flabbiness in eating establishments. A virtue carried too far becomes a vice. In Germany patriotism becomes jingoistic hatred and contempt for others, organization becomes the utilization of servility, obedience becomes willingness to do wrong at command.

I said he *tries*. Turns out there's not much room for sunshine in *The Land of Deepening Shadow*.

My Four Years in Germany was a tremendous hit. It catapulted a little-known judge/ambassador/Tammany operative into the stratosphere of celebrity, where the air can get a bit thin. He set out on a cross-country speaking tour, during which he fomented paranoia about all things German, including Americans of German descent; the low point was a speech he gave to the Ladies Aid Society of St. Mary's Hospital in New York, titled "Loyalty and German-Americans," in which he inveighed:

> We must disappoint the Germans who have always believed that the German-Americans here would risk their property, their children's future, and their own neck, and take up arms for the Kaiser. The Foreign Minister of Germany once said to me "your country does not dare do anything against Germany, because we have in your country 500,000 German reservists who will rise in arms against your government if you dare to make a move against Germany."
>
> Well, I told him that that might be so, but that we had 500,001 lamp posts in this country, and that that was where the reservists would be hanging the day after they tried to rise. And if there are any German-Americans here who are so ungrateful for all the benefits they have received that they are still for the Kaiser, there is only one thing to do with them. And that is to hog-tie them, give them back the wooden shoes and the rags they landed in, and ship them back to the Fatherland.

You'd think that sort of talk would hurt book sales; it didn't. Instead, a fledgling movie outfit run by four brothers named Warner turned it into a film ("I shall stand no nonsense from America after the war" was the pull-quote for the poster) and with it produced their first national hit. Shot in New Jersey, the film adaptation of *My Four Years in Germany* generated some controversy with its depiction of German atrocities in Belgium; it was also, somehow, both wooden and histrionic. Ticket sales were brisk nevertheless.

Knowing that the movie would be coming out in mid-1918 — and also, perhaps, that the war might not last much beyond that — Gerard scrambled to follow up with another book. *Face to Face with Kaiserism* is like *My Four Years in Germany* without the autobiographical material, giving the author more pages wherein to lay Germany and Germans to waste verbally, which he does with vim:

> The German to-day is essentially practical, cold, cynical and calculating. The poetry and the Christmas trees, the sentiment and sentimentality, remain like the architectural monuments of a vanished race, mere reminders of the kindlier Germany that once was, the Germany of our first impressions, the Germany that many once loved. But that Germany has long since disappeared, buried beneath the spiked helmets of Prussianism.

And then there's this:

> It has been at all times the policy of the German autocracy to keep the people of Germany from amusing themselves. I know of no class in Germany which really enjoys life. . . . The houses are plain and, for the most part, without conveniences of bath rooms and heating to which we are accustomed in America. Very few automobiles are owned in Germany. There are practically no small country houses or bungalows, although at a few of the sea places rich Jews have villas.

Hence the Jews' aforementioned "gentle instincts." As for the rest of Germany, their lack of toilets, cars, radiators, country houses, and board games presumably drove them to the crazed impulse to conquer the world, and the delusional notion that they might just get away with it.

Needing to set *Kaiserism* apart from *Four Years,* Gerard decided to focus on what set America and other "good" nations apart from Germany — namely, democracy. There is no equal anywhere in Germany's omnipotent autocracy to President Wilson, Gerard notes, because an autocracy cannot produce men who can temper strength with compassion. Only a democracy can do that. Which is why, of course, America was fighting to Make the World Safe for Democracy.

It didn't help. Gerard's second book didn't sell nearly as well as his first. It did, however, popularize the word "Kaiserism," quite possibly the best neologism that war produced. It almost makes you wish there were still a Kaiser somewhere so you could casually drop it in conversation from time to time.

・　・　・

The Soldiers' French Phrase Book. **Chicago: Felt & Tarrant Manufacturing Company, 1918.**

Remember all those songs about France? "And He'd Say Ooh-La-La! Wee-Wee!"? "Oh! Frenchy"? "You'll Have to Put Him to Sleep with the Marseillaise and Wake Him Up with a Oo-La-La"? (I may have left that last one out before; it's a bear to type.) Everyone Over Here, it seems, was terribly excited at the prospect of millions of Red-Blooded American Boys going Over There. What fun they'd all have! Strolling through the City of Light, eating delicate pastries, drinking bold wines, wooing *les belles femmes* — doing pretty much everything but crouching in muddy trenches, taking the occasional shot at the Hun, and trying hard not to die in the process. No one back home much cared to think about that aspect of the Expedition. And can you blame them? Those were *their boys* out there, their sons and husbands and brothers. Newspapers didn't want to write about it if they could possibly avoid it; bad for morale. The Army didn't disagree — it sometimes told newspapers what not to print, and more often just withheld certain information. Not many went looking for it, either.

Instead, almost everyone chose to focus on the less-hazardous elements of the adventure, conjuring scenes of their Johnny, who'd never left Gage County, Nebraska, before, suddenly in the midst of the most exotic and civilized country in the world, a place where they didn't even speak English. Can you picture Johnny trying to order eggs in one of those fancy cafés on Rue de something-or-other? Would he just crow like a chicken until they figured out what he wanted? Sure, that had worked for Art Fiala, but you couldn't count on it hitting every time.

And so, on page 32: *Apportez-moi deux oeufs à la coque mollets.* "Bring two soft boiled eggs." For hard-boiled, say *à la coque durs.* Those are your two options, according to Messrs. Felt and Tarrant. Of course, even if you're not in the mood for eggs, they've got you covered. "Waiter, bring the bill of fare." "Bring me some fresh bread and butter." "Bring some meat right away." "A rare beefsteak." "I should like some veal chops." "With cauliflower or cabbage." "Where is the cheese?" "Have you wine or cider?" (Hello — it's France.) "Give me a glass of water." "I will now take a cup of coffee." And, of course: "Bring me some stale bread and milk." Ah, *haute cuisine.* Don't forget, as you sit down, to declare, "I am ravenous," or "I have a great appetite." And if anything looks fishy after "Give me the bill," feel free to break out "There is a mistake in the addition."

Over the years I have picked up a number of these dictionaries; I can only imagine how many thousands were published and then given to soldiers or, more likely, sold to their loved ones, who may or may not have passed them along to an actual doughboy. Some, like *First Lessons in Spoken French for Men in Military Service*, are as dry as their titles, offering little more than grammar lessons and basic vocabulary; not a great way to learn a foreign language, at least in my experience. Others, like the Gordon-Detwiler Institute's *Soldiers' French Course*, combine the dry stuff with phrases, many of which are strangely specific: "I shall give him a neck-tie." "You perceive the clamor of the street." "They will visit us the day after to-morrow and will come in the new automobile." "He has a longer right arm than left." "You punish the wicked and the culprits." "Have you paid the customhouse duties on these hats?" "They will start on the way to pass the winter in Cuba." "She will sell her jewels and give the amount of money to the Red Cross." "Is Philadelphia far or near from here?" "Your collar-bone is dislocated." "You have saved my life." Sadly, it's not too much of a stretch to imagine scenarios where those last two, at least, might have proven useful.

I don't know, though, if all these books were about practical French as much as aspirational. (Certainly, it's pretty aspirational to imagine you'll be able to ask someone in Verdun for directions to Philadelphia.) When you're young and male and dropped into a foreign country, you tend to pick up the language on the fly — trying to get something to eat, maybe, or to drink, or to chat up a pretty girl. Or to find shelter during an artillery barrage, although I imagine hand gestures and facial expressions would probably do in that situation.

Still, it must have been fun to imagine that you might need all of those restaurant expressions from *The Soldiers' French Phrase Book*, or many of the others it taught, like, "I shall be in London next week," "Paris is as beautiful as Chicago," "What do you say, Miss?," "I give you full authority to do as you please," "The captain fell from his horse," "You have my sabre," "Long live France!," "Long live America!," and "You will always be in my memory."

And, lest you suspect these books were entirely impractical, there is also: "Tell him the colonel asks for him," "We had a narrow escape," "He has been wounded in the chest," "A piece of shrapnel broke his ankle," and "A bullet pierced his lips."

A Yankee in the Trenches, by R. Derby Holmes. Boston: Little, Brown, 1918.

Like Arthur Guy Empey, Bostonian Robert Derby Holmes sailed off for England and enlisted in the Army there well before America entered the war. Empey did it, he tells us, out of anger at the sinking of the *Lusitania* and a desire to show the Germans what was what; Holmes, on the other hand, explains he joined up because he was afraid of missing out on what was clearly shaping up to be the greatest event of his lifetime. "As the war went on," he tells us in the opening pages, "it became apparent to me, as I suppose it must have to everybody, that the world was going through one of its epochal upheavals; and I figured that with so much history in the making, any unattached young man would be missing it if he did not take a part in the big game."

Holmes and Empey cover much of the same ground: Tommies, trenches, cooties, army food. And each, independently, describes a rather striking phenomenon:

> Daylight movements in No Man's Land are somehow disconcerting. Once I was in a trench where a leg — a booted German leg, stuck up stark and stiff out of the mud not twenty yards in front. Some idiotic joker on patrol hung a helmet on the foot, and all the next day that helmet dangled and swung in the breeze. It irritated the periscope watchers, and the next night it was taken down.

Either the German-boot-with-German-leg-inside-it-sticking-up-out-of-the-ground motif was a widespread urban legend on the Western Front, or it really happened, and often. Horrible as that image is, Holmes outdoes it with a tale he shares about a night he was sent on patrol down to a sloping riverbank:

> Sliding gently through the grass, I kept catching my feet in something hard that felt like roots; but there were no trees in the neighborhood. I reached down and groped in the grass and brought up a human rib. The place was full of them, and skulls. Stooping, I could

see them, grinning up out of the dusk, hundreds of them. I learned afterwards that this was called the Valley of Death. Early in the war several thousand Zouaves [French or French Colonial infantry dressed in old-timey North African–style uniforms comprising open tunic, baggy pantaloons, sash, and fez] had perished there, and no attempt had been made to bury them.

One thing Holmes discusses that Empey doesn't is the proliferation of other Yankees in the trenches prior to 1917; Empey doesn't quite imply that he was the only American there, but he never mentions, even in passing, that he wasn't. Furthermore, to hear Empey tell it, Tommy's only complaints about the war are the mud and the hours; he's long since gotten used to cooties, rats, and army food, and only gripes about them anymore with a grudgingly affectionate twinkle in his eye. Holmes, however, bravely reveals that many English weren't all that happy to be in Flanders just then:

> Some of the opinions voiced out there with more frankness than any one would dare to use at home would, I am sure, shock some of the patriots. The fact is that any one who has fought in France wants peace, and the sooner the better. . . .
>
> I should say offhand that there was not one man in a hundred who was fighting consciously for any great recognized principle. And yet, with all their grousing and criticism, and all their overwhelming desire to have it over with, every one of them was loyal and brave and a hard fighter.

If that passage made readers uncomfortable, it didn't hurt sales; for a time, *A Yankee in the Trenches* appeared on bestseller lists right alongside *Over the Top*. Little, Brown ran ads for the book featuring a glowing blurb calling it "the most entertaining war book that I have read, and I have read many." The blurb's magnanimous author was Arthur Guy Empey.

The Chicago Daily News War Book for American Soldiers, Sailors and Marines. Chicago: The Chicago Daily News Company, 1918.

It's pocket-sized — a bit broader in area than a checkbook, and about as thick — but somehow the *Chicago Daily News* managed to cram 192 pages into such a small package, and a minor encyclopedia's worth of information into those 192 pages. Here's just a sampling: fully illustrated guides to American, French, British, and German military insignia, both army and navy; American, British, French, German, Russian, Romanian, Serbian, Italian, Austrian, Australian, Polish, Portuguese, Belgian, and Scottish headgear — army and navy, officers and enlisted men, regular service and special details; Allied and German aeroplanes; codes and signals; knots and splices; rifles and bayonets; American, French, and German map symbols; and French road signs. There are intricately detailed two-page maps of the Western Front, Europe, the United States, and, most important, Paris; a list of Paris hotels, organized by price; tutorials on the French "75" gun, the metric system, French currency, methods of finding true north and measuring the distance to the horizon, getting your bearings, and "German Poison Gasses"; a three-year calendar; French–English and English–French dictionaries; selected German phrases, including "Surrender!," "Hands up!," "Drop your rifles!," "No talking," "Give me your pay-book, your diary, your note-book," "How many machine-guns are there in this trench, and where are they placed?," "Don't shoot," "I am badly wounded," "Please carry me," "Take me to a hospital," "I am cold," "I know nothing about that," and "I am an American"; and, of course, a selection of American war songs. And the "Marseillaise." And directions for doughboys to the Paris and London offices of the *Chicago Daily News*, "where all the facilities of reading and writing rooms are at their service." And if you don't much care for the *Chicago Daily News*, "the leading American newspapers are on file" there, too. How much would you expect to pay for such a resource? Put that wallet away. "The national uniform," the title page declares, "is in itself an order for a free copy of the book."

It's an impressive little volume — truly, I think, the kind of thing that makes you want to enlist if you haven't already. That may explain how it scored forewords from Secretary of War Newton Baker *and* Secretary of the Navy Josephus Daniels. It also received an endorsement — printed in both English and French — from no less than the head of the Supreme War Council, the newly created Allied central command, who signed his name, simply: "Joffre."

Joseph Jacques Césaire Joffre. Better known as, simply, "Papa." The most beloved and respected general in France.

Now *that* was a real get.

The First Shot for Liberty, by Osborne de Varila. Philadelphia: The John C. Winston Company, 1918.

On October 22, 1917, Corporal Osborne de Varila, serving in the French town of Nancy with Battery C of the 6th Field Artillery, was given the honor of firing the first American shot of the war — fittingly, a 75-millimeter shell, millions of which had already sailed through the air of France during the past three years. Battery C expended a lot of energy wresting that honor from the rest of the 6th FA, all of whom wanted it for themselves; when told another battery was "out to steal the bacon," a gunner cried: "Are we going to let them get away with it?"

"We'd be a sick lot of hounds if we did," replies Corporal "Reddy" (on account of his red hair) de Varila. So he and the rest of Battery C haul their gun "through the storm and pitchy darkness, for a distance of three-quarters of a mile over an almost impassable country — a swamp pocked with mud-choked shell-holes." And yet, when the moment is upon him — "I pulled the lanyard of the little spitfire, and America's first shot of the war went screaming into German territory" — Reddy confesses that he is "filled with a thousand conflicting emotions," though he doesn't tell us what any of them were; back then, emoting was not on a man's menu.

And de Varila, though only eighteen years old, is nevertheless all man. His prose is thoroughly marinated in testosterone. "I will concede that I come of a race of red-headed, freckle-faced fighters, and am proud of it," he tells us on the very first page. In the 1870s, his father served out West in the US Cavalry, where "the Indians dubbed him, 'Red the Brave.'" His paternal grandfather fought for the CSA under Stonewall Jackson; his maternal grandfather for the Union under U. S. Grant. "My mother was of Irish descent, and my father French," he tells us. "Now, you need wonder no longer why I love to fight when the fighting is good. When you get a French and Irish combination, and breed it for several generations on the stimulating soil of the good old United States, you are bound to produce something that absolutely refuses to 'let George do it,' when there is a scrap on deck." He continues:

> I was fifteen years old when the Kaiser and his gang of international burglars set out to crack the safes of the nations of the world, and revive the chain-gang methods of the unholy old Roman Empire.
>
> I wanted to get into it then, honest I did, although I had blossomed out in my first suit of long trousers, and was proudly wearing my first dollar watch.

His mother, though, wouldn't let him go. But then, three years later:

> The bottom dropped clean out of my education when Congress bucked up to the occasion and declared the United States at war with the German Empire.
>
> Wow! Every fighting de Varila in the whole list of de Varilas seemed to rise up before me in spirit and announce:
>
> "Now is the time to get in, my boy."
>
> That settled me; I determined to get into the scrap while the getting was good. I was eighteen then, and big for my age. All I needed was my mother's signature to precipitate me into the biggest war in history. I packed my suitcase, went home and told my mother I was going to enlist in the United States Army.
>
> She was game and didn't even blink a tear. . . .
>
> "You are a de Varila," she said, "and I'd be ashamed of you if you didn't want to go."

So off her son goes to France, and pretty soon he and his buddies in the 6th FA are just about running the war:

> It is true that the American gunners are the best in the world. They have a truer eye, a steadier hand and work more quickly and accurately than the artillerymen of any other nation. We demonstrated that after we had been on the front line but a few days, and when American batteries get going good over there, Germany is going to realize that the Yanks are on the job. American gunners are going to deliver the knockout to Von Hindenburg's forces.

After firing that first shot, de Varila traffics in a fair amount of rather gruesome propaganda, like this tale:

In the little shell-torn village where my battery was quartered when we first moved up to the front line, lived a young French mother with her two-year-old son. Just before this son was born she was taken prisoner by some German cavalrymen, and sent to a hospital in Germany. When her child was born it was taken from her and returned two weeks later, with its sight destroyed.

"If your child had been a girl," explained the brutish German surgeon, "we would not have done this. But we of the Fatherland must make sure that the French will never again take up arms against Germany."

With her face full of woe and tragedy, the mother told me this story, and I swore vengeance against the Hun as the tale slipped from her trembling lips. Nestled in her lap as she gave me every detail was the living evidence of the crime — the poor little two-year-old who is doomed to go through life sightless because of German Kultur.

If the Germans hope to scare Americans by their campaign of frightfulness they are going to be badly fooled. Every time a Yankee boy comes in contact with one of these cases, it simply whets his desire to kill another Boche.

De Varila sees a good bit of combat, but spends the last weeks of 1917 in the hospital, he writes, with "a very bad case of frozen feet." Then, in March of 1918, he tells us, "I got my first bad dose of gas. It was mustard gas too, one of the worst kind the devilish Boches send over. I was pumping away at my gun, when suddenly I felt a choking, stinging sensation, and then I passed out like a baby hit with a brick." He wakes up in a hospital, "blind as a bat. When I discovered there was something the matter with my eyes I was so mad I almost foamed at the mouth." His war is over.

At least Over There. He does regain his sight after six days, but is nevertheless deemed unfit for the front. Instead, he is sent home, a war hero, to campaign for the Third Liberty Loan drive. He's ripe for the new challenge, having already told us, a hundred or so pages earlier: "The food improved wonderfully after the raising of the Second Liberty Loan over in America. The folks at home must back us to their last cent if we are to win this war. Money talks harder right now over in France than at any time in the history of the world. There must be a constant stream of cash from the pockets of Americans if we are to keep men and munitions pouring into the fighting zone." He ends his tale with another appeal:

> I am happy that I played my little part in this big war by firing the first shot for liberty. I think it was fitting that I should be sent to Philadelphia, the birthplace of liberty and the shrine of that wonderful old relic, the Liberty Bell. Every man-jack of us who came over is going back to put in more blows against the Hun. We feel that it is our duty to do this, and besides the fascination of war has its grip upon us.
>
> In Philadelphia I met the best girl in the world, and now I have her to fight for as well as my country when I return to France. The Hun peril is a real one, as every American will soon realize if they do not put their full weight into this war. The boys over on the other side are getting splendid treatment, and since the putting over of the last two Liberty Loans there has been plenty of food and clothing. The Yank who fails to get into this war with both feet is losing the opportunity of his life. I will not rest content until I am fighting with my battery again over there in France on the front line. It is my burning desire to send over many more shots for liberty into the Boche trenches.

Sadly, that desire wasn't the only thing burning within him at that point. According to an old clipping I found from the *San Francisco Call,* Corporal de Varila "died on June 4, 1920, at a government hospital from the effects of mustard gas." He was twenty-one years old, and left no will. The short article, dated October 26 of that year, reports that his mother, Clara de Varila of 224 Bartlett Street, filed a petition in San Francisco's superior court to claim her son's estate. It was, the anonymous reporter noted, "valued at less than $300."

Home Reading Course for Citizen-Soldiers. **War Information Series, No. 9. Washington, D.C.: The Committee on Public Information, October 1917.**

On April 13, 1917, just one week after the United States declared war on Germany, President Wilson issued Executive Order 2594, establishing the Committee on Public Information, "to be composed of the Secretary of State, the Secretary of War, the Secretary of the Navy, and a civilian who shall be charged with the executive direction of the committee." The civilian Wilson chose was George Creel, a reporter for Denver's *Rocky Mountain News*. Reporters are supposed to be objective, more or less; not George Creel. "An open mind is not part of my inheritance," he once said. "I took in prejudices with mother's milk and was weaned on partisanship."

That mindset made Creel the right man for the job. The Committee on Public Information was, quite simply, a propaganda bureau. And, as those things go, perhaps a relatively benign one; unlike some other American institutions of that time, its stated primary objective was not ginning up anger at and suspicion of America's enemies, real and imagined, and disseminating what Creel called "hymns of hate." Rather, it purported more often to accentuate the positive — sometimes going so far as to fabricate it, but still. As Creel wrote in his 1920 memoir, *How We Advertised America,* "In all things, from first to last, without halt or change, it was a plain publicity proposition, a vast enterprise in salesmanship, the world's greatest adventure in advertising."

The Committee pitched stories and press releases across the country and around the world, published its own daily newspaper, called the *Official Bulletin,* produced feature-length motion pictures with titles like *Pershing's Crusaders* and *America's Answer (to the Hun),* and got some of the most prominent artists of the day, including N. C. Wyeth, James Montgomery Flagg, and Howard Chandler Christy, to design posters promoting enlistment, bond drives, food conservation, and other such initiatives. Perhaps most impressive, Creel recruited and trained some seventy-five thousand volunteer "Four Minute Men," who traveled the country giving speeches on patriotic subjects, talks that lasted no more than four minutes, which was believed, at the time, to be the average American's attention span.

The CPI also published two different series of (usually) free booklets — the Red, White, and Blue Series, for civilians, and the War Information Series, for servicemen. The two series deal with similar issues — mostly the whats, hows, and whys of the war — though the latter's execution is somewhat less artful, which makes it a much better read.

From No. 11, *The German War Code:* "The German war code abounds in evidences of unfairness and gross partisanship and appears to have been intended to inculcate hatred in the hearts of the German army against their enemies." (How dare they!) "German army officers are warned against being misled by the excessive humanitarianism of the present age, which the German manual says has too often degenerated into 'sentimentality and flabby emotion.'"

From No. 15, *Why America Fights Germany:* "We are in the war because we had to go in unless we were entirely blind to our own honor and safety, and to the future happiness of the whole world." Clearly, the CPI — in this case, author John S. P. Tatlock, Professor at Stanford University — was not given to understatement. Nor to underselling; that particular sentence is boldfaced. So are many others, like "The net of German intrigue has encompassed the world," "All-Democracy is now waging a supreme struggle against all-Despotism," "Mercy and justice through all the world are at stake," and the curiously familiar "We must fight Germany in Europe that we may not have to fight her in America."

From No. 13, *German Militarism and Its German Critics:* "Some of the characteristics of Militarism are in evidence in all European countries . . . but in no other is the adulation of the soldiery so pronounced as in Germany . . . in no other is Militarism either so exaggerated or so objectionable." I'm not sure if that means America chose the right country to go to war with, or the opposite.

From No. 14, *The War for Peace:* "The Allies cannot concede peace until they conquer it. When they do so, it will be permanent. Otherwise they fail." This cryptic statement was authored by the president of the New York–based League to Enforce Peace, one William Howard Taft. Before he landed that job, Mr. Taft had been, interestingly, secretary of war. Oh, and then president of the United States, at least until he lost his bid for reelection to Woodrow Wilson in 1912.

The first book in the series, *The War Message and Facts Behind It*, presents the text of President Wilson's April 2, 1917, address to Congress, complete with annotations. When Wilson declares, "We are, let me say again, the sincere friends of the German people and shall desire nothing so much as the early reestablishment of intimate relations of mutual advantage between us," the booklet's editor — one Guy Stanton Ford, director of the CPI's Division on Civic and Educational Cooperation — notes: "There are now two Germanies — the old, noble, idealistic Germany; the new, hard, materialistic nation, created by Prussia. Americans would fain love and recall the former." And when the president insists, "The right is more precious than peace, and we shall fight for the things which we have always carried nearest our hearts," Ford contrasts Abraham Lincoln's second inaugural address ("With malice toward none, with charity for all") with choice tidbits from a diatribe from Friedrich von Bernhardi — "German lieutenant general, and acceptable mouthpiece, not of the whole German nation, but of the Prussian military caste which holds the German nation in its grip" — including "Might is at once the supreme right, and the dispute as to what is right is decided by the arbitrament of war," and "The idea is presumptuous that 'the weak nation is to have the same right to live, as a powerful and vigorous nation.'"

So No. 9, *Home Reading Course for Citizen-Soldiers,* is a bit of a departure — kind of an Over There for Dummies:

> In order to make good in the National Army you must, first of all, fit yourself to carry with credit the simple title of "American Citizen-Soldier" — one of the proudest titles in the world. This means that you must develop in yourself the qualities of a soldier. The more quickly and thoroughly you cultivate them the greater will be your satisfaction and success.

The three basic qualities, it tells us, are Loyalty, Obedience, and Physical Fitness, and it ruminates at length on all three. Then there are the three soldierly qualities of Intelligence, Cleanliness, and Cheerfulness; and, finally, the three qualities of battle: Spirit, Tenacity, and Self-Reliance. It's a very high-minded list, and indeed, the whole booklet is quite so. In the very first of its thirty lessons, it teaches the reader that a fundamental tradition of the American Army "is that of fighting fairly and treating even the enemy with as much humanity as his own conduct will permit. As for slaughtering or enslaving the civilian population of captured territory, attacking prisoners, or assaulting women American soldiers would as little commit such crimes in time of war as in time of peace."

There are lessons on army insignia, staff branches, and fighting arms of the service, what to expect of camp life, "The Army System of Training," drilling, guard duty, army courtesy, European warfare, cleanliness, health, equipment and arms, organization, discipline, teamwork. There's an entire lesson, two pages in length, on marching and the care of feet. ("Keep your feet scrupulously clean. A foot bath can be taken, when other facilities are not at hand, by scraping a small depression in the ground, throwing a poncho over it and pouring water into this from your canteen. Even a pint of water will do for a foot bath. You can bathe all over by making or finding a depression of suitable size and using your poncho as for a foot bath." I wonder if anyone ever actually took a full-body poncho-bath, and, if so, how that worked out.) There's the obligatory lesson on "Why We Fight," and one on "Some National Traditions." A section on "The Bearing of a Soldier" breaks it down to ten categories, from heels to head. Lesson No. 23 presents a checklist for "Getting Ahead in the Army." (Number 9: "Ability to sketch and read maps.") A considerate addition, I think.

And Lesson 11, "Playing the Game," includes a section titled "Making Use of Spare Time," which begins:

> The use that a man makes of his time off duty is a good test of his character and of his capacity for growth. The good soldier is self-restrained. Don't spend your time repeating indecent stories. They add nothing whatever to your standing, either with the men to whom you tell them or with your officers. Avoid boisterousness, vulgarity, and profanity.
>
> That doesn't mean at all that you should keep yourself in the background or that you should fail to be a good "mixer." Let your personality stand out. Broaden your influence by every proper method. But use your personality and your influence to help the men in your own squad and company carry on their work and prepare as possible for the big task ahead of you.

That image — of eighteen- or twenty-year-old boys arriving at boot camp, being handed a copy of *Home Reading Course for Citizen-Soldiers,* perusing to this section (page 25, if you're looking for it), and really drinking it in — is enough to make you wish that somewhere, at some point, everyone would be issued a handbook that would spell these things out for us. I can't think of a better use for a printing press than that.

9

Hell, We Just Got Here

THIS NEXT STORY IS ABOUT — well, I'll let you decide that for yourself. I'll just say up front that it's a bit . . . uh . . . you know what? I'll let you decide that, too.

It begins around Veterans Day, 2003, when I came across an article in a small newspaper from a town in upstate New York, near Albany. The reporter profiled, in brief, a few local World War II veterans, then lamented that there were no longer any World War I veterans left in town, and that the only one in the area — which term, thankfully, he defined loosely — was one Eugene Lee, of Syracuse. He didn't say much else about Mr. Lee, except that he was "no longer able to give interviews."

Well. I won't say I took this as a challenge, exactly, but I certainly wasn't going to just accept such a statement until I checked it out for myself. I called the reporter, who reiterated the statement, telling me its source was one Jim Casey, whom he said was Eugene Lee's close friend and sort-of gatekeeper. He gave me Mr. Casey's phone number and wished me luck.

Jim Casey was a Marine Corps veteran (he had served in the late 1950s) who had sought out Mr. Lee some years earlier, having learned of his existence. Mr. Lee hadn't any children; his closest relative, a niece, lived out West. So Mr. Casey befriended him, looked after him, visited him regularly. He told me that Mr. Lee could still hear and speak well enough, but that his memory was dicey — some days it was fair, some days much less so — and that he was prone to getting frustrated when it wasn't working all that well. I said I understood, and that I would be willing to take a chance, drive up to Syracuse, and see what might happen. He said he'd check with Mr. Lee, then called me back a day or two later and told me to come on up at my convenience.

I made the trip on December 2, 2003, and met Jim Casey the next morning in a waiting room at Community General Hospital in Syracuse, where Mr. Lee lived in a long-term-care wing. Jim was a broad-shouldered, burly man with an easy smile and a handshake that was all business. After chatting for a few minutes he led me to Mr. Lee's room: whitewashed and institutional, but filled with pictures and mementos. Hanging on one wall was a collage of photos from his 104th birthday party, which saw him surrounded by Marines in white gloves and dress blues, a splendid-looking group. That same day, he had been presented with a diploma from Liverpool High School in Liverpool, New York, from which he had dropped out in the spring of 1917 in order to join the Marine Corps. That diploma, eight months old now, rested atop a nightstand. Next to all the photos in the room — most of them eighty, ninety, a hundred years old, relatives, friends, a young man who bore a striking resemblance to his father — it looked jarringly white.

William Eugene Lee was a slender man; it would be hard for me to say just how tall he was, because I never saw him standing up. Throughout our conversation he sat in a wheelchair, wearing a brown plaid flannel shirt and, on his ears, a pair of fuzzy headphones, which were attached to some kind of hearing aid that looked like an old Sony Walkman. His hair was decidedly thinner than in those old photographs, and entirely white, but it was there. His speech was extremely halting; he was given to very long pauses, twenty or thirty seconds or more, sometimes two or three to a sentence. His discharge papers recorded his height as sixty-seven and a half inches, his eyes blue, his character excellent.

He was born on March 24, 1899, he told me, in the small town of Salina, New York, which is now a suburb of Syracuse. His parents were named Margaret and Norman; his father, he recalled, "worked for the Mohegan Company, as a meat cutter."

"That's a store chain," Jim explained.

"Did he get to bring home meat from the job?" I asked.

"We would always eat good," Mr. Lee said. He grew up in between a brother, Otis, and a sister named Nell.

"How did you come to join the Marines?"

"They was my favorite, from when I was a kid." His childhood was a time of great glory for the United States Marine Corps, storming beaches in the Caribbean and Latin America, putting down insurrections that somehow threatened American interests (often, purely commercial interests); he would have read about them, or at least heard about them, often. He joined, he said, as soon as he was old enough. His papers show he was inducted at the Philadelphia Navy Yard on April 27, 1917, just three weeks after America entered the war; his actual enlistment probably took place in Syracuse a week or two before that.

In Philadelphia, the Marines assigned him to the 51st Company of the 5th Regiment. After only six weeks of training — much of it spent "on a rifle range there" — the 5th Marines boarded the USS *Henderson* and sailed off for France; it was June 14, 1917. General Pershing had himself arrived in France just days earlier. "We was thirteen days going across, I know that," he said. "They had a lot of ships" — that is, destroyers, subchasers — "following us, so nothing happened until we got across." He vividly remembered two things about the crossing. The first was that "they was giving the fellows a shot in the arm. I can remember it so well that there was one guy, he was watching, he thought they was giving him a big needle, and he jumped around. They took him out of the line, and put him back, back farther." He laughed at that one. The other: "After we landed in Saint-Nazaire [France], we was onboard ship, they paid us fifteen dollars for payday . . . seems to me they paid us in gold. And one of the guys leaned over the ship, he had it in his pocket, and it slipped out. He lost that." I laughed at that one.

But the day of my visit was not a good one for Eugene Lee's memory. He began to get frustrated with himself only a few minutes into our conversation, started interjecting the phrase "How the hell was it?" into just about every answer. He still had a fair amount to say, but not nearly as much, I could tell, as he wanted to. So while he was able to impart some information to me, I had to fill in a fair number of gaps after we spoke, and in doing so I came upon a part of the story, a big part, that he didn't even know about, that didn't even happen until much later, years after he died.

• • •

"On the back of a truck," Eugene Lee recalled, eighty-six years after the fact, "we went to this little town, and — how the hell? — we stayed in this little town, and we done some training there." This would have been the early summer of 1917, shortly after the 5th Marines arrived in France. After a while there, "they put us in the trench up there at Verdun, I think it was." He said "Ver-DOON," offering me a brief glimpse of an archaic pronunciation (or mispronunciation) that was once, I imagine, quite common. "We didn't do anything, just . . . I don't know how long we was in them up there, them big trenches they had. And the next thing — the next thing, I guess, was they took us up . . . they moved us over there by truck. Then we started up the road and we met — there was one Frenchman coming back. He was all alone, but he come, he said: 'Beaucoup Boche.'"

Beaucoup Boche: A lot of Germans.

Now: If you should find yourself at an Oktoberfest one day with an enormous beer stein in your hand, swaying to the deep and soothing tones of an oompah band, do not — please — address your fellow revelers as "Boche." It is not a polite term. I don't think Germans back then cared for it any more than they did "Kraut," or "Heinie," or "Blockhead," or "Jerry," or "Fritz." If you're wondering, the word is actually a shortened version of *Alboche,* which is itself a combination of *Allemand,* the French word for "German," and *caboche,* slang for both "cabbage" (aka "kraut") and "blockhead." It was the favored French term for Germans, and the French *hated* the Germans back then. Deeply. The Germans, after all, had invaded their country twice in less than half a century, tore the place up, and appropriated lots of land and riddled it with concrete trenches and bunkers and gun emplacements to keep the French from taking it back.

Whatever bad things the Germans of World War I may have done, though — and they weren't exactly humanitarians who invaded neutral Belgium to better spread a message of tolerance and love — it's important to remember that they did not build death camps. They weren't the Gestapo, the SD, the SS, or the *Einsatzgruppen.* Maybe I draw this distinction because I know that in the east — Russia, Poland, the Baltics — the German Army of World War I actually served, for a while, as liberators of the indigenous Jewish population, who had been dealing for centuries with dehumanizing anti-Semitic statutes and murderous state-sponsored pogroms; maybe it's because every account I've ever read of the legendary Christmas Truce of 1914 has the Germans courageously initiating it. Maybe it's the stories that Arthur Guy Empey and Frank P. Sibley tell about Saxons deliberately firing over their enemies' heads. Maybe it's all of these things. One thing I can say for sure, though, is that my attitudes on the subject have been shaped, in part, by something Eugene Lee told me that day.

At exactly 11:00 a.m. on the morning of November 11, 1918, somewhere in the Meuse-Argonne sector, he recalled, a German soldier "come out waving a white flag, and he started walking down, and our officer went out to meet him. When they got there, all of a sudden, all the German soldiers come running down, and our fellows — well, we got up, and they got mixed up talking to — some could speak our language, and a lot of our fellows could speak German, so we had a great time changing, trying to talk. And they showed us pictures of their family, you know, and we had a great time to celebrate . . . swapping souvenirs."

A couple of weeks later, "after the armistice," he explained, "we had to follow the Germans back." That is to say, the 5th Marines were part of the Army of Occupation, which was established by the terms of the armistice; they were stationed in the German Rhineland. "We had to follow them back, and in a little town, we stopped for Thanksgiving, and had our Thanksgiving dinner there. It's a little, little place. I forget the name of the place."

"Where did you stay when you were in Germany?" I asked him. "Did you stay in somebody's house?"

"Yes, lived right in the house," he replied. "There was so many men to a house. There was two in our house. We each had separate rooms, bedrooms, beds to sleep in."

"Do you remember the name of the German family that you stayed with?"

"Yes, I did. I did, but I've forgot. It was something like Horteig."

"Did you go hunting when you were in Germany?" Jim Casey had told me that Mr. Lee had hunted back home before he'd enlisted.

"Yeah, we could hunt," he said. "The only thing was we wasn't supposed to shoot was deer. But they had wild boar, anything else you wanted to shoot."

"So what did you shoot?"

"I shot a deer up there." He laughed, and I did. "I left it there and went back down and got a friend of mine. We brought it back down, and this, where I lived, the old man, he come out and took the deer. Let's see, they invited us — the fellow with me — they invited us down for a dinner when they had the deer. We went down and had venison dinner, and we had the one meal after that. We didn't go down [more often] because they didn't get too much to eat, you know."

"Where did the German families get their food?"

"The government allowed them so much each week, I guess."

"The American government?"

"Yeah. Those German people, they were nice people, they were . . . At first we used to have to carry a weapon with us all the time. It wasn't long after that we didn't have to carry any weapons. The German people were good people, and we got to know them."

"They were very friendly to the Americans?"

"They was, when we got to know them. They used to — before, you used to have to wash some underwear, when we was in France, we used to walk out in the stream and wash them and hammer them. Well, [in Germany] I had some dirty underwear, I was going to wash it, and when I came back, the German woman there, she had it all washed and clean for me. And I give her five francs. And Jesus, that was a lot of money to them." He looked down at his hands.

"Were you surprised at how nice the German people were?" I asked.

"No," he said. "No, because I knew a lot of German people where I lived, in Liverpool."

"Did you hear a lot of bad things about the Germans during the war?"

"Oh, yes. I heard a lot of bad things. Something about, they threw some of them in the furnace."

Later, Jim explained to me that Mr. Lee must have been confused by my question, confused in particular about which war I was referring to; that he was thinking I'd meant the Second World War, and that "furnace" meant "crematoria." This was after the interview had ended, after I had packed up my equipment and thanked Mr. Lee and left his room and the long-term-care wing; he was asleep by then, I figured, or maybe having lunch. Whatever the case, I didn't feel I could go back there and ask him the question that Jim Casey's revelation had raised in my mind, which was this: Having heard, many years later, about the furnaces, how did you square that image with your fond memories of the German people from your time in the Army of Occupation?

I'm glad Jim Casey didn't tell me what he did until we were well away from Eugene Lee's room. I'm glad he didn't do so because, if he had explained the "furnace" reference to me while I was still there, I would have asked Mr. Lee that question, would have done so reflexively. Because I would have wanted to know. Very much. It wouldn't have occurred to me, until I had watched him wrestle with words and memory for a bit — something he did even after much simpler, more straightforward questions — that it's a ridiculous question to pose to a 104-year-old man. I was thirty-six at the time, and I couldn't have answered it.

I still can't.

Back to *Beaucoup Boche.*

"So we was going up the road," Private Eugene Lee recalled eighty-five years and six months hence, "and we met the French people walking back, all the old people." It's a scene that was recounted by someone else who was with the 5th Marines that day — William Edward Campbell, writing fifteen years later as William March, telling the story as Private Jesse Bogan of Company K:

> We came to a long hill shaped like a semi-circle and dug in against the protected side. Below us the Germans were shelling Marigny, a small town. We could see people running out of the houses, making funny gestures, and down the narrow streets, until they joined the line that filled the highway. Then we dug in on the off side of the hill and waited.
>
> It was late May and the whole countryside was green and beautiful. Below us, in the valley, fruit trees were in bloom, pink, white and red, running across the valley in strips of color, and spotting the side of the hill. Then a haze settled over the valley, and gradually it got dark.
>
> The Germans had quit shelling the town. It lay demolished below us. Lieutenant Bartlestone came up: "All right, men! Get your things

together. We're going in the wood when it gets dark." Then he spoke to Sergeant Dunning: "The orders are to stop the Germans and not let them advance an inch farther. . . ."

"Well, anyway," said Alex Marro, after the lieutenant had gone, "that's simple and to the point."

"What's the name of this place?" asked Art Crenshaw.

"I don't know," said Sergeant Dunning. "What difference does that make?"

"I asked a Frenchman on the road," said Allan Methot, "and he said it was called Belleau Wood."

"Come on! Come on!" said Sergeant Dunning. "Get your equipment together, and quit chewing the fat!"

Belleau Wood. It's hard to explain just what those words mean to a United States Marine. What "Valley Forge" meant to a former Continental soldier, perhaps. Except that now Valley Forge has been appropriated by all Americans; few who aren't World War I buffs have even heard of Belleau Wood. Every single Marine has, though, and that little two-word phrase is as important to them as just about any other they know. USMC Commandant General James F. Amos told me that Belleau Wood "was the birth of the modern Marine Corps."

You might recall Captain Emerson G. Taylor's description, in *New England in France,* of Belleau Wood: "Shapeless fragments of what once were men hung in the jagged branches of the trees, blown there by shells." There's a good chance that at least some of those fragments had once been Marines. By the time Captain Taylor arrived on the scene, they could have been up there for nearly a month; no wonder he, and the rest of the 102nd Infantry, "came to move and talk as when they know that ghosts are watching them." To the living and already edgy, those woods — blasted to shards and reeking of decomposing corpses — must have seemed haunted.

Six weeks earlier, and for centuries before that, they were the private hunting grounds of a landed French family, a fine place to stalk deer and wild boar. But war is often like a roulette wheel, with battlegrounds being chosen by chance rather than strategy. In the case of Belleau Wood, that wheel started spinning a few months earlier and a few hundred miles to the east. On March 3, 1918, Germany and Russia — the latter in the charge of Vladimir Lenin and his *Bolsheviki* —

signed the Treaty of Brest-Litovsk, ending their part of the war, allowing the *Bolsheviki* to devote their attentions entirely to putting down
the various anti-Bolshevik uprisings, which are now remembered collectively as the Russian Civil War. But the treaty also allowed the Germans to move nearly all the forces they had on their Eastern Front —
most historians say the number was thirty-three divisions, roughly five
hundred thousand troops — to the Western Front, which gave them, at
long last, numerical superiority over the Allies. For the time being, that
is. They believed, as did everyone else, that four million fresh American troops would be arriving in France sooner or later; as they saw
it, their only chance to win the war would be to do so before the bulk
of those American troops could get there. So the Germans, who had
been fighting a largely defensive war since the fall of 1914, mounted a
massive offensive — known to history as the Spring Offensive — just a
few weeks after the treaty was signed, in the hopes that it might punch
through the French and British lines.

It did. So successfully, in fact, that the Germans dramatically over-
achieved their objectives every day. This might sound like a good thing;
it was not. Have you ever gone to break down a door with your shoulder, only to discover, at the point of contact, that the aforementioned
door wasn't even latched? Probably not, but I have, and I can tell you
that when the resistance you've prepared for isn't there to meet you,
you lunge ahead clumsily, and more often than not end up face-down
on the floor. That, in essence, is what happened to Germany during
their successful-beyond-their-greatest-hopes Spring Offensive of 1918.
For one thing, they soon found themselves far ahead of their own supply lines, which can only move so fast. Worse still, they had advanced
so quickly that they hadn't had time to determine an objective beyond
simply advancing; soon, they found themselves deep in enemy territory with no idea where to go next. Their offensive floundered, nowhere more colorfully than the town of Albert, where, stunned by the
sight of stores full of food and wine — they'd been out of reach of their
supply lines for days, and German stores had been all but empty for
years — they stopped marching and instead ate and drank themselves
into a collective stupor.

By this time, though, France was in a panic. The Germans were now
within forty miles of Paris, the closest they had gotten to the French

The German Spring Offensive, 1918

Strait of Dover

Dunkirk

Ypres

Lille

2

Arras

Cambrai

Albert

1

Amiens

Somme R.

Cantigny

St. Quentin

F R A N C E

BELGIUM

Meuse R.

Sedan

Chemin-
des-Dames

Aisne R.

Compiègne

Soissons

4

Oise R.

3

Reims

5

Vesle R.

Belleau
Wood

Château-
Thierry

Meaux

Seine R.

Paris

Marne R.

1	March 21 - April 5
2	April 9 - 29
3	May 27 - June 5
4	June 9 - 13
5	July 15 - 17
——	Line of March 21, AM
- - -	Line of May 26

0   25   50 Miles

capital since the summer of 1914. Thousands of civilians fled the city, clogging the roads. The French government made plans to relocate to Versailles. The Allied high command feared the worst; among themselves, they agreed they were now confronting the gravest threat of the war. The French and, even more so, the British had been trying for months to force Pershing to throw his men into battle — berating him, belittling him, and when that didn't work, going through diplomatic channels in an attempt to have him replaced. Pershing, though, had held firm; his men weren't ready, he said, weren't fully trained. He would not let the British and French use the Americans as they had the Canadians and Australians, the Senegalese and Moroccans. America had entered the war on its own terms; it would fight under its own command, when it was up to the task.

Now the Allies amplified their pleas, told him just how dire the situation was. And Pershing, moved — probably more by the French, who treated him with greater respect than the British did — committed two Regular Army divisions, the 2nd and the 3rd, to the fight: fifty thousand men, nearly all of whom, it seemed, were terribly excited to finally have their chance to get into the action. Numerous contemporary accounts have them marching to the front with chests swelled and chins thrust out, laughing and joking even as retreating French troops scurried by, warning them to follow suit. If there ever really were a time and place where the scene portrayed in the song "The Americans Come!" actually played out, this was probably it.

Slowly, the Allies started pushing back, though it wasn't easy, as the Germans had taken care during their offensive to set up defensive positions at various points along the way. So when the 2nd and 3rd Divisions — the 2nd Division at that point comprised two Army regiments, the 9th and the 23rd, and two regiments of Marines, the 5th and 6th — managed to beat back the Germans at Château-Thierry, less than fifty miles northeast of Paris, the Germans fell back into their nearest fortified position, only a few miles away: Belleau Wood. And there the roulette wheel stopped.

Of course, it was the Germans who stopped there, and that wasn't a matter of chance; the woods offered them an excellent defensive position. You only have to walk through a dense forest to understand why it's not a good place to launch an attack on an entrenched and experienced enemy. Perhaps that's why the French didn't want to go in there themselves, why they asked the Americans to do it, instead. Some historians argue that America should never have undertaken that battle, that they should have known how costly it would be to fight in such conditions, that there were plenty of examples from the previous four years to warn them off. But the Americans were still new to the war and, I would guess, invigorated by the fighting at Château-Thierry, and by news of the 1st Division's success at Cantigny a few days before that; they followed the Germans up to Belleau Wood, dug in, and withstood German attempts to break out. Again, French soldiers urged the Americans to retreat. The Americans would not. Their attitude was famously summed up by one Captain Lloyd Williams of the 5th Marines, who said: "Retreat? Hell, we just got here!"

Instead, they decided to go on the attack.

Now, years of trench warfare had taught the French, British, and Germans the value of softening up your enemy with a heavy-artillery barrage before you launched an attack against them; but General Pershing, who didn't much care for trench warfare, also didn't much care for tactical artillery, at least not at this point in the war. Neither did an old friend of his, James Harbord, who had initially gone to France as Pershing's chief of staff. By June, 1918, Harbord had been promoted to brigadier general and put in charge of the Marine brigade that comprised the 5th and 6th Regiments. So the Americans launched their initial attack upon entrenched German defenses without the benefit of a prolonged artillery barrage beforehand. Not a good idea.

This would be the morning of June 6, 1918, twenty-six years to the day before Americans would launch another attack against fortified and skilled German defenders elsewhere on French soil (or, as it were in 1944, French sand). In order to get to the woods, and the Germans therein, the Americans had to cross a large, open wheat field. "They started us in waves towards the Belleau Woods," Private Eugene Lee recalled eighty-five years later. "In four waves — we'd go along and jump the first wave as they go so far, then the next wave, they kept doing that till we reached the woods up there . . . You'd go so far, and you'd keep firing along there, into the woods until the next wave come

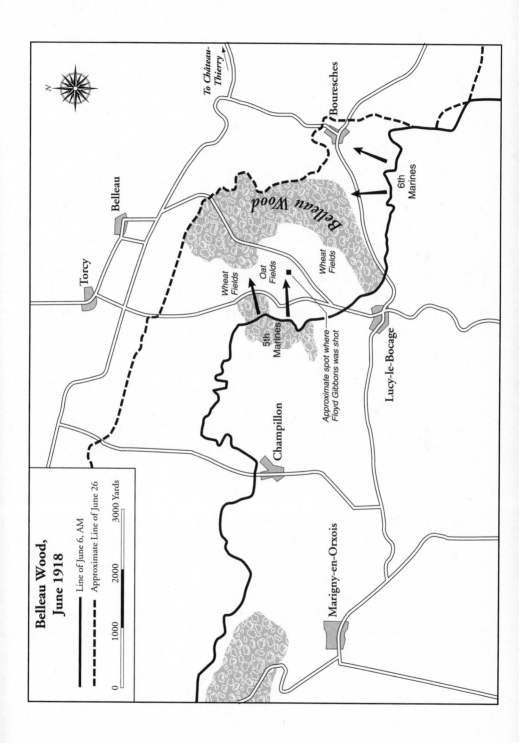

Belleau Wood,
June 1918

Line of June 6, AM
Approximate Line of June 26

0   1000   2000   3000 Yards

N

To Château-
Thierry

Bouresches

6th Marines

Belleau

Torcy

Belleau Wood

Wheat Fields

Oat Fields

Wheat Fields

5th Marines

Lucy-le-Bocage

Approximate spot where
Floyd Gibbons was shot

Champillon

Marigny-en-Orxois

along . . . We kept going so far, and then you'd lie down, and the next wave would come in back of them, jump each one until they got to the edge of the woods. And then they got in the woods, fighting."

That day, and that field, are now iconic elements of USMC lore. First Sergeant Dan Daly, a forty-four-year-old native of Long Island who had been in the Corps for nearly twenty years and had already won two Congressional Medals of Honor — two! — is said to have rallied his squad in the open field that day by calling out: "Come on, you sons of bitches! Do you want to live forever?" That quote — or a toned-down version of it, anyway — was recorded by Floyd Gibbons, a dashing reporter for the *Chicago Tribune* who hurried up from Paris to be with the Marines that day. As he approached the field, a colonel urged him to turn back, warning him it was "damn hot up there." Gibbons ignored his advice and started across a field "covered with a young crop of oats between ten and fifteen inches high." When he was halfway across, a German machine gun opened fire; Gibbons, unarmed, flattened himself against the earth and started crawling forward. He didn't make it very far. One bullet shot through his left bicep; a second nicked his left shoulder. And then a third tore into his left eye, exiting through his forehead. "Just how does it feel to be shot on the field of battle?" Gibbons wrote in his memoir, *"And They Thought We Wouldn't Fight,"* published by Doran later that year. "I always wanted to know." He found out that day, three times over. His judgment: No big deal. "It seemed hard for me to believe at the time, but . . . I was experiencing not any more pain than I had experienced once when I dropped a lighted cigarette on the back of my hand."

In all, the Marines sustained nearly eleven hundred casualties on June 6, making it the deadliest day in the Corps's history to that point. "I never saw men charge to their death with finer spirit," Gibbons would recall in *"And They Thought We Wouldn't Fight,"* but still: *to their death.* Things didn't get much better once they made it into the woods, either. The good news for the Marines was that, if you must fight in a dense forest, it's best to do so with sharpshooters, of whom the Corps had many; "The deadliest weapon in the world is a Marine and his rifle!" General Pershing boasted after the battle. The bad news was that the enemy had plenty of them, too. The Americans did manage to wrest Belleau Wood from the Germans, but then the Germans, famous for counterattacking, did just that, and wrested the forest back. Then the Americans counter-counterattacked, and the Germans counter-counter-counterattacked, and before the Americans could claim victory — on June 26, with a report that stated, simply, "Woods now US Marine Corps entirely" — the forest had changed hands a dozen times. It took the Americans — Army and Marines — twenty days to take it and hold it. The price was 9,777 casualties, of whom 1,811 were killed in action. Among them was Captain Williams, whose refusal to retreat was already famous by the time he was killed on June 12.

Another casualty that day was one Private Eugene Lee, shot through the left wrist. "I was lucky," he told me. "It didn't hit the bone."

"A bullet hit your wrist but didn't break it?" I asked, not even sure how such a thing might be possible.

"No," he said. "That's why I was lucky all the while."

Despite his injury, Private Lee helped evacuate more seriously wounded Marines. "I helped get them back where they could take care of them, get them to an ambulance," he recalled. It was an act that won him the military's third-highest decoration. "The Silver Star," he said. "I don't know why they give it to me."

"I think they gave it to you for bravery under fire," I told him, "and for helping carry other wounded soldiers out even though you were wounded yourself."

"Well," he replied, "you didn't think about that."

Both the Army and the Marines fought at Belleau Wood, yet the battle is today remembered solely as a triumph for the Marine Corps. Responsibility for that fact resides with Floyd Gibbons. General Pershing had instituted a strict prohibition against naming specific units, or even branches of the military, in association with any particular action or location; he didn't want the enemy to have any intelligence about which units were where. But Gibbons, in writing up his coverage of that day's fighting — three bullet holes, one eye, and all — mentioned that Marines had been in the fight, and the military's censors, reckoning that Gibbons was dying, decided to leave intact what they figured to be his final dispatch, as a tribute. Of course, Gibbons did not end up dying, at least not until 1939, but since no one else had been allowed to mention any Army units, the public celebrated Belleau Wood as a victory for the USMC, and the USMC alone. By the time the histories started being published, it was too late. The concrete had set in America's national consciousness.

This didn't help relations between the Army and the Marine Corps, which had never been all that good to begin with; the matter of who deserved credit for Belleau Wood, which General Pershing afterward called "the most considerable engagement American troops had ever had with a foreign enemy," generated no small measure of ill will between the two. Ninety years later, I spoke with several historians who felt very strongly that the Army had been denied its due. One of them even asserted that Belleau Wood was the reason that Marines were kept out of the European Theater in World War II.

The French, though, see no controversy. Their feelings about Belleau Wood are summed up by the fact that, immediately after the battle, they renamed the forest — what was left of it, anyway — the *Bois de la Brigade de Marine.* And they're crazy about the place; over the decades, they've picked it dry, stripping away everything in sight and, with the help of metal detectors, most of what wasn't in sight. The French government long ago banned the use of metal detectors in such circumstances, but ardent collectors still use them anyway. Sometime around the turn of the new century, one even dug up, in the woods near the village of Lucy-le-Bocage, an old American mess-kit cover with the original owner's name scratched into the side: WILLIAM E. LEE. 51 CO. US. Delighted, he did some research and was astonished to learn that William E. Lee was still alive and living in Syracuse, New York, though no longer going by his first name.

Private Lee had presumably dropped it — the canteen, not the first name — in those woods on June 12, 1918, when a German bullet drilled through his wrist. And though he considered himself lucky that it hadn't shattered his bone, the wound was still serious enough to land him in a hospital for four months. He didn't seem to mind; for one thing, no one was shooting at him there. He even got to play some baseball. Back home, he'd played third base, but at the hospital, he explained, "they got me pitching."

"Were you good?" I asked him.

"I didn't have a lot of stuff on the ball," he said, "but I had good control. I could throw where I wanted to throw."

"Did you ever bean anybody?"

He laughed. "Yeah . . . one time . . . they had a second lieutenant playing with them, and I hit him on purpose."

In the hospital, he met another wounded Marine, a fellow named Joe Winook; at least it sounded to me that day like "Winook" — I didn't ask him for a precise spelling. "He was from the 6th Regiment," Private Lee, of the 5th Regiment, recalled; they met not while playing ball, but while throwing dice. "He got in a crap game, and he won so much . . ."

"What'd you do with it?"

"Oh, we traveled." They went to Paris, a good place to spend money, and became fast friends. Eighty-five years later, it was clear that Eugene Lee still thought about his old pal Joe Winook from time to time; he mentioned him often during our visit, spoke of their time at the hospital and in Paris, their return to the front once they'd healed.

It seemed to me that Eugene Lee was a man who didn't mind revisiting the past on a regular basis. His walls, as I mentioned, were covered with old photographs — pictures of friends and relatives, of girls peering through old tennis rackets, and one of himself, alone and in uniform, labeled: "April 1917, Philadelphia." The picture that commandeered my gaze, though, didn't have any people in it at all; it was of a massive airship, broken and resting atop a stand of young trees: a zeppelin. "It'd only landed just a little way, a couple of miles from where we were," he explained. "Crashed. Next morning, they marched the whole company over to that zeppelin there. And I got a piece of it. I tore [it] off, and I got it somewhere in a bunch of things I got." This particular zeppelin, the LZ-49 (aka L49, or LZ-96 — who understands these things?), was returning to Germany from England, where it had dropped more than two tons of bombs, when, on October 20, 1917, French planes shot it down near the town of Bourbonne-les-Bains, in the region of Lorraine. The German crew escaped unharmed, but soon found themselves nearly surrounded by angry Frenchmen; it's hard to crash-land a zeppelin without attracting attention to yourself. The crew was supposed to set the airship on fire, but decided they'd better just flee, instead. And so the Allies captured their first intact zeppelin.

They inspected it thoroughly, took copious notes; zeppelins had been terrorizing civilian populations in England and France for three years. After the war, the US Navy patterned its first rigid airship, the USS *Shenandoah*, after the LZ-49.

Seeing my fascination with the picture of the zeppelin, Jim Casey dug out a photo of that recently unearthed mess kit, the one marked "William E. Lee," and told me about it. And here's where things start to get hinky.

In the movies or a feel-good newspaper story, the fellow who had dug up that artifact, having discovered that its original owner was, incredibly, still living eighty or so years later — that fellow would magnanimously return his find to the aforementioned original owner, who would pass it on to his overjoyed children, or maybe the Smithsonian. In real life, however, the treasure-hunter, realizing that this astonishing historical quirk made his find all the more valuable, put it up on eBay, instead. Jim didn't know what happened to it after that, but he recommended that, if I ever got to France, I should look up a fellow named Gilles Lagin. He might know something about it.

Five and a half years later, I did look up Gilles Lagin. A swarthy man built like a shipping crate, Gilles lives in the nigh-unpronounceable town of Marigny-en-Orxois, near Belleau Wood, and grew up hearing tales of the battle fought there nearly half a century before he was born. He also grew up digging for artifacts there, even before the ban on metal detectors; over the decades he found a great many, enough for a little museum, which he established in the upper floor of an old barn next door to his house. He graciously received me there and showed me around. ˊ

It's not exactly what you think of when you hear the words "French museum." Gilles's place is actually quite small, just a few rooms, and extremely cluttered. Much of his collection is still in boxes, labeled "1995" and the like, waiting to be organized. Most of it is covered in rust — a lot of rust. Some is arrayed in crannies under eaves, so that you really have to bend over to view it. All of that said, the man has just about everything you can imagine, American and German: helmets, bombs, artillery, gun carriages, grenade launchers, rifles, machine guns, pistols, bayonets, trench knives, gas masks, uniforms, cartridge belts, bandoliers, flags, banners, canteens, mess kits, first-aid kits, cigarette cases, keys, whistles, insignia; and not just one of each, but dozens. He has at least a platoon's worth of identification disks.

The front room — the only one that doesn't look like a hoarder's garage sale — features mannequins in uniform and glass cases filled with carefully labeled objects. All of it, fascinating and even oddly beautiful as it is, though, is upstaged by two very large objects that at first glance seem out of place there. One is a segment of tree husk, stretching from floor to ceiling, in the middle of which is a hole large enough, if not quite wide enough, to stick your head through; that, Gilles explained, came off a tree that was hit by a shell that did not explode. Next to it stands an actual tree — or at least a five-foot-tall chunk of one. Carved into its trunk are the words "USMC, 5th Marines, July 17th, 1918," surrounding a rough approximation of the Corps's symbol, an eagle perched atop a globe and anchor. A placard tacked to the top of the trunk reads:

> Tree from Villers Cotterets forest, it was
> carved by a Marine from the 5th regiment
> /2nd Division, on July 17, 1918 after they
> moved from Belleau Wood area to Soissons,
> they debussed in the big forest in the
> afternoon of July 17, 1918 and some of them
> found the time to carve trees before to move
> to the jump line, the same day by night, and
> by the way, to keep the remembrance forever.

I asked Gilles how he had managed to secure this particular artifact. He just smiled and said it wasn't easy. He added that it was particularly popular with former Marines, quite a few of whom, he told me, had visited him over the years. One had even made him an honorary member of the Corps. I noticed he was wearing a USMC T-shirt that day — not for my benefit, I believe, but because he owned a lot of them.

I inquired about Eugene Lee's mess kit. Gilles said he'd tried to acquire it for his museum, but had been outbid by someone else. He thought he knew who the winner was, he added, but declined to furnish a name; for whatever reason, collectors of this ilk often seem kind of shadowy, not the sort of folk whose names you might drop casually. They don't much like each other, either.

The next day, I was in Belleau. It's a very small village, without any shops to speak of, though it does have a little museum dedicated to local history, and particularly to the First World War. I was told I needed to see this museum, and I was glad to get into it, since, like much of small-town France, it keeps odd hours, and not many of them; but by the time I did, I'd been in the area for several days, and there wasn't much in it that I hadn't seen before. I did, however, notice that many of the military artifacts therein were marked as being on loan from one Georges Bailly. I asked the curator for M. Bailly's phone number; the French being not nearly as obsessed with privacy as Americans are, she gave it to me right away. (I may or may not have flirted with her a bit, first. Hey — it was France.) M. Bailly sounded a bit cagey at first, but when I dropped the name Eugene Lee, he invited me over.

Unlike Gilles Lagin, Georges Bailly did not have a museum in his house, or anywhere else; he was just a collector — and, he later acknowledged, a dealer. (In case you're wondering, his last name is pronounced "by-EE." And yes, I did ask him how things were at the Bedford Falls Savings and Loan; he had no idea what I was talking about.) A sharp, silver-haired man who looked more like a dealer of art than militaria, he stored his collection mostly in one very large room on the second floor of his house. Everything in it looked almost as good as new — not a trace of rust anywhere, at least not as far as I could see. He had as many *Pickelhauben* — those German spiked helmets — as Gilles Lagin had identification disks. Every one was different, too, each bearing subtle distinctions indicating rank, branch of service, state of origin, and so on. When I asked if I could take pictures, he looked suspicious, then anxious, and said *non*. I imagine he worried about thieves. His greatest concern, though, was moths; he'd recently routed an infestation, but not before it damaged some of his old uniforms, which otherwise looked pristine on their mannequins. It was a sad thing to see.

Throughout the room, he had sealed plastic tubs and small metal filing cabinets. From time to time he would open one up and show me a drawer or a tub filled with insignia, or identification disks, or other such artifacts, sorted and stored like with like. He tracked everything — many thousands of artifacts — on an extensive set of file cards;

each individual item had a corresponding card. As much as he had, he knew exactly where all of it was.

I asked him about Eugene Lee's mess-kit cover. Yes, he said, he knew all about it. Someone else had it; he heard they'd dug it up with a metal detector. Who had it? A shrug.

So, he asked me, did you really meet Eugene Lee? By this time, Mr. Lee had been gone for more than five years; he'd died on March 25, 2004, less than four months after I'd met him.

Yes, I said, I did.

"Do you know the name Joseph Winook?" he asked. I said I did, that Mr. Lee had talked a lot about his old friend. But how do *you* know about him, M. Bailly? He just smiled and pulled out a small box filled with index cards, flipped through until he found the one he was looking for, withdrew it, then opened a drawer filled with eating utensils and rooted around in it for a few minutes. Finally he pulled out a fork, looked it over for a few seconds, then gingerly passed it to me. It was dark with oxidation, but I could still read clearly the engravings on its handle:

117654
WNUK

The index card read, in part: "WNUK, Joseph F. Fork. Found 5 November, 1993." M. Bailly was an excellent researcher; using nothing more than a fork bearing a serial number and one name, he was able to determine its owner's date and place of enlistment (Philadelphia, April 27, 1917), the date he probably dropped it (wounded June 11, 1918), the term of his hospitalization, the fact that he'd been awarded a Silver Star, and much more. I, on the other hand, have never been able to find out anything about the man. But at least now I know how to spell his name.

Eventually, both William E. Lee and Joe Wnuk returned to the front. By then they were serving together in the 51st Company of the 5th Regiment; I don't know if Joe had requested such a transfer so he and William could serve together, or if it had just worked out that way. They were sent east, to Lorraine, just in time for the great Meuse-

Argonne Offensive, the last great battle of the war. The Argonne — another forest. A very dangerous place to be. They were glad to be fighting together.

"Where was Joe from, do you remember?" I asked Mr. Lee.

"He was from Pennsylvania. I was going to stop to his house after I was discharged," he said.

"Did you get to do that?"

"No. No, I never did. He was killed the last night."

The last night: of the war. November 10, 1918. Twelve, maybe fifteen hours to go until the armistice. "During the night, as we crossed the river . . ." — the Meuse River — ". . . once in a while, they'd throw a shell over, it'd land in the river in back of us. It's one of them that killed Joe," he said. "The very last night."

Tell me, what words can possibly do justice to the notion of a young man, freshly healed and back to fighting strength, being killed anonymously from a mile away by a lone piece of German artillery *on the last night of the war?* My mind, limited as it is, doesn't know what to do with that, with the notion that, by the time the sun set next, the war would be over, yet somehow Joseph Wnuk wouldn't be there to see it. I don't know how to feel about the fact that, seventy-five years after his death, a scavenger dug the man's fork up out of the earth, the ground where he might have died but didn't, and now a collector, a man with no connection at all to Joseph Wnuk of Pennsylvania, keeps that fork in a drawer with scores of other forks and spoons and knives.

Do I even have the right to feel anything at all about a story told to me in the last months of his life by a man who survived Belleau Wood and the Argonne Forest, hunted deer and fed his hosts in occupied Germany, sailed home on the USS *Leviathan* (which, before it was seized by the United States in 1917, had been the SS *Vaterland*), marched in parades in Philadelphia and New York and Washington, returned to Syracuse, married his sweetheart, started going by his middle name, passed nearly half a century working as a traveling foreman for the Syracuse Lighting and Niagara Mohawk power companies, passed another forty years in retirement, and still carried with him, through all of it, through every month of those eighty-five years, the memory of that friend and of his death on the last night of the war? The pain, the

grief, the indignation or cynicism or bitterness or relief or whatever —
that all belongs to William Eugene Lee.

"You wrote a letter to his — Joe's — mother after he was killed?" I
asked him that day in Syracuse in December, 2003.

"Yes, I did," he said.

"What did you tell her?"

"I told them how he was a great friend, and I was going to stop
there."

But he never could bring himself to make that trip.

10

We Didn't See a Thing

W HO IS A WORLD WAR I veteran? It's a simple enough question, I guess; the answer, though, at least in some cases, is not quite so simple. Take Harold Gardner.

In August, 2005, I drove up to Choconut, Pennsylvania (it sounds like it should be a subdivision of Hershey, but actually it's just over the border from Binghamton, New York), to see him, having read about him in a newspaper article. He was 106 years and eight months old at the time, quite sharp and self-sufficient, still living alone in his own house, a slight fellow in wire-rim glasses, red plaid shirt, high gray trousers, and wide suspenders. Before and after we talked he scurried around the house, showing me this and that from his long life. There was a good-sized barn connected to the place, and he had it filled with lots and lots of large and elaborate machinery. He kept it all in fine working order, clean as the day it was manufactured; he was very proud of it, took the time to tell me what each and every machine or engine was and did. Or, I should say, he tried to. I didn't understand a word.

He had grown up in Binghamton, started tinkering with things when he was eight or nine years old, and dropped out of high school in his senior year to go to work as a toolmaker and machinist; "dollars and cents was more important to me than that diploma," he explained, though he quickly added that he regretted never having graduated. Then the country got into the war, and he ended up being drafted into the Army. He was supposed to be sent down to Camp Humphreys, in Virginia, for basic training, but his departure was delayed due to the influenza epidemic; "just shut the place down till they got straightened out with the flu, you know," he explained.

Months passed. Then, one day, he got the call to report for duty at the armory, on Washington Street in Binghamton. "It was over thirty of us, I would say," he recalled. "They gave us a blanket and socks and one thing or another and got us ready to go up. When we got up we got on the train, I had blankets and socks and all that stuff with me. Hadn't gotten a uniform yet."

The train, full of anxious and excited new doughboys, sat in the station for a while. "There were three or four coaches," Harold Gardner recalled. And then, "at, I guess, about half past nine," he said, "one of the Army officers came on the train" with an announcement: "You boys can go home now. The armistice has been signed."

That was it.

Except that, at first, nobody moved. "We couldn't understand it at all," he told me. They thought it could be a practical joke, that they might find themselves in trouble if they really did try to go home. "We found out the next day that the war was over," he remembered.

"Did you keep your blanket and your socks?" I asked him.

"I still have the blanket," he said.

And lest you think that was all the Army gave him for his troubles, they also sent him a check for his service. "One dollar," he announced. "I never cashed it." He still had it, too. Even showed it to me, proudly. From time to time, he said, the government would send him a letter asking him why he hadn't deposited it yet, but he just ignored them; said he'd rather have a souvenir of his service in World War I than the dollar. I guess his attitude about money had changed since high school.

So: Was Harold Gardner a veteran of World War I? Are the blanket and socks and that check for one dollar enough? Or does none of it count because he hadn't been issued his uniform yet?

In the course of tracking down, meeting, and interviewing World War I veterans — a process that occupied me for the better part of a decade — I gathered quite a few unusual stories. Many of them involve people whose service is not easily defined, or even categorized.

Take, for example, Henry Roy Tucker, whom I found off the French

List. Mr. Tucker—he went by Roy—lived in Toccoa, a small town in northeastern Georgia that I knew, from my childhood obsession with the *Guinness Book of World Records,* as the home of Paul Edward Anderson, who was the world's strongest man through much of the 1970s. (It's also the birthplace of DeForest Kelley, of *Star Trek* fame, but since he wasn't in the Guinness book, I didn't know that back then.) Roy Tucker had been born in Alapaha, Georgia, on May 9, 1897, left school after the fifth grade, went to work on his father's farm, married at twenty, and was drafted at twenty-one. The Army assigned him to Company F of the 28th Infantry, 1st Division, which was already in France, having been one of the first divisions to go across in 1917; he was to be a replacement, a stand-in for someone who had been shot or gassed or blown up. He went through basic training in Atlanta, got terribly seasick while going across on the *Leviathan*—"about three days I'd like to have died," he told me—and was greeted, when he arrived, by the worst sight of his life: "The first thing I saw when we got off," he recalled, "there were dead horses and dead men littered around there. Dead to beat the band . . . I don't remember how many. There was a lot of them there, though. They had been fighting all that morning, when I got there."

I visited with him in September, 2003; he was a small man in a brown cardigan sweater and red plaid shirt, large glasses, fine white hair. He had a very gentle, peaceful air about him; he and his daughter, Cassie, bore a striking resemblance to one another. She prodded him along, pointed him in the direction of the stories she had heard growing up, repeated my questions loudly as necessary. She helped him remember the name of the minister who had officiated at his wedding in 1917—it was Stallings—then helped him remember that Reverend Stallings's son had served with Roy Tucker until the younger Stallings came down with influenza. It was implied, though never confirmed, that it had killed him.

One of his favorite stories involved the night that he had been on guard duty when a motorcycle and sidecar came roaring up. He paused, smiled. Who was it? I asked him.

"Pershing," he replied. "Came out of his sidecar, rolled up there, talked to us all a good while."

"What did you say?"

"I don't remember now, it's been so long . . . Nice old man though, he sure was." Pershing had been fifty-eight years old at the time — nearly fifty years younger than the man now telling me that story.

Mr. Tucker had liked the Germans, too, at least those he'd met when he was there as part of the Army of Occupation. "They were just as nice as anybody you'd ever seen in your life," he recalled. "When we camped in this little town here, maybe a week or ten days, and then they'd transfer us to another town, and another town, and there's people that were there, from over there, that would invite us back over to have dinner with them."

I suppose he never put together in his mind those fine dinners and all those dead soldiers and horses he'd seen that first day, though both were, of course, the work of Germans. Maybe he was disinclined to bear a grudge, since he was spared the fate of those corpses. He attributed his good fortune to God, but timing deserves some of the credit, too: As it happened, he arrived in France on November 11, 1918. "The armistice was signed that morning," he explained.

I wonder if Henry Roy Tucker, having just gotten there that very day, understood, entirely, what that meant. We know now, of course; we regard November 11, 1918, as the day the Great War ended, even though, technically, the peace treaty was not signed until the following summer. Few people know the month and date the Treaty of Versailles was effected, much less the time, but everyone knows the eleventh hour of the eleventh day of the eleventh month of 1918. I expect, as years went on, that date grew to mean a great deal to him. And even though he arrived, technically, after the armistice took effect, eighty years later, the government of France decided to give him a pass when they evaluated his Legion of Honor application. He was in uniform on French soil as of November 11, 1918: That was good enough for them. No matter that, unlike all those dead men and dead horses that greeted him, he never stood a chance of becoming a casualty of war.

His family, though, was not spared. Roy Tucker's brother, Quincy, was too young to be drafted, but his sister, Lillie, was married to a fellow who went off to France. He returned just fine; or so it seemed at the time. Turns out, Cassie said, he "brought her a disease back from overseas, from the First World War. That's what killed her." The way she said the word "disease" left no doubt as to what, exactly, she meant.

"She was a beautiful woman," her niece mourned. "Oh, she was pretty."

In November, 2005, I went to Smith Center, Kansas — so-named because it sits just a few miles away from the geographic center of the continental United States — to meet 106-year-old Albert "Jud" Wagner, who had served in the Marines in World War I. Mr. Wagner's son, Junior, was also a Marine Corps veteran, in his case from the Second World War; when we spoke on the phone, Junior told me I was welcome to come see his father, though he wasn't sure the interview would prove fruitful for me. Undaunted, I traveled to (literally) the middle of the country, confident that I could get a good interview out of Jud Wagner. I couldn't. He was able to give me the basic facts of his youth — when and where he was born, his parents' names, his siblings' names, where he went to school, what year he graduated — but very little beyond that. He was working on the family farm when he decided to enlist; "everyone else was," he explained. He chose the Marines because "it was a good outfit," went through basic training in Quantico, Virginia, and then shipped out. According to his discharge papers, which his son sent me later, he arrived in France on October 21, 1918, three weeks before the armistice, but never saw combat. He did, however, serve in Germany from December 12, 1918, until August 6, 1919, as part of the Army of Occupation, though he could give me absolutely no details about that — or anything else.

Homer Anderson, of Pompano Beach, Florida, probably could have answered questions all day long, if only I'd had them. I'd heard that Mr. Anderson, who was 107 when we met in January of 2005, had served in the Balloon Corps, and I really, *really* wanted to meet someone who'd had something to do with aviation in that war. The United States Balloon Corps wasn't exactly the Lafayette Escadrille, but they did make it aloft. Actually, the Balloon Corps is a quirky little footnote of the war: Balloons, typically filled with hydrogen, were used by both sides for observational purposes on the Western Front pretty much from the war's start; you can see a lot more from a balloon, even one that's only fifty or a hundred feet up, than you can from a trench. The problem was that balloons were essentially defenseless — the only

thing an observer could do in the name of self-preservation was franti-
cally attempt to lower the balloon quickly, or, failing that, jump — and
they soon became a favorite target of enemy planes, not only because
they were strategically important and easy to destroy, but because all
that hydrogen burned rapidly and looked beautiful doing so. I imagine
shooting one down must have been pretty satisfying for a pilot, and
guilt-free, too, since most observers wore parachutes.

Homer Anderson — who was wearing a *blue* plaid shirt on the day
I visited him — had grown up in Du Bois, Pennsylvania, in the central
part of that state, and was interested in balloons and aeroplanes, so
when he enlisted he asked for that kind of post; oddly, though, he wasn't
looking for any action. "To tell you the truth," he told me, "I was more
interested in questions and answers, in problems, than I was in carrying a rifle around." So even though he had asked to serve in the Balloon
Corps, he spent most of his time there doing office work, and only went
up in a balloon a half-dozen times, by his recollection. And all of them
were in Pennsylvania. And none of them were at all unusual. "We had
certain areas that we went out in balloons," he explained, "and more or
less inspected the area that the different corps were parked in, and we
just checked the area to see if there was any change or anything, anything moving in or out that wasn't already scheduled. We knew what
was scheduled. It was just more or less a review." Nevertheless, he said,
"it was thrilling for me."

At least, that is, until the Army decided there was no future in balloon surveillance, due to the aforementioned issues, at which point
they converted his unit to infantry.

They never made it to France.

While I never got to meet anyone who flew a plane Over There — or, for
that matter, Over Here — I did get to meet some veterans who worked
with trucks. Sure, trucks aren't particularly dashing or romantic; I
doubt anyone ever wore goggles and a long scarf while driving one. But
those old rigs looked pretty cool, with their enormous square grilles
and absence of headlights. And it's a matter of fact that they were tremendously important in keeping the boys in the trenches well supplied, a task not devoid of danger, since they sometimes got quite close

to the front, and almost always had to lumber long distances on roads that had been rough even *before* they'd sustained three years' worth of shelling. Reuben Law worked on those trucks, trained soldiers to drive them, even drove them himself. Yet, as far as I'm concerned, that fact is actually among the less interesting things he told me when I visited him. And I *love* trucks.

It was July 1, 2004; Mr. Law was six weeks shy of his 106th birthday, living in the dry hills of Carson City, Nevada, with his son and daughter-in-law. Like almost every World War I veteran I interviewed, he looked much younger than he was, although to me he also looked distinctly old-timey; with his firm chin, perfectly trimmed brush mustache, steely gaze, and white hair combed back straight from his forehead, his countenance seemed like it had been lifted whole from another era, one that predated color photography. Then again, I guess it had. He wore a deep red cardigan sweater over a brown shirt, and khakis with banker's cuffs and a crease so sharp it could have cut a crusty loaf of bread. His voice, clipped and gravelly, was the spearhead of a powerful dignity; there was no mistaking it. He was alone at home when I first got there, and seemed, at first, unsure of why anyone would want to interview him. He graciously answered my questions anyway.

He was born in Northfield, Minnesota, on August 14, 1898. His father, Walter Tweedy Law, a Scottish immigrant, worked for the William Pearson Land Company, running trains up to Canada to sell wheat lands; he died of stomach cancer when his son, Reuben, was just starting high school. His mother, born Victoria Augusta Bowler, was the daughter of James Madison Bowler, a native of northern Maine who had moved to Minnesota in 1858. When the Confederates fired on Fort Sumter, J. M. Bowler joined Company F of the 3rd Minnesota and was quickly made a corporal; by the time Victoria, his first child, was born — on September 16, 1863, to be specific — he had been commissioned a captain in the 3rd Minnesota, and then a Major in the 11th United States Colored Regiment. As a baby, Reuben Law's mother "was taken into a Civil War camp by her father," he told me. "A Civil War camp of colored troops. And some people thought it was awful for him to do that. But they took real good care of the baby while it was there. And the family has always been black-oriented, to do the same for a person that is black and a person that is white." Pretty unusual for

1863, when much of the country still regarded black men and women as property.

"So your grandfather was a very progressive man," I said.

"Very progressive," he agreed. "I was grown up when he died, and I spent a lot of time with my grandfather."

The world can get to know James Madison Bowler a bit through his and his wife's many letters to each other, written during the Civil War and since published. He must have passed the epistolary gene on to his grandson, Reuben, who, while in the Army — at least during the nine months before he got shipped over to France — wrote several letters a day to various friends and family back in Minnesota. I know this because he also kept a diary, writing in it every single day, from:

12/19/1917: Visited Chicago Art Museum and walked the dirty city streets. Reported at First Illinois Armory at 1:00 p.m. Left for Florida by special train at 7:00 p.m. on Illinois Central R.R.

to:

11/11/1918: *Le guerre finis.* All flags & colors raised at noon; whistles blown, bells rung & rifles of all guards fired at 4:00 p.m. Men on crutches carried them on their shoulders.

And a bit beyond.

The diary is curt and businesslike but also a fascinating glimpse of his service, which can be said to have begun on June 6, 1917, when he was still in high school. "There was a soldier came to visit us at the school looking for recruits," he explained to me. "And I was in a technical course, and he was kind of impressed with what I'd been doing in school . . . I enlisted there, when he was there, in the Army Reserve. And it was agreed, when I enlisted, that they wouldn't — my graduation, my high school was coming up in a few months, in a month or two — that they wouldn't call me to active duty before my graduation." They actually called him up in December; he'd spent the interim working on a Ford assembly line in Minneapolis, making Model Ts. "I was putting boards together in the little trunk area in the back with screws," he recalled. "It was good work at the time. I think they paid five dollars a day. Anyway, the other automobile companies that were at the time, said Ford would go broke paying that kind of money. And his answer was, if I don't pay them that kind of money, they won't have money to buy my cars."

Reuben Law acquired his diary on December 18, 1917, when he boarded a train from Minneapolis and left for Chicago, and started writing in it the next day. As I said, he never missed a day. Some were more eventful than others. On December 21, he wrote:

In train all day. Took one hour hike at Albany, Georgia. Arrived at Jacksonville 8:30 p.m. Friday, took side track to camp and slept on Pullman that night. Had no supper. Wrote to: Hester, Marion & Deac.

On December 22:

Went into Camp [Joseph E.] Johnston at 8:30 a.m. and ate very light breakfast. Cleaned around barracks and loafed rest of day. Received 1 blanket, 1 comforter and 1 mattress to be filled with hay. Sang at night with Chicago bunch who were gathered around the barracks. Camp fire accompanied by three string instruments. 300 more hungry men came from Fort Thomas, Kentucky. Wrote to: Edith M., & Mother.

And December 28:

Morning cold, but bright. Wrote to: Mother, Jim, & H. Street. Uniforms issued. Spent several hours trading uniforms in order to get a somewhat better fit.
Clothes issued: 1 O.D. [olive drab] coat; 1 O.D. trousers, 2 khaki trousers; 1 khaki coat; 1 pair shoes; 1 pair puttees; 2 shirts; 1 overcoat; 1 poncho; 1 overalls; 1 jacket; 1 hat; 2 suits summer and 2 suits winter underwear; 6 pair sox; 1 belt.

By New Year's Eve, the temperature in Jacksonville — Florida — was down to 10 degrees. "Wish my skates were here," he wrote. "Drilled. Had inspection!! Wrote to: Hester & Mother."

January 1, 1918:

Cloudy, 15 degrees. New Years day; no frill and had no detail duties. Went to Jacksonville to do some errands for myself and the boys.

Tried to look up Mr. C. E. Hillyer; got note at his office. Took pictures along the roadway while hiked to town.

January 2:

Cloudy, 23 degrees. Had a fine morning of drill which loosened up our colds a great deal. Had seven hours of drill today. They are livening things up now and working us harder. Received two very welcome letters from Lois today, the first mail since arrival at camp. Wrote to: Mother & Lois.

He lived in Block G and was assigned to the Motor Transport Corps. All in all, it seems to have been a relatively easy post: A typical day may have included an hour or two of drilling, and maybe some cleanup or patrol. There was a lot of time for visiting family friends in the area, touring around Jacksonville and St. Augustine, and, most of all — except for writing letters — hiking. Reuben Law did a lot of hiking in Florida, so much, in fact, that I wondered if perhaps that was the secret to his longevity. Until, that is, I came across his entry for February 10, 1918: "Six of us hired a Maxwell and drove them to St. Augustine . . . Drank from Fountain of Youth." (Upon further reflection, it occurs to me that his mother, who lived to be 109, probably had something to do with it, too.)

The next day, he wrote: "Rifles were issued to company this afternoon. I now have Springfield 30-30 #739744." He didn't get much chance to train with it, though; the day after that, he was assigned to his truck, a two-ton Pierce-Arrow. His job, he told me, was "training soldiers to drive and drive at night without any lights, and drive by the feel of the edges of the road so that they're on the road but not quite." The trucks "were all Pierce-Arrows and Cadillacs," and were so well made, he recalled, that "we could oftentimes leave the truck overnight and start it in the morning with that little tickler and it'd hit the right cylinder." I have no idea what that means, in case you're wondering.

After about nine months of that — during which time he probably trained hundreds of drivers — Reuben Law was sent to France. Eighty-six years later, he still didn't quite know why. "I imagine they figured they'd trained as many [truck drivers] as they could use," he speculated, but it seems the Army might not have known why they shipped

Private First Class Law Over There, either, because when he arrived at Brest, he recalled, "they seemed to not know where to fit us. I went from a receiving company in France, to an electrical company." But the electrical company didn't have anything for him to do, so eventually they put him back in the Motor Transport Corps and sent him east, to the town of Allerey. On the way, he passed through Reims, the ancient city to which French kings had traveled for centuries to be crowned; the Germans had damaged or destroyed much of the city by the time he got to see it.

In Allerey, PFC Law was quickly promoted to sergeant and put in charge of the motor pool of Base Hospital 26, a large facility comprising three smaller hospitals. "We were sent there to take charge of transportation of all kinds: ambulances, staff cars, motorcycles — the works," he explained. "We had a mobile repair shop that was moved right into a big garage, and we repaired any vehicles that came our way that needed repair — mostly motorcycles. And we gave the dispatch rider a motorcycle that had been repaired and we took his in for repair, ready for the next guy." He was assigned a motorcycle, too — a British model that he didn't much care for. One day, though, a Harley-Davidson came in for repair, and he snagged it.

He told a lot of stories about France, many of which I had heard before in some form or other — of roaming around the countryside looking for supplies, bargaining with farmers for eggs ("the French aristocracy are kind of stiff-necked people, but the peasants are real down-to-earth people and friendly"), celebrating the armistice ("we joined the hubbub in town, and every girl that came by gave you a kiss"). He admired the French, was impressed by what he'd seen Over There; by the time he'd arrived, he told me, France was "a worn-out nation, a worn-out people. They'd been at it so long and there was so much *I'll go over and kill you, you come back and kill me,* and you kept repeating that over and over until eventually both are likely to lose." He said he thought the two nations had forged a bond during that war; "By and large, I think we've had a pretty decent relationship with France," he offered, then added: "Up until just recently, [when] they've disagreed with our activities in Iraq." Two more years would pass before the congressional commissary would stop serving *Freedom Fries.*

In the months following the armistice, the French and Americans gradually broke down that huge hospital in Allerey and its motor pool, until one day, Reuben Law was the only soul still there. "I was the last man scrubbing," he recalled. "And there was an engineer that had charge of the electrical generating system for the camp and he said, 'I'm gonna leave that on and when you're through and leave here, pull this switch and that's the only thing you have to do.'" The last one to leave, he turned out the lights. Eventually he made his way to the coast and sailed back home, a journey that must have inspired in him some ambivalence — not only because of his fondness for the French, but because the trip *to* France, the previous fall, had very nearly killed him.

It wasn't seasickness, either, or the U-boat that forced the convoy to separate into two columns shortly after it set sail. He had boarded the HMS *Corona* in New York on September 29, 1918, and sailed off the next day. "Left the harbor this afternoon," reads his diary entry for September 30, 1918. "Lots of sea." Two days later, though: "Sick as the devil this morning."

"I remember they assigned me to duty at a doorway that goes to the lower deck," he told me, "and an officer came along and I failed to salute. And he checked me out, and I made some vague remark that didn't make any sense to him. And he knew right away that I had the flu and he hospitalized me." Hence his entry for October 3, 1918: "Was taken to the hospital this morning with Spanish Influenza."

Spanish influenza: the great flu pandemic of 1918. It started at Fort Riley, Kansas, in March of 1918, or so it is believed. Unlike other strains of the virus, the 1918 flu preyed mostly upon hearty adults. In eighteen months, it killed off 3 percent of the world's population, around fifty million people; some estimates double that figure. It was so terrifying that just about every country engaged in the war, Allies and Entente alike, censored news of the disease's spread. The Spanish, though — they were neutral — shared their own news of the flu, including that it had nearly killed their king, Alfonso XIII. They were rewarded for their openness by having the disease — one of the deadliest pandemics in all of history — named for them.

The flu spread quickly, tearing through the *Corona* in just a couple of days. "They converted the big, fancy dining room of the ship to a hospital," Reuben Law explained. "And so we slept, we stayed on tables. They put two tables together and there'd be two of us, and I, my head was next to the feet of the guy next to me . . . We had little pads, but they didn't amount to much. I was awfully sick." Conditions in that makeshift infirmary didn't help, either. "I remember the brother of a sergeant that was in our unit was behind me," he said. "And his feet would come to my head. And he kept kicking me in the head. He was just out of it, you know. He couldn't help it, he was just trying to survive. And he finally died." Fortunately for Reuben Law, his bunkmate's replacement "was more gentle with my head."

Things got grim pretty quickly on a ship that wasn't designed to handle a deadly epidemic. "They started putting the bodies along the outside deck," he explained, "but it got to be too many and they reverted to burying them at sea." By the time they arrived at Brest on October 13, ninety-one men on the *Corona* had died. Reuben Law was not among them, although he was still so sick that, as he told me, he had to sleep with "a sergeant on either side of me to keep me warm at night." Even so, he — and everyone else onboard — had to help unload the ship. With their reduced numbers, it took four days.

And through all of it — the delirium, the fever and kicks to the head, sleeping between two sergeants, unloading the ship, and everything that followed — Reuben Law never once failed to write a daily entry in his journal:

10/4/1918: Sick.

10/5/1918: Sick.

10/6/1918: Got my mind streightened [*sic*] out this afternoon. Had been delerious [*sic*] for four days.

10/7/1918: Sick.

10/8/1918: Sick.

10/9/1918: Sick.

10/10/1918: Sick.

10/11/1918: Carried out of the hospital this morning. Weak as the deuce.

Even if you've never been weak as the deuce, or anything "as the deuce," you've got to appreciate that kind of archaic slang. I picked up a fair bit of it in the course of interviewing a lot of men and women whose vocabularies were three generations older than mine, but perhaps the strangest little bit of argot I collected was one I encountered in a letter that Corporal Howard Verne Ramsey of Company C of the 302nd Water Tank Train wrote to his mother from France on November 3, 1918. In its penultimate paragraph, he bemoans his lack of stationery:

> I've sure got to Hooverize on paper as we are unable to get any at the Y.M.C.A. I brought this sheet from the states with me.

Yes, I know, these days we remember Herbert Clark Hoover as the thirty-first American president, a man whose ineffectual dithering in the face of the Great Depression set the stage for the advent of Franklin Delano Roosevelt and the New Deal. But a decade or so before all that, during World War I, Hoover became famous, and universally admired, as the man who saved Europe from starvation.

War, you see, is not good for farming. Land tends to get ruined once people have been fighting over it for a while, especially if those people are digging trenches and firing off hundreds or thousands of artillery shells a day. And the men who would ordinarily work that land are off somewhere in uniform, hunkered down in a trench on someone else's farmland. Oh, and the enemy has probably captured a lot of it, too, so you couldn't even get to it if you somehow managed to escape that trench. All of which added up to a severe food shortage in Europe.

Enter Mr. Hoover, a man of humble origins who had initially attained wealth and prominence as a mining engineer. Working as both an independent consultant and a lecturer, he had already earned a reputation as a man possessed of excellent organizational skills by the time war broke out in Europe, whereupon he was asked to help coordinate the safe return of more than one hundred thousand Americans who were then trapped across the Atlantic. I guess that project gave him a taste for large-scale humanitarian efforts, because as soon as he finished it he started an organization called the Committee for Relief in Belgium. Belgium, of course, had been occupied by Germany since the very beginning of the war; before the invasion, the small, highly urbanized country had only been able to produce about 25 percent of the food it consumed, importing the rest from neighboring countries. The Germans cut off those imports, and confiscated most of Belgium's homegrown food for its own consumption, which left the Belgians pretty hungry. Hoover and the CRB successfully imported nearly six million tons of food into Belgium, feeding more than nine million Belgian civilians — no simple task, considering that the Germans were deeply suspicious of the organization's motives, and the British feared that improving conditions in occupied Belgium, and thus easing tensions there, only helped the Germans in the end. Any man who could manage to appease both of them simultaneously must have been tremendously talented. And perhaps masochistic.

When America entered the fight, President Wilson recalled Hoover from London, where he'd been living since before the war, and put him in charge of the newly created United States Food Administration. The United States was larger in area than all of the European combatants (except for Russia) combined, and had plenty of fertile farmland that was unsullied by trenches and shell holes. Surely, America could feed Europe, or at least its allies, until the war was over and they could start planting again. There were only two challenges: seeing to it that Americans were OK with shipping their wheat overseas so someone else could eat it; and making sure that nobody on either end of the transaction got gouged in the process.

That second objective was relatively easy; the USFA just instituted price controls across the board. Asking Americans to sign off on shipping their own food overseas — effectively, to take food off their own plates — would prove more complicated. For one thing, it had never been done before; sure, Americans had curtailed their food consumption during the Civil War and the Revolution — but not voluntarily. The memories of those experiences were far from pleasant. And this war wasn't even being fought on American soil; it's one thing to cut back because your farm has been burned by the British, but quite another to do so on behalf of foreign civilians you can't even see. Sure, conserving would benefit soldiers, too, even American doughboys. But there is a natural human tendency, in anxious and uncertain times, to hold fast to what you have. Overcoming that, Hoover understood, would take some doing.

And so he launched one of the greatest public affairs campaigns in American history, designed not only to make Americans less uneasy about parting with their edible bounty — and, just to be clear, eating less so others might have something — but to make them actually feel good about it, and righteous, and proud to be doing so. They commissioned America's most renowned artists and illustrators, and produced dozens of posters attacking the issue from every angle. "Don't waste food while others starve!" implored one poster featuring an illustration of a gaunt mother cradling a baby as two emaciated children clutch at her skirts, all against a backdrop of a destroyed cathedral. Another pictured a corpulent plutocrat sitting at a table, smoking a fat cigar while harried servants carry off trays of half-eaten entrées; "Sir," it implored, "don't waste while your wife saves. Adopt the doctrine of the clean plate." "Eat less, and let us be thankful that we have enough to share with those who fight for freedom," advised a poster set in a brimming storehouse; an identical backdrop was employed for the message: "This is what GOD gives us. What are *you* giving so that others may live? Eat less wheat, meat, fats, sugar. Send more to Europe, or they will starve." That was direct.

"Eat more corn, oats and rye products — fish and poultry — fruits, vegetables and potatoes, baked, boiled and broiled foods," declared another poster, in what sounds like a pretty good diet plan; it almost makes you wonder if the USFA was doing the right thing in sending American wheat, meat, sugar, and fats Over There. One poster showed a bunch of lean doughboys — obviously not too much sugar or fats in their diet — charging over the top, bayonets fixed. "They are giving all," it proclaimed. "Will you send them wheat?" Posters urged households to observe "Meatless Mondays" and "Wheatless Wednesdays," women to plant "War Gardens," children to cultivate "US School Gardens," and immigrants to do their bit, too. "Food Will Win the War," proclaimed one poster, under a scene of new arrivals crowding on deck to catch their first glimpse of the Statue of Liberty (under a rainbow, no less). "You came here seeking freedom. You must now help to preserve it. Wheat is needed for the allies — Waste nothing." And just to make sure that even recent immigrants got the message, versions were printed up in Italian, Polish, Yiddish, Hungarian, and Lithuanian, too.

"Hunger breeds madness," Woodrow Wilson once said, and that quote emblazoned a number of posters; so did offerings from General Pershing, Belgian Cardinal Désiré-Joseph Mercier, the late President Lincoln, and eighteenth-century Polish generals Kosciuszko and Pulaski. The most effective entreaties, though, were neither subtle nor high-minded. "Blood or Bread" declared one poster, featuring an illustration of a shirtless doughboy cradling a wounded comrade in his arms. "Others are giving their blood. You will shorten the war — save life if you eat only what you need and waste nothing." As corporations have taken to saying these days: Do more with less.

Hooverize.

It worked. Americans ate more fish, more corn, more potatoes, more fruit; less meat, less wheat, less sugar and fats. They grew their own vegetables, put less on their plates, ate leftovers more often. And Herbert Hoover and the USFA sent $7 billion worth of food across the ocean. Yes, a dozen years later, many Americans would be reduced to living in Hoovervilles. But in 1917 and 1918, they were eager, and honored, to Hooverize. I don't know that Howard Ramsey was among them, but he did it nonetheless.

Mr. Ramsey had been born on April 2, 1898, in Rico, Colorado, a mining town in the western part of that state. Rico scarcely exists anymore, but in 1898 it was a thriving concern, big and lively enough to support Charles Allen Ramsey's dental practice. Charles had been born in Iowa (or, as his son Howard pronounced it, "Ioway"), his wife, Eva, in Kansas (pronounced the regular way). "They came to Colorado in the covered-wagon days," Howard Ramsey told me when I first met him, on October 19, 2003. We were at his daughter Coral's house in Portland, Oregon. Mr. Ramsey lived nearby, in a private home that the owners had converted into a very small assisted-living facility. I was surprised to learn that; he looked about seventy-five, thirty years younger than he was, and seemed quite robust to me. Certainly, talking to Howard Ramsey was no different than talking to any adult, except that, like every other centenarian I met, he was a bit hard of hearing. He had a very high forehead, and full, puffy white hair behind it;

wore eyeglasses so large they could have served as safety goggles, and a white, short-sleeved shirt with two pockets on the chest. Our entire conversation that first day — more than two hours of it — took place at Coral's kitchen table. Her father sat up straight, spoke easily and in a deep voice. His discharge papers said he stood five feet ten and a half inches tall, but he seemed taller than that to me.

"They used to take the kids close," he said of that covered-wagon trip. "The kids who could walk, they would let them walk . . . they'd make them walk close to the covered wagons on account of the Indians. They wouldn't let the kids wander anyplace." Mr. Ramsey wasn't sure why, exactly, his parents' families had migrated to Colorado, but apparently they weren't interested in working in the mines. His father, he told me, "went to barber college after he had four kids. Then he was a barber for a while, and then he went to dental school. He went to dental school for four years when he had four kids. So he became a dentist, and he was a dentist ever after." Howard grew up the third of four children — the oldest was his sister, Hazel, then his brother Erle, and a younger brother named Charlie — in a big house right in town. "'Course, the town wasn't much of a town," he said with a chuckle. "It had one main street, and that's about it. It had a hotel at one time, but the hotel burned down. That took care of that." After his first year of school, the family moved to nearby Telluride, which was then just another mining town, if a somewhat larger one. (In 1889, Butch Cassidy had robbed the bank there, so at least it could boast that much.) At fifteen he moved with his family to Portland; after he graduated from high school, in 1916, they all moved again, to Salt Lake City, where Howard went to work driving a taxi.

His discharge papers actually list his occupation as "chauffeur," a term a bit fancier than "taxi driver," but I don't think he would have minded either title. He'd always loved cars, ever since his father had bought one back in Rico. "We had the first and only car in that little town," he told me.

"What kind of car was it?" I asked.

"A Winton Six," he said. "It was like a . . . let me see, a Pierce-Arrow, the Winton, and the Packard. Those were the three major cars. The big cars." The Winton, he explained, "was a five-passenger car, with two extra seats in the back they added, so that made it a seven-passenger car . . . And everybody in this little town at one time or another had a ride." Eventually, Howard learned to drive on that car; and later, while driving a taxi in Salt Lake, he learned about the war. "We were right near Fort Douglas, you know," he explained, "and so Fort Douglas was all war . . . and we used to pick up a lot of soldiers, you know. They'd be in town visiting a friend, and they'd take a taxi to get back to the fort." On June 19, 1918, he and a friend from work, a fellow named Harry Cleveland, went to a recruiting station in town and enlisted. Or tried to, anyway. "We went up to sign up, and we was underweight," Howard recalled with a smile. "They wouldn't take us. So we went down into town, and we bought a bunch of bananas, and ate these bananas, and drank a lot of water." He laughed. "Then we went back, we weighed in, and we waited.

"We passed," he said.

Good thing, too; the Army needed men who knew how to drive. "Nobody drove in those days, like we do today," Corporal Ramsey explained to me eighty-five years later. "You know, driving was an exception." They were assigned to the 302nd Water Tank Train — Howard to Company C, Harry to Company D. "So after we get in the service, here were these, all these company guys, not hardly one of them could drive. We taught them how to drive, you know," he said. "We taught whole units how to drive."

The 302nd Water Tank Train is one of the most interestingly named outfits I have encountered. If you're wondering what, exactly, a water-tank train is, so did Howard Ramsey's mother; he took pains, in his letter of September 23, 1918, to explain it to her:

A Water Tank Train or motor supply train consists of 75 men and a Captain and a Lieut. 77 all-together. A train consists of 33 trucks making 33 drivers, each driver is a corporal. 33 assistant drivers who are 1st class privates. 1 truckmaster and one head mechanic who are 1st class Sergeants. 3 assistant truckmasters and 3 assistant mechanics who are all Sergeants. The extra man I think is what is called a signal man. This is about all I know about it.

They drove trucks — "white trucks" — fitted with enormous water tanks. "We carried water to the front," Mr. Ramsey told me. But that was months later, after they got to France. In between, the Army sent them to Camp Holabird, in Baltimore, for more training, and then across the Atlantic on the *Leviathan,* where, unfortunately, his experience was not entirely unlike Reuben Law's on the *Corona.* They even landed at the same port. "At Brest," he recalled, "sits a high hill. And here's everybody, half-sick from the flu — well . . . they were sick either from the flu or the seasickness — and they had to carry their packs and walk up this hill. And I'll never forget that. A lot of guys, they didn't make it. They just collapsed on that side of that hill. I'll always remember that. I carried somebody's pack for him so that he could still walk. We weren't there too long. We had, all these — two, three hundred died on the ship, so they had to all be buried there." Fortunately, Howard Ramsey had remained healthy through it all. "I didn't even get seasick," he said. "I got to wandering around one time, and I got to this part of the ship where these sick guys were, and they got me out of there."

Surprisingly — or perhaps not — there was no hint of this in his first letter home from France, dated October 8, 1918:

> We left in the afternoon. For the first few days we had a very quiet sea. Just like a lake. Very few got sick. The last days was very rough. The ships rolled and pitched. A few now got sick. But Harry and neither one felt a touch of it. Not even a headache. We got magazines and found a dandy place on deck and read out loud to each other and ate candy. . . . We were up on deck most of the time watching the flying fish and nothing but water everywhere. We sure had swell eats. I was on K.P. several times and believe me the sailors sure know how to cook. I ate enough pie to sink a ship. It was sure a swell kitchen. The trip was very uneventful as we didn't see a thing.

Not a syllable about influenza. I'm not sure if the Army forbade it, or if he just didn't wish to worry his family. He shared all kinds of other information — so much that some Army censor had to black out the date, time, and location of his arrival in France. They did, however, allow him to discuss the weather:

> It was raining when we landed and we had to march here, to our temporary camps. It was dark and the cobblestone road was full of holes. We stumbled and slipped along wading in mud and stepping in water holes.

We didn't get to see any of the town. The streets are narrow and the houses average three stories. But the lights were out and the shutters up. Occasionally we would see a gray haired woman in a window waving. . . .

Today I have just been laying around. There has been a few French girls and boys around selling nuts and grapes. They look human and we have been practicing our French on them. I have a sheet of French words I have been studying. Harry and I know about a dozen words and its fun to say Hello goodbye etc. But I think as a French-man I'd be a failure. I went to the canteen and got this paper and some American Bull Durham. I'll soon have to be using centimes and francs instead of dollars and cents. But mother I think I'll like it here. So I had better close for this time and I will write you as often as I find time. Give everyone my love.

If it sounds like Howard Ramsey's war was pretty easy, perhaps it was, at least compared to some others'. According to his discharge papers, he didn't arrive at the front until October 16, just twenty-five days before the armistice. He told me he drove a water-tank truck to the front lines exactly once; "then," he said, "they took our tank off and put seats on there, so I carried officers after that." But though, again, he rarely mentions it in his letters home (he begins that November 3 note with, "It is awful hard to write having nothing to write about"), he was, he told me, often in harm's way during those twenty-five days. The 302nd Water Tank Train was stationed just to the rear of the trenches — there was only a "pile of dirt" separating them, he recalled — and billeted, he said, "in abandoned houses and things like that." And "oh, yeah, they got shelled," he added. "All the time, when we was on the front, these shells were landing all around us."

"Did any of them ever get close to you?" I asked.

"Well, yeah, they did. Maybe in the next block, or across the — they were all over."

"This was in daytime, or at night, or both?"

"Oh, all the time. Mostly at night."

"And what would you do to take cover?"

He laughed. "Just roll up the blankets. That's about all we could do, you know."

After a while, he said, they stopped putting on their gas masks; none of the shells, to his knowledge, had ever contained gas. Still, he recalled, "it was tough to get sleep. Because every so often it was 'abandon ship!' We'd have to get up and get going." And in addition to that, he told me, "we used to get bombed every so often" — that is, by aeroplanes. It was an experience that, strangely, he appreciated. "About the only excitement we have is running for the cave or cellar when Jerry flys over," he wrote in that November 3 letter. "We occasionally see an air battle for aeroplanes are quite common here. Of course the anti-aircraft guns always open up and drive back any enemy plane."

Dramatic as that all is, the most memorable stories Howard Ramsey told me that day, and when I visited him again two years later, concerned things that happened between November 11, 1918, when the bombing and shelling stopped, and the following summer, when he left France aboard the USS *Luckenbach* (which, on a previous crossing, had carried Art Fiala home). One takes place just a few days after the armistice, when Private Ramsey was approached by a couple of officers who ordered him to drive them, in his former water-tank truck, to Germany. The reason was never clear; perhaps they were just curious to see the place. So they all drove to Germany. But soon, for whatever reason, the officers lost their nerve. "They decided that we were in too far," he recalled, "so we had to turn around. So we turned around, went back, and we came to the country called Luxembourg." And then, somewhere in Luxembourg — he didn't recall where, exactly, but the entire country is smaller than Rhode Island, so any guess stands a fair chance of being right — the officers had Private Ramsey stop the car so they could get out, perhaps to take some snapshots. "So we parked — I don't know whether we got pictures or not — but we parked along the curb," he said. "And I was waiting for these two officers to come back. Well, while I was sitting there, a little girl come up, a little girl with little blond curls. She jumped on the side of the truck, and sat down beside of me. She talked perfect English. And I found out from her, and I later verified it, that pretty much everybody in Luxembourg spoke English.

"So this little blond girl," he continued, "she sat there, and we visit back and forth. And finally she says, 'Will you give me a souvenir? If you give me a souvenir, I will give you a souvenir.'" Perhaps she had never met an American before, and was hoping for something that might teach her just a little bit about that country across the ocean. Private Ramsey was flummoxed; "I don't have any American souvenirs to give you," he told the little girl. But then, he said, "I looked all through my pockets, and I had a penny." It was the only thing he had to give, so he presented it to her; and she, in turn, pressed something into his hand. And then, he told me, "she jumped down off the truck and ran." What she gave him, he explained, "was wrapped up, it was — like a little package, like this here." He cupped his hands together tight. "So when I open it up, it was a lock of her hair. A lock about that long." He held his two index fingers up, about three inches apart. "I still got it," he said, and laughed. "Someplace, somewhere."

After that, Private Ramsey — he would be promoted to corporal in January, 1919 — took up souvenir-hunting himself back in France. His favorite trophies, he said, were German helmets; sometimes he'd lead parties of several friends and acquaintances out into the field to scavenge for them. They were plentiful, apparently, because he even managed to send quite a few home to friends and relatives. "Tell you what," he wrote his mother in March, 1919, "a Fritz helmet makes a nice flower pot. You might try it. But don't think it was gotten in the mix, for you used to find them everywhere."

"I remember one time," he told me, "I asked one of the other guys, 'Come on, Joe,' or whatever his name was, 'Let's go and get some helmets.'" So they went out and scavenged around; it turned out to be a productive afternoon. "Each of us got four, five, six German helmets," he recalled. "And we came back, and one of our trucks came by. So we flagged him down, and we went around — the panel truck had a high tailgate, like this — we took these German helmets, and we threw them over the tailgate, and then climbed up to get in." He paused, just a beat. "The truck was full of German war prisoners," he said. "We never felt so damn foolish in our lives."

He had a lot of funny stories, but of everyone I interviewed, Howard Ramsey also had the grimmest assignment after the armistice. While others were hunting deer in Germany, or relaxing at Aix-les-Bains, or being inspected by President Wilson, Corporal Ramsey and some unfortunate others were performing a duty that none of them would have requested. "We started a big cemetery in France," he recalled. "We would take the bodies from the grave to this new cemetery." He told me this very early in our first visit; in fact, it was one of the first things he said. Clearly, the experience had left quite an impression on him.

When he said "take the bodies from the grave to this new cemetery," he meant: exhume bodies from what were meant to be temporary burial sites, usually at or very near the spot where the deceased fell, a place typically marked by a wooden stake or the like, and labeled in some manner — the best bet would be to fix one of the deceased's two identification disks to the stake — so that, when a party would return in the future to reclaim the remains, they might know whose remains they were reclaiming. Of course, since lines shifted and artillery fell everywhere, a lot of remains were lost before anyone could reclaim them; and even if they were somehow found later, whatever was left to identify them might since have been blown somewhere else. War produces a lot of corpses but doesn't give you much time to deal with them properly.

The "new cemetery" he referred to is now known as Meuse-Argonne American Cemetery. It is the largest American cemetery in all of Europe, covering 130 acres; more than fourteen thousand Americans are buried there. That's more people than lived in the town in which I grew up, in Westchester County, New York, which seemed like a pretty big place to me at the time. The cemetery is divided into eight sections, each of which are exactly the same size, perfect rectangles with perfect ninety-degree corners. Every row of markers — and you can imagine how many rows there are, with fourteen thousand graves present — is unfailingly straight and evenly spaced. The lawn is the most verdant and meticulously mowed I have ever trod upon; the cemetery is without a doubt one of the three most majestic human constructions I have ever beheld. Like the other two — Hoover Dam and the Empire State Building — its scale is difficult to imagine if you've never seen it, and difficult to grasp even if you have. I spent several long days walking through it — in that part of France, in late June, the sun sets at about 10:00 p.m. — and only managed to read a small fraction of the markers.

The site of the cemetery was selected on October 14, 1918, almost a month before the Meuse-Argonne Offensive, the last great battle of the war, ended; needless to say, nothing else happened until after November 11. Howard Ramsey seemed to indicate that he and others started working on it just a few days later, and I know, from his letters, that he continued to do so until July, 1919. Very early photos of the cemetery show wooden crosses; the white marble markers were installed later. Somewhere I came upon a book of a dozen or so postcards from 1919, each one illustrated with either a different photograph of some aspect of the cemetery's construction, or a shot of the wreckage of the nearby village of Romagne-sous-Montfaucon. The book is complete; not surprisingly, none of the postcards were ever used. I'm not sure whose idea it was to print up postcards featuring scenes of the building of a massive new cemetery and the destruction of a quaint old village, but I doubt he was able to land a job at Hallmark after the war.

One of the reasons Meuse-Argonne, and the other American military cemeteries of that era, turned out so well is that their construction was personally supervised by General Pershing. In fact, he was onsite all the time; on Easter Sunday, 1919, Howard Ramsey wrote his mother that his camp had just been inspected by both Pershing and Secretary of War Newton Baker. "One time General Pershing came to interview us," Corporal Ramsey told me eighty-four years later. "This convoy was bringing General Pershing to view this scene, he came up there. So we all lined up to the back. So here comes this person's car, and another officer's car, and another officer's car, like that, four, five. And as Pershing went by, we were sending a salute. And Pershing was the only guy, the only officer in that whole convoy, that ever returned our salute.

"We always thought about that — how funny that was," he continued. "Yeah, Pershing respected us twice. Another time, we went out to pick up the troops, I forget how many each truck picked up, then we carried them over to the cemetery and let them out, and we went back to the cemetery after the ceremony and picked them up, took them back to the camp . . . [Pershing] had a platform made out where he'd go to talk, and it was over a bunch of trenches, empty trenches. But the trenches had been, you know, dug, but not filled — you know, no bodies in it. So to make this look nice so Pershing could look out over nice bodies, they stuck up planks. They filled these graves, these trenches in again, they put up a flag or a name, you know, so he'd look out over this, and it'd look nice. Soon as he left they dug the trenches up again. Oh,"

he said, laughing, "I never got over that." General Pershing's involvement with the cemetery was hardly ceremonial; he spent the last quarter century of his life as chairman of the American Battle Monuments
Commission, which oversees all overseas American military cemeteries to this day, and personally made a great many decisions regarding
World War I cemeteries' design and maintenance. One of those decisions was that it would not suffice for every unknown American soldier
buried in France to be commemorated with a cross. "He said, 'We know
that a certain percentage of the identified dead buried here are Jewish,
so that same percentage should be represented as Jewish among the
unknowns'" with a Star of David marker, explained Phil Rivers, who
was superintendent of the Meuse-Argonne American Cemetery when
I visited. "World War I was the only war for which this was done. If
you go to a World War II cemetery, all the unknowns are marked with
crosses."

Like many beautiful things, the Meuse-Argonne Cemetery was
the product of a hard, dirty, ugly process; in the beginning, Corporal
Ramsey recalled, "there were no provisions made for going and coming. So I remember one night, it was cold, and we had no blankets,
or nothing like that. We had to sleep — we slept in the cemetery, because we could sleep between the two graves, and keep the wind off
of us, see?" Still, he was fortunate compared to some, and he knew it.
The men of the 302nd Water Tank Train were chosen because they
were truck drivers; "we hauled the bodies from the cemetery to the
graveyard," he said. And while the work was unpleasant — "these bodies had been buried, you know, not in coffins or anything like that, just
in the ground," he explained — there were others working there who
had it far worse. "The colored people did all the work," he confessed.
"We didn't have to handle the bodies or anything like that. They'd put
them on a canvas, put the canvas in the box, and take the box and bury
that." All he and the rest of the 302nd Water Tank Train — every last
one of whom were white — did was drive the bodies from one place to
another.

Of course, that was unpleasant, too. "I am now hauling dead bodies,"
Howard wrote his mother at one point. "We go out on the old battle
fields and colored fellows dig them up and we haul them in here to the

cemetery. This is an enormous job and no telling when we will be thru. 15,000 more to bring in and we bring in between 200 and 300 a day." In his next letter, he elaborated somewhat:

> During the war men were buried in small quickly made and rough cemeteries or out on the field. This was the best that these men could receive during the stress of battle. But now that the war is over these men are being put in a more fitting resting place. And this is partly our job. This is a large camp consisting of mostly truck companies and negro regiments. . . .
>
> I won't write anymore or go into detail about this work as it's something a woman wouldn't enjoy.

And as he wrote that sentence, he knew — having acknowledged it already in his last letter — that he and his buddies didn't nearly have the worst of it. "I don't know how we ever got the colored people to —" he said to me at some point, but never finished the sentence. He didn't really need to.

But I'll get to that part of the story a bit later, when the time is right.

Of all the men I've discussed in this chapter, Howard Ramsey was the only one who experienced what we typically envision when we say the word "war." Reuben Law very nearly died of influenza on the trip across, but once he got to France he was far removed from the front lines. Jud Wagner got there just three weeks before it ended, too late, apparently, to make it to the front. Roy Tucker got there on the very day it ended. Homer Anderson never made it out of Pennsylvania. Harold Gardner didn't get any closer than a seat on a train, a blanket, and some socks.

Even so, that war was very important to all of them. It was such a significant event in their lives, in fact, that they were all willing to take the time, eighty-five or so years later, when they must have known well that their remaining days were few, to discuss it with me. More than just willing; they were *eager* to share these old stories with some-one one last time. Most of them hadn't been told in fifty, sixty years. Some of them had never been told before. These men had lived en-tire lifetimes — *long* lifetimes — since the events they recounted to me had transpired; in some cases, the war had occupied very few days of their existence. And yet, something about it carved in them a furrow so deep that for the remaining eight or so decades of their lives, they needed, now and again, to run a finger of memory through that groove, to feel it again for a few minutes, an hour, two hours. You might suspect, in Howard Ramsey's case, that it was about having been shelled and bombed from the air; but having visited him twice and spoken with him for several hours, I think for him it was more about building that cemetery, seeing thousands and thousands of corpses laid out, and moving them from the sites of their deaths to a burial ground of enormous scale. For Reuben Law it was, perhaps, about the wounded he saw at that hospital, and what he encountered every time he had to clean out an ambulance after transport or a truck that had come under fire, and those who had boarded the *Corona* with him but never disembarked. For Homer Anderson, I'd guess, it was about being up in those balloons and seeing, from that height, the great works of war spread out all around him: cantonments, camp sites, shooting ranges, trenchworks, maneuvers, other balloons. For Jud Wagner, I imagine, it was getting close enough to have a loaded rifle in his hands, a gas mask slung around his neck — close enough, maybe even, to hear the big guns — but not, at the last, sent into the fight. For Roy Tucker, I know, it was about those piles of people and horses that greeted him upon his arrival in France, all of them, as he said, dead to beat the band. And for Harold Gardner, I believe, it was about that feeling I imagine he experienced as he sat on the train that morning, that mix of fear and thrill and anxiety, not the same as but not altogether different from what you probably experience at that moment when the roller coaster car you're sitting in pauses for just an instant at the apex of that first great rise, the one you've just spent three whole minutes ascending, passing every slat of track with a clack-clack-clack: Here we go.

I'd say that makes him a World War I veteran. That, and that $1.00 check.

11

Loyal, True, Straight and Square

I N 1880, THERE WERE fewer than fifty million people living in the United States of America.

Between 1881 and the start of World War I, some twenty million more would arrive as immigrants.

Historians and others regard this period as the golden age of immigration, a time when so many came and so few were turned away. Not all were welcome; Chinese and Japanese, for example, were barred entirely. And not everyone in America welcomed those who were admitted. Often, the new immigrants were most fiercely spurned by first-generation Americans, the children of immigrants. Their resistance to the newcomers took many forms, from boisterous rallies and incendiary pamphlets to employers and landlords who refused to hire or rent to Irish, or to Germans, or Jews, or Italians, or Poles, or Greeks, or Bohemians, or Norwegians, or Russians, or Hungarians, or, maybe, to all of them. Still, if you wanted to come to America back then (and you weren't Chinese or Japanese), chances were very good that America wouldn't make much of a fuss about letting you in.

Once you got through the gates, though, you faced immediate and unrelenting pressure to conform, to assimilate, to stop being whatever you used to be, and all that entailed, and start being American. Proudly, fervently, and *only* American. Even Theodore Roosevelt, that great progressive, had no use for what he (and many others) called, derisively, "hyphenated Americans." He insisted that immigrants should start speaking the language as soon as they arrived; "Every immigrant who comes here should be required within five years to learn English or to leave the country," he once told a newspaper. On another occasion, he declared: "It is our boast that we admit the immigrant to full fellowship and equality with the native-born. In return we demand that he shall share our undivided allegiance to the one flag which floats over all of us." Most did, and gladly.

But even those immigrants who undertook Americanization with zeal, who anglicized their names and mastered the English language quickly and adopted western clothing and slang and attitudes and became more patriotic than most natives, had to contend with a society that saw nothing wrong with mocking them at every turn. Back then, American humor was, essentially, ethnic humor; the most successful vaudeville comedy acts were ethnic acts, in which the players assumed exaggerated accents, acted out stereotypes, and mangled the language. It was tremendously popular, even with immigrants in the audience who didn't happen to be among the groups being made fun of at that particular moment. And, strange as it may seem, even the objects of derision sometimes appreciated it; perhaps they were being mocked, but at least they were being acknowledged. They were represented.

And not just on the vaudeville stage. Since the middle of the nineteenth century, political organizations like Tammany Hall had been courting the immigrants' favor, shrewdly recognizing that, newcomers though they were, they nevertheless would soon represent votes; it took much less time to become a citizen back then than it does today. By the early twentieth century, most of the recent immigrant groups had sent some of their own to city council, statehouse, and Capitol. Perhaps the most notable of these "immigrant" congressmen was Fiorello La Guardia, born in Manhattan in 1882 to an Italian father and Jewish mother, both recent arrivals. La Guardia understood immigrant concerns and, more important, culture; he spent several years working as an interpreter at Ellis Island. And when, in 1916, he first ran for Congress from East Harlem, he addressed his prospective constituents in their native tongues — Italian, Yiddish, German, even Croatian. He won handily.

From the start, La Guardia was a progressive firebrand, not the type one would expect to favor American participation in a conflict between crumbling old empires thousands of miles away. And yet, when America did enter the war, he was commissioned an officer in the United States Army Air Service. Barely five feet tall (his first name means "little flower" in Italian), he flew bombers over Austria-Hungary and Italy. The war, it seems, was all but irresistible.

People did resist, of course. But most often, their resistance — their opposition to the war — proved very troublesome for them. And costly.

Actually, "opposing the war" was so easy that it was entirely possible to do so unwittingly. Before America entered the war, there was lots of room for disagreement on the subject. And those who disapproved of American involvement were by no means a small minority; the notion of getting into the fight was so unpopular in the United States in 1916 that President Wilson liberally deployed the slogan "He kept us out of war" to get himself reelected that year. But just a few weeks after his reinauguration, America was in it, and suddenly, prevailing attitudes changed entirely. Not about the war itself; most people can't change their deeply held beliefs so quickly, especially about a matter so grave. But literally almost overnight, it became unacceptable for people in the United States of America to voice their beliefs if they happened, still, to oppose the war. To be accurate, it wasn't even acceptable to *hold* such beliefs any longer, though if you kept them to yourself and never hinted at their existence, you might just get away with it. Then again, you might not. Even silence was often read as opposition; to be really safe, you had to be openly, loudly, boisterously in favor of the war.

And if, by some chance, you should happen to express an unfavorable opinion about it? Twenty-seven of the country's forty-eight states enacted sedition laws during the war, and most of them were used, among other things, to send dissenters to prison. One case I find particularly chilling is that of a traveling salesman who, while passing through Montana, made the mistake of referring, in conversation, to Mr. Hoover's food regulations as a "big joke"; he was arrested, tried, convicted, and sentenced to a term of seven to twenty years in prison. In all, nearly eighty men and women were convicted of sedition in Montana by the time the war ended. If you find yourself outraged over this, you may be gratified to learn that Montana's governor did, eventually, grant them all pardons.

In 2006.

Montana's law was particularly severe, which might explain why the federal government used it as the model for its own statute, the Sedition Act of 1918. That law, in turn, was actually a set of amendments to the Espionage Act of 1917, which starts off pretty reasonably — no passing on to the enemy any information about fortifications, ships, weaponry, movements, etc. — but then, in Section 3, decrees the following:

> Whoever, when the United States is at war . . . shall willfully cause or attempt to cause insubordination, disloyalty, mutiny, refusal of duty, in the military or naval forces of the United States, or shall willfully obstruct the recruiting or enlistment service of the United States, to the injury of the service or of the United States, shall be punished by a fine of not more than $10,000 or imprisonment for not more than twenty years, or both.

This might seem reasonable too, at least at first; the problem was that it was just vague enough to cover almost any kind of statement that wasn't entirely enthusiastic about the war and every last thing connected to it. Say you were in a bar somewhere, and happened to tell an old friend that sometimes you wondered if this war was worth all that trouble. Theoretically, your comment might be overheard by some young man who had yet to enlist; and if your remark should make him reconsider whether or not he should actually go through with it . . . well, then, you just obstructed the recruiting or enlistment service of the United States. And if, instead, you should call Mr. Hoover's food-conservation initiatives a "big joke," and someone who eats food should overhear you and, as a result, stop observing Meatless Mondays, the resultant smaller portion of beef on a doughboy's plate could lead to a refusal of duty on his part, and that mutiny would be traceable to you.

And the 1918 act cast an even wider net:

> Whoever, when the United States is at war, shall . . . say or do anything except by way of bona fide and not disloyal advice to an investor or investors, with intent to obstruct the sale by the United States of bonds or other securities of the United States or the making of loans by or to the United States . . . [or] willfully utter, print, write or publish any disloyal, profane, scurrilous, or abusive language about the form of government of the United States or the Constitution of the United States, or the military or naval forces of the United States, or the flag of the United States, or the uniform of the Army or Navy

of the United States into contempt, scorn, contumely, or disrepute, or shall willfully utter, print, write, or publish any language intended to incite, provoke, or encourage resistance to the United States, or to promote the cause of its enemies, or shall willfully display the flag of any foreign enemy, or shall willfully by utterance, writing, printing, publication, or language spoken, urge, incite, or advocate any curtailment of production in this country of any thing or things, product or products, necessary or essential to the prosecution of the war in which the United States may be engaged . . . and whoever shall willfully advocate, teach, defend, or suggest the doing of any of the acts or things in this section enumerated, and whoever shall by word or act support or favor the cause of any country with which the United States is at war or by word or act oppose the cause of the United States therein, shall be punished by a fine of not more than $10,000 or the imprisonment for not more than twenty years, or both: Provided, That any employee or official of the United States Government who commits any disloyal act or utters any unpatriotic or disloyal language, or who, in an abusive and violent manner criticizes the Army or Navy or the flag of the United States shall be at once dismissed from the service.

And that *really* covered just about anything you could say or do short of belting out "Over There" at the top of your lungs. You could be arrested for possession of an Austrian flag, or for saying you thought the Navy's uniforms, with those oversized floppy hats and enormous bell-bottoms, were ugly. A lot of people — according to some estimates, as many as fifteen hundred of them — were sent to prison for saying something injudicious within earshot of a government official or informer. The most prominent of these was Eugene Victor Debs, the renowned labor leader who had already run for president four times on the Socialist Party ticket. Debs gave a speech in June, 1918, in which he implied he was dismayed that nearby, three fellow Socialists were rotting in prison for speaking out against the war; a few days later he was arrested, tried on ten counts of sedition, convicted, and sentenced to ten years in prison. He ran for president a fifth time, in 1920, from the federal penitentiary in Atlanta, and won nearly a million votes — 3.5 percent of the electorate. A New York radio station was named WEVD in his honor.

Debs may have been popular with his followers, but his antiwar stance rendered him anathema to a great many others. Even more unpopular was Robert La Follette, a former governor of Wisconsin who was first elected to the United States Senate in 1906. La Follette, who called himself a progressive (technically, his party affiliation was Republican), was an unwavering opponent of the war and everything connected with it, including the Espionage Act, and he was not shy about expressing his opinions on the floor of the Senate. His fellow senators weren't shy, either: They attacked him virulently on that same floor, called him a traitor and a madman and a German agent, likened him to Benedict Arnold and Judas Iscariot, said that he should be hauled off to an internment camp, that he would be better suited to presiding over Germany's parliament. Theodore Roosevelt — a fellow progressive — referred to him as a skunk "who ought to be hung." Almost all of La Follette's friends abandoned him.

The people of Wisconsin didn't, though, and thus his job was secure. Sadly, the same was not true for the hundreds of Americans who were locked up under the Espionage and Sedition Acts, or the thousands who applied for deferments as conscientious objectors, a great many of whom were denied and faced the choice of going off to the trenches or to prison. Others, whose applications were approved, were not sent home but rather ordered to work in war-supportive industries under the auspices of the military; those who refused were also sent to prison, where they were often underfed, beaten, and put in solitary confinement. And countless others, who said and did nothing wrong at all, lost their jobs anyway because they spoke with suspicious accents or were regarded as "slackers."

And while all this was going on, America watched in virtual silence. The newspapers, ordinarily guardians of free speech, didn't condemn the Espionage and Sedition Acts; many, in fact, supported them, having previously secured a promise that the government would leave *them* alone. Intellectuals, by and large, kept mum. Nicholas Murray Butler, president of Columbia University — the main library on campus is named for him — had opposed the war in 1916; in 1917, he called opposition to it "treason," and declared that there was no place among his faculty for anyone who didn't wholeheartedly support it. Senator La Follette's many friends in academia were among the first to distance themselves from him. I guess if Teddy Roosevelt wants to have you hanged, you should expect to be forsaken by professors.

You ask: How could such things happen in America?

They couldn't have without two things: the war; and President Wilson.

The latter seems a strange thing to say given that, at this distance, Wilson is remembered as a progressive, a lone Democrat in a sea of Republican presidents, an idealist who kept the United States out of war as long as he could and then set to work on a plan to prevent all future wars, which he lamentably failed to sell to his more vengeful allies. But Wilson was also prickly and, as a knowledgeable source once told me, "remarkably thin-skinned." Abraham Lincoln, the country's last wartime president (unless you count McKinley, which you shouldn't, as his war wasn't much of one), was famous for being able to take an insult; political enemies and rivals called him everything from an idiot to a demon to a baboon, and worse. But Woodrow Wilson — well, he just couldn't take criticism of any kind: not of him, nor of his war, nor of any of his decisions. He didn't just support the Espionage Act of 1917 and the Sedition Act of 1918; he conceived them. "If there should be disloyalty," he warned, "it will be dealt with with a firm hand of stern repression." And by disloyalty, he meant criticism. Freedom of speech? No, thanks, he said. Those who were less than fully "loyal," as he would have put it, "sacrificed their right to civil liberties."

So, if you're wondering why nobody wrote another "I Didn't Raise My Boy to Be a Soldier" after 1916 — there you have it. Instead, they cranked out stirring numbers like "Our Wilson Is the Greatest Man The World Has Ever Known," and "If You Don't Like Our President Wilson (You Knife the Land That Feeds Us All)."

Harder to sing along with than "I Didn't Raise My Boy to Be a Soldier." But much safer.

The best estimates hold that some two thousand people were tried under the Espionage and Sedition Acts during the nineteen months Uncle Sam was at war with the Kaiser. About two-thirds of them were convicted. Nearly all of those went to prison. And not for sixty days, either; the typical sentence was three to twenty years. The government was methodical and ruthless in pursuing violators: In addition to its own secret agents, it depended upon the services of vigilante organizations with names like the Liberty League, the National Security League, the Home Defense League, the Anti–Yellow Dog League, and, to mix things up a bit, the Knights of Liberty. The Boy Spies of America — really — employed the nation's youth in ferreting out the unfaithful; another posse, the Sedition Slammers, sounds more like a baseball team. (I wonder if they played in the same league with all those other leagues; the Loyalty League, maybe?) My favorite, at least in terms of nomenclature: the Terrible Threateners. Did they make terrible threats, or threaten terrible characters? Or was it that they were terrible at threatening?

The largest of these groups, the American Protective League, or APL, boasted a quarter of a million members in more than five hundred American cities. Founded in early 1917, it was officially sanctioned by US Attorney General Thomas Gregory (as were many of the other, smaller organizations); its members carried badges that read "American Protective League — Secret Service." To those paying attention, though, it might have seemed like they did more attacking than protecting — spying on individuals and groups, infiltrating factories and unions, breaking up labor and Socialist rallies, investigating shopkeepers and customers to make sure they adhered to food and fuel regulations, and stopping passersby and demanding to see their draft-registration cards. Often they would infiltrate bars undercover and try to entrap patrons into making illegal statements about the war, the president, the rules of the day. Not infrequently, they succeeded.

The environment they fostered in 1917 and 1918, saturated with fear and suspicion and distrust, was hazardous enough for average citizens; for immigrants, whose American-ness was new and precarious, things were far worse. Their accents — whatever they might be — rendered them suspect. So did their funny-sounding names, their ridiculous clothing, the weird foods and spices they ate, the cacophonous languages they sometimes lapsed into, the way they couldn't talk softly or without waving their hands all over the place, and the fact that they were here, in America, trying so hard to be just like everyone else — which is, of course, exactly what everyone else told them to do. If all Americans were at risk of being collared by a federal agent or someone from the APL, it seemed that the children and grandchildren of immigrants were at even greater risk, and actual immigrants at much greater risk still. Unless, that is, you were an English immigrant; the English, apparently, were a protected class, in part because they were America's ally, and in part because America has always been infected with a peculiar Anglophilia borne, I suppose, out of guilt over the Revolution. So protected, in fact, were the British that when, in early 1917, a new motion picture titled *The Spirit of '76* cast them in an unflattering light — in 1776 — the government decided to prosecute the insult to its ally. Interestingly, they didn't go after the film's screenwriter or its director — just its producer, Robert Goldstein. An immigrant.

If the film had only been released a year earlier, in 1916, it might have garnered its producer a serious payday instead of a serious prison sentence. Pluggers Howard Johnson and Joe McCarthy had a big hit that year with their song "It's Not Your Nationality (It's Simply You)," the lyrics of which proclaim:

> *Ev'rybody has a native land in the North, South, East or West*
> *And it's only right your native land should be the place you love the best.*
> *Now, it makes no diff'rence what you are, don't wait for fame to come*
> *Just go and get it, and they'll give you credit, no matter where you're from.*

So if you've got the spirit, never mind your name, they tell us at the end of the first verse. *Folks will hear it, if you play the game.*

That, though, was 1916. When the war came to America a few months later, it suddenly made a whole lot of diff'rence what you were. Immigrants weren't merely more likely to be arrested for sedition — they were more likely to be suspected of it, too. On April 6, 1917, the day that the United States of America declared war on Germany, the Honorable Joseph Buffington, senior judge on the Third Circuit Court of Appeals, swore in a group of immigrants in Philadelphia as new citizens and took the opportunity to lecture them on the matter of loyalty; his speech was later reprinted in a booklet (available, according to its back cover, "in Bohemian, Polish, German, Italian, Hungarian and Russian"), published by — who else? — the Committee on Public Information, under the ironically ominous title *Friendly Words to the For-*

eign Born. "To-day there are 14,500,000 of men in America of foreign birth," Judge Buffington's talk begins. "There are 14,000,000 who are the children of those of foreign birth." He himself, he tells us, has been turning immigrants into citizens for a quarter century, through which work he has been brought "into close touch with the foreign-born, have learned to understand them, have believed in them, and have always said that when war faced us that these foreign-born men would prove themselves Americans. **The crux is not the fact of the hyphen, but whether the man's heart is at the American end of the hyphen.**" The CPI chose to boldface that passage, as it did the following: **"Remember what was only foolish and unwise in word and deed last week, in peace, may be treason when war comes."** Buffington's "friendly advice" is:

> to keep clear of any disloyalty; keep clear of any one who counsels or advises it. Indeed, anyone, native, naturalized, or alien, who knows of such disloyal plans, purposes, or schemes is already on dangerous ground, although he may not himself have done a thing; for as your friend I should tell you that **there is not only treason which consists of overt acts, but there is a lesser treason which consists in knowing of treason by others** against the United States and not making it known. . . .
>
> It is not necessary for me to tell you the many forms treason may take, for treason will always find a hundred different secret ways in which it can give aid and sympathy to the enemy. But right can take but one plain course. **Be loyal, true, straight and square to the Government, and you will be sure you are not committing treason. . . .**
>
> My advice to every foreign-born man who comes to me will be: **Put a flag at your door, another on your coat, and above all keep one in your heart.**

That was probably more flags than the typical native-born American even owned, but then again, immigrants felt — were made to feel — that "being American" required much more of them than it did of those who were fortunate enough to have been born on American soil. To the immigrant, it was portrayed as a state of grace that they had to work hard to achieve, and then to maintain; and the government, which fostered this aspiration, wasn't shy about exploiting it, too, most brazenly when it came to selling bonds. "Remember Your First Thrill of American Liberty" beckons one poster for the Second Liberty Loan of 1917, over a scene of immigrants up on deck, catching a glimpse of the Statue of Liberty. "YOUR DUTY — Buy United States Government Bonds." Another, featuring an image of a family — the man's archaic cravat and the woman's headscarf identify them as immigrants, although the ship behind them doesn't hurt — orders: "Remember! The Flag of Liberty — Support It!" That flag fills the top right corner of the poster; the father, clearly moved, holds his exotic-looking hat over his heart and gazes earnestly into the distance. (There's a son, too, who looks like a bit of a dullard: immigrants!) And then there's the poster for the Third Liberty Loan featuring an eagle, a couple of flags, a couple of howitzers, and these words:

ARE YOU **100%**
AMERICAN?

PROVE IT!

BUY
US GOVERNMENT BONDS

Immigrants had to prove it, and prove it, and prove it again. "What Kind of an American Are You?" demanded a 1917 song by Lew Brown and Charles McCarron; the sheet music's cover, with its scowling Uncle Sam pointing a craggy finger right in your face, features the question that was now on every native-born American's mind: "What are you doing over here?" (Interestingly, the song's composer was the Teutonically monickered Albert Von Tilzer; but since he was the younger brother of Harry Von Tilzer, one of the most successful pluggers and music publishers in American history, and since he, Albert, had written the music for "Take Me Out to the Ball Game," I guess he got a pass.) *We welcome ev'ry stranger, and we help him all we can,* the song declares, *and now that we're in danger, we depend on ev'ry man.* That's certainly fair enough, though the song takes it a few steps further when it demands:

If the Star-Spangled Banner don't make you stand and cheer,
Then what are you doing over here?

As another song title declaimed: "Loyalty Is the Word Today — Loyalty to the U.S.A."

That one was written by Dee Dooling Cahill, in collaboration with composer J. E. Andino, whose name must have seemed suspiciously foreign to many. Of course, many of the nation's pluggers were immigrants — a much greater proportion, even, than the American population as a whole, which was 15 percent foreign-born in 1910, and even more so by 1917. There are no such statistics for the denizens of Tin Pan Alley, sadly, but judging from what I've seen and read, I wouldn't be surprised if something very close to a majority of them were immigrants themselves. This makes sense, in its way: The typical plugger lived in a city and was largely self-educated; many of them were men and women whose access to more "conventional" middle-class professions was blocked in some way or other. And the more immigrants who were able to make a good living writing and selling songs — and thus attain a high profile for having done so — the more who flocked to that little, increasingly overcrowded stretch of West Twenty-eighth Street.

The apex of American songwriting was occupied (some would say still is) by an immigrant who had come over from Russia in 1893, at the age of five. Legend has it that little Israel "Izzy" Baline's *shtetl* had been burned to the ground by Cossacks, forcing the family to seek refuge across the ocean. Whether that's true or not — that sort of thing did happen, and not rarely — there can be no doubt that the family fared much better on the Lower East Side of Manhattan than they had in the Russian Pale of Settlement. As Jews in Russia, they had virtually no civil rights to speak of, and could essentially be slaughtered with impunity; in Manhattan, they might be called Kikes and Sheenies by their gentile neighbors, might have to toil twelve-hour days in overcrowded sweatshops and come home to overcrowded tenements, but at least their lives were protected by the law. They could even become American citizens, and own property, and vote.

I don't know if, as an adult and the world's most famous and successful songwriter, Izzy Baline — now going by Irving Berlin — thought about that fact every day. Certainly, no immigrant was ever prouder to be an American. Given how many odes he wrote to his adopted country, and how many of them he just gave away for little or nothing, I don't think you can make a case that he was a patriot for profit. His war, though, was an unusual one. Drafted at the age of twenty-nine, Berlin was sent to Camp Upton, in the town of Yaphank (pronounced "Yap-Hank") on Long Island, along with thousands of other immigrants from the city of New York; unlike all of them, though, he was plucked from the infantry and made the center of a special troupe whose objective was not to get the scalp of Mr. Kaiser Man, but to put together a musical revue. This he did: *Yip-Yip-Yaphank, a Military Musical Mess* debuted on Broadway the following year. It featured a number of songs that have long since been forgotten, including "Kitchen Police," "I Can Always Find a Little Sunshine at the Y.M.C.A.," and "You Can't Stay Up on Bevo," perhaps the only ode to nonalcoholic beer ever written. The show's breakout hit was "Oh! How I Hate to Get Up in the Morning," which is ironic considering that Berlin struck a deal with the Army that enabled him to ignore reveille and awaken when it suited him.

He also wrote a great many war songs beyond *Yip-Yip-Yaphank,* including "For Your Country and My Country," which informs Americans of every background: *It's your duty, and my duty, to speak with the sword not the pen.* Other songs, though, were aimed specifically at Berlin's fellow immigrants, perhaps none of them more blunt than 1917's "Let's All Be Americans Now," the chorus of which ends with: *You swore that you would so be true to your vow / Let's all be Americans now* — that vow, presumably, being the oath of citizenship. It's the second verse, though, where things really get pointed:

> *Lincoln, Grant and Washington, they were peaceful*
>   *men each one,*
> *Still they took the sword and gun,*
> *When real trouble came;*
> *And I feel somehow, they are wond'ring now,*
> *If we'll do the same.*

I'm sure there are other interpretations, but when I hear these words, nearly a century after Berlin wrote them, I feel strongly that the "we" in that last line is not the American people as a whole, but he, Israel Baline, and his fellow immigrants. I think he really believed, palpably, that America had saved his life, that without it some Cossack would have long ago split open his head; he was deeply grateful to his adopted country for every day of life it had given him, and believed fervently that his fellow immigrants — Jew or gentile, Irish or Russian or Greek or Hungarian or Italian or Pole or whatever — should feel the same, and act on those feelings.

And maybe, rich and famous and acclaimed though he was, he felt, too, what every immigrant surely felt on some level: that other Americans, native-born Americans, were disinclined to regard them as *real* Americans, but rather as Micks or Wops or Sheenies or Bohunks or Polacks — and that, to compensate, they would have to do more than just their bit. No matter that nearly 20 percent of the Army's doughboys were foreign-born; Berlin, I suspect, would have liked that figure to have been 80 percent. Let's *all* be Americans now.

He, at least, was subtle. Other pluggers, many of whom had made a good living writing "ethnic" songs before the war, were not. Some of their fruits, like "The Army's Full of Irish," are actually somewhat complimentary toward the groups they mock; others, like "When Tony Goes Over the Top" — well, not so much. The Tony in question is an immigrant from Italy, a barber *who shaves and cuts-a the hair.* When the war caught up with him in America, though, *He said skabooch, to his Marioch, he's gonna fight "Over There."* (I'm guessing his *Marioch* is the woman he married, and *skabooch* is another form of "See ya!")

Tony's a real live one; when he goes over the top, *He no think of the barber shop.* Rather, *He grab-a-da gun / and chase-a-da hun / And make 'em all run like a son-of-a-gun.* No need to question his loyalty; *With a fire in his eyes / He'll capture the Kais' / He don't care if he dies.* And: *With a rope of spagett / And-a big-a-stilette / He'll make-a the Germans sweat.* It almost sounds as if the songwriters — Alex Marr, Billy Frisch, and Archie Fletcher — actually admire Tony. Sure, he talks funny and carries a switchblade; but in the trenches, he's a real corker. An American.

Almost:

> *When Tony goes over the top*
> *Keep your eyes on that fighting wop.*

It wasn't until years after I first stumbled upon this song that I connected it to the fact that the very first World War I veteran I interviewed back in 2003 was, in fact, an Italian immigrant. Named Tony.

He was gone by then.

I had the opportunity to interview three immigrants who served in the American military during World War I. The first, of course, was Anthony Pierro; the other two, men who had never met and who lived hundreds of miles apart, came from very similar backgrounds and had surprisingly similar stories to tell. I met the first of them, Stanley Lane, in late August of 2003, about six weeks after I had first interviewed Mr. Pierro; he was living then in a pleasant nursing home in Silver Spring, Maryland. He'd been born Samuel (or, more accurately, Shmuel, or Szmul) Levine in Warsaw, Poland, on October 1, 1901, which fact makes him the youngest of all the World War I veterans I interviewed. He and his mother, Sarah, and his brothers, Edward and Oscar, sailed to America on the *Mauretania* — the *Lusitania's* sister ship — arriving in New York in April, 1908. His father, Bernard, had come across earlier, settling in the Hell's Kitchen neighborhood of Manhattan, setting up shop repairing shoes and saving his earnings until he had enough to bring over his wife and young sons. It's a common tale, except that Hell's Kitchen was not the Lower East Side; it was, rather, a predominantly Irish and Italian neighborhood. "Where all the longshoremen lived," Stanley Lane explained to me ninety-five years later. The Irish and Italians didn't pick on the Jews, he said, or at least not on him; "I was only a kid," he recalled, "and they didn't bother me." Even so, he told me, when it came time for him to attend school — one block up and another to the east — "my mother would walk us . . . because if you went from one block to the other, the kids might bother you. 'Hey, what block are you from?'" Their apartment, he said, was a tenement — a third- or fourth-floor walkup without heat, or hot water, or electricity. "Gaslights on the stairways," he recalled. "Open flames."

Nearly a decade later, the family had moved up to the Bronx, and Samuel Levine, then a teenager, had left school and "was working as a shipping clerk for a dress manufacturer named Jacobson . . . He only made wedding dresses, so he had a sort of a national reputation." He was making eight or nine dollars a week — good money back then for a boy his age. ("The average only made about five.") The office had a nice view, too; "We overlooked the armory of the 612th National Guard of New York," he recalled. That armory, on Lexington Avenue between Twenty-fifth and Twenty-sixth Streets, is still there, and is undoubtedly one of the most beautiful in the city, and quite possibly the country. In 1913, it was the site of a now-legendary art show that marked the debut of modern art in the United States.

The 612th — the "Fighting 612th," as it was then known — was an old unit. For World War I, it was absorbed into the 42nd Division, known as the "Rainbow Division" because, at a time when most Army divisions — like the YD — were regional in composition, the 42nd contained units from twenty-six states. Its nickname was coined by a young major named Douglas MacArthur. The Rainbow Division went on to become famous fighting at the Marne and Château-Thierry, Saint-Mihiel, and the Meuse-Argonne.

Back to Samuel Levine, working at a wedding dress factory on Lexington Avenue and gazing out the window at that armory. "We could see the roof," he recalled, "and they had just come back from Mexico, and they were lounging around the roof and we could see what they were doing there all of the time. I don't know, somehow it must have interested me. I used to read novels by Bret Harte, and people like that. They wrote about all the western stories, about the guides who, you know, went around with the settlers and showed them where to live and all that. That sort of thing interested me somehow. I read all those novels. And later on in that period, some kid or friend of mine enlisted — I guess he couldn't enlist somehow in the American Army, but he got into the Canadian Army, and he was only fifteen years old. And I heard about it. So I said, it's a pretty good idea. I just walked into the recruitment office in New York, and it was no problem. They didn't ask me anything. And I enlisted there."

I asked him how old he was at the time; "I was exactly sixteen," he said. It was October of 1917. No one at the recruiting station had asked to see his birth certificate, or any other proof that he was old enough to serve.

"And what did your mother think about that?" I asked him.

"I didn't tell them, see," he said. "When I enlisted there in that office, they sent me directly from there to Fort Slocum, where all the recruits went, so I didn't have to go home and tell them anything."

Straight from the recruiting office to boot camp, without a stop at home? I found that pretty surprising, and turned to Mr. Lane's son, Bruce, who was sitting nearby, to see if his face betrayed the fact that his father might be embellishing the tale a bit. It didn't.

Fort Slocum, on an island in Long Island Sound just off the coast of New Rochelle, New York, was only the first stop. As a volunteer, he was allowed to choose which type of unit he wanted to serve with. Having read all that Bret Harte, he said he wanted to be a horse soldier. The Army sent him to Fort Oglethorpe, in Georgia, to serve with the 22nd Cavalry. "Had you ever ridden a horse before?" I asked him.

"Never saw one before," he said, and smiled. He really took to riding, though, and shooting. But then the Army sent the 22nd Cavalry down to China Spring, Texas, and converted it to an artillery unit. Samuel Levine was made a signalman — "I was supposed to handle the radio and the flag, the semaphore; I could do all of that, you see" — which he enjoyed pretty well, too. Then the Army shipped them all back east, to Fort McClellan, near Anniston, Alabama, and Samuel Levine never got any closer to France, at least not in that war. He stayed in the Army for the rest of his career, more or less, serving through World War II — when he did make it overseas — and the Korean War, and rising to the rank of lieutenant colonel. He spent most of that career as Stanley Lane, having changed his name in 1930; in the peacetime Army, he told me, he'd felt he had to in order to move up.

Sam Goldberg, on the other hand, never changed his, at least not after he got to America. His American name — bestowed upon him by his father when, at the age of seven, the son came across from Lodz, Poland — was Samuel Benedict Goldberg. Or, as he pronounced it when I asked: "Sam-ewe-elle, Ben-eh-dic-T, Gol-D-ber-G." The man had the best diction of anyone I have ever met, and he was 106 years old. Back in Lodz, his name had been Shmuel Baruch Goldberg, or, as he pronounced it that day in May, 2006: "SHMU-elle, Bar-OUKKKH, Gol-D-ber-G. And don't laugh at it," he continued — for the record, I hadn't — "because all the Jewish kids I met when I came to Rhode Island thought, 'Oh, Benjamin wasn't good enough for him.' But Shmuel

Anthony Pierro in Swampscott, Massachusetts, July 19, 2003, aged 107.
Left: Anthony Pierro, 1918, aged 22.

Unless otherwise noted, all photographs are reproduced courtesy of the veterans, their families, and the author.

J. Laurence Moffitt, June, 1917, aged 20.

J. Laurence Moffitt in Orleans, Massachusetts, November 11, 2003, aged 106. He is wearing his original Army helmet from World War I.

A publicity shot of Arthur Guy Empey, taken in early 1918 on the set of *Over the Top*, the film version of his 1917 memoir of the same name, the best-selling American book about the war. In addition to starring in the picture, Empey also wrote the screenplay — and, in his spare time, gave demonstrations of trench warfare at Carnegie Hall.

This full-color, full-page ad for the Victor Victrola appeared in American magazines in 1918. "Thousands of miles from home in a land torn by battle, our boys yet listen to the spiritual voice of Art," its text proclaims. If they ever really did, it probably wasn't in a dugout, few of which were as dry and well lit as the one pictured.

Arthur Fiala, 1918, aged 19.

Arthur Fiala in Kewaunee, Wisconsin, April 30, 2005, aged 106.

Lloyd Brown in Charlotte Hall, Maryland, November 18, 2004, aged 103.

Lloyd Brown, 1918, aged 17.

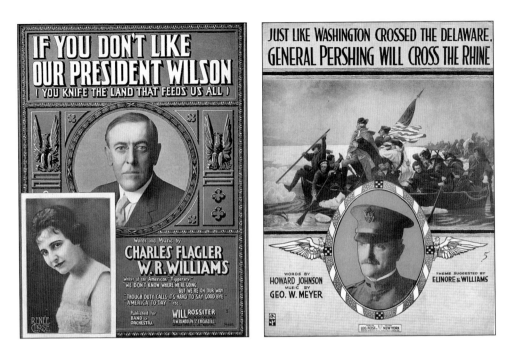

The hundreds (maybe thousands) of songs Tin Pan Alley cranked out during the nineteen months the United States was at war with Germany exalted American leaders, doughboys, and dear old Mom, while vilifying the enemy, slackers and cheapskates.

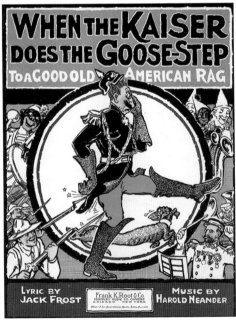

Ernest Pusey in Bradenton,
Florida, June 15, 2004, aged 109.
Left: Ernest Pusey, date unknown.

Eugene Lee, April, 1917, aged 18. *Inset:* Eugene Lee in
Syracuse, New York, December 3, 2003, aged 104.

Yanks in front line Trench
watching No Man's Land-France

During the war, the *Chicago Daily News* issued a series of postcards featuring photographs taken at the front in France. It's not clear who selected these two pictures (and another one titled "American Wounded after Bombardment"), or why they thought the folks back home might like to receive such a thing in the mail.

American advance, wounded and dying Germans
spread along the road. Belleau Wood-France

Howard Ramsey in Portland, Oregon, October 19, 2003, aged 105.

Howard Ramsey (center), 1918, aged 20.

Reuben Law, 1918, aged 20.

Reuben Law in Carson City, Nevada, July 1, 2004, aged 105.

Yeomanettes. In 1917, the Navy became the first branch of the US military to admit women; by 1918, 11,000 had signed up. All were discharged after the armistice, whether they wanted out or not. (*National Archives*)

Soldiers of the highly decorated 369th Infantry Regiment, the Harlem Hellfighters, posing with their Croix de Guerre. The 369th was one of the few colored American regiments permitted to fight the Germans — but only in French uniforms, under French commanders. (*National Archives*)

Samuel Goldberg (with his horse, Chickamauga), 1918, aged 18

Samuel Goldberg in Greenville, Rhode Island, May 16, 2006, aged 106.

George Johnson, 1918, aged 24. The nurse is his sister, Levinia.

Moses Hardy in Aberdeen, Mississippi, January 6, 2006, on his 113th birthday. No photos of Mr. Hardy in uniform, or from the World War I era, are known to exist.

George Johnson in Richmond, California, October 14, 2005, aged 111.

Eugene Lee's mess kit cover, unearthed by a collector in the woods near the French village of Lucy-le-Bocage some eighty years after Private Lee dropped it during the Battle of Belleau Wood. The rough inscription reads: "William E. Lee, 51 Co. US."

Frank Buckles's *Gott Mit Uns* belt buckle (complete with belt). These buckles were the most sought-after souvenirs of the war; few German soldiers willingly parted with them.

A display case filled with unearthed American artifacts at Gilles Lagin's Belleau Wood Museum in Marigny-en-Orxois. It holds everything from a helmet and a boot to first-aid kits and tobacco tins.

This unexploded shell surfaced one morning in a field outside Romagne more than nine decades after it was fired. Nearby were bullets, cartridges, a comb, and a uniform button. These kinds of things pop up every time fields are plowed in this part of France.

William J. Lake,
likely 1919, aged 23.

John Henry Foster Babcock (front row, center), 1916, aged 15, with other soldiers from
Canada's 146th Over-Seas Battalion.

William J. Lake in Yakima, Washington,
October 20, 2003, aged 107.

John Babcock in Spokane, Washington, July 20, 2004, aged 104.

Doughboy and *poilu* shake hands on Thiaucourt's World War I monument.

Soldiers of the 102nd Infantry Regiment captured by the Germans at Seicheprey, France, April 20, 1918. They were photographed by their captors later that day in nearby Thiaucourt.

Homemade memorial mounted on Seicheprey's World War I monument— a common sight throughout France.

Warren Hileman in Anna, Illinois, June 10, 2004, aged 102.
Left: Warren Hileman, 1919, aged 18. The coat and hat were official AEF Siberia issue.

Hildegarde Anderson Schan in Plymouth, Massachusetts, May 17, 2006, aged 107.

Hildegarde Anderson (right) in Washington, D.C., 1918, aged 19.

Wiew of the Argonne Cemetery at Romagne

1919 postcard: "View of the Argonne Cemetery at Romagne." Still under construction, it would eventually contain the bodies of more than 23,000 American soldiers.

Today the Meuse-Argonne contains some 14,000 graves. It is the largest American military cemetery in Europe.

L'Ossuaire, the ossuary at Douaumont, France. It is said to contain the bones of some 130,000 French and German soldiers killed at the Battle of Verdun in 1916.

Homemade memorial in the German military cemetery at Consenvoye, France, to 25-year-old Jakob Berger, killed on May 22, 1916, at Verdun. He is buried in the mass grave underneath.

George and Germaine Briant in Hammond, Louisiana, September 18, 2004, aged 103 and 101.

George and Germaine Briant, date unknown.

Frank Buckles, 1917, aged 16.

Frank Buckles in Charles Town, West Virginia, March 20, 2008, aged 107.

306 F.A. Batt C Camp Upton H 5667 P.N.Cor.

Baruch" — and here he spelled it out for me — "the dictionary said that *Baruch* was 'Benedict.'" *Baruch* means "blessed" in Hebrew.

His mind was no less crisp than his tongue; he had, it seemed to me, near-total recall. He knew the precise date the family had arrived in America (December 27, 1907), the name of the ship that brought him over (the Cunard Line's *Campania*), every address at which he'd lived in America — from Newark to Hartford to Atlanta and, finally, Rhode Island, where he was still living when we met — precisely how long he'd lived at each one, every employer he'd ever had, how long he had worked for each of them, and how much they'd paid him. It was, truly, a thing to behold. He had lots of memories of life in Poland, too, though not many of those seemed terribly positive. (Russia didn't hold the patent on pogroms.) He remembered his father's iron shop, in Newark ("In those days, they made fire escapes . . . There were no fire escapes in this country at that time. Then all of a sudden every city got an ordinance: fire escapes. Too many people were being killed jumping out the window. And if you opened an iron shop and made fire escapes, you had it made."), his stumbles in learning English ("A couple of months after we arrived there, I got a hold of a penny or two and five or six of the kids my age, we went to the candy store and they picked what they wanted and I said, 'I want for two cents these,' and they laughed. And I said 'Well, how do you say it?' And they said, 'I want two cents' worth of these.' Well, after that, I wasn't talking Jewish."), and the time President Taft came to town ("I saw him personally dedicate the statue of Abraham Lincoln. I didn't get too close, but I was looking over.").

He grew up to be a slight young man, five feet two or three and blond. He'd never had any trouble, he said, as a Jewish kid living in a predominantly Irish neighborhood; on the contrary, he told me, he'd actually developed a brogue. He left the public schools to go to trade school, then left trade school to go to work. He was good with numbers, tended to get jobs at manufacturers where he could use his accounting skills. He was working for the Willys-Overland automobile company in Atlanta when he joined up. "May 6, 1918," he recalled.

"Why did you enlist?" I asked him.

"Because the excitement appealed to me," he explained. "You know, I wanted to enlist in the signal corps because that was a dangerous corps. You exposed yourself by sending signals." The recruiting sergeant, though — on orders from above, or maybe his own initiative — tried to steer new enlistees to another branch of the service. "He said, 'Kid, join the cavalry. You know, ride a horse.'" The minimum weight for the cavalry was 116 pounds; Sam Goldberg weighed 104. The recruiter got him a waiver, and assigned him to M Troop of the 12th Cavalry, one of Arthur Guy Empey's old outfits. He went to Fort Oglethorpe for a week — Samuel Levine was long gone by then — and then on to Leon Springs, Texas. But the 12th, unlike the 22nd, was allowed to remain a cavalry unit, and after two months of training in Texas, it moved on to New Mexico, where it was assigned to guard the border against a Mexican invasion.

In those days, there was actually some reason to worry, if not quite fear, that Mexicans might come streaming over the border with intent to do Americans harm. On March 9, 1916, some five hundred armed Mexican revolutionaries, under orders from their leader, Pancho Villa, attacked the border town of Columbus, New Mexico, killing eighteen Americans — ten of them civilians — and burning down much of the place. Historians differ on why, exactly, Villa did this; some say he was angry at the United States for backing a rival of his, or for selling him defective bullets, or both, while others claim he needed provisions. It seems possible that all are correct, but whatever the case, Villa took the worst of it — he gravely underestimated the size of the Army garrison in Columbus, and lost eighty men there, at a time when he had only about two thousand in total. Nevertheless, his raid terrorized the United States, which sent General Pershing and his troops down to capture Villa. But they couldn't, and Villa sent his men over the border several more times, killing a handful of American soldiers in Texas in the summer of 1916. Then came the Zimmermann Telegram incident of March 1917, when Germany was caught trying to entice Mexico into attacking the United States should America enter the war, which it did shortly thereafter. So when the Army sent Sam Goldberg and the 12th Cavalry to Hachita, New Mexico — just fifty miles or so from Columbus — he had reason to think he might actually get to see some action.

He didn't. By the summer of 1918, Pancho Villa was off doing other things, and no one else in Mexico seemed interested, or in any event able, to take Herr Zimmermann up on his offer. Nevertheless, his service in the cavalry did give Sam Goldberg an appreciation of horses; his own didn't have a name — "his number was 93. But I called my horse Chickamauga," he explained, "because he was so old, he was in the Battle of Chickamauga. He was a good horse." More important, though, the cavalry was his admission ticket to the great diorama that was, and remains, America. It was a dying institution, but still proud, and it had an unusual ratio of old-timers to novices. His drill sergeant — "a Polack from Chicago" — was one of the former; when Sam arrived in M Troop, the sergeant, calling out the name "Goldberg" in the roll, laughed and said: "A Jew in the cavalry? That's gone too far." Private Goldberg didn't take it too hard, since the same sergeant, who had served in the Pacific during the Spanish-American War, also picked on him for being so small. "In the Philippines," he told Sam once, "they would issue a blanket with a little boy like you."

"Get it?" Mr. Goldberg asked me. I didn't. "They issue *a blanket*," he elaborated. "A little boy like me would be grabbed by a lot of the Filipinos, like priests do to boys."

"I see," I said.

"I knew what he meant," he continued. "I was quite sophisticated. And I said, 'Well, Sergeant' — just like this, with a smile on my face — 'where I come from, a remark like that coming from you would indicate that you might possibly be a sissy.' In those days we called a homosexual a 'sissy.' And the guy, I could see him flush. Big guy. And he walks toward me, and he says, 'What did you say?' Now, I knew he wasn't going to punch me, that's against the rules . . . so I said, 'Well, Sergeant, I heard what you said and now you heard what I said. I don't need to repeat it. So my best opinion is that you should go back and teach us to be soldiers, not to poke fun at me, because you're going to get it back.' And he walked back." Apparently he'd been no less feisty at eighteen than he was at 106.

There were, he recalled, a great many "Polacks from Chicago" in the cavalry; for some reason, he said, they had gravitated there. "Every troop had a Polish cook," he told me. His troop's cook, Kluzinski, was notoriously ill-tempered. Once, when Private Goldberg hit him up for a piece of pie, Kluzinski responded, "You get the hell out of here! You see this cleaver? I'll chop your head off." The hungry little private, though, was undeterred. "I said, 'All right, all right, OK, Klu, put it down. It's all right.' And I get to the door and I said, 'You know what Blackey Mitchell, the sergeant major, and the four other guys in head-quarters call me?' And he says, 'What?' 'The little Polack.' [In fact, what everyone *really* called him was Goldie.] And he says, 'Why do they call you that?' 'Because Blackey Mitchell looked up my service record and it says born in Poland.' 'Born in Poland?' And I says, 'Yeah,' and he said, 'Where in Poland?' And I said, 'Lodz' . . . And I said, 'See ya later, Klu.' And he says, 'Hey kid, get back here.' There's a big piece of pie . . . I walk into headquarters and they say, 'Where did you get that pie?' And I said, 'Klu gave it to me.' And he said, 'How did you manage that?' And I said, 'Diplomacy.'"

There were all kinds in the cavalry, as he would discover — Irish from New York and "hillbillies" from Tennessee, Australians and English-men, Okies and cowboys, gentlemen from refined families and tough city kids. At one point, he even told me, "We had a homosexual prob-lem." Four men, he explained, were caught fooling around under the bunk one night. "Dishonorably discharged," he recalled. "The leader was given three years in Leavenworth Penitentiary. The other two were given two years." The fourth, he said, got off on "a technicality. Seemed like they punched him around too much, a confession and so on."

Perhaps the biggest surprise, at least at first, was that "each of those troops" — that is, I Troop, K Troop, L Troop, and M Troop — "had one Jewish soldier . . . One was Harry Schneider in one troop, the other was Dan Smith, and the other was Mose Jacobson. Three of them, they all came from Louisville, Kentucky. They enlisted in 1916. They by now were career guys. Smith and the other guy, Schneider, they were tough guys. Not nasty, not at all. They were middleweight champs; they boxed all over the place . . . Jacobson was the obvious *schlemiel*. He couldn't be more of a jerk. He was just, I imagine that they were all on the same street and two of them said let's join — oh, they joined when Pancho Villa shot up Columbus. They joined, and Jacobson said, 'Me, too.' He was the last over the fence. They placed them each in differ-ent [troops], so when I joined, there was one Jew in each troop." And then there was the time when he found himself being trained at the rifle range. "Now, you get a sergeant to coach you," he recalled. "He sits and I'm sitting, aiming so on, and coaches you. And the guy coaching me was a sergeant, didn't give me his name. Handsome sort of guy. If you had to wonder what he looked like, you'd say, well, good-looking Greek, a good-looking Polack, and so on . . . And he sat with me, a couple of hours, no recognition, no hello, no buddy-buddy, nothing." Later, he learned the man's name. "Sergeant Levine," he told me. "L-E-V-I-N-E. Jewish. Handsome. He'd been there ten years, and somebody said, a sergeant said, 'That Levine, best cavalryman in the Army' . . . And he coached me in rifle. Never said to me, 'Oh, you're a Jewish kid.' Never identified himself. I didn't learn his name till quite a while after."

Clearly, it filled Private Goldberg with pride to hear a fellow Jew referred to as the "best cavalryman in the Army." And I'm sure it made him prouder still to hear, that fall, of the exploits of another Polish Jew, Abraham Krotoshinsky, in France. Krotoshinsky had immigrated to New York in 1912 because, he said later, he did not wish to be drafted into the army of the anti-Semitic czar, whom he despised. Five years later, while working as a barber, he was drafted into Company K of the 307th Infantry Regiment of the 77th Division of the Army of the United States of America, in which he was glad to serve. The 77th was a storied division; composed entirely of draftees, most of them from the city of New York, it was the first division of American draftees sent Over There, and was seen as a model for those that followed. Because it came from New York, and because so many of the men in its ranks were immigrants, it was nicknamed the "Statue of Liberty Division," although the press sometimes referred to it as the "Melting Pot Division" or the "Metropolitan Division," and devoted a great deal of space to how well the Irish and Jews and Italians and Poles and Greeks and Ukrainians and Magyars were getting along under the banner of Uncle Sam. The 77th went into action at Château-Thierry in July, 1918, and later played a critical role at the Meuse-Argonne. It was there, on October 2, that 554 men from the 77th found themselves cut off from the rest of the AEF, trapped in a forest ravine and surrounded by Germans. Newspapers, learning of their plight, dubbed them the "Lost Battalion"; they were picked off by both German snipers and poorly aimed American artillery, and had no way of communicating with headquarters except by carrier pigeon, as the Germans killed every runner they tried to send through the lines. Desperately short of food, water, and medical supplies — they took bandages off the dead to use on the wounded but still breathing — their position looked hopeless, not least to the Germans, who couldn't believe the Americans wouldn't just surrender. On October 7, they sent back a captured American, blindfolded and bearing a note that read, in part:

> It would be quite useless to resist any more, in view of the present conditions. The suffering of your wounded men can be heard over here in the German lines, and we are appealing to your humane sentiments to stop. A white flag shown by one of your men will tell us that you agree with these conditions.

It was signed: THE GERMAN COMMANDING OFFICER.

The American commanding officer, Major Charles Whittlesey, ignored the plea. Instead, he called once again for a volunteer to try to make it through the German lines and bring back reinforcements. Given what had happened to the previous runners, he must have wondered what kind of man might volunteer for such a mission. Private Abraham Krotoshinsky did.

Krotoshinsky managed to evade German fire, though it wasn't easy; at one point, sensing he was surrounded, he lay down on the ground, pretending to be dead. A German patrol came upon him. The American certainly *looked* dead. A soldier stepped on his hand anyway, just to make sure. Nothing. They moved on. Krotoshinsky waited a while, then hopped up, shook out his hand (or so I imagine), and was able, somehow, to find a hole in the German lines; he made his way through to headquarters, and led a rescue mission the next day. The Lost Battalion was saved. Nearly 200 of them had been killed; another 150 or so had been taken prisoner or gone missing. Only 194 of the original 554 were able to walk out of that ravine.

There's a lot more to the story, of course, but many of the newspapers focused on Krotoshinsky — the private, the barber, the immigrant, the hero. He was exalted as a symbol of the New American, the man who came here by choice and made good, who proved his Americanness with blood, or at least tremendous courage and resourcefulness and a crushed hand. In New York, before the war, he may have been a greenhorn, a Polack, a Yid; in the Army, he was a Yank. And if he took any abuse in the ranks on account of his origins, it was nothing compared to what immigrants were still dealing with back home.

And that, strange as it seems, made them — all of them — feel better.

I visited with Sam Goldberg for more than four hours that day in 2006, and he told me quite a few stories. I've shared some of them here. The one that has stuck with me the most, though, was this one:

> One day, I'm alone on the parade ground, there wasn't much of anything around. There was one soldier, Sergeant Moellering, you might say the handsomest soldier in the US Army. He had unusual white, silver-blond hair, white-like, if you've seen that color. Light complexion, blue eyes, about five-eleven tall. Ten years in the service. He was twenty-eight years old. M troop, my troop, hundred-yard dash he could outrun everybody. He used to be a bugler in Washington, and once in a while taps would blow and you'd hear this bugle almost sing, somebody would say Moldie was up . . . He was a soldier's soldier. Middleweight boxer, but a gentle sort of a guy. He's standing about that distance away from me, we two were alone, and he says to me, "Hey, Avrumchik." Avrumchik is, "Avrum" is Abraham and "chik" means, like, "Jimmy" [i.e., a diminutive]. And I walked over and said, "Hey, Sergeant." Sergeants don't talk that way to recruits. And I said, "How come?" He said, "Well, I'm from St. Louis and that's a German city. We lived next door to a Jewish family." And he says, "I can speak Jewish." And he did. And we started, we became friends. It was the most peculiar friendship. It just didn't happen, normally. Here's a ten-year soldier and he's the best buddy with a guy who's in a little less than a year. It just didn't make sense. And I remember how proud I was when somebody said in my presence, "Whenever you see Moldie, you see Goldie." We were buddies . . . we became absolutely like he was my big brother.

It was bad to be German in the United States of America in 1918, worse by far than to have been British in 1776, or a Southerner (or Yankee) in 1863, or Spanish in 1898. Never mind that Germans had lived in America in large numbers since colonial times. Never mind that in 1918 more Americans could trace their ancestry to Germany than to any other country. (This is still the case today, actually.) America was at war with Germany, and all things discernibly German — no matter how faint or tenuous the connection — were suspect. In a move that foreshadowed 2003's "Freedom Fries" craze, sauerkraut producers even renamed their product "Liberty Cabbage." Fortunately, that trend didn't survive the war.

And I don't think many sauerkraut magnates were hurt too badly, at least not compared to ordinary Americans of German extraction. It's safe to say that a disproportionately large number of those targeted by the American Protective League and its fellow vigilante organizations — probably quite disproportionate — bore suspiciously Teutonic surnames. They didn't have to say, do, or even think anything suspicious; often it was enough merely to have that blood in you somewhere. German American professors and teachers were pulled from the classroom, or even fired; symphonies let German American musicians, and even conductors, go. They also stopped playing music by German composers. (Mostly Wagner, from what I've read, so that actually may have worked out well.) Libraries pulled German books off their shelves. The American Red Cross refused to hire anyone with a German surname, even as a volunteer; it was rumored that German American saboteurs were putting ground glass into bandages. I suppose it never occurred to anyone at that organization that a really good German American saboteur might adopt, say, a Scottish *nom de guerre*.

The entire state of California banned the teaching of German in its public schools, decreeing it "a language that disseminates the ideals of autocracy, brutality, and hatred." (Maybe it's all those guttural consonants?) Nebraska, not satisfied to leave it at that, made it illegal to teach any language other than English. Iowa banned foreign languages — not just the teaching of, but the speaking of — in schools and other public places. In Minnesota, a minister was dragged outside and tarred and feathered after being overheard praying in German with a dying woman. And in southern Illinois, across the river from St. Louis, a German immigrant named Robert Prager — who had tried to enlist in the US Navy but was turned away because he had only one eye — was lynched by an anti-German mob of about two hundred shortly after midnight on April 5, 1918. Prager, a former baker and miner, was described by many who knew him as ornery, which was not, at the time, a hanging offense in Illinois. Being German, though, apparently was. Before they strung him up, the mob allowed him to write a brief note to his parents back in Germany, and then say a prayer. How nice; perhaps that's why the dozen men who were later tried for the lynching were summarily acquitted. "The lesson of [Prager's] death has had a wholesome effect on the Germanists of Collinsville and the rest of the nation," wrote a local newspaper publisher after the trial.

Good Americans never had to lynch another German after that. Instead, untold thousands of German Americans, many of whom just couldn't get work or even credit to buy bread, anglicized their names — names that had, in some cases, remained unchanged in America for two or even three hundred years.

But not Sergeant Edward Moellering, of the 12th United States Cavalry. He didn't need to.

It is strange to think of the Army, an institution that is by definition hierarchical and authoritarian, as being more progressive, more sensitive, more caring than the society it protects; and yet, that's exactly how things were in America during the First World War. In those days, in peacetime, when the Army was small, it was also thoroughly native; it was illegal, at those times, for anyone who was not a citizen to serve in the American military. But in wartime — especially big wars, like that one — that restriction evaporated. It didn't happen slowly, either; in April, 1917, the War Department changed its policy almost overnight from eschewing immigrants to actually soliciting them. The impetus wasn't philosophical or ideological. It was strictly practical. These immigrants, these men, these warm bodies — they were needed, very badly. As I said, nearly 20 percent of the troops in the American Expeditionary Forces were not born in America; had the war dragged on longer, that figure surely would have grown larger. Twenty percent of even four million is an awful lot of manpower.

To its credit, someone at the War Department realized this fact very early in the war, and did more than just decide to let foreign-born men serve in the AEF; they did more even than actively recruit immigrants for service. They actually set out to make immigrants feel welcome, and valued, and *comfortable* in the United States Army. They didn't merely train recruiters to speak Italian, and Yiddish, and Magyar, and Polish, and Greek, and Czech, and Serbo-Croatian, and even German; they set up an entire bureau — specifically, the Foreign-speaking Soldier Subsection (or FSS), part of the Military Morale Section of the department's Military Intelligence Division — dedicated to servicing the particular needs of immigrants. The FSS recruited ethnicity-specific clergy, brought in specialized foods and foreign-language newspapers (carefully screened, of course — at least, the newspapers were), worked with organizations like the Jewish Welfare Board, the Knights of Columbus, and the Order and Liberty Alliance (dedicated to assisting "foreign-speaking men"), and even sought, whenever possible, to commission foreign-born, foreign-speaking officers from the ranks. You know those World War II movies where the heroic platoon is composed of one of everybody? That ethic, that aspiration, was borne out of the previous war. Only the accents changed in the interim.

In 1917, it took an immigrant to the United States at least five years to earn American citizenship; unless, that is, he was serving in the military. Immigrant Army recruits were offered a fast track to citizenship and strongly (if benignly) encouraged to accept it, not as a test of their loyalty or even a reward for their service, but because it was believed that they would fight harder for a country in which they were fully invested.

Even Germans.

In some cases, German-born United States Army soldiers — or those born in other enemy lands, like the Austro-Hungarian Empire — had to have their commanding officer vouch for their loyalty in order to stay in the service; and a few were yanked out of their units temporarily while their loyalty, often without cause, was investigated. But many German immigrants did go to war for their adopted country, as did many, many more who, like Sergeant Moellering, were born in America of German ancestry. They made a profound and invaluable contribution to the war effort. They all did — immigrants and the sons and grandsons of immigrants — no matter what country they'd been born in.

How strange to think that, while everywhere else in America they were subject to scorn and suspicion and derision and detention and even violence, these huddled masses, wretched refuse, were, all in all, being treated infinitely better in the Army. And so, too, were the destitute, the hungry, the unemployed and orphaned and directionless and, in general, downtrodden.

With one really big exception.

12

Old Dixieland in France

O F THE HUNDREDS OF PIECES of World War I sheet music in my collection, one of the strangest — and this is saying quite a lot — is a composition titled "Indianola." The song, with words by Frank H. Warren and music by S. R. Henry and D. Onivas, is not, as I initially imagined, about the Delta town of Indianola, Mississippi, near which I once lived; the cover illustration, of a warrior wrapped in a striped blanket and sporting a large feather headdress, tells you that much. The gentleman pictured, it turns out, is one Chief Bug-a-Boo,

> *a Redman who, Heard the call of war (aw-aw-aw),*
> *Swift to the tent of his love he went,*
> *Sighing for his little Indianola.*
> *"Come be the bride of a chief," he cried,*
> *"Keep me wait no more (aw-aw-aw),*
> *Come and help me make my war paint fit,*
> *I do my heap big bit."*

Chief Bug-a-Boo explains his war fever to sweet Indianola:

> *Me hear cannon roar, Me help Yank win war,*
> *Me much like to kill, Scalp old Kaiser Bill;*
> *Me go to fight in France,*
> *Me do a big war dance,*
> *Me love a maiden so, wed Chief 'fore he go.*

I told you it was strange. It clearly wasn't written by Native Americans for Native Americans; I doubt that market ever registered in the collective mind of Tin Pan Alley. But then — who was it written for? Did white people actually play this song at parties? Did they wear a headdress while doing so, dance around in circles and whoop? How did they render the *aw-aw-aw*? I kind of like the image of a bunch of goofy small-town Midwesterners acting out "Indianola" in their Victorian parlors. At the same time, I kind of don't.

Less than thirty years earlier, it had been official American policy to suppress the Redman in every meaningful way, and to exterminate him when and where suppression proved impossible, or perhaps just inconvenient. So when I listen to Chief Bug-a-Boo sing about how he would like to scalp old Kaiser Bill, I can't help but think of what Muhammad Ali is reputed to have replied in 1966 when someone asked him why he didn't care for the prospect of being drafted to serve in Vietnam: "No Vietcong ever called me *Nigger.*" And Kaiser Wilhelm, deeply flawed man though he was, never stole an acre of Native American land, or ordered the relocation, or killing, of a single American Indian. At least not until they showed up in France, wearing the uniform of the American Expeditionary Forces.

Which they did — anywhere from ten thousand to eighteen thousand of them, depending upon which estimate you believe. No small numbers, those, considering that a great many Native Americans, perhaps even a majority of them, weren't even American citizens at the time — they were, as a class, the only group not covered by the Fourteenth Amendment's clause granting citizenship to anyone born in the United States. Yet they served anyway, as volunteers or draftees, fighting for a country that had usurped theirs. Some attribute their participation in the AEF to a great Indian "warrior culture" or the powerful ethos of traditionally protective clans, others to the hope that going Over There might earn them better lands, more rights, a vote. Whatever their reasons for enlisting, they served in regular Army units, alongside everyone else — bringing quite a few city kids, who knew of them only from Bret Harte novels, into contact with their first real live Indian.

And so, to all the other plaudits I've already accorded the AEF, add this one: It was about as effective a melting pot as you could find in a country that fancied itself one great big melting pot. Indians were sequestered throughout the nation, but not in the Army. Chinese may not have been welcome at Ellis Island, but they were welcome in the Statue of Liberty Division. American cavalry may have been patrolling the border to keep Pancho Villa and his minions out, but Mexican Americans could — and did — serve in those very cavalry units. Whether the War Department did this out of a sense of fair play or merely necessity is, in the end, irrelevant; bunking, eating, and fighting beside a Native American, a Chinese American, or a Mexican American makes it harder to continue regarding him as a Redskin, a Chink, or a Wetback.

There was, however, one group of Americans that the War Department could not accommodate, no matter how acute its manpower needs. Ironically, it was a group that the United States had been able to count on in every war since it had become the United States, and a few even before that. And according to the best estimates, more than 350,000 African Americans were willing to accommodate a military that was unwilling to accommodate them.

Now, when I say "accommodate," I'm not talking about desegregation; that was never for a moment considered. While plenty of black soldiers had served on both sides during the Revolutionary War, afterward, the Army became an entirely white institution, and remained so until the Civil War. The Marine Corps was even worse in that regard — it remained entirely white until *World War II.* Only the Navy enlisted black seamen for almost all of its existence, mostly because it couldn't afford to be racist; the Navy was always short of men. So in 1917, needing to raise an army of millions in mere months, the War Department set out to recruit and draft the services of hundreds of thousands of black American men — and keep them entirely separate from everyone else. But segregation is just the prologue to the very strange tale of how the Army dealt with African Americans in World War I.

Immediately following the end of the Civil War, the government of the United States dedicated itself, at least in word, to making sure that the millions of recently emancipated slaves weren't harmed or exploited or marginalized, but rather were treated fairly, represented, and given the same opportunities to succeed that everyone else in the country had been born with. And for twelve years, freedmen were educated, registered as voters, and even sent to Congress and the United States

Senate. The Thirteenth, Fourteenth, and Fifteenth Amendments enshrined these protections in the Constitution. But in 1877 all federal troops were hurriedly withdrawn from the former Confederacy, and white resistance, somewhat stifled during Reconstruction, roared into the open and quickly rolled back all of the advances of the previous twelve years. In 1896, even the Supreme Court gave racial segregation its imprimatur, in its ruling on the case of *Plessy v. Ferguson.* "Legislation," the Court decreed, "is powerless to eradicate racial instincts or to abolish distinctions based on physical differences. . . . If one race be inferior to the other socially, the Constitution of the United States cannot put them on the same plane."

White Supremacists — they called themselves such, and proudly — had a higher objective than merely keeping African Americans out of their schools, parks, restaurants, libraries, museums, theaters, swimming pools, doctor's offices, hospitals, funeral homes, and cemeteries; they didn't want them anywhere at all, unless they were there to pick crops, carry bags, cook meals, or mop the floor. So when Theodore Roosevelt invited the renowned black educator and leader Booker T. Washington to dinner at the White House in 1901, in honor of the publication of Washington's new autobiography *Up from Slavery,* many whites, especially in the South, took the news rather badly. James K. Vardaman, a future governor of Mississippi, bellowed that, merely by having Washington there, Roosevelt had rendered the White House "so saturated with the odor of the nigger that the rats have taken refuge in the stable." Senator Benjamin Tillman of South Carolina, getting right to the point, predicted that "the action of President Roosevelt in entertaining that nigger will necessitate our killing a thousand niggers in the South before they will learn their place again." Roosevelt, a man not easily cowed, never invited another black man to dine at the White House; decades would pass before another president would. In 1913, just days after he took the oath of office, President Woodrow Wilson issued an executive order racially segregating all offices and agencies of the federal government. Many black government workers lost their jobs in the process.

It was a time when racial discrimination thoroughly pervaded American life from Main Street to Pennsylvania Avenue, when African Americans were incessantly mocked and humiliated not only privately but also on the vaudeville stage, and in Tin Pan Alley, and on every newspaper's funny pages, and on the packaging of everything from pancake mix to toothpaste. Worse even than all that, though, it was an era of the most horrible interracial violence, all of it happening in only one direction. There were, for one thing, quite a few "race riots" — Irving Berlin might have recognized them as pogroms — in which white mobs rampaged through black neighborhoods and towns, killing and maiming residents and destroying homes and businesses; and there were lynchings. A lot of lynchings. In the twenty years between 1896 (the *Plessy* decision) and 1916 (Woodrow Wilson's reelection), 1,830 people were lynched in the United States of America; 1,575 of them were black.

And it was in that time, and in that America, that 350,000 black men entered the American Expeditionary Forces.

In 1919, Emmett J. Scott, a former newspaper publisher and personal secretary to the late Booker T. Washington, published *Scott's Official History of the American Negro in the World War*, the definitive contemporary account of the subject. As Scott recalls early on, it very nearly came to pass that there was no American Negro in the World War. At the start of the conflict, the Regular Army had just four colored regiments, comprising some ten thousand men. (Two of those regiments, the 9th and 10th Cavalry — Buffalo Soldiers, as they were known — served with distinction in Cuba, charging up San Juan Hill alongside Theodore Roosevelt's Rough Riders, although Frederic Remington chose not to include them in his famous painting of that battle.) Ten thousand more were serving with National Guard units, including the 15th New York, the 8th Illinois, the 1st Separate Battalion of the District of Columbia, the 1st Separate Company of Maryland, and so on — many of which had just recently spent time patrolling the Mexican border. That was fine for peacetime; but then, Scott tells us, "at the beginning of the war the War Department apparently was uncertain as to just exactly what attitude it should take with reference to having Negroes enlist. Eager youths of the race volunteered their services, but . . . Negro enlistment was discouraged." Scott quotes an Associated Press dispatch a few weeks after America entered the war:

Richmond, Va., April 24 — No more Negroes will be accepted for enlistment in the United States Army at present. This was the order
received by Major Hardeman, officer in charge of the recruiting station here, from the War Department. "Colored organizations filled,"
was the explanation.

Fortunately, the War Department soon changed its mind, in part
because of protests led by some of the country's most prominent black
citizens (including W. E. B. Du Bois, who became America's highest-
profile black leader after Booker T. Washington died in 1915), and in
part because military leaders understood that they needed every man
they could get. In the end, actually, blacks served in greater numbers
proportionate to their population than whites during that war, and
were granted fewer draft exemptions.

Black leaders, for the most part, strongly urged young black men
to enlist. Du Bois himself declared: "If this is our country, then this is
our war." Thousands stepped forward, which pleased the War Department, though many in it soon started asking vexing new questions:
Should black doughboys serve under white officers, or black? Should
they be trained in the South, where most of them were from but where,
presumably, a large mass of armed black men might touch off a panic
among local whites? Should they even be armed at home, like all other
troops, or not issued weapons until they reached France? Or not at all?
If they were to be trained at the same camps as whites, what would be
an optimal "safe ratio" of white troops to blacks?

A tremendous amount of energy went into addressing these questions, most of which were never really resolved. General Tasker Bliss,
the Army's chief of staff, favored a plan that would forestall drafting
black men as long as possible, give them minimal training at camps
close to home once they were drafted, and then ship them right off to
France.

The War Department, savvy about public relations as it was, knew
it might have some issues with the black community; when General
Bliss's proposed plan started leaking out, black leaders took their concerns directly to Secretary of War Newton D. Baker, who quickly appointed Emmett Scott to the newly created post of Special Assistant
to the Secretary of War, even giving him a five-man staff. The official

announcement, carried in a CPI newsletter, reported that Scott would serve as a "confidential advisor in matters affecting the interests of the 10,000,000 Negroes of the United States, and the part they are to play in connection with the present war." In truth, I suspect, he was supposed to be a lightning rod to insulate Secretary Baker from the anger and dissatisfaction of black leaders. Some, like Du Bois, continued to take their grievances directly to Baker anyway; in December, 1917, Baker assured Du Bois that black troops were being treated no differently than white troops.

But of course they were. Every facet of black army life, from enlistment to discharge, was kept entirely separate from white army life, and very little of it could be called equal. Housing at black army camps often consisted of tents that lacked heat and even floors. Sometimes there was no housing at all for black troops, who were left to find their own shelter wherever they could, like under trees and in dugouts. Medical care — what there was of it — was subpar, to say the least; black soldiers who presented with serious ailments were often sent away with nothing more than a spoonful of castor oil, and sometimes with simply an admonition to work through the pain. Black soldiers never got nearly as many passes and furloughs as white soldiers did. Often, they got none at all. They rarely had access to in-camp comforts like YMCA huts. There were no accommodations in or near camps for black female visitors from home — wives and mothers — until very late in the war. Even then they were rare.

African American soldiers were undertrained and underequipped; the first batch of black stevedores sent to France was actually issued blue uniforms left over from the Civil War. They were assigned work deemed "unfit" for white soldiers, and ordered into factories as strikebreakers. They were warned, in the most menacing of terms, to stay far away from French women, not to enter French homes or eat in French cafés. (French citizens, for their part, were asked by American authorities to honor American "cultural sensitivities" by adopting a policy of racial discrimination for the duration of the war.) They were, as a class, labeled — in official reports — as lazy, or simpleminded, or devious, or all three. Contemporary accounts report that they were subjected to an extraordinary amount of verbal and even physical abuse in camp, just in the course of an ordinary day. When they left camp, they were

subject to discrimination and abuse by local merchants, business owners, police officers, and, for good measure, much of the rest of the local
white population—even if they were in states, like Kansas, where
racial segregation was technically illegal. Their opportunities for advancement were severely limited; because it was considered unthinkable that a black man might issue orders to a white man, relatively few
blacks were commissioned as officers, none of them outside combat
units. As a matter of policy, none could rise above the rank of captain.
In labor battalions, even sergeants had to be white. No situation where
soldiers of different races might serve together as equals — never mind
a black soldier holding command over a white soldier—was allowed
to stand: If two soldiers of different races and identical ranks should
happen to find themselves in the same outfit, one of them—almost
always the black soldier — was transferred out. Black soldiers who entered the war as officers, from National Guard units, were often de-
moted, or transferred, or both. Lieutenant Colonel Charles Young of
the 10th Cavalry Regiment, the third African American to graduate
from West Point and the highest-ranking black officer in US Army
history to that point, was discharged for fabricated "health issues" in
the spring of 1917 to keep him from being promoted to brigadier general.

Tin Pan Alley, which had been profitably publishing "coon songs"
for decades, now seized on the opportunity to churn out a whole lot
of songs on the theme of "Guess Who's Coming to France?" There was
"Mammy's Chocolate Soldier," and "Goodbye My Chocolate Soldier
Boy," and "They'll Be Mighty Proud in Dixie of Their Old Black Joe,"
and "When I Gets Out in No Man's Land (I Can't Be Bother'd with No
Mule)," but for bitter irony, it's hard to beat Grant Clarke and George
W. Meyer's "You'll Find Old Dixieland in France," in which a white
traveler, perplexed by Swanee's sudden emptiness, queries Mammy
Gray, who informs him that all the local darkies—including Dancin'
Mose (*folks all called him "Tickle Toes"*), Old Shimme Sam (*famous
boy from Alabam'*), and every last member of Alexander's Band—have
already left for the trenches. She explains:

> *Instead of pickin' melons off the vine,*
> *They're pickin' Germans off the Rhine.*

And that line actually backs into the tragic and profoundly frustrating truth about the African American in the First World War. For, despite the greatest hopes of W. E. B. Du Bois and others, the black doughboy's khaki uniform did nothing to shield him from racist stereotyping; and because of that, he was not, for the most part, even allowed to fight the Germans.

There was one final component to General Bliss's plan for what to do with black men in the AEF, in addition to keeping them out of it for as long as possible, before giving them minimal training and shipping them off to France at the first opportunity: Once they're in France, he proposed, they should be used, exclusively, in what was then called Services of Supply, or SOS. Have them unload ships, dig latrines, build barracks for white troops, staff white mess halls — anything, really, but man the trenches. Unless it was to dig them, or shore them up.

At that time in America it was generally believed, among white scientists and laymen alike, that a black man's brain was only about three-quarters the size of a white man's; now, studies were hastily commissioned that "proved" blacks were inferior to whites in every measure of intelligence. Surely, many said, these simple souls do not, as a group, have the raw material needed for a fighting man. And the one person who might have possessed the power to single-handedly quiet all of this nonsense — General Pershing, who knew from personal experience that black men fought every bit as well as white men — remained largely silent on the question, leaving that matter to the folks back home.

Many whites, of course, used the inferiority argument as a cover for deeper fears. A man with a rifle, after all, has a certain measure of power, authority — of dignity. He also has a weapon. Even if you don't end up sending him overseas to kill white men, they worried, he might come home with a taste for it. Or at least with a distaste for being kept in his station, which was decidedly beneath theirs. "I know of no greater menace to the South than this," said James K. Vardaman, by this time a US senator from Mississippi. He didn't want blacks in the Army *at all.*

There was, in fact, so much controversy surrounding the use of black troops in the AEF, so much disagreement about how and where to train them and what to do with them afterward, that the Army still didn't have a set plan or policy in place by the time the war ended. The result was part chaos and part social engineering; white commanders in France often took it upon themselves to convert black infantry regiments into labor battalions. If they didn't do so expressly to demoralize the troops in question, they probably weren't terribly disappointed that that's exactly what happened. Not that there was any lack of honor or utility in having your rifle taken from you and replaced with a shovel; but if you joined up in part to advance your own case for equality — the equality given to you by the Constitution but taken away from you by lawmakers and judges — then it can be hard to perceive how you are advancing that case by simply doing the same thing abroad that you were doing at home.

And that, I believe, was the real reason so many whites were opposed to having blacks fight in the trenches. Yes, a man with a rifle has power, authority, dignity; but a man who uses that rifle to fight — for you — also has pride. You owe him your gratitude. And he knows it. And when this man comes back home again after putting his life at risk to defend your freedom, perhaps he'll be satisfied to just return to the way things were before. But perhaps not.

In the end, only 20 percent of all African American troops sent to France in World War I were used as fighting men. There were two colored combat divisions in the AEF, the 92nd and the 93rd, although the latter was not a true division in terms of strength. Every other combat division the Army sent to France in that war consisted of infantry regiments and artillery, but the 93rd had no artillery component of its own; there was a great deal of debate at the time over whether or not black men possessed the intelligence to man artillery. To this day, the 93rd bears the qualifying descriptor "provisional" in history books because it was always under normal divisional strength. It was the first of the two colored infantry divisions to head Over There, although, unlike most white divisions, its troops did not ship across, or even train, as a division. It contained one regiment, the 371st, of draftees; the other three comprised black National Guard outfits that were already in existence before the war started. The first of these to go across was the 15th New

York. It had been sent to train in Spartanburg, South Carolina, but after tensions arose between the soldiers and the local white population, the Army quickly shuttled the 15th NYNG to France, where they were renamed the 369th United States Infantry Regiment. They were shipped out so quickly, in fact, that when they arrived overseas, no one knew what to do with them, and for several months they were used as a labor unit. The rest of the division came across gradually, until, in April 1918, the 93rd was deemed complete (if "provisional"). And then something really strange happened: General Pershing gave them to the French.

Pershing, you may recall, put both his reputation and his popularity at great risk — at least among his British and French counterparts — with his adamant refusal to allow his divisions to be broken up and distributed, piecemeal, to foreign armies, where they would serve under foreign commanders who might deploy them wherever and however they pleased. For some reason, though, at one point he did promise the French one division; and when the 93rd was consolidated, he recognized an opportunity to simultaneously fulfill that promise and deal with the tricky question of what to do with this lone colored outfit. He seized it.

The British, who had helped train some newly arrived white American soldiers, didn't seem to care for the colored troops any more than the Americans did, and refused to help train them. The French, though, were happy to have them. For one thing, many of their colonial troops were sub-Saharan Africans; they knew that the Germans feared them terribly, particularly the Senegalese, who were reputed to collect German ears as souvenirs. But the French were also somewhat more color-blind, at that time, than the Americans and British. Not that the French were free of vile bigotry, mind you — a quick visit with Lieutenant Colonel Dreyfus at Chemin des Dames would disabuse you of that silly notion. But many French only halfheartedly honored the Americans' request to enforce racial segregation in their shops, cafés, and nightclubs, and many more ignored it entirely. And their military understood, as the saying goes, that one body can stop a bullet as well as the next. It was their country, after all, that had been turned into one enormous battlefield. So the French Army welcomed them — and immediately split them up again, scattering the four regiments among three different divisions.

The French gave them French gear (including overcoats with many pockets — much more useful, if confusing at first, than the American version), French Lebel rifles (which were inferior to American Springfields and Enfields; the Americans traded them for captured German Mausers whenever they could get away with it), and distinctive French "Adrian" helmets, which quickly became the symbol of the division. They took to each other, too, especially the 369th — nicknamed the "Harlem Hellfighters" — which had a particularly distinguished record: 191 days at the front; approximately 1,500 casualties; some 170 men awarded the Croix de Guerre; and a regimental Croix de Guerre, awarded for the Hellfighters' role in wresting the strategic town of Sechault from the Germans. The 369th also produced the country's first black World War I heroes, Sergeant Henry Johnson and Private Needham Roberts, who, while out on patrol on the night of May 14, 1918, ran into a German raiding party of more than two dozen men. Roberts was badly wounded, but when the Germans tried to drag him away, he and Johnson fought them off using everything they had — rifle, bayonet, grenades, and even a bolo knife. They managed to kill four Germans and wound a number of others before the rest ran off. The French awarded Johnson the Croix de Guerre with Star and Gold Palm; he was the first American to win such an honor in that war. His own government would later award him the Distinguished Service Cross.

In 2003.

He had died in 1929.

Another soldier of the 93rd, Corporal Freddie Stowers, would be awarded the Congressional Medal of Honor for heroically leading, on September 29, 1918, a charge on a German machine-gun emplacement after all of his officers and noncoms were killed. Stowers, too, was killed that day; he was awarded the Medal of Honor posthumously. The president who presented the medal to Corporal Stowers's two surviving sisters was not Woodrow Wilson, but George H. W. Bush; he made that presentation on April 24, 1991. At least it was still the twentieth century.

Stowers, a farm hand from South Carolina, served with the 371st Infantry Regiment, which, unlike the other three regiments in the 93rd,
was composed of draftees. It was the second-most-decorated regiment
in the division, disproving the then-common belief that the colored
Regular Army units (none of which ever got sent to France) and colored National Guard units (which made up the other three regiments
of the 93rd) had snapped up the cream of black American manhood,
leaving only the dregs for the draft board. Nevertheless, that belief
remained current throughout the war, to the great detriment of the
Army's other colored division, the 92nd, which was composed entirely
of draftees.

The 92nd had other strikes against it, too, the greatest of which was
a feud between its commanding general, Charles C. Ballou, and his
superior, General Robert Lee Bullard. Military feuds, as the soldiers
of the Yankee Division had already discovered, can prove harmful to
the troops under the command of the feuding officers, especially the
officer of lesser rank; in addition, Ballou, who was not without his
own racial insensitivities, believed — and many historians agree — that
Bullard (whose name at birth had been William Robert Bullard; he'd
changed it in honor of Robert E. Lee) was an ardent racist who resented the existence of the 92nd Division and was determined to see
it fail. The division was dogged by absurd rumors that it was full of
rapists and other criminals; its black officers, unfairly accused of in-
competence, were often transferred out and replaced by white officers,
many of whom didn't care for their assignment or the men under their
command. Still, in late August, 1918, the 92nd was sent to a sector in
the Vosges Mountains, near the German border, where they replaced
a French unit. There, over the course of a few weeks, they fought off
nearly a dozen German raids, all while being bombarded with shells
containing high explosives, shrapnel, and gas. And, on at least one occasion, something else.

On the morning of September 12, part of the 367th Infantry Regiment, crouching in trenches, donned their gas masks when they heard
the Germans start sending shells their way. Soon, though, it became
apparent that these particular shells actually contained leaflets — in
English. Scott quotes them in their entirety:

TO THE COLORED SOLDIERS OF THE AMERICAN ARMY

Hello, boys, what are you doing over here? Fighting the Germans? Why? Have they ever done you any harm? Of course some white folks and the lying English-American papers told you that the Germans ought to be wiped out for the sake of Humanity and Democracy.

What is Democracy? Personal freedom, all citizens enjoying the same rights socially and before the law. Do you enjoy the same rights as the white people do in America, the land of Freedom and Democracy, or are you rather not treated over there as second-class citizens? Can you go into a restaurant where white people dine? Can you get a seat in the theater where white people sit? Can you get a seat or a berth in the railroad car, or can you even ride, in the South, in the same street car with white people? And how about the law? Is lynching and the most horrible crimes connected therewith a lawful proceeding in a democratic country?

Now, this is all different in Germany, where they do like colored people, where they treat them as gentlemen and as white people, and quite a number of colored people have positions in business in Berlin and other German cities.

Why, then, fight the Germans only for the benefit of the Wall street [*sic*] robbers and to protect the millions they have loaned to the British, French, and Italians? You have been made the tool of the egotistic and rapacious rich in England and in America, and there is nothing in the whole game for you but broken bones, horrible wounds, spoiled health, or death. No satisfaction whatever will you get out of this unjust war.

You have never seen Germany. So you are fools if you allow people to make you hate us. Come over and see for yourself. Let those do the fighting who make the profit out of this war. Don't allow them to use you as cannon fodder. To carry a gun in this war is not an honor, but a shame. Throw it away and come over into the German lines. You will find friends who will help you along.

Whoever wrote that clearly had a powerful understanding not only of the English language, but of American history and society. I don't know how good the black people of Germany had it in 1918, or how many of them there even were, but it's hard to argue with that second paragraph; I can't imagine it didn't resonate with the men of the

367th. And yet, Scott writes, "Be it said to the honor and credit of the many thousands of Negro officers and soldiers to whom this propaganda was addressed, the invitation had no effect other than to present an intimate view of German methods and to confirm in our men a loftier conception of duty."

No one in the AEF thought to include the 92nd Division in the massive Meuse-Argonne Offensive until someone noticed, on a map, a gap in the lines in between a French unit and the American 77th Division, at which point it was decided that another French unit and the American 368th Infantry Regiment be used to fill it. At last, it seemed, black American troops were going to get to play a part in a major battle while serving under American command. As it happened, though, their performance was used by many to discredit both them and black troops in general. In truth, they never really had a chance to make good.

It would be too much to say that they were set up to fail; it's hard to believe that any military commander, no matter how racist, might ever want to see an American military unit fail in a major battle, especially considering that such a failure might potentially jeopardize other troops — white troops — not to mention the battle's resolution. On the other hand, it doesn't seem as if much consideration was given to helping them succeed, either. They were rushed to the front without much notice or adequate supplies. Many of them rode there on open flatcars, for a hundred miles or more, in the pouring rain, arriving just two days before the attack was to commence. Their officers didn't have time to do any scouting or familiarize themselves with the area. According to testimony some of them gave afterward, they weren't given specific objectives, either, or even maps. Their artillery batteries were sent to support other divisions; they did not receive essential equipment, like grenade launchers and signal flares, for several days after the battle commenced. And they were given the wrong wire cutters — instead of the heavy-duty cutters they needed to slice through entanglements the Germans had been laying down for four years, they were issued light tools that weren't up to the task — which meant that they could advance only very slowly (if at all) and in small groups, rather than with full regimental strength.

Things did not go well. Morale was low to begin with, and dropped quickly. Communications broke down between the many small units.

Orders were confused or contradictory or incomplete. Artillery support was promised (from the French) but not delivered. Some units were ordered to retreat for no apparent reason, only to be sent forward again. A few managed to break through, penetrating so far beyond the German lines that they lost contact with regimental headquarters. And the commanding officer of the lead battalion, Major Max Elser, appears to have suffered some sort of mental breakdown in the midst of the battle, withdrawing from command without actually relinquishing it. In the end, the 368th failed in its overall mission, which was to achieve liaison with the 77th Division. They were pulled from the field after five days, having suffered more than 250 casualties.

Word spread quickly: The black troops were a bust. They did not hold up under fire, but fled; they could not keep order. There was no discussion of wire cutters or artillery, of jumbled orders, of the white Major Elser. The entire 92nd Division was deemed incompetent, despite the fact that three of its four regiments had been held in reserve, kept out of the battle entirely. It was pulled from the Argonne and sent to another sector, where its troops performed admirably, but it didn't matter: They were already tainted. There was to be no redemption for them — or, in the eyes of many, any black combat troops, despite the heroic accomplishments of the Harlem Hellfighters and the rest of the 93rd Division. Detractors would cite the "failed" 92nd Division as proof that black men were unfit to serve in combat, through the next world war and right up until President Harry Truman desegregated the armed forces in 1948. And even for a while after that.

Even if few cared to investigate further the charges against the 92nd Division, the successes of the 93rd were not so easily ignored. For one thing, their exploits had been covered by newspapermen during the war, including a number of white journalists who had been disinclined, beforehand, to look favorably upon black soldiers, but who were won over after seeing the 93rd in action. Irvin Cobb, a well-known southern writer who covered the war for the *Saturday Evening Post*, was so impressed with the 369th after visiting them in France that he wrote: "A word that has been uttered billions of times in our country, sometimes in derision, sometimes in hate, sometimes in all kindliness — but which I am sure never fell on black ears but it left behind a sting for the heart — is going to have a new meaning for us, South and North too, and that hereafter n-i-g-g-e-r will merely be another way of spelling American." He was trying, anyway.

The 93rd got an awful lot of good press in America during the war, especially the 369th. As it happened, the Harlem Hellfighters were the first New York troops to return home, and on February 17, 1919, they were cheered by huge crowds of black and white spectators as they marched through Manhattan, a parade that could be regarded as the point of origin of the civil rights movement. There is, indeed, a case to be made that the movement had its genesis in that first World War, which not only afforded many thousands of African Americans the dignity of a uniform and service but took them to a country where, more often than not, they were treated just like everyone else, at least by those who weren't American. "We *return*," Du Bois wrote in the NAACP's magazine, *The Crisis*, in May, 1919. "We *return from fighting*. We *return fighting*. Make way for Democracy! We saved it in France, and by Great Jehovah, we will save it in the United States of America, or know the reason why."

In 1993, I met a very old black man in Memphis who had served in the First World War. His memory had retreated too far for him to share very much of that experience, except for one tantalizing swatch of a story: that he and all the other black soldiers at whatever camp he'd trained at had had to wear tin cans on strings around their necks as spittoons, lest they spit on the ground. I had never heard of such a thing; certainly, no one had made white soldiers do anything like that as a matter of policy. It was as if I had pressed my eye against a pinhole in a door and beheld one tiny detail, grotesquely magnified, of the pageant going on behind it. So ten years later, when I set out to find and interview America's few surviving doughboys, I wanted very badly to find and interview several who were also black. In the end, I managed to interview only two. And the second denied that he was actually black.

His name was George Henry Johnson; I learned about him from some brief newspaper article that Google brought to my attention in the fall of 2005. He lived in Richmond, California, near Oakland, and was then 111 years old. I did not know, from that article, that Mr. Johnson was African American. I did not know it, either, from the lengthy telephone conversation we had before I booked a flight to Oakland to go see him. He told me, in fact, that his mother had been born in Sweden, and that his father, a native of northern New England (or, he later said, Delaware), was of mixed European and Mohawk ancestry. But then he told me something else: that because his father had been part Mohawk and had passed on to George a somewhat swarthy complexion, when George was drafted, in 1918, the Army put him in a colored regiment.

Two weeks later, I was there.

Census records do confirm that he was, as he claimed, 111 years old, having been born in Philadelphia in May of 1894. But of all the things he told me, that little bit of information is one of the few that I know without reservation to be entirely accurate. George Henry Johnson's story comprised a great many claims and anecdotes that, I have come to understand over time, may or may not have been true; and some, I am certain, were not at all.

Now, there is plenty about George Henry Johnson that was truly remarkable. He was, after all, 111 years old, and lived on for another ten and a half months after I met him. At the time of his death, at age 112, he was among the oldest men who had ever lived. He was married to the same woman for sixty-eight years. When I met him he was blind but still lived alone in a house he had built himself seventy years earlier, mostly with wood he had salvaged.

And yet, it became apparent to me very soon after I arrived at that house, on October 14, 2005, that George Johnson was a man who could, shall we say, spin a yarn.

Take the story he told me, over the course of twenty minutes, about his childhood adventures at sea, which began when he and a friend, Charlie Porter, went across the Delaware River to the shipyards at Camden, New Jersey, to poke around a huge ship that was about to be launched — only at some point Charlie disappeared, and by the time George made it back on deck, the ship was far out at sea. So young George embarked, he said, on an odyssey that took him to South America, then South Africa, then back to South America, then England — and I'm probably missing a few stops in there; it's a hard tale to follow, even though I have a transcript of it — until finally, he said, "I arrived home on a Christmas Eve Day . . . and I got home and my mother opened the door. So now I had been gone three years. They didn't know where I was, and to stand there and see me at the door of the home, she was just amazed." That's right: From that day he'd gone off to Camden with Charlie Porter, he said, his parents had had no idea where he was. "I tried to write but I couldn't," he explained. "Didn't have enough papers or enough pencils to write." And so, "when I finally got home I was about seventeen years old . . . and we had a wonderful Christmas Day that year."

Or something like that. There were several tales of that nature; at various times, for instance, he told me that his father, or maybe his grandfather — he vacillated on this point — had been the illegitimate son of President Andrew Johnson, and that both were present on the platform at Abraham Lincoln's second inaugural address ("With malice toward none, with charity for all"), although apparently he told others it was the Gettysburg Address. He was clearly proud of his father, a "very distinguished-looking man, a very uprighteous man" who "looked like the king of England" and worked for six decades for the Baltimore & Ohio Railroad, calling trains on the platform of Thirtieth Street Station, a position of a certain prestige. That much can be verified. I even examined a picture of his father: dark three-piece suit, watch chain, wire-rim glasses, perfect posture, impeccably trimmed Vandyke, stern expression. He did bear a passing resemblance to George V, in a way.

He did not, however, look at all like a white Vermonter (or Delawarian) with a bit of Mohawk in him; nor did his mother, in the same picture, look like a Swedish immigrant. And they weren't, at least not according to the United States Census Bureau, which recorded in 1900 that James Edward Johnson had been born in Kentucky in November, 1861, Corona Mason Johnson in Maryland in October, 1864. Her parents had also been born in Maryland; James's parents had, like him, been born in Kentucky. All were listed as black. And, as far as the Army was concerned, George Johnson was colored, too.

To be honest, I don't know all that much about his military service. As I said, he never made it to France, although he told me that they were getting ready to ship out when the war ended, and that he was glad it did. He told me — and also told several other people who interviewed him on different occasions — that he was sent down to Camp Greene, North Carolina, and assigned to the "14th Company, 154th

Battalion." There was a Camp Greene near Charlotte, and some two thousand black inductees were sent there for training in the summer of 1918, exactly when Mr. Johnson was inducted into the Army; but there was no "14th Company" there (Army companies were typically lettered, not numbered), and no "154th Battalion." He gave that unit in response to a question, and gave it quickly, reflexively. Whether he had become confused over the years or was deliberately obfuscating, I don't know. He did not, he told me, have his discharge papers anymore. I can only say for certain that he served because I saw, in his house, a photograph of him in uniform.

Whatever his unit, he said he was eventually made "a postal agent" at the camp, assigned to sort and deliver the mail. When I asked him if he'd liked the Army, he replied: "No, of course not." He said it "mostly was drilling, drilling, drilling, drilling." The officers, he recalled, "treated us well." "They were all white," he told me when I asked him. "All white — that is, as far as I know." He refused to acknowledge, though, that his fellow soldiers were all black. Or even that any of them were. I asked him every which way about this, yet he always avoided using the *B* word somehow. One of his close friends was "a brown-skinned man," while another "was a kind of mulatto." The rest of his unit, he said, "were different-looking nationalities . . . there was so much of a mixture . . . that is, so far as general looks were concerned — light, brown, dark, what have you."

"Right," I said. "But there were no white soldiers in there?"

"Not that we knew of," he answered. "But there might have been."

Not really, but never mind. It wasn't just about the Army for George Johnson; he seemed unwilling or unable to comprehend the notion of blackness, or at least to acknowledge it. His father, he stated, "was a light, light brown-skinned man." Of his mother, he said: "Of course, she was naturally Caucasian." His brothers and sisters "all looked Caucasian." He described himself as "a very light brown-skinned man." (He was; in old pictures I spotted around his house he looked Caucasian, though in person, at age 111, he did, indeed, look like he was at least part Native American.) His wife's family, the Dulaneys, were also "very light brown-skinned." Ida, his wife, had had "very light brown skin — you could take her for a, oh, French — average French." He seemed mystified that I was even asking him about this. "What I can't under-stand now," he said at one point, "here in America, right here, I have so many people that come in here and ask me, 'What nationality are you?' . . . You know, in the last couple months I've been asked several times . . . and I don't know why. All my life there I was, a young man born and raised in Philadelphia, you know what I mean? The color I am — never have I . . . just like you, right here right now, you have asked me more questions about nationality than I was ever asked in my life. Back in Philadelphia, we traveled with everybody. I went to school, there were German Jews and French, and Germans and Mexicans, everything, and we never — so God have mercy on my life — I never heard a single word spoken about what nationality were they, whether they were this or that. We never thought about it!"

An unlikely story — I'll just go ahead and say impossible — from a man who was already sixty years old when the Supreme Court handed down the *Brown vs. Board of Education* decision. I'm sure he thought about it, for instance, when he was inducted into the Army, which didn't assign soldiers to colored units simply because they were swar-thy. Like the rest of America, the Army determined race by blood, not appearance. Some light-skinned African Americans, I am sure, passed for white in the AEF; but George Johnson, I discovered years later when I found a copy of his draft-registration card, didn't even try: On the blank space next to "Race," he wrote, "African."

At some point, though, between 1917 and 2005, he decided to change his answer; and over the course of several hours' conversation at his house that day, he inadvertently hinted, here and there, at why. There was the story, for example, about a fellow named Clarence with whom he used to work in the 1940s and '50s, "and he was from Mis-sissippi somewhere, and he was with me for ten or fifteen years and used to get me down . . . the way he would act — he would always act as if he was subservient to a lot of the people that come around. I don't care how light or how dark they were, if they were considered white, he always acted subservient to them. And I used to say to him, 'Clarence, why do you always act submissive? You don't have to be like that, you're just as important as they are. I say that day and time is gone. They fought a war for it. Just stop it, don't bring it back for Christ's sake!'"

But it could be that the most traumatic thing, the episode that really shook his equilibrium to the point where he had trouble even recognizing the notion of race, at least for non-Caucasians, was something that actually happened to his younger brother, Herbert, who also served in World War I — in the Navy.

Now, as little as you hear about the Navy in World War I, you hear even less about African Americans in the Navy in World War I. And, in some cases, nothing at all; Emmett Scott doesn't even mention it in his 511-page *Official History of the American Negro in the World War*, an omission that might just lead you to believe that the American Negro did not serve in the Navy at all then. But he did. As Kelly Miller, a Howard University professor and editor of *The Crisis*, wrote in *Kelly Miller's History of the World War for Human Rights* (embossed at the bottom of its front cover is the subtitle: "It is Fair to the Negro") in 1919, "During the World War, there were approximately ten thousand Negroes who voluntarily enlisted in the navy of the United States." Miller devotes an entire chapter to the Navy, in fact, most of it comprising tales of the heroism of individual black seamen. He lauds the Navy as an institution, contrasting it with the Army, "where segregation and discrimination of the rankest type force the Negro into distinct Negro units; the navy, on the other hand, has its quota of black men on every vessel carrying the starry emblem of freedom on the high seas and in every shore station." He continues, in a passage titled "Work of Colored Seamen":

> He formed a part of the crew of nearly two thousand vessels that plied the briny deep, on submarines that feared not the under sea peril, and wherever a naval engagement was undertaken or the performance of a duty by a naval vessel, the Negro, as a part of the crew of that vessel, necessarily contributed to the successful prosecution of that duty; and, whatever credit or glory is achieved for American valor, it was made possible by the faithful execution of his duty, regardless of his character. For, on a battleship where the strictest system of co-ordination and co-operation among all who compose the crew is absolutely necessary, each man is assigned a particular and a special duty independent of the other men, and should he fail

in its faithful discharge the loss of the vessel and its enterprise might possibly result.

True enough; but the Navy had its own system of segregation in place, designed to marginalize the colored seaman, and even though Miller is much more realistic in his assessment of institutionalized racism than Emmett Scott—going so far as to acknowledge that every black cadet who'd ever been admitted to the United States Naval Academy had been run out before graduating (Annapolis wouldn't graduate an African American until 1949), that "the awarding of commissions was made to inexperienced white boys with no prior naval experience or demonstrated ability in preference to the Negro," that in fact no black man had yet been commissioned as an officer in the history of the United States Navy—even he does not present the full story, which is this: The Navy, unwilling or unable to build and launch separate colored warships, instead created an unwritten but rigid caste system that kept the races separated onboard shared vessels by assigning them different duties. With just a handful of individual exceptions (all of them sailors who had already been in service before the war), blacks were consigned to kitchen and mess duty and, in a few cases, to engine and boiler rooms; and whites to every other station onboard. As Secretary of the Navy Josephus Daniels explained it in a letter to a New Jersey congressman: "As a matter of policy . . . to avoid friction between the two races, it has been customary to enlist colored men in the various ratings of the messmen branch; that is cooks, stewards, and mess attendants, and in the lower ratings of the fireroom; thus permitting colored men to sleep and eat by themselves." In other words, no colored seaman manned any guns, swabbed any decks, or otherwise worked out in the open air on any United States naval vessel during the First World War—and of course, none worked side by side with white men. And here is where Herbert Johnson got himself into trouble.

Nearly nine decades later, George Johnson recalled that his younger brother, Herbert, born in Philadelphia in 1896, "was lighter than me. Nobody would ever question him as to whether he was . . . everyone just figured he was completely white. He looked like a Caucasian." And so, Mr. Johnson explained, Herbert, "being of a light color, when they went and drafted him, sent him to the ship, they asked him what was he; just like you ask me. He says, 'I don't know exactly,' but he looked . . ." His voice trailed off.

It's questionable whether or not Herbert Johnson was drafted; the Navy generally relied on volunteers. And whether or not the conversation in question happened that way, on Herbert's draft-registration card he crossed out the other three options under race — White, Indian, and Oriental — leaving just Negro standing; but the type is very small, and perhaps the Navy overlooked it. Or, more likely, Herbert didn't wait to be drafted, but went ahead and enlisted in the Navy and, when asked his race at the recruiting station, decided on the spot that he would try to pass for white. However it happened, he was taken for white, and assigned to a battleship (his brother no longer remembered the name), which eventually set sail for France. "They had him working on the deck," George Johnson told me that day in 2005. "Him being on the deck, he was there with most of the American soldiers." *American*: i.e., white. "On the deck," he said again, a minute or two later, "completely white sailors." And Herbert.

So there he was on some American battleship in 1917, far out at sea, "scrubbing decks," his brother explained, "and washing the decks, and washing clothes on the main deck," until, at some point, a rumor started circulating onboard regarding Herbert Johnson. "They probably suspected in some way that he wasn't completely white, you know what I mean?" is how his brother chose to articulate it. And this rumor persisted, until, finally, four officers approached Herbert Johnson and asked him about it. "I guess they asked him his different nationality insofar as country was concerned," George Johnson put it, in that strange, tortured way of his. And, asked about it directly, Mr. Johnson recalled, Herbert "said he wasn't white."

"Why did he say that?" I asked Mr. Johnson.

"I don't know why," he replied brusquely, then proceeded to put himself in the minds of the officers: "'Oh my God, no, you can't put him in the kitchen,' because most of the people in the kitchen were all black," he declaimed. And Herbert, he reiterated, "was like a white boy." Hence the dilemma. "You're too dark to be down there on the deck; you're too light to be in the kitchen, because they're all black in the kitchen." And so, he explained, "the best thing they could do was take him, and 'have you as our own, and let you take care of us.'" In other words, feeling that they couldn't very well return him to work among the white seamen, but also unwilling to have him go work among the other black seamen, those four officers sent him, alone, upstairs to their cabins, and made him their valet. "Up on the very top deck . . . He had to fix their arrangements, their meals, take care of them and wait on them," his brother explained. "Making up the beds . . . keep their clothes and everything clean and dusted." It was an elegant solution for everyone — except Herbert.

"Many a time," his older brother told me, "he'd sit there and look down and see the men working on the deck, and wish he could do a little work . . . He wanted to get down there. He said they all weren't just working like dogs — [they were] laughing and joking and having fun. He said he just felt so isolated." He spent the better part of two years that way; became depressed. "You know, he felt kind of dreary up there by himself all the time . . . That was just like being in a prison," George Johnson said of his brother's "promotion." "All the work he could do he would do in a couple of hours; and then, all day long, doing nothing but sitting up there, looking down at them."

This tale, of the bizarre contortions four Navy officers put themselves through in the name of White Supremacy, seems even stranger when you remember that it was Navy Secretary Daniels who first opened a branch of the armed forces to women. He even admitted a few black Yeomanettes. But just as all of the Navy's women were discharged after the armistice, so were all the black seamen who had enlisted during the war. African Americans would not be allowed to enlist in the Navy again until 1932.

As I said, George Johnson was actually the second African American World War I veteran I interviewed. Two years earlier, after months of fruitless attempts, I had found the first, one Moses Hardy of Aberdeen, Mississippi. Of the fifteen Mississippians on the French List, he was the only one still living. I had tried the other fourteen first, saving him for last because, at 110 years and eight months, he was by far the oldest in the lot. He was not listed in the phone book, so I dialed a number of other Hardys in Aberdeen until one — Frederick — answered. I told him who I was and why I was calling, and then asked, in a tone that strongly hinted that I knew the effort was futile, if he knew Moses Hardy and, more important, if there was any chance he might still be alive.

"He's my grandfather," Frederick told me. "And he is."

I got down there in a hurry.

Aberdeen is near the Alabama state line in northeastern Mississippi, a few hours from where I had lived in the Delta; it's a pretty little antebellum village on the Tombigbee River, with a quaint downtown (featuring a great old movie house) and a sprawling historic cemetery filled with big old trees. As I strolled through that old burying ground the first time, thinking about the visit I was about to make, I noticed that a lot of the graves therein belonged to veterans, men who had served in every American war going back to the Revolution. Quite a few were Civil War stones, markers for men who had fought for states' rights and the Confederacy, but also, whether they cared for the notion or not, to keep Moses Hardy's ancestors enslaved.

Did I say his ancestors? I meant: his parents. Morris and Nancy Hardy had been born slaves. And not just born; according to the 1900 census, Morris had been born in Texas in 1830 (or Tennessee in 1834, depending upon which census you believe), and Nancy in Mississippi in 1849, meaning they had been thirty-five (or thirty-one) and sixteen years old, respectively, when the Civil War ended and the Thirteenth Amendment officially abolished slavery. When they were married, on February 19, 1868 — Frederick later sent me a copy of the marriage bond for "Mr. Morris Hardy, Freedman, and Miss Nancy Reynolds, Freedwoman" — Andrew Johnson, who had ascended to the presidency upon Abraham Lincoln's assassination, was still in the White House, where he was doing his best to keep Reconstruction from proceeding. And now, in the age of cellular telephones and broadband Internet and HDTV and DVRs, I was about to interview their youngest son, Moses, named for that first Great Emancipator.

Moses Hardy resided in a nursing home a few blocks from the old cemetery. It was a nice enough place, and the staff were friendly and helpful in that Mississippi kind of way; and yet it troubled me for some reason that, while they all liked the man pretty well, no one seemed to think it was any great shakes that he was there. Perhaps they might have had the same feelings about, say, the fact that I walk by the Empire State Building all the time without looking up; but this was a man, one of the oldest in the world, the son of former slaves, a World War I veteran. Surely, that was more remarkable even than King Kong's erstwhile perch. Which I do look up at, sometimes.

Frederick, who was in the process of moving to Tennessee at the time, couldn't be there that Sunday afternoon, nor could his father, Haywood (who had served in World War II) — nor, possibly, Frederick had warned me, any other family members. I felt a bit concerned about interviewing a veteran without any relatives or friends present to help facilitate; someone or other had always been there in the past, and none of those men had been 110 years old. Worse still, soon after I arrived and set up and started talking to Moses Hardy, it became apparent to me that no one had even told the man I'd be coming to see him, much less why. He seemed a bit confused, if not wary, that first time — I would visit him twice more, the last time on the occasion of his 113th birthday — but he talked to me anyway. The second time I came by, about nine months later, he was much more comfortable; he seemed to remember me, though it's entirely possible that I'm flattering myself. He was dark-skinned and almost entirely bald, with just a dusting of white hair on the sides of his head. I never saw him but that he was lying flat on his back, head propped on a pillow, blanket drawn up almost to his shoulders. Every once in a while, a thin hand would emerge from underneath that blanket and run its long, bent fingers across his forehead or stroke his chin. Aside from that, the only times I ever saw him move at all were when he would lift his head off the pillow in order to hear me better, an act that always made me feel slightly guilty. People at the nursing home told me they'd never seen him get out of that bed in the several years they'd been working there, and yet he never developed bedsores. Like Fred Hale, it would seem, Moses Hardy was some kind of a superman. Did I mention that he had worked his farm *and* held two other jobs his entire adult life? That he drove until he was 106, and stopped only because his children started hiding his car keys? That he served as the superintendent of the Mount Olivet Missionary Baptist Church's Sunday school for *seventy-five years?*

Maybe there's something to all this clean-living business. Moses Hardy was raised on the 274-acre farm outside Aberdeen that his parents had purchased in 1874 for a dollar an acre, an act that in itself made them far more fortunate than most of their fellow freedmen and -women. They worked hard, ate and had only what they grew or harvested or made themselves. When I asked him what kind of farm chores he had done most often while growing up, he said: "Picked cotton and corn." He ate carefully — a lot of vegetables, sweet potatoes and cabbage and peas, some cornbread, some buttermilk. Never drank or smoked. His one indulgence was Dr Pepper; he liked to tell people that was the only doctor he cared for. He didn't go in for medicine. He was devoted to his wife. He was usually the first person to show up for Sunday-morning services at Mount Olivet, which he had helped found, and where he was also a deacon. "He didn't put up with any mess," his son, Haywood, once told a reporter.

He was born, he told me, "January sixth, but I don't know the year." The 1900 census says it was 1894, while the 1920 census says 1891. The family, though, generally believes the 1910 census, which reports that he was born in 1893. "Might have been," he himself said of that theory. "I don't know." He never came around on the matter; when I asked him about it during subsequent visits, he would only acknowledge, "That's what they say." And add, usually: "They don't know." (He also refused to acknowledge that he actually lived at the nursing home, insisting: "I'm just staying here for a while, until I get better.")

I never could get him to tell me anything about his parents' time as slaves; I got the impression that they hadn't spoken of it all that much. But they had certainly been beneficiaries of Reconstruction while it lasted, marrying, buying that farm, and, whether or not they managed to prosper, at the very least being in command of their own lives. Moses was the youngest of nine children, born after a quarter century of marriage, when Nancy was forty-four and Morris nearly sixty, or maybe sixty-three. He may have been the baby, but he was not spoiled. He went to work on the farm at a very young age, even as he went to school, which he left, he told me, only when he was "good and grown." He stayed there even after he was married, at the age of twenty-five, to a nineteen-year-old woman named Fannie Lou Marshall. And then, just three months later, he was in the Army. "I didn't join," he explained. "They just — they drafted me." And quickly put him on a train. "Camp Funston, Kansas," he told me. "Way up yonder."

Someone at the draft board must have seen something in Moses Hardy, because he was put in a special kind of regiment, somewhat different from the labor battalions that caught the vast majority of black draftees. It was known as a Pioneer Infantry unit — the 805th PI, a freestanding regiment. The term "Pioneer Infantry" fell out of use long ago; these days, they're known, at least in the United States Army, as combat engineers — soldiers who build things, like bridges and railroads, that their army needs, while destroying similar things that the enemy needs. I once came across a quote from an officer in such a unit in the AEF, who explained that Pioneer Infantry "did everything the infantry was too proud to do, and the engineers too lazy to do." And they did it all right up at the front, often following very closely behind advancing combat troops. There were white PI regiments and colored PI regiments, and because they worked so close to the enemy, all of them were issued rifles and gas masks, just like regular infantry. Outside of the 92nd and 93rd Divisions, PI regiments contained the only armed African American troops in France; the vast majority of black soldiers in the AEF were SOS, service troops, and thus issued not so much as a slingshot. Those rifles meant a great deal to the men of the colored PI regiments — more, perhaps, than many of their white commanders understood. "Oh, it was long," Moses Hardy recalled, fondly. "Yeah, it was a long rifle."

"Did they teach you how to shoot?" I asked him.

"I already know how to shoot when I went to the Army," he replied.

"How did you know?"

He looked at me quizzically. "Shoot a gun?" he asked.

"Yes," I said. "How did you know how to shoot a gun?"

He stared at me for a moment, perhaps in disbelief. "I come up on a farm!" he declared. "I knowed how!" A friend who had come along for that visit laughed out loud at my urban ignorance; she was from Alabama, and knew better.

Mr. Hardy didn't have much to say about Camp Funston — named for Pershing's superior who had died suddenly, opening the way for Black Jack to take command of the AEF — except: "That's where I got my clothes and everything." I asked him how long he was there. "Oh, it wasn't no time," he told me. "They sent us right on." For the record, it was a bit more than two months. They boarded trains on August

27, 1918, and made a stop at, curiously, the Canadian side of Niagara Falls, where the troops paraded through a town; and then at Camp Upton, on Long Island, where they were outfitted before moving on yet again, this time boarding a train at 2:00 a.m. Mr. Hardy did not speak of any of this, only of reaching the train's destination, Quebec (which he pronounced "QUEE-bec") City, and boarding a transport ship, the *Saxonia* (which he pronounced "Sax-OH-nee"). "We went over from Quebec, Canada, to Liverpool, England," he told me. "We stayed there for a while, and then we crossed the English Channel, and *then* we got in France."

"And what did you do over in France?" I asked him.

"They drilled us," he said. "They drilled us."

"Did you go into battle?"

"No, we didn't get into battle. They just drilled us all the time, so if they needed us, we'd know."

"What was the drilling like?" I asked him at one point. "What did they make you do?"

"We did a lot of walking," he said. "Walking. And then they had us use our rifles and everything. That's what training was for — we used our rifles, so when they needed us on the front, we'd know what to do."

"Did they make you carry a heavy pack?" I asked him.

"Yeah," he said, nodding.

"How heavy was it?"

"Ninety pounds," he replied matter-of-factly.

To hear him tell it, there wasn't much to his time in France. As he remembered it, army life was mostly "drilling. That was all we had to do." They drilled six days a week, he said; "they let us off some Sundays, just sit around the house, around the camp, that's all. There was nothing to do." On another occasion, he told me, "When we was in camp, we would be in the house . . . We wouldn't sit out. We didn't sit out. We sat inside the camp all the time." He seemed to recall that other men left camp at times, but he never did. He did write letters, he said, and got one from his wife nearly every day. "And if I didn't have time to write a letter," he said, "I just wasn't doing nothing."

Well, not exactly *nothing*. There was the work for which he and the rest of the 805th were sent to France. And yet he either didn't remember it or chose not to speak of it. But whatever that work was, it wasn't drill; and it didn't happen in camp. "Did you ever get close to the front lines?" I asked him.

"Pretty close," he said. "I was close enough to hear the guns fight." If things had gotten to that point, he believed, they would have been sent into battle themselves; but they never did.

"Were you in danger ever?" I asked.

"No, no," he said, dismissively. "Not too much." The worst of it for him, he seemed to think, was that "I got sick. One time." Just that once, and he couldn't remember what it was exactly that ailed him, but it made quite an impression on him nevertheless, because, he told me, it was the only time he was ever sick in his life.

It's quite unlikely I would have ever learned enough about the 805th PI to question Moses Hardy's minimized version of his service were it not for the regiment's adjutant, a Wisconsin-born, Harvard-educated newspaperman and poet named Paul Southworth Bliss. I own a slender volume of his verse, *The Arch of Spring*, a collection of poems about trees that he published in 1932; my copy is inscribed by the author, "Merry Christmas to Maj. A. V. Wortman," a nice reminder of a time when military men both read and wrote poetry without embarrassment. After the armistice, Captain (later Major) Bliss undertook to compile and publish a record of his regiment's experience in the war, *Victory: History of the 805th Pioneer Infantry, American Expeditionary Forces;* as far as I know, no other PI regiment, colored or white, produced such an account. Bliss wrote much of it himself, but handed off individual companies' histories to officers from those companies. Lieutenant Orlie E. Ooley (not a pen name, though it would make a great one), of Spencer, Indiana, begins his history of Company E with this high-minded introduction:

> When in the course of a nation's existence it becomes necessary to take up arms in defence of rights or principles, that defence often calls into service many types and colors of citizens. This was the case when the United States declared war on the German Empire and set about getting together a cosmopolitan army to defend the rights of Democracy and Humanity.

Lieutenant Ooley, like all of the officers in the 805th PI, was white; all of the enlisted men in the regiment were black. It was, in that way, thoroughly segregated. And yet, reading *Victory*, you get the strong sense that the 805th PI was different, somehow, and that credit for that, in large part, belongs to the regiment's commander, Colonel Chauncey Benton Humphrey, a West Pointer who was recalled from the Panama Canal Zone in June, 1918, at the age of forty-six, and sent to Camp Funston. "The regiment awaited his coming with interest," Bliss writes. "He arrived July 23, tanned with three years in the tropics, a tall, powerfully built officer light on his feet as a cat, giving the impression of tremendous nervous energy." From the beginning, his men idolized him.

And he, apparently, regarded them very highly in return. It was often the case in those days that white officers resented being assigned to black units; it was an insult, they believed, to be put in command of colored troops. C. B. Humphrey, though, appears to have taken on his command with eagerness and vigor, and no sense that his couldn't be the finest regiment in the Army, period. Bliss tells us:

> All that he asked of his officers and men was — perfection. His expression, "Why not Excellent?," which often appeared on his memoranda to company officers, was the hammer with which he drove home his points. He asked that bricks be made — and somehow the straw was found.
>
> In his first talk to his men he told them he wanted them to be "Bearcats." It was a name that stuck. The regiment was known in Funston as the "Bearcat" regiment.

And the Bearcats, it would seem, met his high standards. "Personally," he wrote shortly after the war, "I consider that I had about the *best* Pioneer Infantry regiment in France. I saw all of them and inspected several." Like Private Hardy — and, presumably, every other man in the regiment — Colonel Humphrey believed that the 805th would be used in combat should casualties at the front rise sufficiently; he even went so far as to have nearly a hundred of his men trained in what he called "machine gun work." And though they never saw the inside of a trench, they were certainly put in harm's way, sent to the Meuse-Argonne and assigned the unenviable duty of marching into sectors and villages that the Americans and French had just recaptured from the Germans in order to secure ammunition dumps and repair roads and railheads.

What made this assignment unenviable was the fact that the Germans, who had held most of these villages for four years, were known for counterattacking after they'd seemingly been driven off; they regularly sent in planes to bomb roads and tracks — and especially ammunition dumps — they'd just lost. So Lieutenant Ooley discovered when Company E — which included a twenty-five-year-old private from Aberdeen, Mississippi — was sent "to Auzeville, a small village near Clermont, to work on a railhead. The camp," he writes, "was a poor one, and many men were sent to the hospital with dysentery or fever." Perhaps this was where that twenty-five-year-old private, Moses Hardy, became sick for the only time in his life. "It was also at Auzeville," Ooley reports, "that Company 'E' received its introduction to 'Jerry,' as the German airmen were called. Here also they could hear the big guns on the front, some twelve kilometers away, and see the ambulances carrying back the wounded." Moses Hardy heard those guns, he told me; he probably saw the ambulances, too, and wondered how many more would have to pass through before the 805th would be sent up to take the place of all those lost men.

After a week in Auzeville, Company E moved on to Varennes, a picturesque town best known as the place where Louis XVI was captured in 1791 while fleeing the French Revolution. There Company E "took up the repair of the roads and railhead," Lieutenant Ooley reports, adding, coolly: "Here we were under nightly bombardment by Hun planes seeking to destroy the railhead and hospital, also the ammunition dumps between Varennes and Cheppy. Here Sgt. Hayden made his famous assertion that, 'It's a hell of a war where a fellow has to work all day and run all night.'" That's "Sgt. Hayden," you'll note, not "Harry," as white folks would have invariably referred to him back home in Bedford City, Virginia.

"They'd just fly overhead, way up — you couldn't hardly see them, so far up," Mr. Hardy recalled, and shook his head in response when I asked if they'd frightened him. He never mentioned being bombarded — only talked, indirectly, of seeking shelter "in the house" when German planes were heard or spotted. "We never did go take a good look out," he told me. "We was just in the house." They ducked German planes nightly for a full month, until, on November 7, they moved on to Saint-Juvin to repair the roads there. Four days later, the war ended.

That occasion he remembered well, at least during our second visit. "When the armistice was signed, we was at near thirty miles to Germany . . . We was on our way to Germany, then," he told me that day. I asked if he was glad to get the news; "Yeah, I really was," he replied. So, he said, were his fellow soldiers: "They all jumped up and shot their rifles. And then there was a lot of hollering and going on." The shooting, he added, went on "in the air and in the house." He made sure to add: "I didn't shoot none . . . hollered, that's all."

"Immediately the men began to celebrate by using their rifles and proceeded to fill the roof of their quarters with holes," Lieutenant Ooley writes, by way of confirmation. "No thought of future rains entered their heads." Which is surprising, because they'd already seen quite a lot of rain; Ooley describes their first week in France, at the end of September, as "a most miserable period . . . the men pitched pup-tents on rain-soaked fields, and slept in them with nothing but a blanket between them and the ground." ("It was always raining," Moses Hardy told me the last time I saw him; he, too, remembered it as "miserable.") Such, I suppose, was the joy of the armistice.

The Bearcats enjoyed a rather distinguished postwar career, with visits from American generals, congressmen, and other dignitaries. In the spring of 1919, still in France, they put together a baseball team (the players all enlisted men, the coach a captain from Birmingham, Alabama) that beat all comers. And on June 4, 1919, while stationed at Brest on their way home, they were inspected by General Pershing himself. Pershing, Major Bliss writes, "wanted the men sent home erect, vigorous, well-clad." "He'd come on, check with us," Moses Hardy remembered eighty-six years later. "Have us all in the line and check with us." The general, Private Hardy recalled, "looked nice. He looked like a nice man."

"Did he talk to you?" I asked.

"No," he said. "No. It wasn't right for him, to talk to him. He just have us all in a line and inspect us, that's all."

That's all. Were it not for Lieutenant Ooley, I wouldn't have known that Private Hardy had come under fire every day for a month; were it not for Major Bliss, I wouldn't have known much at all about what the 805th Pioneer Infantry did in France, nor that sixty-one of them — including seven privates and one corporal from Company E — died doing it. Neither Bliss nor Ooley, though, told me what I regard as the most remarkable thing about the 805th. Mr. Hardy hinted at it while telling me about how the Bearcats sometimes staged plays; "they were good plays," he recalled. "I enjoyed them." There were concerts, too — "all kinds of playing, all kinds of music . . . couldn't name them all. It was in a very big room."

"Were they just for black soldiers?" I asked him. "Or were there black and white?"

"All mixed together in there," he said. "All of us in there together."

"Did you sit together, or did you sit separately?"

"Sit together. No different in there. Go in there, if you could get in there, you could sit anywhere you wanted to."

"Is that right? So you could sit right next to a white soldier?"

"Oh, yeah. No difference there."

"Really?"

"Yeah," he said. "It's just — you were in the Army. There's no difference in the Army." Yes, he did concede that "officers didn't sit with us." And since all the officers were white and all the enlisted men black, the men were segregated in any event. But when I asked him, "Did black soldiers and white soldiers get along with each other?" he said: "Oh, yeah. They got along nice. See, there was just one there. You didn't need to separate. There was nothing, ever."

Now, we know, of course, that that wasn't true. And maybe it's just a reflection of his personality, of the mindset that helped enable Moses Hardy to survive to within one month of his 114th birthday; but I don't think so, not entirely, anyway. Maybe it was the openness of France, or the experience of ducking German planes together; maybe it was being away from home, or serving under the command of Colonel Humphrey. Maybe it was the nickname "Bearcats," or the undefeated baseball team, or the Enfield rifles everyone was issued. Whatever it was, I can't but imagine that something special existed within that regiment. Major Paul Southworth Bliss still had enough of it in him, several months after they were all discharged and sent home, to write that the 805th was "undoubtedly the greatest colored regiment in the history of America." Maybe you discern paternalism in those words; I just hear pride.

• • •

Remember Corporal Howard Ramsey of the 302nd Water Tank Train, the fellow who was given a lock of hair by a little blond girl in Luxembourg in exchange for a penny right after the armistice? I started to tell you a story about him a couple of chapters ago, then stopped and said I'd finish it at the appropriate time.

Well, this is it.

Very shortly after the armistice, the 302nd Water Tank Train was, you may recall, assigned to help build the new Meuse-Argonne American Cemetery, which would eventually contain the graves of more than twenty-three thousand Americans killed in that last great battle of the war. Corporal Ramsey and the rest of the 302nd shuttled bodies — some two hundred to three hundred a day — from the battlefield, where they had just been disinterred, to the cemetery, where they would be reinterred. And that, Mr. Ramsey pointed out to me when I visited him in 2003, was all they did. "We didn't have to handle the bodies or anything like that," he'd said. "They'd put them on a canvas, put the canvas in the box, and take the box and bury that." By "they" he meant "the colored people," and by "the colored people," he meant black troops in the AEF. Six thousand of them.

"The colored people did all the work," Howard Ramsey had readily admitted. And it was unpleasant work, to say the least: What they were digging up was *not* pine boxes. The war dead, he recalled, "had been buried, you know, not in coffins or anything like that, just in the ground." Many had decomposed considerably; and some had not, which was, perhaps, even worse. One civilian witness — a nurse, no less — called it "a gruesome, repulsive and unhealthful task." (Howard Ramsey, you may recall, wrote his mother at one point: "I won't . . . go into detail about this work as it's something a woman wouldn't enjoy.") It would have been bad enough to have to do it in open, unhindered fields with no other hazards about; but the colored troops assigned to it didn't have that luxury, since they were working on ground that had very recently hosted a fierce seven-week battle. In his account of the 805th PI's Company L, First Sergeant Joseph A. Thornton (who had been given the honor of chronicling his company's war even though he was an enlisted man — not to mention black) reports that, starting November 21 — just ten days after the armistice — he and his men spent four months in the vicinity of Romagne and Cunel:

This area was to be cleared of the debris of the war. Clothing, rifles, machine guns, shells, cannon, and in fact all of the implements of warfare were to be found in this area.

The men were cautious, but it was inevitable that some of them should be injured. Pvt. Fred D. Lytle had his hand mutilated by explosion. The cause will never be known, as the explosive was hidden in firewood used in Lytle's quarters. Pvt. Robert Anderson and Pvt. Frank Sartin were severely burned by mustard gas from a leaky shell.

Getting gassed after the cessation of hostilities is bad enough; but imagine retiring in your bunk after a long, cold day of clearing live ordnance and dead bodies from a shell-shattered and barbed-wire-strewn forest — only to have your fire explode. You can understand why morale might be low.

And it was. The men assigned to "mortuary affairs" felt ostracized, reviled because they had been given such a detail. It wasn't all in their heads, either; some white American soldiers told French townsfolk that the black men had been assigned this wretched work because they were already diseased. Resentment grew; bad things were in the air, a mood as poisonous, in its way, as the gas in those leaky shells. At one point, the Army, eager to calm tempers, even allowed the YMCA, for the first time, to bring in black women workers. It didn't want six thousand angry colored troops on its hands. No one wanted to find out what that might look like — especially, I imagine, the 302nd Water Tank Train, including Corporal Howard Ramsey. Yet, to hear him tell it eighty-five years later, they very nearly did. The trouble, he said, started with one particular class of black soldier. "They had labor battalions and they had Pioneer Infantrymen," he explained. "And they were the same group of people, except the Pioneer Infantrymen carried a rifle."

It isn't clear which PI regiment he meant. Most records seem to indicate that the 813th, 815th, and 816th PI regiments all worked on the cemetery at one time or another; a contemporary magazine account also mentions the 806th and — yes — the 805th. (That account calls the work "a task which seemed too sacred to leave to German prisoners"; I'm sure the men actually doing it would have gladly passed the honor on to the Germans.) Curiously, there's almost nothing in the Bearcats' history about it; Bliss writes only that "two of the 805th Pioneer Infantry companies had the honor of helping build" the cemetery, and never gets any more specific about it. So I don't know who, exactly, was involved in what Howard Ramsey witnessed there. I wish I did.

"So, they decided that, after the war and all, these guys don't need any guns," Mr. Ramsey told me that day in October, 2003, sitting at his daughter's kitchen table in Oregon. "So the major they had took their guns away from them. Said, 'You don't need guns.' . . . They had two big units, with two, three thousand colored troops . . . So when they took the Pioneer Infantrymen's guns away, that made them a labor battalion." Those rifles meant a great deal to Pioneer Infantrymen. As Colonel C. B. Humphrey, commander of the 805th PI, explained in a report he wrote in 1920: "The fact of their being equipped with arms did not impede their work in the slightest, and, at the same time, vastly increased their Morale, as it made them feel that they were soldiers and not slaves." These were men who were but one or two generations removed from slavery to begin with; it was not an abstraction to them.

"Well," Howard Ramsey continued, "these colored guys didn't want to be called a labor battalion; they were Pioneer Infantrymen. So they mutinied. And I mean mutinied! They all had rifles. Of course, they'd taken our rifles away from us. So we were going to fight a war, a race war. So we went all over the battlefield, and we got any kind of a gun that we could find that had matching ammunition. So we'd take back this gun, take it back, clean up the gun, and get ready for this war that we were going to have. And the ammunition. After everything was settled, we were supposed to throw these guns away, or get rid of them. I never did. I brought mine home . . . It was a German Mauser or something like that." He said his son-in-law still had it.

He smiled from time to time as he told the story — not because he thought it was amusing, I believe, but rather by way of saying: *Look what I barely got out of.* "I was there when a colored sergeant was cussing out a colonel," he said. "White colonel, you know. And the colonel wasn't doing anything about it. And another guy and I, we walked down, we just wanted to give the colonel some support." He laughed. "And he told us, he said, 'You get back.' He says, 'I'm fine. If I need your help, I'll call on you.' And that was as close as we got. But there could have been a real race [war], because these guys were shouldering their rifles."

I asked Howard Ramsey if he had been surprised to see all of this transpire. "Oh, you better believe it," he said. What he didn't say, but which became obvious in hearing him tell of it, was that he'd also been terrified. "We went out on the battlefield, we got any kind of gun we could find — Springfield, Enfield, Mauser, one of these English guns," he said. "There were only, I think, about two hundred of us, or something like that. They'd win in a walkaway." Maybe so; but should black troops draw any white blood in a "race war," there could have been no "winning" for them beyond that. Retribution would have been swift, irresistible, merciless. In the end, other black troops would have been called in to bury *them*.

Howard Ramsey was no Southerner — in fact, he had grown up in the West and Pacific Northwest — and yet his attitudes on race were not, let us say, terribly enlightened. For one thing, in witnessing what he did that day, he perceived not unrest among fellow soldiers, but the advent of an all-out "race war" — and scrambled to arm himself and his fellow white men. For another, in his letters home from France, he refers four times to African American soldiers simply as "the niggers"; a fifth time he calls them "colored fellows," which just shows you that he knew better. The second time I saw him, two years after our first visit, I asked him what had been his impression of the black soldiers he'd worked with. He was 107 at that point, and a great deal more frail than he had been at 105; his memory was failing. But this much he remembered: "We didn't like them." He said it twice, actually.

"Why not?" I asked.

He laughed. "We was white troops."

Even so, however unknowingly, Mr. Ramsey told me a story — otherwise lost to history — about the birth of the modern civil rights movement, a tale of black men standing up for themselves, speaking out against an order that consigned them to the grimmest work one can imagine while white troops were kept at a safe and sanitary remove, responsible only for driving the trucks. (He himself told me, during our second visit: "The black troops, they decided they weren't going to handle the bodies anymore.") Even just to say no to a white man — much less cuss one out — would, back home, have meant a certain beating, and perhaps even a lynching, for any or all of them. And, in the years after the war — when terrible "race riots" would sweep through Chicago, and Tulsa, and Omaha, and Rosewood, Florida, and dozens of other American towns and cities, a reaction against the new confidence and assertiveness whites perceived in black men home from the war — it did. But not that day, in Romagne, France, for those Pioneer Infantrymen who'd finally had enough. I wish I knew who, exactly, they were — them, and that white colonel who just stood there and let a black sergeant cuss him out, jeopardizing his reputation in order to defuse the situation.

The black narrative of that war, like the white narrative, is strongly biased in favor of combat, the Harlem Hellfighters and Henry Johnson and Needham Roberts and, now, Freddie Stowers. In his history, Emmett Scott devotes more than 150 pages to the exploits of the two colored fighting divisions, and only 13 pages to SOS troops, even though the latter comprised 80 percent of all the African Americans who served in France then. If that page count alone doesn't illustrate Scott's own prejudice on the matter, he starts the slender chapter about SOS thus:

> War is not all "death and glory." For every soldier who gets even a glimpse of the enemy or risks his life within range of shell-fire, there must, in all modern warfare, be from twenty to thirty men working at such commonplace and routine tasks as loading and unloading ships, building piers, laying railroad tracks, making roads, in a thousand other ways making it possible for the fighting men to get to the front, and for the necessary food, ammunition and other supplies to reach them. But what man would want to render such service?

The overwhelming majority of African American men drafted into the AEF were never given that choice. They were, however, given a uniform, and a passage to France, and an essential, if not always dangerous, job to do. And whether or not, like Pioneer Infantrymen, they also got rifles and gas masks and, like a few now-forgotten Pioneer Infantrymen in the town of Romagne, a chance to step forward and demand they be treated with dignity — many came home with a taste for it. Just as James K. Vardaman had feared they would.

Even so, I am obliged to tell you that this particular story does not have a happy ending. Another thirty-five years would have to pass before the United States Supreme Court would even begin the process of undoing what it had done in *Plessy*. In that time, there would be those "race riots," in which hundreds of African Americans would perish. Hundreds more would be lynched (seventy-six in 1919 alone). Henry Johnson would descend into alcoholism and possibly drug addiction, grow estranged from his family, and die, broke and alone, in a VA hospital at the age of thirty-two. Needham Roberts would hang himself. George Johnson, traumatized by his brother's mistreatment in the Navy and who knows what else, would decide he couldn't even stand to think of himself as a black man anymore.

Despair, though, isn't racist; many white veterans succumbed to it, too, among them Major Paul Southworth Bliss of the 805th Pioneer Infantry. In "The Arch of Spring," he had written:

> *Life comes prancing,*
> *Shot with glee,*
>
> *Head flung back,*
> *And high of knee;*
>
> *Death goes down side*
> *Lanes, back stairs,*
>
> *Life comes up wide*
> *Thoroughfares.*

Eight years later, on New Year's Eve, 1940, sitting alone in his room at Kansas City's YMCA, he picked up his army sidearm and shot himself. "I greatly regret doing this," he wrote in the note he left, "but my nerves have snapped and it is impossible for me to go on." Some thoroughfares, it seems, get shelled to the point where no one can repair them, not even a Bearcat.

Fortunately, Private Moses Hardy's road remained passable, and led him back to Aberdeen, Mississippi, where he reunited with his wife, started a family and a church Sunday school, worked his farm and drove a school bus and sold health and beauty products door-to-door, and lived on another eighty-seven years. The first time I met him, in 2003, I couldn't help but run the numbers in my head: The man was already seventy-one years old when Freedom Summer came to the Hospitality State.

"A lot has changed in Mississippi for black people since you were young," I said to him. "Did you ever think you'd live to see that?"

"No," he said.

"Do you think things are better now than they were when you were young?" I asked — worried, as the words were departing my lips, that it sounded like a stupid question.

But Moses Hardy, at least, didn't seem to think so. "I can't tell," he replied. "Might be, and might not be."

13

L'Ossuaire

THERE'S A REASON it became known, even before it ended,
as the World War. Yes, it started out as the Great War, and
some still call it that. But for many, "great" just didn't do the
thing justice. Other wars had been broad in scope; this one was ubiquitous. There was action in Namibia, Tanzania, Kenya, Uganda; Ara-
bia, Mesopotamia, Persia, Anatolia; Polynesia, Samoa, Guam, New
Guinea; East Prussia, Galicia, Transylvania, Latvia. Naval battles were
fought off the coasts of China, India, Chile, Denmark. Men shot at each
other on the veldt, in the jungle, across the desert, atop mountains;
killed and died in the snow-covered Italian Alps, mosquito-infested
African swamps, ice-encrusted Siberian harbors, and the clear blue
waters of the Red Sea. It really did scar the entire planet.

But if you know anything at all about the World War, you know that
one country in the world, more than any other, was consumed by it.

Battles — epic, heroic, iconic battles — were fought in Belgium, Russia, Turkey, Italy. But France — France *was* a battle. And it never let up
for a single day in more than four years. Elsewhere, sections of cities
or towns may have been badly damaged, a village largely destroyed;
in certain parts of France, just about every settlement was entirely destroyed. Some would eventually be rebuilt where they had stood, others on a different spot not too far away. But many — often within a matter of hours — simply ceased to exist, forever.

In much of the country, the landscape remains altered even now. In
some areas, just about every patch of woods is riddled with trenches;
narrow but deep, twisting sharply this way or that every ten yards or so
(to prevent enfilading fire should the enemy make it into your trench),

dappled with leaves and pocked with branches and roots, you might take them for dry creek beds but for the fact that they intersect, at fairly regular intervals, with other narrow, deep, jagged depressions. Near Verdun I walked through a section of forest — just one of many in that part of the country — where the grassy floor undulates so much that there doesn't remain even a square yard of flat ground: shell holes. Here and there you will find massive craters, some the size of a large amphitheater. Desperate to break the stalemate, both sides took to tunneling beneath No Man's Land, carving out large chambers under the enemy's trenchworks, packing them with explosives, scurrying out and then, at a predetermined hour, detonating them. Someone thought to film one such event, the detonation of forty thousand pounds of ammonal (a particularly nasty explosive) by the British Royal Engineers' 252nd Tunneling Company at Hawthorn Ridge, near the village of Beaumont-Hamel, at precisely 7:20 a.m. on July 1, 1916. It was the start of the Battle of the Somme, but the footage — somehow more terrifying for being silent — makes it look more like the end of the world. The blast left a crater 80 feet deep, 450 feet long, and 300 feet wide. Eight minutes later, the Royal Engineers set off another mine, this one packed with forty-eight thousand pounds of ammonal, south of the village of La Boisselle. That hole, now known as the Lochnagar Mine, is even larger; it has been preserved as it was, and is a tourist attraction today. When I visited I saw a couple of men parked nearby in tiny trailers, selling World War I artifacts.

After a few such blasts everyone, out of necessity, became very good at listening in and detecting each other's tunneling efforts. Thereafter, they usually knew when and where the other side ceased digging, giving them plenty of inadvertent warning to evacuate the targeted area. These colossal explosions, then, spectacular and fearsome though they appeared, did not claim all that many lives. Still, neither side stopped tunneling.

The average World War I soldier spent an awful lot of time below the surface of the earth. There were those trenches, to begin with — fire trenches up front, support trenches in the rear (not too far in the rear, though — maybe two or three hundred yards at the most), and the communications trenches that ran in between the two. No one knows how many miles of them were dug in France between 1914 and

1918; many thousands, at the least. The typical fire trench was about twelve feet deep when freshly dug; rain, water seepage, and bombardment filled them in pretty quickly, though, and they required almost constant maintenance. Then there were dugouts, earthen basements (minus a house) where men who were lucky enough to have access to them might seek shelter during a bombardment or, if they were off the front line, sleep a bit. Dugouts were scarcely more habitable than trenches. Both were always wet (the water table in much of France was rarely very deep), riddled with rats and cooties. You had to be pretty tired, or frightened, to spend much time in a dugout; at least in a trench you could look up at the sky. The British and French carved their dugouts about a dozen or so feet beneath the surface. The Germans often burrowed two or three stories for theirs, even outfitting them with concrete stairways.

The Germans seemed to have a special affinity for subterranean life. In some areas, like the hills of the Argonne Forest and the heights above the Meuse River, they built large underground hospitals and convalescent wards, linked and supplied by an impressive network of tunnels. Both sides took shelter for months at a time in the old mines that lined the Chemin des Dames, but the Germans actually electrified theirs; you can still see the wiring in them today. If you walk around certain areas, you quickly come to understand that the Germans brought to the war a distinct technological edge. They ran electrical lines through just about every place they went, and laid countless miles of narrow-gauge railroad track, too. Most of it is still out there; the track, at least, has aged quite well. So have their trenches, many of which were fortified with concrete — no mistaking any of them for a dry creek bed. The French, on the other hand, were not allowed to build concrete trenchworks; concrete implies permanence, and the French were always supposed to be pushing forward, attacking until they had driven the invader from their country. To use concrete, the high command believed, would be bad for morale. The *poilus* — slang for French infantrymen (*poilu* literally translates as "hairy one") — crouching in those dirt trenches might have disagreed.

The Germans, though, were not only concerned with pushing forward, but with holding what they had already taken. So they trucked in lots and lots of concrete and used it to build lots and lots of supply cellars and sewer systems, pillboxes and bunkers, dugouts and trenches, a great many of which are still there, more or less. In the Argonne, where he was commanding the German 5th Army, *Kronprinz* Wilhelm, the Kaiser's oldest son, built himself a bunker that looked like a posh chateau, complete with marble fireplaces. It remains there, set into a slope in the forest, and still projects hints of its former elegance, even though souvenir-hunters long ago carried off the last of the marble.

The Germans' technological edge extended to their weaponry. They invented the flamethrower. Their Mauser rifles were superior to the French Army's Lebels. Their barbed wire was thicker, with more barbs. Their wire cutters could easily cut through British wire, but not vice versa. Their Luger was better than any pistol a French officer might carry; their machine guns were better than those the French had. Their artillery fired 77-millimeter shells, while the French guns fired 75-millimeter shells; this meant the Germans could fire captured French shells back at the French, while the French couldn't cram German shells into their own guns. You can't help but get the sense that Germany really should have won that war.

And yet it didn't. The French did. But it was France, not Germany, that was largely destroyed in the process.

France certainly didn't volunteer to host a war that would drag on for four years and, in doing so, lay much of the place to waste. The strange thing is that Germany didn't plan on it, either. Actually, its grand war plan promised the conquest and capitulation of France in just a matter of weeks. Ironically, it was only because the French managed to thwart that plan that so much of their country was destroyed.

The roots of the First World War went back four decades, to the Franco-Prussian War of 1870–71. The French started that one, but it didn't end well for them: In just six weeks, the Prussians killed or captured a huge chunk of France's army, including Emperor Napoleon III. Paris fell after a four-month siege. France, which had prided itself on having the finest military in the world, was humiliated. The Prussians held a grand victory parade in Paris, occupied much of the country until the French paid them five billion francs in reparations, and annexed part of the French province of Lorraine and almost all of the province of Alsace, France's industrial heartland and the source of almost all of its iron ore. France, devastated and demoralized, seethed to strike back at the hated *Boche.*

Germany knew it, too, and gave a lot of thought to preparing for the next war. At first, the Germans were expecting just another one-on-one fight, and had no reason to worry things might go differently for them the second time around. But Kaiser Wilhelm II, prickly fellow that he was, managed to alienate once-friendly Russia and Great Britain, both of whom then entered into alliances with France. Uh-oh: Russia bordered Germany to the east and had the largest army in the world; Britain ruled the seas. Alarmed, the Kaiser asked the chief of the Imperial German General Staff, Count Alfred Graf von Schlieffen, to work up a plan that would enable Germany to fight a war on two fronts simultaneously and win both. The result became known as the Schlieffen Plan, one of the most storied strategies in modern military history.

The Germans believed that the French, faced with overwhelming military opposition, would fold quickly, as they had in the last war, and that the real war would be fought in the east, against the "Russian Steamroller," 150 divisions strong. An army that large in a country that vast, though, would take time to mobilize, so Schlieffen's plan was to send 90 percent of Germany's troops — including reserves — into France immediately following a declaration of war, not only across their shared frontier but also through the neutral countries that sat in between them elsewhere — namely, Belgium, Luxembourg, and the Netherlands. Sure, violating Benelux neutrality wasn't very nice, but doing so would enable a huge German force to sweep into France along a very wide front (Schlieffen famously called for "the last man on the right [to] brush the Channel with his sleeve") and, swinging around like a scythe, encircle the French Army and precipitate a general surrender, just as they had thirty-five years earlier. Schlieffen determined that French military surrender would be achieved in six weeks, whereupon the bulk of German troops would be shipped east, in time to confront the steamroller. The diplomats would have plenty of time to step in and smooth things over with the Benelux countries after that.

Count Schlieffen retired in 1906, shortly after submitting his plan, which proved unfortunate for Germany, because the count's successor, Helmuth von Moltke — nephew and namesake of the great hero of the

Franco-Prussian War — started to tinker with the established order, as successors are inclined to do. He moved troops around, even sending some of them to the eastern frontier, weakening the offensive army in the west; he also scrapped plans to pass through Holland and Luxembourg, opening up the potential for bottlenecks in the assault. Many historians believe Moltke's revisions doomed the Schlieffen Plan to failure. It certainly didn't help matters that Belgian resistance proved tougher than expected, throwing off Germany's timetable. Moltke, trying to recover, made several more alterations to the original plan, all of which weakened it; while heading for Paris, he swerved off to envelop retreating French armies, and in doing so exposed his right flank (a year earlier, a dying Count Schlieffen had uttered, as his last words, "Remember to keep the right flank strong!"), a mistake the French and, now, the British, rushed to exploit. (In a famous episode, some ten thousand French reserve troops were shuttled from Paris to the front in taxicabs.) To everyone's astonishment, they stopped the Germans at what would become known as the First Battle of the Marne. And so, six weeks after the start of their great offensive, the Germans found themselves not accepting a complete French surrender, as Schlieffen had envisioned, but retreating and digging the first trenches of the war. The lines they all established at that point would scarcely move over the next four years.

The news from the Eastern Front was much better. It turned out that the men chosen to drive the Russian Steamroller, the czar's top generals, were incompetent, a fact that effectively neutralized their great numerical superiority. The Germans trounced them regularly — an early defeat, at Tannenberg in August, 1914, was so spectacular that after the battle was lost the commanding Russian general, Alexander Samsonov, skulked off into the woods and shot himself — and, though Russia would stay in the war until March, 1918, the Germans never had to worry about them too terribly much after those first few weeks. Instead, they focused on France, where the war ground on, month after month, year after year, never advancing much in either direction but quite deadly for all present nonetheless.

And also terribly destructive for France. When I visited Reuben Law in Carson City, Nevada, in 2004 — he was the truck driver and mechanic who had barely survived a bout with influenza while sailing to

France in the fall of 1918 — I found in his photo album a snapshot of the Cathedral of Notre-Dame de Reims, taken at the precise moment when a German shell struck it: medieval construction meets modern firepower. I don't know how he came upon it, but Reims, which dates back to Roman times, unhappily found itself near the front lines during the war, and well within range of enemy howitzers. The Germans did not spare it. Whether or not they took aim specifically at the cathedral — where French kings had traveled for centuries to be coronated — they hit it an awful lot, doing so much damage that it took twenty years to restore the edifice afterward. To this day, perhaps two-thirds of its windows are clear; the stained glass they once housed will never be replaced.

Reims and its cathedral are, of course, just one example among an innumerable litany, but for many they came to symbolize the country's losses. Owen Johnson, an American writer who traveled through war-torn France before the United States entered the conflict, writes, in his 1916 book *The Spirit of France:* "Nothing has sown more bitterness in the French mind than this incomprehensible destruction of the treasured monuments of the past. A thousand men dying under the barbarism of asphyxiating gases are nothing to burning Rheims . . . for what is being destroyed there is France itself." Perhaps those thousand men and their families might have felt otherwise, but what happened to Reims — what the Germans did to Reims — was truly outrageous. "No photographs can adequately visualize what has been wrought," Johnson says of it.

That remains true to this day of France and that war, even though Notre-Dame de Reims looks much better now than it did in 1915. The earth is constantly regurgitating the detritus of that war. One morning, in a small, freshly plowed field outside Romagne, I found five identical bullets sitting atop the loose brown soil. Later, I brought them into a gun shop in Augusta, Maine, to see if I could learn anything about them. The owner picked up one of the bullets — a bit shorter than the first segment of my thumb, with a very sharp point — examined it for a minute or two, and smiled. "It's a 7- or 8-millimeter," he told me. "German. Probably from a Mauser 98. It wouldn't make a big hole, but it was designed to go through you and the person behind you and the person behind him." The Mauser Gewehr 98 was the primary, and by far the most popular, rifle among German infantry units in the First World War.

In addition to those bullets, I found several five-cartridge clips — known as stripper clips — in that field, as well as a button from a Bavarian uniform, and a piece of a comb. Oh: and an unexploded shell. It was reddish-brown and almost as large as my foot; like the rest, it was just sitting atop the soil, as if it had all been dropped there that morning. My guide told me, politely but firmly, not to kick it or attempt to pick it up. Even now, a few people are killed or maimed every year by World War I shells. They are prized as souvenirs; the French often take them home to display atop the mantelpiece. Sadly, my guide, Jean-Paul de Vries, called the sighting in to the police instead. He knew better, and besides, he already had a garage full of souvenirs.

M. de Vries is a slight, dark-haired, and energetic fellow who spends a tremendous amount of his time exploring the terrain of the old Meuse-Argonne battlefield, whether accompanied by a fellow World War I buff or alone. (Among other notable traits, he possesses an alarming *sangfroid* when it comes to the status of his fuel-tank gauge.) There's a great deal of that terrain — the offensive ranged over a fair chunk of Lorraine — and though he seems to know just about all of it as well as most people know their favorite corner of their own backyard, he is always out exploring and inspecting this area or that because he knows it is, all of it, perpetually changing. In just a few hours he had us zigzagging through a network of French trenches, still around eight feet deep; scurrying up a hill to inspect several shallower American trenches, just deep enough, he told me, for doughboys to gain some cover while kneeling and firing at the Germans (some of the action was moving so quickly at that point that there was no time to dig deeper trenchworks); ducking into part of a German waterworks; poking around the cement entrance to a large German dugout; examining, mixed in a patch of ivy, a great tangle of barbed wire (probably German); and stumbling upon artifacts almost everywhere, like a cluster of three rusted conical shell-caps — again, probably German. At one point he led me to a patch of woods where the forest floor seemed tiered, like a grand staircase in which each step was a quarter the size of a football gridiron. Well before the Americans came through during the last great battle of the war, he explained, this had been the site of a German rest camp, where soldiers might be furloughed for a couple of weeks to relax, visit baths, get medical attention if they needed it, eat well, drink well, and enjoy the company of willing French ladies, of whom, he assured me, there was no shortage. The Germans occupied this area for four full years; they weren't the only ones who just assumed they'd stay forever. Compliant French girls were welcome to share the Germans' gastronomical bounty (as evidenced by an empty wine bottle we found nearby) and, of course, their *Papiermarken,* which were then accepted as currency throughout the area.

M. de Vries described this enormous furlough camp so vividly — gesturing about, "this was all beds, and that was a spa, over here a tavern," etc. — that I actually started to see some of it, faintly. He could see it all in detail, it seemed, and occasionally I found myself wondering if he had, somehow, actually been here when the operation was still in full swing. At one point, spotting an old tree that had just been felled during a storm, M. de Vries darted over to it and gestured excitedly for me to follow. Beckoning me to the thicket of gnarled old roots, he pointed: There, resting in the tangles, were bullets. A lot of them. The roots, he explained, drew them up out of the soil along with the water, then held onto them until the old trees fell and offered their buried treasure up to the world. We picked them out and he gave them all to me, along with that wine bottle and everything else we'd found that day. He had no room for any of it; his garage, in Romagne, was, as I said, already full of things he'd been finding for decades.

I call it a garage because it had a vehicle door in front and sat in the midst of a village, but inside it was much more like a barn with a large loft. Whatever it once was, it is now full of locally found bayonets, rifles, grenade launchers; trench knives, "persuaders," entrenching tools; helmets, gas masks, wristwatches; mess kits, eating utensils, pots, pans, jugs; horseshoes, saddles, harnesses, ammunition crates, wicker shell carriers; Bibles and religious statuettes; enough bottles to supply several bars and pharmacies; and many, many photographs — wallet- and wall-sized, framed and loose — of men in uniform. On one wall hangs an old propaganda poster featuring a huge photograph of a kindly German soldier feeding a little girl who sits on his knee; the caption reads: "An infantryman shares his lunch with a hungry French child, recorded on October 22, 1914 in Romagne." The title, up top, is simply: "A German 'Barbarian.'" The text is German; who was this poster meant for?

Walking through the building — which you have to do carefully, as stuff is strewn everywhere and the passages are narrow and serpentine — you find yourself asking some variation of the question "who was all this meant for?" over and over again. You can't help but wonder: Why did so many men carry so much stuff to the battlefield with them?

It's a museum, now, like Gilles Lagin's near Belleau Wood: haphazard and compelling, wondrous and sad. M. de Vries accepts donations but does not charge admission. Everything he has here was offered up to him, for free, by the earth. Experts say France's World War I battlefields will continue to regurgitate artifacts of that war for another two or three centuries.

The garage — or barn, or whatever — that houses Jean-Paul de Vries's museum looks like it has been there since the time of the Bourbons. All of Romagne does. Drive through little villages in that part of Lorraine, and you'll see they all look that way — old, quaint, untouched by the passage of hundreds of years.

It's all a lie.

None of the buildings predate the war. Whatever had been there before the fall of 1918 was destroyed by November 11 of that year. In the case of Romagne, I have the postcards to prove it.

What the French did here, typically, was rebuild villages so that they looked pretty much the way they had before German, French, and American shells reduced them to rubble, with only certain subtle improvements — cement lintels over windows, iron braces along mortar walls. I'm not sure whether they did this out of reverence for what had been destroyed, or simple necessity; there wasn't a lot of money to spread around for rebuilding, especially when Germany fell behind on its reparations payments, as happened often during its period of postwar hyperinflation. Fortunately, the French got a bit of help from their transoceanic allies, who apparently didn't consider their debt to Lafayette fully squared when the guns stopped firing. Americans, it turned out, had a proprietary feeling toward the places they'd liberated (and sometimes helped destroy in the process), and so the 37th Division constructed a new hospital in the village of Montfaucon-d'Argonne; the Yankee Division rebuilt the church at Belleau; the 315th Infantry Regiment put up a public bathhouse in Varennes; and so on, hundreds of times over. All of it was paid for by the units' veterans' organizations, which included soldiers, wives, parents, and neighbors back home. Sometimes, they'd send a delegation back to France for the ribbon-cutting ceremony.

Perhaps the grandest such project was the Temple Memorial, a church built in Château-Thierry in the 1920s that features, as its centerpiece, a large stained-glass window depicting General Pershing arriving in France and being greeted by the Marquis de Lafayette. Parents of slain doughboys donated to build the place; so did institutions that lost members or alumni. Ursinus College, in Pennsylvania, gave a pew; Mercersburg Academy, also in Pennsylvania, donated the church bell. An association of military chaplains built the altar in honor of their colleagues who did not survive the war. And Edith Carow Roosevelt, wife of the former president, donated a large Bible in memory of their youngest son, Quentin.

Everyone seems to agree that Quentin was the family's favorite; TR, who worked hard to maintain his image as a tough guy, nevertheless doted on his youngest, calling him "Quentyquee" and "Quinikins." Smart and witty, cheeky and mischievous, young Quentin pummeled unsuspecting Secret Service agents with snowballs from the roof of the White House (history is mum about whether or not they fired back) and dispensed irreverent quips to reporters. TR's other sons all served in the infantry — Theodore Jr. and Archie with the 1st Division, Kermit in the British Army — but Quentin dropped out of Harvard to join the new Army Air Service. (Daughter Ethel Roosevelt Derby also served in France, as a nurse.) For the most part, only wellborn young men became aviators in that war, largely because there were only a few dozen training aircraft in the entire country in 1917, and money tended to buy access to those kinds of things. Quentin was quite myopic; he never should have been allowed to fly. But he was. It is said that he memorized the eye chart in order to pass muster, but I seriously doubt anyone would have turned away President Roosevelt's youngest son no matter how poorly he did on the test. On July 14, 1918 — Bastille Day — Quentin's plane was shot down near the village of Chamery, not far from Reims; he was dead before he hit the ground, two German machine-gun bullets in his head. The official story is that Quentin's squadron had engaged a German squadron and he had been downed during a dogfight. Another version, though, holds that after a tussle, both sides, having lost no one, turned and headed back toward their lines — but that Quentin, nearsighted as he was, accidentally followed the Germans, who turned on him when they realized his mistake. They buried him with full military honors where he fell; the spot is still marked today.

His father, who had fiercely advocated for America's entry into the war as early as 1914 — and was so disgusted with President Wilson's refusal to fall in line that he actively campaigned for Wilson's opponent, Charles Evans Hughes, in 1916 — was devastated. He himself would be dead within six months, snatched in his sleep by a coronary thrombosis; the family called it a broken heart, which, if you think about it, it kind of is. They built a monument to Quentin right in the middle of Chamery, a big, wide fountain bearing an epigram from Lieutenant Roosevelt's father, one of the least equivocal declarations I've ever encountered:

ONLY THOSE ARE FIT TO LIVE WHO ARE NOT AFRAID TO DIE.

Lots of famous people served in that war. Some were already famous beforehand, like Quentin and his brothers — one of whom, Archie, was badly wounded in both World War I *and* World War II. (He was forty-nine years old the second time around.) Alfred Joyce Kilmer, who went by his middle name professionally, had already made a name for himself as a journalist, critic, and poet; he is best remembered today for a bit of verse that begins

I think that I shall never see
A poem lovely as a tree.

and perhaps for the rest stop on the New Jersey Turnpike that bears his name. Kilmer was thirty-one years old and serving as a sergeant with New York's famed "Fighting 69th" Infantry Regiment (under Major William J. Donovan, who would go on to found the OSS, the precursor to the CIA) when a German sniper killed him at the Second Battle of the Marne on July 30, 1918. With his education — he was a graduate of

Columbia — and prominence, he could easily have been commissioned an officer, but he chose instead to enlist as a private. Even before he set sail for France, he had contracted with a publisher to write a wartime memoir, to be titled "Here and There with the Fighting Sixty-Ninth." Sometimes I wonder how it would have measured up against *Over the Top*.

New York sent quite a few men of celebrity to France, including thirty-eight-year-old Christy Mathewson, the New York Giants' star pitcher who was so clean-cut and admired that his nickname was the "Christian Gentleman" — and, at the other end of the scale of renown, forty-two-year-old Monk Eastman, a legendary Manhattan gangster and opium addict. (The story goes that when Eastman stripped for his induction physical, the army doctor, stunned by Monk's collection of bullet and knife scars, asked him what war he'd gotten them in. "Oh," he replied, "a lot of little wars around New York.") Eastman, serving (under an assumed name) with the 27th Infantry Division (composed of New York National Guard units and volunteers), is said to have performed heroically, bringing in wounded comrades under fire and single-handedly wiping out a German machine-gun nest; Mathewson, assigned to the Army's new Chemical Warfare Service, was accidentally gassed during a training exercise. He never recovered, dying seven years later at the age of forty-five. Monk Eastman also died at forty-five, gunned down on a Manhattan street just a year after being honorably discharged from the Army.

Walk around the Meuse-Argonne and you also hear a lot about people who were not yet famous when they served there: Captain Harry Truman of the 129th Field Artillery's Battery D, who had also memorized the eye chart in order to enlist, and who once corralled his men, scattering in the face of a German attack, by unleashing upon them a wave of profanity the likes of which they had never heard; Colonel George S. Patton, who commanded the 1st Provisional Tank Brigade, and whose life was once saved by his orderly, Private First Class Joe Angelo; Brigadier General Douglas MacArthur, of the 42nd Infantry Division (the Rainbow Division), who eschewed military uniform regulations, preferring to lead his men into battle wearing a cardigan sweater and carrying a riding crop, and who was gassed twice and once taken prisoner by another American division, which mistook him for a

German general; and Colonel George C. Marshall, a favorite of General Pershing's, who played a major role in planning the offensive.

And one more name. Standing at the edge of a large field outside Romagne, Jean-Paul de Vries pointed out a lonely farmhouse several hundred yards away; in 1914, he told me, as the Germans were first taking the area, a twenty-two-year-old second lieutenant named Erwin Rommel stopped with his men at this farmhouse to eat and drink and rest a bit. Moving on, he came across some German infantrymen who had become separated from their units, and then some more, and they all fell in under his command, until he was leading a band of some 350 men. When he finally caught up with his colonel, the man did not commend Rommel, but rather excoriated him for having so many men under his command; he was, after all, a lowly lieutenant. "To my intense regret, an older officer was given command of this outfit," Rommel wrote in a memoir twenty-three years later. The colonel sent Rommel away, and went back to doing whatever it is colonels do. I wonder if that long-forgotten senior officer ever shared that story with his grandchildren.

Rommel would return to France a quarter century after that first visit; Patton would be back, too, while Marshall oversaw the whole operation from Washington. World War II was also fought in this area, but you'd have to look pretty hard to see any evidence of that. It's as if the First World War has consumed all of the local memory. The military cemeteries are all World War I cemeteries; the military monuments are all World War I monuments. When people here speak of battles, they are World War I battles. "The War" is the first war, not the other one. Lorraine bled out during the First World War, and never really recouped its strength. Even so, that war is a tremendous source of pride there — there, and throughout France.

After the armistice, the French government allotted funds for every town and village and hamlet in the country to construct a monument. In all of France, I am told, only five settlements — five — failed to do so. In many places — like, say, the village of Richecourt in the old Toul Sector, which was occupied by the Germans for four years and completely demolished — the World War I monument is the only thing of note: a giant, old-style Cross of Lorraine bedecked with flags and laurels, in front of which, on a stone, sits a *poilu*, his rifle, bayonet, and helmet all resting on the rock beside him, his head thrown back onto his left shoulder, eyes gazing skyward; I think he's supposed to be dead. The monument bears only about a dozen names — a great ratio of splendor to fallen.

Occasionally, in these towns, you'll find that someone, a generation later, updated their monument to add a new name to the roll of the dead — *victime*, as the appendix in Seicheprey reads, *de la barbarie Nazie*. In Dun-sur-Meuse, one of the larger towns in the old Meuse-Argonne Sector, someone added two Second World War *victimes* — a Celine Thierion, and *Les Familles Salomon*. I don't know about Mme. Thierion, but I have a pretty good idea of what happened to the latter. More often, though, you'll see nothing at all; it's as if the Second World War didn't even occur. Which, in a sense, it didn't: The Battle of France, which began with Germany's invasion on May 10, 1940, ended just six weeks later with France's surrender — an even more spectacular, and humiliating, defeat than the one the Germans had dealt them in 1871.

A drive through Lorraine, though, will certainly lead you to question the stereotype that the French cannot fight. Should you take that trip in the right company, you will hear stories; a retired French soldier named Patrick Simons gestured to a vast field just outside the town of Flirey (pronounced "Flea-Ray") and told me that after a battle there in the fall of 1914, you could walk from one end of the field to the other, a mile or more, treading upon the body of a dead French soldier at every step. This was the early war, before trenches, when things moved quickly and surprise carried the day. The Germans had attacked so swiftly on September 19 that a mother and two of her children, who had unsuspectingly left their farm that morning to do some shopping in the nearby village of Limey ("Lee-May"), were trapped there when the Germans stormed through, and could not reunite with the rest of their family for four years.

Quite a few villages in this part of France, like Montfaucon-d'Argonne (where the 37th Infantry Division built that hospital) and Flirey — to name two that I just happen to know about — were rebuilt after the war in a different location, their original sites having been destroyed or contaminated beyond reclamation. Quite a few more were completely demolished during the war and never rebuilt. What Lorraine seems to have gotten in exchange for all those lost villages are cemeteries, a lot of them. You can't drive very far in any direction without passing some field or park or walled-in yard full of war dead. America took great care with its cemeteries; General Pershing, even before he became chairman of the American Battle Monuments Commission, took a significant personal interest in them. They are among the most perfect public green spaces you will ever see. The fourteen thousand or so markers at Meuse-Argonne, the largest American cemetery in Europe, are precisely spaced and aligned. Even the angles at which the grass is cut are beautiful. After the armistice some twenty-three thousand Americans were buried in this one cemetery, but in the 1920s a campaign was launched — by the funeral industry, I am told — that used fear and guilt to persuade many Americans to repatriate their loved ones' remains to the United States, at government expense. Many of them now repose in small, obscure cemeteries, unvisited by relatives who have forgotten about them, or moved away, or both.

The French, who had a great many more bodies to bury, did not have the luxury of building vast, wonderfully landscaped cemeteries; theirs tend to be flat, plain affairs, studded with thin, tan concrete crosses. (The markers at the American cemeteries are all plump white marble.) There are quite a lot of them; the largest, with some sixteen thousand marked graves, is at a place called Douaumont. Before and during the war, Douaumont was the site of the biggest and most strategically important of the nineteen French forts that protected the city of Verdun, which, in the wake of the defeat of 1871, came to be seen by the French as an essential bulwark against future German invasions. Whether it really was or not is a question that military historians have debated for decades; what's indisputable is that Verdun was tremendously important to the French people, even if that importance was, in fact, no more than symbolic. Its fall would have damaged French morale immeasurably. Even so, France's high command came to understand, early in the war, that Verdun's defenses, once believed impregnable, could not withstand an indefinite German assault and bombardment. In 1915 the French started to transfer Verdun's armaments elsewhere, and even to plan the demolition of that ring of nineteen forts.

The Germans, with their superb network of spies, discovered what the French were up to and decided to launch a massive attack on Verdun, reasoning that French public opinion would never stand for the loss of — much less the abandonment of — Verdun. The Germans, you see, knew that the old city wasn't all that valuable in and of itself; their objective, as they put it, was to use Verdun not to achieve a strategic victory, but to force the French to defend it at all costs and thus, in the parlance of the day, "bleed them white." And the French obliged them by taking the bait, especially after, on February 25, 1916 — only the fifth day of the battle — a small German raiding party snuck into the impregnable Fort Douaumont and, without firing a single shot, captured it from the even smaller French defending party. Well, then: All of France now rose up under the cry "They shall not pass!" They threw everything they had into defending Verdun, shuttling men and materiel around the clock along a slender forty-five-mile road that would become known as *La Voie Sacrée* — The Sacred Way.

The battle lasted nearly ten months. In that time, each side dropped more than twenty million shells on the other; it is believed that 70 percent of the casualties at Verdun — more than 700,000, in all — were caused by artillery. The Germans very nearly did bleed the French white, killing more than 160,000 of them. But 140,000 of their own were killed in the process. The French retook Douaumont, at a very high cost, after eight months; in the end, they held Verdun. Whether, strategically, it was worth all that — to either side — is another matter for debate. To the French, though, the fact of having saved Verdun — and the memory of all they had to do to save it — were of immeasurable value to their morale. Even today, to many French, Verdun *is* World War I.

Just knowing that much, you could be forgiven for looking at that enormous graveyard at Douaumont and wondering: *Is that it?* But of course, if you were there, you'd know that it isn't, because the whole thing — all sixteen thousand or so graves — rests in the shadow of what is commonly known in that part of the continent as *L'Ossuaire*. The French claim that the bones of 130,000 men repose in the underbelly of the massive Douaumont Ossuary, and I'm certainly not going to challenge them on it. The only other ossuary I am familiar with, at Arlington National Cemetery, is said to hold the bones of 2,111 Civil War dead. That one — they call it a "vault" at Arlington — is about the size of a large delivery van. What they have at Douaumont is, well, not like that, or like anything else you've ever seen, for that matter. To my eyes it resembles a giant stone submarine, 137 meters long, with a 46-meter-high periscope rising up in the center. The periscope is a tower; you can climb to the top and look out over the cemetery and the battlefield beyond it. The hull is a cloister, with an area for religious services — a Catholic Mass was being held there when I visited — and alcoves containing the bodies of unknown soldiers, arranged geographically according to where on the vast battlefield they were recovered. Just about every little block of stone in the place is inscribed with the names of those who went missing at Verdun during those ten months in 1916. It makes quite an impression.

But that's not why this ossuary is here. The real reason for its existence is mostly out of sight, kept below the place's stone floors: the skeletal remains of those 130,000 men, French and German, recovered from the battlefield after the war. If you walk around the outside of the building, you will see, embedded at around the height of your shin, little windows that peer into the chambers where the bones are kept. Press your face against the glass and you'll discern seas of them: femurs behind one window, ribs behind another. In one chamber I saw nothing but skulls; one, very close to my own face at that moment, had a large hole in it, above the eye sockets. I don't know who came up with the figure of 130,000, or how they did so, but having looked into some of those windows it sounds conservative to me. No one knows how many men are still out there, unrecovered as of yet; some estimates put the number at around 100,000. When remains turn up — and they still do — they, too, are taken to Douaumont.

L'Ossuaire is the only place I know of in France where French and German soldiers' remains commingle, or even rest in the same general vicinity. There are, though, a whole lot of German military cemeteries from World War I in France; in certain areas, they are a more common sight even than French cemeteries. The ones I saw were, without exception, lovely spaces, quiet and green, sometimes hosting among the tombstones a number of large old trees, the kind that lend a natural dignity to everything around them.

Some of the cemeteries contain a few small monuments dedicated to this or that fallen soldier (*Hier ruht in Gott unser Kamerad*) during the earlier part of the war by his surviving comrades — many of whom, I imagine, died themselves just a year or two later, when there were no longer enough of the living remaining to pay for such personalized memorials, and no room for them in any event. Most of the rest now lie under a simple black cross shared with three other *Soldaten gefallen.* Some German war cemeteries also contain large cement slabs marking mass graves; one I saw, in the cemetery at Consenvoye, near Verdun, bears a cold metal plaque stating that it contains the bodies of 2,537 German soldiers. Of those, 933 are unknowns; the names of the rest are listed, along with their service title and date of death, on other cold metal plaques, a long line of them. Resting on one on the day I stopped by, held in place by four stones, was a vellum sheath, inside which had been placed a greenish old photograph of a German infantryman: rifle in hand, *Pickelhaube* on head, trim mustache above upper lip. He looked off to the left, away from a bit of prose that some other German, nearly a century later, composed and printed on the page next to him. It read, in perfect twenty-first-century typeface:

In Sacred Memory
Prayers in honor of the respected departed
Jakob Berger
Baker's son from Endorf
Sergeant in a Bavarian foot artillery regiment
Knight of the Iron Cross

Who died heroically for the Fatherland
Far from home and his loved ones
On the 22nd of May 1916
On the heights near Verdun
In the 25th year of his life . . .

And then there was a poem about the Iron Cross, which I won't even try to translate. It was maudlin and overwrought, but my! I could not look away for a long time. I stopped by just about every German cemetery I passed in France — and I passed a good number of them — but never saw anything else like this. I was, as always, completely alone in the place, and yet I only realized that fact when I came upon this little homemade memorial to one of the 11,148 German soldiers buried at

Consenvoye. To many in Germany — and in France, and plenty of other countries, too — it sometimes feels as if the dead of that war are not long gone. Their absence is experienced yet, even though they would have been dead by now anyway; even though they are, in truth, so long gone that probably no one survives who carries any living memory of them.

Neat and orderly as these German cemeteries are, they are not uniform. Some contain personal monuments, and some mass graves. Some contain fewer than a thousand bodies, others more than ten thousand. In some the crosses are thin and iron, while in others they are fat and stone. One thing they all have in common, though, is a scattering of other markers, always stone, shaped like one of the tablets containing the Ten Commandments. These are the Jewish war dead.

Their discovery surprised me so much that even now, years later, I'm not quite sure what to say about them. It saddens me that I even feel that I must say something; surely, the men themselves saw nothing unusual or ironic in their military service, nothing tragic about it but the risk of death that attached itself to them no more or less than to their fellow soldiers who did not happen to be Jews. They served in every *Korps*, in every branch of service, enlisted men and officers, *Kanonieren* and *Musketieren* and *Grenadieren* and *Infanteristen*, doctors and stretcher-bearers, career soldiers and reservists and volunteers for the war. None of that is what surprised me, continues to surprise me; Jews had been in Germany since Roman times, were well integrated and even assimilated into the population at large, enjoyed many more civil rights than did their coreligionists in Russia, say, and certain other parts of Europe.

No, it's not the presence of the bodies that surprises me. It's the presence of the markers. Because the Germans came back a generation later, and stayed another four years, this time as instruments of the Third Reich; and wherever else they went in Europe in those years, they made a point of tearing up Jewish cemeteries, defiling them, carting off the stones and using them to pave roads and line sewers. Their objective was to degrade the Jewish people as a whole, to confiscate their humanity and obliterate their dignity and, ultimately, to erase even their memory. And yet, though they had four years to do so, they never touched those Jewish markers in their own military cemeteries, never tried to destroy this evidence that Jews were a part of Germany, too, and just as willing, and able, to die for their country as anyone else. I have no explanation to offer you.

But what's all this about Lorraine? What's all this about Verdun? What about the Somme? What about Flanders Fields, Where Poppies Grow? Where are the men going over the top wearing kilts and kicking soccer balls? Where are the bagpipes? Where are those guys who wrote poetry in the trenches?

They were all a part of the war; but they were not *the* war. Not even in France. The Somme offensive, while enormous and deadly, was actually launched as a diversion to relieve German pressure on Verdun. And yes, quite a lot of blood fertilized the ground in Flanders — but certainly not more than was spilled in Lorraine, where poppies did not grow.

If this comes as a surprise, it is probably because the image of World War I in the American consciousness has been shaped, for the most part, by sources that are not American; or, for that matter, French, or German. The most influential sources of information about that war in America — the greatest fashioners of World War I imagery in American minds — have been British. Americans wrote an awful lot about that war while they were in it, but for whatever reason, once it ended, they mostly stopped writing about it. The British, though, never did. If anything, they wrote much more about it afterward than they had while it was going on. The French and the Germans wrote a lot about it, too — but not in English. And so, when it came to America's memory and understanding of that war, the British pretty much had the field to themselves. And, understandably, British historians tended to focus on places like Flanders and the Somme, where Tommies fought and died.

In doing so, though, they often engendered, by implication, the false impression that not much went on in places like Verdun and the Argonne, and that what did wasn't terribly important to the war. And when they did choose to mention the AEF at all, they typically wrote that America arrived in France too late and too slowly and utterly unprepared for war; that American officers were poorly trained, incompetent, incapable of command; that American soldiers were cocky, unruly, lacked skills and discipline; and that America's contribution to that war — beyond selling materiel to the Allies, which it did not for any altruistic purpose but simply to make money, a great big pile of it — was negligible. Britain, you see, bore a bit of a grudge against America, because, unlike Canada and Australia and New Zealand and South Africa — which were all British dominions at the time, and had no choice in the matter — the United States did not enter the war when Britain did, in 1914; and once it did enter, in 1917, its supreme commander refused to break up his divisions and have his doughboys fight in smaller units under British commanders, having seen already what the British did with their dominion troops. Those grievances wrought an anti-American bias that infected British histories of that war for decades — some would say it still does — and, by extension, the Americans who read them, including, tragically, the parents and widows and fatherless children of some of the 117,000 or so doughboys who never came home.

I'm not going to tell you that America "won" that war. But neither did Britain, nor France. Britain's naval blockade of Germany, and France's refusal to stop fighting and surrender, were both essential to breaking the German war machine in 1918; but so was the threat of four million fresh American soldiers charging onto the battlefield. From the time America entered the war, in April, 1917, Germany knew time was short. In the spring and summer of 1918, having dispatched the Russians at last, the Germans threw everything they had into a few great offensives on the Western Front, gambling on winning the war before a handful of Americans turned into a horde. But the thing about gambles is: They don't always pay off. Those offensives ultimately failed — due, in no small part, to that "handful" of Americans — and, come fall, left the Germans in a precarious position. At which point there were enough Americans in France to capitalize on that precarious state and, along with the rest of the Allies, actually win the war.

Sadly, America has forgotten that. Instead, decades of British histories and voices have convinced Americans, for the most part, that they got into it too late, that they arrived just in time for the war's end but didn't do very much to bring it about. And that, I believe, is why America has all but forgotten World War I.

You know, though, who hasn't forgotten that America played an essential role in winning that war?

The French.

If you don't believe me, just go to Saint-Mihiel.

In September, 1914, just weeks after the war began, the Germans launched an offensive in Lorraine that is now known as the Battle of Flirey. It proved to be a tremendously successful endeavor for them. Not so much for the French, who left all those bodies strewn about that vast open stretch of farmland, so many that you could walk from one end to the other without touching the ground; but for the Germans? Tremendous. Not only did they kill all those *poilus*, but they seized some two hundred square miles of French territory — and not just any two hundred square miles. For one thing, they contained Montsec, strategic high ground that commanded the entire area; more important, though, they jutted into French lines, creating what became known as the Saint-Mihiel Salient. ("Salient" is a cartographical term for a bulge in a line that protrudes into neighboring territory like a hernia. If you want to see a good example of a salient on a map, look up Browns Valley, Minnesota.) The Saint-Mihiel Salient bedeviled the French; it cut off the main route connecting Nancy, a major French supply center, with Verdun and Paris. Over the course of four years, the French tried repeatedly to drive the Germans back and reduce the salient, but they never could. The Germans held those heights, and had fortified their position heavily. They did like their concrete.

Four years later, after a summer of brutal fighting that started at Belleau Wood and trudged through Château-Thierry, and the Marne, and Soissons, and the Oise-Aisne — throughout which American troops, though under American commanders at the divisional level, ultimately served under French high command — Pershing, bristling at what he and many others perceived as a number of misuses of American troops by the French that resulted in heavy American casualties, decided that the AEF had earned the right, and now had enough troops in country, to fight in cohesive and independent American armies, composed entirely of American divisions and under entirely American command. Having spent much of the past several months eliminating large German salients at Amiens and the Marne, Pershing set his sights on the last one left: Saint-Mihiel. From there, he intended to push on across the German border and capture Metz, which the Germans had seized

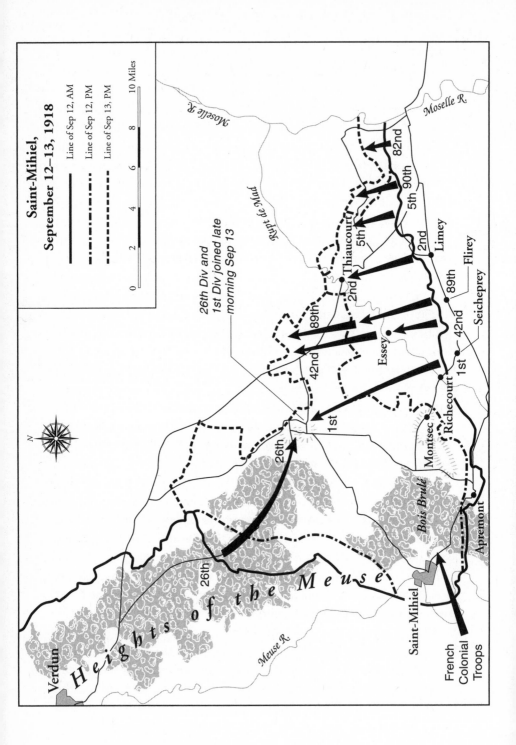

**Saint-Mihiel,
September 12–13, 1918**

Line of Sep 12, AM
Line of Sep 12, PM
Line of Sep 13, PM

0   2   4   6   8   10 Miles

*26th Div and
1st Div joined late
morning Sep 13*

N

Moselle R.

Moselle R.

Rupt de Mad

Thiaucourt

82nd

90th

5th

5th

2nd

2nd

Limey

Flirey

89th

89th

42nd

Seicheprey

42nd

Essey

1st

1st

Richecourt

Montsec

Bois Brulé

Apremont

26th

26th

Heights of the Meuse

Verdun

Meuse R.

Saint-Mihiel

French
Colonial
Troops

from France in 1870 and annexed. The French said: Godspeed. They would even lend him artillery, aeroplanes, tanks, and French colonial troops to support him.

But then, just days before the Americans were to launch their first independent offensive, France's Marshal Ferdinand Foch, the Supreme Commander of all the Allied armies on the Western Front, changed his mind. Now he said he wanted to split the force Pershing had assembled for the offensive — fourteen American divisions in all, collectively the American First Army — into three pieces, two of which he would pull from the offensive and assign to a new one he was planning elsewhere. Pershing refused; instead, he offered this compromise: The First Army would remain intact and launch its offensive on the Saint-Mihiel Salient as planned; once the salient was eliminated, instead of pushing on to Metz, they would hustle up in time for the launch of Foch's new offensive, at a place called the Meuse-Argonne.

Despite their elaborate intelligence network, the Germans knew nothing of this; conversely, the Allies did not know that, in one of those marvelous coincidences of history, General Erich Ludendorff issued orders on September 8 — four days before Pershing's offensive was to commence — for the German Army to begin withdrawing from the salient in order to strengthen their fallback defensive position, the Hindenburg Line. That's the thing about salients: While they vex your enemy, they require a lot of men to hold, since you're surrounded on three sides. And so, on September 11, the Germans started what they reckoned to be the long, slow process of packing up and moving on out. The very next day, more than two hundred thousand American troops, joined by nearly fifty thousand French and French colonials, attacked them on three sides at once.

It started at 1:00 a.m., with a four-hour artillery barrage; at 5:00 a.m., supported now by another barrage that rolled forward ahead of them — and by nearly fifteen hundred aeroplanes, the largest air assault in the entire war (and, to that point, history) — a quarter million Allied troops, all under American command, poured into No Man's Land. It was muddy ground — it had been raining steadily for days — but the troops moved quickly, surpassing their objectives in many cases. (One exception to this was the Yankee Division, which, attacking from the west, met particularly fierce German resistance.) Many of them must have been surprised at how well it all went.

Not nearly as surprised as the Germans, though; Ludendorff, it is said, was rendered inarticulate upon receiving the news. On the morning of the second day, American troops attacking from two sides linked up, enveloping those German troops who remained. By evening, every objective for the offensive had been achieved. The Americans and French had completely eliminated the Saint-Mihiel Salient in less than forty-eight hours — capturing, in the process, some fifteen thousand prisoners and 450 big guns. It was one of the shorter battles of the war.

Pershing had planned the offensive meticulously; without that, it would almost certainly have lasted much longer, perhaps even come out some other way. But in war, well-laid plans that come off almost without a hitch still exact a price. Even with those meticulous plans — and that added bit of luck that had the Germans inaugurating a withdrawal almost simultaneously — that price was 7,000 American casualties; 4,153 of them are buried in the St.-Mihiel American Cemetery, just outside the town of Thiaucourt.

If that name sounds familiar, it's because Thiaucourt was where the Germans had marched some two hundred American prisoners from the 102nd Infantry Regiment, mostly Connecticut men whom they had captured when they'd stormed Seicheprey nearly five months earlier. The Germans hadn't held Seicheprey for more than a few hours; they'd held Thiaucourt for almost exactly four years, having taken it, along with two hundred square miles' worth of other towns and villages, during the Battle of Flirey. The Americans liberated all of those places on September 12, 1918. To this day, no one in any of them needs to have the significance of that date explained to them. The town of Essey, liberated by the 42nd Division — under the command of Douglas MacArthur (who, against orders, wanted so badly to go on and capture Metz that Pershing took pains to restrain him) — even renamed its main thoroughfare *Rue du 12 Septembre.*

You probably wouldn't know that, though, unless you traveled to Essey and saw it for yourself. You probably wouldn't know that in Flirey, after the war, they took the government's allotment and built *two* monuments — one to the French soldiers, local and otherwise, who perished in the war; the other to the Americans who fought in the region. You probably wouldn't know that in Thiaucourt, they used their allotment to build just a single stone pedestal, upon which stands a life-sized statue of two soldiers shaking hands: a *poilu*, holding a rifle; and a doughboy, carrying the Stars and Stripes. You probably wouldn't know that, though America has largely forgotten what Americans did Over There — what a difference it made in the war and how much it meant to France — the French haven't.

And you certainly wouldn't understand, without seeing the place for yourself, just what a hell the heights above the Meuse River and the depths of the Argonne Forest were for four years. And how, though it could hardly have seemed possible to the French and Americans coming off their exultant victory down at Saint-Mihiel — and to the Germans, still stunned from their defeat — things were about to get much worse there.

14

A Wicked Gun,
That Machine Gun

IN SEPTEMBER, 2003, having returned from a swing through the South and a trip to Wisconsin, I began planning a visit to the Pacific Northwest. I wanted to get to Portland to meet Howard Ramsey—formerly of the 302nd Water Tank Train—and had a few more prospects lined up, mostly in the Seattle area. Still, I felt that I needed more; I suspected that some of those prospects might not pan out. I was correct: The 107-year-old who'd served with the 1st Engineers and now lived near Tacoma—he had been gassed in France, I'd heard, but had fully recovered—turned out to be unable to answer any questions beyond his name and date of birth; and the 104-year-old cavalry veteran at the Soldiers Home in Orting, Washington—he'd served in the Panama Canal Zone—told me I was an idiot for imagining that he might remember anything at all about his youth or military service, and that the secret to his longevity was nobody else's damned business. I may have mentioned him before.

Fortunately, before I headed west I went through the French List and tracked down every prospect listed as living in Washington and Oregon. Unfortunately, they were all dead.

The day before I departed for Seattle, though, I went through the list again, just to make sure I hadn't missed anyone. I'd called everyone recorded as living in those two states, with one exception: one William J. Lake, of Yakima, Washington. I hadn't even bothered with Mr. Lake, since his date of birth was listed as October 30, 1885, which would have made him 117 years and eleven months old. No man, I knew, had ever lived to that age. But as I looked over his application one last time, it occurred to me that he would have been 113 years old when he'd been awarded the Legion of Honor, at which point he would have already been one of the oldest men who'd ever lived. Yet I had never heard of Mr. Lake, had never seen his name on any of the lists of the world's oldest people, which lists I had been studying quite frequently of late. I wondered: Was 1885 a typo?

I confirmed as much after I called his last listed place of residence, a retirement manor in Yakima, and learned, to my delight, that he was still alive and healthy and clearheaded and would be equally delighted, I was told, to visit with me. Some group, in fact — the Boy Scouts, maybe, or the American Legion, something like that — had not too long before come and presented him with something or other, and everyone had had just a fine time. I got there as quickly as I could.

Yakima is not what most people envision when they think of Washington. That image — green, mountainous, rain-soaked — is accurate, but only in the western part of the state. When you head east, you hit a certain point — I'd peg it just past Cle Elum, a nice little town about eighty miles southeast of Seattle that boasts a telephone museum and a gas station convenience store that sells every kind of jerky one can imagine — where that Washington disappears pretty quickly, leaving you in a Washington that is a lot flatter and strongly beige, a desert without cacti. Yakima, which sits in a valley surrounded by ridges about sixty miles beyond Cle Elum, is the largest city in this particular Washington, but it's actually a fairly compact place, one of those settlements in the middle of a whole lot of nothing that begins suddenly and ends just as quickly. Don't let all that beige fool you, though — they grow a lot of apples there. Hops, too, I am told.

The retirement home in which William J. Lake lived was, like Yakima, earth-toned and compact, but it was a pleasant place. His particular room, right up front, was large and bright; I don't know if he got it just because he was nearly 108 years old and a World War I veteran, but I like to think so. A friendly attendant led me to it when I showed up, and even knocked on his door for me. Mr. Lake opened it himself, as I remember, grinned charmingly, and shook my hand. He had a great smile, understated and just a bit wry, and wore a pair of almost-comically-oversized aviator eyeglasses that seemed to accentuate his baldness somehow. And he was a small man, five feet six and a

half inches tall in 1919, according to his discharge papers; the succeeding eighty-four years, and a stoop he had developed at some point in
there, had shaved off a few more inches. Someone had told him I'd be
coming, because he was dressed sharply, in a plaid cotton dress shirt
and chinos with a solid crease. He had his citations all laid out for me,
too: the grand, impressive Légion d'Honneur certificate; a Certificate
of Congratulations from the Veterans of Foreign Wars; the large medal
that the Boy Scouts or American Legion or whoever had presented to
him; and a handful of smaller medallions. He seemed excited to talk to
me; I got the impression that, despite all of those awards and honors,
no one had actually asked him about his service in a long time. It was
October 20, 2003.

I had to concentrate pretty hard just to hear Mr. Lake, since he spoke
softly and had, besides, another one of those old-timey accents that are
all but extinct now. In his case, it was a gravelly-old-prospector type
of voice — he sounded a bit like the elderly Jack Crabb as portrayed by
Dustin Hoffman in the film *Little Big Man*. It was, at first, a jarring
contradiction to his clean-shaven and ironed appearance. Adding to
the dissonance of the atmosphere was his large recliner, also beige; it
utterly dwarfed him, made him look like a child, sitting in it as he did
slouched over to one side. Still, I stopped noticing all of it just as soon
as we started talking.

"When were you born?" I asked him.

"October the thirtieth, eighteen ninety-five." And there it was.

"And where were you born?" I asked.

"Missouri," he said. Or, more accurately: "Missoura."

"What part of Missouri?"

"Hannibal. Mark Twain's old town." On October 30, 1895, Mark
Twain was in the midst of a worldwide lecture tour.

Actually, Mr. Lake added quickly by way of clarification: "Well, I was
in New London, which is only ten miles from Hannibal."

"What were your parents' names?" I asked him.

"My dad's name was . . ." He pursed his lips and looked off to one
side for a moment. "My dad!" he said suddenly, seeming startled at
the mention of the man, or, perhaps, the fact that he could no longer
remember his name. I looked away for a moment, not wanting to em-

barrass him — or, if I'm being really honest, to catch a glimpse of what it must feel like to discover that you have forgotten such a thing.

"You know," he continued, undeterred, "he died when he was very young. He went to Oklahoma and opened that Indian Territory for homesteading. And he got pneumonia and was home just a week when he died. Left my mom — a wife and seven kids."

"And were you the youngest?"

"No, there was two younger than I, and then one brother and three sisters older than I was." He was the last of them left, he said — not surprising, since his youngest brother, Graydon, had been born in 1899.

"What did your father do for a living?" I asked him.

"He had a ranch there in . . . Missouri, but he went to Oklahoma. That's when they opened up that Indian Territory for land," he said. His father, he explained, had gone on ahead to Oklahoma on his own to stake a homesteading claim, but had fallen ill there and hurried back to Missouri just in time to expire. "He just — he died," his son recalled more than a century later. "And so we had a pretty rough time." He was six years old then.

His mother, Emma, was left alone with seven children under the age of twelve; the youngest was still a baby. So she did what people did in those days, if they could: she farmed her children out to kin. "I stayed with my uncle and aunt for a while," Mr. Lake told me. "Some of our relations took at least one of us, because our mother couldn't do it. Our granddad [also named William J.], my mother's folks, they built us a house — they had a big son, they built us a house, and then we lived there. But then, soon as I got big enough to work, I had to go to work quick. There was nothing else to do."

"How old were you when you went to work?" I asked him.

"I think I was about eight years old when I started working," he replied.

"What kind of work did you do, at first?"

"Well, I would drive and shoe the horses . . . I drove — well, the most horses I ever drove was eight, eight horses at one time. Plowing and just doing things like that. In Montana." And here's where the chronology gets fuzzy for a bit, because at some point — 1915 or 1916, as he recalled — the family moved from Missouri to Montana. "Some of our relations was out there," he explained, "and they was talking about the difference in the two states." Apparently, the relations convinced them to make the move, which they did when Bill was nineteen or twenty years old. That doesn't mean that he really didn't start working at the age of eight, but I suspect he didn't leave school then, because the 1910 census records fourteen-year-old William J. Lake's occupation as "None." The family was living in Saverton, Missouri, then, a little town on the Mississippi just eight miles downriver from Hannibal; they are listed as working a home farm. I'm sure young Bill had to do a lot of work around that farm, and quite possibly more elsewhere. I don't doubt he started doing so at eight years old.

And I imagine it was a hard life for all of them, too, since they did eventually move all the way to Montana, no small undertaking, and "leased a farm out there," as Mr. Lake remembered nearly nine decades later. "Hay and grain," he explained. "A small one. No corn, too cold for corn. The season was too short for corn." He added: "That's where I was when I went into the Army."

"When did you end up joining the Army?" I asked him.

"I didn't," he said. "I wanted to join the Army, but Mother said don't do it. She said maybe it'll blow over, so I went to work. But then I was drafted." This, he told me, was in the fall of 1917, about six months after the United States entered the war. Almost exactly, as it happens: His service record shows he was inducted into the Army at Livingston, Montana, on October 4 of that year. "Yeah," he said, "my mom — I wanted to enlist, but she talked me out of it . . . She said, 'Well, maybe the war will be over soon, and maybe you won't have to go.' But — there was four of us boys, and I'm the only one that went." He explained: "My oldest brother, apparently he had, he was farming and he had a daughter. And my other two brothers — they, of course, I mean they was drafted, but neither one of them passed. I was the only one that did."

"Is that right?" I asked. "They didn't pass the physical?"

"I don't know why," he said, still sounding genuinely perplexed. "But neither one did."

The Army put Bill Lake on a train in Livingston and sent him west, to Pierce County, Washington. There, about ten miles from Tacoma, they were building a new training base for sixty thousand soldiers: Camp Lewis, named for explorer Meriwether Lewis, whose Corps of Discovery had passed through the general vicinity on its way to the Pacific Ocean more than a century earlier. Today, Fort Lewis is the largest military installation in the Pacific Northwest; it is said to be the most requested posting in the United States Army.

In the fall of 1917, men from eight states — Washington, Oregon, California, Nevada, Utah, Idaho, Montana, and Wyoming — and the territory of Alaska streamed into Camp Lewis to be gathered into a new division, the 91st, nicknamed from its conception the "Wild West Division." Its symbol was a pine tree. The 91st was the highest-numbered white division in the Army at the time. The two colored divisions were the 92nd and 93rd. The Army used a system of ordinal numbering that had some logic to it, but not much. Single-digit divisions were Regular Army; 26 through 42 were regional National Guard, starting in New England and moving, as the digits rose, south and west — at least until the high 30s, when they spiraled hither and yon, culminating in the 42nd, which comprised National Guard troops from twenty-six states and the District of Columbia; and the last stretch, 76 through 91, being draftees, once again starting east and moving west, ending at Camp Lewis with the 91st. There were a lot of unused numbers; I don't know why. I have heard it speculated that these were "ghost divisions," used to intimidate and mislead the enemy. Perhaps.

But back to Camp Lewis, still under construction when a farm hand from Montana showed up, just days before his twenty-second birthday. "It's the most beautiful place on earth," Mr. Lake opined eighty-five years hence. "When we was there, it was all wooden barracks. We had to sleep in tents for a few days till they got our barracks finished. Now it's all brick buildings." He was put in the 362nd Infantry Regiment — composed entirely of Montana men — and assigned to the Machine Gun Company.

The term "Machine Gun Company" brings to mind the image of a trench full of doughboys firing Tommy guns at the Hun, and in fact the Thompson submachine gun — that icon of gangland Chicago and the FBI's Most Wanted list, with its distinctive drum magazine and wooden stock and grip, which became notorious after the Saint Valentine's Day Massacre of 1929 — was developed for use in World War I by a retired Army colonel named John T. Thompson (his middle name, Taliaferro, was the same as Booker T. Washington's), who had served in the Spanish-American War with a young lieutenant named John Henry Parker, a man whose supreme faith in that weapon ultimately earned him the nickname Machine Gun. If the name "Machine Gun Parker" sounds familiar, it's probably because twenty years later, as a colonel, Parker would be commanding the Army's 102nd Infantry Regiment when they came under attack by German *Stosstruppen* at a French village called Seicheprey. It really was a small world.

Colonel Thompson's weapon — its original nickname was the "trench broom" — came along a bit too late to be used in the war, but it's interesting to think about what it might have done had the armistice not preempted its career in the military. It was truly revolutionary: relatively small and light, it could be fired by one man from a standing position, and reloaded in mere seconds. The machine guns of the war — Vickers and Hotchkiss and Browning and Maschinengewehr and all the rest — were large and heavy and, whether cooled by water or air, prone to overheating and jamming. Cumbersome affairs, they were mounted on tripods or sledges, and thus could be fired only from a prone position. They were belt-fed and required entire crews to operate and maintain; the nature and demands of the weapon rendered those crews less mobile than regular infantry, which is why machine guns were often corralled into their own companies or battalions, which were distributed strategically. Unable to relocate as easily as regular infantry, they had to dig in, construct defenses, and camouflage themselves as best they could, which often was not very well at all. In one of those odd little quirks of war, operating a terribly intimidating weapon left you terribly vulnerable, too.

This was Private William J. Lake's assignment.

"How did you end up in a machine gun company?" I asked him in 2003.

"Well, that's where they put me!" he said. "So that's where I was."

"Did you have any experience with guns before?"

"Well, just rifles and shotguns, is all. There, of course, we had to practice. Do a lot of shooting with the rifles at different distances, and the machine gun. They had, there at Camp Lewis — well, now they call it Fort Lewis — they had a Colt, which is a very light machine gun, but

I was shooting and I forget how many yards I was shooting, but I got forty-five out of fifty shots out there at I think it was three hundred yards, I think is what it was if I remember right. And then we had the Browning, which was a water-cooled gun. And that was fast — three hundred shots a minute."

"Did you prefer that to the Colt?" I asked.

"Yeah," he said.

"You liked it better?"

"Oh, yes," he said. "A lot better. It was a heavier, a bigger machine. And it was faster; I think it was three hundred shots a minute, or something like that. Terrible." The Browning sat on a tripod and was belt-fed; "they had targets," he recalled, "which I had to practice on all the time — rifle and machine gun both. And I done pretty good." Once he got to France, though, he was assigned not to fire the gun, but to run back and forth from the nest to a depot behind the lines to fetch ammunition for it, which was quite possibly the most dangerous job in the crew. But I'll get to that a bit later, because first there's the story of the thing that happened to Bill Lake even before he made it to France, the thing that seemed pretty awful to him at the time but which might just have saved his life.

Private Lake and the rest of the Wild West Division trained at Camp Lewis, he told me, for nine months before they boarded trains for Camp Merritt, New Jersey, whence they would head up to New York and ship out for France. According to the unnamed author of *The Story of the 91st Division,* published in 1919, the land portion of the trek took about six days. It was early summer; they traveled through a lot of areas that were probably quite hot at the time, and I doubt there were showers on those trains. Nevertheless, it was a spirited journey:

> On their trip across the continent, the soldiers from the Far West had an excellent opportunity to acquaint themselves with the patriotic unity which ultimately was to bring about the defeat of Germany. After witnessing demonstrations from coast to coast, the men of the 91st felt that they were backed by an undivided nation. The motherly gray-haired old woman standing in front of her little cottage on the broad prairie of Montana, alternately waving a flag and brushing

away the tears she could not restrain, contributed as much to this feeling as did the impromptu receptions tendered the men in the great cities through which they passed.

The journey also gave many citizens, especially in the East, a better conception of the high quality of manhood the West was contributing to the United States Army.

If it sounds like the men of the 91st had a grand old time crossing the country by rail, Private William J. Lake, at least, did not. He was sick the whole way across; was sick even before he left Camp Lewis.

"I got the measles," he explained.

Eight and a half decades later, that continued to mystify him: "I don't know where I got them," he told me. "*Still* don't know where I got them!" No one else seemed to have them; there was no word of measles in the camp, or on the train. Not even from him: Bill Lake traveled six days on a hot, crowded troop train, from Washington to New Jersey, sick with measles — and never told anyone. "I didn't say anything until we got on the boat," he confessed. "I was out on the water." The boat, he recalled, was the *Empress of Russia*, a British/Canadian mail ship that was used as a troop transport during the war.

"Why didn't you say anything?" I asked him.

"Because I know if I did," he said, "and it leaked that I did have something, I might be out of the company or something, and I didn't want that, so I didn't say nothing." He smiled, and then laughed.

Eventually, out at sea, he told his captain. "I was laying down," he recalled. "He came around, he says, 'What's the matter?' I says, 'I don't feel good.' He sent the doctor down there, told me I had the measles. Still don't know today where I got them."

"Nobody else had them?"

"Nobody else had them far as I know. So they put me in the hospital on the boat, hospital room . . . and then they got over there" — that is, Liverpool, where the 91st disembarked before shuttling across the Channel to France — "and they left me [in a hospital] over there for six weeks. Wanted to be sure I was all good before I went back to the company."

"Six weeks?"

"Yeah. And they'd been in two battles before I got there."

That last bit is not quite accurate: The 91st Division — minus Private Lake — arrived in France in late July, 1918, and proceeded directly to "its training area in the Department of Haute Marne," the divisional history reports, where "the nature of the terrain could not be surpassed for training troops in the open warfare in which they were to participate later. . . . The entire month of August was passed in this area while the Division received its final training. Incessant drilling, long marches and frequent exercises were the schedule for the entire Division." In early September they moved over to Saint-Mihiel, but were held in reserve until that offensive ended, at which point they moved again, to Meuse-Argonne, where they were assigned to a central place in the line, between the 35th and 37th Divisions, near the village of Cheppy. And it was from there that they were sent forward at 5:25 a.m. on September 26, 1918, the start of the offensive. Private Lake arrived at the front on September 29. He missed out on a lot of training that might have proven useful to him at some point; but he also missed out on his division's first three days of battle, and, though he probably didn't feel this way at the time, the historical record shows that those were good days to miss.

"The 91st had never been in any except a practice trench, or heard a bullet or shell fired in battle, when it went into position for the attack," Frederick Palmer writes in his 1919 account of the Meuse-Argonne, *Our Greatest Battle.* Palmer had heard many bullets and shells fired by that time; an American war correspondent — like many reporters of the time, he jumped papers pretty frequently, as it suited him — he had seen a good bit of the war by the time the United States entered it, and managed to write and publish three books about it while it was still happening. In the last of these, 1918's *America in France,* he predicts that a fight must take place in the Meuse-Argonne, and that an Allied victory there would be essential to an ultimate triumph over Germany. "The German must resist our advance or endanger his line of communications to Champagne and Picardy," he explains. "The area from Verdun to Holland formed the mouth of a pocket, although a broad one, for all the German army on the soil of northern France. Steady pounding from Verdun to the Argonne must be a part of any great plan which sought, whether in the hope of swift results or in the deliberate expectation of slow results, to force the German army back to German soil, or to draw reinforcements from the Rheims-Flanders line under its threat."

Marshal Ferdinand Foch, Supreme Commander of the Allied Armies, envisioned a "Grand Offensive" against Germany's fearsome Hindenburg Line, its back-against-the-wall defensive position. It would take the shape of a trident, its three points being Ypres, in Belgium, where the Belgians, British, and French would attack; northern France, where mostly British and Australian troops would strike, abetted by two American divisions; and the section of Lorraine, northwest of Verdun, that encompassed the Argonne Forest and a stretch of the Meuse River, where ten American divisions (plus the 368th Infantry Regiment of the 92nd Division) and two French armies (including two regiments of black American troops, the 371st and 372nd) would attack. Ypres had been the site of four previous battles during the war, while northern France had been overrun by the Germans during *their* great offensive that spring; both were largely flat, and had been blasted clear in the course of four years of war. The Argonne Forest, though, was largely intact and quite dense, and the entire area was full of hills and valleys, with sharp heights above the Meuse. The landscape alone made the place a difficult one in which to launch an assault; the Germans had taken it in the opening weeks of the war, and had promptly augmented nature's defenses with bunkers and trenchworks, barbed wire and machine-gun nests, tunnels and electric lines and narrow-gauge railroads and lots and lots of concrete. A great many French and Germans had died there in the succeeding four years — sniping and shelling, dropping bombs from aeroplanes or detonating them in subterranean chambers — but France hadn't launched a major offensive there since 1914. The Germans' defenses, natural and manmade, were just too formidable.

Now, though, with Germany weakened from its losses during the summer, the Americans would try it. Despite the fact that German defenses there were still very strong, perhaps even as tough as ever, Pershing wanted the Meuse-Argonne for his troops, and had fought hard for it; he'd even agreed to rush his men up there from Saint-Mihiel as soon as that battle was won, though this meant transporting hundreds of thousands of troops in the dark of night — surprise was seen as an essential element of the new offensive's success — along with guns,

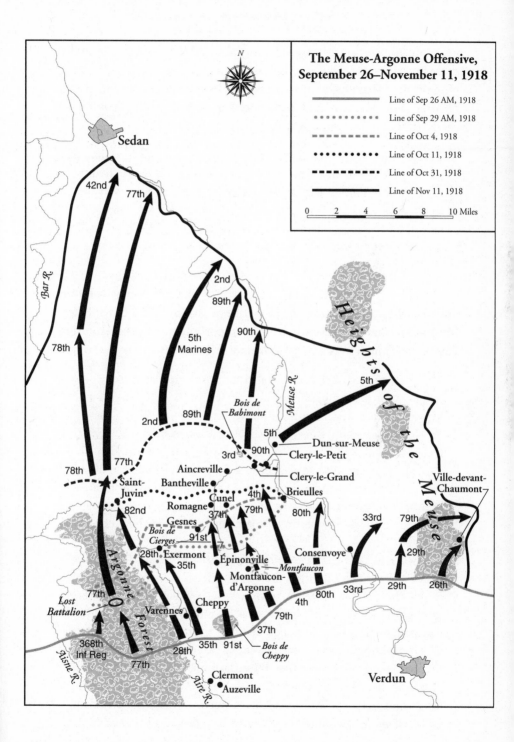

The Meuse-Argonne Offensive,
September 26–November 11, 1918

Line of Sep 26 AM, 1918
Line of Sep 29 AM, 1918
Line of Oct 4, 1918
Line of Oct 11, 1918
Line of Oct 31, 1918
Line of Nov 11, 1918

0   2   4   6   8   10 Miles

N

Sedan

Bar R.

42nd

77th

78th

78th

77th

2nd

89th

5th
Marines

2nd

89th

90th

Bois de
Babimont

Meuse R.

5th

5th

Dun-sur-Meuse

Clery-le-Petit

Saint-
Juvin

3rd

90th

Clery-le-Grand

Brieulles

Aincreville

Bantheville

82nd

Cunel

4th

79th

80th

Romagne

37th

Gesnes

Bois de
Cierges

91st

28th

Exermont

35th

Épinonville

Montfaucon

33rd

79th

29th

Ville-devant-
Chaumont

Heights of the Meuse

Consenvoye

Lost
Battalion

77th

Varennes

Cheppy

Montfaucon-
d'Argonne

4th

80th

33rd

29th

26th

368th
Inf Reg

77th

28th

35th

91st

79th

37th

Bois de
Cheppy

Argonne Forest

Aisne R.

Aire R.

Clermont

Auzeville

Verdun

tanks, ordnance, and all manner of supplies, all of it (and them) on just three muddy roads. That it somehow managed to succeed, without tipping off the Germans, says a lot about Colonel George Marshall, who planned the operation, and about the men he was moving around. As Frederick Palmer writes in *Our Greatest Battle:*

> Officers who had hoped for a little sleep once the Saint-Mihiel offensive was under way received "travel orders," with instructions to reach the Argonne area by hopping a motor-truck or in any way they could. Soldiers, after marching all night, might seek sleep in the villages if there were room in houses, barns or haylofts. Blocks of traffic were frequent when some big gun or truck slewed into a slough in the darkness.

Somehow, though, they all made it into place in time, including the Wild West Division, which hadn't been put into the fight at Saint-Mihiel but was now installed in an important position in the line. Palmer held them in high regard from the first:

> The Pacific Coast men had traveled far, clear across the Continent and across the Atlantic. Traveling was in their line. If distance had kept them from reaching the front as soon as some of the eastern divisions, noticeably those praised New Yorkers of the 77th, they would show that they could move fast and stick in the war to the end. The pioneer heritage was theirs; they were neighbors to Alaska, who looked toward Asia across the Pacific: big men who thought big and were used to doing big things. Their people depended upon them for great deeds worthy of their homes beyond the Great Divide....
>
> They had the stamina which their climate breeds. They were under no apprehension that their inexperience in battle would not enable them to take care of the Germans they met, once they were through the trenches and in the open. As men of the distances, they had imagination which applied all their training to the situations which they would have to encounter. No veterans ever went into action with more confidence than these draft men. The roar of the surf on Pacific beaches, of the car-wheels from the Coast to New York, of the steamship propellers across the Atlantic, was the song of their gathered energy suddenly released in a charge.

If I'd known that simply hailing from the West infused one with such a romantic persona, I would have arranged to have been born out there instead of in the land of the 77th. It's a good thing that the men of the 91st didn't read Palmer's paean to them before they started forward on the morning of September 26, 1918; such effusive advanced press can be intimidating.

As it was, they got off to a slow start that morning, having to contend with uncut tangles of German wire, but they benefited from a massive artillery barrage the night before, "so vast, so stunning," the divisional history records, "and the noise was so overwhelming that no one could grasp the whole. The German trenches were marked in the darkness by a line of leaping fire, punctuated now and then by the higher bursts of some particularly heavy shell." Hundreds of those shells contained phosgene and mustard gas; yes, America used them, too. By the time the men of the Wild West Division came upon those German front-line trenches, the next morning, they were empty.

Beyond them, though, the 91st ran into stiff resistance, first in the dense Bois de Cheppy (or Cheppy Woods), and then while crossing an open ravine raked by German machine-gun fire. Still, they advanced, knocking out machine-gun nests one by one, taking prisoners along the way. They took a lot of casualties, too, yet they advanced more rapidly than the 35th Division, on their left, and the 37th on their right. Fastest of all was Private Lake's regiment, the 362nd, which advanced some five miles that day, and by late afternoon had reached the strongly defended village of Épinonville, an act that won them the praise of the regiment's new commander, Colonel John Henry "Machine Gun" Parker, formerly of the 102nd Infantry Regiment, who had, in the space of four days that summer, been awarded two more Distinguished Service Crosses to supplement the one he'd earned at Seicheprey.

The Montana men now under Parker's command had done well for themselves on the first day of the offensive. Unfortunately, they did so well that the troops on their flanks — the Wild West Division's 361st and 363rd Infantry Regiments to their left, the 37th Division to their right — couldn't keep up. The 362nd had thus created a salient in the German lines that proved difficult to defend; the Germans counterattacked, drove them back out of Épinonville, and promptly set about reinforcing their defensive positions all around the village. The next day, the Montanans tried to take the village again. And again. "Three separate assaults on Épinonville were made, but each was repulsed," the divisional history reports. "When the attack moved forward it met an enemy reinforced and strongly located in a multitude of machine gun nests, supported also by a well-directed and cruel artillery fire that grew in intensity throughout the day." Under different circumstances they might have tried something less dangerous, instead, but they were ordered to push forward as hard and as far as they could in the hope of drawing German firepower away from two American divisions to their right, which were trying desperately to take Montfaucon, having failed in their attempt the day before. At eleven hundred feet, Montfaucon — its name translates to "Falcon Mountain" — was the high point in the sector; it commanded views of the entire area. Like everything else they held in the vicinity, the Germans had taken it in 1914, and had fought off determined French assaults in the months and years that followed. It was essential ground; *Kronprinz* Wilhelm used it as his personal lookout station, and the Americans knew they couldn't move forward without it. They took it that second day. Today there is an American monument there, a stout column some two hundred feet high.

The 362nd spent the night of September 27 in the same spot as they had the night of the 26th, south of Épinonville. There were fewer of them this time. The following morning, the rest of the division joined the assault, extending itself out almost into other sectors in an effort to flank the village, which they finally took, and held. The 362nd was then given the unenviable task of keeping the Germans from encircling the Wild West Division's other three regiments, the 361st, 363rd, and 364th. The farther they all advanced, the farther their salient stretched, leaving them increasingly exposed to German attacks, which in turn became more and more fierce as the Americans advanced, first into the Bois de Cierges — woods filled with barbed wire and machine-gun nests — and then the open fields approaching the village of Gesnes. "The [German] artillery fire had become much more severe from morning on; it continued throughout the night," the divisional history recalls. "A heavy rain had also come on and increased as darkness closed in. The men had been fighting steadily for three days, had had no blankets to protect them from the cold September nights, and because of their rapid advance it had been impossible to serve them any hot food since before the jump-off."

Those were the three days that the measles had spared Private William J. Lake.

He arrived at the front on the fourth day, September 29, 1918. His six weeks in that hospital in Liverpool had given him a view of the war that no one else in the Wild West Division had experienced, yet. As the lone American among ailing Tommies, he told me, "it was like a different universe. They talked different. And they told me, they didn't seem to have any money; they was always asking me for money. Well, I didn't have any money to give them guys. That's the way it was — they was just left behind and broke."

"Were a lot of them wounded?" I asked.

"Yeah," he said. "I saw several of them with their arms and legs off."

When he was deemed well enough to fight, he was put on a train for Southampton, then a transport for Le Havre, and then, he said, "I had to walk a day to get to the unit," carrying a fifty-pound pack all the while. When he arrived, the first person to greet him was his captain, a man he and the rest of the Machine Gun Company held in very high esteem. Instinctively, he went to salute, but the captain caught his arm and stopped him; shook his hand, instead. Private Lake was perplexed. "He said, 'Don't salute me,' he says. 'You don't know who's looking.' And so I didn't. That's true — you didn't know," he told me.

And then he added, softly: "And he was killed that night."

"He was killed that night?" I repeated, a bit stunned. "How? By a sniper, or . . .'"

"I don't know," he said. "All I know is he got killed." He shook his head. "Well, that hurt me. He was a good guy. He was easy to get along with, but he wanted you to do what [he told you to do] . . . He was one of them guys who wasn't afraid of nothing." He added: "He wouldn't ask you to do anything that he didn't."

"Do you remember his name?" I asked.

He was quiet for a moment, pursed his lips. "No," he said softly. "I cannot remember his name." It seemed to pain him as much as not being able to remember his father's.

"So what was it like when you got to the front?" I asked him. "What did it look like?"

"Well, I'll tell you," he said as he closed his eyes and shook his head again. "Bullets zipping around you all the time. You just never knew when you was going to get hit. But I was lucky . . ."

He was. The corps commander's orders for the 91st Division on September 29, the day Private Lake arrived at the front, were to advance and advance, "pushing the attack with utmost vigor and regardless of cost." For the 362nd, that meant leaving the cover of the Bois de Cierges, crossing a mile or so of open fields, and taking Gesnes. Since the American divisions on their left and right were still way behind them, those fields would be subject to German fire — artillery, machine gun, rifle, mortar, poison gas — from three sides. Machine Gun Parker, who is said to have strongly questioned the wisdom of the orders, nevertheless led the attack himself.

He didn't make it to Gesnes.

Colonel Parker displayed great gallantry and fearlessness in leading and directing his front line with utter disregard for personal safety and urged his men forward by his personal example, all under heavy machine-gun, high-explosive, gas-shell, and shrapnel fire. He was abreast of his front line until he fell, twice wounded, but thereafter remained in active command for a period of five hours, when he was relieved by the lieutenant colonel of his regiment.

So reads the citation for his fourth Distinguished Service Cross (a record for that war, by the way); it was not awarded posthumously, which implication makes him more fortunate than many of the men under his command that day, who died somewhere in that mile between the woods and the village. More fell in and around Gesnes itself. "This attack was very costly to the 362nd Infantry," the divisional history offers, with typical understatement. "Colonel Parker and Major Bradbury of the 362nd were wounded, a number of valuable officers were killed, the total loss of regiment in killed and wounded being at least five hundred."

Still, by day's end, the 362nd had, somehow, found a way to attain their objective, slowly advancing against terrible resistance to take Gesnes. By nightfall, though, their position was deemed indefensible, and they were ordered to retreat. At least they could get a hot meal, since a few rolling kitchens had finally caught up with them, though they had to be set up in the cover of the Bois de Cierges, and even there could only operate at night. "It was impossible to use these kitchens in the daytime without exposing the vicinity to heavy shell fire," the history explains. "Some of the men serving the kitchens were killed and wounded, and some men going to the kitchens for hot coffee were wounded."

The history ends its account of September 29, 1918: "In four days the Division had lost 8 field and 125 company officers and 3,000 men." Two days later, the figure was 150 officers and 4,000 men. And they would be there nearly another two weeks beyond that.

As he said time and again eighty-five years later, Bill Lake was lucky. He was not among those thousands of casualties. The Germans sure did try to include him, though. Like artillery, machine guns were high-priority targets for the enemy because of the damage they did. ("That machine gun was a wicked gun, that machine gun," Private Lake recalled. "Oh, man.") But there are only a few ways to silence a machine gun, since you can't really assault them directly without exposing yourself to their terrible fire. One is to hit them with artillery; for that you have to know exactly where they are, and you have to be able to hit them quickly enough that they can't just scuttle away once they figure out what you're up to. Another way is to crawl up on their flanks undetected — and already you're getting into a high level of difficulty, as machine-gun nests were often well-protected — and blow them up with grenades. Or, finally, you could kill the guys who run back and forth between the machine gun and its supply depot, fetching ammunition.

Private Lake was one of those guys.

"That's what they were after," he told me, "they" being the Germans. "After the guys hauling the machine-gun ammunition."

"They wanted to keep you from —"

"Getting ammunition in there."

"So what would you do?" I asked. "You would have to ride back and forth between the front line and the ammunition depot?"

"Yeah," he said. "But we did that at night. We didn't do it during the daytime." Too dangerous.

He was given the job, I imagine, because of his experience driving teams of horses. "They didn't have this mechanized stuff at that time at all," he explained.

"So when you would go back and forth between the front and the ammunition depot, you were driving a horse cart?" I asked.

"Mule," he said.

"What were the mules like with the artillery? Did they get spooked?"

"They would get killed once in a while."

"How did you find your way?"

"Well," he said, "we knew about where our front line was. And we'd haul it up there so far, and they'd come and get it and carry it in by hand. Because it came in belts."

"How many belts would you bring back at a time?"

"Oh, maybe four or five."

"And how many bullets on each belt?"

"A hundred and fifty, I think it was."

A machine gun can go through 600 or 750 rounds pretty quickly in the heat of battle. Private Lake had to make quite a few runs every night, and flashlights — and lighters, and matches, and anything else that might help illuminate the way — were, of course, forbidden. "Was that difficult?" I asked him.

"Well, yeah," he said. "Sometimes it was, 'cause that's some pretty rough country to go over."

I asked him if he got used to it at some point. "Well, you kind of get used to it," he told me, "but it's pretty scary, I'll tell you, because you don't know when you're going to get it."

"How did you cope with that?"

"Well, it kind of bothered me at first, but I got used to it — well, as near used to it as I'd ever get, because you'd hear bullets hitting off, zipping all around . . ."

"What would you do when bullets were zipping around? Would you hit the ground, or would you just keep on your way?"

"No," he said, "I just kept going."

"So you really just had to be very lucky?" I posited.

"That's right," he said. "Very lucky, that's true." One night, he told me, "a piece of shrapnel just missed my left arm," while another one tore through his coattail, he said, "about two inches from my back." If it had hit him, he reckoned, "I'd have been gone . . . that's how close I come to getting it." The following night — "I was just standing there," he explained, "waiting for something, I guess, I don't remember what it was" — he had a close encounter with a German bullet. "It was either machine gun or rifle," he told me. "Whichever it was, I don't know, I couldn't tell you. But it hit the heel on my shoe." And tore it off. He got off a few shots himself — some at a low-flying German aeroplane, others at an enemy gunner — but he didn't believe he'd hit either.

Another time, he recalled, "I got a little gas" — that is, mustard gas, not the kind we all get from time to time. "Not enough to do any harm, really," he told me.

"What kind of effect did it have on you?" I asked him.

"Well," he said, "it makes you sick. It makes you feel terrible."

"You threw up?"

"Oh, yeah."

"Did you lose your voice?" I asked, thinking of Laurence Moffitt.

"No," he said, "we had gas masks, so we wore them all the time." Everyone in his company was exposed to gas at some time or other. "Some of them got it pretty bad," he said. "But I didn't . . . It could have killed me, but I didn't get that much."

I asked him what it was like at the front when there wasn't any shooting going on. "Well," he said, "it wasn't very often. Up at the front there was shooting all the Goddamned night."

"How did you handle the stress?" I inquired at one point.

"Well," he replied, "I took it the best way I could. I just — I know it was going to happen, so what could you do?" Just two options, really: adapt somehow, or break. Plenty of men, sadly, broke.

"They called us one day," he remembered, "a couple of us, and they had what they called a paddy wagon. Some guy lost his mind, and they had to take him to — I forget where it was they took him to. And they said, 'You don't know what he's going to do.' One of us had a loaded rifle, the other didn't. And they said, 'If he gets out of hand, kill him.'"

"Really?" I said.

"Thank God we didn't have to do it."

"He just cracked?"

"Yeah, that's right. They put him in a padded cell. I never did hear any more from him. But boy, I was glad I didn't — one of us had a loaded rifle, the other one didn't, and we just . . ."

"You didn't know which one had it?"

"No."

"They told you both to shoot him?"

"Yeah."

"Was he shell-shocked?" I asked.

"I think so," he said. "I think that's what did it." He said he knew of several cases, but that this was the only one he'd encountered personally.

"Shell shock" is just a phrase, of course; "battle fatigue" may be more accurate. There were any number of things that might make a man crack after being at the front for a while. Some of them, like bullets, were utterly random; shells, at least, gave you a little bit of notice. "You could tell by the way, the sound of the artillery, you could tell pretty close to where it was going to land," Mr. Lake explained. Still, he recalled, "you just never knew when you was going to get hit. But I was lucky, as I said," he mused. "Now, another guy and I were sitting on a bank." He paused, lowered his chin, pursed his lips; his voice dropped. "And a sniper shot him instead of me."

I looked at him for a moment. "You were sitting next to each other?"

"Yeah. No more than two feet apart. And he picked him instead of me. He killed him, of course." They had been sitting on a little dirt rise, near a trench. And this, I'm pretty sure, is the reason Bill Lake kept saying he was lucky. "They picked him instead of me. I was lucky, that's all . . . we were sitting there side by side and he picked him instead of me."

We were quiet for a moment. "They got him," he assured me. "They found him, they found the sniper."

"Oh?" I said. "They killed him?"

"Oh, yeah," he said. "They didn't take him prisoner, not a sniper, no. He was up in a tree when they found him, and they let him have it. And he fell out of the tree, dead. And that's all there was to it."

He said it with aplomb; the passage of eighty-five years had not dulled his sense of righteous outrage. There was a very hard feeling about snipers then, even though everybody used them. "They didn't take a sniper prisoner," he explained. "They was dirty. They would shoot you in the back as soon as they would in the face, you know. They didn't care as long as they got you. But they got *him,* of course." He told this story several times over the course of our two-hour conversation, and though he never had anything new to add, he kept returning to it: They picked him instead of me.

Like almost every other World War I veteran I interviewed, William J. Lake was stoic; if thoughts like those plagued him, he didn't let on much, besides revisiting the incident again and again. But he saw plenty of people get it, as he said, and knew of many more. The buddy who had enlisted with him in Montana was killed in a railroad accident even before the division shipped out for France. Also with him in Camp Lewis, he recalled, were "three guys from Salt Lake City . . . they went home and got married [before shipping out]." His voice dropped again. "Every one of them got killed."

"Every one of them?" I asked.

"Every one of them got killed," he repeated, twice. "Well," he continued, "I didn't even have a girlfriend, but if I had, I never would have done that."

"You wouldn't have married her before you went?"

"No. I would not have married anybody. No way."

"Why not?"

"Well, you think: too much pain. You didn't know if you were going to get back or not." He added: "Well, see, I didn't even have a girlfriend, so that was all right."

He told me that men in his company were killed just about every day; and he saw a lot of death on the other side, too. "We killed so many of them," he said. "They had concrete bunkers in there . . . but we fixed that and just — I don't know how many got killed, I was told but I don't remember how many. Just completely wrecked it, demolished it."

"With artillery?" I asked.

"Yeah," he said, "with artillery. We had six- and eight-inch artillery. They started in at, I think it was six o'clock in the evening, and kept it up all night. And that was it."

"And that was it. They destroyed the bunker."

"Just completely destroyed it. And I don't know how many it killed. I was told, but I can't remember how many it was, killed and wounded.

I saw a lot of dead ones and a lot of wounded." He shook his head and pursed his lips.

"A lot of dead and wounded Germans?" I asked.

"Yeah," he said. "And that's what ended the war."

I wish I could tell you that things got better for the Wild West Division after those awful first four days at the Meuse-Argonne. But they didn't. The enfilade fire kept coming; the shells kept falling. New plagues started coming around, too. "Many men were suffering from diarrhea due to exposure . . . without warm food or overcoats and blankets," the divisional history — which is supposed to be a positive recounting — reports. "Most officers and men had raincoats, and some had found German blankets in dugouts. The men built shelter from small-arms fire by excavating the northern edges of shell-holes. But they were observed by hostile planes and subjected to heavy fire (shrapnel and shell) from German artillery. . . . Although many casualties resulted, the morale was undisturbed." I guess that last clause was the positive part.

The divisions on their flanks — the 35th on the left, 37th on the right — never could seem to catch up with the 91st, or even get within a couple of miles of them, so the Westerners continued to get hit — hard — from three sides. Often men would seek shelter in safe spots called splinter-proofs, only to learn, the hard way, that they were neither safe nor splinter-proof. The 362nd, the history records, "suffered heavy losses because of lack of overhead shelter." The farther they advanced, the stronger the German defenses became. By October 4, the 91st had been battered so incessantly that they — as well as every other division in the First Army's V Corps — were relieved and ordered into reserve. Their corps commander took pains to write to the 91st: "This relief results solely from a realization by higher command that your Division has done its full share in the recent success, and is entitled to a rest for reorganization." Two days later, higher command, realizing it couldn't spare the entire division after all, ordered half of it — the 181st Brigade, which included the 362nd Regiment — back in to fight alongside their replacements, the 1st Division.

It was apparent from the start that the Meuse-Argonne wasn't going to be another Saint-Mihiel. The terrain alone would have made it a much more difficult fight, but that terrain was nothing compared to the heavy German fortifications. If the doughboys had hoped they might hit some weak point in the enemy's defenses going forward, a critical soft point that would start the process of bringing the whole thing crashing down before them — well, they were disappointed. It seemed, in fact, that the farther they managed to advance, the fiercer the resistance they encountered. Every step they took forward brought them closer to the Germans' ultimate line of defense; every step the Germans took backwards brought them closer to the point where they would no longer be able to take any more steps backwards. Rather than just give up in the face of that prospect, the Germans threw more and more reserve divisions into the fight, working feverishly by night to rebuild those defensive points that had been damaged or destroyed during the day's fighting and to strengthen those that hadn't. Dough-boys would push off in the morning fog expecting to build on gains they had made — often at great expense — the day before, only to find themselves fighting to take the same ground all over again. Soon, a very hard feeling developed toward all German soldiers — not just snipers. "Everybody hated them," Mr. Lake told me at one point; "that's just the way it was." I've read, here and there, reports of newly captured German prisoners at Meuse-Argonne being executed rather than sent back behind the lines. There were reasons the French hadn't attempted a major offensive in the area in years.

On October 12, 1918, the 181st Brigade was pulled from the Meuse-Argonne for good. By then, the divisional history reports, the 91st had suffered 25 percent casualties. They had also advanced farther than just about any other division in that first phase of the offensive; liberated a number of villages and farms; and captured more than twenty-three hundred prisoners and, the divisional history notes, the follow-ing "hostile material":

440 Machine Guns
24 Field Guns, caliber 77
1 Field Gun, caliber 105
6 Field Guns, caliber 150
5 Minnewerfers [*sic;* a *Minenwerfer* was a short-range mortar]
500 Rifles, Mauser
266 Rifles, Luger

46 Pairs Field Glasses
1,105,000 Rounds Rifle Ammunition
963,000 Rounds Machine Gun Ammunition, in belts
12,000 Rounds Field Gun Ammunition, Caliber 77
1 Tank
5,000 Hand Grenades

None of which the Germans could spare at that point.

The battle would continue, without the 91st, right up to the very minute the armistice took effect. The Americans never stopped pushing forward; it never got close to anything you might call easy. In the end, 26,277 doughboys would die there, including 1,019 from the Wild West Division. Another 95,786 — including 3,916 men of the 91st — would be wounded. When Palmer called it "Our Greatest Battle," he wasn't merely employing hyperbole: More Americans died at the Meuse-Argonne than in any other battle in the country's history, before or since.

The Germans, with their terrestrial advantages and extensive fortifications, gave up a lot of territory during the six weeks between the offensive's beginning and the armistice. They lost about as many men as the Americans did, too, and they *really* couldn't spare them. They were down to reserves by then, whereas the Americans had hundreds of thousands of unused troops on French soil, and another two million just waiting to cross the Atlantic. The great gamble the Germans had taken with their Spring Offensive had failed them, and then broken them. Many historians believe the Meuse-Argonne Offensive dealt Germany its *coup de grâce*. Private William J. Lake, who was there, certainly thought so. "At Argonne Forest," he told me, "the Germans were on one side and the French were on the other, and they said they couldn't drive the Germans out. And we drove them out." He understood why the French had been unable to do it on their own: The German prisoners, he said, "the ones we had, was in pretty good shape"; but the French soldiers he saw, "they was pretty ragged. They'd been in pretty bad shape." The difference, he must have believed, had to be the AEF. As he told me, more than once: "We ended the war. In fact, our division ended the war."

I'm not sure how many historians would sign on to that statement;

but with everything he saw and did Over There, you could certainly understand why Bill Lake might think such a thing.

The Meuse-Argonne was not the end of the Wild West Division's war. After they were pulled out of that sector, they were sent up to Belgium — a rare assignment for doughboys in that war — where they were given more than four thousand replacement troops and then put back into the field on October 31, alongside British, Belgian, and French units, and the American 37th Division, which had fought on their right flank at the Meuse-Argonne. I'm not sure how it came to pass that these two American divisions were sent up to Flanders — I've seen it speculated that Foch wanted a token American presence at that northernmost offensive, for some reason — but I imagine they found it a preferable site for fighting: it had been blasted all to hell over the course of four years, but at least it was flat and open. Private Lake certainly found it less exciting; the only thing he had to say about Belgium, eighty-five years later, was that that was where he was when he got word that the armistice had been signed. "We was on our way up to the front," he recalled, "not talking, no smoking, no noise of any kind, and a guy come along and stopped us and said you could talk and you could smoke and do what you want to do. And he says there'll be another runner along in about a half an hour, and he didn't say what he was going to do. And this guy come along and told us the armistice has been signed, and that was it."

In fact, in the last twelve days of the war, as part of the Ypres-Lys Offensive, they helped drive the Germans back across the Scheldt River, and liberated nine towns and villages, all of which cost them another 929 casualties, including 215 killed. Not an easy stretch by any measure — except, perhaps, compared to what they had been through earlier that fall.

It all stopped suddenly on that November morning when that runner came along and told them the armistice had been signed. "Oh, it was just like you had a fit, I'll tell you for sure," Bill Lake recalled, meaning that in the good way. "Everybody was so happy." After that, he said, "we stayed in Belgium until I think it was the first of the year, and then we went back to France — doing nothing — but they kept us there. And they had the Army of Occupation, and we was supposed to be in that, and they changed it; otherwise I'd have been over there for another six months. But they had us doing nothing. . . . Just relaxing." Not that he was complaining.

"They must have had you doing something during the day," I said.

"Well," he offered, "we drank a lot of wine."

Someone high up must have decided that the 91st had had a really rough time of it, because they weren't assigned any duty at all, not even the guarding of prisoners. The divisional history confirms Private Lake's recollection that the 91st did time after the armistice in both Belgium and France; it reports lots of rain and uncomfortable billets, neither of which he mentioned. He did meet French women, he told me, but added: "I couldn't understand their language, so . . ."

"Did you try to talk to any of them?" I asked him.

"I tried to," he said, "but it didn't get very far. We had a translator tell me what they said."

"Were they friendly?"

"Yeah, most of them were, yeah."

"Were they pretty?"

"Some of them. And some of them looked like old men. You see," he explained, "the French drink a lot of wine, but they heat it. That takes alcohol out of it. And they drink so much of it that their dang teeth just all fall out."

"Is that right?" I asked.

"That's the way it was," he asserted.

On one occasion, he told me, a Sunday morning, he and some buddies found themselves in a little town in France where, he said, "they wore wooden shoes — everybody wore wooden shoes." That morning, he explained, they came upon the town's church during Mass; all the wooden shoes were lined up outside. He grinned. "You know what we done?"

"What did you do?"

"Go up there and mixed them up," he said, tumbling into a laugh. "Boy, you talk about jabbering!" He laughed harder.

I don't know if that little stunt had anything to do with it, but the Wild West Division was shipped back home in March, 1919, earlier than most. Private William J. Lake was mustered out at Fort D. A. Russell in Wyoming on May 5, and returned home to Montana. "How were you received there?" I asked him.

"Pretty good," he said. "Oh, yeah."

"Your mother was glad to see you?"

"Oh, you bet your life."

"Were your brothers all there, and your sisters?"

"Yeah." He confessed that he hadn't written anybody very often when he'd been in the Army. "Boy, they got after me for that."

"They were upset?" I asked him.

"Yeah," he replied. "They'd want to know where I was and what I was doing. And somebody wrote and told them — I don't know who did — said I'd been wounded and I was in the hospital, and I wasn't wounded and I wasn't in the hospital. I don't know why they did that." He said he got a lot of letters when he was Over There, mostly from his mother and his sisters; he still remembered his address: APO 776, France.

He went back to work on the farm, got married, had a daughter, and moved the family to Puyallup, Washington, because he had fond memories of the area from Camp Lewis. His wife, though, missed Montana, moved back without him, and divorced him. He met another woman, to whom he was married for fifty-two years; they had a son and another daughter. He worked for a sash-and-door company in Tacoma, made doors and windows, but "I didn't like it, so I come over to Yakima, and I've been here ever since." That was in 1924. "First thing I done was pick apples," he explained. Then he went to work somewhere firing a kiln to dry hops. He dug ditches for the government's Reclamation Service. Worked on telephone lines and water gauges.

"What were you doing during the Depression?" I asked him.

"I wasn't doing nothing," he said.

"You weren't working?"

"I did some, but not a heck of a lot . . . it was rough."

At one point he ran into a fellow he knew who owned an apple orchard; he went to work for the man, harvesting apples, for five years. Later in life he worked in a warehouse, then drove a truck, hauling fruit. He finally retired at the age of seventy-five, and only then because he was in an accident and crushed two vertebrae in his back. When I met him, he'd been on disability for more than thirty years. His mother had died at age seventy-five; no one in his family, he told me, had lived to be much older than that. His longevity was a mystery to him. His only son died in his late forties or early fifties; his older daughter lived in Oregon. His younger daughter lived in Yakima, but he only saw her, he said, twice a year or so.

At one point he pushed himself out of his chair, walked over to a chest, opened a drawer, and pulled out his Légion d'Honneur. He smiled proudly, handed it to me: It is a very beautiful medal. He pointed out his stationary bicycle, said he rode it every day. He told me he walked, too, every day, to a certain street and back again. "If the weather's bad I walk back and forth in the hall," he said. He had visited, at their invitations, the governor of Washington and the commanding general at Fort Lewis; went out for breakfast or lunch every Saturday and Sunday, and occasionally during the week, too, with a couple of friends in Yakima, younger veterans. They didn't necessarily stay in town, either. I could tell that was important to him. "Some of these people," he said sadly, referring to his fellow residents, "never go out at all." Not that he didn't like the retirement manor, mind you. "They come in every morning and make your bed, and then they come in and vacuum the carpet and dust the furniture and clean the bathroom and everything and wash your clothes, and if you have to visit the doctor they take you to it, so what else can you ask for?"

If your father dies before your seventh birthday, you start working at the age of eight, get drafted into the deadliest war the world has ever seen, ride clear across the country on a train for six days with a case of the measles that you're scared to tell anyone about, sail across an ocean with the same case of measles, spend weeks in an English hospital full of fellows who have lost an arm or a leg or a set of lungs or a face in that war you're on your way to, arrive at the front just in time to see your beloved captain get killed, see lots of others get killed all around you, get so close to death yourself that it puts a hole in your coat and knocks the heel off your shoe and makes you vomit besides, see a buddy shot dead by a sniper while he's sitting not a yard away from you, manage to return home somehow only to have to scratch and scrounge for work, marry a woman and have a child with her only to have her tell you she's going home to Montana and then never return, marry another woman and have two more children one of whom dies young and well before you, have to continue to scratch and scrounge for work and often come up short throughout the Great Depression and still be working well into your seventies and only stop then because you have an accident and crush two of your vertebrae — really, what else could you ask for, ten days short of your 108th birthday?

And that would be a fine place to end the story of Private William J. Lake of Yakima, Washington, but for the fact that about six months later, I unexpectedly found myself back in the vicinity, and went to visit him again. Visit: not interview. Because I hadn't planned to be there much in advance, I had not brought along my video camera. I did, however, have with me a copy of *The Story of the 91st Division*, the existence of which I had only discovered recently. Though this was not a regular practice for me, I asked him to sign it, and he did, in a very shaky hand:

> *Bill Lake*
> *362 M G CO*

He was 108 years old now, halfway to 109, and while he himself didn't look all that much older, everything around him somehow seemed to have aged in the interim, especially his shirt, the same one he'd been wearing the last time I'd seen him, a sharp plaid which had impressed me as crisp in October but which now, in April, looked worn and a bit ragged. You don't think the mere sight of a shirt can make you feel sad, but it can.

He seemed a bit more tired at first, too, than he had been before, but as we started talking he perked right up. We discussed all manner of things, past and present, touching on something new here and there but mostly revisiting ground we'd covered the previous fall. At one point, he told me once again about how his father had gone off to look for land in the Indian Territory and returned just in time to die of pneumonia; and for some reason, right then, I decided to try again. "What," I asked him, "was his name?"

"Richard," he answered immediately. "Just like yours."

And then, a few minutes later, when Mr. Lake started telling me again about his captain — how he'd been the first man to greet him upon his arrival at the front after six weeks in an English hospital with the measles; how he'd caught Private Lake's hand when he went to salute and shook it instead, cautioning, "You never know who's watching"; how, at Camp Lewis, he'd told his men time and again, "I don't want any cowards in my company; I can't stand a coward"—I asked him for the man's name. And again, he answered without even a pause: "Worsham." Some days, I guess, you just get really lucky.

That night, I picked up my copy of *The Story of the 91st Division* and turned to the section in the back titled "Those Who Have Fallen"; it's thirty-eight pages long, if that gives you some idea of how many men of the Wild West Division did not return from France. The list includes one colonel, two majors, and eight captains, the last of whom is listed as: Worsham, Elijah W. I opened my laptop and googled Elijah W. Worsham. There weren't many hits, but the top of that short list was a page on someone's genealogical website that contained the transcript of a letter sent by Worsham's replacement, Captain Ray W. Hays, to one William R. Heilman, a childhood friend of the late captain's back in Evansville, Indiana, who had inquired after him. It is not dated, but Hays does specify that he is writing from "Oostletern, Belgium"— probably Oostvleteren—which would make it sometime around the end of the first week of November, 1918. Captain Hays writes:

> While Captain Worsham was in command of the machine gun company, I was one of his officers. Since his death I have had the honor of commanding his company, and it is his company, known universally as Captain Worsham's company, and not the machine gun company. Inspired by his ideals and teaching, I am trying to run the company as he did, but no one can take his place.
>
> We first went over the top at Rendevous de Chasse and the first day advanced about ten kilometers. We met with stiff resistance at Ejenonville [Épinonville] the next morning, and it was largely due to the Captain's courage, tactics and machine gun company that our division held out while divisions on our flank were forced back.
>
> During the two days of fierce fighting we advanced some eight kilometers, until, on the 29th, we were held up. A small town, by the name Gesnes, seemed to be the point of resistance, and about 3 o'clock in the afternoon of September 29 the battalion to which we were attached was ordered to take the town. The magnificent manner in which it was charged and taken will never be forgotten by the

surviving participants. Led by our Captain, we followed the assault wave, and, under his direction, mounted our guns on a ridge commanding the town, where we could use direct fire over the heads of our own troops.

We had some wonderful targets, but were subject to direct observed artillery fire, front and flank, the flank organizations having failed to gain their objective.

After getting my guns in action, I found the Captain firing a machine gun, the crew of which had become casualties. Under the cover of the gun he was firing and three others from my platoon, I removed the remainder of the guns forward to escape the heavy enemy barrage.

Then I rejoined the Captain. Shortly he gave the order to cease firing, our troops having advanced so far that it was dangerous to continue to fire over their heads.

We continued to observe, waiting for dusk to advance. I left the Captain to give orders to one of my gun crews. When I found him a few moments later he was dead, shot with a rifle bullet. He had started forward, field glass in one hand, rifle with fixed bayonet in the other.

We advanced with leaden hearts and heavy feet to help reorganize and consolidate the line for the night, because that is what he would have had us do. It was two or three days before the body was recovered and laid to rest in a grassy meadow in the Forest of Argonne, beside that of one of his Lieutenants, who gave his life the same day.

He was your dear friend, you say. To us he was more — peerless leader, boon companion, comrade, instructor and friend. We mourn his loss in a way that words cannot express. His men and officers loved him as he in his whole-hearted way loved them. The fateful German bullet cost the army a valiant leader and officer, a true soldier in every sense; robbed the government of a valuable citizen, and deprived all who were privileged to know him in the future society of a beloved friend and always cheerful companion.

Pardon me, sir, for so much detail about an action that I was in, but I loved and admired the "Old Skipper," as he will always be to us, that it is a relief to talk to one who, likewise, knew and loved him. I dream of him by night and think of him by day, and always, in my plans for his company, I wonder if he would approve of my actions were he here. Most of my military education, all my machine gun experience, was received from him, and perhaps his invisible hand is still guiding me in my effort to take his company home as he would have taken it.

Even your high regard for Lige Worsham, the citizen, would have been increased had you known the Captain E. W. Worsham that I knew and served under. He understood men and by his own high ideals brought out the best in them. I truly sympathize with you in the loss of a friend,

Sincerely yours,
Capt. Ray W. Hays
M.G.Co., 362 Inf., A.E.F.

Elijah William Worsham had been captain of the football team at Purdue, and later moved to Seattle, where he'd started a brokerage firm. He was thirty-one years old when he died, and was buried at the Meuse-Argonne Cemetery. His marker there mistakenly records his date of death as September 26, 1918.

I left Bill Lake that afternoon in April, 2004, with a promise that I would come see him again in July, when I planned to be back in the area. I told myself that I would be sure to bring my video camera the next time. And I did.

But I didn't get to interview him again; in June, he went into the hospital to have surgery for a perforated ulcer, contracted pneumonia post-op, and died. His obituary got his unit wrong, but it did mention the name of his daughter who lived in Yakima, something he never had. In July, passing through town as expected, I called her — her name was Pat — and asked if I could stop by.

She hadn't known about my visits with him, and I got the sense, in talking with her briefly, that they weren't exactly distant but weren't exactly close, either. She showed me his original discharge papers, gave me an official copy someone had requested decades later, perhaps in support of a pension application. I told her in general terms about what we'd discussed; and then I mentioned how he couldn't remember his father's name the first time I'd visited him, but that the second time, when I'd asked again, he'd replied, without hesitating, "Richard, just like yours."

She raised a hand to her mouth, stared at me for a moment. "I never knew his name," she said. She was then seventy-three years old.

We took a moment to go through the names of her father's mother and sisters and brothers, just to make sure I had gotten them all right. And then I asked her if she knew why her father's two younger brothers — Downing, who was twenty years old in 1918, and Graydon, who was eighteen — had been turned away when they'd tried to enlist. She told me that she didn't. But she did know, she said, that Downing had taken it very badly: He went home afterward and killed himself.

15

Wasn't a Lot of Help

Three stories.

I.

ON JULY 20, 2004, I left Yakima and drove two hundred miles to Spokane to visit with a man who was, I already knew, different from any other veteran I had interviewed, or planned to. His name was John Babcock, and he had served in the CEF: the Canadian Expeditionary Force.

Now, like many Americans, you may regard Canada as a very large fifty-first state, or perhaps America Lite. Block out the weird spelling ("humour," "centre," "grey"), odd nomenclature (z = "zed"; bathroom = "washroom"; macaroni & cheese = "Kraft Dinner"), funny-looking currency, clean city streets, bilingual highway signs, excellent public transportation, ubiquitous Tim Hortons doughnut shops, and even more ubiquitous national symbols — I once bought a dozen eggs and found a tiny maple leaf stamped on each one — and you might not be able to tell the difference. But make no mistake: Canada is *not* the United States of America. Its entire identity, it often seems to me, is based upon this fact.

Canada's so-very-not-American-ness goes all the way back to the American Revolution. Before that little disagreement, the big chunk of North America up yonder was overwhelmingly French, at least ethnically; Britain had seized New France from old France some years earlier, but there still weren't all that many Britons living up there. After the Revolution, the 20 percent of the population of the Thirteen Colonies who had harbored Loyalist sympathies during the rebellion found themselves in a rather awkward position vis-à-vis the other 80 percent. Many Loyalists, who had been among the more affluent American colonists, now found themselves, shall we say, relieved of their property. Others were harassed and menaced by Yankee Doodle ruffians.

Canada — still British — beckoned.

It is estimated that around one hundred thousand Loyalists fled across the new northern border after American independence was secured. This is why, today, Anglophone Canadians sound much more like Americans than Englishmen. It is also why being not-American is still terribly important to Canadians. And, most important to this story, why Canada remained a part of the British Empire well into the twentieth century. What that meant in 1914 was this: When England declared war on Germany at 11:00 p.m. on August 4 of that year, Canada necessarily went to war, too. If there was a lot of opposition to that state of affairs, I don't know of it. Canada, after all, was the good child, the one who didn't rebel.

They didn't have much of an army on August 4, 1914; the entire country had fewer than eight million people in it at that point, and hadn't faced a serious threat in a century. By the end of the war, though, more than half a million Canadians had served in uniform. The great majority of them were volunteers; Canada didn't even have a draft until 1918.

Canada's war got off to a rough start. Newfoundland's lone regiment — Newfoundland wasn't technically part of Canada until 1949, but it was close enough — was sent to Gallipoli, a notorious meat grinder; and CEF troops were present at Ypres (which Canadians, like the British, still pronounce "Wipers") in the spring of 1915 when the Germans unleashed their first large-scale chlorine gas attack. The Canadians got hit particularly hard, taking thousands of casualties at Wipers; a couple thousand of them died there.

Nevertheless, the following winter, back in Ontario, John Henry Foster Babcock made a spontaneous decision, one evening, to enlist.

He was fifteen years old.

All of the veterans I interviewed looked younger than their actual age, but none of them looked younger than John Babcock; he looked like he was about seventy. And a youthful seventy, at that. He resembled Mr. Tate on the TV show *Bewitched:* thick white hair brushed straight back, trim mustache, bulbous nose. On the day I stopped by, he was wearing an off-white polo shirt over a bright white T-shirt, and dark pants. While we talked, he sat in a dark red armchair; his wife, Dorothy, hovered nearby and offered up a detail or two when he was slow to recall them, which was rare. They had an easy, playful rapport, the kind you hope you'll have with your spouse at that age, or any age. I was surprised to learn that Dorothy was actually his second wife; they had met in 1976, when she'd cared for his first wife, Elsie, in the hospital as Elsie lay dying. John had been married to Elsie for forty-four years.

John Babcock was born on July 23, 1900, he told me, "twenty miles north of Kingston, in Ontario"; his service records list the specific town as Holleford, which is actually a bit farther away. Kingston, a picturesque old city that is home to both the Royal Military College of Canada and what seems like every prison in the country, sits at the spot where Lake Ontario empties into the St. Lawrence River. It was originally settled by Loyalist refugees, who named it for George III. Later, it became the capital of the Province of Canada, which eventually grew to become just Canada. John Babcock's mother, Anne, was born in Ottawa, the current national capital; his father, James T. Babcock, grew up in the same area as his son John, who was born on the family farm. "What kind of farm was it?" I asked him.

"There was three hundred and fifty acres," he recalled, "and there was about a hundred acres that was farm. It was patches and all. And most of it had timber on it. There was a small lake on it." His father, he said, "had this farm, and he had a sawmill on it. He was doing very well." Then one day, he explained, "he was getting out timber, and they were felling a tree, and he took the young man's place at the saw, and" — he raised his hand and then swatted it down — "tree fell, and it hit a cedar tree, a dead cedar tree that was leaning diagonally across the path of that tree they were felling, and it broke off and come down and hit my father on the shoulder." He touched his own right shoulder. "And he lived for two hours. They brought him in on a sleigh, one of the sleighs and a horse blanket. He lived for two hours," he repeated, staring straight ahead and starting to rock in his chair. "He died."

James Babcock was forty-three years old. His son John, not yet six, was the eighth of ten children left behind; his father's first wife had died in childbirth, one of those things that, like deadly farm accidents, happened a lot back then. James's death was a real hardship to his second wife, Anne. "The in-laws didn't like my mother, because she had a high school education, and very few people had that much of an education at the time," her son explained. "And the half brother and sisters, they drifted away. And finally just we five of the second family was on the farm. So my mother milked thirteen cows, night and morning." Eventually she put the farm up for sale. "And my half brother bought it for twenty-one hundred dollars." John continued to live there for about a year, until, one night — well, I'll let him tell it.

"I was in a little town called Perth Road," he recalled. "And there was a lieutenant and a sergeant came. And we were having a kind of a dance in the upstairs of the house, and they were trying to get people to enlist. And they asked me if I wouldn't like to." He laughed, an unusual variation on "Ha!" that started silently but then suddenly burst forth with great volume, like a sonic boom. "And I, of course, said, 'Why, yes!'"

"At fifteen and a half!" his wife declared.

"And they — you didn't lie about your age?" I asked.

"No," he said.

"They didn't ask your age?" I asked.

"Yeah, they did," he replied. But it seemed they didn't care; Canada needed soldiers, and recruiters have quotas. "They were hard up for men," he told me. "Very hard up." He laughed again. "They had to be, to [take me]," he explained. For him, though, it seemed like a good deal: He had dropped out years earlier — "I didn't care about school," he explained — and was working as a laborer on the farm that now belonged to his brother. He didn't particularly enjoy the work; the war seemed like an adventure. Why not go?

According to his attestation paper — the Canadian version of an enlistment form — young Mr. Babcock joined up on February 1, 1916, and did, indeed, offer his real birth date. (Interesting: At that time, the standard Canadian attestation paper did not record the enlistee's weight, though it did note *two* chest measurements — "girth when fully expanded" and "range of expansion.") After he enlisted, he recalled, "I went to Sydenham the next following Monday morning. It was about fifteen miles; I walked." He was assigned to the 146th Over-Seas Battalion, and sent to Kingston. "We drilled there for a few weeks," he said, "and then they sent us to Sydenham and we spent the winter there. And men kept enlisting — we had about thirty-five or forty men there." Come spring, they were sent to Valcartier, Quebec, where the Canadian Army had just built a large training camp. And it was there, as the 146th was preparing to ship across, that John Babcock's youth first emerged as an issue.

"Before they went overseas," he recalled, "everyone got a physical. And I was turned down. 'A-4.' I was physically fit but underage."

He had never, to that point, tried to fudge the matter; and yet, the Army had had no problem enlisting him, training him, clothing and feeding him, and moving him around as it suited them. At one point, his mother, unhappy that John had enlisted, even wrote his colonel asking that her son be discharged on account of his age; but John demurred, and the colonel dropped the matter. Again: "They were pretty damn hard up for men, let me tell you," as he put it. So I don't know why, suddenly, his age became a problem for the CEF. Perhaps there was a change in policy, or personnel; perhaps the wrong person just happened to get a look at his records at the wrong time. Whatever the reason, he was pulled from the corps. Resourceful fellow that he was, though, he quickly found a loophole, of sorts. "For some reason or other, my name wasn't published with the guys that were turned down," he explained. "So I put my pack on, and got on the train and went to Halifax. And the company commander knew my status, so when I went to get on the boat, he made me step aside, and sent me up to Wellington Barracks. That was a peacetime barracks, in Halifax. And they put me on a truck, wrassling freight there, and I didn't care for that."

He bided his time, waiting for an opportunity to make a move; and one soon presented itself. "They called for a draft of thirty or forty men to go to the RCRs," he told me. "That was the Royal Canadian Reserves, that was peacetime reserves. I volunteered. They asked me how old I was, and I said, 'Eighteen.' And went — got to England, went over on the old *California*. That's a cattle boat; they converted it." He confessed, "I did a lot of vomiting." Still, he was relatively fortunate: A year later, the German *U-22* torpedoed the *California*, sank it.

John Babcock finally got across in October of 1916, which by then was looking like an even worse year for Canadians in that war than 1915 had been. On July 1, the Newfoundland Regiment had suffered a casualty rate of *90 percent* in the first few hours of the Battle of the Somme. If you think that's bad, then I won't tell you that their officer corps suffered a casualty rate of 100 percent. But it did. The Canadian Expeditionary Force, which entered the battle a few months later, would take more than twenty thousand casualties at the Somme that fall. It's enough to make you wonder why young John Babcock kept trying so hard to get into it all. I asked him: "Were you eager to get overseas?"

"Oh, yeah," he said. "I wanted to go over there."

"You were eager to go fight?"

He laughed. "Well, I didn't want to get killed."

"But you wanted to get into the action."

"Yeah, I did," he said. When he first arrived in Liverpool, though, he was given a six-day leave, which he spent in London. It was full of soldiers, he told me — not just British, but Australians, New Zealanders, and Canadians on leave. There was a lot of rivalry among them, too. "Everybody thought they were the best," he told me. "The Canadians and Australians thought they were the best. And the English *knew* they were the best," he said, laughing. "The English people have great self-confidence." He saw that in their civilians, too, who, he recalled, simply "went on with their work," undisturbed by the war, except for the occasional zeppelin. "Seemed to me," he recalled, "they had an air raid while I was there. And I think we went into these places, you know . . . these air-raid shelters." There would be a lot more of that sort of thing there the next time around. Young Babcock spent much of his time in the city at a train depot; "They had a free lunch in the Victoria Station. That's where I did most of my eating," he said with a laugh. "I only had two pounds. That was equivalent to ten dollars. When I got back to camp I had two shillings in the pocket; that was equivalent to fifty cents."

Later, to his surprise, he discovered that he had family in the area. "My half brother had gone with the outfit," he told me. "With the 146th Battalion. And he was stationed just a few miles from where I was."

"In England," Dorothy clarified.

"England," he agreed. "I went down to see him, and he asked how the hell I ever got over there." Later, Mr. Babcock said, his brother — Albert Manly Babcock, eight years John's senior — transferred to the engineers, where he was made a sapper: "The people [who] would tunnel under the enemy lines, and put a lot of explosives there and blow them up," he explained. One time, he told me, his brother "dug into a German sap where some people got — the tunnel had been blown in behind them. They were just sitting there; they were dead." Sapping was a dirty job in every sense; it wore on his brother terribly. "He had a nervous breakdown," John Babcock recalled. "He got buried one time up to his waist. They were putting a narrow-gauge railroad across a shell hole, and they were driving the wooden piling down to support this railroad. And they'd just hit a couple of licks and the Heinies zeroed in on that, so they'd hit a couple of licks and have to get back and hide because those three-inch shells — whizz-bangs, they called them — would come over there." One of these whizz-bangs landed close enough to Albert Manly Babcock to bury him up to his midsection in earth. He was lucky: Plenty of soldiers in France were buried alive entirely by artillery blasts. One day, during the Battle of Verdun, an entire French company disappeared in an instant. They were discovered shortly after the armistice when their bayonets, still fixed to their rifles, poked up through the earth. The bodies were never exhumed, but rather left where they sat, still awaiting orders to go over the top; today the *Tranchée des Baionettes* is something of a shrine at Verdun.

Being half-buried was quite enough for Albert Manly Babcock. "He had a nervous breakdown," his brother reiterated. "They discharged him, sent him back to Canada. And his church got ahold of him, and they sent him to Montreal, to McGill University, a few months after that. And he became a minister."

He was lucky.

John Babcock was lucky, too, in a way, and he knew it. "We lost a lot of fellows that was in the little detachment that I was in, in Sydenham," he told me. "Quite a few of them got killed."

Though they had gone over too late for the carnage of 1916, there was still ample opportunity for Canadians to die in France in 1917. In April of that year, the CEF — all four Canadian divisions, united for the first time in one Canadian Corps — was assigned to take a strate-

gic high point at the northern flank of a British offensive that would
come to be known as the Battle of Arras, in order to protect nearby
British troops from that pesky German enfilade fire. It was a tough
assignment; the Germans, aware of the position's importance, were
well fortified. Nevertheless, the Canadians delivered, taking some ten
thousand casualties but capturing all of their objectives in four days —
including that high ground, which was named for a nearby town: Vimy
Ridge.

Now, here's another difference between Canada and the United
States: If you're American, it's likely you've never heard of Vimy Ridge.
If you're Canadian, though? Not a chance. Vimy Ridge is to the nation
of Canada what Belleau Wood is to the United States Marine Corps.
The address of Canada's very fine national War Museum in Ottawa is
1 Vimy Place. The British general who commanded the Canadian
Corps at Vimy, Julian Byng, was appointed governor-general of Can-
ada after the war — a largely ceremonial but high-profile position that
comes with lots and lots of juicy perks. The British also made Byng
First Viscount of Vimy.

Canadians who fought at Vimy (which is pronounced "Vimmie")
could dine off that fact back home for the rest of their lives. John Babcock, though, had to remain satisfied with the free lunch at Victoria
Station, because he never got out of England. While the CEF was fighting at Vimy — and, later, at Passchendaele, and Amiens, and Cambrai — he was unable to get into the action. The issue, once again, was
his youth. At some point before the RCRs were sent on to France, he
told me, "my service record came through . . . and they found out I was
sixteen." So he was plucked out of the RCRs and reassigned to the 26th
Reserve. Many of the men in the 26th — all Canadians, as he recalled —
had already seen action in France, and were recovering from wounds,
physical or psychological or both. "Did you get to talk to a lot of them
about what they had done and seen?" I asked him.

"Oh, sure," he said. "Yeah."

"And what kind of stories did you hear?"

"All kinds of stories . . . I remember, one thing that struck me as
rather cruel. When the Canadians would take a bunch of German prisoners, somebody would be detailed to take them back. To the prison
area. Most fellows didn't want to be bothered taking them back, [so]

they'd take them into the reserve trenches and they'd shoot them. I thought," he said, shaking his head, "I thought that was terrible." He cast his eyes downward. "I think of that to this day. But when you get in the Army and fighting, you get pretty damn callous, I guess. And shooting somebody" — he looked back up at me — "of course, the Germans, they were just as cruel as our guys were."

"You think that was pretty common?" I asked him.

"Yes," he said. "I do."

There were a great many stories told, he added, that he didn't get to hear. "We had what was called a 'wet canteen' in the area. And the men would go there and drink beer at night. And some of them would drink as many as eight or nine of those imperial pints of beer, and they would talk about their experiences."

"What else would they talk about?" I asked.

"Oh, I don't know," he said. "I didn't go to the wet canteen."

"You didn't?"

"I didn't care for beer." Very unusual for a Canadian, in my experience. Even an expatriate.

This is not to say that he didn't enjoy other pursuits. "I got acquainted with one of the WAACs when I was in Edinburgh, in Scotland," he said — the Women's Army Auxiliary Corps, founded in Britain in 1917. He was drawn to one in particular, a Scottish sixteen-year-old with the unusual name of, as he recalled it, Isabel Hailstones. He met her, he told me, "one evening on Prince's Street, in Edinburgh."

"Did she show you around?" I asked.

"Oh . . . not really," he said.

And then Dorothy said to her husband: "Tell him the story."

"What story?" he asked her. She offered just a bit of guidance; "Oh!" he exclaimed, and looked incredulously at his wife, then let loose that sonic boom of a laugh and turned to me. "We were going to have sex," he said. "And I had, I was in this little cul-de-sac, and I had my overcoat down [on the ground] and she was on it, and we were going to have sexual intercourse. And a policeman walked in. And that kind of stopped that." He laughed again; we all did. "So I came home a virgin," he said, in summary.

"I thought you told me," Dorothy prodded him, "she was the one that had the bloomers on, and you couldn't get her bloomers down or something?"

"Oh, they had bloomers and long johns," he said. "And I got her bloomers down around her ankles — I couldn't get her legs apart. So I came home a virgin." He laughed again, and so did Dorothy and I, though I will confess to you now that I'm pretty sure my laugh was a good bit more awkward than theirs.

Things improved on that front once he came home to Canada after the war and returned to school. "The girls that I had gone to school with, they learned about the birds and the bees," he explained. "So I got taken care of then."

I once had a Canadian woman — a professor at Queen's University in Kingston, Ontario, as it happens — tell me that Canadians are much more sexually liberated than Americans. At the time, I thought she was just coming on to me.

After six months in the 26th Reserve, Mr. Babcock told me, "they rounded up everybody in the Canadian Army that was underage and put us in one outfit. There were thirteen hundred of us. And we were at Bexhill-on-Sea; that was in Sussex. And they drilled us eight hours a day. And when you became nineteen, you went into D Company, and you went from there to France." This new unit, he recalled, was known as a Young Soldiers Battalion, and its formation was a curious byproduct of the war. The British, it seems, did not discharge an underage soldier from their army (or from the armies of their dominions) once his true age became known; rather, they transferred him to one of these Young Soldiers Battalions and kept him there, in the service, until he came of age, at which point he would be sent to some front-line unit as a replacement. If it were discovered that you were, in fact, underage in the Army, you would be plucked out of your unit and transferred to a Young Soldiers Battalion immediately — no matter where you happened to be at the time, even if that should be a fire trench in Flanders.

In his battalion, John Babcock told me, "about a third of them had [already] been to France . . . We had one kid who had won the DCM — the Distinguished Conduct Medal," a British decoration for extreme bravery, second in prestige only to the Victoria Cross. The brave boy soldier's name was Kinley; he was sixteen years old and, according to John Babcock, "wilder than a March hare." There was also, he recalled, "an Iroquois Indian that had been to France, and he came back — they took him out of the trenches and sent him to this Young Soldiers Battalion when I was there. His brother got killed. And his father, who was also in the Canadian Army, he got wounded."

John Babcock had hoped he would get sent across; "I wanted to 'do my bit,' as they called it," he told me. And he got pretty close: When the boys in his Young Soldiers Battalion "were six months from being nineteen, they put them in D Company, and they trained them," he explained. And then, as soon as they turned nineteen, "they shipped them back to France." When the war ended, John Babcock was about ten weeks away from being sent to D Company.

While he never made it to France, he did manage to get some fighting in, thanks to his highly decorated friend, Kinley. One time after the armistice, he said, "when we were in Kimmel Park Camp in North Wales and some of our guys got thrown out of a dancehall by the British, he says, Kinley says, 'You know, we should go up there and clean them bastards.' And so up we went, thirteen hundred strong." A heated discussion ensued, and then "somebody picked up a bench and threw it through a window," he recalled. "That's when the old sergeant came out and said, 'Don't hit me, I'm an old man!' Then he was socking everybody he could." I laughed, picturing the scene with that music from *The Benny Hill Show* playing in the background. "This big sergeant major," he continued, "a soldier like that" — he spread his arms wide to indicate a man of some size — "said, 'Don't you hit that old man.' Someone hit him with a one-by-four alongside the jaw, crack!" He chuckled. "And I thought, 'Well, this is no place for me.' And I just kind of faded away and went back to camp. One of our guys had a bayonet thrust through his thigh. And they had us — in less than two weeks they had us on a boat back to Canada." It seems Britain tired of that particular group of Young Soldiers. And I suspect it was mutual; when I asked Mr. Babcock if everyone onboard the RMS *Aquitania* with him seemed to be glad to be going home, he replied, simply: "Oh, hell, yes."

He was formally discharged on January 11, 1919. He returned to Holleford, enrolled at the same school he had left as a child, but dropped out again after a few months; "I decided I wasn't going to make it through the entrance [exams] into high school," he explained, quickly adding: "I graduated from high school when I was ninety-five years old. I'm considering now taking a college course." Back in 1919, though, having left school again, he went to work "in the Adirondack Mountains in a lumber camp. And they gave Canadians a vocational training." That training enabled him to get a job in Sydenham, "running a light plant . . . I'd read the meters." After a while he moved west, to Saskatchewan, to work the harvest; and then in 1921, he told me, "I enlisted in the American Army, and came to Camp Lewis, Washington." The same place where Bill Lake had gone through boot camp a few years earlier.

"Why did you do it?" I asked him.

"Well, hell," he said. "I didn't have any money, and I didn't have a trade."

But with his three years in the CEF, he told me, army life came easily to him. "In a month I was a corporal," he recalled. "And in another month I was a sergeant." He liked America, decided to stay; after moving around the Northwest a few times, he landed in Spokane in 1932. Eventually he became an American citizen, which, at the time, meant he automatically forfeited his Canadian citizenship. I'm not sure how much thought he ever gave that fact.

We visited for a few hours that day in Spokane; I never saw him or talked to him again, but I did keep an eye out for his obituary. Years passed, until, in May of 2007, I came across a different death notice, for a fellow named Percy Dwight Wilson, which stated that Mr. Wilson's passing left exactly one living Canadian veteran of the First World War, a man named John Henry Foster Babcock.

And here's another difference between the United States and Canada: Just as soon as John Babcock achieved that status, he became quite famous throughout the land of his birth. Canadian journalists — newspaper, television, magazine, radio — descended upon Spokane, Washington, to interview him, and sometimes just to meet him. The government decided that, upon his death, he would be given a state funeral; he declined that honor, though he was happy to have his Canadian citizenship restored. Government officials, including at least one member of Parliament, visited him at his home. He received birthday greetings from the prime minister, the governor-general, and Elizabeth II (who still retains the title of Queen of Canada for some reason). The honors continued to accumulate for several years, until he died in February, 2010, at the age of 109.

Sometime during the first week of November, 2008, I was on a train riding from Montreal to Cornwall, Ontario, when I observed a couple of well-dressed, distinguished-looking older gentlemen sitting across the aisle; both had large red plastic flowers affixed to their lapels. I had seen quite a few such flowers while visiting Montreal, and wondered what was up, so I asked these two gentlemen about it. They were poppies, they explained, sold to raise money for veterans' causes every year in the weeks leading up to Remembrance Day: November 11. Veterans Day. Armistice Day.

They were veterans themselves; I noticed one had some sort of military decoration pinned to his jacket near the poppy. We talked a bit more, and then for some reason I told them that I was American, and that I had once met John Babcock. They — these proud, dignified, accomplished old men — suddenly looked at me with awe, then admiration, and started talking effusively, something I couldn't have imagined (much less expected) from two Canadians of such bearing. One of them told me he had served in Mr. Babcock's unit, by which I think he meant the 146th Over-Seas Battalion; when I rose to leave the train a few moments later, he removed the poppy from his coat and pinned it on mine.

II.

My visit with 102-year-old Warren Hileman on June 10, 2004, was another singular experience. Like most of my interview subjects, he was quite hard of hearing; unlike the rest, though, he refused to wear his hearing aids. After a few minutes of shouting questions at him (with his caregiver repeating them, even louder and right in his ear), I came to understand that I was going to have to write them down on my legal pad and just hand that to him, instead. It made for an interesting conversation.

Not that I'm complaining, mind you, because that conversation almost didn't happen at all. When I learned of Warren Hileman's existence, from an article in a small-town newspaper, I called up the Illinois Veterans' Home in Anna, Illinois, where the article had said he lived, and asked if he was capable of giving me an interview. He was certainly capable, I was told, but also disinclined; several television crews had shown up at the home with similar intentions, only to be turned away. Nevertheless, they said, if I happened to be in the area, I'd be welcome to come by and try for myself. I wasn't anywhere near the area — Anna is in extreme southern Illinois, so far downstate that it's only about a three-hour drive from Memphis — but I decided I'd take a chance, because Warren Hileman had a story that I knew no other living veteran could tell me. So I flew to Memphis and made the drive.

I'm not sure why he decided to see me. To tell you the truth, I'm not even sure he actually did. When I showed up at the Veterans' Home I was directed to a sort of conference room and told to wait; a few minutes later, he was wheeled in. It seems possible to me that he wasn't told what was going on until we were in each other's presence, at which point it might have proven a tad awkward for him to just leave without talking to me. However it happened, I'm grateful that it did; and he didn't seem to mind much, either.

He was born, he said, on September 29, 1901. When I asked him where, exactly, he replied: "Well, as far as I can recall, I was born on one of Grandpa's daughter's farms . . . out about eight miles east of Anna." He spoke quite deliberately, taking plump pauses here and there, often in the middle of a sentence. His voice was deep; you couldn't tell, just by his accent, what part of the country he'd grown up in, but you could tell that it was rural. His discharge papers listed his height as five feet seven, but he seemed much taller than that, sitting down though he was. His facial features and torso created the impression that he had been stretched out at some point. It suited his voice, and vice versa. And that voice lent itself to rambling. Often, when I posed a question to him in writing, he would answer it and then just continue on talking, unraveling a string of anecdotes and details that were no less interesting for being, at times, not entirely relevant. For instance, after telling me where he was born, he continued:

And there was a little country store out there where it used to be . . . And Dad rented it one time. And as you don't know, though, back then in an old country store, wasn't a lot of help. And transportation then wasn't what it is now. The car back then was a curiosity. There was the old dirt road — you could tell when cars were coming right down a country road, you could see a big trail of dust. And in the wintertime, that'd become mud. And people would — first big rain all year, they'd put the car in the garage or someplace. Then they'd take the tires off the car and put them upstairs.

When I asked him, out loud, what his father's name had been, he stared at me for a moment and then said, with a chuckle, "We're not communicating at all." That was when I decided to start using the legal pad. I wrote the question down and slid it across to him; he read it, took another pause, and said: "Aaron." He didn't have many memories of the man, though: His father, who worked on a farm, was killed in an accident when Warren was very young. "His brother run over him with a thrash machine," he explained. "The engine didn't run over him, just the separator. Right on the rear wheel, run across his chest."

"How old was he?" I asked.

"He was thirty-five years old."

"And how old were you?"

"I was three years old. And my sister was five. And I think the baby was eleven months." A month later, I would hear a somewhat similar story from John Babcock; that world, in a lot of ways, was a more dangerous place than ours is today. Mr. Hileman made this same point rather colorfully a minute or so later, while telling me about his grandfather's farm. "Grandpa bought land for twenty-five cents an acre," he recalled. "The old barn is still standing — it's got hand-built walls. And it's been there over a hundred years, but dry rot is getting into them walls." At one time on that farm, he recalled, "there was five buildings, and all built out of hand-hewn logs. You ever see what they call a broadaxe?" he asked me.

"Yes," I said.

"You ever tried using one?"

"No."

"You had to be a little careful with one," he said. "If you didn't watch what you were doing, you'd chop your foot off. And Uncle John, he had a guy that'd give him railroad ties ... and he was hewing away! And he just set his broadaxe down beside the log, sat down on it, took his shoe off, took his sock off, shake it like that . . ." He mimicked the motion of shaking out a sock; a wry grin spread over his face and then dissolved in a laugh. "Three white toes fell out," he said.

After his father died, Warren Hileman told me nearly a century later, his mother, Alvena, "got married again before too long." She had moved in with her late husband's father and was working as a farm hand; and her father-in-law had a single son at home. "She married a Hileman the second time," her son recalled, a practice so old it's actually mandated in chapter 25 of Deuteronomy; they call it Levirate marriage. "And she's buried at Mission Chapel," he continued. "That's down there — you know where St. John's Church is?"

"No," I said.

"You don't?"

"No."

"I thought everybody knows where St. John's was," he said. He was a funny fellow and had a lot of funny stories — like the time, when he was three years old and ran excitedly to see his first cow, and the cow hooked one of its horns under his suspenders, lifted him off the ground, and thrashed him about. He was even funny, sometimes, in talking about his military service, although, knowing a bit beforehand about where he had served and when, humorous anecdotes were not what I had expected to hear that day. You see, Warren Hileman enlisted at the age of seventeen and was assigned to the 27th Infantry Regiment, one of two Army regiments in the American Expeditionary Forces that were given a special assignment. They fought overseas — but not in France. Or Europe.

"I'm a World War I veteran," he said, when I first asked him about his service. "And I served in a place that a lot of people . . ." He paused for a moment, perhaps contemplating how he might finish that sentence.

He never did. Instead, he just said: "Siberia."

And that's why I went all the way to Anna, Illinois, on the off chance that he would grant me an interview: Warren Hileman was the last surviving veteran of the AEF Siberia, a chapter in American history as strange as it is now obscure.

The Treaty of Brest-Litovsk, in March, 1918, took Russia out of the war against Germany; but Russia was still quite far from peaceful at that point. The *Bolsheviki,* who had made that peace with the Germans several months after seizing power in the October Revolution, had allied themselves with various leftist, pro-revolutionary, and anti-czarist groups, collectively calling themselves the Workers and Peasants Red Army, more often known as the Red Army or, simply, the Reds. But the Reds didn't yet have control over the vast expanse that was (and is) Russia; there were still a great many groups, organizations and individuals, united by little more than their hatred of the Reds, fighting together in a loose confederation known as the White Army — or the White Guard, or just the Whites. The Reds and the Whites fought each other in a savage civil war that raged for years and claimed hundreds of thousands of lives. The Reds executed many innocent civilians as "enemies of the people"; the Whites slaughtered many innocent civilians, too, including lots of Jews — to whom some Whites, being steeped in centuries of good old-fashioned Russian anti-Semitism, assigned blame for the whole revolution — in some of the worst pogroms the country had ever seen, which is saying quite a lot. The Whites played on the West's fear of the Reds (not hard to do) and the Allies' desire to reopen the Eastern Front and draw German troops away from France and Belgium (also not hard to do), and quickly lined up French, Italian, and especially British support. The British, in turn, were quite keen to draw the Americans into the effort. President Wilson and Secretary of War Baker, though, weren't particularly interested at first; while they weren't terribly fond of the *Bolsheviki* — who had, after all, made a separate peace with the Germans — they didn't see Russia as their fight. Nevertheless, the British kept trying, and in the summer of 1918, they conjured just the right combination of incentives.

The first was essentially financial. When America entered the conflict in the spring of 1917, it started shipping war materiel — everything from guns and shells to locomotives and boxcars — to its new ally, Russia; by the time Russia left the war the following spring, nearly a billion dollars' worth of American materiel was sitting in two Russian ports: Arkhangelsk, above the Arctic Circle in the north-central part of the country, and Vladivostok, in the extreme far east, near Japan. The British presented a simple case: Go in with us and help make sure the *Bolsheviki* — or, worse, the Germans — don't get their hands on your stuff. Pretty straightforward. And persuasive.

The second argument, though, was more emotional, and it might just have been the one that really swayed President Wilson. It involved a curious band of men — I've seen estimates of their numbers ranging from forty thousand to seventy thousand — who captured imaginations and won admiration throughout the West in 1918: the Czech Legion.

In 1914, the areas that are now known as the Czech Republic and Slovakia were part of the Austro-Hungarian Empire. As ethnic minorities, though, many Czechs and Slovaks had no great love for the empire. Some fled east rather than be conscripted into the emperor's army; others, who had already been conscripted, deserted. Still others were captured by the Russians in battle. At some point, someone hit upon the idea of forming a military unit, composed largely of these displaced Czechs, that would fight alongside the Russians in the east, against the Germans and Austrians. And it did — at least until Russia signed that treaty and left the war. The Bolshevik government couldn't allow the Czech Legion to continue the fight on their own, at least not in the east, but it did permit them to leave. The problem was that they couldn't head west — the Germans were there. The only way out of the country was through the Pacific Ocean port of Vladivostok. Five thousand miles to the east.

At first, things seemed to be going somewhat smoothly. For a while, the Czechs were able to ride east on the Trans-Siberian Railway — the only way to get to Vladivostok from Europe — more or less unmolested. But then some *Bolsheviki* decided they should try to disarm the Czechs. This did not go well. Soon the Czechs found themselves thoroughly embattled, mixing it up with Reds and German POWs and various bands of brigands. Nevertheless, they were astonishingly successful, plowing east in armored trains, defeating the Reds at almost every turn, and liberating towns and villages. They also established and ran a bank, built a theater and mounted productions, and secured a printing press that they used to publish books and a regular newspaper — none of which are easy to do even if you're *not* on a moving train that is constantly coming under attack. They were celebrated internationally as heroes, but the battles took a great toll on them; they needed help. The British made the case for intervention to President Wilson who, though he may not have believed in racial equality, did believe passionately in the right of self-determination, at least for white men. He agreed to send troops to Russia, even adding a directive that, in addition to securing American war materiel and aiding the Czech Legion, American troops should offer support to "any efforts at self-government or self-defense in which the Russians themselves may be willing to accept assistance." Which Russians, exactly, was never clear, and even if it had been, the doughboys couldn't have done much about it; they had quite enough to do already in pursuit of the other two, less vague, directives.

There were actually two AEF actions in Russia. The first was in Arkhangelsk, where there were no Czechs, but lots of American war materiel. And Reds. American troops — some five thousand of them, mostly from Michigan — arrived there in early September, 1918, and almost immediately discovered that the Bolsheviks had already moved the American arms out of the city; the AEFNR (American Expeditionary Force North Russia) went after it. They also went after the Reds, especially along the railroads. But Russia is a very large place, and it soon became apparent to the AEFNR that they were overstretched, at which point they stopped advancing and tried to hold what they had already taken. But Russia is also a very cold place, and the men of the AEFNR didn't know how to fight in a Russian winter nearly as well as the Russians did. After the Bolsheviks went on the attack, driving the Americans back, pressure from family in America to bring the men of the AEFNR home started to build; the men themselves — cold, besieged, and unsure of their objectives — started grumbling. Fear of mutinies arose. In February, 1919, President Wilson decided to start shutting the mission down. By summer, they were gone. The Bolsheviks had killed more than a hundred of them; disease had killed scores more.

You'd think the experience would have ended America's adventurism in Russia. It didn't. Even as the last of the five-thousand-man AEFNR was sailing out of Arkhangelsk, there were between seven thousand and ten thousand American troops of the AEFS — the American Expeditionary Force Siberia — still on Russian soil way out east. They had been sent across the Pacific, to the port of Vladivostok, with the same objectives as the AEFNR: secure American war materiel, and support the Czech Legion. But if North Russia had been a mess, Siberia was utter chaos. The acronym FUBAR, coined by American troops during the following war, would have fit the situation quite nicely.

To start with, no one really had control of Siberia at the time; different towns and villages were in different hands. And there were a lot of hands in Siberia: In addition to the Americans, there were Canadian, French, Italian, and even Polish forces there. The British sent a relatively small force, but nevertheless tried to take command of the situation as they had in North Russia (where they had dispatched a much greater number of men), and put a lot of pressure on the American commander, General William S. Graves, to seek out and attack Red forces. And then there were the Japanese, who sent more than seventy thousand troops to Siberia — ten times the number the Allies had requested — ostensibly to protect their borders. I often wonder why anyone bought that argument to begin with — isn't Japan a series of islands? — but in any event, it soon became evident to Graves and others that Japan's real objective was to grab up as much land in the area as possible. This meant that, contrary to its stated objective, it was actually in Japan's interest to keep the state of affairs in Siberia as unstable as possible. The Japanese did this, primarily, by arming, abetting, and supporting a number of roving gangs — "armies" is too dignified a word — of Cossacks.

That's right: The guys who had tried to kill young Irving Berlin were in Siberia, too, although, to be fair, they probably weren't the same men (though you never know). While those earlier Cossacks had been organized mounted units serving (more or less) the czar, the Cossacks who were major players during the Russian Civil War were more akin to Attila's Huns (with better technology), ranging about the lawless expanse of Siberia, hunting Reds when they felt like it but more often attacking lonely villages unfortunate enough to fall in their path. If such a band were to visit your town, you could expect to be robbed of all you had of value — including, almost always, your young daughters — and quite possibly killed in the bargain. Like the Czech Legion, they advanced on their own armored trains, although it must be said that the Czechs — who did not, as a rule, rape or plunder — had a much better record versus the Reds.

Add various itinerant elements of the Red Armies, which were not always hostile, and the White Armies, which were not always friendly, and, well: FUBAR. It's hard not to feel bad for General Graves, an honest and honorable man who had hoped to be given a command in the trenches. Instead, Secretary Baker literally sent him to Siberia, and with little more than this advice: "Watch your step; you will be walking on eggs loaded with dynamite." Not the sendoff he was hoping for, I imagine. Nevertheless, though it seems he regarded the mission as a mistake from the outset, he did his best, resisting British pressure to go after the Reds — there was nothing about that in his orders, he insisted — and trying to keep the Japanese in check. His best, though, wasn't nearly good enough; nobody's could have been. This was Siberia, and it was a terrible, awful, dangerous mess.

And freezing.

Private Warren V. Hileman arrived there on September 6, 1919. He was not quite eighteen years old.

"The only thing good I seen about it," he told me when I first asked him about Siberia, "when it got cold, it stayed cold. And I mean *cold*. People around here complain: '*Zero?* Whoa, it's so cold!' I say, 'Well, what would you do if it was thirty below?'" He cinched his arms and shook his head, mimicking someone shivering pathetically: "Ooh, wub-wub-wub-wub!"

He went on: "How do you think we did at thirty below zero? And it *stayed* thirty below zero. And we had from a foot to three and a half, four foot of snow."

The cold was a subject he returned to again and again during our conversation, whether I asked about it or not; then again, if you'd been through something like that, I'm sure it would occupy a prominent place in your personal narrative, too. "I slept under nine blankets," he told me at one point. "I wore nine pair of regular socks. I'd have wore more, but I couldn't get them on. And over that we had lumberman's socks, heavy wool, and they come up to below your knees, and had an elastic band, and you'd fasten that. Oh, and I could have wore wool underwear. Well, this, what they issued, it was good, it was good high-quality wool. Now, some wool itches you; this didn't . . . [we] wore that next to our body. Of course then you add that, uh, wool trousers, and that wool underwear, a wool OD [olive drab] shirt . . . that went all over your body, your arms, over that. And then over your face, you had another wool helmet." He gestured around his face, then drew a hand across his mouth. "And you had another piece that come across here. That buttoned. And when you walked guard duty, you was on it for two hours. Two hours, and off four." After a shift on duty, he said, "you would have thought they'd have hot coffee." He smiled faintly, shook his head. "Not a thing. You got into quarters, then, and start peeling all this stuff off." He told me he slept in most of it, too.

Memories of the recent influenza pandemic, coupled with the extreme cold, led the Army to take special steps in an attempt to keep its Siberian doughboys healthy, though sometimes they had unintended consequences. "Every night just before bedtime, we'd spray our throats with some kind of an antiseptic," Private Hileman recalled eighty-five years later, at the climate-controlled veterans' home. It worked—sort of. "Nobody had a cold," he told me, but "one guy, one night, they got their stuff mixed up and he sprayed his with fly spray." I don't think I laughed harder at any point in all of my interviews. "He felt a little uncomfortable," he added, wonderfully deadpan. "But he survived."

To hear him tell it, the cold was always the Americans' biggest concern; it was going to get you one way or another. One time, he said, after several shifts on guard duty as an MP, walking from 4:30 to midnight, "I got to where I couldn't walk. My legs just quit." That landed him in the hospital for a spell. And then there was the night he and three other men were on outpost duty. "It was snowing and sleeting . . . miserable," he recalled. Finally, he said, "we got relieved, more or less, and we got in and they served us supper, in them old aluminum mess kits." No sooner had they sat down to eat, though, than they were ordered to assemble outside at once. "And they mean *at once,*" he explained. "And we all lined up . . . Then they said, 'We called you out just to let you know that somebody come in drunk, and don't let it happen again. Dismissed.' Course, I got back and that food was froze solid. I just took that old mess kit over to the garbage can." He shook his head. "Of course some fool would have to pull a stunt like that." When they found the guy, Warren Hileman assured me, "first thing they did, they worked him over. And good. He was more or less battered after that."

He seemed satisfied that justice had been done. "There's always some fool," he declared.

An army, as Napoleon (who had his own experience of Russian winter) is reputed to have said, travels on its stomach, and if the food in Siberia sometimes froze — and not just the food; coffee often froze in the cup before you could finish drinking it — at least Private Hileman found it interesting. "The old-timers didn't like it . . . but I thought it was pretty good!" he told me. "They had cabbage soup, black bread, and vodka." The Russians were resourceful; "they'd take ten or fifteen medium heads of cabbage and make a hundred gallons of soup," he recalled. "That black bread . . . you'd smell it going by. It had an odor!" And if vodka wasn't your thing, "they had another one," he said, "an alcoholic drink called 'spud juice,' made out of a fermented horse potato." He shook his head. "Boy, that'll knock your hat off." There were two brothers, he told me, assigned to the same company, who took it upon themselves to set up a still with a third man and cook up some moonshine. "They went out and they thought they was buying spirits," he explained, "and they got wood alcohol, and loaded up with that. And one of them died before they could get him back to quarters, and the other two went to the hospital, got them pumped out." A lot of people would make the same mistake back home a few years later, during Prohibition.

The alcohol served more as a source of warmth than as a social lubricant. "We didn't fraternize too much," he told me, with the Russians. "They didn't encourage that fraternization." By "they," he meant the United States Army.

"Did you encounter any Japanese soldiers in Siberia?" I asked him.

"Well, plenty!" he replied. In one area, he explained, "the Russians were first in the head of the valley. Then the Japanese. Then us. The Russians had a cemetery up on their end of it. When they had a body, they'd take it up, to the Japanese. And then you stopped." He jabbed an extended finger straight down, to signify how abruptly one would have to halt. "The Japs wouldn't let 'em across."

"Did you encounter any Bolsheviks in Siberia?" I asked him.

"*Everybody* was a Bolshevik," he said with a grin. Apparently, they didn't much trust the Russians, either; in truth, there wasn't much of a Bolshevik presence in that part of Siberia at that time. General Graves later testified that there had been none at all, though that seems rather unlikely.

I asked Mr. Hileman what he had done in Siberia. "We was on that Trans-Siberian Railway," he replied. "We was eighteen hundred miles in the northerly direction — we landed at Vladivostok, and then we went up to Lake Baikal. It was eighteen hundred miles from Vladivostok. We was on that Trans-Siberian." Protecting American property and the Czech Legion meant protecting that railroad. It was the central artery of the entire region, and everyone was scheming, maneuvering, and often fighting to control it: Reds, Whites, Czechs, Allies, Cossacks. When the men of the AEFS ran into trouble, it usually involved the railroad somehow or other. And it usually involved not the Reds, or the Whites, nor even the Japanese; but the Cossacks. "The Cossacks," Warren Hileman said, pronouncing the word "Coe-Sacks." "They wasn't supposed to be armed, but they had sabers — in addition to machine guns — about, oh, three to four and a half feet, about that broad" — he measured off a section of his hand about four inches wide — "and a cutting edge."

"Did you encounter any Cossacks?" I asked him.

"Any Cossacks?" He laughed. "Plenty of them . . . The Cossacks machine-gunned that troop train when I was on it. But I didn't get hit." He was referring to a deadly encounter on January 20, 1920, between soldiers of the AEFS and Cossacks, the latter subservient to the notorious warlord (or *ataman*) Grigoriy Semyonov. That incident is known today in certain circles as the Battle of Posolskaya. Sometimes spelled Posol'skaya. Or, in the case of Mr. Hileman's discharge papers, "Posloraya."

In a time and place that saw more than its share of unsavory characters, *Ataman* Semyonov was one of the most unsavory of all. He was also one of the most powerful; the supreme commander of a heavily armed and violent horde, he knew just how to play the Whites and Japanese for maximum personal gain, which was his primary — perhaps only — concern. Semyonov's Cossacks marauded through Siberia in a fleet of armored trains, at least one of which was said to contain an entire car full of girls they'd forcibly taken from their families for, well, personal use. They were known to shoot men in large groups and leave the bodies where they fell, to be consumed by wild animals. Semyonov was too brutal even for some of his own men, who were no sweethearts themselves. At one point, according to Lieutenant Colonel Charles H. Morrow, commander of the 27th Infantry Regiment, five hundred of the *ataman*'s Cossacks fled to Morrow's camp, outside the city of Khabarovsk, seeking refuge and bearing tales. Among those Colonel Morrow shared with a committee of the United States Senate in 1922: "Sixteen Austrian musicians who were playing in the *Chaska Chai* [a teashop] were executed in the public gardens in full daylight and the remains left there for public show. These musicians had not committed any crime deserving such bestial treatment." And: "By order of *Ataman* Kalmykov [Ivan Kalmykov, one of Semyonov's top generals] some employees of the Swedish Red Cross, among them one lady, have been shot. *Ataman* Kalmykov wanted to rectify this murder by charging them with espionage, but the real reason was that he got a chance to get hold of 3,000,000 rubles and of a large stock of different goods." And: "Prisoners of war who are detailed to work in town have been forced to deal the last death-bringing stroke to wounded citizens for Cossacks."

What Semyonov wanted most of all was control of the railroad. Morrow's men — among them, Private Hileman — were there to protect it. It was just a matter of time before something unpleasant happened between the two forces. Reports of intimidation and violence against railroad employees reached Colonel Morrow regularly; several tense encounters between the Americans and the Cossacks very nearly escalated to violence. Finally, the AEFS banned Semyonov's armored trains — there were believed to be nine in all, with such endearing names as *Terrible, Horrible, Merciless,* and *Destroyer* — from its sectors entirely. Things calmed down a bit, at least until several armored trains requested permission to pass through the sector, and Colonel Morrow consented. One of these trains was the *Destroyer,* which, Colonel Morrow later testified, had fifty-seven men and officers aboard, ten machine guns, and four small artillery pieces; its cars were clad in steel armor reinforced with eighteen inches of concrete. On the evening of January 10, 1920, it pulled into the station at Verkhne-Udinsk, where Colonel Morrow happened to be stationed. The Cossacks, Morrow later testified, "arrested the station-master, robbing him all of his property, including all the clothing of his wife, broke up the furniture in his house, and took him aboard." Someone sent word to Colonel Morrow, who boarded the *Destroyer* and confronted the general in charge, Nikolai Bogomolets. After "a rather heated argument," Bogomolets released the stationmaster (he had at first told the colonel he planned to execute the man), and the general, humiliated and very angry, ordered the *Destroyer* to move on.

Sixty miles up the line, it pulled into the station at Posolskaya. Colonel Morrow's testimony tells the next part of the story thus:

A lieutenant named Paul Kendall was posted at Posolskaya with a detachment of 38 men. They were sleeping in box cars. The armored train, Destroyer, moved into Posolskaya . . . moved back from the American box cars and opened fire. This was between 12 and 1 o'clock at night. It was about 40 or 50 degrees below zero and there was about 8 inches of snow on the ground.

Kendall and his men turned out with hand grenades and rifles and began the battle against the armored train. They threw a hand grenade into the engine, very seriously damaging it, so that it could only move down the track about five versts. Here Captain Ramsay closed in on it from the east and the armored train was captured in the morning.

During the fighting that occurred Sergeant Robins was killed, Private Montgomery died later of wounds, and Private Towney was knocked from the armored train when he attempted to board it, and his foot was cut off. . . .

General Bogomoletz [*sic*] and his officers and men were brought under guard and placed in the guardhouse by my command.

Shortly thereafter, though, Colonel Morrow was ordered to leave Siberia, at which point he had no choice but to free the man who had caused the deaths of two doughboys. By April 1, all of the Americans in Siberia, including Colonel Morrow, had left.

The Cossacks, though, didn't have much time to revel in their absence. Less than two months after Posolskaya, with the Reds closing in on him, Kalmykov fled to China; the Chinese Army quickly arrested him and held him for six months, trying to figure out what to do with him, until he attempted to escape and they shot him. *Ata-man* Semyonov fled Russia a year later — first to Korea, then Japan, and then to Shanghai, where a team of Bolshevik assassins tried to kill him. They failed, but Semyonov figured he'd better leave China, anyway, and landed in, of all places, the city of New York. He was not warmly received in Gotham; actually, he was arrested as soon as he stepped off the train. General Graves and Colonel Morrow testified at his deportation hearings. Not content to wait for the ruling, Semyonov jumped bail and fled, first to Canada and then the Far East. He eventually ended up in Manchuria, where the Soviets caught up with him at the end of the Second World War. Despite the passage of a quarter century, there were no bygones; they hanged him.

Nearly two hundred Americans died during the AEFs's nineteen months in Siberia. I have no idea when, where, or how they perished, other than Sergeant Robins and Private Montgomery, killed at Posol-skaya on January 10, 1920. Private Warren Hileman, eighteen years old, was in one of those boxcars that night when Semyonov's Cossacks opened fire on them. But aside from confirming that he'd been there and hadn't been hit, he didn't care to say much about it. At one point, he told me: "I wouldn't take anything for the experience, but I wouldn't give a plug nickel for it . . . I'm lucky. The only thing I got to show for it, I got a bad scar on my left shoulder here, covered with a tattoo. But now we're getting too close for comfort."

"How did you get the scar?" I asked him.

He shook his head. "No way," was all he would say.

At one point, just after telling me about the night his dinner froze, he said, in response to nothing: "We had several that didn't make it. They had a one-way trip." But he wouldn't elaborate on that statement. Instead, he talked about how the Army sent him to the Philippines and Hawaii after Siberia (he didn't care for either — said they were too *hot* for him), how he went home afterward and took up farming, took a wife and finally had a daughter after twenty years of marriage. He told me that when it came time for them to leave Siberia — his papers mark the specific date as March 10, 1920 — the ice in Vladivostok's harbor was still so thick and solid that they had to blow it apart with hand grenades before the ship could move. As I was about to leave that day — seven months before I would come upon his obituary in the newspaper — I decided to try one more time.

"How did American soldiers in your unit die in Siberia?" I wrote on the yellow pad.

He took it from me, read the question, set the pad down. He was quiet for a moment. "Well, I'm going to cross that last one out. That's zeroed-out information," he said at last, smiling apologetically. And I must tell you: In all these interviews, hundreds of hours of conversation, that's the only time anyone ever said anything like that to me. I don't know what it was that he didn't want to revisit after eighty-five years, but it must have been bad.

"Well," he said, "that about covers it. That's just hittin' the high spots." He folded his arms, and smiled.

And then added: "You ever try that Japanese beer, that *sake*?"

III.

She giggled at her own name. That was really something; if the sound of a 107-year-old woman giggling doesn't stir your heart, then it's time to reach for the defibrillator.

"Can you tell me your full name?" I'd asked her.

"My *full* name?" she replied. She paused for a second, then said: "Hildegarde Lillian Eugenia Anderson Schan." And giggled.

"That's quite a name!" I said, and she giggled again. I would have traveled a significant distance for that, but as it happened, I'd only had to go as far as an assisted-living facility in Plymouth, Massachusetts. It was May 17, 2006; once again, I had traveled to hear a story that I imagined I wouldn't be able to hear anywhere else. And once again, I was right: though Hildegarde Schan had not served in the armed forces in World War I, she was drafted into it nevertheless.

She'd been born, she told me, on January 13, 1899, in the Bronx — 145th Street and Willis Avenue. Her parents, Carl and Charlotte, had both come from Sweden; according to census records, they immigrated to the United States in 1887, when they were in their midtwenties, and married in 1891. "My mother had two boyfriends," Mrs. Schan explained. "And one of them did all of the talking, and the other was very quiet. So she didn't know which one to marry. So she decided to marry the quiet one, because she liked to do the talking." She giggled again, fluttering her wavy white hair and the string of pearls she wore over a dotted blouse.

"Why did they come to America?" I asked her.

"Because they were going to find gold on the streets," she said, smiling. "Everyone said, you go to America, you'd find gold." Instead they found each other, and started a family: three daughters and two sons. Her father, she told me, had been an inventor. "He invented the first shoe with a zipper in it," she said. "Men's shoes used to have buttons. And this was a zipper, and you pulled it up on the shoe. And then he painted on glass. He did a lot of painting on glass."

"And he had the milk route," her daughter, Joan, prompted.

"And then he had the milk business," she agreed. "You know, with the old milk wagons and the horses. I remember I used to step on the back, and we all liked to ride on that." The newspaper article that alerted me to her existence stated that Carl Anderson had had the very first milk route in the Bronx. Back then, the Bronx was relatively pastoral; when she was a child, Hildegarde Schan recalled, 145th Street "was a beautiful street, only three houses. But then they started to bring apartments and spoil the whole thing . . . We had a beautiful house. It was sixteen rooms."

"Two sides," Joan clarified.

"Eight rooms on each side," her mother said. "So we lived in one end, and they rented out the other. Imagine — twenty-five dollars a month. For an eight-room house." She laughed.

She attended PS 37, right up the street, but left school after the eighth grade and enrolled at Bird's Business Institute, on 149th Street. "What did you study there?" I asked.

"Oh, everything," she said. "Typing, shorthand, bookkeeping, everything for business."

"Did you like it?"

"Oh, yes."

"And then what did you do?"

"Then I got a job with Funk & Wagnalls. They're the ones that run the *Literary Digest*." While it's largely forgotten today, the *Literary Digest* was a tremendously popular and influential weekly magazine in its day, a combination of *Time* and *Reader's Digest* with a circulation that exceeded one million at its peak. Funk & Wagnalls, the magazine's publisher, was also known for its reference books, particularly its encyclopedia; working there, even as a secretary — as Hildegarde Anderson did — would have been a source of some prestige. She enjoyed the job, too. "I liked the typing," she said. "And we had a very nice superintendent. She was lovely." She was there for about a year, she said, and was earning $125 a month. This was in 1917.

"When the war came," Mrs. Schan explained, "every company had to pick so many employees and send them to Washington. So I was picked to go to Washington."

This is how she remembered it: At some point in the fall of 1917, she and four other women were told to go take a civil service examination. "Where was that?" I asked her.

"I don't know," she said. "In a government building." In New York. Of the five of them, she told me, "only the two of us passed the civil service."

"Why do you think they picked you to take the test?" I asked.

"I don't know," she said. "They must have thought I could do it." The test proved them right; and then, shortly thereafter, the government sent for her. "We got the telegram at one o'clock in the morning," she recalled, "for me to report on December seventeenth. The next morning, I called them in Washington, and asked if they could wait until after Christmas, you know. And no, they said I had to come right away."

A knock on the door from Western Union at one o'clock in the morning was not the kind of thing anyone ever hoped to hear. I have to wonder why the government chose to do it that way: Was it cheaper to send a telegram in the middle of the night? Or were they — that is, whoever sent the telegram — trying to convey a sense of urgency, even crisis? Whatever their reasons, that knock reverberated throughout the house — or at least the eight rooms on the Andersons' side. "They woke everybody up?" I asked.

"Yes," she said. "And I got all excited — going away from home — and I was crying."

"You were only eighteen, too," Joan said to her mother.

"Did *all* of the companies have to send women down to Washington?" I asked her.

"Yes," she said.

"Why?"

"They needed help."

For years after that conversation, I asked all kinds of people, including quite a few historians, about this. I read everything I could find on the subject of women and the war, followed serpentine information trails, looked up footnotes, and worked every search engine I knew of to find a definitive answer to the question of what, exactly, had happened to Hildegarde Anderson in the fall of 1917.

I never found one. Over time, I came to understand that her belief — that, as she had put it, "every company had to pick so many employees and send them to Washington" — was mistaken. If such a program had ever existed on that scale, there would be some record of it. There is none. There were plenty of government agencies and bureaus and offices that were concerned, at least in part, with drawing women into the workforce for the war effort, whether at the War Department or munitions plants, but none of them were given the mission, or the authority, to actually conscript women for work. Still, Hildegarde Anderson had received that telegram at one o'clock in the morning. She reported to Pennsylvania Station in Manhattan on the morning of December 17, 1917, and boarded a train for Washington, D.C. "Who decided that you should go to Washington?" I had asked her that day in Plymouth.

"My boss," she said. "The woman at Funk & Wagnalls."

To understand why, exactly, her employer might do such a thing to her, you need to know a few things. First, there was a severe labor shortage at that time in Washington; much of the government's male clerical staff had either volunteered for, or were drafted into, the AEF. There weren't nearly enough qualified women remaining in the city to fill all those jobs. There might well have been had President Wilson not, several years earlier, instituted a policy of racial segregation in federal offices; but he had. And now the government — particularly the War Department — was in trouble.

When America entered the war in April, 1917, some men, successful executives and the like who were too old or otherwise unfit for military service, chose instead to act upon their patriotism by taking leaves of absence from their jobs and offering their expertise to the war effort, in some form or other, for free. Actually, it wasn't quite for free: The government typically paid their expenses — and, to sweeten the deal, a stipend of one dollar a year. They were known as Dollar-a-Year Men, and though they are largely forgotten today, they made an important contribution to the war effort. I cannot imagine that a company like Funk & Wagnalls, a high-profile member of what we would now call the mass media, would not have sent any Dollar-a-Year Men to Washington in 1917. Certainly, they would have understood that such a visible gesture could pay dividends in any number of ways after the war. Perhaps one of Funk & Wagnalls' Dollar-a-Year Men worked at the Department of Labor (or at least knew someone who did) and, hearing that the War Department was having a difficult time finding good clerical help, thought to himself: *Well, I know where there are lots of fine secretaries!*

"I'll never forget that train ride," Mrs. Schan told me, eighty-nine years later. "We had a train, it was filled of soldiers. And they were singing, and they were so happy on the train, so nobody slept all night. We had to sit up all night on the train. Then we got to Washington, the Union Station, and they gave us a list of all the different places where we could go to see to live, and that morning we checked everything in Union Station and went out and took the trolley to look at the names of all these places they gave us, and it was snowing, and we were two people that had never been there. So we went from one place to another, and finally picked one place. I don't remember the street now, but it was across the street from the German Embassy. Fourteen [th Street] Northwest." The embassy, of course, was closed down at that point. "So it was a great big apartment house with an elevator, and there were three of us in one room. Another little French girl came from France. I don't know why they brought her from France. And she was very homesick; she was crying all the time."

"Was she very young?"

"She was about eighteen or nineteen. Marcelle Briere. She was a very nice girl, but she was so homesick."

I asked her who was the other woman from Funk & Wagnalls. "Grace," she said. "Grace Shea. And every time she would read in the paper that her husband's battalion was here or there, then she'd start crying. It was a sad time and a happy time." Grace, she said, had been about twenty-three years old then.

I asked her where she had worked in Washington. "On Pennsylvania Avenue," she said, then specified: "I was in the Engineering Department." In fact, she worked as a clerk in the Office of the Chief of Ordnance; she saved a copy of the memorandum, dated April 29, 1918, informing her that, "having completed three months satisfactory service," she was given a raise, from $1,100 to $1,200 per annum. Even after the raise, it was significantly less than she'd been making at Funk & Wagnalls; and she'd been living at home then, too.

That memo was just one of many slips of paper she kept in a scrapbook of her time in Washington. It was nine decades old when I saw it, yet still in good condition; she must have taken very good care of it over the years. She kept everything: certification of her smallpox vaccination; postcards and valentines from beaux in camp and overseas; photos of herself and a friend (Grace Shea?) posing in front of a monument; clippings of articles ("May Beat Germany by Christmas Time"; they did) and cartoons; snapshots of Charlie Chaplin at a Liberty Bond parade. Perhaps he made an impression on the young clerk, because her scrapbook also contained a subscription to the Fourth Liberty Loan, which took a dollar from each of her $55.00 paychecks. The Belgian Children's Fund took another fifty cents.

"Was the work interesting?" I asked her.

"Oh, yes," she said. "Yes. Very hard though. Big words, we never knew. We had a lovely boss. The boss we had came from the same town [as] my girlfriend. So he got me to work in his department after we got down there. They came from New Jersey."

I asked her what her hours were. "One month we worked days, and the next month we worked nights," she said.

"When they sent you down to Washington," I asked, "did they tell you how long they were sending you down there for?"

"Oh, no," she replied. "Until the end of the war."

"And when they put you in that apartment, did they pay the rent, or did you have to pay the rent?"

"Oh, we had to pay the rent . . . we had to pay all of our own expenses."

The War Department eventually solved its labor shortage and then some, it seems, because, as Mrs. Schan recalled, "they had built a lot of barracks on Pennsylvania Avenue, and that's where we worked, in those barracks . . . big, open space," room enough for a hundred women, maybe more. Some, like her friend Grace Shea, were married; and some were not. It wasn't a bad time and place to be an unattached woman, because, despite the existence of a severe shortage of manpower to work clerical jobs in Washington, somehow there were always a lot of men in uniform around. She remembered with special fondness "the French soldiers, from France. They had the most beautiful outfits, and they were so polite. So we went out with them quite a bit . . . we'd go to nightclubs," she said. "And they could all speak English."

"What did their outfits look like?"

"Green pants and a white shirt." Not what comes to mind when you think about French soldiers from that war, but maybe these were special troops; they were in Washington, after all.

They went out with American soldiers, too — "they were nice," she said, leaving me with the distinct impression that she'd preferred the French — to nightclubs and restaurants and the like. And by "they," I don't just mean the single girls. "My girlfriend was married, you know," she said, referring to Grace Shea. "She wouldn't take off her wedding ring. So" — she giggled again — "when we'd go out on a date, she'd bandage her hand up to hide the wedding ring!"

Miss Anderson had had a boyfriend, she revealed (with yet another giggle), a Bronx boy named Theodore Ross who was also in the Army. "Did he go to France?" I asked her.

"Yes," she said. "He had the mustard gas and all of that."

"Did he come back home after that?"

"Yes, he came back. And Grace's husband came back." Two happy endings. But, as you know, the name "Ross" did not figure anywhere into Mrs. Schan's impressive monicker. "I liked this guy better," she explained. This guy: the late Mr. Schan.

Miss Anderson had been told, at Funk & Wagnalls, that she was to go to Washington "until the end of the war." And she was there on November 11, 1918, when word of the armistice reached the capital. "And we rushed out," she said, "and everybody — an automobile would come, and everyone would get in, and then this big coal wagon — do you remember a coal wagon driven by horses?" I said I did, even though I didn't; it seemed the polite thing to do. "And a big, high seat?" she continued. "Well, Grace and I got up on this big, high seat, you know, on the coal wagon, and this coal man, filthy dirty from the coal, and we got in the parade and drove up Pennsylvania Avenue. And we'd gone a little ways and this coal man saw a florist! So he got up and went into the florist, and he got each of us a great big chrysanthemum with the oak leaves. So, up we got on the wagon again, and here we're sitting up on a big seat with a dirty coal man, and a big chrysanthemum on [do I even have to mention that she giggled yet again?], and driving up in the parade on Pennsylvania Avenue." Sounds like it was an impromptu procession. And quite a celebration.

Miss Anderson understood that the war's ending meant that she was free to return to her job at Funk & Wagnalls. But here's the interesting thing: After she'd gotten settled in at the Office of the Chief of Ordnance, she found that, despite the cut in pay, she actually *liked* working for the government; preferred it, even. So she stayed with it, even though there was no longer any need for her in Washington. "They transferred me to New York," she told me. "To the Veterans Bureau."

The Veterans Bureau was the predecessor to the Department of Veterans Affairs. Created by Congress in 1921 to provide care, rehabilitation, and vocational training to several hundred thousand wounded veterans, many of whom were blind or disfigured or missing a limb or two, the Veterans Bureau was also charged with administering disabled veterans' War Risk Insurance claims. The insurance had been strictly optional for doughboys, and though all were urged to purchase it — General Pershing personally issued several such pleas — many did not, meaning that after the war they got nothing at all in terms of an annuity, no matter how grievous their wounds. Unfortunately, many who did purchase the insurance also got nothing at all, because the man President Warren Harding appointed to head the new Veterans Bureau, a decorated veteran (and Harding crony) named Charles Forbes, was almost unthinkably corrupt (even by Harding administration standards), and fleeced the new agency voraciously, embezzling more than $200 million from it in just two years. This meant that planned facilities were never built, a lot of medical supplies and equipment "fell off trucks" (to use the technical term), and, worst of all, many thousands of legitimate benefits claims were unjustly denied. Eventually, Forbes — who also availed himself liberally of bribes, kickbacks, and an expense account that probably wouldn't have passed an audit — was forced to resign and face prosecution. He ended up serving less than two years in Leavenworth, and paid a fine of $10,000. I don't imagine he had trouble coming up with it.

Needless to say, the Veterans Bureau didn't really get to do much good in those early years. Still, it tried, at least at the most personal level, which was where Hildegarde Schan had worked. Its offices in Manhattan were on West Thirty-fourth Street, right across the street from Pennsylvania Station, whence she had departed New York for Washington some years earlier. She was a benefits administrator, meaning that she handed out money to wounded and disabled veterans. That might sound like a very easy and satisfying job; it wasn't.

"It was very sad," she told me. "Because we paid them there, you know every month, and you'd see them coming in with one leg or one arm . . . It was awful to see them come in, you know, and borrow. They'd borrow on their check, and then they'd have to pay it back next month, and they wouldn't have any money *then*. So the poor things, it was very sad to see how they were trying to get along. These nice, good-looking men with their arm off, their leg off. Ohh."

"A lot of the veterans who came back, they had a very hard time?" I asked.

"Oh, yes," she said. "To get a job and all, they had a *very* hard time."

I asked if a lot of the men she saw at the bureau hadn't had enough money to live. "That's right," she said.

"So what did they do?" I asked

"Well, they had a lot of charity," she said. "A lot of charity. And neighbors and them helped, you know." But even that was rarely enough, and many of the men had to borrow against their small monthly benefits check, which always seemed to lead to worse hardship down the line. "They came in, and you know, if they owed money, we'd hold the check," she recalled. "And then they'd have to come in and we'd take the money out of that check and give them what was left. And it was very sad to have to take money from them, you know, when they were giving up so much."

"Did you ever talk to any of them?" I asked.

"Oh, yes," she said. "They'd tell us all of their sad stories. You know, how they were very sad. And they didn't like the way the government was treating them, you know, just bring them home and let them go on their own . . . After they'd go, I'd sit there and cry and cry, you know. I felt so sorry for them." Mrs. Schan — she would die later that year, a few weeks before Christmas — dropped her gaze to her lap, and I looked away, too. I don't like seeing people get sad; especially 107-year-old women.

A lot of people were more than merely saddened by the situation; they were angered. It seems impossible to us now that hundreds of thousands of men who'd taken bullets or shrapnel or gas for their country, and who had yet to fully recover — who might *never* fully recover — could return to a country, full of people who wanted to help, that just couldn't seem to manage it. And they weren't the only ones who needed help: Hundreds of thousands more, maybe even millions, had lost their livelihoods while Over There. Farms had gone to rot; businesses had been shuttered or failed for lack of attention. Many had no homes left to which they might return, much less available avenues by which they might improve their lot. In his 1932 memoir *I Am a Fugitive from a Georgia Chain Gang!*, Robert E. Burns writes bitterly of his homecoming from the war:

> I had dreamed those happy dreams all soldiers have when lying in the mud and muck of trenches, ducking "Fritzies," "whiz-bangs," and "potato mashers," and machine gun bullets. But the promises of the Y.M.C.A. secretaries and all the other "fountain-pen soldiers" who promised us so much in the name of the nation and the Government just before we'd go into action turned out to be the bunk. Just a lot of plain applesauce! I found that being an ex-service man was no recommendation for a position — rather it was a handicap. Really an ex-soldier was looked upon as a sucker. The wise guys stayed home — landed the good jobs — or grew rich on war contracts. . . .
>
> In trying to find a position in society and earn a decent, honest living, I found that ex-soldiers were a drug on the market. The position I left at $50 a week was filled. But I could get a job at $.40 per hour — $17.60 a week. I thought of a few of my buddies, dead, forgotten, pushing up poppies and with nothing but a little white cross to mark the spot somewhere in France, and thought, Is this how my country rewards its volunteers — the men who were ready and willing to sacrifice life itself that democracy might not perish?

President Harding, a Republican who had succeeded Woodrow Wilson in 1921, had promised a "return to normalcy," and though a lot of people protested that "normalcy" wasn't a real word, he won pretty handily nonetheless, and then brought in an administration so corrupt that it didn't accomplish much beyond making a few old pals the richest men in the penitentiary. Harding might well have landed there, too, but for the fact that he died suddenly, in August, 1923; some whispered that his wife, who would not allow an autopsy, had poisoned the president to spare him the impending ugliness. During Harding's time, various bills had arisen in Congress to address the sort of thing Hildegarde Anderson witnessed at her job every day by extending some form of compensation to veterans, but the president had thwarted them all, claiming such a plan would be fiscally irresponsible. (I guess he didn't want to take money out of his friends' pockets.) When he died, proponents of the idea, including the American Legion, were hopeful that Harding's successor, Calvin Coolidge, might feel differently. But Coolidge was a man who didn't care for the notion of government doing much of anything at all, and who seems to have done his best to set an example in that regard, reportedly sleeping twelve hours a night. He didn't much care what other people thought of him, either; and when, the following May, Congress presented him with a bill called the World War Adjusted Compensation Act, which would have granted onetime monetary "bonuses" to veterans of that war, Coolidge — who had never served in the military himself — vetoed it, declaring: "Patriotism which is bought and paid for is not patriotism."

Coolidge's apparent callousness toward four million American World War I veterans, many of whom were in need, outraged many, including Fiorello La Guardia, who had returned from the Italian front with the rank of major and was quickly reelected to his seat in the House of Representatives. The Little Flower was (forgive me) no shrinking violet, and with characteristic vitriol he led the effort to override Coolidge's veto. It succeeded. Veterans and millions of other Americans cheered its passage, even knowing as they did that there was a codicil to the law — first proposed by New York congressman Hamilton Fish Jr., who had served as a white officer with the Harlem Hellfighters — that postponed payments of the bonus until 1945. Fish, a Republican (as were La Guardia and Coolidge), had put it in there in the hope that it might preclude Coolidge from vetoing the bill, but it stayed in even after the veto.

That seemed fine, at the time; it had been hard enough to get anything passed in any form, after all. But by the end of the decade, with the country suddenly plunged into a terrible economic depression, and millions suddenly without work, many veterans came to the conclusion that they just couldn't wait another fifteen years for the money the government had promised them. They needed it now. (Most so-called bonuses were calculated at the rate of $1.25 per day of service overseas and $1.00 per day of service in the United States, minus the $60 bonus everyone had already received upon discharge, plus 4 percent interest; with that interest, the average payout in 1945 would have been around $1,000, or so I have read.) The new president, Herbert Hoover — who, you may remember, had saved Europe from mass starvation during the war — refused them; a deal was a deal, he said, and besides, to make the payout now would require raising taxes, and the frail economy, he asserted, couldn't support that.

Then, in the spring of 1932, another war veteran in Congress, Texas Democrat Wright Patman, put up a bill that would pay the veterans their "bonuses" immediately. At first its prospects didn't look very good; Hoover was sure to veto it, and he seemed to have enough Republican supporters in Congress to prevent an override. But then something unusual happened: Around the country, groups of veterans started assembling to discuss Patman's Veterans' Bonus Bill and what they might do to help it pass. A group in Portland, Oregon, decided to ride boxcars all the way to Washington, D.C., and present themselves at the Capitol. They started calling themselves the BEF — the Bonus Expeditionary Force. As they rode across the country, they attracted notice, and other groups of veterans decided to follow their example. Politicians and crowds greeted them as heroes; people who were themselves suffering donated food, clothing, supplies. By June, a "Bonus Army" — estimates of its size range from ten thousand to twenty thousand veterans, plus their families — had converged upon the capital. They set up camps throughout the city; the largest was in Anacostia Flats, former swampland where the BEF laid out streets, established health facilities and sanitation infrastructure, and built huts from just about anything they could salvage. Eight decades before the Occupy movement, they occupied D.C. And they welcomed *all* honorably discharged veterans: In a thoroughly segregated city, the BEF's camps were racially integrated.

The presence of twenty thousand or so unemployed veterans congregating outdoors in the heat of summer was bound to make some people nervous; among them was Army Chief of Staff Douglas MacArthur — the man who had led his men into battle at the Meuse-Argonne wearing a cardigan sweater — who suspected that the Bonus Army was nothing more than a mob of communists and pacifists, although he didn't take pains to distinguish the two in his own mind. He was mistaken on both counts, though no one could convince him of that. In fact, the BEF had only one issue — benefits for veterans. And they were far from a mob. They drilled daily, even in the sweltering heat, and observed strict rules: no drinking, no begging, no radical condemnation of the government. Despite MacArthur's view of them — and he wasn't alone in his thinking on the matter — the Bonus Army attracted many admirers, among them politicians, policemen, socialites, and high-ranking military men. Quite a few visited the camps to offer moral support; plenty donated food, clothing, sundries, and medical supplies. They got a lot of press. Many allowed themselves to believe that their cause might prevail.

And for a while, it seemed like it actually would. On June 15, 1932, the House of Representatives passed Congressman Patman's Veterans' Bonus Bill by a margin of 35 votes. Thousands of veterans thronged the Capitol and held a vigil on the lawn, in anticipation of the Senate's vote on the bill. But the Senate lacked the courage to take that vote; instead, it voted, 44 to 26, to table the bill, taking it off the agenda for the rest of the year. Everyone expected the BEF, defeated, to pack up and go home.

It didn't. Rather, the veterans vowed to stay where they were until the Senate actually voted on the bill. More veterans flocked to the capital. More donations and supplies poured in. Despite all the support, though, morale wasn't always high; it can be hard to remain cheerful in Washington in the summer, even if you're not out of work and living in a Hooverville. Lloyd Brown — you might remember him as the gentleman who had an eighty-six-year-old USS *New Hampshire* tattoo on his arm — was working as a fireman in the city at the time, and he saw Bonus Marchers every day. He told me he was sympathetic to their cause — "I'm a World War I veteran, myself," he reminded me — but said they "looked like people in need . . . they looked pretty rough, some of them." They looked, he often recalled, just like hound dogs.

This went on for six weeks: the BEF unsure of what, exactly, to do next; the government unsure of what, exactly, to do about the BEF. Tensions mounted. Finally, on July 28, Hoover's attorney general, William D. Mitchell, ordered the eviction of Bonus Marchers wherever they could be found. Police fatally shot two men while clearing out a building on Pennsylvania Avenue. Then General MacArthur literally called in the cavalry — and the infantry. As thousands of government employees watched, a phalanx of soldiers marched against the veterans, forcing them out of their camps at bayonet point. And just to make sure, tanks were deployed, too — under the command of Major George S. Patton — as well as gas. Yes, it's true: Soldiers of the United States Army gassed veterans of World War I in the streets of the nation's capital in the summer of 1932.

The veterans fled across the river to their largest camp, in the Anacostia Flats. President Hoover, starting to worry about, in more modern terminology, the "optics" of the situation, sent word to MacArthur not to pursue them any farther. MacArthur — and this was confirmed years later by one of his aides that day, a Major Dwight Eisenhower — just ignored the president and sent his men charging into the huge camp. Everyone was expelled; the camp was burned. Dozens of veterans were injured in the attack. Scores were arrested. A three-month-old infant, exposed to the gas, died.

One of the expelled veterans was an emaciated forty-three-year-old private first class from Camden, New Jersey, named Joseph T. Angelo. If that name sounds familiar, Angelo was the aide who, fourteen years earlier, had saved George Patton's life at the Meuse-Argonne. Angelo had been awarded the Distinguished Service Cross for his heroism, but that didn't spare him the ravages of the Great Depression. A year earlier, he had walked all the way from New Jersey to Washington to testify before Congress about veterans' need to receive their bonuses immediately, and not fourteen years hence. Now, a day after the Battle of Anacostia Flats, Angelo convinced a sergeant in the 12th Infantry to take him to Patton, telling the man he was an old friend of the major's. It's not clear what Angelo hoped to say to Patton, because he never got the chance to speak with him; according to newspaper reports, when Patton spotted his former aide, he became enraged. "Sergeant, I do not know this man," he spat. "Take him away, and under no circumstances permit him to return!"

And so the Bonus Army was scattered — and yet, not quite defeated. It had drawn attention to the plight of indigent veterans and the government's indifference to them; Americans were very angry about it. And they stayed very angry: angry enough to vote President Hoover out of office three months later; angry enough to pass the GI Bill of Rights in 1944. To be fair, people had plenty of other reasons to be angry at Herbert Hoover in November, 1932, and to take a chance on New York Governor (and former Assistant Secretary of the Navy) Franklin Roosevelt. But it would also be fair to state that the GI Bill didn't square things in a lot of people's eyes, either, at least not right away. In the 1945 movie *Pride of the Marines*, there's an eight-minute scene in which a group of men, wounded in the Pacific and convalescing at a hospital in San Diego, discuss what awaits them back home after the war is over. Many of them are afraid — as afraid as they were at Guadalcanal. One, a fellow with the clever nickname "Irish" who tells us he has "a silver plate in my head," snarls to his buddies: "Twice in his life my old man got his name in the papers. The first time in 1917 — he was the first to enlist in Milwaukee. The second time in 1930 — he was the first vet to sell unemployed apples."

Other wounded Marines take up the cause. One speculates: "So maybe we'll even have prosperity for two years after the war while we catch up on things. Like making diaper pins and autos — things the poor civilians did without. But what happens after two years? Answer me that!"

Al Schmid — the hero of the film, a real-life Marine who was blinded by a Japanese grenade and is portrayed by the great actor John Garfield — offers: "A bonus march!"

"I'll put a little handwriting on the wall for you," Irish says. "We don't want no apples. And whoever's running the country better read it, too — no apples, no bonus marches!"

They did read it. The Bonus Army ultimately won their quixotic battle — maybe too late for themselves, but for their children, the Greatests, and beyond.

The First World War was doughboys in trenches and flyboys in aeroplanes, gas masks and machine guns, bayonets and barbed wire, kilts and soccer balls and poetry and mud. But it was also adolescent boys drilling on a green in Sussex until they were old enough to be shipped to the trenches, young women being summoned to the War Department in the middle of the night, men fighting off cold and Cossacks from inside a Siberian boxcar, passionate congressmen being outmaneuvered by indifferent presidents, middle-aged veterans and their families being gassed in a swamp in their nation's capital. And much more, even, than all that. A world more.

16

The Last Night of the War

I N THE YEARS AFTER the war ended, Americans built a whole
lot of monuments in France. There's that enormous column on
Montfaucon, to commemorate the Meuse-Argonne; a beautiful
marble rotunda atop Montsec, for Saint-Mihiel; a massive double col-
onnade situated on a hill looming over Château-Thierry. All of Belleau
Wood is, in essence, a monument. There's the huge Temple Memorial
in Château-Thierry, and the little fountain that the 102nd Regiment
installed at Seicheprey, and hundreds of others that fall somewhere
between the two in both size and location. Former battle sites are littered with markers installed years later to commemorate some position held at some point by this division or that; near Limey, I came
across a little concrete obelisk commemorating the 5th Division, dated
September 12, 1918, to which had later been affixed a bronze plaque,
dated September 1944, for . . . the 5th Division. I wish I could have
been there to see those GI Joes stumble upon a monument to their
doughboy predecessors. I suspect it happened often, especially to the
men of the 5th Division; so many of their markers are scattered about
that one American guide told me: "The saying goes that the 5th put up
a monument every time they stopped to take a piss."

About forty miles northeast of that obelisk I found what is, in my
opinion, the most poignant monument of that war, maybe the most
poignant monument I've ever seen anywhere. I say I "found" it, rather
than "came across" or "stumbled upon" it, because in fact I went out
searching for it, and had to look very hard. To see it for yourself, you
must first find the tiny and unceremoniously named Ville-devant-
Chaumont — literally, the village in front of Chaumont — which rests in

a pleasant green dale. If you see someone walking about, ask them for directions; you may have to ask several people before you find one who knows of the thing you're looking for. If they do — and if they know, for sure, where exactly it is — you'll be directed to a hard-to-spot road, narrow and overgrown as a cow path, that snakes up a rounded hill. It will probably occur to you at some point that the villager who gave you the directions is having a laugh at your expense; it doesn't seem like the kind of road that leads anywhere at all, much less to something you'd want to see. But stick with it, and eventually you'll arrive at a place where the hill levels off. To the right is a beautiful vista of farmland so lush it seems impossible that a war was ever fought here. I assure you, one was. Just look to your left.

Planted upright in a small sandpit is a stone, a rough-hewn tablet just a few feet tall. Standing behind it is a modest white flagpole. The American flag — at least on the day I visited — was tattered all along the far edge, and looked like something had taken a couple of bites out of it, besides. In the fall of 1918, this area, only ten miles or so north of Verdun, was the far-right flank of the Meuse-Argonne Offensive. There were two American divisions assigned to it in early November: the 26th, the Yankee Division; and the 79th, the Liberty Division, composed of draftees from Pennsylvania, Maryland, and the District of Columbia.

The 79th was credited with taking the eastern half of Montfaucon on September 27, the second day of the battle. By the end of October, having seen some of the offensive's worst fighting, they were moved to this section of the battleground, deemed to be quieter. It may well have been, but it wasn't by any means quiet. In what turned out to be the final days of the war, the 79th managed to wrest a number of French villages from the Germans, including, in the early hours of November 11, Ville-devant-Chaumont. Later that morning, some soldiers from one of the Liberty Division's regiments — the 313th, known as "Baltimore's Own" — were crouched atop this hill outside town, facing stiff German resistance. "The Boche fire was very heavy, and no sooner had the troops come into view than a barrage was put down," writes Henry C. Thorn Jr., in the regiment's history, published in 1920. "The soft, marshy ground was all that saved the Battalion from appalling casualties, as the shells sunk very deep upon impact. . . . The bursts seemed to throw mud, water and iron straight up into the air." Then, Thorn writes, at 10:44 a.m., a runner from headquarters arrived, bearing "orders to cease firing at 11:00 a.m. French time, hold the lines at the spot, and neither advance nor give way to the rear. The Armistice had been signed and fighting was to stop." The men hugged the earth; sixteen minutes to go.

Among them was a twenty-three-year-old private named Henry Nicholas Gunther. Photographs of the time show Gunther to be a handsome, mustachioed gent with thick, dark hair and a wry grin, a man you can easily picture hoisting an enormous stein of pilsner in a Baltimore beer garden. Like much of that city, and most of his neighborhood, he was of German descent; all four of his grandparents were immigrants. In 1917, he was drafted, left behind a good bookkeeping job at the National Bank of Baltimore and a fiancée named Olga, and headed off for Camp Meade, about twenty miles south. The following July, he sailed for France on the *Leviathan*, the same ship that later brought Howard Ramsey and Henry Roy Tucker to France, and that later yet brought Eugene Lee home. The *Leviathan*, you might recall, had started life as the German ocean liner *Vaterland*.

By the time he shipped out, Gunther had been made his company's supply sergeant, a position of considerable responsibility that would seem to indicate he was a dedicated and capable soldier. Nevertheless, when he got to France, he did something pretty stupid: In a letter to a friend back home in Baltimore who had yet to be conscripted, Gunther advised the man to stay out of the service for as long as he could, as conditions in the Army were very bad. Gunther must have known that all soldiers' letters passed through censors' hands before they were delivered; he should have figured that such a written sentiment would attract unwanted attention, especially given the author's Germanic surname. That letter cost Sergeant Gunther his stripes — all of them.

He took it very badly. According to an interview that Ernest Powell, Private Gunther's platoon sergeant — and, before the war, his close friend — gave to the *Baltimore Sun* in 1969, Gunther was humiliated by the incident; once a gregarious fellow, he became sullen and withdrew into himself. Eventually, though, he started stepping forward, volunteering for dangerous missions and assignments. At one point, he was wounded badly enough that he could have been sent back home, or at least away from the front; but he refused, insisted on returning to the 313th. He seemed determined to redeem himself in the eyes of his comrades, and the United States Army. That, though, would take time. And, as he'd just learned, the war was about to end — and with it, his best chance at redemption. Perhaps that explains what Private Gunther did that morning, atop that hill outside Ville-devant-Chaumont. The little monument that sits there now tells the story in French, German, and English. The English text, translated by Christina Holstein from Pierre Lenhard's original French, elaborates:

> Emerging from a bank of fog, Private Gunther and his friend, Sergeant Powell, found themselves confronted by two German machine gun squads manning a road block. The Germans watched in disbelief as the Americans came forward. Powell and Gunther threw themselves to the ground, as the bullets cracked overhead. The Armistice was imminent and the Germans ceased firing, believing that the Americans would have the good sense to stop. Their sacrifice would not change the war.

Indeed, no one fighting in those last few hours of the war could have known how little their potential sacrifice would have meant; according to the terms of the armistice, which had been signed almost six hours earlier, all German troops would have to evacuate France entirely — including Alsace and Lorraine — within fourteen days. In other words, where the lines ended up being drawn at 11:00 a.m. meant exactly nothing.

Even all these years later, historians still wonder why so many men fought so hard in those last few hours — to the point where hundreds of them died, within sight of the war's end. It is without a doubt one of the most tragic and mystifying elements of a cataclysm that was almost unthinkably tragic and mystifying. I certainly don't have an explanation to offer.

Instead, I offer you George Briant.

I found him, too, off the French List, which seems appropriate because he was, he would tell you, French himself. By way of Louisiana. Whether his ancestors arrived there directly from France, or from Acadia or somewhere else, is unclear; all he could tell me was that they were "local people — local French people, you know." They hailed from St. Martinville, Louisiana, the heart of Cajun country (and site of the legendary Evangeline Oak), but he was born more than a hundred miles to the east, in the city of New Orleans, the fifth of nine children; the others were Ferdinand, Hamilton, Rose, Lassaline, Gabriel, Walter, Pearl, and Ruby. Lassaline was named for his paternal grandfather, Paul Louis Lassaline Briant, who had served in the 22nd Louisiana during the Civil War. If you think Paul Louis Lassaline Briant is one cool monicker, his next-door neighbor in St. Martinville in 1870 was named Oneziphore Delahoussaye.

I found all of this information in census records, where I also discovered that, in 1900, Paul Louis Lassaline Briant's son, James Philippe Briant, lived at 1434 North Roman Street, in New Orleans; his neighbors, two doors down at number 1438, were a black family, which fact alone made that block one of the more integrated in the South at that time. The man of the house at number 1438, a Mr. Homer Plessy, was the Rosa Parks of his era. In 1892, he boarded a train in New Orleans, sat in a whites-only first-class car, and promptly summoned a conductor and informed the man that he was, in fact, what the law in Louisiana then called "colored," or possessed of mixed-race ancestry. The conductor must have been surprised; Plessy, who was what was then known as an "octoroon" — that is, he was one-eighth black by ancestry — was quite light-skinned, and certainly capable of passing for white. But he chose to challenge the law instead, got himself arrested for it, and took his case all the way to the Supreme Court, where it did not fare well. That's right: James Philippe Briant's neighbor on North Roman Street was the Plessy of *Plessy v. Ferguson*.

The 1900 census lists Homer Plessy's occupation as "day laborer"; James Briant's is "dry goods (clerk)." His son told me later — 104 years later — that the dry goods store was in fact D. H. Holmes, a legendary (and now, sadly, defunct) emporium on Canal Street in New Orleans. That son, George Leon Briant, was born in that city on March 3, 1901. A few months later, another child named Louis Armstrong would be born in New Orleans. Though they grew up in very different parts of the city, their childhoods did bear certain similarities, none of them felicitous. Louis Armstrong, for instance, was abandoned by his father at a very young age; his mother — just a teenager when she'd had him — was unable to care for him, and he was shuttled around between various relatives. I don't know what, exactly, happened to George Briant's family when he was a child, but I got the impression that it was more than just one thing. "My schooling was very limited," he explained, "because I was — so many deaths in the family, the disruptions in the family affairs. Everything is tipsy-topsy. Nobody knew where — you go your way, I go my way, do the best I can do, that was it. Most of us had to bring ourselves up, to a certain extent." He even spent time in an orphanage, he told me. His tone was steady, but the words came out haltingly; part of that was just the way he spoke, but I got the distinct sense that there was something inside him that I hadn't perceived in any of the other veterans I'd interviewed.

George Briant seemed sad.

A little housekeeping:

Mr. Briant pronounced his last name "BRY-ant." I visited with him at the nursing home in which he was then living, which was in Hammond, Louisiana, about an hour north of New Orleans. We talked in an empty common room; he was seated in a wheelchair throughout. He looked to be a slight man in large wire-rim eyeglasses, with perfectly white hair, thinner on top, crowning a somewhat oblong head. He wore a tan jacket over a gray shirt and trousers, and an abbot-sized crucifix that hung down well below his sternum on a long leather thong.

George and his wife had had but one child, a son named George Hamilton Briant, born in 1923. George H. had served in the Army Air Corps during World War II, earning the rank of captain, and afterward went to work as a stunt flier for the movies; word is he was a dashing fellow. Around 1947 or 1948, he was killed on the set during some sort of accident — I've seen it described as a parachute jump, though it may have been a plane crash.

In 1921, a friend of George's introduced him to eighteen-year-old Germaine Thibodeaux at her cousin's house in St. Martinville; the friend was dating one of Germaine's sisters. When George asked her out, though, Germaine informed him that she was already engaged to another fellow. Nevertheless, as they liked to tell the story, it was love at first sight, and Germaine quickly broke off the other engagement. She and George were married four months later, on July 20, 1921.

They were still married when I visited, on September 18, 2004 — *eighty-three years* later. He was then 103 years old; she was 101. I don't know what she was like at eighteen, but at 101, Germaine Thibodeaux Briant was a handful. I was told as much even before I made the trip. "I'm going to have to distract her while someone brings Papa to you," their goddaughter, Irma, advised me on the phone. "She doesn't like to let him out of her sight."

"You don't have to do that," I said. "I find it helps to have someone else present when I'm doing an interview. I want her to be there."

"No, you don't," Irma replied. "Trust me."

She was right. Germaine Briant was jealous of any attention that wasn't directed entirely toward her. She insisted on answering just about every question I posed to her husband (Irma's attempt to keep her godmother away during the interview had failed), and doing so in a voice that was, petite and aged though she was, much louder than his. Her Cajun accent, too, was much thicker even than his. It all made for one of the more difficult interview experiences I've ever had, and one of the most memorable; if George Briant hadn't been so determined to share his story with me despite all the distractions — and if his story hadn't been what it was — I might have just given up, gone to New Orleans, and gotten drunk instead.

But enough of my trauma; back to his.

"Where were you living when you joined the Army?" I asked him.

He laughed, smiled broadly; I got the impression that he'd had to move around quite a bit in those days. "Let's see," he said. "Where was I then?"

"Mrs. Garcia's house!" Germaine Briant called out, pronouncing it "GAW-shuss."

He didn't even seem to notice she'd said a word; eighty-three years is a long time in which to learn how to tune someone out. "I think I was living with my mother and my sister —"

"And an old lady," his wife interjected. Irma whispered to her to be quiet.

"— and her husband, at the time I joined the Army. I think I was fifteen years old when I joined the Army." Actually, he was sixteen, and looked it; the recruiters turned him away, several times, before he made such a pest of himself that they finally just let him enlist. "The guy says, 'What are we going to do with him?' And the [other] guy says, 'Take him!'" he recalled with a laugh.

I asked him: "Did you have to lie about your age to get into the Army?"

"Yes, I did," he declared.

"How old did you tell them you were?"

He laughed again. "I had to tell them I was about seventeen, I think," he said. "They found out afterwards, but they cast me over, let me pass over because I was anxious to join." I cannot explain why the Army did this, except that I doubt "the Army" did anything at all; it seems to me that recruiters were given a great deal of individual discretion when it came to enlistment. "And I was in the war from then on," he told me.

"Did you tell your parents when you joined the Army?" I asked him.

"My parents weren't alive," he said. "My parents were dead."

I asked him why he'd joined up. "To become a man," his wife declared; he, though, just chuckled at the question, and considered it for a moment.

"The conversation," he said finally, "was generally on warfare at that time, you see. This one was going to join, that family was going to join — in other words, families were being separated right and left. Young people — young people wanted to join because of youth, age. They all wanted to know what warfare was. So did I. And I sure learned too much about it."

I asked him where he had gone to enlist. He said he couldn't quite remember; "I think he told me Jackson Square!" Mrs. Briant announced.

He turned and asked me: "Why does a person, fifteen years of age, want to go to war? You tell me."

"For adventure?" I offered.

He laughed. "I was anxious to join the war," he told me. "I wanted to go to war. Of course, I only knew about the war what I'd heard, you see. You know what I'm saying? And what I could visualize. But after I was in it, I learned a hell of a lot more."

"You said you wanted to be a man," Germaine Briant called out. "You told me."

"I was tickled to the death that they let me [enlist]," he recalled with a smile at one point; but then, suddenly, he grew serious. "But let me tell you, it was no fun," he said, leaning forward as his voice softened a bit and started to waiver. "War is hell, it's real hell. It's nothing to joke with, nothing to laugh with. You might think it's a journey, having fun or something." He shook his head. "There's no fun in war. War is do or die. It's you or me. And who can pull the trigger faster."

And with that, he fell back into his wheelchair.

"How did you choose the artillery?" I asked him.

His response was one I'd heard before. "First, I wanted to be a rider," he said. "I wanted to be a horse rider; I wanted to join the cavalry. So I went to join the 18th United States Cavalry. And if I remember right, they sidetracked me because of my age, you see. They put me into some smaller department. I wound up in the 18th United States Cavalry, and I learned how to ride horses." He chuckled. "And I mean, you had to *learn*. Yeah. They'd take you rough — through woods, like a roughrider. They'd turn your horse loose with you, and your horse followed the leader, that's all. He'd pay no attention to you at all." He laughed. "One after the other. I liked it. I never tried to get out of it. That's what I wanted."

"So how did you get into the artillery?" I repeated.

"Well, at the time, they had no use for riders, you see. So the Army organized . . . the 76th Field Artillery. They organized that organization, and I was in that, see? And I was in that until the war ended . . . At my age, everything was wild," he said, spreading his arms wide. "Name and assignment, I didn't care. Put me in here, put me there — made no difference what it was, make sure I was in the Army . . . I was at the height of my glory then."

By now he was quite animated — smiling, laughing, gesturing. "Yeah, it was the same outfit," he recalled. "It was the same thing, but they changed the name, that's all. In other words, instead of training with horses, we trained with guns . . . but it didn't make no difference, as long as I was in the war. I was satisfied that I was fighting, and doing what I was supposed to do. And that was it. I had the young persons' ideas, you know, and the ability to do what the young persons do. And that was all I wanted to do. I didn't care if it was the artillery, the cavalry, or what. So between the cavalry and the artillery, I became a soldier." He laughed again, and I began to notice that his laugh almost always arrived in the company of a singular smile, wide and thin and light, like a melon rind. He had started off our discussion by warning me that "quite possibly, I've forgotten much of it," then adding: "It's not a good thing to remember." But now it seemed that remembering it was reviving him; he was becoming more and more energized the deeper he bored into that old reserve, which I suspect he hadn't approached in a very long time. Compared to the other veterans I'd interviewed, George Briant seemed to have an entirely different vocabulary at his disposal. He was able to speak not only of what he'd done, but how it all had made him feel. Alone among the rest, he stood out for being human in a way that most of us can actually relate to much more than we can to the stoicism that characterized almost all of his remaining contemporaries: He was *emotional*.

And, as it turned out, he was just getting started.

The day after its official designation as an artillery unit, the 76th FA was assigned to the 3rd Infantry Division. Although the 3rd was one of a handful of Regular Army units that had existed before the war, it didn't get to France until April of 1918, ten months after elements of the 1st and 2nd started showing up Over There, and six months after the Yankee Division arrived in full. Still, the men of the 3rd Division were early American guests to the party, and first rushed into action to stop the Germans at Château-Thierry a few days before Belleau Wood got under way. They never really got a break after that, either. According to E. B. Garey, O. O. Ellis, and R. V. D. Magoffin, the excessively initialed authors of 1920's *American Guide Book to France and Its Battlefields*, "The history of this division is unique. It had no service in a quiet sector. It learned how to fight by fighting."

I haven't said very much about what went on in France in the summer of 1918, the time between Belleau Wood and Saint-Mihiel. The truth is, that summer is often overlooked in histories of the war. But it saw the last of Germany's five great pushes that are now collectively remembered as the Spring Offensive of 1918; in effect, it was the last time the German Army would go on the attack in that war. It was Germany's last hope for the great gamble it had undertaken back in March, after finally knocking Russia out of the war and shifting a half-million seasoned German troops to France, its last attempt to break through the lines, take Paris, and decisively defeat France, Britain, and the United States before millions of fresh American doughboys could get into the fight. Had the Spring Offensive succeeded, it might have done just that. Instead, many historians believe, the failure of this final push, in the summer of 1918, mortally wounded the German Army — and Germany itself. Yes, Bill Lake and lots of others who were there believed the war was won that fall at the Meuse-Argonne; but many of those who take a long view of the war, who have the distance and perspective to do so, believe the Meuse-Argonne merely *ended* the war, and that it was, in truth, *lost* after weeks of vicious combat at the place where, nearly four years earlier, it began in earnest: the Marne River. Even some who didn't have the benefits of distance and perspective believed as much: As the authors of the aforementioned *Guide Book* wrote just two years afterward, "During these battles the German Army had not lost its morale and the fighting was even more bitter than during the Argonne-Meuse Battle." And that's pretty bitter.

The stakes could hardly have been higher. When they launched that last push, right around midnight on July 14, 1918, the Germans were only about forty miles from Paris. Panic once again flared up, terror that the hated Boche were about to storm into the French capital and do God-only-knows-what when they got there. And some believe they might have made it had it not been for George Briant's 3rd Division. So many felt that way at the time that, after the battle, after the Germans had been turned back and the panic began to subside, people started calling the 3rd the "Rock of the Marne." They still do. The division itself adopted the nickname the "Marne Division." It, too, still stands.

They earned these titles by holding steady in the face of a terrible attack on that first day. The Germans started off with a massive bombardment, high explosives *and* gas, that killed or incapacitated thousands. (One report I've read says that hundreds of American soldiers were blinded by gas that morning.) Then they sent *forty divisions* rushing forward into the French lines on either side of Reims. They were effectively stopped east of the city by superb French defenses, but to the west — the side closer to Paris — they enjoyed great initial successes, crossing the river where they'd been halted four years earlier. Veterans later reported watching from atop the opposite banks as the Germans flung themselves at that river with tireless determination, using whatever they had handy — rafts, pontoons, wooden beams — to help them across. When the enemy blew up their new bridges, put up in a hurry under fire that morning, the Germans hastily rebuilt them, perhaps in the same spot, perhaps a few hundred yards up- or downstream. Accounts of the fighting that morning are among the most chilling I've ever read. The French and Americans (and there were some Italian troops present, too) brought an awful rain of shells and machine-gun fire down upon the Germans; still, they kept coming. The only way to stop them, it seemed, would be to kill them all.

And that, more or less, is what the 3rd Division did at the western edge of the line, just east of Château-Thierry — so close to Paris that many people now commute from one to the other every day — on July 15, 1918, and on into July 16. Two other American divisions, the 28th ("Keystone") and 42nd ("Rainbow") were elsewhere in the line that day, but they'd only just been moved there in anticipation of the attack; the 3rd had been holding its ground ever since they'd taken it six weeks earlier, before Belleau Wood. It had been a fairly quiet six weeks, until then; they lost more men on that one morning than they had since they'd first arrived at the front. But they held the line. The Germans did not successfully cross the Marne in their sector. Many of those Germans never crossed any body of water — or stretch of ground — again. By the next day, according to the division's commander, Major General Joseph T. Dickman, "there were no Germans in the foreground of the Third Division except the dead." A lot of dead.

On that first day of the battle that is now known as the Second Marne, the 3rd stopped the Germans at the western edge of the latter's line. By the third day, the Germans had been stopped everywhere. On the fourth day, the French and Americans launched a counteroffensive, their first of the year. From that point until the armistice, the Germans would be on the defensive; but while many now view that battle as the beginning of the end, the Germans were far from beaten at that point. They fought ferociously. The battles that followed that summer

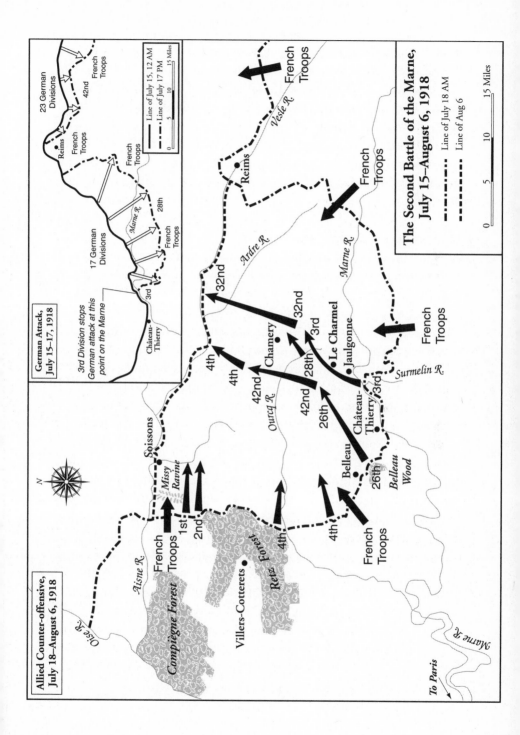

**Allied Counter-offensive,
July 18–August 6, 1918**

**German Attack,
July 15–17, 1918**

23 German
Divisions

French
Troops

42nd

Reims

French
Troops

French
Troops

17 German
Divisions

French
Troops

3rd

Château-
Thierry

28th

Marne R.

3rd Division stops
German attack at this
point on the Marne

Line of July 15, 12 AM
Line of July 17 PM

0   5   10   15 Miles

N

Soissons

Aisne R.

Oise R.

Missy Ravine

French
Troops

1st

2nd

Compiègne Forest

Villers-Cotterets

Retz Forest

4th

4th

French
Troops

Belleau

26th

Belleau
Wood

Château-
Thierry

3rd

26th

42nd

28th

3rd

Le Charmel

Jaulgonne

Surmelin R.

French
Troops

Ourcq R.

Chamery

32nd

4th

4th

42nd

32nd

Ardre R.

Marne R.

Reims

Vesle R.

French
Troops

French
Troops

To Paris

Marne R.

**The Second Battle of the Marne,
July 15–August 6, 1918**

Line of July 18 AM

Line of Aug 6

0   5   10   15 Miles

would claim Joyce Kilmer, the journalist and poet and would-be author of "Here and There with the Fighting Sixty-Ninth"; and Quentin Roosevelt, aviator and favorite son of the former president; and Major George Rau, of Hartford, Connecticut, hero of Seicheprey; and thousands of other Americans.

And Private George Briant — Battery B, 76th Field Artillery, 3rd Division — would come very close to joining their ranks one afternoon in late July, just outside a pretty little farming village in Picardy named Le Charmel.

Field artillery regiments were assigned to specific infantry divisions, but since infantry and artillery can't really be commingled — artillery units need a lot of space, and you wouldn't want to be entrenched near them even if you could be, for any number of good reasons ("We had to be at least three miles behind the lines," George Briant explained) — artillery's location and movements are much more difficult for historians to pin down. Often, they were dispatched to some third point, distant from both the enemy and their own infantry; and sometimes they were loaned out to support other divisions — even other armies. I only know that the story I want to tell you happened near Le Charmel because I happened to find a remarkable little book.

It's called *Roll of Honor of the Seventy-Sixth US Field Artillery*. Small and thin, with a dark red cover that is plain but for the title embossed upon it in simple gold letters, it looks at first glance like a children's reader. It doesn't much resemble any of the other regimental or divisional histories I've ever seen from that war. There are no pictures, or illustrations of any kind; no sentimentality, no nostalgia, no ribbing or swagger. More than twenty of the book's seventy-four pages are occupied by a roster of every last man who served in the 76th FA, from Colonel E. St. J. Greble Jr. to Private William B. Zolinski of Battery F. Thirty-six are given over to a list of every citation recommended for any soldier in the regiment, including nine Distinguished Service Crosses and more than a hundred Distinguished Service Medals. Each is accompanied by a detailed description of the action or actions for which the citation was considered appropriate, like this one, for Second Lieutenant Henry W. Clark of Battery F:

Near Chateau-Thierry during the Second Battle of the Marne he maintained an exposed observation post throughout the most intense series of enemy bombardments. His steel helmet was partially torn from his head by a large shell fragment but he refused to quit his post until his operator was severely wounded. Finding himself unable to accomplish communications of any kind with his battery he saved his comrade from bleeding to death by carrying him through intense fire to a dressing station.

The book opens with a memorandum from Colonel Greble, titled "Recommendations for Distinguished Service," that begins: "In compliance with Memorandum Headquarters 4th Army Corps dated Dec. 18th, 1918, there are submitted herewith lists of names of officers and men of this organization whom the Commanding Officer has seen fit to specially recommend to higher authority for their continuous, meritorious, and distinguished service in action. . . . It is to be greatly regretted that every member who has helped compose a regiment, which has been able to perform the services which this regiment has rendered, does not receive from the Government some fitting recognition worthy of those services."

Colonel Greble goes on, in the next couple of pages, to furnish a skeletal accounting of the 76th's history, concluding: "The regiment continued its fighting constantly with practically no rest during its entire operations nor a chance to re-equip or rehabilitate. It cheerfully and willingly at all times underwent its privations and suffered its hardships doing its duty as it saw it." It really does read like a memo; perhaps it was conceived as a service document instead of a regimental history. Before it was published, though, probably in early 1919 (the frontispiece records that the book was printed by Lithographie von Deinhard & Co., Coblenz, Germany), some anonymous soul undertook to add and compose a short section titled "Brief Narrative of the engagements in the Great European Conflict participated in by the 76th Field Artillery."

According to the "Brief Narrative," the 76th first went into position on the night of July 5–6, 1918; the following afternoon, "Battery 'D' sent the first message from the Regiment to the Boche." Still, their initial ten days at the front were pretty quiet — until, the narrative declares, "On the night of July 14th–15th the Germans launched their grand offensive from Rheims to Soissons that was to prove their Gettysburg. The heaviest pressure came just to our right in the now famous bend of the Marne at Jaulgonne. At 11:50 p.m. on that night the following message was received at Regimental Headquarters: 'Enemy crossing at Gland, fire your general OCP [offensive counter preparation — that is, a barrage you lay down on the enemy before he attacks you, to dissuade him or at least render him less effective] until further orders.' We fired it without a moment's intermission until about noon the next day. For the remainder of that night the whole sky was lit by the flashes of the guns, as though there was some tremendous fire extending for miles." Compare that to what Mr. Briant told me when I asked him if he remembered how he'd felt that first night he went into battle.

He laughed, and leaned forward. "I'll tell you," he said, "the first battle is something you never forget in your life, you see? Everything is *Ssssh!*" He raised a finger to his lips. "*Ssssh!* No noise. No noise." He dropped his voice to a loud stage whisper for a moment, looked around and gestured with his hand here and there, as if addressing men standing all around him. "'Quiet! No noise. Quiet.' And you worried all the time, 'What's going on? What's going on?' But if you only knew what was going on" — he broke into a chuckle — "you were dying. So we finally caught on, the reason we were being shushed down was because *our life was at stake,* you see?"

I nodded.

He leaned in closer. "The enemy had secret posts out in the fields, you see," he said, extending a hand and sweeping it across a pasture only he could see. "And they knew every move we was making. And every time we moved the troops another mile, a half a mile, they knew all about it. They knew more than we did, because we didn't know we were going to be moved. But they knew in advance we were going to move, and they were waiting for us, you see." He punctuated that thought with a deep nod. "Our officials should have known there were going to be secret listening posts out in the fields and everywhere, taking messages all the time," he asserted. "And that's one of the reasons we got shot up. Because the enemy knew what we were doing all the time, better than we did. We were standing in an open field, and then they were sitting there waiting for us."

I thought he was speaking metaphorically. "They were tough, the Germans," I said.

"Yeah. Between the *boom-boom-boom-boom,*" he continued, stretching out his hands to mimic the motion of firing a machine gun, "and they was always up there dropping those bombs, we didn't know which way to run."

"Were you scared the first time you went into battle?" I asked him.

He was silent for a beat. "Yeah," he said soberly, then shook his head. "It's a funny feeling. There was a *thrill,* you understand?" he explained, raising both hands. "You knew you were in *real* action then, you see. They wasn't saying, 'We're going to train you,' or nothing." He raised his hands again, pointing both forefingers to form rifle barrels. "You're going to take those guns and you're going to fight *for your life.* Man to man, him or you. So we grew to be adult persons at that age of fifteen years old. In other words, it was do or die." He shook his head. "And even though we were kids, it was do or die. And me, I got my share."

None of the other veterans I interviewed, before or after, had ever gotten near a word like "thrill" when describing combat. They all must have understood, on some level, that such a composite of terror and excitement is an awfully heavy thing to carry with you throughout a life, and that you'd better find a way to set it down and move on without it if you wanted yours to be a long one.

But not George Briant. He had borne an awful lot of pain in his life, not just during the war but throughout what sounded like a wretched childhood — and then he lost his only child, his son, his namesake, at a terribly young age. Any one of those is the kind of thing you might never get over; all three together could kill you. But they didn't kill George Briant; in fact, by all accounts he led a happy, fulfilled, godly life. He never had much money — eventually, after passing through several other jobs, he set up shop as a sign painter — and spent most of his retirement living in a trailer. But I read, in one of his obituaries, that he and Germaine were in the habit of plucking old toys out of the trash, repairing and restoring them, and then giving them to needy children.

A crushed man doesn't do that sort of thing.

So I wonder if, maybe, George Briant managed to do something that seemingly no one else I'd met had — that perhaps like them he had, a ways back, set down his load, but that he had also, somehow, always kept track of where he'd left it, always knew where it was so that he could, if the occasion should call for it, run back and fetch it.

And now, having picked it back up, he never put it down, at least not that afternoon. That potent cocktail, terror and excitement — once he sipped from it again, for the first time in who knows how many years, the taste stayed with him. "But I'll tell you, that's a thrill," he said at one point, using for a second time that word I'd never heard anyone else utter in this context, "that's a thrill you should never want. Because your life is at stake every instant. I mean, every instant! You know which[ever] way you turn, you're going to get shot at. But we didn't realize that at the time, you understand? You're in the war, and you never was in war before. And first thing you know, you're being shot at from all directions." He laughed.

"I'll tell you something," he said once, after a long pause. "There's two things about warfare. You want to be there, but you don't *want* *to* be there. But you've got to be in both places, and you can't do it. So you try to" — he moved his hand around from point to point, mimicking with his pinched fingers the dance one might do in trying to avoid incoming fire — "and you keep trying. But of course, you wind up in the graveyard."

It was a point he kept returning to, this uneasy marriage of two extreme emotional states; it seemed terribly important to him that I understand. At first I thought it was the fear he wanted me to comprehend, but the more he revisited the subject, the more I started to wonder if in fact he was more concerned that I grasp just how *exciting* he'd found it all. The 76th had spent the second half of July on the offensive, chasing the Germans across the Aisne-Marne Sector. They moved often, almost always under cover of darkness. "Jumping from place to place," Mr. Briant recalled. "You're moving as fast — I mean, you're here now, and three hours later, you get all packed up and be ready to leave. They don't tell you where you're leaving for, but be ready to leave in three hours. So you get all the equipment together, pack it all up, and in three hours you're standing out there in the open field, like that, waiting, waiting. If they [the Germans] ever come down and see you there, they're going to half-kill all of you." He shook his head. "It's something you can't explain, it's something — you're in a warfare that you were never in before. In other words, you're not a *war man,* you know what I'm saying? You're just a soldier. And here you are, in *the World War I.* All of a sudden, overnight, you're in World War I. 'Pack up, pack up and get your things.' Twelve o'clock at night. No sound. No noise. Everything's quiet." He raised a hand to his ear, then waved it in front of him. "Most mysterious things you ever seen in the war. You never see that, you never see a thousand men standing out there, all the packed-up guns and everything, waiting up there. *Shhhhhh! Shhh!* Three, four hours, standing there, waiting there. Then you get to line and march." He silently swept an arm around, like a pinwheel: *Hurry up!* "A thousand men moving, and the enemy don't know it. He don't know it because he don't hear a sound. He got sound equipment all over there, he hears everything, you see. But being it's so quiet — we kept the sound down, you see. And it saved many of our lives. We'd have got killed by the animals. And everything is mysterious. Everything is *Shhhhhh!* No sound. You know they've got a thousand men out there with guns and everything, all the equipment, cannons and everything that they're ready to fire. There's a thousand men out there waiting — you don't hear nothing. You don't hear a sound. All of a sudden a guy comes in, he says" — he paused, slowly swung his arm across his chest twice: *Move along!* — "'Go, march, march, march,' until you get to three miles within that front line there, you see? Then you unload, pack up, dig in. Get your guns in position to fire, get that other stuff — you don't hear a sound. A thousand men digging holes, preparing for war, and you don't hear a sound. Everything mysterious. Every move you make is mysterious. And that's what makes it so thrilling to young people. The movements — you never see the movements. You're in the movements, and you don't know it. All quiet, no sound. Don't you dare light a light, a cigarette, because they could have shot at you." He laughed, took a drink from a water cup he'd been holding in his left hand. I hadn't noticed it there until that moment.

Reviewing the tape years later, I hear his wife, Germaine, interjecting comments here and there, though at the time he'd just talked over her, and I, transfixed by his story, hadn't perceived she'd said a word.

Now, though, as he took a pause, she seized her opportunity. "I've lived his life, over and over, what he told me," she cried out. "Years ago. Every bit of it is true. How he went through all that, only by the grace of God, all without being mentally ill, I don't know. And the best husband in the whole world! To the people! To one another! A wonderful marriage!"

She was shouting; but none of it seemed to register with him. "I'll tell you one thing," he finally said to me. "You dead, and you don't know it. All of a sudden you're marching, you're marching, you're marching. And soon you slow down, it slows down, it slows down. And you hear the *Shhhhhh!*" He turned his head here and there, hushing ghosts in every direction: "*Shhhhhh! Shhhhhh!* Why so quiet? You better be quiet till you know what's buried there, you know what's hidden over here, see. They got listening posts all over. They know just where you at. They hear you talking. And they don't want to shoot because they don't want to expose their position. They could kill us all at any time, see, but they want to know more about us, what we after, see?" He was even more animated now; he leaned forward, his eyes wide, looking into mine.

"That's enough, Papa!" his wife called out.

"There's action and danger," he continued, unheeding. "There's a *thrill* attached to it."

"The nerves!" Germaine said.

"What's thrilling about it — you know you're going to *die!*" he concluded, but his hands kept moving after his lips fell silent; he was in the thrall of that thrill even yet.

And that thrill — it was not, as Winston Churchill once described it, the thrill of being shot at to no effect. The war, you see, had very nearly claimed George Briant's life. He wasn't waxing philosophical when he told me that he had sure learned too much about war, nor poetic when he recalled: "We were standing in an open field, and then they were sitting there waiting for us." He really had; he really was. And they were, really.

It happened on July 28, 1918, two weeks after the Germans launched their last great offensive, ten days after it had faltered and the French and Americans launched their own. There had been quite a lot of fighting in and around the village of Le Charmel by then; the French and

Americans would take part of it, then lose it to a German counterattack, then repeat the process again and again. "Le Charmel was probably reported captured as many times as any town in France," the *Roll of Honor*'s "Brief Narrative" reports. On July 27, it seemed the Germans had finally been chased off for good. The narrative continues:

> Le Charmel . . . had been before the war a quiet little farming town snuggled down under the hills with the inevitable Chateau on a small hill across the valley. It was quite a strong point for the Boche and was held by many Machine Guns. The regiment moved on July 27th, the day it was captured, the batteries taking position along a hedge near the Roncheres road.

I know two versions of what happened there the next day. "On the morning of July 28th the 1st Battalion limbered up and moved to the road preparatory to changing position," the narrative reports, "then received orders to return and fire a barrage." As George Briant remembered it, though, his battery — Battery B — was ordered to move in daylight; and then, already dangerously exposed, they — well, they got stuck in traffic. "We were changing positions," he recalled. "We were going to take a French position, you see, and they were supposed to have moved. But when we got there, they had never moved. They left us out in the open." Literally: Battery B was stuck standing in an open field, the sun high overhead, illuminating them, as if an artillery battery surrounded only by grass and hay needed further illumination. They could do nothing but stand there and wait, wondering which would reach them first — orders that they could finally move, or something very bad.

And then they heard it: something very bad.

The "Brief Narrative" is almost cavalier about what happened next. "It was while we were in this position that we made our first real acquaintance with the Boche 'planes," it records, and you can't help but marvel, nearly a century later, that aircraft were still so new at that point that "planes" required an apostrophe up front to remind you that it was short for "aeroplanes." Planes themselves were also still objects of marvel for many; but for the men of Battery B on July 28, 1918, they were just objects of terror, moving unfettered overhead as you were trapped down on earth, as free to kill you as were those unseen German soldiers hiding just off the road in the dark of night. Unlike those soldiers, though, the planes didn't hold their fire; they already knew where the Americans were headed. "As 'B' Battery was going in a plane came quietly sailing over and let go four bombs that got 28 horses and 34 men," the narrative explains.

"They couldn't help it," George Briant told me. "They were flying over; they saw us out in the field. And when they saw us out in the field, they were all ready with the bombs. All they had to do was drop their bombs."

"However," the "Brief Narrative" continues, undaunted, "everyone stuck to his post, including many of the wounded; put the battery in position and fired the barrage. It was excellent work and the 'B' Battery officers deserve great credit, particularly Lieut. Hopkins, who, though severely wounded, took command and stuck to his post until the battery was in position." Sounds like a happy ending, or sort of. But then, the very next sentence: "Encouraged by this success several other 'planes came over bombing during the day and dropped many bombs." The unnamed author then closes his tale with a true masterpiece of understatement: "It was a bad day."

I'll say; George Briant did say. "They got about, I don't know, I think about seventy-five Americans," he said. "Me, I was all shot up. My teeth were shot out. I got shot in the eyes. I was shot in the shoulders. I was shot — I think seven, seven shrapnel wounds from that one attack."

"How many bombs did they drop on you?" I asked.

"I tell you," he said, "we weren't counting." He started taking an assessment again: "I got my teeth knocked out. I got some — I got poked a hole in my shoulder about the size of a dollar . . . where else?"

His wife couldn't stand it. "That's a real, real man!" she called out.

"I forgot," he continued, as calm as she was agitated. "I was walking around with blood running all over me — my face, my shoulders . . . they picked me up and took me to the hospital." But he didn't forget, not at all; rather, he returned to it time and again. "I had seven holes in me," he repeated at one point. "Biggest one was the size of a silver dollar, right in here." He touched his right shoulder. "Then I had one over the eye" — he raised a hand to his left eye — "how I didn't lose my eyesight, I don't know. It was a miracle. Right inside the eye, right alongside the eyeball, without damaging the eyeball. It was a miracle." Later, he said that he'd been hit in one of his hips, too.

I have stood on a road just outside Le Charmel and looked out over that field where Battery B's bad day played out. I found the spot with the help of Jeffrey Aarnio, superintendent of the Oise-Aisne American Cemetery, where some six thousand of the doughboys killed during that last German offensive and the subsequent Allied counteroffensive, including Joyce Kilmer and men from Battery B, are buried. Though he had never heard the story of Battery B, Mr. Aarnio knew the area well; Le Charmel is still a quiet little farming village, a pretty spot with narrow old streets that wind around buildings and up hills. The field is like something out of a Van Gogh painting, the kind of place you might stroll through lazily, hoping to get lost in thought and the scent of tall grass.

On July 28, 1918, young men, Americans, died in that field. George Briant, seventeen years old, was not one of them. Red-hot shrapnel tore through a shoulder, a hip, an eye socket of his that day; it knocked his teeth out. But it did not kill him. "They picked us up," he explained, "brought us over to the hospital, and they dressed the wounds. Then they put us right back in the war again." He laughed, perhaps because he knew quite well it wasn't like that at all; he spent three months in the hospital, and even after that, the Army was inclined to just ship him home. He pleaded with them to send him back to the 76th, instead. "I said, 'I didn't come here to go home, I came here to see what the war was like.'" The Army, though, wasn't convinced by that line of reasoning. They still wanted to send him back to Louisiana.

"Let me tell you here," he said, eighty-six years later. "I really rethought that conversation many times. Because many times I thought to myself I should have went back. I should have gave up."

But he didn't. Instead, he offered another argument. "I said, 'I never saw the beginning of the war, and I want to see how the war ends.'"

That one worked. He was discharged from the hospital on October 20, 1918, and was back with Battery B within the week. And he saw how the war ended.

For the rest of his long life, though, he wished he hadn't.

• • •

While George Briant was in the hospital recuperating from his wounds, Germany's were festering. One by one, its allies, worn down by relentless assaults that culminated in grave military defeats, signed separate armistices with the Allies: Bulgaria, on September 29, 1918; the Ottoman Empire, on October 30; and, worst of all, Austria and Hungary, on November 3. It was the Austro-Hungarian Empire that had, arguably, started the war four years earlier, and then dragged Germany into it. At the end, there was no empire, and no Austria-Hungary; in the face of its final humiliating defeat, at Vittorio in northeastern Italy, the whole thing had split apart, Czechs and Slavs and Magyars going their own ways. Austria and Hungary sued for peace separately from one another. Germany remained, alone.

It wasn't so much that Germany had relied on its former allies for their military prowess, but they *had* been invaluable for their resources, especially oil and food. Without them, Britain's naval blockade would have smothered Germany years earlier. As it was, Germans were starving; they didn't have their own Herbert Hoover working tirelessly to supply them with wheat. Chronically hungry people are disinclined to just go along quietly, especially when that hunger is accompanied by the news that the war effort for which you are doing without is slowly failing. Such news started reaching the German people in the fall of 1918. The streets quickly filled with grumbling. In an example of what would later come to be termed "blowback," the revolution that Germany had fomented in Russia started to seep back across its own eastern borders. At the same time, General Erich Ludendorff, one of Germany's two top military commanders, was slowly being undone by bad news from the front. On September 28, 1918, Ludendorff suffered a breakdown; one account I read has him collapsing to the floor during a meeting, literally foaming at the mouth. That night, frantic, he convinced Germany's other top military commander, Paul von Hindenburg, that Germany must try to effect a truce immediately. Ludendorff then brought his case to the Kaiser, warning also that President Wilson, from whom the Germans expected they'd get the best terms, would not even begin to negotiate with Germany until that country put into place a more democratic system of government. The Kaiser, with great reluctance, signed an order replacing his government with one more closely resembling a parliamentary system, to be headed by his cousin, the relatively liberal Prince Maximilian von Baden. Ludendorff — who would, after the war, become an early supporter of Hitler's — later changed his mind, deciding to continue prosecuting the war with great vigor. He later changed his mind about Hitler, too.

In both cases, he was too late. The turmoil in Germany never abated; and as news from the front became worse, the calls for revolution at home grew louder and more insistent. Morale within the Army plummeted, too, and desertions climbed. German sailors, ordered to take the fleet out to sea for one great last battle, mutinied instead. Prince Max, as he was known, wanted the war ended immediately; he reached out to President Wilson, careful not to divulge how weak Germany's position was. Privately, the Germans' most hopeful scenario was that they would withdraw to pre–August 1914 lines, and from there negotiate terms from a position, if not exactly of strength, then at least not of desperation, either. Germany couldn't claim to be victorious, but it could claim to still be undefeated.

Poor Prince Max. How do you even start a conversation like that? *I'm not saying we want to stop this war — why should we want to do something like that, with everything going so well for us? — but let's say, just for fun, that we did . . . ?* Caught between German pitchforks and French bayonets, he did his best, but no one was particularly eager to work with him. If the French or British had detected a hint of weakness, they would have borne down mercilessly; they'd been in this thing for four years, and had lost more men than they cared to count. And President Wilson, well, he was high-minded enough in word, but when it came to actually talking peace — a real, immediate cease-fire — he dithered, waivered, changed old terms, added new ones. Finally, he grew cold, told the Germans he was seriously considering demanding something like unconditional surrender, and implied that they'd better just go talk to the French directly. They did.

The French received the German negotiating party less than graciously. They didn't see them as coming to negotiate a truce, but rather a surrender. Prince Max assembled an armistice-negotiation party devoid of high-profile German military figures, and headed by a civilian, a forty-three-year-old politician and member of the Catholic Centre Party named Matthias Erzberger. A former schoolteacher, Erzberger had initially supported the war, but in the past year or so had grown sour on it, and had since been speaking out loudly in favor of peace; Prince Max calculated that the French would be more likely to deal respectfully and fairly with such a man than with, say, von Hindenburg. He was wrong. The French delegation, headed by Supreme Allied Commander Marshal Ferdinand Foch, regarded the prince's gesture only as a sign of weakness, and Erzberger as a sapling easily trampled.

The German delegation was to meet its French counterparts at a spot in the Compiègne Forest. When its motorcade crossed into French territory, on the evening of November 7, its appearance touched off rumors of an armistice — not negotiations, but an actual, already-existing truce — that raced to the coast and appeared, as fact, in American newspapers the next day. The Germans were not warmly welcomed; the French didn't do that thing where they spread their arms wide and then kiss you on both cheeks. Rather, Foch wordlessly looked over their credentials and then said: "What is the purpose of your visit? What do you want of me?" Erzberger, flustered, replied that they had come to receive the Allies' proposals for arriving at an armistice, the implication being that Germany had its own proposals, and the final terms would be a compromise of the two. Foch, though, had no interest in compromise. "I have no proposals to make," he spat, adding that he was perfectly satisfied to continue the fighting. The Germans were speechless. Finally, another member of their party humbly asked Foch for his conditions for an armistice. "I have no conditions to give you," Foch replied, haughtily, then added: "Do you wish for an armistice? If so, say so — formally." He intended to humiliate the Germans, make them grovel. With Germany on the brink of collapse into anarchy — as far as its negotiators knew, it might already have collapsed while they were en route to Compiègne — they were in no position to deny him that, or pretty much anything.

Foch's terms were severe; he recognized the strength of his bargaining position, and the desperation of Germany's. He also wanted to make sure that Germany was rendered so weak that it would not be in a position to fight again at the end of whatever armistice period was agreed to, and so impotent that it would be in no position to resist any terms that might come out during future peace-treaty talks. He demanded that Germany *immediately* evacuate all occupied territories — including Alsace and Lorraine, which it had annexed nearly a half century earlier; that all Allied prisoners of war immediately be liberated and returned to their units, despite the fact that no German POWs would be liberated immediately; and the surrender of specific numbers of materiel — guns, aeroplanes, ships, etc. — including *all* U-boats. *And* they reserved the right to issue further demands in the future, including reparations. Oh, and the Kaiser had to go. The French gave these terms to the German delegation at around eleven o'clock on the morning of November 8, with a deadline of seventy-two hours hence. Erzberger asked that a cease-fire take effect immediately, to spare soldiers' lives while he secured approval for the terms. Foch refused. He intended to press the Germans as hard as possible until they gave him every last thing he asked for; never mind that many of the lives that might have been spared in those last seventy-two hours were French. And British. And American.

The Kaiser abdicated the next day and fled to the Netherlands; good thing Germany hadn't invaded it, too, as the original Schlieffen Plan had called for. The German government considered the terms, but there was little to discuss, beyond the fact that in some cases Germany did not actually possess as many of this or that as the Allies demanded they surrender. On the night of November 10, they radioed their delegation in Compiègne, authorizing them to sign the agreement; it was signed, in a railroad car, shortly after five the following morning. Erzberger, who hadn't wanted to be a part of the delegation at all and had been thoroughly demeaned during the "negotiations," attempted, at the last moment, to salvage some dignity for himself and his country with a brief statement written for the occasion: "The German people, which held off a world of enemies for fifty months, will preserve their liberty and unity despite every kind of violence. A nation of seventy million people suffers, but it does not die." Foch, refusing to grant Erzberger or any other German even the slightest comfort, merely replied, *"Très bien,"* the 1918 French equivalent of "Whatever." The Germans filed out, wordlessly; no one shook hands. Three years later, a right-wing German terrorist death squad assassinated Erzberger for his role in the affair. They literally shot the messenger.

Officially, the armistice was signed at 5:00 a.m. on November 11, 1918; for some reason, though, the cease-fire was set to occur six hours hence, at 11:00 a.m., the original seventy-two-hour deadline. I don't know why this was done, except, perhaps, for symmetry. That symmetry carved out for the First World War the singular distinction of terminating at a precise moment, one that everyone knows, even if they know nothing else about the conflict. It also carved out an additional six hours of fighting, six hours in which hundreds of men died. Of course, that pales compared to the thousands — German, British, Australian, Canadian, Italian, African, American, and French — who died in the last seventy-two hours of the war, thousands who would have been spared had Foch been moved by Erzberger's fervent plea to cease firing immediately while he procured Germany's approval of the Allies' severe terms.

But he hadn't been.

"You said you wanted to see what the war was like," I said to George Briant that afternoon in September, 2004. "But by the time you got to the hospital, you'd already seen what the war was like, hadn't you?"

He laughed. "I saw all of it!" he said. "North, south, all directions."

"So why did you want to go back to the front after that?"

"I don't know — it's just in you. It's something that's in you. You have no fear. You're facing the guns, you know it. Young as you are, you know you can get killed. So there you are. I went back again. The guy that passes you to go back home, he says, 'Look, I ain't supposed to pass you. You're supposed to go back home. . . .'" But he knew young Briant would find some way or other to get back to the front; so he passed him. "And when I went back, many a day I realized that I was a fool to go back. Because I risked my head so many times it was pitiful."

He had missed the latter part of the Aisne-Marne, and all of Saint-Mihiel, but the Meuse-Argonne — where the 76th was when he caught up with them — was a place where one could easily risk one's head. The 76th had already helped take Montfaucon, and afterward set up its command post on the slope's north face, which act earned it special attention from the Germans. According to the *Roll of Honor*'s "Brief Narrative," around the time George Briant returned, Battery B and the rest of the regiment's 1st Battalion were set up just east of the village of Cunel, where Bill Lake's Wild West Division had also spent time, and where Moses Hardy's Bearcats would very soon. Battery B and the rest of the 1st Battalion were there primarily to support infantry attacks on nearby German strongholds, villages like Bantheville and Aincreville and Clery-le-Grand and Clery-le-Petit, and a troublesome stretch of woods called the Bois de Babimont. From there they would move northeast to help infantry cross the Meuse River at Dun-sur-Meuse (literally, "Dun on the Meuse"), the town where, twenty-seven years later, finally liberated from a very different breed of Germans, someone would think to append the civilian *Familles Salomon* to the local World War I monument.

The fighting was hard; the Germans weren't giving away anything at that point. Perhaps they sensed the end was near; perhaps they feared that they didn't have anything left to go home to, or at least not anything they would recognize. Or perhaps they were just keeping their heads down, hoping that if they fought really hard, their dedication might pay off somehow. Whatever the reason, every one of those villages and scraps of forest had to be wrested from tightly clenched German hands and then held firm, with tightly clenched American hands, in the face of the inevitable counterattack. So did the patches of ground the batteries had to seize, and hold, so that those villages and scraps of forest could be taken to begin with. The Germans threw everything they had at the Americans: high explosives, shrapnel, gas, bullets, grenades, sharpened steel. "Everybody's shooting at you," George Briant recalled, with another of those thank-God-*that's*-done laughs. "I got gassed — let's see — maybe once or twice," he said. It made him feel weak, "like there's something wrong with you," but that wasn't the worst. The worst was the relentless onslaught of H.E. shells. "It's 'kill, kill, kill, kill,'" he said. "The dog kills the cat, the cat kills the dog."

"Let's go, Papa!" his wife called out; I don't know if he willfully ignored her or just didn't hear, but he laughed at the lethal absurdity that is war. One time, he told me, during a bombardment, he made for "a clump of bushes about fifty feet [around] . . . I figured I'd go behind it. The shrapnel flying through there, the trees would stop it, you see?"

I'd come across a similar tale before. In the book *Company K*, a lieutenant orders a sergeant to take some men and head out to "an isolated clump of trees. 'That grove should be a good place for a squad of machine gunners, if the Germans should attack.'"

"I wouldn't do that, Lieutenant," the sergeant, a career Army man, cautions. "That clump stands out like a sore thumb. The Germans are sure to figure we'll put men there, and shell the hell out of it — I been expecting that all morning."

"I'm sorry," the officer replies, "but I think you understand my orders."

The sergeant takes the squad out; the Germans shell them for twenty minutes. The lieutenant hurries out there afterward, finds the sergeant "lying across a fallen tree, his body ripped from belly to chin." All the men but one are dead; the lone survivor "stood upright looking down at his hand, from which the fingers had been shot away." Before the war, he had been a concert pianist.

Fifteen years before those words were written, Private George Briant, caught in a German barrage, spotted a clump of bushes that promised shelter. "So I went to hide there," he recalled. "And it wasn't long before they notified me to get the hell out of there, because it was under shell fire. It was under gas flare." Gas: in this case, not to poison you, but to illuminate you in the darkness. "In other words, the enemy knew we were going to be hiding there, see? And it was your life if you didn't go."

"I've had enough!" his wife called out; but he was smiling. It seemed to me that, pregnant with emotions and sensations as these memories of his were, he wasn't doing too badly with them. Indeed, the cues — occasional smiles, laughter, the urgency in his tone — led me to believe that it was in fact doing him good to air these things out. It didn't occur to me that these questions of mine might take him someplace he really shouldn't go. So I asked him a few more, and he answered them, just fine; and then I asked: "Do you remember the last night of the war? The last day of the war?"

"Yeah," he replied, his voice seeming to drop an octave or two. "It was a *funny* thing. The night before, you understand?"

He took a pause, appeared to be struggling to remember, or at least to convey the memory adequately. It didn't help that Germaine Briant was shouting: "That's enough!" I leaned forward, straining to hear what her husband was trying to say. He appeared to be doing the same thing. Irma and Mrs. Briant were now squabbling in the background; Irma told her godmother that if she didn't quiet down, she'd wheel her out of there. "You're not going to take me back, 'cause I'll come right back!" Germaine spat.

Her husband closed his eyes for a moment. "I have to remember this right, now," he said. "The night before . . . the night before, it was us that . . . us . . . we fired — we knew the war was going to end, you understand?"

"That's enough!" his wife repeated, ever louder. Just a few minutes earlier, she'd let loose a loud, histrionic sigh, to indicate that she was terribly bored; now, apparently, she'd reached her limit.

"So we suddenly — they had the artillery shells laying on the ground, so they could shoot them back at us," he explained. "We shot all the shells, all the ammunition, shot it at them that night. So we shot at them —"

"That's enough on Papa's mind!" Mrs. Briant shrieked.

He turned, looked at her for a second or two, then turned back to me. "We shot all our ammunition at them that night. And during that night, they shot what they had at us. In other words, instead of moving it, we emptied it at each other. I'll always — there was more men unnecessarily killed — I'll always remember that, as long as I live."

Germaine started to sputter. "Papa's mind!" she cried.

"Why?" he asked. "Why kill the last man? What did you gain by killing the last man?"

"You knew the war was ending," I said.

He nodded, gravely. "Yeah. But that's what they did." He dropped his head. His lips pursed, bitterly. He turned away, looked down for an instant; but then, suddenly, his head snapped back up. He looked at me — and smiled. "What's she want?" he asked me, laughing.

"Shut up, already!" his wife moaned. I turned the camera off for a moment, swapped out the tape. Mrs. Briant moved closer to her husband and threw an arm in front of him.

"So you were telling me about the last night of the war," I said to Mr. Briant, the camera rolling again. "That you emptied all your shells, and they emptied all their shells . . ."

"Yeah," he said. "We went out to see what damage was done on the outside, because we were hiding in the woods, you see? And we got to the edge of the woods to see what happened. And we got out there, walked along the edge of the woods, and there were dead Americans that took shelter at the edge of the woods." He'd stumbled over the word "Americans," made himself repeat it. "And that was exactly where the enemy was shooting at, you see? They knew they were going to hide there." His wife tried to protest, but he wouldn't stop now. "There were more American soldiers killed there than at one time during the war, because they hid in — they hid in the wrong place, you see? And the enemy knew they were going to hang there. And at twelve o'clock at night, the enemy opened fire, you see?" He swept an arm in front of him. "And all the edge of those woods there, they fired. And there was American soldiers hiding all up in those woods there." He shook his head. "It was a *sad* affair, when I went along there and saw these men laying there, dying — six, seven, eight at that time. And I — I cried for their parents. That was sad."

And he cried — again, now, eighty-six years hence, in that common room in Hammond, Louisiana. He turned away, narrowed his eyes and tensed his lips — and sobbed. "The last day of the war!" he gasped. "They sacrificed their life!"

"You think it's good for him, this?" his wife asked their goddaughter. "Now see what's coming on!"

"Papa," Irma said, "if it's upsetting you, we will quit, OK?"

He looked at her, and wept, rubbed an ancient hand on his ancient scalp and fell back into his chair. "It was too sad," he uttered over his wife's protests, and leaned forward again, looked at me, shook his head in grief; it was almost more than I could bear. "The last — the last night of the war. Such — these fine, big healthy men — had to lose their lives!" He cried so that his body shook, and fell back again, deflated.

"That's the real stuff!" Germaine shouted. "You're coming up with the real stuff. Y'all shouldn't do that. That's a mortal sin!"

I asked him if any of his friends had been among the dead; he didn't seem to hear me. "That's so sad," he said. "It's too sad." He sat up again, still weeping, and looked right into my eyes. "On the edge of the woods, figuring they were safe — and they sacrificed their lives without knowing it . . . I had nothing to do."

And then George Briant stopped weeping as suddenly as he'd started. "I had nothing to do," he said, and that was it. He was done crying. His voice reverted to normal; so did his expression. You couldn't tell he'd been sobbing just a few seconds earlier; in fact, his mood was better than it had been all afternoon. "At eleven o'clock exactly, everything stopped dead," he said. "No more fire. It was all over."

"And what did you do at eleven o'clock?"

"Nothing." He laughed. "We had nothing to do." It was the opposite of what he'd meant when, just a minute or so earlier, he'd said, "I had nothing to do," by which he'd meant: There was nothing I could do for them. Now: "We had nothing to do" — nothing more needed to be done. "You put the guns and cannons in a safe place in case, you never know if it would start again, you see," he said. "But after eleven o'clock it was all over . . . Yeah, everything looked funny." He smiled. "You looked like you was in a new land. You couldn't believe that everything is quiet. You just didn't believe you were there. It was a different place. Everything is so different during war . . ."

"All the sorrow is unnecessary!" Germaine Briant declared.

He said: "It's so funny to walk out in the open. I mean, it wasn't real. It wasn't real, you're out there walking in the open, and nobody's shooting at you. You couldn't believe that! But that's what happened. Eleven o'clock. Eleven o'clock, the last shot was fired, the last man was killed."

And most accounts I've read, or heard personally, are pretty much like that. There was firing; then, suddenly, there was none. In many of those accounts, at 11:01 a.m., doughboys and German soldiers poured into No Man's Land and celebrated with the men who had been their enemies exactly one minute earlier — shaking hands, dancing, sharing pictures, exchanging souvenirs. Even Eugene Lee, who had lost his best friend just hours earlier to a German shell — even he recalled doing so.

But George Briant did not. For one thing, his battery, like most artillery, was not within sight of German soldiers. "We celebrated by walking around," he told me; but that was it. They could have gone in search of German troops with whom they might rejoice, but as far as he was concerned, at least, "we were still enemies."

I started to ask him about his experience in the Army of Occupation, but by then Germaine Briant seemed to be edging close to hysteria. When I asked her husband about the German prisoners he saw, his wife squawked at their goddaughter: "You tell him he better quit before I have a . . . a . . . a *suit* on his hands!"

This made her husband laugh. "I'll tell you later," he said to me.

Irma wheeled her godmother out of the room, over Mrs. Briant's loud protests. "I'm sorry it broke up like this," Mr. Briant said, as soon as she was gone. "You lost the interview."

I assured him that everything was fine, and that there was certainly no need for an apology; but I couldn't seem to convince him of that. "I'm sorry it happened this way," he said. "But Mama — Mama's a very upset woman . . . and I'm sorry for her, and I'm sorry for all of us. In her condition, she can't help it . . . I hope you can forgive her."

"There's nothing to forgive her for," I said. But now he was preoccupied, unable to think about German prisoners and the Army of Occupation. Afterward, when I wheeled him back to their room, I saw that she was just fine. Actually, it was as if she had forgotten the entire episode; sweet as pecan pie, she asked me where I was from, how I liked it down here in Lew Z. Anne. At one point she tried to get me to promise her I would become a Catholic. "How do you know I'm not one already?" I asked her. It worked; she changed the subject, prattled on about this or that, asking me more questions but not really pausing to wait for an answer. At some point I looked at her husband; he just sat there, oblivious to the conversation. But he was smiling. All he needed was to be near her. Perhaps, at times, that was all he could take; but it was enough for him, after all he had endured in his long life. Four months later, she passed away. It was a Friday. He died the following Monday.

Before all that, though, back in the common room, I was just about to turn off the video camera when he started answering another question, one I hadn't asked. "Most people," he said, "most people hate our enemies — either side. You know what I'm saying? I hate you because you hate me . . . You killed my father-in-law, and I killed yours, see? So we're mad at each other and want to kill each other. But it's the wrong thing to do, and we've got to look at it as warfare, and not as a grudge in life for the rest of our lives. We must try to be friends, and help each other. German or Frenchman, it makes no difference. We all suffered." His voice started to break. "We suffered in war together. I suffered. You suffered. And I know very well you suffer because you hurt someone, your enemy. And I suffer because I hurt my enemy. And enemies . . . that's bred into war. We teach each other to hate each other, when we're living; and we try to outdo the other, unbeknownst to the other fellow. We try to overcome these things as we live along life's pathway."

At the time, I thought he was talking to me; but watching him on that tape now, years later, I wonder if he wasn't really speaking to his ancient enemies, the airmen who'd dropped bombs on him, the artillerymen who had killed his comrades on the last night of the war. I think it was a dialogue he'd been carrying on in his head for many years — and I wonder if that may have been what enabled him, at some point, to negotiate an armistice with his memories, the two of them moving through the decades together without wearing each other down. Private Briant did not hate. He understood.

I don't think Private Gunther, in those last minutes of the war, hated. But I don't think he understood, either. That takes time; and, as he had just been informed, he was all but out of time, time to redeem himself — if not to others, like his former friend Sergeant Powell, hugging the ground next to him, then at least to his parents back home, and his fiancée, Olga, and maybe even to himself. How he must have despaired at that moment.

And then — well, I'll let the monument tell it:

Suddenly, Gunther got up and ran at the enemy. Sergeant Powell ordered him to stop. The German gunners signaled to him to go back but Gunther kept advancing. One of them fired a five-round burst. Gunther was struck in the left temple and died instantly. It was 10:59 a.m. One minute later, the Armistice took effect and silence descended on the front. . . .

General Pershing's Order of the Day recorded Henry Nicholas Gunther as the last American soldier to die in the First World War. He was posthumously promoted to Sergeant and received the Distinguished Service Cross. In 1923, Gunther's body was returned to Baltimore and buried in Section W of the Holy Redeemer Cemetery.

Yes: It worked. Henry Gunther got his stripes back, and a DSC to boot. No one cares to remember that the last man killed in World War I — an American from the Liberty Division — was a suicide.

17

The Last of the Last

A ND SO: Frank Buckles.

People are fond of saying that truth is stranger than fiction; every once in a while, you'll hear someone remark of a particular real-live human being that if he or she hadn't existed, someone would have had to invent them. Neither of these clichés can touch Frank Buckles. No one could have invented him; "strange" does not approach the truth that was his 110 years and twenty-six days on this earth. I will just tell what I know.

Of all the men and women in this book, perhaps the only one you may have heard of before opening its covers is Frank Buckles. For the last three years of his life, which concluded on February 27, 2011, he was the only surviving veteran of the American Expeditionary Forces of the First World War. Back around the turn of the new century, he was appointed national commander of the awkwardly named Veterans of World War I of the USA. For much of his term, he was the organization's only member, too. I asked him about that once; he chuckled and said it didn't bother him at all.

If you perform that weird exercise I described a while back and subtract 110 years, Frank Buckles's ultimate age, from 1901, the year in which he was born, you get 1791, the year the Bill of Rights was ratified. Pretty impressive, I suppose; but that's not the real story here. It's not even, really, that Frank Buckles was the last of the last of the doughboys, or the last surviving Army veteran of that war anywhere in the world, or, if you take into account every last human being with even the faintest claim to such status, the third-last World War I veteran to leave the planet. More than any person I've ever met or expect to,

Frank Buckles's consciousness embraced the entirety of American history; and more than any other person I've ever met or expect to, he personally experienced the entirety of the twentieth century.

He was born exactly one month after the mathematical commencement of that century, on February 1, 1901, not all that far from what was then the geographical center of his country, in Harrison County, Missouri, near the town of Bethany. When I first visited him, on August 30, 2003 — and every time thereafter — he was living on an old farm outside Charles Town, West Virginia. Charles Town is not what you think of when you think of West Virginia; there are no mountains or hollers there, and no coal. A lot of sheep, though. And round, verdant hills. And people who commute to work in Washington, D.C., just about ninety minutes away. About fifteen minutes away is Harpers Ferry, West Virginia. Back in 1859, when both were still part of Virginia, John Brown was tried and hanged in Charles Town for what he had done at Harpers Ferry — or, more accurately, for what he had tried to start at Harpers Ferry.

Ninety-five years later, Frank Buckles had come there for another, more obscure historical reason: Two centuries earlier, his earliest American Buckles ancestor — "Robert Buckles," he told me, "who was born May the fifteenth, seventeen hundred and two" — moved to the area from an English Quaker settlement in Pennsylvania, on the Delaware River just north of Philadelphia. At that settlement, his great-great-great-great-grandson told me, "he married Ann Brown, whose grandfather was one of the original members of William Penn's colony. And with his family and fifteen others, they came down to this area in 1732. Robert Buckles, according to the history of that time period, and his will, had 2,090 acres of land . . . near Shepherdstown." Shepherdstown was about ten miles away from where we then sat; about a hundred miles away, in a different direction but also in 1732, George Washington was born.

Frank Buckles was a genealogist; he cared about family, and lineage. After he died, I discovered, plucking around records online, that he had filed at least six different applications for membership in the Sons of the American Revolution, each one for a different ancestor, all of them successful. "My grandmother," he told me, early in our first meeting, "my father's mother, whose name was Harriet Caroline Ripsom,

R-I-P-S-O-M, said that her great grandfather, Mathias Riebsomeer — Holland Dutch — was killed at the Battle of Oriskany. And his name is up on the monument. On the Bicentennial, I went up to Oriskany to attend the ceremony. And Nelson Rockefeller" — then vice president of the United States — "gave the address. After it was over, I complimented Rockefeller on giving the address, and he said it was one of his favorite stories when he was a boy. So he knew it without looking at his cuff." The story is this: On August 6, 1777, a band of Continental soldiers and Indians under the command of General Nicholas Herkimer, hurrying to the aid of the besieged Fort Stanwix (now Rome, New York), were attacked by a larger band of Loyalist troops and other Indians outside what is now the town of Oriskany, about seven miles from the fort. The Continentals took the worst of it, losing three times as many men as the Loyalists, among them General Herkimer.

Mr. Buckles spent a good bit of time during our first visit telling me, in great detail, about his forebears. And I was reminded, as he talked, of the many autobiographies I have read of Americans of note — from Benjamin Franklin to Ulysses S. Grant and beyond — that begin with detailed accounts of their lineage, not to make any kind of point, I think, but rather to put themselves in some form of context. And that, I believe, is what Frank Buckles was doing for me that afternoon in August, 2003. There was history to his tale, and he wanted to make sure I had all of it.

He began and ended his life on farms. The last of these, three hundred or so acres outside Charles Town, was called Gap View: rolling meadows, lovely vistas, solid stone house built before all those ancestors fought for independence. The first — well, I don't even know if it had a name. He just described it as "my father's farm, north of Bethany, in Harrison County, Missouri."

"What were your parents' names?" I asked him.

"James Clark Buckles and Theresa Keown Buckles. K-E-O-W-N. Scotch-Irish." They were married September 14, 1881, in Illinois; "They soon after that came to Missouri," he explained, "because my mother's family had already moved there from Illinois . . . My father was born November the twentieth, 1857, in Jersey County, Illinois. My mother was born in the next county, Madison County . . . on April the twenty-fourth, Easter Sunday, 1859." Eventually they had five children. "Three boys, and two girls." Roy was the eldest, born in 1882; then Grace in 1884, Gladys in 1886, and, after a long break, Ashman in June, 1899. Twenty months later, Theresa Buckles, a few months short of forty-two years old, gave birth to another son. She and her forty-three-year-old husband named the baby Wood. No middle name, just: Wood Buckles.

In January, 1904, four-year-old Ashman died of scarlet fever. Wood, who was not yet three, got the fever, too, but did not die of it. He lived most of his youth, he told me, effectively as an only child. "The elder brother," he said, speaking of Roy, "left home from high school. Why, his son told me, was because he wanted to play in the band, and his father didn't want him to. I can understand that, because my father was a farmer, and you don't want the boy spending his evenings with the — as a musical student."

"Because he wouldn't be able to get up for farm work the next day?" I asked.

He laughed. "Probably." He said he had no idea what instrument his brother had played, but music ran in the family. "My father, when he was at Illinois State, played the flute," he told me. "And his five sisters all played some musical instrument . . . and his brothers both had musical instruments. And they, in their home, my grandfather would have assembled the eight members of the family and have his own concert."

He had pictures of various relations framed and displayed on a shelf in a curio cabinet that stood in a little sitting room filled with artifacts from his long life and books that dealt with the things he had lived through. That was where we sat and talked that day, and every time I came to visit him after that, he in a large red wingback armchair, facing his side yard, the sun illuminating his features as it set, though it never seemed to irritate him any. He was somewhat on the shorter side, in part because of a stoop, with white hair, a high forehead, and sharp features — sharp in the way FDR looked sharp, which is to say he always looked to be entirely alert, and interested, and thinking about something. He greeted me that first time in a cream-colored linen suit and bright blue-checked dress shirt, open at the neck; he hadn't been interviewed all that much up to that point, and I suppose he wanted to make a good first impression. It was important to him, I would learn, to look good — not for anything as petty as vanity, but for his own dignity, and that of the occasion, whatever it might be.

Almost as significant to him as dignity was luck; he had a lot of it, he would have told you, going back to his birth, an unexpected baby to parents already in their forties. The illness that took his brother Ashman had spared him. His father, having lost one son to music and another to the fever, gave up farming for a while, sparing young Wood those kinds of chores for a good part of his childhood. As the baby of the family, fifteen years younger than his next surviving sibling, he was indulged a bit, too, allowed to pursue his interests. And his interests then all seemed tied closely to the future, what would much later be dubbed the Next Big Thing. When I asked him what the earliest historical memory he had was, he said, "Well, of course, at that age, a young age, I wasn't particularly interested in history. I do remember the first automobile . . . I would have been less than four years old." It was in Bethany, the county seat; the car, the only one in town (and possibly the county), belonged to a Mr. Roleke, he recalled, a businessman who had a park in town named for him. "He needed some repair," Mr. Buckles recalled, and had to bring it into a shop in town. So he hooked it up to "a team of horses, and drove throughout the town, so that people would be accustomed — *horses* would be accustomed. The big problem with automobiles when they first came out was for the horses to adjust. They were afraid of automobiles . . . that would be about 1904 or 1905." I guess it's the kind of sight you don't forget, even after ninety-nine years.

Inventors were *the* great celebrities and heroes when Wood Buckles was a child; Thomas Edison was revered as a new kind of George Washington. It was a time when so many new inventions came along, one closely following the last, that there was scarcely time to grasp their magnitude, if it could even be grasped at all: the telephone; the electric light; the phonograph; the automobile; the airplane; broadcasting. I can barely envision a time before cell phones and the Internet, and I was a fully grown adult before I first encountered either; imagine how different the world of Wood Buckles's childhood was from the one his parents had grown up in, back in the 1860s.

That new world was just coming into focus when Wood saw that car being pulled around by horses, but it grabbed hold of him at that moment — or, I should say, he grabbed hold of it, and clutched it tightly ever after. He seems to have had a remarkable presence of mind from a very young age, coupled with a drive to seek out the kind of *new* that would prove important, and the ability to recognize it when he found it. "Do you remember the first time you saw an airplane?" I asked him at one point.

He smiled. "I sure do!" he said, interlacing his fingers and sitting up straight; we had been talking for nearly four hours by then, and his posture was holding up better than mine. "It would be . . . when I was about seven or eight years old. And my mother, when we moved from the farm, every summer took a vacation, visited some of her relatives. We were in Decatur, Illinois . . . Lincoln Beachey with his biplane was coming into Decatur and going to exhibit at the racetrack. He was going to fly around the racetrack, and somebody — it wasn't Barney Oldfield, but it was somebody of importance — was going to race around with the car, and he was going to beat the biplane. Well, we boys figured out the baseball park is next to it . . . So we went to the baseball park, climbed over the fence, and walked right over there to Lincoln Beachey. And it was close — well, you could touch his biplane . . . That would be about 1908." Beachey, a pioneer aviator, was killed while flying a stunt over the Pan-Pacific Exposition in San Francisco in 1915; he was a daring pilot who raced trains as well as automobiles, flew loops and even upside down. Among his many fans was said to be Orville Wright. Frank Buckles would have seen Beachey fly just a few years after the Wright brothers first flew at Kitty Hawk.

From the start, Wood Buckles was what we now call an early adopter. He was the first person in his family to cotton to the automobile. "I started driving when I was twelve years old," he told me. "The reason for that, they had been bothering my father, coming to my father with automobiles, trying to get my father to buy an automobile. And finally, the agent said, 'Well, Mr. Buckles, I'll just trade you this new automobile for the steers that are over in that lot there.' Well, he says 'Oh.'" He smiled. "He knew that he couldn't say that it was too expensive. So he bought the automobile. [The agent] brought it out. My father said, 'This is the biggest harvesting season, busy season — I just don't have time for it now. But — you can teach the boy.' So, until my father had time to spare, I drove the automobile." And he was happy to do so. The car, he recalled, was a Ford, and had an electric starter. "And that was unusual," he told me. "A Grand Davis starter, almost as big as the motor. And the batteries were on the running board." He learned how to make batteries himself; this before his house even had electricity.

A year or so after he learned to drive, he developed a fascination with another nascent technology. "I read about Marconi," he explained. "He was only forty years old at the time." There were stories of David Sarnoff and the *Titanic,* and Lee De Forest, visions of a day not too far off when voices would fly through the air for hundreds of miles — maybe even across an ocean. Wood Buckles was captivated. "I took every magazine — well, there weren't many of them — anything that had to do with wireless," he recalled. "And somewhere I saw an advertisement for a company in New York that produced and sold these machines . . . Well, it had to be about 1914, I suppose."

"So you sent away for it?" I asked him.

"Yes," he said. "And I'd be going to the post office every day to find out." He chuckled.

"What did it look like?"

"It's an oak base. About, not very long, eighteen inches long. And the green coil. The tuner on top. And the key . . . and a little buzzer. So you could work that, a buzzer. And that part of it never worked. And I'm not too sure whether that one was any advantage over the one I already had."

"You had already made one yourself before you sent away?" I asked.

"Oh, yes, sure," he replied. "I took a . . . a medium-sized oatmeal container, and, let's see, varnished it over first. And then wound it with wire, copper wire. And the terminals at the beginning and the end. And then with a, a little adjustment key that you moved it back and forth on that drive. So that would — the total sound of the wires, including the lead-in, would finally bring it over to whatever was on the transmitter. And one of the transmissions that we used to get was from Arlington."

"Arlington, Virginia?"

"Yeah."

"You used to get that out in Missouri?"

He nodded. "We got that in Missouri."

That wasn't just luck. He'd gotten some pretty extraordinary help from his father; another dividend of being an indulged youngest child. And growing up on a farm. In those days, you see, a radio set — and they were still crystal sets, no tubes yet — needed an extremely large aerial to pick up anything at all. The magazines suggested they run as high as fifty feet off the ground. "There was a problem getting sticks that were long enough," he explained, ninety years later. "So my father arranged to get over to the river and had somebody cut two trees, fifty-five feet long, and trim them down. And we went over on a wagon, with the wagon seat in front, and then he took that and extended it — two wheels in the back and two wheels up the front, where the seat was. And that wagon was fifty feet, fifty-five feet long." Then his father — who was already in his midfifties by then — sank the two poles five feet into the ground, spaced 225 feet apart, and then somehow ran six wires back and forth between the two poles, spaced out two feet apart, starting all the way up at the top. That's what you had to do to make a good antenna back then.

"Where else did you pick up from?" I asked him.

"That was about the only one," he said. "Nobody else was sending out." "That" was the United States Naval Observatory, and they made exactly two transmissions every day: a time signal, one at precisely 11:00 p.m. Central Standard Time, the other at precisely 11:00 a.m. "You could set your time by it," Frank Buckles said. A little dry by today's standards, but terribly exciting in 1913, seven years before the first commercial radio broadcast. Especially to a twelve-year-old boy. The only damper, he told me, was that "I had no one to talk to about it."

A couple of years later, another person in town, a jeweler, finally got a set. Wood Buckles showed him how to use it. By then, he himself had a newer model, that kit he had sent away for; he would often listen to it well past the point where a schoolboy should have gone to sleep. "My parents were very nice about that," he said fondly. "Let me stay up late and do that thing." One day, a traveling photographer stopped by the farm and made a portrait of young Wood sitting at his wireless set, headphones on. He'd even donned a necktie for the occasion. Both the photo and the wireless set were on display in that sunroom the next time I visited. The latter was one of the most beautiful things I'd ever seen.

Like many things, the birth of radio looks nothing but romantic at this distance. To Wood Buckles, it was mysterious, exotic. People were talking about it; maybe not in his particular corner of Missouri, but out there, in the world. Someday, he believed, it would bring that world, and everything in it, to him. And someday, he believed just as fervently, he would be out there, in that very world, a part of things that people in little corners like his would hear about on the wireless.

Soon enough.

In 1916 — "for reasons I don't know, because parents didn't always confide in the children, and children . . . sometimes didn't ask too many questions" — Wood Buckles's father, James Clark Buckles, decided to move the family to Dewey County, Oklahoma, in the western part of that state. (Mr. Buckles later told me: "I know from some of his associates that he was expecting an oil strike.") He had already bought some land in Dewey County, and decided to send some draft horses on ahead to sell there — the price they fetched would have been much higher in western Oklahoma than in Vernon County, Missouri, where the family was then living and farming — in order to help prepare their arrival. James Buckles had planned to send a hired man to do it, for twenty dollars and round-trip fare; but his son, Wood, fifteen years old, sensed an opportunity for adventure. "So I talked to him allowing me to make the trip," he recalled. "I made the trip alone with the horses. It took four days to get to western Oklahoma." His parents would follow, eventually; for a while, though, he was on his own, in the small town of Oakwood.

He loved it. "I lived at the hotel," he told me, "worked at a bank, and went to school."

And after that, I imagine, it was just a matter of time. Wood Buckles wasn't going to go back to living with his parents again, and doing farm chores; not for long, anyway. Something, sooner or later, was going to lure him away again. Something bigger.

"It was April the sixth, 1917," he said, setting the scene. "We declared war. And naturally, the posters appeared on the post office, and the newspapers were full of it, full of the news. So I was quite aware of it. And I had been aware of the World War since it started in August, nineteen hundred and fourteen."

"You had been reading the news accounts?" I asked.

"I don't think that was unusual then," he said. "People around the country were quite well-informed about what's going on in the world." Years later he would add that he had known from its inception that the war was "an important event": "The world was interested," he told me. "*I* was interested." He wanted to be a part of it; waited for his chance.

"Well, the summer vacation came," he continued. "And a rancher nearby in this place — Oakwood, Oklahoma — his son, about my age, invited me to stay with him for the Kansas State Fair, in Wichita. I went up to Wichita, and while there, went to the Marine recruiting station. The Marine sergeant was very nice to me, but he says, 'You're too young.' I gave my age as eighteen. So he says, 'You have to be twenty-one.' Well, I went then out to Larned, Kansas." He had an aunt and uncle living there; they owned a bank nearby. He spent some time visiting with them and his ninety-two-year-old grandmother, Harriet, who took the occasion to tell him, for the first time, about her great-grandfather, Mathias Riebsomeer, killed at Oriskany in 1777.

A reminder like that of the potential price of military service might make some people less likely to enlist; not Wood Buckles. As soon as he was back in Wichita, Mr. Buckles told me, he returned to that recruiting station. This time, there was a different sergeant on duty. "He very graciously gave me the examination, which I passed with no question," he recalled. "But he says, 'You're just not heavy enough.' So then I tried the Navy, and the Navy gave me an excuse. Said I was, flatfooted." In retrospect, he understood that they had known all along he was under-age — if you see pictures of him from that time, there's no mistaking it; he looked about twelve years old — and were making excuses that would either spare him some hurt feelings, or them some paperwork. Or both.

"Well," he continued, "what am I going to do? I'm going to get in someplace. So, I went to Oklahoma City, tried the Marine Corps, the Navy, with no success. Then — I decided, well, I'll try the Army, then. And there the sergeants wouldn't — they had to get permission from the captain. The captain interviewed me, and asked about a birth certificate. I explained that in Missouri, where I was born, there were no — they had no public record of births, and that it was in the family Bible."

"Is that true?" I asked.

"Yes," he assured me. "And I told him, 'I'm not going to bring the family Bible down here.'" He smiled. "OK. They accepted me." Years later, he would add: "If I hadn't have made it in Oklahoma City, I would have gone to St. Louis." And from there, wherever he had to.

"After the recruiting station," he continued, "I went with thirteen men out to Fort Logan, Colorado. Those of us who were qualified . . . they wouldn't at that time accept married men, you had to be a certain age, and quite, quite strict about it. Well, that was the Regular Army. My serial number by the way, 15577 . . . that's the Regular Army. An older sergeant told me that if I wanted to get to France in a hurry to go into the Ambulance Corps. Because the French are just, are asking for ambulance service. So he said to go that way."

"When was this?" I asked. "What month?"

"I was sworn in on the thirteenth of August, in Fort Logan, Colorado." The whole process — being turned away, going elsewhere, trying and trying again until he found someone who would enlist him — took nearly two months. As badly as the AEF needed men, at least some recruiters remained reluctant to sign up boys who still had baby fat on them.

The story goes that, when he gave that captain in Oklahoma City his full name — Wood Buckles — the captain informed him no one could enlist who didn't have a middle name. Perhaps this was one last gambit to turn him away — I personally know of several men who entered the Army in 1917 without a middle name — but whether or not the captain was doing a bit of fudging himself, Wood went ahead and changed his name right there and then to Frank Woodruff Buckles. It wasn't too radical an amendment; he'd been named for his uncle, Frank Woodruff, anyway.

"How did your parents feel about you going off to join the Army?" I asked him.

"Well," he replied, "the first they knew about it, I was on the way to Bordeaux. I sent a postcard, that I was in the Army, on the way to Bordeaux."

"Did your grandmother know, when you were staying with her in Kansas?"

"She knew. She told me that she approved of it."

I asked again about his parents: "When they got that postcard, and they found out you had already enlisted . . . did you hear back from them?"

"No," he said.

"They were upset."

"I don't know." Years later, he told me that his father would have known there'd be no point in trying to talk his son out of enlisting, or anything else. "We weren't that kind of people," he explained. "We made a decision and that was it."

"Why were you in such a hurry to enlist and see action?" I asked.

"Well, why not?" he said, and smiled. "I knew all about the war, had for several years."

"Why did you think America was getting into the war?"

"Well, I don't know. It might have been influenced by the year previous, when General Pershing was down in Mexico chasing Pancho Villa. I knew all about that. I knew the position of our Army — very small. And of course, now, you're thinking about patriotism, well . . . I didn't know anybody whose . . . family hadn't lived in this country for maybe a century or two. So, we just — we didn't talk about those things."

"But I mean," I said, "did you join up because you wanted adventure, or did you believe strongly in the cause? Or both?"

"Oh, well," he said, and shook his head, silently, for a moment. "I wanted action, of course."

For a while, it certainly seemed like Frank Buckles had chosen wisely in following that older sergeant's advice about joining the Ambulance Corps. He was sent to Fort Riley, Kansas, and placed in the First Fort Riley Casual Detachment. In army parlance, a casual detachment was a discrete group of men, separated from a larger unit, that could be sent out on its own, or even attached to another unit, for specific duties or assignments. In the case of the First Fort Riley Casual Detachment, there were 102 men in all. Mr. Buckles had a group picture of them, one of those old, oblong photographs you associate with that war, framed and hanging in his sitting room.

The training was exciting from the start; "at Fort Riley," he told me, "there were officers there from France and from Britain, who had you build trenches, similar to the trenches in Europe." Once that was done, they got into more serious matters. "The training that we had there was 'trench retrieval,' they called it," he explained. "A man was lying here, and they'd teach you how to go crawl up to him, take off your belt — you'd want to use [that], you didn't have anything else — put it over his arm, and turn a certain way, and you could put him right on your back, he'd come up." He mimicked some of the actions as he described them. "It was a very tricky thing, I knew. But I could do it. And I probably weighed 125 pounds." He added: "But men weren't so big then, too . . . Well, we were soon well-trained, and they made up the unit; the top-ranking officer in that group was going to go overseas with me, with the sergeant."

They rode the train from Fort Riley to Hoboken, and sailed from there. "On the *Carpathia*," he specified. "His Majesty's Ship the *Carpathia*, which rescued the *Titanic*, the survivors of the *Titanic*, on the fifteenth of April, 1912. And which I knew all about from reading the newspapers and listening to the stories." It was winter; he remembered that specifically, he told me, because from Hoboken they'd sailed up to Halifax, Nova Scotia, arriving just a few weeks after that city experienced a terrible disaster: In the busy port, the French freighter *Mont-Blanc*, loaded with munitions, collided with another ship, caught fire, and exploded. "Exploded" doesn't really do it justice, though; it was the biggest manmade blast in history to that point, destroying every structure in a vast area and causing a tsunami that did even more damage. Some two thousand people were killed, with many times that number injured; more Nova Scotians died that morning in Halifax than on the battlefield during the entire war. Bodies kept turning up for years afterward. Even though he wasn't there at the time, Frank Buckles never forgot the date. "December the sixth, 1917," he recalled. The devastation was still fresh when he came through, weeks later. "There were great woods in there, cedar trees, and all you would see is the stumps," he said.

From there, the *Carpathia*, which was also carrying a unit of Marines, sailed off to Europe — though not to Bordeaux. "Our unit was stopped in Winchester, England," he explained. "And the Marines went on to France. And as a unit I don't know what happened to them."

At first, England was exciting to Frank Buckles; it was certainly a long way from Missouri and Oklahoma. "The first day that I had a case to go down to Winchester," he told me, "I saw the statue of King Alfred the Great. It says: 'Died in Nine Hundred and One.' I said, 'My gosh, that's a thousand years before I was born!' And I saw men on the streets with long robes and a hat, almost like a bishop's hat . . . they were soldiers of the Crimea. The Crimea was 1853. That impressed me. And then, of course, the history of the place — the museum, and the cathedral. And you go in the cathedral, and there's a [seat] next to Jane Austen." Or her body, anyway. It's buried under the aisle.

Even more than the history of the place — how ancient it all was, compared to America — he was struck by how grave everybody seemed in England. "All the men," he recalled, "well, not all the men, but all the officers, all the officers in uniform would have the black band. It meant that a member of the family [had been killed in the war]. And women — all in somber black. Some of them even looked dead, with veils, black veils."

Somber as England was at times, young Private Buckles seems to have had a fine time there. "First I drove a motorcycle," he recalled. "As the dispatch — you know, they didn't use the telephones then, just sent a boy on a motorcycle or a bicycle. Then I drove a car. And mostly, in that car, I was driving distinguished people around . . . And then, some of the time [I drove] an ambulance." Years later, he clarified: "I didn't care for the darn thing; but I enjoyed the motorcycle and sidecar."

As he had been back in Missouri, Frank Buckles was somewhat indulged in England, perhaps because of his youth. He managed to get away with a degree of cheekiness (if not quite insubordination) toward British officers, and even got chummy with a certain aristocratic one-armed lieutenant general who terrified most of the other soldiers. He might well have been happy to spend the entire war in England, but for one thing: The war wasn't in England. It was in France. And he had signed up to be in the war, not simply nearer to it.

Unfortunately, it didn't appear as if the First Fort Riley Casual Detachment was going to get to leave Winchester anytime soon, so Private Buckles decided he was going to have to detach himself from the detachment. "I let any person who had any influence at all know that I wanted to go on to France," he told me. "I contacted one of the field clerks and told him that I wanted to see the colonel." Colonel Jones, the top-ranking American officer in the area, was particularly indulgent of him — privately, he found the young private's antics entertaining, especially when they flummoxed the British — but this wish he could not grant. "Colonel Jones said he'd like to go to France, too," Mr. Buckles recalled, eighty-five years later. "But he said, 'When the Army tells me I've got to do something, I've got to do it.'"

Perhaps that should have put the matter to rest, but it didn't. Private Buckles kept scheming; at one point, seeing lots of other doughboys stop at Winchester briefly en route to France, he developed a plan and pitched it to three would-be collaborators. "When there were a sufficient number to fill up a craft for transportation across to France, they would march down to the railway station, always at night," he explained. "And I'd watch them. So . . . I explained to these folks what happened, when they come to a certain place, and nothing in between, when they are marching along there, what we'll do is just merge right into them. Go on the train, and these lads are just not sharp enough to check everybody. We'll be on the boat, and we'll be over in France."

"Wouldn't that have meant going AWOL from your unit in Winchester?" I asked him.

"Well the way I was calculating," he said, "we got in France, we'd stay there. But what happened was, I had somebody I had to take down to, I think Plymouth, England, or some distance, and I couldn't get back in time. So here I left these poor fellows, three of them, without their leader."

"So they went to France and you didn't."

"They went to France. And they came back."

"They sent them back?"

"Under patrol."

"Because they had gone AWOL," I said.

"And they had a trial," he recalled. He went and sat in on it, in the company of a major; fortunately, the three were only given work detail. And Frank Buckles kept scheming to get across.

And then one day, after he'd been in Winchester for about six months, he said, "finally came an order, here's a unit going through, and I believe it was an airplane unit. And it left this officer in Winchester, and they had to send him on to France. And I didn't know why — it didn't matter to me, I wanted to get over." The Army needed a volunteer to escort the officer across. It got one very quickly.

It soon became apparent to the volunteer why such an escort was needed. The officer — Mr. Buckles always referred to him as "Lieutenant Nick" — was a bit eccentric. After boarding ship with the lieutenant in Southampton, Private Buckles was told by a deck hand that they wouldn't be departing for several hours, so he went back ashore to do some shopping; when he returned, he recalled, the lieutenant "wanted me to write a letter to President Wilson and General Pershing asking my pardon for going off the ship that day. So I knew there was something wrong with that guy." Fortunately, he added, "I was in charge. I realized that because *I* had the orders." When I asked him why he had been put in charge instead of the officer, he replied: "Because the guy was nuts."

The orders were to bring the lieutenant to Paris. Once there, they waited for further orders. Private Buckles didn't mind; he was in France at last. He stayed at a hotel near headquarters, visited the Eiffel Tower and Notre Dame, ate well. Finally, after a week or so ("You know," he explained, "the Army used to work awfully slow"), new orders came through: Bordeaux. "And the same thing worked over there," he recalled. "Stayed at a small hotel . . ." He and Lieutenant Nick worked out a routine: "If I wanted money, all I would have to do is ask him for it. I'd ask him for twenty francs or whatever it was, and go down below and get a bottle of cognac. Bring up a little flask. Feed it to him until he's about ready to pass out, and make sure he had his boots off — he sleeps in his clothes, but I felt the poor guy should have his boots [off]." He chuckled.

It was in Bordeaux that Private Buckles first learned what, exactly, his charge's role in the war was supposed to be: dentist. A week later, the two of them were ordered on to the port of Bassens, a few miles away. "He was sent there to set up a business and I was to be his assistant," Mr. Buckles explained. "I don't know how they figured I was a dental assistant."

In Bassens, another routine quickly took shape. "A patient would come in — he handled his business very well," he told me. "But soon as the patient left, he'd sit up in a chair, in the dental chair, and I'd light a cigarette for him. And sometimes he'd go, he had a little washroom — I never was in it, just a tiny little place, and he'd go in there a few minutes and come out feeling fine." He smiled knowingly. "Among other things, he had a trunk full of quarts of ethyl alcohol . . . and you mixed ethyl alcohol with water and you could really get a high. Oh, my. And you don't have a headache afterwards." Private Buckles didn't partake; "I wasn't very strong on ethyl alcohol," he said. "But a lot of my friends enjoyed it."

That interesting work environment lasted for about a month. Then, one day, an American colonel came to the office, accompanied by a lieutenant, who promptly took Private Buckles aside and advised him: "Get the hell out of here quick. Don't let the colonel see you, because he'll raise hell with you." The party, apparently, was over. "So I beat it out," he said; later, "I found out what happened. That morning, or that night, the lieutenant had walked on his hands and knees, and walked into the major's office, major's room, barking like a dog." It would seem ethyl alcohol does produce some sort of hangover, after all.

And that was the end of Lieutenant Nick. "So," Frank Buckles added, smiling, "I went back to my usual occupation — motor crew." The Army sent him to Saint-André-de-Cubzac, about ten miles from Bassens. "What would you do in the motor pool there?" I asked him.

"Nothing much," he said. "Drive a car, a motorcycle. Drive a Ford ambulance. Not much."

"Not much" is hardly the first phrase that comes to mind when you think about what ambulance drivers do in wartime; but, like Bassens and Bordeaux, Saint-André-de-Cubzac wasn't at the front. Or near it. The front, in fact, was hundreds of miles away. Still, Mr. Buckles said, there was no mistaking the fact that you were in a country that was at war, and had been for a long time. In France, he recalled, *everybody* seemed to be wearing black. But that was only the most obvious indicator; there were hundreds, thousands, of only slightly more subtle ones. For instance, he explained, "there were no lights at night. And it wasn't because they were afraid of an air attack. It wasn't that at all. It was because they were saving the lights."

Even so, four years of devastating warfare hadn't managed to rob the French of everything. Sometimes, he recalled, "in the village there would be a group of French soldiers . . . They were leaving, and they sang the 'Marseillaise.' Well, I made some inquiries, to find out: What's the purpose of this? They were called up, going back to the front." He paused and nodded respectfully, still a bit awed, nearly a century later, by such a display. "And that was a surprise to me," he continued after a moment. "Not that they were going to be called back, because they had to go, [but that they were] approaching it in the right manner."

The sight only made him more eager to get to the front, but time did not indulge him as others had. November 11, 1918, found him still in Saint-André-de-Cubzac. The celebration there, as he later remembered it, was subdued: "It didn't seem to me quite as joyous as some of the people say," he told me in 2006. Perhaps, though, that was just a projection; a few years earlier, when I'd asked him how he'd felt at the war's end, he'd answered: "Well, very disappointed, of course. I felt like I hadn't been anyplace. I didn't get to the front . . . That's what I felt I went over there for."

Just because he never got to fight the Germans, though, doesn't mean he didn't get to see them up close. Because he did, in fact — much closer, even, than many of the men who, right up until 11:00 a.m. that morning, had been trying to kill them. And though he didn't realize as much at the time, the experience he did end up having actually suited him much better.

For a few weeks after the armistice, nothing changed for Frank Buckles. He was still in Saint-André-de-Cubzac, still shuttling the sick and wounded around in a Ford ambulance. But then, for some reason, he was sent to the village of Saint-Sulpice-de-Cognac, seventy or so miles to the north, and given a new assignment. "I was attached to a POW company," he recalled. "Prisoner-of-war company . . . Our principal job was taking the prisoners back to Germany." And it was at the prison camp that Frank Buckles finally got his first look at the dreaded Hun. It was not what he expected.

"They were behind barbed wire," he recalled, "but they had an orchestra that they had formed. They made their own instruments and so forth. And on the outside of it we put up some lumber and made some seats, and the Americans would sit outside and listen to them . . .

"I wish I had a camera," he said. "Or I wish I could have sketched it . . . An American soldier would take a group, of maybe twenty, out on the different assignments. And this was an assignment up in the nearby woods, and they had their equipment with them. And here the [American] soldier has a side[arm], a gun. But this day, it must have been a payday or something with the soldier, because — now, the French peasants, all they have to do to start a café is just [get] a table, a chair, and a bottle. So wherever they are, if there is a soldier there with any money in his pocket, he has access to a café. And here it came time to quit, and the picture that I saw was, coming along, here were soldiers, all in formation, a German soldier with . . . the American's sidearm, and an older German smoking his pipe and pushing a wheelbarrow with [the American] soldier in it. That was something."

I'll say. "So the Americans and the Germans after the war — there wasn't a lot of animosity between them?" I asked.

"No," he said. "None whatsoever. One evening — my reason for going into the German barracks I don't know, it was some communication, I guess. Like I told you, we didn't have telephones, so we moved the information around by letter. And in there — I don't have the vaguest idea [anymore] what the argument was about, but there was a young German, maybe about my age, and he and I got into an argument. And it looked like it was going to be pretty serious. Well, just then, two big older Germans stepped up. One of them pinned the other fellow's arms behind his back; the other one pinned mine. And they started talking to us, and telling us what would happen, that we'd all get in trouble if we had any fisticuffs in there. They made us shake hands." Just a few weeks earlier, they would have been obligated to try to kill each other.

Eventually, orders came down for Private — now Private First Class — Buckles to escort 650 German prisoners back to Germany, by train. "The first town we came into in Germany," he recalled, "they had the train stop there, and what they had — the equivalent of Red Cross, or whatever it was, to receive them. So the prisoners all lined up with their cups to get some coffee" — a mischievous grin spread across his lips — "and I did too. I was the only escort who would; I was always ahead, I never missed a thing." He smiled. "So I lined up with them. So when it came to me, they gave me the coffee. I just stood there [before] an old gentleman with a beard, and I said, *Danke schön, das Kaffee ist sehr gut*. With that, he reached behind the counter, gave me a slice of potato bread. And I said, *Danke schön, das Brot ist sehr gut*. Well, I got a piece of baloney in addition to that. See, that's where early I learned the advantage of foreign language." He laughed.

The prisoners were confined to boxcars at the rear of the train, while the guards rode in a coach close to the locomotive; but after one stop, PFC Buckles, having dallied a bit too long, arrived back at the station just in time to see his coach roll by. "I couldn't catch up," he explained. "So Germans sitting in the boxcars [rolled up], the doors open, and the Germans signaled to me — I was running, trying to catch up, and he reached down and grabbed me and brought me aboard. So I stayed in their car the rest of the way." Again: the old enemy was clearly no longer a danger; but, he soon learned, the old allies just might be. "While I was in this [boxcar]," he told me, "I don't know how long — it was some time before we stopped the cars again — but in the distance was a French guard with French prisoners. And he took a potshot at the car." Five or six years later, Frank Buckles was down in Brazil when he made the acquaintance of a photographer. "And the man was a German, and he had an American accent," he told me. "He spoke English with an American accent. And I asked him where he picked that up. He said he was a prisoner during the war, and he'd perfected his English. So I asked him about, if anything unusual happened." Why yes, the man said: After the armistice, he was being transported back to Germany in a boxcar, with an American guard onboard, when a French soldier in the distance had taken a potshot at the car.

The German prisoners were very fond of their captor, apparently, and he of them. I'm not sure what he had to barter — perhaps nothing more than chocolate and cigarettes; he couldn't remember — but he came home with plenty of souvenirs, including a gray uniform cap, "a knife which had Von Hindenburg's silhouette on the side of it," and even a *Gott Mit Uns* belt buckle, the most prized German souvenir of all. After the war, at the YMCA in Oklahoma City, another veteran offered him twenty-five dollars for it. He really could have used the cash right then; but when I visited him at Gap View Farm nearly nine decades later, it was still there, on a shelf in that curio cabinet, along with the cap and knife.

The Army sent him home the following fall, formally discharged him with the rank of corporal on November 13, 1919, at Camp Pike, Arkansas.

He was eighteen years old.

• • •

While Frank Buckles was guarding German prisoners, the leaders of the victorious Allied nations were gathering in Paris to formalize the peace. Or so they said. What they really did was redraw the maps of much of the world, divvy up fallen empires, appropriate certain choice properties, spin others off into brand-new countries, and, most of all, punish and humiliate Germany. Severely. It lost all of its overseas possessions. Big chunks of its home territory were lopped off and given to France and Belgium and several new nations, including Czechoslovakia, Poland, and Lithuania. Germany was forced to shrink its military to the point where it would be, effectively, a ceremonial entity. It was ordered to pay pretty much the entire cost of the war, an amount equivalent to nearly half a trillion of today's dollars. (They made the final payment in October, 2010.) And it and its allies — the bloc known during the war as the Central Powers — were awarded complete responsibility "for causing all the loss and damage to which the Allied and Associated Governments and their nationals have been subjected as a consequence of the war imposed upon them by the aggression of Germany and her allies." A nice little flourish, that. The victorious Allies alone worked out the details of the treaty; Germany was given three weeks to read and sign it.

In Paris, the other Allies rejected the first thirteen of Woodrow Wilson's Fourteen Points, an idealistic plan for establishing and maintaining global peace, allowing only the creation of a "League of Nations" that would safeguard borders and settle international disputes. Back home, an increasingly isolationist United States Congress rejected both the peace treaty and the League of Nations. (The United States would sign its own individual peace treaty with the Central Powers in 1921.) Attorney General A. Mitchell Palmer rounded up and deported hundreds of foreign-born men and women, many of whom had done nothing more than speak out in favor of anarchism, communism, or some other leftist ideal — or, in some cases, merely keep company with those who did — and the country soon found itself caught up in its first Red Scare. In 1921, Congress passed a temporary immigration-restriction act; three years later, it passed a new one that tightened the restrictions even further — limiting immigration from eastern and southern Europe to a tiny fraction of what it had been, while greatly favoring immigrants from northern and western Europe — and made them permanent. President Calvin Coolidge, who would later display an execrable callousness toward impecunious veterans, eagerly signed it into law. The golden age of immigration was dead.

Frank Buckles would have read about all of this in the newspaper, but for a while, at least, most of it must have seemed as much of an abstraction to him as had the European war before April 6, 1917. From Camp Pike he went back to Oklahoma, $139.50 of discharge pay in his pocket; he visited with his parents for a bit, and enrolled at Hill's Business College in Oklahoma City to study shorthand and typing, skills he figured would be valuable for whatever course he might embark upon next. One day, he heard that General Pershing was to be speaking at the city's Hotel Skirvin. Oddly, he told me, he was unable to convince any of the veterans he knew at the college to go along, so he went alone. And in uniform. "I don't remember seeing any military men," he said. "There may have been earlier in the evening. But when I came along, the sergeant followed me and said the general requests me to come back. He said, 'He would like to talk to you.' So General Pershing asked a number of questions . . . He asked where I served . . . and also he asked where I was born. Of course, I told him, 'North of Bethany, in Harrison County, Missouri.' He said, 'Just forty-two miles as the crow flies from Linn County, where I was born.'" It was a story Frank Buckles would repeat many times in the years to come; he always told it exactly the same way. He was, he declared, "very impressed" with the general.

After a few months at the college — during which time he was also working 4:00 p.m. to midnight at the post office, for sixty cents an hour — he felt stuck. "I was not progressing too well," he explained. He was also coming to understand, he said, that "I had to get out of that atmosphere of association, associating only with Army men . . . nobody wanted to talk to me. Nobody knew my story." Veterans, he realized, were "the only people I knew." He was also sick of the heat. He thought about heading up to Montreal and getting work at the seaport, but a fellow he knew recommended Toronto, instead, so that's where he went. "Well," he recalled, "I hadn't the vaguest idea as to how to get a job. I didn't know you could look in the newspaper for want ad jobs. They didn't tell me that in the school. [!] But the nice Irish couple at the place I roomed would cut out the items from the newspaper and paste them on a board for me to answer. I rented a typewriter, for three dollars a month, for a month. Started answering the advertisements. One of them was from the White Star Line. When I saw the flags on there . . . I said, 'That's the job I want.' And I was going to get that job." And he did. It was in the line's freight soliciting department; he made sixty-five dollars a month. He got a second job working nights across the street, at the Great Northwestern Telegraph Company, looking up old accounts for thirty-five cents an hour. Later he left to work for an automobile dealership in town, at the salary of twenty-five dollars a week. "It wasn't very long until I had money enough," he said, "I went to the best tailor in Toronto, on Yonge Street, and had a suit of clothes made." That was the second lesson he learned, after the utility of knowing foreign languages: It pays to look sharp. Or, as he put it: "I recognized that the important thing was the appearance."

In those days, cold weather more or less killed automobile sales in Canada, so in the winter of 1921, Frank Buckles took his new suit and savings — "forty-nine dollars and a half" — and boarded a train for New York. He arrived at Grand Central Terminal, walked over to the YMCA on West Fifty-seventh Street, and took a room, a share, for five dollars a week. He found a job at an advertising agency down by Union Square, then quickly found another one in the bond soliciting department of Bankers Trust Company, on Fifth Avenue at Forty-second Street. "It was a prestigious bank," he told me. "It was formed in nineteen hundred and three. And they were rather particular about their clientele. You had to have some money to belong there. And most of the bond salesmen, I even remember their names, practically all of them, right from Seward Prosser, the president of the bank, on down." One of them, a sixtysomething senior vice president named Wyckoff, befriended the young bond salesman; Mr. Wyckoff, the scion of an old Knickerbocker family, shared tales of old New York with him. "Well, he said that when he was a boy, about ten years old, he used to play over there" — that is, across the street, where the big library, the one with the lions out front, is now — "because it was the city reservoir." From time to time, he recalled, "we went down to the Murray Hill Hotel, which at that time was the aristocratic hotel. And we were treated nicely of course, and had one of those nice ten-course dinners."

Frank Buckles had always been very fortunate in his associations, but in New York they ascended to a new stratum. He was living at the Hotel Elite, on West Fifty-seventh Street across from the Y, and going to a gymnasium, where he met a couple of men who took it upon themselves to help him get integrated into the life of New York. They advised him, among other things, to join a National Guard unit, so he did: the 7th New York, an old outfit sometimes called the "Silk Stocking Regiment" because of the affluence and prominence of its members. (In 1861, it is said, they marched off to the Civil War carrying lunches from Delmonico's, the finest restaurant in the city.) Their armory, opened in 1880 and occupying an entire city block on the Upper East Side, was constructed and furnished entirely with private funds; the members wanted the likes of Louis Comfort Tiffany and Stanford White to be able to work on the project, and a government budget just wasn't going to cut it.

The regiment, Frank Buckles said, was primarily a social organization in those days, with a few military trappings. "Once a week we had a meeting," he recalled. "I was the secretary of my company." Occasionally they would drill, though even that was a social event. "After each drill," he said, "we'd go up to the mess room on the fourth floor and have a beer . . . even though this was Prohibition." There was a brewery in the neighborhood owned by a colonel in the regiment, a fellow named Jacob Ruppert; "he made sure that we had plenty of beer," Mr. Buckles explained. Colonel Ruppert also owned a professional baseball club, and was just then in the process of building it a new ballpark across the river, in the Bronx.

Every day, walking to and from work, he would pass by an automobile dealership on Fifty-seventh Street at Eighth Avenue. "On the main floor, the big windows in there, that's where his showroom was," he told me in 2006, noting that the owner was always there each morning. "When I came back in the evening, very likely he'd be in there. I don't know how he spent all of his time there, in the showroom." The dealership belonged to the Rickenbacker Motor Company; its owner, the man standing in the showroom every morning and evening, was Eddie Rickenbacker, a former racecar driver who became America's top air ace of the war, with twenty-six confirmed kills. "And he liked to talk to me," Mr. Buckles explained. "I guess because I was probably the one ex-soldier . . ." His voice trailed off; I knew what he meant to say.

In 1921, he heard about a Bible class being given at a Baptist church in Manhattan, and decided to start attending — not for religious reasons, but because the class was being taught by the future vice president's father, John D. Rockefeller Jr. "I sat about how close we are now," he told me, also in 2006. "There were never more than forty, if there were that many, in the class. I always sat down in the front, in the old-fashioned pews. And he would sit there with his feet on the seat, and I would be facing. That would be the first row I would be in."

"Did you get to know him?" I asked.

"I sure did," he said. "And I remember, I was clearly impressed by the frankness with which he could speak. And the ease, and such a relaxed person. He was a little bit different than the reporters tried to make him out to be. Because they made him to be a statesman, but a young man has a better way of analyzing the situation than some reporter."

"He was quite a philanthropist."

"That is what he talked about." His father, John D. Rockefeller Sr. — still alive then, at eighty-two — had made the money, his son liked to say; and now, he said, it was his time, to "utilize that money in the right way, to help people out." He told Frank Buckles, "'I have an entire staff whose job it is [to read through the many letters he received], and we look seriously at every one.' Then he described some of them — [for instance,] a woman who needed money so her son could go to college. Naturally, and some of them were more private nature, but still, [he said,] we never bypassed any of them."

In 1923, Frank Buckles, now twenty-two years old, decided he was ready for another change, so he got a job with the Munson Steamship Line, as a purser. "Now, as the purser on a ship," he explained, "you're dealing with all of the crew, right from the captain to the lowest boy. You're dealing with all the passengers. In the ports, you're dealing with all of the officials. It's the job where you know everybody. So that was the place where you learned."

And he learned well. In his spare time he studied Spanish, as he'd become fascinated with the idea of seeing South America. In 1924 he moved over to the W. R. Grace Line, which made him purser on the SS *George Washington,* a luxury liner that had been seized by the government after April 6, 1917; it had been launched in 1908 by the North

German Lloyd Company, which had christened it . . . *George Washington*. Really. "I probably did twenty or thirty ports in South America," he told me. "I was in Brazil, and Uruguay, and Argentina . . . then I went to the west coast of South America." Through the Panama Canal, too. After that, he decided he wanted to see the Orient, and traveled from port to port, China and Japan, for a while. One day, onboard, he was approached by a very distinguished-looking Japanese gentleman who engaged him in conversation. As a young man, this gentleman had left Japan to live and study in Portland, Oregon, returning to Japan in 1902, at the age of twenty-two, having earned a law degree. He was drawn to the young American. "And he asked questions. Where I was going? What I was going to do on the boat? . . . Are you going to Japan? And I said . . . I probably will. And I said, of course, if I go there, I'll go to Tokyo. And he said, 'When you come to Tokyo . . . come to my office and I will take you around Tokyo and show you the sights. Now, if I'm not there' — and he wrote on the back of it — 'you just present this card, and you'll get a chauffeur, and an interpreter, and taken around sightseeing.' He signed it — and I have it somewhere if I could find it — Yosuke Matsuoka." He added: "Look him up."

I did. Matsuoka was a successful businessman turned diplomat; in 1933, some years after his encounter with Frank Buckles, he stood before the League of Nations in Geneva and, disgusted by international condemnation of Japan's invasion of Manchuria, delivered a scathing address condemning that body, then led his country's delegation out, never to return. He then went into politics, and was eventually named Japan's foreign minister; he conceived and vigorously campaigned for a tripartite alliance with Nazi Germany and Fascist Italy, which was realized and became known as the Axis. He tried to get Japan to invade Siberia (because that had gone so well the last time), but was unsuccessful; after the war, he was arrested and charged with war crimes, but died in prison before he could be tried.

October, 1929, found Frank Buckles back in New York, living at 111 Bedford Street in Greenwich Village, walking distance from the West Side piers and across the street from poet Edna St. Vincent Millay, whom he often ran into at a certain restaurant. His job protected him, personally, from the economic chaos that was descending upon the country, but there was no mistaking that a depression was underway; "nobody had any money to spend, that's one thing," he said. Perhaps because of that, he started thinking about Europe again. He had been to England with the Munson Line, but a 1928 trip to Bremerhaven revived fond memories of Germany, and he sought a position that would take him there. He found one, and traveled back and forth between New York and Hamburg many times over the course of seven years, from 1931 to 1938, on the SS *City of Norfolk*, which had a mail contract.

It soon became apparent that something was up. Much of the crew of the *George Washington* had been German, friendly fellows who taught him the language. During one visit to Germany, he told me, he'd met a German gentleman and his father-in-law, who had been, respectively, a captain and a major in the last war; they invited him to visit them down at the family estate — he was moving in lofty circles again; or, more accurately, had never stopped doing so — where, in the course of entertaining him, they took him into their confidence. "And they said, 'We are going to tell you something that will surprise you — that we are preparing for another war.' He says, 'It's not the wish of the officers who have been through the war, but still . . . we are going to get into another one.'" On another occasion, he said, he was visiting a baron's estate in Hungary and enjoying lunch on the lawn, "and there was a plane flying over. And he says, 'We never know, when a plane is flying over, when we might get a' — I forget how he expressed it, but — 'get a visit from Germany.'" But few people did much more about it than just nod knowingly, and shrug: *What can you do?* Even the newspapers, he said, didn't report such things. Many people felt guilty about the harsh terms of the peace treaty, and few could bring themselves to contemplate the prospect of another war so soon after the last one.

The iconic image of post–World War I Germany is people pushing wheelbarrows full of money to the bakery just to buy a loaf of bread; but by the time Frank Buckles first saw Hamburg, "in 1931, they had, they did an excellent job of recovery," he told me. "And Germany was doing quite well." Two years later, though, Adolf Hitler was made chancellor, and things started to change. He first took notice at an antiques shop in Hamburg that he had started frequenting on his first visit; it was owned by a Jewish lady. "She would invite me to have tea," he said. "So I would go up in the center dais and have tea. And this time I came, and she saw me, and came right over to the door and said, 'I'm sorry, my situation has changed. I won't be able to talk to you. I can't invite you in to have tea.'" She was, she said, being watched.

"Then I went into one of the very fine big stores," he continued. "And they had put up signs in front of it." Signs: Don't Buy from Jews, or some equivalent sentiment; "signs against the Jews, against the Jewish people," is how he put it. (One of his earliest memories, he once told me, was of a Jewish peddler coming by his family's farm in Missouri; "Every place they went, they were received . . . they always sold something . . . [and] they never went hungry.") One time, he said, he was at a party, enjoying the company of a young Jewish woman — "the life of the party, always cheerful," he recalled — until "she went to the telephone to call her family, who I think were in Hanover . . . and, my gosh, when she came back, she was just broken up. She said nobody could believe what they . . . what was happening there, what was happening to some of her family." He added: "And there were Americans going over to Europe, making a trip around, telling [people back home] what a wonderful time they were having in Germany." And not just older folks, who perhaps didn't know better; "I had students during that period," he said, "who had traveled around in Germany and stayed at youth hostels, and came back and said it was wonderful."

For years after that first visit, I had a terrible time trying to reconcile the things Frank Buckles had seen in Nazi Germany — and, looking at the entire picture, I know he'd seen almost nothing of it, but not quite nothing — with those stories he'd told about his encounters with the German prisoners, with those tired, underfed men who had fashioned musical instruments out of scrap and gave concerts behind barbed wire, with those big, older fellows who had pinned his arms behind his back and whispered for him to calm down until he did, when just as easily they could have strangled him and buried his body out in the woods. In 2006, three years after our first conversation, I asked him: "The Germans that you knew right after World War I seemed like very decent people; was it hard for you to imagine them then following Hitler?"

"No," he said. "I knew how it was done. Hitler wrote in his book *Mein Kampf,* which is, if you read that, you can see what, that he had to have somebody [for a scapegoat], and the way he got control of the people — Germany wasn't all . . . it wasn't *Germany* speaking in their attitude toward the Jews; it was a certain group, and they got you either for them or against them." It was, he said, very effective; as he told me during another visit, "When they get control — boy. And I'll tell you something: You have difficulty keeping your hand in your pocket when they said 'Heil Hitler.'" Most historians, political scientists, sociologists, and anthropologists would probably agree with that; but that doesn't make it any more satisfying an explanation. One thing is certain, though: Without the previous war — and the peace treaty that officially ended it — none of it would have happened.

Frank Buckles made his last trip to Germany in August, 1938. "Our company could see what was happening," he said, "and we diverted all our ships." The signs — literally — were everywhere, now, even at the elegant hotels at which he stayed. That spring, Germany had annexed Austria, in what is now known as the Anschluss. Austria capitulated without a fight; indeed, many Austrians were thrilled with the development. In September, in an act that has become synonymous with the word "appeasement," Western Europe sold out Czechoslovakia to the Nazis, allowing them to seize the Czech territory known as the Sudetenland without uttering a syllable of protest. In November, the Nazis unleashed a night of terror — Irving Berlin might have recognized it as a pogrom, but for its massive scale — upon the Jews of Germany and Austria, during which nearly a hundred Jews were killed, tens of thousands more were arrested and sent to concentration camps, more than a thousand synagogues were burned to the ground, and many thousands of Jewish-owned shops and businesses were destroyed. It has since come to be known as Kristallnacht, or the Night of Broken Glass, an unmistakable harbinger of what was to come.

After Germany's invasion of Poland on September 1, 1939, dragged Europe back into another war, Frank Buckles knew he wasn't going to be sailing there anytime soon. Nevertheless, he didn't have any trouble finding work. Actually, "I had two jobs offered to me," he told me. "One of them was to go to Buenos Aires with the Captain of the Port, and the other one was to go to Manila. But the one in South America was with the McCormick Line, and wouldn't give me any advantage coming back to the United States. If I went out to the Orient, I could use that advantage in San Francisco," where the other company, the American President Line, was based. "So I took that," he said. His job, he explained, would be "to expedite the movement of cargos in the port of Manila." He arrived there in January of 1941, he told me, and "expected to be out in a year."

And here Frank Buckles chose unwisely.

In 1931, Japan had invaded the northern Chinese region known as Manchuria, an act for which Japan was strongly criticized around the world. (This criticism, you will recall, led Frank Buckles's former Tokyo tour guide to lead his country's delegation out of the League of Nations, never to return.) The Japanese didn't leave Manchuria, though; instead, they fortified their position there and then started pushing farther and farther into China, until the situation developed into an all-out war in 1937. The world took this turn of events rather badly, particularly the United States, which had significant interests in China, not to mention a residual wariness of Japan from their dealings in Siberia a couple of decades earlier. The farther Japan pushed on, the more the United States restricted sales of critical supplies to it, including machinery, oil, and gasoline. (As a small island nation, Japan was quite dependent on the United States and other nations to provide it with such necessities.) The more the United States withheld supplies, though, the more the Japanese felt the need to push on into China and other territories (like French Indochina) in search of new sources. In July, 1941, six months after Frank Buckles arrived in Manila — capital of the Philippines, then an American commonwealth — the United States cut off all oil sales to Japan. At that point, people on both sides of the Pacific who understood these things figured that it was just a matter of time before something bad happened.

December 7, 1941, was a Sunday. Across the International Date Line, it was already Monday, December 8; and so, while you might think that people in the British Crown colony of Hong Kong, or the Dutch East Indies, or Thailand, or British Malaya, or the Philippines — all of which, history records, were invaded by Japan on December 8, 1941 — had at least a day's notice of what was coming, they didn't, really.

Being the kind of person he was, Frank Buckles had, after his arrival in Manila, made the acquaintance of the commander of the US Army Forces in the Far East, headquartered there: Major General Douglas

MacArthur, former commander of the Rainbow Division, commandant of West Point, Army chief of staff, and conqueror of the Bonus
Expeditionary Force. "I met him on occasions when they would have
meetings at the Manila Hotel," Mr. Buckles recalled. When Japan invaded, he said, he tried to enlist, but was turned away, an act that, depending upon how you look at it, either saved his life or very nearly
took it. I'm not sure even he, more than six decades later, knew for sure
which it was. "I was trapped," he said, "because MacArthur's headquarters said that I was more valuable to them staying where I was than
being in the Army. I could see that, because we were congregating the
people in the Philippines." "The people" he was referring to were citizens of countries then at war with the Axis — Britons, French, Dutch,
and Americans, among others — who had fled there from other Pacific
points under attack. "We were telling them that was the safest place in
the Orient." He added: "We knew damn well better than that."

He surprised me with that; it wasn't like him. "Why would they do
that?" I asked him.

"To keep a good impression of the Orient," he said. A few months
later, he told me that a Captain Hatfield, who worked for another
American shipping line, managed to sail out of Manila and escape after
the invasion; "he told me to fetch a bag and come along," Mr. Buckles
recalled. But, he added, "I had already told MacArthur's headquarters
that I was going to stay there . . . They told me that I would be more
valuable to stay there in case we decided to take the people out and to
take the cargos out."

The American force in the Philippines was far too small to keep the
Japanese at bay. There wasn't much they could do, though they certainly did try. One afternoon, Frank Buckles recalled, he was walking
in Manila when he spotted "a Japanese plane flying over, very high."
Suddenly, he said, an Army truck pulled up, "and a sergeant and his
squad of eight men hop out and start firing, shooting at the planes.
So I tell the sergeant, 'Sergeant, what's the extreme range of your
rifle?' He knew right off. I said, 'Well, now, how high do you think that
plane is?' It was about twice it. And he said, 'Mister, I've just got to do
something.'"

Everyone now knew what was coming. MacArthur left Manila,
moved his headquarters to the fortress of Corregidor, on an island in

Manila Bay, and then to Australia. The Japanese marched into Manila — left defenseless, as an "open city" — at the beginning of January, 1942. The city was full of foreigners who had fled there seeking sanctuary; in addition to the aforementioned British, French, Dutch, and Americans, there were, Frank Buckles explained, Canadians, Australians, and New Zealanders, too. "Many of these people," he recalled, "had no residence in Manila at all. They had just been staying at the hotels." Now, he said, the Japanese "gave word that everybody was to present themselves . . . at the Santo Tomas University [in Manila], and to bring provisions for three days." He didn't, deciding instead to wait until they came and got him.

It didn't take very long. They found him at his apartment: a Japanese soldier — "big, bad" — and "two Japanese civilians, nice little people." After they took him to Santo Tomas, the Japanese civilians returned to his apartment, "took a mat I had, about this size, and put all my canned goods and stuff in it, bound it up and took it out there for me." It was one of the few lucky breaks he would catch over the course of the next few years.

I asked Mr. Buckles why the Japanese had told people to bring along only enough provisions for three days; what did they expect to happen after that? "They thought you would go back to your home," he replied. In Manila. "Japanese were not accustomed to taking prisoners. They didn't know how to handle them. They didn't want prisoners. Even their own people. If their own people were taken prisoner, they never wanted to see them again. He's marked off . . . It was a disgrace to be taken a prisoner. They said they would die for the emperor, and so forth." Consequently, he said, "they hadn't made any provision for it." Apparently, it hadn't occurred to the Japanese that taking prisoners also meant feeding prisoners. "At first there wasn't anything," Frank Buckles explained, during our second visit. "Then a man who had a warehouse full of coffee and so forth managed — you get permission to do a lot of things — to go outside and bring in coffee. And he brought in enough coffee for the whole [camp] . . . In the beginning we were only a thousand people there; eventually, there were three thousand. And then we negotiated with the Japanese. The Japanese began to give a certain amount of foodstuffs."

In some ways, the walls at Santo Tomas were porous; the Japanese recognized that the more food prisoners could have brought in to them from the outside, the less food their captors would have to provide. But you had to have connections. Fortunately, Frank Buckles did; he'd actually had the presence of mind to make the arrangements as the Japanese were escorting him out of his apartment. "I told my Filipino houseboy — I gave him money, I told him, 'You just stay here.' He lived someplace nearby; I said, 'You just move in, you and your wife move into this apartment and stay here' . . . The people who lived in Manila all had servants . . . *loyal* servants. And they came right down bringing food. So finally the Japanese allowed an arrangement where they could come down and put it in an apartment inside the wall in Santo Tomas. Then my houseboy would right away bring . . . little containers; there would be one, two, three, four, five of them, and then a handle at the top. And he would bring about, more food than I could eat. And I had two or three friends there. One of them . . . was from the Shell Oil Company. And he didn't, he couldn't immediately find any contact; and he was a big man, too. So I kept him alive for the first few months." Despite such arrangements, though, food was never plentiful; "even the first few months, we were suffering from hunger," he explained.

That wasn't the only problem at Santo Tomas, even in the early days. "We were in this building, well, I guess about seven hundred in that building," Frank Buckles told me during our first visit. "The ruling was, you had to be in at seven o'clock, seven o'clock out in the morning. Well, men were getting stiff, and complaining about everything . . . and they wanted some exercise. I said, 'I'll give you some exercise.' So I took about forty men, lined them up, and started giving them stick drill. The Japanese commandant came along with his crew. And everybody thought I was going to get into trouble. The Japanese said: 'Put up a notice on the bulletin board — everybody should take exercise.'" The incident earned Frank Buckles some measure of renown among the prisoners; one day, he told me, he was approached by another American, a man whose family had owned a large sugar plantation on the Philippine island of Luzon before the invasion. "Name of Walter Weinzheimer," he recalled. "Was in there with his family, and the little daughter, nine years old, had the polio. And [they'd] had an Austrian doctor, a woman, who was taking care of her." Austria, of course, had been annexed by Germany in 1938; as a German citizen, the doctor would not have been interned by the Japanese. But at a certain point, he explained, "she could no longer come in [to Santo Tomas]. So she asked if somebody could take care of the daughter. And the father came to me and asked if I could . . . So every morning, I gave her exercise, and I walked her around the place." They'd stayed in touch ever since; he showed me a letter he'd just recently received from her.

Others started coming to him for help, too. But though he appreciated the responsibility that came with his position in the community, internment grated on him; so when, after a year or so at Santo Tomas, the Japanese announced that they would be moving eight hundred men to a new camp at another university in Los Baños, about fifty miles away, Frank Buckles stepped forward. "It had been part of the Philippine Agricultural College," he explained. "I volunteered to go because I knew the mountains around there and thought that I would be able to get out. Well, I thought it was a possibility." He was quiet for a moment. "But I didn't make it."

"You tried to escape?" I asked.

"No," he said. "We have very good reasons why you don't."

"What are they?"

"They'd take the next twenty people around you. Execute them." Their allies, the Nazis, were known for doing the same thing.

Life had never been comfortable at a Japanese internment camp. Food was always scarce; the soldiers, officers, and commandants always indifferent, and often cruel. As the war started turning against the Japanese, though, things got much worse for their prisoners. Rations were cut, and cut again, and again, to the point where they were almost nonexistent. Brutality surged, became the norm. Prisoners died of disease or starvation; others were taken away by soldiers and never seen again.

Frank Buckles was not spared. Though he continued to lead his daily calisthenics class, his body was breaking down. Before the war, he'd been a healthy 150 pounds; now — well, he didn't know, exactly. "They had scales there," he said, but after a while he stayed away. "When I got down to a hundred pounds," he explained, "I quit weighing." He developed beriberi, a disease of the nervous system caused by malnutrition, which would affect his sense of balance for the rest of his life; whenever we walked somewhere together — across his lawn, into a restaurant — I had to gently press one hand into the small of his back. It got to the point, he said, where "you can't get any worse, or you die." He added: "Lots of them did."

News had a way of filtering into the camp, through civilians outside the walls and secret radios inside them, and when Allied forces started liberating parts of the country toward the end of 1944, prisoners' hopes and spirits rose. "We were accustomed to seeing planes fly over, cargo planes," Frank Buckles recalled. "And we knew Americans were there somewhere, because . . . here a Filipino would appear with a package of American cigarettes." But the Philippines is a large place, spread out over many islands, and the Japanese were tough defenders, known for fighting to the death; the process of liberation took time. By early February, 1945, the prisoners of Los Baños were hearing rumors that the Japanese were killing prisoners wholesale before the Americans could free them. It's difficult to imagine the sense of anxiety the prisoners must have experienced, wondering which set of rifles would get to them first; it must have been hard for many of them even to get out of bed. Except they had to, from 7:00 a.m. to 7:00 p.m., every day.

"The morning of the twenty-third of February, 1945," Mr. Buckles recalled, during our second visit, "most of us were out. You'd go out early, maybe have a folding chair or something to sit on . . . [We] saw a plane fly over, and the paratroopers started dropping out . . . Most people in there had never even heard of a paratrooper. And the guerillas had been hiding up in the trees in the background along the mountain. They came out with their wire cutters and opened up the wires, the fences. And the paratroopers" — that is, men of the 1st Battalion, 511th Parachute Infantry Regiment, 11th Airborne Division, United States Army — "started coming through. About 180, about the same number of Japanese in the camp. And fortunately for the paratroopers, it was just calisthenics time. The Japanese all do calisthenics, and not all would be out doing that, but many of them were. So paratroopers came through and killed the Japanese — except those who escaped. And plenty of them got out, too; they are not all as brave as they try to tell you." The prisoners, he said, were elated, bordering on hysterical. "After you have been in prison camp three years, you're a little bit stir-crazy," Frank Buckles explained. "Some of them were trying to take all their possessions with them."

And by *them,* he meant: us. "When the paratroopers started going through the barracks," he recalled that same day, "my bunk was up high. I reached up on the wall and grabbed my rucksack, and put a mat on the floor. And I reached into the rucksack and I took out my shirt, that I'd had made, and shorts. And there was still starch on them, where my boy had starched them when I was back in Manila a couple of years before . . . I had a pair of knit socks, and I was one of the few men who had a pair of shoes. I dressed up, put on my shoes, put my rucksack on, and just as I walked out the door, the roof was on fire. Just as I walked out the door, the roof fell in." He wanted to honor the occasion accordingly; you can't teach that kind of dignity. Or style.

"Did you know that the roof was on fire when you were getting dressed?" I asked him.

"Well," he said, with a wry grin, "I sort of suspected it."

Add poise to that list.

He returned home, visited his eighty-eight-year-old father in Oklahoma (his mother had died of cancer in 1936) and a lot of other people here and there who'd believed for years that he was dead, took that job in San Francisco, and married a woman he'd met there before the war. In 1953, he moved to West Virginia; the following year, he bought Gap View Farm. A year after that, at the age of fifty-four, he became a father. Gap View was always a working farm; when I first met Frank Buckles, he still drove the tractor, still hired and supervised the hands, still kept the farm's books and paid all its bills himself. He never really retired.

But, though farming was much harder than he had imagined it would be when he bought the place, he never withdrew from the outside world, not a bit; never even limited his scope at all. He still read the newspaper, remained active in his community, traveled. And though his gaze now extended backwards, too, he never lost his fascination with the new. At one point, toward the end of our first visit, I said to him: "You have lived to see so many changes. What kind of things have you seen that you never could have imagined?"

He didn't hesitate: "That little instrument you have there in your pocket," he said. My cell phone. I had forgotten to turn it off, and it had rung while we were talking.

"I was calling on an elderly gentleman in the county," he told me. "And while I was there, his grandson was in Singapore onboard of an oil tanker, the chief engineer, [and] he gets on a telephone and calls his grandfather." He laughed. "*That's* the change," he declared.

We talked, as I said earlier, for more than four hours that day, and only stopped because I got tired. I came back a few months later, and many times after that, until he became too frail to receive visitors, a turn of events that, despite his greatly advanced age, surprised me. When I'd gone to see him in 2008, he told me he wasn't at all surprised that he'd lived to be 107, his age then. "I had been warned by my two aunts, both of whom made it past 100," he explained, "to be prepared — that I was going to live past 100 years old." His father's mother, Harriet Ripsom, the great-granddaughter of Mathias Riebsomeer, killed at Oriskany in 1777, had lived to ninety-six; born the same year that the House of Representatives elected John Quincy Adams president (thus infuriating Andrew Jackson, who'd won the popular vote), she lived long enough to hear the election of Warren G. Harding called on the radio. His father, James Clark Buckles, had lived to ninety-five; born three and a half years before the rebels fired on Fort Sumter, he had lived long enough to watch *I Love Lucy* on television. And he, Frank Buckles, born a few months before Theodore Roosevelt was verbally lynched for inviting a black man to visit the White House, lived long enough to vote for Barack Obama, and to see him sworn in as his country's first African American president.

His wife, Audrey, had died in 1999, leaving her husband a widower at the age of ninety-eight. She was nineteen years his junior, and somewhat self-conscious about the age gap; while she was alive, he told me, he never really told their friends and neighbors about his experiences in the Great War, "partly [because] Audrey wouldn't allow me to . . . she didn't want to let anyone know that I was that old. Her father was overseas [during World War I]." So, he said, "I never talked about it." Still, he maintained, his time in the Army "was [important] for me . . . it started my independence." In lieu of friends and neighbors, he shared stories with his daughter, Susannah, and joined the Veterans of World War I of the USA, which had been founded in 1948, the year General Pershing died. He told me that in the 1970s, when he joined, the organization had tens of thousands of members; decades later, when he was made national commander, there were but a handful. For the last five or six years of his administration, there was just one. "Someone has to do it," he told me once, smiling. Still, he conceded, "it kind of startles you."

About six weeks before our 2008 visit, the death of a 108-year-old Florida man named Harry Richard Landis, who had enlisted in the Army a few weeks before the armistice and never completed basic training, left Frank Buckles as the United States of America's sole surviving veteran of World War I. I asked him if he'd ever thought, years earlier, that he might one day be the last of the last. "I had an idea that I would be *among* them," he said. His status didn't seem to please or sadden him; rather, he took the small modicum of fame it afforded him and used it to draw attention to the fact that there was no national World War I memorial in Washington, D.C. He testified before Congress, was received at the White House, rode in parades with celebrities. He continued to speak out for an appropriate memorial, was written up in newspapers and magazines for doing so. Senators and congressmen issued statements to the effect that they would make it happen. It still hadn't when he died, three years later. It still hasn't.

He was buried in Arlington National Cemetery, the required special permission having been obtained before his death. Newspapers across the country ran obituaries; his name was always spelled correctly. The United States Senate passed a resolution in his memory: Senate Resolution 89, "Relating to the death of Frank W. Buckles, the longest surviving United States veteran of the First World War," by name. It was sponsored by sixteen senators.

Whereas Frank Woodruff Buckles is the last known American World War I veteran, who passed away on February 27, 2011, at the age of 110, and represents his generation of veterans;

Whereas America's support of Great Britain, France, Belgium, and its other allies in World War I marked the first time in the Nation's history that American soldiers went abroad in defense of liberty against foreign aggression, and it marked the true beginning of the "American century";

Whereas more than 4,000,000 men and women from the United States served in uniform during World War I, among them 2 future presidents, Harry S. Truman and Dwight D. Eisenhower;

Whereas 2,000,000 individuals from the United States served overseas during World War I, including 200,000 naval personnel who served on the seas;

Whereas the United States suffered 375,000 casualties during World War I, including 116,516 deaths;

Whereas the events of 1914 through 1918 shaped the world, the United States, and the lives of millions of people in countless ways; and

Whereas Frank Woodruff Buckles is the last veteran to represent the extraordinary legacy of the World War I veterans: Now, therefore, be it *Resolved*, That —

(1) the Senate recognizes the historic contributions of all United States veterans who served in the First World War; and

(2) when the Senate adjourns today, it stand adjourned as a further mark of respect to the memory of Frank W. Buckles, the longest surviving United States veteran of the First World War.

It was an honorable gesture, perhaps even an indication of how far things had come since the days, just seven or eight years earlier, when no one at the Department of Veterans Affairs seemed to know or care how many doughboys yet survived, much less who or where any of them might be. And that, I suppose, is about as much as one can hope for in a congressional resolution of that nature; certainly, it's not the United States Senate's job to tell us why that war mattered, why the passing of its last veteran was significant. But having spent some time with him, and with a few others who passed before he did, I feel that I should at least try.

The significance of the passing of the last veteran of that war is obvious, if perhaps a bit difficult to articulate. It creates additional degrees of separation between us and the event; reshapes it in our consciousness, breaks it down and reassembles it in a somewhat less solid state, one that is harder to grasp, and to carry. You can read yellowed old books, watch grainy old silent films, peruse monuments verdant with decades of oxidation; you can stroll upon a forest floor still dimpled with shell holes, poke around crumbling concrete bunkers, zigzag through shallowed trenches, fill a grocery bag with jagged shrapnel picked from a freshly plowed field. None of it is anything like talking to someone who was there; or just looking at him as he lies in a hospital bed before you, mute; or even, simply, knowing that he is still alive out there, somewhere.

The significance of the war itself, though: that's much harder, not because it's difficult to discern, but because it's so vast that you have to wonder how you can manage to step back far enough that you'll be able to take it all in. You can't, really; the best you can hope for is to stumble upon a crevice, a fingerhold somewhere on its surface that might offer you a place to commence.

Frank Buckles gave me that, too. It started with what seemed, in the moment, to be a fairly stupid question, which I posed toward the end of our first four-hour interview. (In my defense, though he could have talked for another four hours at that point, I was quite tired.) "Do you think," I asked, "that the world in some ways is a much smaller place than it was?"

Ask a hundred people that question, and a hundred of them will tell you: Of course it is. Cell phones. Satellite television. Jet airplanes. The Internet.

But Frank Buckles was not one person in a hundred. He was Frank Buckles.

"Ah," he said, and shook his head once. "No."

I was startled. "You think it was smaller then," I said, not asking a question so much as reciting the words, hoping to make sense of them.

"Yes," he said. "Smaller then. At least, it seems that way to me."

That was in August, 2003. It took me years, and many more conversations with World War I veterans — including quite a few more with him — to begin to understand what he meant by that, and more years still to understand that that's the greatest legacy of the Great War. It made the world a much larger place for everyone involved: French and British and German, Russian and Austrian and Czech, Italian and Serb and Turk, Senegalese and Berber and South African, Australian and New Zealander and Indochinese, Newfoundlander and Canadian and Canadien. And American: native-born and immigrant, black and white, affluent and middle-class and indigent, southern farm boys and kids from Hell's Kitchen, gardeners and lumberjacks, Connecticut Yankees and men of the West, drivers and mechanics and bakers and laborers and secretaries and students, people in search of adventure and people in search of a job, volunteers and draftees, the eager, the willing, the reluctant, the resigned. They left the world they knew — Livingston, Montana, or Kewaunee, Wisconsin, or Aberdeen, Mississippi, or Anna, Illinois, or Salina, New York, or Philadelphia, or New Orleans, or Harrison County, Missouri — for far-off places they'd never heard of, much less imagined, and there beheld things that even the people who'd always lived in them had never seen. They set off for a world war, and came back with a world. A much larger world.

And left it to us.

18

We Are All Missing You Very Much

WHEN WE LEFT 107-year-old Anthony Pierro, many pages ago, he was standing on his front steps, waving and calling out "Adios, amigos!" as I drove off, my head occupied at that moment by the solitary thought that I would probably never see him again.

But I did.

It was May 17, 2006, nearly three years later. He was 110 now, a supercentenarian, and I drove up to Swampscott, Massachusetts, from Greenville, Rhode Island, having just interviewed Samuel Goldberg (he of the exquisite diction), to see Mr. Pierro again. I had learned a lot since I'd first interviewed him in July of 2003 — about the war, and the battles he'd fought in, and artillery, and the America of 1917 and 1918, and the immigrant experience, and how to interview the very, very old. I had many questions for him, and the confidence — bordering, perhaps, on delusional — that he'd be able to answer them all. I had not forgotten how difficult, in some ways, that first interview had been; but now, almost three years on, having conducted dozens of subsequent interviews, I mistakenly attributed the difficulties of that interview to my own inexperience at the time, and not to the frailties of a 107-year-old man's memory and expressiveness. Of course, quite a few of the interviews I had done since July 19, 2003, had been even more difficult than that first one, but you don't remember those quite as well in looking back as you do the ones that went much better than you expected, the instances where you could converse with a 106-year-old man as you might with anyone, the discussions where you heard a few fantastic stories, learned a couple of startling things. It was those memories, those boldest and most felicitous ones, that informed my expectations for my second visit with Anthony Pierro. Maybe, I hoped, he'll even remember that story about the fellow who called him a greedy Wop on the mess line.

He didn't. He didn't remember much of anything, anymore, beyond the most basic information — his parents' names, the country of his birth, things like that. His baby brother, Nicholas, who was then ninety-seven, was there, too, and tried his best to fill in the gaps. Among the things Nicholas told me that day was that several of his brothers — not just Anthony — had served in the AEF. The firstborn, Michael, four years older than Anthony, was badly gassed in France, and never recovered; the 1930 census lists Michael's occupation as "Retired — Disabled in War." He died in 1951, not yet sixty years old. (His parents both survived him, living into their nineties.) I'm not sure why Anthony Pierro didn't choose to share any of that with me the first time we'd talked. Perhaps I just didn't ask him the right question.

The second time we talked, he could no longer remember anything about the war, except for Madeleine. I'm kind of glad it worked out that way; if I had lived his life and could pick only one memory from that period of it to carry until I died, I might have chosen that one. Even so, I was disappointed: Not only did I not hear any new stories, I didn't hear most of the old ones again, either. I know I shouldn't have been surprised — at that age, three years is a long, long time — but I was. It bothered me that he might not have at 110 what he'd had at 107. I had come to think of him, and the rest of them, as supermen, and supermen don't slow down, don't deteriorate. They just live, right up until they die. In my defense, a lot of them did exactly that. Still, I shouldn't have expected as much from him, or from any one of them. I shouldn't have been disappointed. But I was.

In time, though, I would come to understand — I'd like to say it happened after just a few days, but in truth it was much later, probably sometime after he died, the following February, one week short of his 111th birthday — that he had, really, told me a lot of stories during our first visit: the time a tree saved his life by catching a German shell; how he climbed up into it to retrieve that shell and then brought it to his captain, who had jokingly ordered him to fetch it and was terrified when the order was actually carried out; the time a horse saved his life by stopping, with its body, shrapnel from another German shell before it could tear into his; burying that horse, and many others, to keep the wolves from getting at them; the fellow in his battery who once slapped a horse on the rear and paid for it with his life; "Upstairs, two dollars." For years after that first visit, I spent a lot of time wondering about the stories I had come by too late to hear, not just from him but the rest of them, too; and about the veterans, centenarians and supercentenarians, that I never got to meet at all — because I didn't start looking until 2003, or because I couldn't arrange the trip in time once I did find them, or because they or their family felt uncomfortable for some reason, or because a cantankerous administrator at the Bay Pines VA hospital in Florida was in a bad mood and decided to abuse power he shouldn't even have had. That last bit might have tipped you off to the fact that I still do think about it, sometimes.

But much more often, now, I think about the stories — astonishing, frightening, heartbreaking, hilarious — that I did get to hear. And I think about the remarkable men and women I did get to meet, about how few of them there were, and how hard they were to find. It amazes me, still, that there were so many wonderful characters, and so many great stories — and so much *history*, otherwise lost — remaining yet in such a small pool. I imagine it always will.

Boy: Was I lucky.

In a park outside the public library in my hometown, in Westchester County, New York, stands a World War I monument. When I was a kid, I made great use of that library (it's said the new wing was funded entirely by my overdue fines), and, in the process, got to know that monument well. It's a life-sized statue of an American infantryman, standing between two tree stumps. His left hand, hanging down at his side, clutches his rifle. (There's no bayonet on it; even in those pre-litigious days, I guess someone knew that would be a bad idea.) His right, raised over his head, cradles a pineapple grenade. A legend in the base reads: SPIRIT OF THE AMERICAN DOUGHBOY. The term "doughboy," in case you're still wondering after all this time, is most commonly used as a nickname for a soldier of the American Expeditionary Forces. Its origins are obscure and contested: Some say it refers to the phenomenon of infantry, covered in dust after a long march down dirt roads, looking as if they had been rolled in flour; others attribute it to the popularity of doughnuts — distributed by the Salvation Army and other organizations — among soldiers of the AEF. There are still other theories, too.

I was quite intrigued by that statue back then, spent a lot of time looking at it. There was nothing else like it in town — the closest thing was a plaque in the post office listing the names of local residents who'd fought in the Revolution, but that was small and plain and upstaged by a huge WPA mural of some guy trying to get control of a runaway team of horses — and though, in my elementary-school days, I didn't know exactly what it was about, I knew it was something important. And I knew, too, that though it stood right out in the open in a corner of the park near a busy intersection, it was ignored. I never saw anyone else stop to look at it, or even slow down as they walked by. Once or twice a year a wreath would appear propped up against its pedestal, sit there for a while, and then disappear. That was it. I didn't care: *I* loved that monument.

I'm not sure when, exactly, it happened, but at some point — probably after I left for some years and then returned as an adult — I discovered that it was ugly. Really ugly. My hometown is small; perhaps they couldn't raise the money for a nicer monument, or perhaps the selection committee was just one person whose taste wasn't very good. However it happened, we ended up with a dopey-looking doughboy. His uniform is entirely correct, but inartfully rendered so that it all looks wrong, somehow: His helmet is dangerously close to a derby; his puttees appear to be telescoping calves. His gas-mask bag resembles a man purse slung around his neck, and his ammunition belt reminds me of an ill-chosen 1960s accessory. His posture is odd — neither standing still nor running, he appears to be taking a casual stroll among the tree stumps, holding a grenade over his head for some reason. His eyes betray no emotion, no urgency, and, frankly, no intelligence. And his mouth is wide open. What could he possibly be saying? "Hey, Captain! What am I supposed to do with this, again?" No wonder nobody ever looked at it.

But you know that isn't quite true, because I already told you that I did. A lot. Before I ever read a word about soccer balls and kilts and trenches and barbed wire, before my mother told me about the old men at the Bronx VA who'd never recovered from being gassed — before, even, I first encountered Snoopy and his Sopwith Camel — that monument *was* World War I to me. It told me: This is something you need to know about. *Remember.* And so it did its job.

Most things don't age as well as the men and women I interviewed over the course of several years in the first decade of the twenty-first century. Monuments weather, and slowly — but, sadly, not uniformly — change color. (The last time I saw him, my guy looked like a bank dye pack had exploded on him.) Sheet music can fade, and sometimes crumble to confetti. Book bindings can crack, and spill out yellowed pages. Posters can crease, split, dissolve. Reputations and fame can diminish, or evaporate entirely. And memories can become corrupted well before they've even had time to start dissolving. In the last chapter of *Company K,* Private Sam Ziegler, the war some years behind him, is taking a summer road trip with his wife and children when he decides "to go see the old training camp again." Perusing a roster, he discovers that his old sergeant, "Pig Iron" Riggin, is still stationed there, and asks to see him; "I'd like to talk to him about old times," he tells the post commander, and soon he and Pig Iron are walking through the camp together. Inside his old bunkhouse, Sam notices that someone has put up metal plaques next to each bed, indicating who had slept there during the war; he quickly finds his own name, and then begins browsing through the others, reminiscing with the sergeant. Or trying to, anyway: The two of them can't seem to remember any of the same men, or anecdotes, colorful though they were. In the book's final paragraph, Ziegler tells us:

> I stood there thinking, trying to bring up the faces of the men I used to soldier with, but I couldn't do it. I realized, then, that I would not have remembered the face of Riggin, himself, if I hadn't known who he was beforehand. I began to feel sad because it had all happened so long ago, and because I had forgotten so much. I was sorry that I had come to the camp at all. Pig Iron and I stood there looking at each other. We didn't have anything to talk about, after all. Then we locked the old building and went outside.

Some might consider that sort of memory loss a blessing; the author of Ziegler's words, William Campbell (writing as William March) surely would have. But he was not so graced. The war tormented him for decades after it ended. Perhaps he had hoped that writing *Company K* might enable him to let go of it at last. It didn't. The book itself went out of print after its initial run. Campbell battled depression and writer's block for decades, and suffered a nervous breakdown at one point. Subsequent novels — all of them literary, none dealing with war — failed to gain much attention. In 1952, the Lion Press brought *Company K* back into print; my copy, a twenty-five-cent paperback edition, features a cover illustration of a trio of exhausted, battered infantrymen slogging through ruins, past a dark-haired, barefoot chippy trying unsuccessfully to beckon them. The men are all wearing World War II uniforms.

In April, 1954, March published *The Bad Seed*, a novel about a sociopathic, homicidal eight-year-old girl. It became a phenomenal success, a bestseller that would be adapted for the stage by the renowned playwright Maxwell Anderson, and later made into a movie — twice. Campbell, though, didn't live to see any of that; he died of a heart attack on May 15, 1954, just a few weeks after the book's release. He was sixty years old, and had been living in New Orleans, not far from George Briant.

My grandfather Abraham Rubin was born in 1890 in Minsk, in what was then known as Byelorussia, or White Russia, in the old Russian Empire. In January, 1906, at the age of fifteen, he left home, traveled to Berlin, caught a train to Hamburg, then made his way to Cuxhaven, where he boarded the Hamburg America Line's SS *Amerika*, arriving in New York on February 16, 1906. When the war broke out in Europe, the *Amerika* was docked in Boston; it sat there, trapped, for two years and eight months, until the United States entered the war, seized it, rechristened it the USS *America*, and commissioned it as a troop transport.

A couple of months later, my grandfather, having just opened his own business in Manhattan after a decade of working very long hours and saving up, was drafted. He was sent to Camp Upton, in Yaphank, on Long Island (where Irving Berlin got to sleep late while writing *Yip-Yip-Yaphank*), and inducted into the 77th Division — specifically, into Battery C of the 306th Field Artillery. Despite the fact that a great many of the men in the Statue of Liberty Division were also immigrants, a lot of them from backgrounds very similar to his — and despite the efforts of the Foreign-speaking Soldier Subsection of the Military Morale Section of the Military Intelligence Division of the War Department — it was, I believe, a difficult adjustment for him. He was twenty-seven years old, had lost his nascent business, and, though he had not yet married and started a family of his own, he was probably pretty homesick for the city, and his life there, and the people he'd had to leave. Those people knew it, too.

My grandfather died in 1978, at the age of eighty-eight; not quite Fred Hale territory, but respectable. I was eleven years old at the time, and hadn't known him all that well, since he and my grandmother had been living in Miami Beach for most of my life. I had a vague sense that he had served in the Army at some point — there were old photographs here and there, including one fairly large portrait of him in uniform — but for some reason I failed to connect him with that monument by the library. It didn't occur to me then to ask him about his service, and the war; by the time it did, he was long gone.

In 2000, my parents sold the house in which I had grown up, and were cleaning it out when they found, down in the basement, a cardboard box full of things my grandfather had saved, going back to his childhood in Russia. There were school notebooks and drawings, his passport, his train ticket from Berlin to Hamburg, a piece of stationery from the *Amerika*. Postcards addressed to him in Yiddish and Russian. His draft notice; furlough passes; railroad passes from Yaphank to Pennsylvania Station. A mezuzah and prayer book from the Jewish Welfare Board. A canvas rifle case. (Sadly, there was no rifle in it anymore.) Some uniform buttons. An Army-issued razor kit, and wristwatch. A pair of identification disks; a copy of the CPI's *Home Reading Course for Citizen-Soldiers*, too. There were no letters that he'd written, but there were a few that he'd received. Most were official correspondence. One wasn't.

Addressed to "Abraham Rubin, 306 Field Artillery, 16 St. and 4th Av., Battery C, Camp Upton, LI," it was sent to him by his uncle, Morris Abramson. Like my grandfather, his mother's brother, Morris, was an immigrant. He was somewhat older than my grandfather, I imagine, when he arrived in America, and English was not his native language.

But he wrote in English. I have corrected his spelling and punctuation, but nothing else:

New York, Oct. 16/17

My Dear Abe!

Your postal and letter received!

And in reply will say that I have so much to tell you, so much to write to you, that I can't start it at all.

All I know is that I set down with the intention to write you a cheerful letter. But if he, that is my letter, will not come up to the standard of cheerfulness, do not blame me for it. For there are times in life when emotion controls reason, when the heart controls the brain and hand. I really mean to write and send you nothing but cheers. But my uncontrolled heart jumps out and dictates to my hand to spell it "Tears." . . .

So as I have said before, do not blame me for it! What I really want to tell you is that we are all missing you very much. And let me tell you, dear Abe, that I would rather serve in the Army, and struggle and suffer and even die on the field of battle, but to be liked and beloved by everybody as you are, than to live and enjoy all the pleasures of civil life and to be hated and despised by everybody — for instance, as your dear brother-in-law, A.R. So you see, dear Abe, even now you are a million times better-off than he is. And I want you to put that in your pipe and smoke, and watch the twists and turns of the smoke, and you will see that it will spell for you: "Cheer Up!"

Cheer up. For if you will look up the history of the world, you will find that from our great teacher, Moses, up to the present great men, all of them fought for the rights of others. And that's what made them great. And I think it is a privilege, an honor, a glory, to fight for other peoples' rights. Especially we Jews, who are charged by the enemies of mankind with being leeches and money-lenders, must show to those Rats of Darkness that we can sacrifice our fortunes, our blood, our lives for the rights of humanity. And we must show to the world that when it comes to fight, that the spirit of the Maccabees is in us as strong today as it was centuries ago!

In short, dear Abe, no one knows better than I the sacrifice you have made for our beloved country. But money could never buy the honor and glory when, in years to come, in the Roll of Honor will be found the name of Abraham Rubin, a Jew, a soldier, who was a credit to his country, a credit to his nation, a credit to his family, and a credit to himself. Don't you think it's worthwhile to fight for it?

I want to tell you, dear Abe, you have been a good boy. A good son. A good brother. A good nephew. A good friend. So keep it up, boy, and be a good soldier!

And don't forget, that wherever you will be, in Yaphank or in the trenches of France, the hearts of your country, the hearts of your nation, the hearts of your family, will always be with you. And my tears which roll between these lines are dumb witness, that every word I say to you, every advice I give to you, comes from the bottom of my heart, and are meant for your good!

Now, dear Abe, let me know at once if we need a pass to see you. And also let me know before Saturday if you are coming to New York. If not, I will come out to see you next Sunday. And let me know what you need, so I could bring it to you.

With love and good wishes to you, and to all your friends in arms, I remain yours,

Morris Abramson

P.S. Lena tells me to tell you that she is sending you her best regards and her best wishes and xxxxxxxxxxxxxxx.

Morris

When I read this letter sometimes I think of the tiny, bright blue flowers I once spotted peeking out of the charred plot of earth where a dignified old building had recently burned to the ground. That war was a terrible thing; people understood that then as well as they do now. Minsk sat near the edge of the Eastern Front for much of the war, and saw a fair amount of action; Morris's sister, my grandfather's mother, was still there then, as were my grandfather's father, two of his sisters, several nieces and nephews, and countless aunts and uncles and cousins. I am sure that few of them, perhaps none at all, had been heard from for years by the time Morris Abramson wrote that letter. Some of them, I imagine, had already been claimed by hunger, or disease, or German guns. Others, perhaps many others, would not live to see the end of the war, or of the civil war that immediately followed.

That war should never have happened; you can argue, as did my old history professor Bruce Kuklick at Penn, that once it did start, the United States should never have entered it. But it did, and then it did, and since it did, you embark down a sure path to cynicism, and perhaps depression or even despair, if you don't try to find at least some little green shoots among the millions and millions of dead, 117,000 or so Americans among them, not to mention the uncountable number of lives that might have been spared, technically, but were ruined nonetheless, and the many millions more (including those two sisters, all those nieces and nephews, and who knows how many of those aunts and uncles and cousins) who perished during the second war that the first war wrought. And so you contemplate all those doughboys who marched off in high spirits with high ideals, who brought America to the world, and to a seat at the dais of nations for the first time, and brought back perhaps even more than that; and you think about the people at home, searching amid uncertainty and anxiety and fear to find something higher, something eternal, that might possibly, in the best of all cases, come out of this awful calamity — and then pass it on to one of those doughboys. Maybe your nephew.

So, in addition to all those veterans and their stories, in addition to all the books and posters and sheet music and other artifacts of that war, I take this letter and pin it to that wheel, taking care to leave some space for all the letters and identification disks and booklets and everything else out there that remains yet in some old cardboard bin in a basement, or locked in a keepsake box that no one has tried to open for decades, or pressed between the yellowed pages of some aged book that is itself pressed between other aged books high up on a shelf. Though the last of the doughboys are now gone and will never return, I like to think that, like the battlefield detritus that pops up every time a field is plowed in certain parts of France, these things will continue to surface for at least a few centuries more.

I don't particularly believe in an afterlife, and have never considered it a constructive exercise to spend time thinking about the world to come rather than the one we know for certain exists and have to live in for a while; but if you meet and get to know even a little bit some two or three dozen very old men and women who share their rich and complex stories with you and then die shortly thereafter, you come to understand why other people choose to believe in, and dwell on, such things. More than I can say, I like the thought, the image of all those men I met who lost their fathers before their tenth birthday, reuniting with them after a century's separation; of Art Fiala cooking up a mess of pancakes and bacon with that French woman who nursed him back to health; of Reuben Law and his grandfather, James Madison Bowler, swapping tales of army life; of Eugene Lee once again throwing a base-ball, or maybe a pair of dice, with Joe Wnuk; of Frank Buckles pull-ing up on a motorcycle with a sidecar and offering a ride to John J. Pershing or Eddie Rickenbacker; of Moses Hardy and the rest of the 805th Pioneer Infantry all sitting together, soldiers and officers, and taking in a show; of the men of the 102nd Infantry Regiment, one by one, filing past Corporal J. Laurence Moffitt as he checks off their name in his register; of Private William Lake, after a long hike, cresting a hill and coming upon Captain Elijah Worsham, and the two of them shak-ing hands vigorously and then saluting each other, because there's no reason not to; and of me, seeing all of them, the whole lot, again once more, if only for a few minutes.

I wouldn't even ask a single question.

Appendix

Typical U.S. Army Infantry Units in World War I

Unit	Size	Commanding Officer
Platoon	40 men	Lieutenant
Company	180 men	Captain
Battalion	800 men	Major or Lieutenant Colonel
Regiment	3,500 men	Colonel
Brigade	8,000 men	Brigadier General
Division	25,000 men	Major General

A corps comprised several divisions; an army comprised several corps.

A Note on Methods

All of the World War I veterans featured in this book were interviewed in person; all of the interviews were conducted by me.

On a couple of occasions, the interview subject said something of note at a time when the camera was off or the tape was being changed; these were written down by me immediately. On one occasion, I called a veteran on the telephone several months after our visit to obtain a little more information on a specific matter.

The very old (and the rest of us, too) often speak haltingly, repeating words, clauses, and even entire sentences while grasping for what to say next. The transcript has for the most part been scrubbed of such interjections as "um" and "uh," and of fragments and repetitions that were not part of the subject's chosen way of relating their story (or of my chosen way of posing a question). I also, on a handful of occasions, took the liberty of correcting an uttered mistake within a quote, such as when a subject confused 1917 with 1918, or vice versa. I would be grateful, should the need ever arise in the future, if someone would do the same for me.

I did not correct subjects' grammar or word choices. At the same time, I did not feel the need to render their dialect phonetically (with a few exceptions, as noted).

Finally, I should note that the various topics of conversation are not necessarily presented in the order in which they were discussed. The conversations were rarely linear. In constructing a narrative that would tell the veteran's story in a way that would prove most meaningful for both the reader and the legacy of the interviewee, I have sometimes altered the order in which some topics are presented here relative to when they were discussed during the interview(s). Great care has been taken to preserve the context of all quotes, statements, and discussions, and to avoid misrepresentation.

— Richard Rubin

Selected Bibliography

Abbot, Willis J. *Pictorial History of the World War*. New York: Leslie-Judge, 1919.

———. *The United States in the Great War*. New York: Leslie-Judge, 1919.

Altschul, Charles. *German Militarism and Its German Critics*. War Information Series, no. 13. Washington, DC: Committee on Public Information, 1918.

American Battle Monuments Commission. *American Armies and Battlefields in Europe*. Washington, DC: United States Government Printing Office, 1938.

Anonymous [John MacGavock Grider]. *War Birds: Diary of an Unknown Aviator*. New York: Grosset & Dunlap, 1926.

Arthur, Max. *Forgotten Voices of the Great War*. London: Ebury Press, 2002.

Axelrod, Alan. *The Complete Idiot's Guide to World War I*. New York: Alpha Books, 2000.

Azan, Paul. *The Warfare of To-Day*. Boston: Houghton Mifflin, 1918.

Barbeau, Arthur E., and Florette Henri. *The Unknown Soldiers: Black American Troops in World War I*. Philadelphia: Temple University Press, 1974.

Barrett, Michèle. *Casualty Figures: How Five Men Survived the First World War*. New York: Verso, 2007.

Bates, Brainless [Brainard Leroy Bates]. *Doughboy Ditties: Popular Parodies for the Battle Hims of the Republic*. Boston: A. M. Davis, 1918.

Beatty, Jack. *The Lost History of 1914: Reconsidering the Year the Great War Began*. New York: Walker, 2012.

Bent, Christine, ed. *The New York Times Book of World War I*. New York: Arno Press, 1980.

Bernstorff, Johann Heinrich Graf von. *My Three Years in America*. New York: Charles Scribner's Sons, 1920.

Bet-El, Ilana R. *Conscripts: Lost Legions of the Great War.* Gloucestershire, UK: Sutton, 1999.

Bisher, Jamie. *White Terror: Cossack Warlords of the Trans-Siberian.* New York: Routledge, 2005.

Bliss, Paul Southworth. *The Arch of Spring.* St. Louis, MO: published by the author, 1932.

———. *Victory: History of the 805th Pioneer Infantry, American Expeditionary Forces.* St. Paul, MN: published by the author, 1919.

Brittain, Harry E. *To Verdun from the Somme.* New York: John Lane, 1917.

Brook-Shepherd, Gordon. *November 1918: The Last Act of the Great War.* Boston: Little, Brown, 1981.

Buffington, Joseph. *Friendly Words to the Foreign Born.* Loyalty Leaflets, vol. 1. Washington, DC: Committee on Public Information, 1917.

Burns, Robert E. *I Am a Fugitive from a Georgia Chain Gang!* Abridged ed., with an introduction by Alex Lichtenstein. Savannah, GA: Beehive Press, 1994. Originally published 1932.

Callahan, Arthur D. *Rhymes and Official Data of the American Army in the World War.* Kansas City, MO: published by the author, 1919.

Call, Arthur D., ed. *The War for Peace: The Present War as Viewed by Friends of Peace.* War Information Series, no. 14. Washington, DC: Committee on Public Information, 1918.

Captain X [pseud.]. *Our First Half Million: The Story of Our National Army.* New York: H. K. Fly, 1918.

Carey, Neil G., ed. *Fighting the Bolsheviks: The Russian War Memoir of Private First Class Donald E. Carey, US Army, 1918–1919.* Novato, CA: Presidio Press, 1997.

Chicago Daily News. *The Chicago Daily News War Book for American Soldiers, Sailors and Marines.* Chicago: Chicago Daily News, 1918.

Committee of Welcome. *Welcome Home YD: In Commemoration of the Foreign Service and Home-Coming of the 26th Division.* Boston: Committee of Welcome Appointed by the Governor of Massachusetts and the Mayor of Boston, 1919.

Committee on Public Information. *American Loyalty by Citizens of German Descent.* War Information Series, no. 6. Washington, DC: Committee on Public Information, 1917.

———. *The War Message and Facts Behind It: Annotated Text of President Wilson's Message, April 2, 1917.* War Information Series, no. 1. Washington, DC: Committee on Public Information, 1917.

Cowan, Sam K. *Sergeant York and His People.* New York: Grosset & Dunlap, 1922.

Creel, George. *How We Advertised America: The First Telling of the Amazing Story of the Committee on Public Information That Carried the Gospel of Americanism to Every Corner of the Globe*. New York: Harper & Brothers, 1920.

Current History: A Monthly Magazine of the New York Times. Vol. 11, part 1, no. 3 (December 1919).

Curtin, D. Thomas. *The Land of Deepening Shadow: Germany-at-War*. New York: George H. Doran, 1917.

Davies, Alfred H. *Twentieth Engineers, France, 1917–1918–1919*. Portland, OR: Twentieth Engineers Publishing Association, 1920.

Davis, Richard Harding. *With the Allies*. New York: Charles Scribner's Sons, 1917.

De Varila, Osborne. *The First Shot for Liberty*. Philadelphia: John C. Winston, 1918.

Dickson, Paul, and Thomas B. Allen. *The Bonus Army: An American Epic*. New York: Walker, 2004.

Drinker, Frederick E. *Our War for Human Rights*. Washington, DC: National Publishing Company, 1917.

Eisenhower, John S. D. *Yanks: The Epic Story of the American Army in World War I*. New York: Simon & Schuster, 2001.

Empey, Arthur Guy. *First Call: Guide-Posts to Berlin*. New York: G. P. Putnam's Sons, 1918.

———. *A Helluva War*. New York: D. Appleton, 1927.

———. *The Madonna of the Hills*. New York: Harper & Brothers, 1921.

———. *Over the Top*. New York: G. P. Putnam's Sons, 1917.

———. *Tales from a Dugout*. New York: Century, 1918.

———. *Troopers Three*. New York: A. L. Burt, 1930.

Flanagan, Edward M., Jr. *The Los Baños Raid: The 11th Airborne Jumps at Dawn*. Novato, CA: Presidio Press, 1986.

Fleming, Thomas. *The Illusion of Victory: America in World War I*. New York: Basic Books, 2004.

Folks, Homer. *The Human Costs of the War*. New York: Harper & Brothers, 1920.

Ford, Nancy Gentile. *Americans All!: Foreign-Born Soldiers and World War I*. College Station: Texas A&M University Press, 2001.

Freidel, Frank. *Over There: The Story of America's First Great Overseas Crusade*. New York: Bramhall House, 1964.

Fussell, Paul. *The Great War and Modern Memory*. Oxford: Oxford University Press, 1975.

Garey, E. B., O. O. Ellis, and R. V. D. Magoffin. *American Guide Book to France and Its Battlefields*. New York: Macmillan, 1920.

Gerard, James W. *Face to Face with Kaiserism*. New York: George H. Doran, 1918.

——. *My Four Years in Germany*. New York: Grosset & Dunlap, 1917.

Gibbons, Floyd. *"And They Thought We Wouldn't Fight."* New York: George H. Doran, 1918.

Gilbert, Martin. *The First World War: A Complete History*. New York: Henry Holt, 1994.

Gordon-Detwiler Institute of New York. *Soldiers' French Course*. New York: Foreign Trade Press, 1917.

Graves, Robert. *Good-Bye to All That: An Autobiography*. London: J. Cape, 1929.

Hagedorn, Ann. *Savage Peace: Hope and Fear in America, 1919*. New York: Simon & Schuster, 2007.

Halévy, Daniel. *President Wilson*. New York: John Lane, 1919.

Hallas, James H., ed. *Doughboy War: The American Expeditionary Force in World War I*. Boulder, CO: Lynne Rienner, 2000.

The Heroic 26th YD: Its Deeds and Valor Over There. Boston: Ball, 1919.

The History of the 306th Field Artillery. New York: Knickerbocker Press, 1920.

History of the Seventy Seventh Division: August 25th, 1917–November 11th, 1918. New York: 77th Division Association, 1919.

Hochschild, Adam. *To End All Wars: A Story of Loyalty and Rebellion, 1914–1918*. Boston: Houghton Mifflin Harcourt, 2011.

Holmes, R. Derby. *A Yankee in the Trenches*. Boston: Little, Brown, 1918.

Hurley, Edward N. *The Bridge to France*. Philadelphia: J. B. Lippincott, 1927.

Jewish Welfare Board. *Abridged Prayer Book for Jews in the Army and Navy of the United States*. Philadelphia: Jewish Publication Society of America, 1917.

——. *Jewish Welfare Board, U.S. Army and Navy: Its Work, Purpose and Scope*. New York: Jewish Welfare Board, 1917.

——. *Readings from the Holy Scriptures for Jewish Soldiers and Sailors*. Philadelphia: Jewish Publication Society of America, 1918.

Johnson, Owen. *The Spirit of France*. Boston: Little, Brown, 1916.

Josephy, Alvin M., Jr., ed. *The American Heritage History of World War I*. New York: American Heritage, 1964.

Jünger, Ernst. *Storm of Steel; From the Diary of a German Storm-Troop Officer on the Western Front*. Translated by Basil Creighton. Garden City, NY: Doubleday, Doran, 1929.

Keegan, John. *The First World War*. New York: Alfred A. Knopf, 1999.

——. *An Illustrated History of the First World War*. New York: Alfred A. Knopf, 2001.

Kennedy, Dick, ed. *Fun from France*. Vol. 1, no. 1. New York: Victor W. Brunall, 1918.

Landau, Henry. *The Enemy Within: The Inside Story of German Sabotage in America*. New York: G. P. Putnam's Sons, 1937.

Lansing, Robert. *The Peace Negotiations: A Personal Narrative*. Boston: Houghton Mifflin, 1921.

Laskin, David. *The Long Way Home: An American Journey from Ellis Island to the Great War*. New York: Harper, 2010.

Lengel, Edward G. *To Conquer Hell: The Meuse-Argonne, 1918*. New York: Henry Holt, 2008.

Lewis, John E., ed. *The Mammoth Book of Eyewitness World War I*. New York: Carroll & Graf, 2003.

Liggett, Hunter. *Commanding an American Army: Recollections of the World War*. Boston: Houghton Mifflin, 1925.

Macmillan, Margaret. *Paris 1919: Six Months That Changed the World*. New York: Random House, 2002.

March, Peyton C. *The Nation at War*. Garden City, NY: Doubleday, Doran, 1932.

March, William [William Edward Campbell]. *Company K*. New York: H. Smith & R. Haas, 1933.

Mead, Gary. *The Doughboys: America and the First World War*. Woodstock, NY: Overlook Press, 2000.

Meyer, G. J. *A World Undone: The Story of the Great War, 1914 to 1918*. New York: Delacorte Press, 2006.

Miller, Kelly. *Kelly Miller's History of the World War for Human Rights: It Is Fair to the Negro*. Washington, DC: Austin Jenkins, 1919.

Millman, Chad. *The Detonators: The Secret Plot to Destroy America and an Epic Hunt for Justice*. New York: Little, Brown, 2006.

Moore, Frederick F. *Siberia To-Day*. New York: D. Appleton, 1919.

Moss, James A. *Privates' Manual*. Menasha, WI: George Banta, 1917.

National Committee on Army and Navy Camp Music. *Army Song Book*. Washington, DC: United States War Department Commission on Training Camp Activities, 1918.

Nelson, James Carl. *The Remains of Company D: A Story of the Great War*. New York: St. Martin's Press, 2009.

Nelson, Peter M. *A More Unbending Battle: The Harlem Hellfighters' Struggle for Freedom in WWI and Equality at Home*. New York: Basic Civitas Books, 2009.

New York Bible Society. *Active Service Testament: The New Testament of Our Lord and Saviour Jesus Christ*. New York: New York Bible Society, 1918.

Palmer, Frederick. *America in France.* New York: Dodd, Mead, 1918.

——. *Our Greatest Battle.* New York: Dodd, Mead, 1919.

Palmer, Svetlana, and Sarah Wallis, eds. *Intimate Voices from the First World War.* London: Simon & Schuster UK, 2003.

Peat, Frank E., and Lee Orean Smith. *Legion Airs: Songs of "Over There" and "Over Here."* New York: Leo Feist, 1932.

Peat, Harold R. *Private Peat.* Indianapolis: Bobbs-Merrill, 1917.

Pershing, John J. *My Experiences in the World War.* New York: Frederick A. Stokes, 1931.

Persico, Joseph W. *11th Month, 11th Day, 11th Hour: Armistice Day, 1918: World War I and Its Violent Climax.* New York: Random House, 2004.

Pitt, Barrie. *1918: The Last Act.* New York: W. W. Norton, 1963.

Powell, E. Alexander. *Fighting in Flanders.* New York: Grosset & Dunlap, 1914.

Putnam, Elizabeth C. *On Duty and Off: Letters of Elizabeth Cabot Putnam, Written in France, May, 1917–September, 1918.* Cambridge, MA: Riverside Press, 1919.

Rawls, Walton. *Wake Up, America! World War I and the American Poster.* New York: Abbeville Press, 1988.

Reed, John. *The War in Eastern Europe.* New York: Charles Scribner's Sons, 1917.

Remarque, Erich Maria. *All Quiet on the Western Front.* Boston: Little, Brown, 1929.

Review of Reviews Editorial Staff. *Two Thousand Questions and Answers About the War.* New York: Review of Reviews, 1918.

Roberts, David E., and Dewitt M. Benham, eds. *Sayings & Songs for Soldiers & Sailors.* New York: National War Work Council of Young Men's Christian Associations, 1917.

Roll of Honor of the Seventy-Sixth U.S. Field Artillery. Koblenz, Germany: Lithographie von Dienhard, 1919.

Russell, Thomas H. *America's War for Humanity.* New York: L. H. Walter, 1919.

Scott, Emmett J. *Scott's Official History of the American Negro in the World War.* Washington, DC: published by the author, 1919.

Scott, George Winfield, and James Wilford Garner. *The German War Code: Contrasted with the War Manuals of the United States, Great Britain, and France.* War Information Series, no. 11. Washington, DC: Committee on Public Information, 1918.

Sibley, Frank P. *With the Yankee Division in France.* Boston: Little, Brown, 1919.

Slattery, Margaret. *The Second Line of Defense: A Plea for the Men and Women of To-morrow.* New York: Fleming H. Revell, 1918.

Slotkin, Richard. *Lost Battalions: The Great War and the Crisis of American Nationality.* New York: Henry Holt, 2005.

Smith, Gene. *Still Quiet on the Western Front: 50 Years Later.* New York: William Morrow, 1965.

The Soldiers' French Phrase Book. Chicago: Felt & Tarrant, 1918.

Songs the Soldiers and Sailors Sing. New York: Leo Feist, 1918.

Sterba, Christopher M. *Good Americans: Italian and Jewish Immigrants During the First World War.* New York: Oxford University Press, 2003.

Stone, Geoffrey R. *Perilous Times: Free Speech in Wartime: From the Sedition Act of 1798 to the War on Terrorism.* New York: W. W. Norton, 2005.

The Story of the 91st Division. San Mateo, CA: 91st Division Publication Committee, 1919.

Strachan, Hew. *The First World War.* New York: Viking, 2004.

Strickland, Daniel W. *Connecticut Fights: The Story of the 102nd Regiment.* New Haven: Quinnipiack Press, 1930.

Sullivan, Mark. *Our Times: The United States, 1900–1925.* New York: Charles Scribner's Sons, 1933.

Tank Corps, N.A. *Treat 'Em Rough.* Vol. 1, nos. 8 (July 15, 1918) and 9 (July 29, 1918). Gettysburg, PA: Tank Corps, N.A.

Tatlock, John S. P. *Why America Fights Germany.* War Information Series, no. 15: Washington, DC: Committee on Public Information, 1918.

Taylor, Emerson Gifford. *New England in France: 1917–1919, A History of the Twenty-Sixth Division U.S.A.* Boston: Houghton Mifflin, 1920.

Thisted, Moses. *Pershing's Pioneer Infantry of World War I.* Hemet, CA: Alphabet Printers, 1981.

Thomason, John W., Jr. *Fix Bayonets!* New York: Charles Scribner's Sons, 1925.

Thompson, Holland, ed. *The Book of History: The World's Greatest War.* New York: Grolier Society, 1920.

Thorn, Henry C., Jr. *History of 313th U.S. Infantry, "Baltimore's Own."* New York: Wynkoop Hallenbeck Crawford, 1920.

Tuchman, Barbara W. *The Guns of August.* New York: Macmillan, 1962.

Tumulty, Joseph P. *Woodrow Wilson As I Know Him.* Garden City, NY: Doubleday, Page, 1924.

United States Navy, *The U.S. Navy: Enlistment, Instruction, Pay, and Advancement.* Washington, DC: Bureau of Navigation, Navy Department, 1917.

United States Senate. *Deportation of Gregorie Semenoff: Hearings Before the*

Committee on Education and Labor, United States Senate, Sixty-Seventh Congress, Second Session, Relative to the Deporting of Undesirable Aliens, April 12, 13, 17, and 18, 1922, Part I. Washington, DC: United States Government Printing Office, 1922.

United States War Department. *Home Reading Course for Citizen-Soldiers.* War Information Series, no. 9. Washington, DC: Committee on Public Information, 1917.

———. *Regulations for the Army of the United States, 1913, Corrected to April 15, 1917.* Washington, DC: United States Government Printing Office, 1917.

———. *Rules of Land Warfare, 1914, Corrected to April 15, 1917.* Washington, DC: United States Government Printing Office, 1917.

Wallgren, Abian A. *The A.E.F. in Cartoon.* Philadelphia: Dan Sowers, 1933.

Wharton, Edith. *Fighting in France: From Dunkerque to Belport.* New York: Charles Scribner's Sons, 1917.

Whitehouse, Arch. *The Years of the Sky Kings.* New York: Doubleday, 1959.

Wilkins, Ernest H., Algernon Coleman, and Howard R. Huse. *First Lessons in Spoken French for Men in Military Service.* Chicago: University of Chicago Press, 1917.

Willmott, H. P. *World War I.* New York: Dorling Kindersley, 2003.

Wilson, Woodrow. *In Our First Year of War.* New York: Harper & Brothers, 1918.

Wood, Eric Fisher. *The Note-Book of an Attaché: Seven Months in the War Zone.* New York: Century, 1915.

Acknowledgments

This book would not exist without the generous assistance of a great many people who contributed to its development and progress over the past ten years. First and foremost on that list are all the veterans and others I interviewed, men and women between the ages of 101 and 113 who graciously invited me into their homes and offered me as much of their time as I wanted. Frankly, if I were 107 years old and some guy I knew nothing about wanted to come talk to me about things I did eighty-five years ago, I'm afraid I might be too aware of just how few were my remaining hours to readily offer up some of them for such a purpose. Yet if any of these people felt that way, I never perceived even a hint of it. I am honored to have made their acquaintance, and grateful that they chose to share their stories with me.

Their children and grandchildren, and friends and neighbors and caregivers, were every bit as gracious, and often expended a lot of effort on my behalf: furnishing introductions, making arrangements, sitting through interviews in order to make the interviewee (and the interviewer) more comfortable, suggesting lines of inquiry, prodding memories, and taking the time to scan old photos, letters, and documents and send them to me. I could not have done it without them.

I would not have found a great many of these veterans without the help of a few individuals. Even after I discovered the French List online, I was having a difficult time tracking down people on it: Although the list noted their city or town of residence, there were no street addresses provided, and few of them were listed in the phone book; most, I would eventually discover, were living with a relative or in a residential facility. Frustrated and discouraged, I phoned the French embassy in Washington and was fortunate enough to be put in touch with an adjutant there named Nam Do Cao, who expressed a strong desire that "everyone who fought for liberty in that war should be recognized." Although he was to be transferred back to Paris in a few weeks, he undertook to photocopy, on his own time, every single American application for the Legion d'Honneur going back to 1998, some 550 documents, each of which contained a full name, a recent address, a date and place of birth, and other information that proved invaluable in my search. (He also refused to accept any recompense whatsoever for the copying and mailing costs involved; this at a time when many Americans were cursing the French, serving *Freedom Fries*, etc.) Not long thereafter, I made the acquaintance of Ellen Lovell and Peter Bartis at the Library of Congress. Both were then working on the library's fine Veterans History Project, and offered me very useful guidance on both finding and interviewing veterans; Peter has continued to be a source of wisdom ever since. Eventually, two men at the Department of Veterans Affairs, John Buck and Chris Scheer, also lent their efforts to the search—in Chris's case, for several years.

Having secured all those interviews, I could not have done much with them were it not for the help of ten student interns, history majors who cheerfully undertook the tedious yet essential task of transcribing and indexing seemingly endless hours of video, and also helped with research: William Schlavis, Dana Love, Jacob Croke, Mara Ravitz, Dean Zingmond, Mary Pilon, Matthew Murphy, Jessica Rofe, and Jordan Benge at New York University; and Patrick Kelley at Fordham University. Jake Croke and Dana Love continued their efforts on behalf of the project even after their internships ended, and Bill Schlavis is still helping me with it today, years later. They all have my gratitude, as do Jackie Biello and Mona Huegel for administering the internships at NYU.

I had cause, on many occasions, to seek out those who knew much more about something than I did; all proved exceedingly generous with their time and expertise, including Major Jason P. Clark, Colonel James T. Seidule, and Colonel Lance Betros at the United States Military Academy; General James F. Amos, Major Joseph Plenzler, and historian Annette Amerman of the United States Marine Corps; Dr. Thomas T. Perls of the New England Centenarian Study at Boston University; Dr. L. Stephen Coles of the Gerontology Research Group at UCLA; Jane Naisbitt at the Canadian War Museum; professors Robert F. Engs, Geoffrey R. Stone, Nancy Gentile Ford, Christopher Capozzola, Gerald Early, Lawrence Moe, and Maurine Greenwald; Gene Smith, Susan Ziegler, Tim Bingaman, Joni Kesler, Julian Beale, Jim Fuglie, Thomas Fleming, Joan Larson, Jeff Lowdermilk, Joe Pomainville, David Laskin, and Randal Gaulke; Tim Nosal at the American Battle Monuments Commission; Jonathan Casey at the National World War I Museum; and the wonderful staff at the National Archives. Thanks also to Marjorie Silver, JaeMi Pennington, and Stacy Andersen at the New England Centenarian Study for their help.

I am grateful to Karl Schonberg and Val Lehr at St. Lawrence University for helping me get to France, and to the following people for helping me get the most out of it once I was there: Joseph P. Rivers and Dominique Didiot at the Meuse-Argonne American Cemetery and Memorial; Jeffrey Aarnio at the Oise-Aisne American Cemetery and Memorial; David Atkinson at the Aisne-Marne American Cemetery and Memorial; Bobby Bell at the St.-Mihiel American Cemetery and Memorial; and Jean-Paul DeVries, Gilles Lagin, Georges Bailly, Patrick Simons, Stan Bissinger, and that nice woman at the museum in Belleau, whose name I never caught. Thanks, too, to Mike Conley at the American Battle Monuments Commission.

Although I would have had a much larger pool to work with had I started my search for World War I veterans a decade before I did, that search—and the accompanying research—would doubtless have been a great deal more difficult back then, as it would have been undertaken without the benefit of the Internet, and all the search engines and other tools it offers. Scarcely a day passed when I did not consult the vast database of census records, military records, newspaper clippings, and ephemera at Ancestry.com. I am grateful to Mike Ward and Heather Erickson for facilitating my access to that indispensible resource.

More of this book was written at the Patten Free Library than anywhere else; they provide a beautiful and quiet space in which to work, not to mention free WiFi, electricity, heat, and an excellent interlibrary loan network. And the staff is always cheerful, even when it's three minutes to lights out and you haven't yet begun to shut down your laptop. The same is true of the Curtis Memorial Library, where I spent many hours working when PFL was closed. I also availed myself, on many occasions, of the facilities of the New York Public Library, the Skidompha Public Library, the Lithgow Public Library, the Maine State Library, the Owen D. Young Library at St. Lawrence University, and, on quite a few late nights, the Hawthorne-Longfellow Library at Bowdoin College.

I have been the beneficiary of kindnesses, great and small, from friends, acquaintances, and erstwhile strangers, people who read through a troublesome passage or chapter (or, in some cases, the entire manuscript), listened while I worked out a passage or an argument or a notion aloud, shared their own perspective on matters historical or literary or both, drove with me for hours (and even, in some cases, days) to visit veterans, gave me guidance, loaned me equipment, offered me a place to sleep and a home-cooked meal when I was tired and far from home, or otherwise supported a very long and involved venture in some way. For any or many of these I am grateful to Shelby Foote, Sheldon Hackney, Leslie Epstein, Stephanie Wagner, Steve Theodore, Kellie Maske, Julieta Cristal, Colby Smith, Rebecca Weinstein, Julia Addison, Peter

Bailey, Svetlana Yanina, Adam Fox, S.E. Brown, Michael Greenwald, Meg Guroff, Rick Klugman, Jo-Ann and Jeff Smith, and Will Vandenburgh. Special thanks to Joy Maske for an extraordinary and unsolicited act of beneficence, and to The Babe, for whose grace even special thanks are not enough.

My agent, Kristine Dahl, was an enthusiastic supporter of this project from the beginning, even though I had originally told her, after my last book, that the next one was going to be on an entirely different subject than this, one that had nothing at all to do with World War I, and which I strongly suspected would have been much more popular. For that, and for keeping me calm and focused most of the time, I thank her, as well as Laura Neely, Liz Farrell, and Katie O'Connor at ICM. Gillian Blake was an early, tireless, and patient champion of this book; her vision and encouragement helped shape it, and keep me going, at a critical time. Bruce Nichols ably nurtured and edited the manuscript, and helped whip it into shape. Melissa Dobson's efforts as copy editor can aptly be labeled heroic; Chris Robinson managed to render the maps despite having to work with a cartographically-challenged author. Ben Hyman and Sarah Iani at Houghton Mifflin Harcourt did a lot of heavy lifting on this book's behalf. Thanks also to Jill Lazer, Melissa Lotfy, Patrick Barry, Megan Wilson, and Katrina Kruse at HMH.

Finally, I would like to thank all of the people who helped in some way or other over the past decade but whose names, for one reason or another—most likely my own poor record-keeping and organizational skills—do not appear here. Please accept my apology, and feel free to email me at thelastofthedoughboys@gmail.com (or approach me in person should our paths cross somewhere) and make me feel guilty about it. I am susceptible to that.

Index